Wireless Security

Wireless Security

Models, Threats, and Solutions

Randall K. Nichols
Panos C. Lekkas

McGraw-Hill
New York   Chicago   San Francisco   Lisbon   London
Madrid   Mexico City   Milan   New Delhi   San Juan   Seoul
Singapore   Sydney   Toronto

Cataloging-in-Publication Data is on file with the Library of Congress.

McGraw-Hill

A Division of The McGraw-Hill Companies

2 3 4 5 6 7 8 9 0   DOC/DOC   0 7 6 5 4 3 2

ISBN 0-07-138038-8

The sponsoring editor for this book was Marjorie Spencer and the production supervisor was Sherri Souffrance. It was set in ITC Century by MacAllister Publishing Services, LLC.

Printed and bound by R.R. Donnelley & Sons.

Throughout this book, trademarked names are used. Rather than put a trademark symbol after every occurrence of a trademarked name, we use names in an editorial fashion only, and to the benefit of the trademark owner, with no intention of infringement of the trademark. Where such designations appear in this book, they have been printed with initial caps.

 This book is printed on recycled, acid-free paper containing a minimum of 50 percent recycled de-inked fiber.

Dedication

From Randall K. Nichols:

To: Montine, Kent, Phillip, Diana, and pumpkin Michelle—The Bear is still going!
To: Gladys and Chuck—It is clear that you have not retired.
To: My Grandkids—Brandon, Scott, Ryan, and Kara—take the future into your hands.
To: Dr. Lile Murphree—For your mentorship and advice, I am indebted.
To: My GWU students—I am honored and blessed to have worked with you all.
To: Waldo T. Boyd—Who remains the best editor in the country.

From Panos C. Lekkas:

To: The memory of my father Chrysostomos, spellbound for words of gratitude and appreciation, for everything he taught me about life and people, integrity and perseverance, and for instigating in me an unquenchable thirst for knowledge.
To: my mother Maria, with my deepest love and respect. Thank you for pushing me relentlessly forward, for teaching me how to keep the right perspective, and for always being there, especially when I stumbled. God bless you and may He give you many more years with us!
To: RÉgine, my beloved wife, my best friend, and unconditional partner in life. You and our precious four, Jean-Chrysostome, Marie, Marina, and Nicholas are the meaning of my life and the only reason I am doing what I do every day.

To our fallen comrade, Naidu Mummidi, we will miss you and pray for your family.

Special Dedication:

On 11 September 2001, the United States suffered the cowardly attacks of terrorists. More than 6000 innocent human beings were killed in the attacks on the World Trade Center buildings and the Pentagon. We dedicate our book to the Firefighters and Policemen and Rescue-workers who gave their lives so selflessly and honorably in the performance of their duties. We pray for comfort for families that lost loved ones in these terror attacks. A portion of our book royalties will be donated to the American Red Cross to help the families affected by these unspeakably violent acts.

Contents

2 Wireless Information Warfare 37

13 Optimizing Wireless Security with FPGAs and ASICs   *503*

Foreword

The safeguarding of information traveling over wireless technology has quickly become one of the most important and contentious challenges facing today's technology innovators. With the advent of *third generation* (3G) Internet technology—a capability that connects mobile devices to the Internet and allows users to send and receive detailed information over wireless and fiber networks—the security measures necessary to protect critical data on these wireless networks have become even more elusive and complex. The issues surrounding proper security in the use of networked wireless devices have played out in a contest between individual, business, and government interests. While protecting the privacy of individuals is of utmost importance, many would argue individual privacy must be balanced with the interests of public safety and law enforcement's ability to monitor the private communications of suspected criminals. Moreover, the business costs associated with providing the appropriate security measures are often substantial.

Current security issues are further clouded by the merging of the private and public information infrastructure sectors, areas previously guided by separate regulatory measures that now exchange information and operate in a common framework known as the *public switched network* (PSN). Wireless technology has evolved to carry increasing amounts of valuable information that require higher privacy and security levels. Some refer to the PSN as the "Interstate Highway" system for telecommunications; however, wireless increasingly serves as the "on-and-off ramps" to this vast and global information infrastructure.

From my vantage point of a career in Naval and National Intelligence focused on developing intelligence on the former Soviet Union and hot spots impacting U.S. national security interests, the interception of wireless communications was key to our successful intelligence operations. This was true during World War II, throughout the Cold War, and it continues today. Data in the form of wireless communications in the days before digital, computer-based networks was vulnerable only during the moment of transmission. It was in that instant of transmission that the intelligence needed to be collected, or the opportunity was lost. Intelligence officers learned to rely on communications intelligence from wireless systems as a means of providing invaluable strategic and tactical intelligence. Experience taught us that wireless communications had to be protected at the precise moment that tactical, and even critical, strategic information was being communicated. The successes of Desert

Storm in the Gulf War further demonstrated how wireless communications could be turned into immediate actionable intelligence unavailable from any other source. Today, massive networking, with data created, transmitted, and stored online, has made connected nations the world's most vulnerable target for information attack. These vulnerabilities include capture of information for intelligence purposes, disruption or corruption of information, or destruction of data in the network. Because this networking capability, which has added to productivity, efficiency, and wealth creation, carries so much vital data, such nations have significantly more to lose than their less developed counterparts. For example, terrorists potentially could target the monetary system, a networked infrastructure that moves and records financial transactions. The vast majority of this wealth is stored in a database, which is vulnerable to disruption from a sophisticated and determined adversary.

As we expand and enhance our connectivity, our vulnerability to hostile attack inside the homeland will only increase. Military superiority will not entirely provide the protection we have become accustomed to in the past. Rogue states, terrorists, and other disaffected groups have the ability to acquire cyber weapons of mass disruption, and the means of their implementation have multiplied. As the recent Hart-Rudman Report on National Security for the 21st Century ominously predicted, without adequate safeguards, a catastrophic event inside the U.S. will occur. With new digital network information technology, our borders will become more porous; some will bend and some will break. U.S. intelligence will face more challenging adversaries, and even the best intelligence measures will not prevent all surprises. Reliance on unprotected networks carries with it the risks of loss of government services and military failure, as well as catastrophic economic consequences.

The military is increasingly dependent on the private information infrastructure to conduct its essential operations. This dependence is complicated by custom, culture, and statutes that focus the military on foreign operations and would restrict any attempt to prevent or contain asymmetric attacks within borders. In the future, collaboration and coordination between civil, military, and private sectors will become essential. In time, data will have to be shared for rapid integration into information products to be useful to operational decision makers. Likewise, government supplied information will have to flow to the private sector to ensure appropriate awareness and decision-making.

Increased mobility has become a key benefit to an Internet-working society. With the past and current proliferation of mobile technologies and devices, vendors have moved aggressively to extend the wired network through mobile pathways that businesses and service providers can operate with confidence. The value for mobile wireless users resides with the ability to communicate over great distances, while in motion, at a relatively modest cost. With so much of our national wealth riding in the networks using wireless devices for entry and exit, it is clear that more attention needs to be paid to building in the required security features. Furthermore, a new security culture needs to emerge across the entire Internet user community. We must resist the glorification of the hacker ethic, in which destructiveness poses as inquisitiveness. In a personal vein, we need to develop a culture that emphasizes responsibility and accountability on the part of every user—from school child to CEO.

Proper online security habits must become second nature to protect our privacy and the broader interests of society. These include all of the obvious things that we should do, but often don't: changing passwords; disconnecting from the Internet when it is not in use; running anti-virus software daily; changing the default password whenever a new device is purchased; and using appropriate security and encryption services. In addition to personal action, corporations must understand and adopt proper security technology to safeguard the future. Nowhere is the development of this new security culture more important than in the wireless theater of operations.

Wireless Security addresses these evolving security concerns by providing deep insights in a readable and effective manner. The broad practical and academic backgrounds of the authors have allowed them to seamlessly present the most current state of information protection and vulnerabilities related wireless security in a balanced, easy to understand and fully documented treatise. The cases presented are real and topical, and flow seamlessly with the theme of the subject matter presented. The authors tell the reader the risks, examine cases where people and systems have fallen victim, and provide remedies to those who have been victimized by these risks.

Readers will find that the authors have taken an approach of best business practices to present their material—a balanced identification of technologies combined with a systems approach to the problem of wireless communications security. The book is designed for readers who operate at the executive, policy, or managerial level and who have responsibility for protecting their organization's information assets, intellectual property, and communications systems. The content presented is equally valuable to both private sector and government managers.

Wireless Security provides a reasoned approach to making sound decisions about how to expend scarce resources in order to achieve a balanced multidisciplinary approach to wireless security. The end result is a necessary and attainable security response for organizations and government alike.

J. M. (Mike) McConnell, Vice Admiral, USN (Retired)
Vice President, Booz • Allen & Hamilton, Inc.
Former Director of the National Security Agency (NSA), 1992–1996

About J. M. (Mike) McConnell

As a Vice President at Booz·Allen & Hamilton, Inc., Mr. McConnell leads assignments in Information Assurance for departments and agencies of the federal government and for commercial clients. In addition, he oversees the firm's Information Operations assignments for the Department of Defense. From 1992 to 1996, Mr. McConnell was Director of the *National Security Agency* (NSA), the U.S. agency responsible for Signals Intelligence and all security services that protect classified Government information. He also served as the Intelligence Officer for the Chairman, Joint Chiefs of Staff during the dissolution of the Soviet Union and Operation Desert Storm.

At Booz • Allen & Hamilton, Mr. McConnell has led assignments for the Presidential Commission on Critical Infrastructure Protection focused on security standards in the Banking and Financial Industry. He also led work with the U.S. *Critical Infrastructure Assurance Office* (CIAO) for the White House; his team developed the National Infrastructure Assurance Plan design and planning guidelines. Mr. McConnell helped the Department of Justice/FBI develop the new *National Infrastructure Protection Center* (NIPC) concept of operations and was instrumental in the Navy's recent information assurance initiatives.

Preface

Cellular systems have evolved through several generations characterized by analog or digital technologies. *First generation* (1G) refers to analog systems, *second generation* (2G) to digital, and *third generation* (3G) to enhanced digital. Each generation moved the industry into a more advanced stage of wireless communications.

The 1G systems were an alternative when a user needed to be mobile or wired systems were not available. The 2G digital systems were partially competitive with wired services in some markets and were complementary to wired in more mature markets. The goal of today's 3G markets is to drive the wired mature markets into saturated ones in which mobile terminals are ubiquitous.

William Webb in his excellent text, *The Future of Wireless Communications*, suggests that future sustained growth in the wireless global theater will be accomplished by aggregating large numbers of different kinds of networks into an enormous number of virtual personal area networks. *Content* in these systems will be very different from that of 3G systems. Enabling devices to talk to each other is what allows more wireless devices to be sold and the impetus for many new products in adaptive personal areas.[1]

One common evolving backbone network, which is the glue to most new wireless applications, is the Internet. It is not a proprietary wireless infrastructure as is the basis of 2G or 3G technologies. The Internet will continue to evolve through new features and protocols that enhance its usability for mobility access. A complete replacement of real-time circuit-switched connections for all applications through IP and packet-switching at high data rates should be technically feasible. Radio spectrum requirements will increase and be provided to meet increased bandwidth demands posed by increased users, usage, and new wireless services. Webb predicts that a convergence and thorough integration of mobile communications and the Internet makes future wireless growth possible.[2] Mobile Internet usage will far surpass stationary Internet access, as we know it today, through desktop PCs and modems or PCs connected to corporate servers and routers.[3]

Two factors that threaten the growth of wireless systems are standards and security. Standards traditionally expand markets and lower costs by assuring equipment to be interoperable, but they can be confining too. The *wireless applications protocol* (WAP) proposed for secure wireless systems using the Internet backbone is an example of a confining standard. It assumes the one terminal-for-everything model of traditional cellular practice. Wireless multimedia implies many different kinds of application-specific terminals and appliances. The standardization process must change from one that assures compatibility to a process that enables incompatibility such as generic digital networks and proprietary applications.[4]

Security will be both the enabler and inhibitor of the post-3G world. All this expected wireless growth implies a huge assumption that the telecommunications industry, regulators, and governments will accept open standards, processes, and security features and freely share them across international borders. It is also a fact that practically every proprietary encryption system protecting 3G networks has been cracked. Even this interesting fact has not stopped the proliferation of security by obscurity that is accepted practice and prevalent in today's telecommunications systems.

Fraud has been an enduring problem, especially for mobile radio. Much of the impetus for the move from 1G to 2G mobile phones was the increasing fraud occurring because of relative simplicity of stealing mobile identification numbers and making illegal telephone calls. Digital cellular systems overcame these problems but enabled a number of other fraudulent mechanisms, such as stealing a phone and setting up call forwarding before the phone theft is reported and then making international calls on the forwarded path at local rates. As the capabilities of wireless systems increase along with the range of services offered, the opportunities for fraud increase—and so do the attendant costs. As systems designers close off the known loopholes (or don't, which is the typical case), fraudsters seem to devise new schemes to make money. Fraud will not stop the development of wireless technology and services. It may even speed up the overall development by providing strong incentives to introduce new secure technologies.[5]

Wireless Security

A review of the research about wireless communications systems and current best practices turned up more than 500 references in the design, technology, management, and marketing of wireless and mobile communications systems. However, there was not one reference devoted to wireless security. That then became the goal of our book. We have endeavored to provide a balanced approach to wireless security and wireless security solutions for commercial, government, and military organizations.

Target Audience

Wireless Security is for the manager and policy maker, the designer and the project lead. It was written for the benefit of those who must exercise due diligence in protecting the valuable wireless information assets and systems upon which their organizations depend. Among IT practitioners, it is valuable to CIOs, operations managers, network engineers, network managers, database managers, programmers, analysts, EDI planners, and other professionals charged with applying appropriate INFOSEC countermeasures to secure wireless applications and devices. *Wireless Security* is suitable for a first-year graduate course in wireless computer security, for computers-in-business courses, and for Engineering/MBA programs. There are plenty of resources in the bibliography, URL references, and textual leads to further reading.

Structure of This Book

The goal of *Wireless Security* is to explore the vast array of wireless technologies, techniques, and methodologies; to provide relevant analysis and understanding; and to improve the thoughtfulness and longevity of implementations. *Wireless Security* is divided into four parts:

- *Part I: Wireless Threats* presents a basic overview of wireless communications and societal impacts of wireless, telecommunications, cellular network, and bearer technologies. Wireless security is then presented in terms of the model of Wireless Information Warfare. Two chapters inspect the air-to-ground interface and vulnerabilities that are prevalent in both telephone and satellite systems.
- *Part II: Cryptographic Countermeasures* covers a wide range of encryption technologies from stream ciphers to *elliptic curve cryptography* (ECC) to Rijndael, the *advanced encryption standard* (AES) winner that may be applied effectively to wireless communications. The limitations of encryption and need for robust authentication systems are discussed. The fascinating science of speech cryptology is introduced to balance the cryptographic countermeasures applied.
- *Part III: Application Solutions* is a practical section covering the security principles and flaws of popular wireless technologies such as wireless LANS, WAP, TLS, Bluetooth, and VOIP.
- *Part IV: Hardware Solutions and Embedded Design* focuses on hardware considerations for *end-to-end* (E2E) security and optimizing real-time wireless communications security. E2E implementations with advanced integrated circuits; namely, using specialized *field programmable gate arrays* (FPGAs) for rapid prototype development and technology validation and *very-large scale integration* (VLSI) *application-specific integrated circuits* (ASICs) or *intellectual property* (IP) cores for the solution implementation in state-of-the-art *systems-on-a-chip* (SOC) are discussed.

Endnotes

[1] William Webb, *Wireless Communications*, Artech House, 2001, pp. 245–246.
[2] Ibid., p. 277.
[3] Ibid., p. 277.
[4] Ibid., p. 266.
[5] Ibid., pp. 133–134.

Acknowledgments

Books such as this are the products of contributions by many people, not just the musings of the authors. *Wireless Security* has benefited from review by numerous experts in the field, who gave generously of their time and expertise. The following people reviewed all or part of the manuscript: Mike McConnell, Vice President for Booz • Allen and Hamilton and previous Director National Security Agency; Edward J. Giorgio, Principal for Booz • Allen and Hamilton and previous Chief Cryptographer and Cryptanalyst for the National Security Agency; Joseph Nusbaum, Senior Manager for Booz • Allen and Hamilton; Professor Alfred J. Menezes, author of *Handbook of Applied Cryptography*; and plenty of colleagues and friends at THLC. More specifically, Bruce Young, CEO; Chad Rao, Vice President—SW Engineering, Ronald H LaPat, Vice President—Systems Engineering; Edward D'Entremont, Vice President—Business Development; Krishna Murthy, Director—SW Engineering; Thomas J. Petrarca, Executive Vice President. Also GWU-SEAS Department Chair, Professor Tom A Mazzuchi; Professor Lile Murphree at GWU-SEAS; Professor and attorney Daniel J. Ryan, at GWU-SEAS; Professor Julie J.C.H. Ryan at GWU-SEAS; Dorothy Denning, Professor of INFOSEC Technology at Georgetown University; Emeritus Professor Dr. I. J. Kumar; Professor Shri Kant; Professor Emeritus, Charles M. Thatcher, UARK; Professor R. W. Serth, TAMU; Waldo T. Boyd, senior editor, Creative Writing, Pty. and senior cryptographer; Robert V. Klauzinski, intellectual property attorney for Mintz, et al; Marjorie Spencer, senior editor for McGraw-Hill Professional Books; Beth Brown, project manager for MacAllister Publishing Services; Mark Luna at RSA Security.

Special mention is made of THLC's "California" team. We appreciate their efforts, reviews, comments, and hard work on our behalf. Specifically we thank: Sujatha Durairaj, Ramana Anuganti, Srisailam Narra, Prasanthi Tallapaneni, Sirisha Kota, Shiva Shankar Manjunatha, Venu Anuganti, and Sridhar Choudary Chadalavada.

Our dear friend Naidu Mummidi is especially remembered. While we were writing this book, Naidu left this life so prematurely and so unexpectedly at the age of 30, filling the hearts of all of us who knew him and worked closely with him with tremendous sorrow. May he rest in peace! We pray for his soul and for his family. We will never forget him.

We also respectfully acknowledge the help of Dr. John Burroughs, previously Chief Cryptographer of the National Security Agency, for his many constructive comments on our work. Shayle Hirschman deserves a special note of thanks for his hard and diligent work as well as for his hawkish eye for circuit detail. Kevin Bruemmer of Natural MicroSystems has been gracious in sharing thoughts and his impressive expertise. Some extremely interesting discussions with him are sincerely appreciated. Professor Joe Silverman from Brown University and NTRU, as well as Professor Christof Paar, Worcester Polytechnic Institute, Professor Cetin Koç and Dr. Erkay Savas, both of Oregon State University, as well as Professor Yusuf Leblebici, Sabanci University, Istanbul, all provided insight and shared thoughts on specific approaches to embedded security systems. Our thanks go to Thomas Wollinger and Professor Kumar Murthy. The authors are grateful to Professor Ingrid Verbauwhede of the Electrical Engineering Department at the *University of California, Los Angeles* (UCLA) and to Professor Kris Gaj of the Electrical and Computer Engineering Department at George Mason University, in Fairfax, Virginia, for their permission to refer extensively to their impressive research work regarding optimal implementations of cryptographic algorithms in efficient hardware. We thank Professor Dr. Guang Gong of the Center of Applied Cryptographic Research, University of Waterloo, Ontario, Canada, for extensive consultations and numerous hours of problem solving and coding. Our thanks also go to Dr. Käri Kärkkäinen of the Center of Wireless Communications, University of Oulu, Oulu, Finland, and to Thomas Wollinger of the ECE Department at WPI, Worcester, Massachusetts. Last, we thank Professor Emeritus, Dr. Mihály Toth, AZ Kando College, Budapest, Hungary, for his encouragement and reviews.

Many of Professor Nichols' INFOSEC certificate, masters, and doctorate students from his 2000–2001 Fall, Spring, and Summer graduate courses in *INFOSEC* and *Cryptographic Systems: Application, Management and Policy* at The *George Washington University* (GWU) in Washington, D.C., voluntarily formed teams, performed intensive research, and assisted with the writing of several chapters of *Wireless Security*. We worked passionately and cooperatively toward the goal of making *Wireless Security* the premier textbook for a new elective course in the information security Masters and certificate programs at GWU. Special mention of these talented and dedicated professionals is made in the List of Contributors section.

Finally, Montine Nichols deserves a commendation for her help on the final drafts and copy edit for our book. Joe Schepisi did a fine job on the Glossary, and Dennis Kezer was the prime mover for the collection and aggregation of our References. We thank Andrew Downey for his assistance on our material presentation for RSA 2001, RSA ASIA 2001, and GWU INFOSEC 2001 tune-up. To these and many others to whom we may have failed to give appropriate credit, we are grateful for their relevant ideas, advice, and counsel. Any mistakes or errors are, of course, our own. Please advise the authors of errors by e-mail to comsec@epix.net or crypto@gwu.edu and we will do our best to correct the errors and publish an errata list.

Randall K. Nichols
Professor, The George Washington University
School of Engineering and Applied Sciences (SEAS)
Washington, DC
&
Chief Technical Officer
INFOSEC Technologies, LLC
Cryptographic / Anti-Virus / Anti-Hacking
Computer Security Countermeasures
Carlisle, PA
November, 2001
Website: www.infosec-technologies.com
Email: cto@infosec-technologies.com
Voice: 717-258-8316
Fax: 717-258-5693
Cell: 717-329-9836

Panos C. Lekkas
Chief Technology Officer & General Manager
Wireless Encryption Technology Division
TeleHubLink Corporation (THLC)
wireless_security@attglobal.net
Marlboro, MA
November, 2001

List of Contributors

The authors express their gratitude to the talented review teams and The George Washington University research teams from the *School of Engineering Management and Applied Science* (SEAS), Washington, D.C., who contributed so much of their time and expertise to make *Wireless Security* a success. With deepest respect, we present the qualifications of our teammates.

Authors

Randall K. Nichols
Managing Author/Editor

Randall K. Nichols (a.k.a. LANAKI) is Chief Technical Officer of INFOSEC Technologies, a consulting firm specializing in Cryptographic, Anti-Virus, and Anti-Hacking computer security countermeasures to support the information security (INFOSEC) requirements of its commercial and government customers.

Previously, Nichols served as Vice President—Cryptography, for TeleHubLink Corporation (THLC). Nichols led TeleHub-Link Corporation's cryptographic research and development activities for the company's advanced cryptographic technology. He was co-author of THLC's patented HORNET™ SHA-based encryption technology, which is embedded into a family of advanced application-specific integrated circuits (ASIC's), field programmable gate arrays (FPGA) and IP cores that THLC sells to wireless and telephone industry customers.

Prior to joining TeleHubLink Corporation, Nichols was CEO of COMSEC Solutions, a cryptographic/anti-virus/biometrics countermeasures company that was acquired by TeleHubLink Corporation. COMSEC Solutions provided customer support on INFOSEC to approximately 1,200 commercial, education, and U.S. government clients.

Nichols serves as Series Editor for Encryption and INFOSEC for McGraw-Hill Professional Books. Nichols previously served as Technology Director of Cryptography and Biometrics for the International Computer Security Association (ICSA). Nichols has served as President and Vice President of the American Cryptogram Association (ACA). Nichols is internationally respected, with 38 years of experience in a variety of leadership roles in cryptography and INFOSEC computer applications (in the engineering, consulting, construction, and chemical industries).

Professor Nichols teaches graduate-level courses in INFOSEC, Cryptography, and in Systems Applications Management and Policy at the School of Engineering and Applied Science (SEAS), at the prestigious George Washington University in Washington, D.C. He has taught cryptography at the FBI National Academy in Quantico, VA. Nichols is a professional speaker and regularly presents material on cryptography and INFOSEC at professional conferences, international technology meetings, schools, and client in-house locations.

Wireless Security is Professor Nichols' fifth title on cryptography and INFOSEC. *Defending Your Digital Assets Against Hackers, Crackers, Spies, and Thieves* was his best-selling book on the subjects of cryptography and INFOSEC countermeasures (McGraw-Hill Professional Publishing, 1999, ISBN: 0-07-212285-4). *Defending* is used as the graduate INFOSEC textbook at the George Washington University, James Madison University, Rowan College of New Jersey, Iowa State University, Eastern Michigan State University, and Yonsei University, Korea. Nichols' previous books, *The ICSA Guide to Cryptography* (McGraw-Hill Professional Books, 1998, ISBN: 0-07-913759-8) and *Classical Cryptography Course, Volumes I and II* (Aegean Park Press, 1995, ISBN: 0-89412-263-0 and 1996, ISBN: 0-89412-264-9, respectively), have gained recognition and industry respect for Nichols. Expect Nichols' next title, *INFOWAR and Terror* to hit the bookstores in early 2002.

Panos C. Lekkas

Mr. Lekkas is the Chief Technology Officer of TeleHubLink Corporation, and General Manager of its Wireless Encryption Technology Division. Prior to his association with THLC, Mr. Lekkas held several technical and business management positions with cutting-edge high-tech companies.

He was cofounder, President, and CEO of wireless Encryption.com, a startup company designing communications security integrated circuits, which began development of the HORNET™ security technology before being acquired by THLC. Prior to that, he was VP of Engineering for ACI, designing and simulating advanced communications security and digital signal processing microchips, and Director of Business Development with TCC, supervising new product definition and engineering for hardware encryption and key management systems used in high-speed government and commercial communications worldwide.

As Director of International Sales & Marketing with Galileo Corporation, Mr. Lekkas developed new applications and markets for advanced electro-optics and fiber optics technologies used in image-intensification systems for military night vision, heads-up displays for military avionics, and scientific detection systems used in mass spectroscopy and nuclear science. He was instrumental in the launch of their WDM, rare-earth-doped-fluoride fiber telecom amplifier technology and online fiber optic FTIR spectroscopy in Japan and Europe.

Mr. Lekkas originally joined Galileo to establish their European branch, which he ran successfully for several years. Before that, Mr. Lekkas spent several years at IBM, a company in which he has held many positions both in the United States and Europe. As Lead Systems Engineer in Austin, Texas, he helped introduce the RISC architecture that ultimately became the heart of the famous RS/6000 supercomputers. Earlier in his career, he was a VLSI design and EDA applications engineer with Silvar-Lisco.

Mr. Lekkas did graduate research in laser quantum electronics and semiconductor engineering at Rice University in Houston, Texas. He has two graduate degrees in electrical engineering, one in wireless communications and antennas and one in VLSI design. Mr. Lekkas has also pursued M.B.A. work in Corporate Finance at the Catholic University of Leuven in Belgium. His undergraduate degree in electrical engineering was earned at the National Technical University of Athens in Athens, Greece. He is a Licensed Professional Engineer in the European Union and a member of the *Institute of Electrical and Electronics Engineers* (IEEE) and of the *American Mathematical Society* (AMS).

Mr. Lekkas has worked in Europe, Japan, Asia, and the Middle East. He is fluent in 18 languages, including French, German, Dutch, Swedish, Finnish, Russian, Hebrew, Persian, Japanese, Urdu, Indonesian, Malay, Spanish, Hindi, Bengali, Korean, Mandarin, Chinese, and, of course, Greek. Married with four children, he lives in the Greater Boston area. In his precious free time, he is an obsessive classical music lover and enjoys studying world history, advanced linguistics, cognitive neuroscience, and airplanes.

The George Washington University Research Teams

The authors are indebted to the superb graduate students of Professor Nichols' EMSE 218 and EMSE 298, INFOSEC, Cryptography and Systems Applications Management and Policy courses from Fall 2000 to Summer 2001 at The George

Washington University, Washington DC, for their voluntary contributions to *Wireless Security*. It became a joint mission for these dedicated and talented people to help create a book that would serve as the first textbook for a new elective course in wireless security proposed for use in the *School of Engineering Management and Applied Science* (SEAS) INFOSEC Masters and Graduate INFOSEC Management Certificate programs. Graduate students were divided into teams and worked in co-operative rather than competitive mode. The research results were outstanding. The management of this talented team was a significant effort. Presented in alphabetical order are personal vitas of these talented people:

GARY L. AKIN is a program/project management official for acquisition, communications, satellite, and automated data processing systems with over 36 years in government service. Twelve of these years were spent abroad in Europe, Africa, and the Middle East. Currently, he is employed with the Defense Information Systems Agency, Information Assurance Program Management Office. He is a graduate of the Army Management Staff College, class 97-2, Certified level III, Army Acquisition Corps, and undergraduate studies in EE.

CHRISTOPHER T. ALBERT has 10 years of experience in the design, testing, and evaluation of shipboard machinery isolation systems. He designs shipboard automation systems for the U.S. Navy. He holds a B.S. degree in Electrical Engineering from Virginia Tech and a Master of Engineering Management from the George Washington University.

EUGENIO V. ARIAS is a Senior Information Operations planner with the Northern Virginia Operations Center of Syracuse Research Corporation. He is a retired United States Air Force Lieutenant Colonel and has served in the areas of Special Operations, Special Technical Operations, and Acquisition Logistics.

MICHAEL ARMEL is a recent engineering graduate from Penn State University. He is UNIX systems engineer and information security analyst for Lockheed Martin, Management & Data Systems.

EUPHRASIE ASSO-ATAYI is an Internal Information System Auditor at GEICO Corporation. Previously, she has served as an External Information System Auditor for various U.S. government agencies. She also has had Financial Audit experience with nonprofit organizations as well as state government agencies.

LINUS BAKER is an Information Assurance Analyst for Syracuse Research Corporation. He is a veteran of the United States Army where he served as a Military Intelligence Analyst. He holds a B.S. in Computer Science from Brewton-Parker College, and has five years experience in information systems security.

SCOTT BATCHELDER is a technology teacher at Stone Bridge High School and President of Ramsco, Inc. He holds a B.S.Ed. from George Mason University. His graduate work was completed at Stayer University and George Washington University.

JOHN R. BENTZ is a retired U.S. Navy Captain who served 28 years as a Naval Intelligence Officer and now works for a major defense contractor in the Washington, D.C., area. During his naval career he was involved in planning many naval operations that included heavy emphasis on electronic warfare.

CHERYL BILLINGSLEY has a B.S. in Information Systems from Strayer University. Ms. Billingsley is currently a Senior Systems Security Engineer with Mitre Corp.

MASTER SERGEANT ANDRÉ L. BROWN is a 20-year member of the United States Air Force and currently serves as the Directorate Security Manager for the Office of the Chairman of the Joint Chiefs of Staff. His experience includes risk management, emergency planning, and administering DoD Security Programs. He holds a B.S. degree in Economics from Strayer University and is a member of the Operations Security Professional Society.

ROCCO J. CALDARELLA is a senior policy analyst and program manager with SCITOR Corporation. He has an extensive background in the fields of Information Operations, Command and Control and Intelligence. He is a former *Senior Intelligence Service* (SIS) Officer and U.S. Navy Captain.

KRISTINE J. CAMARA is a graduate of Hartwick College, Oneonta, NY. She currently serves as a Senior Systems Analyst with Doctors Community Healthcare Corporation.

DAVID S. COLEY received his B.S./B.A. in computer information systems and finance from American University in Washington, D.C.. He is currently a Lotus Notes Messaging Engineer at United Messaging, Inc., where he is responsible for the development of messaging solutions based on Lotus Notes and Domino. Mr. Coley was formerly Lead Lotus Notes Engineer for Arnold & Porter in Washington, D.C., and has been in the industry for five years.

HILLARY P. COLEY, CPA, received her B.S./B.A. in accounting and finance from American University. She is currently a Senior Associate with Lane & Company, CPAs, where she is responsible for managing all services for nonprofit organizations.

STEPHEN DAVIS is a Senior Program Manager for Telos Corporation, where he provides consulting services in IT infrastructure planning and operations for the federal government. He holds a B.S. degree in Information Systems and Decision Science from Virginia State University and MCSE and CCNA Certifications.

LYNN DECOURCEY is the Manager of Information Systems for the *Software Productivity Consortium* (SPC) at the Center for Innovative Technology in Northern Virginia. Ms. DeCourcey is responsible for the provision, implementation, administration, evolution, and security of SPC's corporate information systems and operations infrastructure. She holds a B.A. in Politic Science from Ithaca College, and earned an M.S. in Information Management from Marymount University.

ALEX DOUDS spent the last two years as a database administrator for SAIC in Vienna, VA. He holds a B.S. in political science from James Madison University.

ANDREW DOWNEY received a B.A. from the University of Calgary. He is currently a project manager at Citizens for a Sound Economy, a nonprofit educational foundation. He writes on privacy and encryption issues.

LANCE C. DUBSKY earned a B.S. in Information Systems from the University of Maryland, an M.A. in International Relations from Creighton University, and is working on his Ph.D. in Engineering Management at George Washington University. A veteran of the U.S. Air Force, he has 20 years of experience in Information Systems Security, Physical Security, Risk Management, System Certification & Accreditation, Network Systems Administration, and Management. He presently serves as an Information Assurance Policy Analyst for the National Reconnaissance Office.

DONNA EBLING is a senior consultant with Booz • Allen & Hamilton, Inc. A member of the National Security Team, she works in the Risk Management Group, in the areas of training and security awareness. Her background includes a Master's of Education degree in Guidance and Counseling and over 10 years working as a defense contractor.

MIKE ENGLE is a Senior Systems Engineer with Lockheed Martin Technical operations in Springfield, VA, where he has spent the last year involved with secure networking. Mr. Engle holds a Bachelor's degree in Mechanical Engineering from Pennsylvania State University, University Park. He also has his MCP and is a pilot in the National Guard.

LT. MICHAEL FAWCETT has 22 years in the U.S. Coast Guard and is currently serving in the Architecture and Planning division of the Coast Guard's Chief Information Officer. He holds a B.S. in Telecommunications from SUNY Institute of Technology.

E. TIMOTHY FLYNN is a Senior Information Systems Engineer for Mitre Corp. Prior to this, Mr. Flynn gained fifteen years of experience as an Intelligence Officer for the Central Intelligence Agency. He holds a B.S. from Virginia Commonwealth University.

REGINALD J. FRANCE has been a Special Agent for the Department of Energy Office of Inspector General since April 1999. He holds a B.S. degree in Finance from State University of New York at Old Westbury.

CHRISTOPHER J. FUHS has over 17 years experience in the design and implementation of automated information systems. He holds an A.A. in CIS and a B.S. in Computer Networking. He is a Senior Network Engineer with Computer Sciences Corporation in Fairfax, VA.

JOHN GARDNER was a member of The National Security Study Group (USCNS/21) as Information Technology Manager, a Gunnery Sergeant, United States Marine Corps, Network Control Specialist/Computer Specialist, and Information Security Analyst and Communication Center Chief, Desert Storm. He holds a Bachelor of Science from Strayer University and multiple computer certifications in computer technology. He proudly served and was awarded the Navy Commendation Medal for Communication Watch Officer during Desert Storm, Desert Shield, and Cease Fire 1990, as well as Commanding General Certificate of Commendation for Communication Center Chief 1992.

BARRY GARMAN, B.S., M.A., specializes in IT and Internet projects. He has served on many committees for e-commerce, Internet security, and infrastructure. He is an active advisor to the Internet City, a multibillion dollar venture for e-commerce, VOIP, and WAP projects in Dubai, UAE.

REZA GHAFFARI has a B.S. in Electrical Engineering from The Citadel and also an M.S. in Electrical Engineering from University of Alabama at Birmingham. He works as an Information Security Officer for a Washington-based consulting firm.

WILL HOFF is a security specialist with WorldCom, Inc., in Northern Virginia. He has been involved with numerous security disciplines and positions during his 13 years in the industry.

TRISTAN HOLMES is a Security Engineer with five years in cable and wireless networking. He holds a Sociology/Criminology B.A. from James Madison University and various INFOSEC Certifications, including one from The George Washington University.

C. KEN HORTON, JR., has worked in the computer field for over 20 years. His experience includes consulting services, systems analysis, user requirements, and customer training in the mailing industry and factory automation. He currently works as a consultant for Zerone, on a project for the United States Postal Service.

FRED A. HUFNAGEL, III, is a Program Manager and Senior Systems Engineer with *Science Applications International Corporation* (SAIC). He has a B.S. from the *University of Virginia* (UVA).

AHMED M. HUSSEIN has worked for Enterprise Security Strategy Business Unit of Litton-TASC as Senior Member-Technical Staff for four years. He currently manages the Enterprise Security Strategic Distributed Laboratory. He holds a B.S. in Engineering Master of Science in Engineering Management from The George Washington University.

LEON JACKSON JR. serves as the Director, Information Technology Security, for the District of Columbia government. Prior positions include *Chief Information Officer* (CIO) for the District of Columbia Metropolitan Police department and as Chief of Staff, Office of the Chief Technology Officer, District of Columbia government. Prior to working in the Washington, D.C. government he served 21 years in the Navy as a Deep Sea Mixed gas diving officer and as an Explosive Ordnance Disposal Technician. He holds a B.S. in Operations Analysis (Computers & Statistics) from the U.S. Naval Academy, an M.P.A. from Troy State University, and an M.A. in Strategic Studies from the U.S. Naval War College.

MACKARTHUR JAMES has been the Program Manager for *Information Technology* (IT) Operations, Bureau of Economic Analysis. He retired from the United States Air Force after 22 years. He holds a B.S. in Computer Science from Strayer University.

KRIS KANE is a lieutenant colonel in the United States Air Force where she serves as a communications computer officer. She holds a B.S. degree in Physics from the University of Pittsburgh and an M.A.S. degree in Information Technology Management from the Johns-Hopkins University.

ANIL KATARKI is a Senior Associate with PricewaterhouseCoopers in their technology security practice in Tyson's Corner, VA. He has six years of the data communication industry experience and has spent the last three years working on information security. Anil holds a B.S. in Electronics and Communication Engineering from Karnatak University in India.

HELÉNE GROVE KENNY has over 30 years of diversified technical and professional management experience with demonstrated expertise in program assessments and strategic planning. She is a SAIC Project Manager. She is a University of Maryland graduate with a Graduate Certificate in Computer Systems Applications from the Center for Technology and Administration at the American University.

DAVID T. KERR is a Senior System Analyst for ANSER Inc. He is the Project Manager for Joint Tactical Radio System Architecture development. He has 30+ years experience in communications, command and control systems, electronic warfare systems, operations plans development, and flight operations. He holds an M.S. in Systems Management from The George Washington University and an undergraduate degree from University of Southern California.

DENNIS KEZER is a Senior Systems Administrator with the Applied Technology Systems Group of Science Applications International Corporation, an employee-owned company that is a key source of leading-edge technology solutions and integration for clients worldwide. He has been working in this capacity for five years. Prior to that he spent 26 years with the U.S. Army as an intelligence analyst and computer security specialist. He holds a B.S. from the University of Maryland. He has earned the MCSE and Comp-TIA Network + certifications. He is a recipient of the Bronze Star and a member of American Mensa.

KIM Y. KELLY has over eight year's broad range experience in Systems Engineering, Project Management, Business Analysis, Process Improvement, Systems Accounting, and Information Security. She holds a B.S. degree in Computer Information Systems and is pursuing a Master of Science Degree in Engineering Management from The George Washington University.

SUZANNE E. KIMBALL, a graduate of The George Washington University, has 20 years experience in the computer field in federal service and as a consultant with experience including Information Management Test Officer, System Designer/Analyst, Software Developer, and Data Manager.

SCOTT KISSER, Information Security Engineer for SAIC, specializes in vulnerability assessments, penetration testing, and security analysis. He holds a B.A. in Political Science from Denison University and certification from the SANS Institute.

STEPHEN KRILL JR., a Senior Program Manager at SAIC, has 12 years of progressive management and technology consulting experience, supporting government programs in counter-terrorism, critical infrastructure protection, and nonproliferation. His areas of technical expertise include risk management, decision analysis, environmental assessment, and emergency management. Mr. Krill holds a Master of Environmental Engineering and a Bachelor of Science in Nuclear Engineering.

STEVE LAZEROWICH holds an undergraduate degree from the University of Massachusetts. He has done graduate work at both Worcester Polytechnic Institute and Harvard University's Graduate School of Business. Mr. Lazerowich has held several sales and management positions in the IT industry and is currently employed by Entegrity Solutions Corporation.

CARLOS L. LEE is a Senior Systems Engineer with five years of experience on intrusion detection and systems analysis/design for Lockheed Martin. He received a B.S. degree from Winston-Salem State University in Computer Science/Math. He received an M.S. in Management Information Systems and a Systems Analysis/Design Masters Certificate from Bowie State University.

RAYMOND L. LEMANSKI holds the position of Deputy Director of Civilian Operations for Creative Technology, Inc., an IT consulting firm where he has worked for the past four years. He has over 11 years of IT experience focusing in the areas of software development, networking, network applications, and information security. He received his B.S./B.A. in Finance from the University of Delaware.

JOHN C. LEON (Major, U.S. Air Force Retired) is MIS Program Manager for *Science Applications International Corporation* (SAIC) and has 25 years experience. He is responsible for Technical and program implementation support to *Defense Intelligence Agency* (DIA), *Defense Threat Reduction Agency* (DTRA), and the *Defense Advance Research Program Agency* (DARPA). He holds an M.A. in Computer Resources and Information Management from Webster University, St. Louis, MO, and a B.A. in Economics from Virginia Military Institute, Lexington, VA.

ERIC MILLER is a Systems Security Engineer with five years of professional experience. He works on a unique corporate intrusion detection team for Lockheed-Martin. He holds a B.S. in Information Systems Management from University College, University of Maryland.

BENTON S. MIRMAN is the Information Security Officer for the International Finance Corporation, Washington, D.C.. He holds a B.S. from McGill University and an M.MSc., from the University of Ottawa.

MATTHEW I. MITCHELL has worked for *Science Applications International Corporation* (SAIC) for the last five years as an Information Security Engineer. He holds a B.S. in Industrial Technology from East Carolina University.

CRAIG NEWTON is a Naval Flight Officer currently assigned to the Office of Naval Intelligence Operations and Tactics Analysis Division. He is a graduate of the U.S. Naval Academy.

ANNA NOTEBOOM completed her undergraduate degree in Computer Science at Hawaii Pacific University. She is a field security manager with Nortel. She is currently enrolled in the Engineering Management graduate program at The George Washington University in Washington, D.C.

JOHN PARK is originally from Korea. He has a B.S. in Information Systems from Virginia Commonwealth University. Currently, he is a Network Engineer at ACS Government Solutions Group working on a U.S. Senate contract. He also holds a first-degree black belt in Tae Kwon Do.

GREG PARMA, with 30 years of combined business, military, and government experiences, currently works for the National Communications System. He is knowledgeable in the areas of Operational Testing and Evaluation, Developmental Test and Evaluation, Independent Verification and Validation, Systems Integration, Configuration Management, Network Design, Integrated Network Management, Operations Research, Project Management, Transmission Systems Engineering, Software Development, Modeling and Simulation, and Information Security. He holds a B.S. in Engineering from the University of Illinois, an M.B.A. in Marketing, and an M.S. in Computer Science from DePaul University.

JANKI PATEL is a lead Network Planning Engineer at Cable and Wireless with their Global Modeling and Simulation group in Reston, VA. Earlier, she was with MCI in Cary, NC, involved with customer support for Industry Data Exchange Association, a private electronic commerce group for electrical industry. Janki has a B.S. in Telecommunications from State University of New York, Institute of Technology at Utica/Rome.

STEVEN PECK is an analyst at an information assurance-consulting firm in Falls Church, VA. He has nine years of experience in policy analysis, contingency planning, *public-key infrastructure* (PKI), telecommunications, energy, and international security. He has an M.A. in International Studies from the University of South Carolina.

"MO" PETITT is a retired Naval Officer with over 25 years experience. During his career he served as a Navy S.E.A.L., salvage diver, and healthcare administrator. He is presently employed by DynCorp, IS, LLC to provide consultative services to the military on command and control and healthcare delivery issues. In 1999 he earned his Masters degree in the Management of Information Technology from Johns Hopkins University in Baltimore, Maryland.

MARK POIRIER has been the Deputy Director of Corporate Security for *Science Applications International Corporation* (SAIC) for over five years. He has worked for SAIC since 1996. Before SAIC, Mr. Poirier worked 10 years for the Central Intelligence Agency. He is an English major from Stonehill College in Easton, MA, and is currently pursuing a Masters degree in Information Security through The George Washington University.

ROYAL PURVIS has been a Sr. Systems Engineer with Veridian for the last three years. He holds a B.A. in Organizational Management from Warner Southern College, Lake Wales, FL, and a Masters Certificate in Information Security Management from The George Washington University.

JOSEPH H. SCHEPISI is a 30-year veteran of the United States Marine Corps and was a command and control, communications, computers, and intelligence, surveillance, and reconnaissance (C4ISR) specialist. He has a B.A. in Computer Science from East Carolina University, an M.B.A. with an emphasis in Human Resources Management from Hawaii Pacific University, and a *Masters in Education* (M.Ed.) with an emphasis in the *Master Teachers Program* (MTP) from Regent University.

RYAN SHAW is an Associate with PricewaterhouseCoopers. He has five years experience working on Information security. Mr. Shaw earned his undergraduate degree in Computer Information Systems from James Madison University.

MARTIN V. SHERRARD is a senior systems analyst with SCITOR Corporation with extensive background in information operations, naval aviation, electronic warfare, command and control, and intelligence systems. He recently retired as a Captain in the U.S. Navy.

MICHAEL A. SPANN is Technical Program Manager at Engineering System Solutions, specializing in implementing VPNs and DOD PKI systems. He has over 25 years in the IT field. Mr. Spann holds a B.S. in Computer Information Systems.

RONALD J. TOUSSAINT is a Senior Information Assurance Analyst on the staff of the Joint Chiefs of Staff (JCS/J-4, Logistics Information System Division). He is responsible for facilitating information assurance within the J-4 Directorate and the Global Combat Support System Family of Systems community.

BILL WASIELAK is an Associate with Booz • Allen & Hamilton. He leads a team of instructors designing and delivering INFOSEC awareness classes at the user, administrator, and manager levels. He has a Bachelors degree in Management and has served nine years in the U.S. Air Force.

JAY A. WILSON works for *Syracuse Research Corporation* (SRC). He is a Network Engineer with more than 27 years experience in communications and computer systems planning and systems security engineering.

ROBERT L. WYATT is an Information Technology manager for the U.S. Department of Defense. He has a B.S. in Computer Information Systems. He has served as a computer systems analyst/programmer and as an engineering manager in several different capacities.

ROBERT YOUNG holds a degree in Computer Science from New York Maritime College. He spent nine years on active duty, primarily with Special Warfare Units, and is a senior officer in the Naval Reserve/Merchant Marine Reserve. He currently works for Commander, Military Sealift Command.

KEITH ZIELENSKI has been with Booz • Allen & Hamilton, Inc., as a Senior Consultant with the National Security Team. He holds an undergraduate degree from George Mason University in Fairfax, VA.

Editor-at-Large

WALDO T. BOYD was not always owner-proprietor of Creative Writing (Pty). The U.S. Navy early on converted his typing skills into shipboard radio operating and maintenance. After attending Navy technical and engineering schools, he was appointed Warrant Radio Electrician and assigned to Sydney University (Australia) *Council for Scientific and Industrial Research* (CSIR) for research in aircraft, ship, and submarine *electronic countermeasures* (ECM). Waldo resigned his commission in 1947, and became technical writer and teacher of ECM to Air Force officers and service members during the Berlin Airlift. He spent nine years at Aerojet-General Rocket-Engine plants as manager of the technical manuals department, producing over 100 missile tech manuals on Titan and other missile systems. He has edited computer texts and undersea detection manuals under contract and has authored six books for Simon & Schuster, H. W. Sams, and others. He "retired" at age 62 and has continued to write and edit selectively.

Why Is Wireless Different?

Wireless communications is the process of communicating information in electro-magnetic media over a distance through the free-space environment, rather than through traditional wired or other physical conduits.[1]

Wireless messages move through the free-space environment on certain spectrum allocations, which are scarce, heavily regulated, and often unattainable resources.

Wireless devices such as cellular phones, *personal digital assistants* (PDAs), and pagers are inherently less secure than their wired counterparts. This is due in part to their limited bandwidth, memory, and processing capabilities. Another reason is that they send their data into the air where anyone with the technology can intercept it.

Wireless technology, by its nature, violates fundamental security principles. It does not ensure the identity of the user and the device (*authentication*), nor prevent the sender of the message from denying he or she has sent it (*nonrepudiation*).

Wireless technology is hardly new, but its application space is immature and quite possibly disruptive.

Introduction

Access to information and its means of distribution have been steeply accelerated through the Internet explosion of the 1990s. Initially the province of an exotic community of radio buffs and phone phreaks, cellular and Internet communications are now in common use among people of all ages, in all professions, with all sorts of interests.

This shift in the user base has changed society. Pervasive in business and increasingly preferred for personal communications, wireless appliances are well on their way to becoming ubiquitous personal accessories.[2] As successive generations of users are born into and grow up within a wireless world, the average individual in our society no longer regards such devices as luxuries or toys but as part of the public infrastructure—in other words, as an *entitlement*. The Internet too has ceased to be a medium of challenges and rules and has become instead a rather casual tool for retrieving and presenting information.[3] The laws of economics dictate that as usage becomes more common, it becomes more affordable.

Today wireless voice and data services are on the verge of attaining the economy of scale of true mass media, incurring all the desirable and undesirable cultural impact that characterizes mass media.[4] As we continue to change our technology, it begins to change us. It has, for instance, made us more reckless about what we say and to whom. A primary question for anyone looking at communications technology today is whether we intended its far-reaching effects along with its immediate conveniences. That question may not be what the practice of information security is about, but it is a context for many decisions about security. One question is "Can we?" Another is "Should we?"

Protecting the Means Of Communication

Infrastructure as infrastructure has always been vulnerable. In that respect wireless is no different (unless it turns out to be resistant to our efforts to secure it). Wireless has in fact fewer physical assets to protect, but, at the same time, there is no locked door on the airwaves so it is far easier to *hack*.

The primary responsibility for safeguarding communication infrastructure generally falls to the government and its military offshoots. In part this is because it is regarded as a public asset and enabler of our constitutional freedoms. In part this is because it is a necessary weapon in making war or defending against attack. The services government provides are in many respects regulatory, but in addition the products of legislation, the needs of law enforcement, and the national security must be upheld.

When it comes to wireless, note that the digital battlefield is a mobile battlefield. The military is not apt to perform its duties in the clear, using unprotected communications circuits. It is a highly distributed organization with highly synchronized missions. Any technology solution adopted by the government for defense purposes must be as mobile as possible. At the same time it must contain mitigation strategies for the use of potentially exploitable wireless technology. The military is often the originator of digital security measures that work, for the best of reasons—it needs the protection. The military, however, is not subject to the same budget constraints and risk tolerance factors that tend to govern business decisions about security. Where infrastructure is privately owned, it can more easily be safeguarded, and the threats it faces are less dire.

Protecting Privacy

Regulations are as likely to thwart privacy as to enforce it. Privacy always has been a concern for modern society. It is an inalienable right not to have people or government intrusion on its citizens. In recent years our sensitivity to privacy has grown even as we have embraced technology capable of infringing on some of the privacy we enjoy. Why is our awareness of privacy heightened? Maybe it's from movies about the long arm of the 'net, news reports about online fraud, or the suspicions awakened by learning what the FBI's powerful Carnivore program is capable of. *Carnivore* is a computer automated snooping tool developed by the FBI that is capable of intercepting and sorting out millions of text messages from many sources such as telephone conversations, Internet, e-mail, radio's and satellite downlinks to reduce to *intelligence take*. Federal law enforcement authorities have the ability to expand the use of the controversial FBI monitoring system to email, *short message service* (SMS), which is extremely popular overseas, and other text messages sent through wireless telephone carriers, as well as messages from their Internet service providers.[5]

Privacy advocates come out of the woodwork for good reason. Our virtual world of banking online, paying bills online, doing anything we want online comes at a price: *we have to share our vital information with virtual persons*. Credit card numbers, date of birth, mother's maiden name, buying habits, naughty Web sites visited—to name but a few—are no longer locked away in a file cabinet; they are open secrets in the virtual world. We know that privacy issues are not unique to wireless technology, but we're fascinated by the question of how wireless can change the way we view privacy.

You are now being asked to look at the expense and inconvenience of doing business beyond the confines of your offices. You must make a conscious decision to:

- Limit the unabashed use of wireless devices
- Add security/privacy via countermeasures or through the formulation of policies and procedures
- Risk interception by continuing to go anywhere and do anything over radio networks

Current laws are not effective in protecting private communications. Cordless phones can access others' conversations if both phones are tuned to the same channel. People regularly use scanners to legitimately or accidentally listen in without fear of consequences. Where it can't be proven that the intention was to eavesdrop, no action can be taken against that individual. Consumers submit credit card numbers over a cell phone, with no guarantee that they won't be picked up by interlopers and stolen. *There is no immediate solution.* To mitigate the threat of interception, some phone companies offer scrambling devices as an option, but this barrier is ineffective against the digitally adept individual who really wants to obtain your private information.

It's not necessarily just a matter of waiting for technological enhancements to come along. It's also a question of priorities. Thousands of cell phones are sold each year to satisfy the convenience society craves, but at the sacrifice of privacy. What if there were a method to *absolutely* ensure calling privacy? Would society be willing to pay more to ensure the privacy of phone calls? A variety of public encryption solutions (basically telephone/fax add-on boxes) have been suggested as a means to secure privacy, yet phone companies have not embraced the technology because it is expensive in practice and offers low *quality of service* (QoS). Society expects privacy, yet society does not demand it of wireless telephones. Encryption-enabled wireless telephones, whether offered by phone companies or manufacturers, is one viable solution and may prove to be cost effective in selected markets.[6]

Promoting Safety

Wireless growth has brought with it an unprecedented improvement in public safety. Consider two groups who are likely to have the least opportunity for equal access to communications: the inner city and rural communities. In the inner city, wireless communication is already cutting down on crime. Through *Communities on Phone Patrol* (COPP), the wireless industry has donated wireless phones and airtime to 13,000 neighborhood watch programs.[7][8] Those 13,000 patrols and other forms of street monitoring are making sidewalks safer—if not necessarily more private—by reporting 52,000 crimes and emergencies each month. Rural communities are also benefiting from wireless, primarily to gain access to services that wouldn't be profitable delivered over wired lines. That makes for more telemedicine, more e-learning, and more business opportunity. A good example is the 911 service which is the only way to help people in emergency situations in rural areas.

But the premium safety application is emergency response. Today in the United States more than 115 million wireless users are making over 140,000 emergency calls a day (Table 1-1). That's close to 96 calls per minute, yet 50 percent of the United States is still without emergency communications systems. *Wireless enhanced emergency service* (E9-1-1) is not just a way to penetrate underserved areas; even more interestingly, it's a way to find the victim. In Phase II of the federally mandated Wireless E9-1-1 compliance, wireless carriers will be required to "provide subscriber informa-

Table 1-1 Number of Wireless 9-1-1 and Distress Calls in the U.S.[10]

Year	Ending Subscribers	Annually	Monthly	Daily
1985	340,213	193,333	16,111	530
1986	681,825	649,659	54,138	1,780
1987	1,230,855	1,202,336	100,195	3,294
1988	2,069,441	2,382,855	198,571	6,528
1989	3,508,944	4,311,497	359,291	11,812
1990	5,283,055	5,914,653	492,888	16,205
1991	7,557,148	8,007,586	667,299	21,939
1992	11,032,753	12,641,470	1,053,456	34,634
1993	16,009,461	15,491,344	1,290,945	42,442
1994	24,134,421	17,910,620	1,492,552	49,070
1995	33,785,661	20,059,894	1,671,658	54,959
1996	44,042,992	21,659,967	1,804,997	59,180
1997	55,312,293	30,517,327	2,543,110	83,609
1998	69,209,321	35,805,405	2,942,910	98,097
1999	86,047,003	43,298,856	3,608,238	118,627
2000	115,000,000*			140,000*

Sources: Cellular Carriers Association of California, (CTIA) California Highway Patrol, New York State Police, and other state officials and wireless carriers.
*estimated

tion upon a bona fide request."[9] This means that a wireless company will provide the location of the caller to the 9-1-1 operator who requests it. (It also suggests that your location will become another datum you've agreed to share with the virtual world.)

The Personal and the Public

The continuing wireless revolution will lead to sweeping changes in how and when business gets done and how phone companies will serve consumers in the future. As wireless evolves from a secondary means of communication to our principal means of communication, it also changes how individuals conduct both their personal and business affairs.[11] The continuing wireless revolution will also lead to the graying of lines between personal and business relationships and transactions. There will be less need for duplicative equipment and systems in fixed locations; in fact, wireless will reduce the need to impose definitions of time and space between personal and professional. For instance, in the wired world, when workers leave their offices, their options to remain *tethered* are limited. They may pack up their portable computers and palm pilots and go. However, they do not pull out their cell phones, which are connected to the organization's PBX or communication server, and then go. They do not have access to the data and information on their personal computers until they tether it to the network again. In the wireless arena, 21st century workers will be afforded true mobility.

Wireless advances will require new strategies and business models to maintain some separation between wired and unwired, as well as to separate personal from professional. We want these distinctions precisely because the opportunity to work at anytime, from anywhere, and to communicate *untethered* via voice or data is so alluring. Wireless affords the capability to send, receive, and respond to business matters while on the road, at the bank, in line at the grocery store, at the park, at the gym, on a bike, in a boat, at the doctor's office, and so on. Wireless will ultimately add free time to our lives and thereby improve the quality of work life by offering truly flexible work hours. We can begin to integrate personal life with professional and experience less conflict between them.

Some hitherto personal realms are already becoming ad hoc offices. It is interesting to note that the hospitality industries have embraced 802.11 (the 1997 IEEE Standard Specification for Wireless Protocol for Homogeneous Systems) more quickly than corporate America. Many hotel chains now offer wireless access to a *local area network* (LAN) upon check-in. Airports, restaurants, and coffeehouses are increasingly offering wireless access to the Internet and LANs for use by their patrons and customers.

The flip side of all this access is that what used to be personal information becomes publicly available. What does privacy mean to us when the personal is no longer inviolate? This debate is crystallizing around the issue of location-based services. Competing groups' battle to reconcile privacy and safety in wireless technology. Privacy advocates fear that location will open up a host of problems. Adam Keiper, president of the Center for the Study of Technology and Society in Washington, D.C., says that while the intent of location technology may be admirable (to provide distress assistance, for instance), the implications demand that we also place limits on who gets access to information about people's physical location. Keiper says marketers and advertisers would relish consumer-location information. So would law enforcement. And if the cops can use it, why not the criminals? According to Keiper, location technology is still too immature to forecast all possible uses and abuses of location technology, although he predicts that there will be at least a couple of "egregious abuses" of location technology in the next decade.[12]

Jim Schlichting, deputy chief of the FCC's Wireless Telecommunications Bureau, says that aside from Enhanced 9-1-1, setting policies that protect consumer privacy is the major regulatory role the government will play in this arena. One of the first steps was amending the Wireless Communications and Public Safety Act of 1999 to include location in its definition of proprietary network information.[13]

Shaking Up the Status Quo

Wireless communication is changing by how and what information can be readily exchanged by whom. Countries without a wired infrastructure are able to establish communication with few resources; countries with outdated or minimal wired infrastructures have an option of allowing technology markets to expand into the area by means of service provision, both in hardware and software. In addition, the industry is developing new uses for voice communication, wireless interaction with other technologies, wireless Web interaction, and e-commerce in the form of business-to-business, government-to-citizen, business-to-customer, and customer-to-customer transactions.

Although the growth and pervasiveness of wireless appears to be inevitable, the path and speed of growth of this technology is not so predictable. Current wireless communication systems use radio waves of many differing frequencies. Wireless communication is facilitated by transmit and receive antenna facilities, which may be within a single building or separated by thousands of miles, as with satellites. Wireless communication interchanges traffic with wired or physical communications networks. The closer the wireless antennas are from user to user, the lower the power requirements, yielding greater volume use of limited radio spectrum. This generally narrowband cellular capacity is expanded by putting up more antennas, creating minicells and microcells, or by launching more satellites.[14] The exchange of information may occur one-way, or two-way, or be limited-party interactive communications. Another of the diverse possibilities is the use of sound waves such as sonar and infrared signals, including laser signals for intersatellite relays in space.[15]

The advantage of radiating signals into a free-space environment is that anyone can receive the signal in the broadcast area whether at a fixed location or a mobile one. This advantage means new links can be established at a moment's notice since physical links do not have to be installed. *Wireless does not conserve frequency.* It is for this reason that so-called cellular transmissions have become important; the signal is low in power or flux density and is confined to a small zone. Thus, the use or consumption of the assigned frequency is geographically limited to a small area. Creation of many small zones for frequency use in wireless applications allows for higher levels of spectrum use by duplicating the frequencies used within the overall service area. This in turn effectively boosts the capacity and effective bandwidth of wireless systems.[16]

It is important to note that *intensive reuse concepts* are critical to the future growth and expansion and security of wireless service. The two most important factors with regard to the future development of wireless communications are likely to be *hyperintensive frequency reuse techniques* and *advanced digital compression techniques.* New and innovative reuse techniques in the field of satellite communications may prove critical to our ability to deploy large numbers of geosynchronous, medium earth orbit and low earth orbit satellites needed to respond to new market demands in the future.[17]

The proliferation of wireless technologies is not only offering competition to traditional communications services; it is also providing modern telecommunications to the developing areas of the world. The burgeoning types of wireless infrastructure being implemented or on the horizon offer a wide range of voice, data, image, and video services. While wireless services cannot currently meet the exploding demand for high-bandwidth Internet services, wireless users will, before long, easily eclipse the number of traditional narrowband wireline telephony users. Eventually, broadband wireless carriers may be able to compete effectively with cable TV and established telecommunications carriers, offering a full multimedia compliment of voice, data, image, video, and Internet access faster than any service available today.[18]

Understanding Wireless Forecasts

Wireless communications is unlikely to replace traditional wired networks, but there are numerous areas and applications in and for which it can be useful. Wireless has not yet matured to the point of being suitable for a data-intensive corporate environment; however, this has not prevented a wireless entrepreneurial spirit and corporate embrace to implement wireless.

According to the CTIA, wireless mushroomed in the U.S. through the 1990s from 2.7 million subscribers in June 1989 to over 76 million users in June 1999. Many analysts predict that the number could more than double in the next five years. Over the same period, estimated for worldwide cellular *personal communications services* (PCS), subscribers range as high as 1.1 billion users. This would represent a telecommunications density of 18 percent of the world's population.[19] With this kind of proliferation, it is unlikely that most consumers will choose to limit their wireless usage in the absence of effective security. Consensus (at least as expressed in actions) has it that while security is a problem for wireless, it is not a showstopper. Nearly every list you see of hurdles for wireless to overcome includes security, often under the guise of consumer confidence. Businesses know that the price differential between good security and barely adequate security can be millions of dollars for each increment. Under these conditions, changing consumer behaviors on the phone may be our direct route to safer communications in the short term.

Reasonable Degrees of Security

If *Chief Information Officers* (CIOs) are going to make policy, manage enterprise solutions, determine best practices, and carry out strategic planning, they first have to weigh risk. In the midst of a swirl of enthusiasm for new technology and the desire to implement immediately, someone must maintain a level head. Most often the question to be answered is not *can* we implement, but *should* we? *Level of Risk* in its simplest terms equates to *Threat* times *Vulnerabilities* divided by *Counter-measures applied* times *Impact*.[20] Although attributing precision to wireless security or any security of an information system is naïve in its purest sense, much can be done to reduce the level of risk to an acceptable security level. If a business case can be made for the implementation of wireless communications technology, a concerted effort must be made in the budgeting, design, and implementation phase to build security in.

Policy provides the foundation, rules, and guidelines for business processes with respect to system development, configuration management, access management, and so forth. Business and government have only recently faced the weighty task of deciding what to allow in their facilities and how wireless technology will be used. *Information Technology* (IT) staffs can attest to the spike of system problems they face each winter just after the holidays, when Christmas gadgets show up at work with executives, engineers, and technocrats, investigating their toys in a high-speed computing environment. This kind of purchasing and implementation decision typifies decisions made in the absence of policy. Employing new technology must take into consideration the safeguards necessary to protect corporate assets. For security managers, compromising security is not an option, yet detecting and disallowing the use of personal devices or software has proven to be equally difficult. Added to the difficulty of maintaining a secure computing environment, introducing extra policy technologies nearly always increases the difficulty of supporting the environment by reducing its degree of standardization.

Several organizations and agencies in government are working on policy addressing wireless use. Proponents of wireless tout increased productivity through access to unlimited information not dependent on a worker's whereabouts. Security analysts are not so sure how to weigh benefits against risks. The question, again, is not can we, but should we? The creation of the Internet has enabled hackers, crackers, spies, and thieves—in many cases with the benefit of anonymity—to challenge the security of persons, companies, and municipalities. The Internet is the battlefield. The attacks are real and come in the form of malicious code such as viruses, worms, and Trojan horses. Web sites are often takeover targets for those seeking publicity or revenge, and frequently those attempts prove successful. The Internet is a minimally regulated entity, and much of its critical infrastructure remains minimally protected.

The Internet and wireless are so closely related that whatever affects the Internet in one way or another affects the wireless environment. As wireless and Internet environments become truly interoperable, the threats and vulnerabilities affecting the Internet will face wireless networks in equal measure. We acknowledge the wireless challenges and begin our explorations into securing them.

Regulatory Environments and Issues

Over the next 20 years, the regulations and policies that evolve will shape the development of the wireless industry. Some of the areas that these regulations will address include:[21]

- Differences between public and private networks
- Differences between regulating content for broadcast networks and the Internet
- Differences between national and international rules for data protection
- Spectrum pricing and allocation schemes
- Levels of security

The questions of data protection, spectrum pricing, and security are especially important to the continued growth and health of the wireless communications industry. Security may become the most crucial of the regulatory issues facing the wireless industry over the next two decades. Consumer confidence in online transactions will be predicated on the perception of security in the wireless medium. Security includes not only the protection of data but also protection from monitoring. Distaste for surveillance is widely believed to be a potential inhibitor of wireless network usage.[22]

Security-Related Regulations

As members of the wireless industry strive for advantage in the marketplace, competitors are beginning to share some resources as a means of reducing operating costs. While lowering the costs passed on to the consumer is considered good for business, sharing resources poses problems for regulatory organizations with respect to security and redundancy. The primary factors that must be considered are:[23]

- Wireless communication, because it does not require physical connectivity, has a better chance of surviving natural disasters such as hurricanes, floods, earthquakes, volcanoes, and tornadoes.
- Wireless transmissions are easier to intercept than those running over fiber or wireline connections. Although fiber is also subject to interception, it is a harder hack than wireless, and the public has a perception that physical connections afford an inherent amount of protection. Digital encryption techniques can be used to protect the wireless transmissions, but public concerns about privacy will need to be addressed.
- The use of fiber and wireless technology are among the best available alternatives for ensuring high levels of system availability.
- The U.S. *Department of Defense* (DoD), the *National Telecommunications Information Administration* (NTIA), and the industry-created national policy and regulatory guidelines for backup capabilities and the restorability of U.S. telecommunication services. These guidelines may require strengthening and must be updated as the technology evolves.

If the industry adopts the shared resources model wholesale, it could create single points of failure for large portions of the telecommunications infrastructure. Government policies and regulations must ensure there is adequate redundancy for the infrastructure.

Security-Related Market Factors

Another driving force for the future of wireless communications is the new application space. Currently, wireless applications are concentrated in mobile Internet, mobile commerce, mobile entertainment, and mobile location.

Quite possibly the most critical element in the growth of *wireless local area networks* (WLANs) will be the development and implementation of wireless security measures to ensure the confidentiality, integrity, and availability of consumer communications. In other respects the outlook for WLAN technology is bright. It is recognized as a viable and often cheaper alternative to hardwired *local area networks* (LANs). In the United States, the WLAN market is nearing $1 billion in revenues according to the *Wireless Ethernet Compatibility Alliance* (WECA).[24] Industry improvements in the areas of cost, management, and speed have greatly contributed to WLAN success. A study conducted by the *Wireless LAN Alliance* (WLANA) demonstrated that installation costs are usually recouped in less than 12 months, but security is still seen as problematic. In response WLAN vendors joined to create the *Wireless Equivalent Privacy* (WEP) encryption scheme to protect WLAN data transfers. Originally, WLANA projected a tenfold jump in the number of WLAN users by 2003, from 2.3 to 23 million. However, the cryptography basis of WEP protocol was decimated in two separate studies, one by internationally known Adi Shamir and Itsik Mantin of the Weitzmann Institute in Israel and the other by AT&T Lab researchers headed by Aviel Rubin at Florham Park, NJ.[25] This has had a chilling and far-reaching effect on the WLAN industry.

The location services market segment is expected to experience slow growth over the next few years, in large part because of concerns about how the inherent privacy issues will be addressed and received by the consumer population. In late 2000, the *Cellular Telecommunications & Internet Association* (CTIA) joined with the Wireless Advertising Association to propose a set of wireless privacy and spamming guidelines to the FTC. One framework for this arena is known as *locate, inform, save, alert* (LISA). LISA is already employed for tracking cars, trucks, and goods in transit. The extent to which this functionality can be implemented to allow tracking of individuals is questionable at this time.[26]

Guidelines for Security Measures

The very nature of most wireless communications makes security a significant factor that must be understood and addressed for wireless communications to achieve its vast potential. Today, the majority of wireless communications use the RF spectrum. Since the signals are being broadcast over the airwaves, anyone in the vicinity with a receiver tuned to the proper frequency can intercept a communication. Cell phones are really just small radios that work on a particular subset of the RF spectrum and are subject to interception and interference from a number of other RF sources. This inherent porosity will not be acceptable as we move into the world of real mobile commerce and the convergence of multiple devices into a single personal communicator.

Security is the combination of processes, procedures and systems used to ensure the confidentiality, integrity, or availability of information. *Confidentiality* is the protection of information from unauthorized readers. *Integrity* protects the data content from unauthorized modification. *Availability* is the process of ensuring that a system or data will be accessible when needed.[27] Within this model, some of the current security challenges for wireless devices that require security measures include lost and stolen devices, insider attacks, man-in-the-middle attacks, and device cloning.[28] Additional security concerns include viruses, denial of service attacks, enhanced radio interception devices, and protection of wireless LANs.

In general terms, a secure mobile solution is one with the following functionality:[29]

- **Authentication**   Validating; the identity of the user
- **Encryption**   Shutting out eavesdroppers on a data conversation
- **Access Control**   Ensuring that users see only the information for which they are authorized
- **Theft and employee termination**   Centrally disabling devices when the device falls into the hands of an unauthorized user

Mobile commerce customers must develop a good degree of trust that their communications and data are being adequately protected before they will embrace the technology. For example, many people use the Internet to research product information, but they do not trust the Internet enough to transmit their payment information. This is true even though many if not most credit card companies guarantee the safety of credit card information and that the consumer has only a $50.00 liability. One of the issues with Internet commerce is authenticity, and the same concern translates readily to wireless commerce. Simply put, consumers want to know that they are connected to whom they thinks is connected. Additionally, they'll demand significant traceability for inappropriate use of networks.[30]

Let's look briefly at some major security initiatives now underway in the wireless arena—*Wired Equivalent Privacy* (WEP), *Wireless Applications Protocol* (WAP), and Bluetooth.

The goal of the WEP model is to prevent casual eavesdropping or unauthorized data modification.[31] WEP uses an RC4 40-bit stream cipher to encrypt and a 32-bit CRC. Unfortunately, according to a paper published by the ISAAC, WEP has a faulty algorithm, and several specific attacks are noted, that can be mounted against WEP.[32] The problem with the algorithm is that RC4 is subject to keystream reuse, which violates a prime precept of any encryption scheme. The attacks against WEP described in the paper include collecting frames for statistical analysis, use of SPAM to decrypt frames, and bit flipping to modify messages.

A good deal of effort is being invested in improving the effectiveness of WEP. Modifications include a transparent upgrade to 128 bits and a highly secure upgrade mode based on the *Advanced Encryption Standard* (AES).[33] Newer versions will also have improved authentication and authorization utilities.

The development of WAP security products is mandated by the number of WAP products for wireless Internet users—approximately 25 million of them worldwide.[34] The WAP security model has four components:[35]

- *Wireless Transport Layer Security Protocol* (WTLSP) provides confidentiality, integrity, and authenticity.
- *WAP Identity Module* (WIM) provides credential portability and client authentication.
- WMLScript CryptoLibrary facilitates cryptographic applications to transmit, store, forward or receive signed data from clients.
- *WAP Public Key Infrastructure* (WPKI) is a wireless implementation of PKI techniques.

The idea of a personal communicator that can phone, compute, calendar, and entertain is quite attractive. But how many people will use such a data-intensive device if anyone with the necessary equipment can retrieve, modify, add, and delete the information it contains without the owner's knowledge? This is especially an issue with the pending explosion in use of Bluetooth-enabled devices and applications. (Bluetooth is covered in detail in a future chapter.) Where a device can also be used to locate its owner, consumer concern about privacy and security converge. By October 2001, the U.S. Federal Trade Commission required all cell phones manufactured to have the ability to pinpoint the location of a cell phone within 50 meters.[36] While this is a desirable feature when there is a need to call emergency services, it may also mean that others may be able to track your movements with less benign intent.

Cellular Networks and Bearer Technologies

In January 1917, German foreign minister Arthur Zimmermann sent an encrypted Western Union telegram to his embassy in Mexico City. The message was intercepted and successfully cryptanalyzed by British codebreakers, revealing a potential Mexican and German alliance supposed to culminate in Germany "returning" the lands of New Mexico, Texas, and Arizona to Mexico. Shortly after the British delivered this message to President Woodrow Wilson, the United States declared a state of war against Germany.[37]

During World War II, *National Security Agency* (NSA) decryption of Japanese communications led to American naval victories at Midway, the Coral Sea, and the Solomon Islands. Less than two years later, NSA eavesdroppers picked up the flight schedule of Admiral Yamamoto, commander-in-chief of the Japanese Navy and the man who authored the Pearl Harbor attack. American fighters subsequently shot his plane down. In the Atlantic, the Allies' decryption of German communications led to devastation of the U-boats, which had been wreaking havoc on Allied naval assets. Another NSA project, Vern, intercepted and decrypted Soviet diplomatic intelligence cables from 1942 to 1946. That project exposed Russia's vast American spy network and led to the arrests and convictions of Julius and Ethel Rosenberg, who had supplied the Soviets with intelligence information on the atomic bomb and details of jet aircraft, radar, and rockets.

These historic incidents and events, all premised on wireless security holes, have led us up to and into the world of wireless communications. Modern wireless communications is viewed in first-, second-, third-, and fourth-generation technologies. With enhancements emphasizing security, which is thwarted mostly by the military and government agencies, and customer service demands, telephony usage rates have dramatically increased with telegraphy considerably falling off.[38]

To begin to understand what drove the development of several distinct generations of wireless technology, we need to look at the infrastructure upon which it operates. Microwave and satellite communications are without wires, but those technologies are considered to be high-speed, network backbone, or access technologies that are point-to-point, point-to-multipoint, or broadcast in nature.

Typical transmission ranges are estimated to be as follows:

Cordless Phones	Several Hundred Feet
Cellular Phones	Several Thousand Feet
Citizen Band Radios	Several Miles
FM Radio Station	20 to 100 Miles
Television Station	One Hundred Miles or more

The term *cellular* is used extensively to describe wireless communication devices. A cell is defined as "a geographic area or zone surrounding a transmitter in a telephone system."[39] You can think of a cell as a kind of predetermined broadcast area within which a signal can be transmitted without producing interference in other cells. With higher frequency technologies, power consumption requirements for a signal to traverse distances drops proportionately. Cellular phones in themselves have the capability to transmit a few thousand feet at best. Through the use of cells, with underlying cellular switching technology, thousands if not millions of mobile users maintain their conversations across cell boundaries. This is a prima facia reason why security of wireless is difficult.

Bell Telephone conceived the cell design in 1947, when engineers arranged arrays of numerous low power send-and-receive antennas deployed to increase the effective subscriber areas almost without limit (Figure 1-1). Cellular design allows each frequency to be reused in nonadjacent cells. Cells generally fall into three possible categories: *macrocells, microcells,* and *picocells* (Figure 1-2). As the cells shrink, the advantages of frequency reuse increase significantly. However, costs of deploying multiple cellular networks increase dramatically, and the difficulty of switching traffic between the mobile users and their phones also increases considerably. Nevertheless, the increase in traffic-handling capacity (and attendant security problems) can be very significant, with an associated increase in revenue.[40]

Macrocells cover the largest service areas and in theory by themselves might only support 12 channels and only 12 simultaneous conversations. Using a typical seven-cell reuse pattern (Figure 1-3), each cell covers a radius of roughly 11 miles. No improvement is seen here; only 12 simultaneous conversations can be supported.

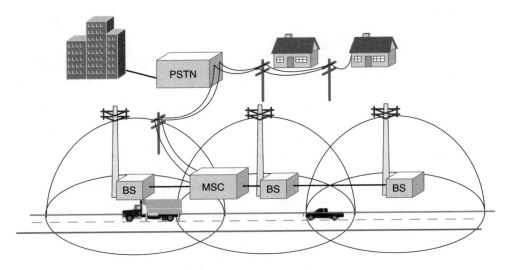

1-1 Cellular network: Switching a user between different cell sites. [41]

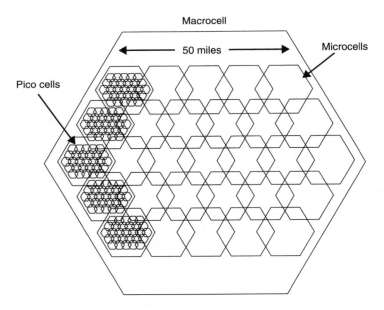

1-2 Cellular example: Picocells, microcells, and macrocells.[42]

The reason is due to the fact that cells must overlap. Therefore, conversations on the same frequency channels in adjacent cells cannot interfere with each other.

Microcells cover a somewhat smaller area comparable to a several-mile radius. Employing a seven-cell reuse pattern and dividing the macrocell into seven microcells, a reuse factor of 27 = 128 is realized. Considering the potential

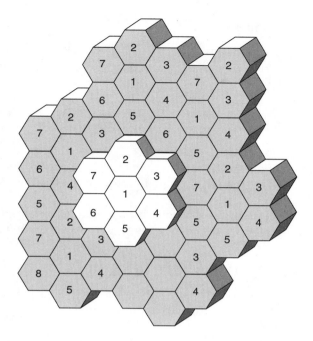

1-3 Seven-cell reuse pattern.

for 12 simultaneous conversations per microcell, we can now support 1,536 simultaneous conversations.

Picocells cover a very limited area of only a few blocks, a stadium, or an urban area. Continuing to consider the seven-cell reuse pattern, with each cell covering a radius of approximately one-half mile, the reuse factor climbs to 514. We now have the capability to support thousands of simultaneous conversations from the initial 12 channels.[43]

We can also compare this reuse factor to current landline telephone number structure. While it would remain somewhat simple to dial your boss's extension while at work, a four number extension would not serve on a global basis. This cellular structure was designed to supply many devices, such as computers, faxes, and cellular phones, with numbers—and this functionality unfortunately portends security issues for the user.

Macrocell = Area Code 10 digits 10,000,000,000 Combinations (123) 456-7890
Microcell = City Code 7 digits 100,000,000 Combinations (XXX) 123-4567
Picocell = Extension
　　　　　　　Code 4 digits 10,000 Combinations (XXX) XXX-1234

The technologies that distinguish the various generations in Table 1-2 are the bearer technologies that transmit wireless communications. A generation plateau

Table 1-2 Technologies to Generation

Generation	Architecture	Example Technologies
1st [1G]	Analog	AMPS, N-AMPS, NMT, TACS, FDMA
2nd [2G]	Digital	CDMA, TDMA, GSM
3rd [3G]	2nd Generation Digital	SMS, EDGE, GPRS, USSD, WCDMA, WATM
4th [4G]	3rd Generation Digital	Builds on CDMA, TDMA, GSM

was created to identify dramatic improvements and changes to technology within each sequential step, and can prove useful in tracking wireless security motivations and measures.

Currently most of the world is attempting adaptation to third-generation technologies or at an intermediary between second and third generations (Figure 1-4).

First-Generation Wireless (1G)

There are many cellular standards currently in use, both analog and digital. Analog cellular standards were the original approach and are best categorized as *Generation 1* (1G) wireless systems. Although the future clearly belongs to digital wireless systems, 3G and beyond, analog systems are still widely deployed, are still the incumbent technology, and serve a vital function, especially in largely undeveloped areas. Generation 1 analog systems consist of AMPS, N-AMPS, NMT, and TACS. All use *frequency modulation* (FM) for radio transmissions.[45,46,47,48,49]

Second-Generation Wireless (2G)

The single most significant problem with first-generation cellular communication systems is found in its lack of resourcefulness when one considers the minute frequency bands allocated for cellular phone usage. When an analog call is being placed, it locks onto and uses a selected frequency band until that call is terminated. While this inefficiency grew to overwhelm the analog infrastructure, a much-needed improvement was then being sought in an improved digital system. Digital cellular systems took advantage of this lack of resourcefulness by chunking the voice into selected fragments of frequency, time, and code for transmission in a more efficient means. These access technologies, *Time Division Multiple Access* (TDMA) and *Code Division Multiple Access* (CDMA), make up the infrastructure of most of the digital wireless communication systems today. *Packetizing* analog radio signals for digital transmission effectively uses the channels' bandwidth potential, see Figure 1-5.

Communication networks also take advantage of the concept of *Demand Assigned Multiple Access* (DAMA). DAMA enables the possibility for multiple devices to share access to the same network on a demand basis—that is, first come, first served. A number of ways exist to access a wireless network; these technologies are replete with their security strengths and weaknesses.[50]

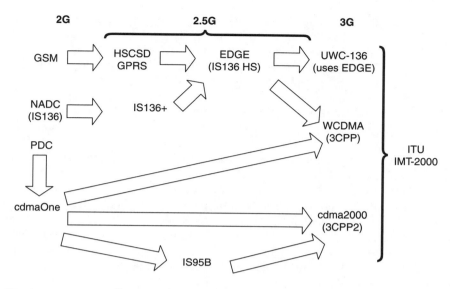

1-4 Wireless Transitions.[44] (Courtesy of CMP Media Diagram)

Analog Call

xxxxxxxxxxRadioSilencexxxxxxxxxxxxxxxRadioSilencexxxxxxxxxxxxxxxxxxx
xxxxxxxxx

30 kHz of Channel Bandwidth—Sinusoidal

Digital Call

xxxxxx,yyyyyyy,xxxxxx,zzzzzzzz,yyyyyyy,xxxxxxx,zzzzz,yyyyy,zzzzzz,xxxxx
xxxx

30 kHz of Channel Bandwidth—Sinusoidal as digital steps

x = data from cellular user #1

y = data from cellular user #2

z = data from cellular user #3

1-5 General Analog vs. Digital Concept.

Digital cellular systems can ordinarily accommodate several wireless users simultaneously on the equivalent in a single user analog channel. The actual amount, typically 3 to 20 users, is characterized by the access technology used in the network, either that of a *time division* or *spread spectrum* variant. This significant increase in user capacity is accomplished in compressing and digitizing of the voice information into packets of time and code, allowing the communication channel to be divided into subchannels that can each serve an individual user for a more efficient use of the wireless network.[51]

The first successful second-generation wireless technology deployment was that of the TDMA-based *Global Systems for Mobile Communications* more commonly referenced as GSM. The Pan-European countries were the initial supporters of GSM and pushed this technology as a standard. GSM development began in the early 1980s and was recognized by The European *Conference of Postal and Telecommunications Administrations* (CEPT) in 1987 as a digital wireless standard with successful infrastructure deployment in 1991.[52] GSM shares the available channel time and bandwidth allowing up to eight users per single 200 kHz band. GSM is not backward compatible with the previous analog infrastructure. With the enormous growth results seen by the analog markets, American industry also sought a way to more efficiently use the limited resources and airwaves regulated by the FCC. As early as 1988, the American wireless industries realized the situation that they would soon be in. Since they were reluctant to accept GSM, a new technology was desired that would increase network capacities by a magnitude of at least 10-fold. With the backing of a new technology marketed and perfected by Qualcomm, the American providers were promised what they desired in a standard. Though *cellular division multiple access* (CDMA) did not have the maturity and years of hardening that GSM/TDMA had, it had been successfully used in military operations. While the world might have been a simpler place if the American service providers had backed and deployed GSM/TDMA networks, Americans chose CDMA, with more growth potential than GSM had offered, along with the promise of backward compatibility.

With the advent of digital wireless technologies, service providers often try to multiply the available capacity of their networks, offer customers lower rates, improve call clarity, improve call security and most importantly generate greater revenue potentials for themselves. Many of the vendors began to find ways of limiting the wasted airtime usage by adding *Digital Signal Processors* (DSPs) to filter background noise and other ambiences that would normally be transmitted in the analog world. This would allow in itself an increase in system capacity by permitting more chunks of digitized packets to traverse the airwaves more efficiently.[53]

Most consumers remain uninformed to the fact that analog cellular conversations were as easy to listen to as a *Citizen Band* (CB) radio conversation. Any owner of a 900MHz-band scanner manufactured roughly before April 1994 was fully capable of receiving and eavesdropping on any analog cellular phone conversation, and at least fragments of any digital cellular phone call.[54] Cellular phone calls are vulnerable to being intercepted as they traverse the air between the user's phone and a nearby microwave transmission and receiving tower. At this point the call is transferred to a wired route and tied into the public switched telephone network. The digital signals are much more complex and encryption is often employed to make conversations unintelligible without knowledge of the secret key. The FCC became aware of this problem and ordered manufacturers—namely Uniden and Motorola, the largest manufacturers of these products—to engineer countermeasures into their products to lock out these bands.[55]

There have been several reported incidents involving the use of scanners, including some that exposed the most intimate of conversations of public figures. In 1995, a retired bank manager in Oxford intercepted and taped a cellular phone call placed between Princess Diana and close friend James Gilbey, who called her "my darling Squidge." The entire 23-minute conversation was transcribed and published in supermarket tabloid *The Sun*. Prince Charles was also embarrassed by the disclosure of recorded cellular conversations; in one, he discussed his sex life with his then mistress Camilla. In 1996, House Speaker Newt Gingrich had been conversing with members of the Republican congressional leadership. Unknown to him, he was being taped and found his call released to the media. In New Hampshire, an antinuclear activist picked up calls made from the operations room of the Seabrook nuclear plant, including one where an employee stated, "I've got a bad feeling about these valves."[56]

At hearings of the U.S. House of Representatives Commerce Committee's telecommunications subcommittee, the chairman of the committee, Billy Tauzin, demonstrated how easy it was to modify a scanner and pick up a phone call. Bob Grove, whose company offers such modification services, testified that of the 10 million legal scanners sold in the United States, a few hundred thousand had been estimated to be altered to intercept cellular frequencies.[57]

Radio Shack, which was perhaps the largest merchant of scanner related products, was required to recall all their on-shelf scanners and to perform modifications disallowing them to listen in on cellular conversations. Once corrected the products were redistributed to the stores with an orange dot to signify they had been modified. Some if not most of these modifications were lackluster; one mobile model manufactured by Uniden for Radio Shack required simply a jumper to be clipped to reestablish the cellular band scanning capabilities.

While today's designs do not offer a simplistic approach to being modified, plans are globally available to any user with soldering skills and desire by accessing forums on this subject on the Internet. With a device called a Celltracker, an eavesdropper can zero in on the conversations occurring over any particular cellular phone within a nearby cell site.

Spread Spectrum

Spread spectrum communications are a means of spreading information signals, typically digital signals, so the frequency bandwidth of the radio channel is much larger than the original information bandwidth. There are actually various forms of spread spectrum communications. The most prevalent forms of spread spectrum radio include *frequency hopping multiple access* (FHMA) and *code division multiple access* (CDMA).[58] Spread spectrum radio spreads the bandwidth of the transmitted signal over a set of radio frequencies that is much wider than required to support the narrowband transmission. It commonly is known as *wideband radio* technology. Spread spectrum primarily uses two techniques: *Direct Sequence* (DS) and *Frequency Hopping* (FH). *Direct Sequence Spread Spectrum* (DSSS) is a packet radio technique in which a narrowband signal is spread across a wider carrier frequency band. The information is organized into packets, each of which transmits across the wideband carrier frequency in a redundant manner. A *PseudoNoise* (PN), 10-bit code sequence for each packet known in advance by the transmitter and receiver, is used to support, prevent interference, secure, and identify multiple transmissions against a noisy background. *Frequency Hopping Spread Spectrum* (FHSS) involves the transmission of short *bursts* of packets over a range of frequency channels within the wideband carrier, with the transmitter and receiver hopping from one frequency to another based on a carefully choreographed *hop sequence*.[59] This hop sequence generally is under the control of the base station antenna structure. The individual sequence uses a particular frequency for a minute instance of time, typically less than 400 ms in the United States. This instance may be the only time interval required to transmit the data packet or even a single data bit. Large numbers of other transmissions will typically share the same frequencies simultaneously, each using a different hop sequence. However, the potential remains, for the overlapping of data packets. The receiving end has the ability to distinguish each packet in a stream by reading the prepended 10-bit code allowing competing signals to be filtered out.[60]

Code Division Multiple Access (CDMA)

Qualcomm defines CDMA as a digital wireless technology that uses a spread spectrum technique that spreads a signal across wide-frequency bands.[61] CDMA offers increased system capacity, increased voice quality, fewer dropped calls, and IP data services. CDMA is the technology of choice for third-generation systems.[62] The CDMA operating frequencies are:

Cellular, CDMA	824 to 894 MHz
PCS, CDMA	1,850 to 1,990 MHz

CDMA was the first digital technology to meet the desired 10-fold call-carrying capacity originally sought by the industry. The technology improves bandwidth utilization because a greater number of users can share the same wideband radio frequency channel. CDMA also speculatively offers the potential for up to a 20 times capacity increase over AMPS. Practical results are seen in a three-to-one or four-to-one range in cellular telephony applications.

The way that CDMA technology is able to reach its potential is by assigning a unique 10-bit code between each call known as the Identifier or CDMA Identifier. Every CDMA code packet has an identifier, so the base station is able to recognize the content of the packet, whether it is voice or data, and process it accordingly. CDMA further allows every customer (which can include a multitude of users) to use the 1.25-MHz cell frequency allocation entirely. The identifier can be located across this broad 1.25-MHz spectrum and the data fished out accordingly, presuming both ends of the communication possess the CDMA identifier. The originating CDMA encoded stream is then locked into the receiver, which then continually scans only for this unique code. The phones will ignore any and all other codes except that one that has established the call (Figure 1-6).[63]

Many of these first-generation digital product enhancements were marketed to the consumer as clarity and quality of service technologies. Most consumers remained unaware that most of these product and vendor enhancements insured a much more secure conversation. Second-generation technologies were sought to create a more efficient use of the radio airwaves; TDMA did not support the analog

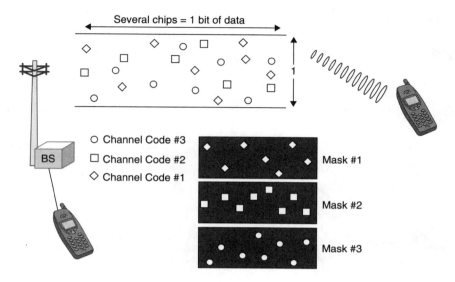

1-6 Locating the CDMA Identifier.[64]

infrastructure and failed to yield the high multitude of callers as compared to infrastructures built on spread spectrum CDMA networks.

With this young but promising technology, we can see why the United States had faith in it and accepted it with a known degree of risk and deployed this newer immature technology. The larger sampling pool and the CDMA unique identifier code certainly offer a more secure alternative than that of the GSM equivalent. As the push has continued to add more features to make our lives more convenient, the wireless or cellular phone has become a necessity to some. With the advent of online stock quotes, traffic reports, sports scores, and weather reports, wireless definitely has added convenience to our lives.

Time Division Multiple Sccess (TDMA)

Time Division Multiple Access (TDMA) is a technology based upon dividing each frequency channel into multiple time slots, each of which supports an individual conversation. When a wireless device communicates within a TDMA network, it is assigned a specific time position on the radio channel. By allowing several users to use different time slots on a single channel, TDMA increases its network capacity by supplying a single channel to several users. TDMA multiplexes up to three conversations over the same 30-kHz transmission channel as an analog system. To allow TDMA networks to provide a continuous voice communication to a wireless device that can only transmit for a short period of time, TDMA systems use digital signal processing to characterize and compress digital signals into short time-slices (Figure 1-7).

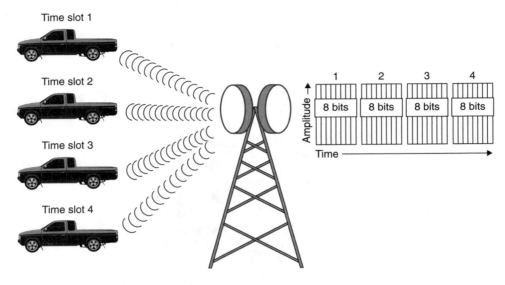

1-7 Time Division Multiple Access.[68]

You can understand TDMA by considering the following example (Figure 1-8). The two mobile phones can communicate on the same bandwidth that a single analog phone once used, with mobile phone #1 communicating on time slot 1 and mobile phone #2 communicating on time slot 3. This leaves the availability of a third call to be supported on time slot 2.[65]

TDMA failed to meet the then desired 10-fold capacity demand to the analog networks, likely one of the major deterrents to early vendor support in the American markets. TDMA offered skeptical magnitudes in capacity at best but it did offer a means to start the digital infrastructure build up.[66] The most popular TDMA-based systems are found in that of GSM network infrastructure. Recent statistics find that one in twelve people on the face of the Earth are using a GSM phone.[67]

Global System for Mobile Communications (GSM)

GSM provides for digital use only and was not engineered with analog backwards compatibility in mind. This TDMA-based technology also uses the idea of time-sharing that allows for the capability of several users, up to eight maximum on a single 200-kHz band. Two 200-kHz waveforms are required for duplex operation.

The GSM operating frequency spectrum is:[70]

GSM 400	450.4 to 457.6 MHz paired with 460.4 to 467.6 MHz
	486 MHz paired with 488.8 to 496 MHz
GSM 900	880 to 915 MHz paired with 925 to 960 MHz

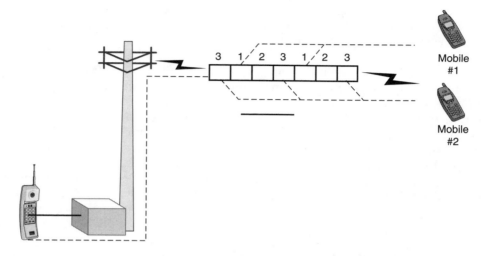

1-8 Time Division Multiple Access, using three time slots and two phones.[69]

GSM 1800   1710 to 1785 MHz paired with 1805 to 1880 MHz
GSM 1900   1850 to 1910 MHz paired with 1930 to 1990 MHz

The GSM system has various types of signal control channels that carry systems and paging information, and coordinates access like control channels on analog systems. The GSM digital control channels have extended capabilities as compared to analog counterparts, offering features such as broadcast message paging, extended sleep mode, and various others. Since the GSM control channels use one or more time slots, they typically can coexist on a single radio channel with other time slots used for voice communication. Potentially, voice channels can either be full rate or half rate. Full rate GSM systems assign only one time slot per frame to each user, each allowing eight simultaneous users per radio channel.

GSM was engineered to easily accommodate any future half-rate speech coder, which is expected to emerge within the next couple years. With a half rate GSM system only one time slot is assigned to every other frame, thereby potentially allowing a maximum of up to 16 users at once per channel. A GSM carrier bit rate is 270 Kbps allowing each less than one-eighth of the total capacity due to synchronization bits and other noninformation material.

Time intervals of full rate GSM channels are divided into frames with the two radio frequencies each broken into eight time slots. Each of these two signals is for send and receive purposes. During a voice conversation at the mobile set, one time slot is used for transmitting, one for receiving, and the remaining six are idle. The idle time slots are used to measure the signal strengths of the surrounding cell carrier frequencies. For the 900-MHz band, GSM digital channels transmit on different send and receive frequencies characterized by 45-MHz of offset, and the transmission does not occur at precisely the same time. On the 1900-MHz band, the difference observed between transmit and receive channels differentiates by a total of just 80 MHz. The mobile telephone transmits bursts of data at one frequency and receives corresponding bursts at another remaining briefly idle in-between a repeat of the process.[71]

GSM offers functionality by means of a *subscriber identification module* (SIM), which plugs into a card slot in the phone unit; this is similar to that of a PCMCIA (PC Card) slot in a laptop computer. The SIM contains user-profile data, a description of access privileges, and an identification of the cellular carrier in the home area likely where the phone was activated and its number assigned. The SIM is universal and can be used interchangeably between any GSM set, allowing the subscriber to be completely mobile throughout any GSM environment in the world as long as a mutual billing environment exists between the vendors.[72] The information contained within the SIM is sensitive, and cryptography (albeit weak) is employed to assure its protection.[73,74,75]

Third-Generation Wireless (3G)

Where consumers looked to add more features and conveniences, industry and users pushed for the adoption of third-generation technologies. Third-generation technologies offer a launching pad for ideas such as wireless Web, email, and paging services, along with improvements to the core of second-generation technologies. By far the most important and globally accepted 3G technology is *short message service* (SMS). Other 3G technologies such as EDGE, WCDMA, USSD, GPRS, and WATM are emerging technologies supported by various vendors. They are briefly highlighted in the endnotes.[76,77,78,79,80]

Short Message Service (SMS)

Billions of SMS messages are sent every month.[81] According to the GSM Association, "SMS as we know it will be used to the year 2005 at least, since the phones, infrastructure, specifications, market development, and awareness are in place today."[82] There are a number of reasons for the growth of SMS to this point, but also a number of obstacles to be overcome if growth is to continue. Not surprisingly, security is one of those challenges. SMS is no more secure than other wireless communications, but can pose more of a threat because it is embedded in services where people don't expect to find it. It has become commonplace, in situations where placement of a *plain old telephone system* (POTS) line to vendors is impractical, to send the purchaser's credit card information via SMS to a central location for authorization.

Today almost every major cellular provider around the world provides SMS. This service allows cellular phone subscribers to receive short text messages consisting of various sizes around 160 to 180 characters. SMS has also been developed for use on most other major wireless networks as shown in Table 1-3.

While security is being applied to SMS data, wireless represents a unique challenge in that, given the right equipment, the wireless signal could be intercepted

Table 1-3 Availability of SMS[85]

Mobile network Standard	Type	SMS Availability	Message Length	Deployment
GSM 900	Digital	Yes	160	Widely
GSM 1800	Digital	Yes	160	Widely
GSM 1900	Digital	Yes	160	North America
TACS/ETACS	Analog	No	N/A	N/A
NMT	Analog	Yes	N/A	Eastern Europe
TDMA/D-AMPS	Digital	Yes (MT only)	N/A	North America
NAMPS	Analog	Yes	14 alphanumeric 32 numeric	North America
CDMA	Digital	Yes (MT only)	256	North America
PHS	Digital	Yes	N/A	Japan
PDC	Digital	Yes	N/A	Japan
IDEN/NEXTEL	Digital	Yes	140	North and South America
TETRA/Dolphin	Digital	Yes	256	Parts of Europe
Iridium	Satellite	Paging	200/20	Truly global
Globalstar	Satellite	Yes	160	Truly global

and/or modified far more easily than through the use of a conventional POTS line. SMS traffic is checked for changes through the use of *cyclic redundancy check* (CRC) to ensure that no changes have been made to the information in transit. The data itself, unless encrypted using the smartcard embedded in the device, is "encrypted using the IA5 algorithm" according to Mobile Lifestreams.[85] This, however, would seem to be insufficient, since IA5 is not so much an encryption algorithm as it is an encoding format similar to ASCII. If users were aware of the level of security that might be a point in favor, however, without the awareness that true encryption is not being used, SMS subscribers are likely to transmit sensitive information which they might not otherwise disclose.

Wireless by definition travels through the air and thus gives many users ready access to the transmission medium and a valuable target in the form of credit card information. Conventional credit card authorization is still potentially vulnerable, although it requires physical access to the transmission medium, which is far more difficult to accomplish. A thief walks through a mall with a wireless receiver in his backpack: Over a few hours of "shopping" he could intercept potentially hundreds of transactions from kiosks throughout a mall and then decrypt the contents of the transmissions at a later time from his recordings, which were made at the mall.

Another potential security and/or privacy issue revolves around the usage of wireless data and advertising. Wireless devices can be triangulated using three or more base stations and then, using this data, the wireless subscriber can be sent advertisements for nearby goods and services. This could be problematic if subscribers begin to be tracked and their patterns stored or analyzed. It could also be problematic depending on who has access to such data, potentially making crimes against individuals easier to commit due to knowledge of their location or movement patterns. If nothing else it raises privacy issues as well as concerns about payment for such messages given that many operators charge for messages received as well as messages sent.

Mobile devices using SMS can also be prone to denial of service attacks, spamming, or mail bombs because of their connections to the Internet. Many SMS networks today contain a gateway to the Internet allowing Internet mail to be sent to the phone. This also allows spammers who obtain this email address to send junk mail to the phone, potentially creating and selling databases of addresses specifically for mobile phones. Mail bomb applications can also be a problem. These applications, originally intended for use on the Internet could as easily be used to flood a mobile device with SMS messages. Depending on the pricing plan of the subscriber, either scenario could bring large bills due to the volume of messages that could be sent. Viruses are also a concern due to the connection to the Internet. Web2Wap, a Norwegian company has recently discovered a way to cause certain Nokia phones to crash due to the formatting of the message.[86] Viruses also have been created to send SMS messages. The Timofon.A virus, similar to the LoveLetter worm, sends SMS to random subscribers in Spain[87] and Kapersky Lab in Russia discovered that someone had created a program to take advantage of an SMS bug, which could flood a network with harmful messages.[88]

Finally, mobile banking is a potential use for SMS, however, just like remote point of sale, there is valuable information to be found inside such wireless communication making it a more rewarding target to someone with the right tools. Security issues may pose a significant problem for SMS as it becomes used for commercial activities rather than just quick messages among friends, and, due to its wireless nature, more people have access to the transmission medium making interception easier. Mobile banking is quickly becoming a key wireless tool allowing subscribers to access account information, pay bills, and move money around. Two examples of this service are found in Canada with the Royal Bank Financial Group and in Hong Kong with Citibank where along with M1 they claim security through "Telephone *Personal Identification Number* (PIN) and 128-bit encryption of messaging data over the wireless communications link provided via GSM."[89]

Use of a SIM Toolkit to create SMS applications for mobile phones will help in the security arena. The SIM Toolkit is based on the use of a smartcard to store applications as well as to identify the cellular subscriber. Smartcards, which are already used for banking and other financial applications, therefore represent a known and understood technology that can be used to provide security for sensitive transactions. The SIM Toolkit allows operators to create applications, distribute them to mobile devices, and remove them when desired. Solutions for mobile phones can include such things as wireless banking and trading and can use encryption based on triple DES.[90]

SMS will likely see future growth for some time to come, especially as it is adapted for and implemented on more networks. As more businesses integrate use of SMS into daily routines, use will certainly rise and new uses of SMS will be forthcoming. On the horizon are major changes to SMS, some of which are being used on a limited basis right now. *Enhanced Messaging Service* (EMS) and *Multimedia Messaging Service* (MMS) are two similar technologies based on SMS that allow users to do more with messaging.

Fourth-Generation Wireless (4G)

What will drive technology past the current status of 3G technology are the usual forces of bigger, better, faster, and more secure. 4G technology implements designs that will take the wireless telecom industry beyond 2010. There is considerable speculation on exactly what fourth generation will entail. Many of the proposed improvements and features are as follows. This infrastructure will function atop the current existing CDMA, GSM, TDMA, and other wireless networks.[91,92]

Reasons to Have 4G
1—Support interactive multimedia services: teleconferencing, wireless Internet, and so on.
2—Wider bandwidths, higher bit rates.
3—Global mobility and service portability.
4—Low cost.
5—Scalability of mobile networks.

What's New in 4G
1—Entirely packet-switched networks.
2—All network elements are digital.
3—Higher bandwidths to provide multimedia services at lower cost.
4—Tighter network security.

3G
Back compatible to 2G.
Circuit and packet switched networks.
Combination of existing and evolved equipment.
Data rate (up to 2 Mbps).

4G
Extend 3G capacity by one order of magnitude.
Entirely packet-switched networks.
All network elements are digital.
Higher bandwidth (up to 100 Mbps).

Researchers claim that some services costing thousands of dollars with 3G services, like wireless real-time video links, won't be as expensive with 4G. The 3G systems have consumed billions of dollars in investments but have not yet delivered the smooth interoperability that a 4G infrastructure will provide. The possibility of having base stations everywhere in the world ensures phone users connection to a high-speed network anywhere anytime. These claims have been promised by the marketers of 3G technologies but are not likely to be found anywhere in the near future.[93]

The high bandwidth capacities that will be available with the 4G infrastructure, greater than 20 Mbps, will offer the availability for music downloading, in-car video games, high-speed data transfer, video conferencing, tracking and monitoring of fleet vehicles, and intervehicle communication.

This 144 Kbps theoretical maximum being the most frustrating downfall of 3G has found some 2G vendors moving directly to 4G. These vendors have offered extremely limited services in a futile attempt to bring the wireless Internet to the mobile user. Particularly because of bandwidth limitations, the 3G wireless Web services only provide minimal amounts of information through a generic graphical user interface, displaying only a skeletal version of the Internet.[94]

Summary

Wireless communications have evolved substantially from their early beginnings in the late 1890s and early 1900s. Over the years businesses and consumers have demanded greater and greater flexibility in where and when they work. This desire has manifested itself in a demand for wireless technologies to allow them the freedom they need or desire. The result of this has been four distinct generations of wireless technologies with each progression providing the consumer with more flexibility and greater reliability. As consumers began to move away from the traditional wired networks, the need for security became apparent. Communications in the wireless world are not limited to traversing the wires upon which they once flowed. Now communications are available to anyone willing and capable of intercepting them.

The evolution of cellular and wireless technologies has been seen through a progression of four apparent generations. The first generation saw the adaptation of the analog cellular telephone. Indicative of this generation was interference, minimal security, large handsets, and short battery life. A need for improved service, increased efficiency with frequency use, more security, and better phones paved the way for second-generation technologies in which improvements in service, security, and network capacities were seen. The third-generation products look to extend features and improve on the first-generation digital products, including adding more overall functionality and greater bandwidth. The fourth generation will continue to improve upon the infrastructure and may interconnect the globe, perhaps one day allowing a cellular phone to be used from the International Space Station. All of this will be accomplished more securely than ever before as various methods for protecting information are integrated into wireless networks and applications—from frequency hopping to data encryption. It is foreseeable, that the upcoming fourth-generation technologies will take security and bandwidth to an entirely new level allowing ubiquitous use of wireless devices with high bandwidth needs anywhere in the world.

Endnotes

[1]Pelton, Joseph N., *Wireless and Satellite Telecommunications*, Prentice Hall, 1995.

[2]Christensen, Gerry, *Wireless Infrastructure Technologies*, Faulkner Information Services, 2000.

[3]Webb, William, *The Future of Wireless Communications*, Artech House, Boston, 2001.

[4]Ibid.

[5]www.washtech.com/news/regulation/12051-1.html, Robert O'Harrow, Jr., August 24, 2001.

[6]RSA ASIA 2001, by Professor Randall K. Nichols, *Optimizing Wireless Security with FPGAs and ASICs*, Singapore, July 10, 2001.

[7]http://www.wirelessfoundation.org/04copp/results.htm

[8]www.apcointl.org/newsreleases/pressreleasearchive.htm#312001

[9]www.wow-com.com (See Table 1-1. Authors have extended data to 2000)

Another timely quote from this site (9/26/01): Wireless Phone Use Soars after Attacks on U.S. Telephone networks, wired and wireless, strained to meet calling demands after aircraft crashed into the World Trade Center, the Pentagon, and a field near Pittsburgh.

"I am grateful for the tireless and heroic efforts of those in the telecommunications industry who are working hard to keep our most fundamental communications systems, such as telephone service, wireless phone service and television service, operating efficiently under the circumstances," said Michael Powell, chairman of the U.S. Federal Communication Commission.

[10]www.wow-com.com/industry/stats/e911/

[11]Christensen, Gerry, Op cit., *Wireless Infrastructure Technologies*, Faulkner Information Services, 2000.

[12]Worthen, Ben, "Location, location, location," *CIO* Magazine, Vol. 14 No. 14, May 1, 2001, p. 108.

[13]Ibid.

[14]Christensen, Gerry, Op cit., *Wireless Infrastructure Technologies*, Faulkner Information Services, 2000.

[15]Pelton, Joseph N., Op cit., *Wireless and Satellite Telecommunications*, Prentice Hall, 1995.

[16]Ibid.

[17]Ibid.

[18]Christensen, Gerry, Op cit., *Wireless Infrastructure Technologies*, Faulkner Information Services, 2000.

[19]Ibid.

[20]Nichols, Randall K., Daniel J. Ryan, Julie J.C.H. Ryan, *Defending Your Digital Assets Against Hackers, Crackers, Spies and Thieves*, McGraw-Hill, November 2000, p. 70. The elegant risk equation was the direct work of Professor Daniel Ryan at George Washington University, Washington, D.C.

[21]Webb, William, Op cit., *The Future of Wireless Communications*, Boston: Artech House, 2001, p. 297.

[22]Radding, Alan, *Fly and Be Free*, Midrange Systems, May 12, 1995, Vol. 8, No. 9, p. 299.

[23]Pelton, Joseph N., Op cit., *Wireless and Satellite Telecommunications*, Prentice Hall, 1995, p. 78.

[24]Byrnes, Cheryl, *Telecommunications: State of the World*, Faulkner Information Services, 2001.

[25]www.extremetech.com/article/0,3396,s%3d201%26a%3d11271,00.asp, *802.11 Wireless Security Holes Exposed* by Dennis Fisher, *eweek*, August 7, 2001.

[26]Webb, William, Op cit., *The Future of Wireless Communications*, Boston: Artech House, 2001, p. 294.

[27]Nichols, Randall K., Daniel J. Ryan, Julie J.C.H. Ryan, Op cit., *Defending Your Digital Assets Against Hackers, Crackers, Spies and Thieves*, McGraw-Hill, November 2000, pp. 44–45.

[28]Vergara, Michael, *Securing the Mobile Internet*, Presentation at Networld+Interop 2001.

[29]Pinna, Bob, *It's the Transaction Stupid*, Wireless Business & Technology, March/April 2001, 54.

[30]Webb, William, Op cit., *The Future of Wireless Communications*, Boston: Artech House, 2001, p. 299.

[31]O'Hara, Bob, *Security and 802.11*, Presentation at Networld+Interop 2001.

[32]Ibid. Also see note 23 supra.

[33]Ibid.

[34]Vergara, Michael, *Securing the Mobile Internet*, Presentation at Networld+Interop 2001.

[35]Ibid.

[36]McKee, Jake, *Unwired Design*, Wireless Business & Technology, March/April 2001, 62.

[37]Denning, Dorothy, *Information Warfare and Security*, Addison Wesley Longman, Inc., December 1998, p. 174.

[38]http://www.cwhistory.com/history/html/FacFigSix.html

[39]*The American Heritage® Dictionary of the English Language,* 4th Ed., Houghton Mifflin Company, 2000.

[40]Horak, Ray, *Communications Systems and Networks*, IDG Books Worldwide, 2/E, 2001, p. 446.

[41]Harte, Lawrence, Tom Schaffnit, and Steven Kellogg, *The Comprehensive Guide to Wireless Technologies: Cellular, PCS, Paging, SMR and Satellite*, APDG Publishing, Fuquay-Varina, North Carolina, August 1999, p.65. In the figure, BS = Base Station, PSTN = Public Switched Telephone Network, and MSC = Mobile Switching Center.

[42]Ibid.

[43]Ibid.

[44]CMP Media, Diagram, http://www.csdmag.com/main/2000/01/0001edge1.htm, copyrighted 2001, July 4, 2001.

[45]*Analog Cellular Systems outside the US TACS Variants,* http://www.iit.edu/~diazrob/cell/tacsvar.html, July 4, 2001. *Advanced Mobile Phone System* (AMPS) was the first analog cellular system developed by AT&T. Although largely used in the United States, the most widely deployed wireless system, AMPS has worldwide use also, with systems operating in over 72 countries. Today, more than half the cellular phones in the world operate according to AMPS standards, which, since 1988, have been maintained and developed by the *Telecommunications Industry Association* (TIA). "AMPS allocates frequency ranges, within the 800 and 900 *Megahertz* (MHz) spectrum, to cellular telephone. Each service provider can use half of the 824–849 MHz range for receiving signals from cellular phones and half the 869 through 894 MHz range for transmitting to cellular phones. The bands are divided into 30 kHz subbands, called channels."

AMPS uses a 3 KHz (standard landline telephone line bandwidth) voice channel modulated onto 30 KHz FM carriers (one frequency for transmit, another for receive). The total of 50 MHz of bandwidth is divided between two operators, each of which uses half of its bandwidth for the forward channel (from base station to mobile) and half for the reverse channel. The B *band* (or *block*) is assigned to the local telephone company ("wire-line carrier"), and the A band is assigned to a nonwire-line carrier. The division of the spectrum into sub-band channels is achieved by using *frequency division multiple access* (FDMA). The two channels supporting a single conversation are separated widely to avoid confusion on the part of the terminal equipment. On average, the AMPS cell site has a radius of approximately one-mile. Based on FDMA transmission and data duplexing methods, AMPS does not handle data well, with transmission generally limited to 6,800 bps.

[46]Harte, Lawrence, Tom Schaffnit, and Steven Kellogg, *The Comprehensive Guide to Wireless Technologies: Cellular, PCS, Paging, SMR and Satellite*, APDG Publishing, Fuquay-Varina, North Carolina, August 1999, pp. 79–81. *Narrowband Advanced Mobile Phone Service* (N-AMPS) is an analog cellular system that was commercially launched in late 1991 by Motorola. Although similar to AMPS, N-AMPS uses analog FM radio for voice transmissions and features increased performance. N-AMPS acquired its name and differs from AMPS in that it uses "narrow" 10 KHz bandwidths for radio channels, one-third the size of AMPS channels. More of the narrow channels can be installed in each cell site and therefore serve more customers without the need to add additional cell sites. System capacity is improved by splitting a 30 KHz channel into three 10 KHz channels, thereby tripling AMPS capacity. Some of the control commands (signaling frequencies) are shifted to the subaudio, below the audio bandwidth for speech, 300 to 3,000 Hz, to facilitate simultaneous voice and data transmissions. Motorola equipment is necessary and only a small number of U.S. carriers deploy N-AMPS.

[47]Harte, Lawrence, Tom Schaffnit, and Steven Kellogg, Op cit., *The Comprehensive Guide to Wireless Technologies: Cellular, PCS, Paging, SMR and Satellite*, pp. 79–81. "*Nordic Mobile Telephone* (NMT) was developed and placed into service in the 1980s by the telecommunications administrations of Sweden, Norway, Finland, and Denmark to create a compatible mobile telephone system in the Nordic countries." NMT consists of two systems, the NMT 450, low capacity system, and the NMT 900, high-capacity system. Nokia, the leading supplier, with more than three million customers served in almost 60 networks, made the NMT 450 commercially available in late 1981. Although the NMT 450 had very good initial success the original design had limited capacity, which spurred the development of the NMT 900 and its subsequent introduction in 1986. "The NMT 450, operates in the 450 MHz range, has excellent signal propagation and is especially suitable for sparsely populated areas supported by few cell sites—such as Eastern Europe—where distances to base stations can be several tens of miles. NMT 900 operates in the 900 MHz range, and is appropriate for more densely populated areas." Few nations outside of the Scandinavian countries use the NMT 450, whereas the NMT 900 has services available in over 40 nations, including certain Asian countries. The NMT system standard includes services such as caller ID, *short message service* (SMS), and voice-mail indication. The NMT system has an assortment of anti-fraud protection schemes that are not found on other systems. Most NMT systems will eventually be displaced by GSM.

[48]Rappaport, Theodore S., *Wireless Communications: Principles and Practice*, Prentice Hall PTR, New Jersey, 1995. "The *Total Access Communication System* (TACS) was developed for use in the United Kingdom in the 900-KHz band. Its primary differences include changes to the radio channel frequencies, smaller radio channel bandwidths, and data i.e. original analog cellular signaling rates." Improving the efficiency of the AMPS cellular system radio channels produced the TACS system. There are multiple other variants to TACS, with each being derived from the basic U.S. AMPS cellular system. The frequency ranges of most TACS systems are 890 MHz to 915 MHz for the uplink and 935 MHz to 960 MHz for the downlink. The TACS system was initially allocated 25 MHz although 10 MHz of the 25 MHz was reserved for future pan-European systems in the UK. TACS has found acceptance in only a few nations, and it is not considered a long-term technology solution. The TACS is being replaced by new digital cellular systems such as GSM.

[49]Horak,Ray, *Communications Systems and Networks*, IDG Books Worldwide, 2/E, 2001, pp. 452–454. *Frequency Division Multiple Access* (FDMA) is a bearer technology conceived upon the idea of splitting the assigned frequency range into multiple carrier frequen-

cies to support several conversations. All wireless communication methods employ these principles since all communications within a given cell must be separated by a guard frequency to avoid their mutual interference. FDMA uses these select guard channels to act as a boarder to prohibit the possibility of signal interference commonly referred to as crossover.

[50]Ibid, Ray Horak. p. 449.

[51]Op. cit., Lawrence Harte, p. 74.

[52]"Welcome to CEPT: What is CEPT?" From the Web page of http://www.cept.org/, "the European Conference of Postal and Telecommunications Administrations—CEPT was established in 1959 by 19 countries, which expanded to 26 during its first ten years. Original members were the incumbent monopoly-holding postal and telecommunications administrations. CEPT's activities included cooperation on commercial, operational, regulatory and technical standardization issues.

In 1988 CEPT decided to create ETSI, The European Telecommunications Standards Institute, into which all its telecommunication standardization activities were transferred.

In 1992 the postal and telecommunications operators created their own organizations, PostEurope and ETNO respectively. In conjunctions with the European policy of separating postal and telecommunications operations from policy-making and regulatory functions, CEPT thus became a body of policy-makers and regulators. At the same time, Central and Eastern European Countries became eligible for membership in CEPT. CEPT with its 43 members now covers almost the entire geographical area of Europe.

As of June 1999 administrations from the following 43 countries are members of CEPT:

Albania, Andorra, Austria, Belgium, Bosnia and Herzegovina, Bulgaria, Croatia, Cyprus, Czech Republic, Denmark, Estonia, Finland, France, Germany, Great Britain, Greece, Hungary, Iceland, Ireland, Italy, Latvia, Liechtenstein, Lithuania, Luxembourg, Malta, Moldovia, Monaco, Netherlands, Norway, Poland, Portugal, Romania, Russian Federation, San Marino, Slovakia, Slovenia, Spain, Sweden, Switzerland, The former Yugoslav Republic of Macedonia, Turkey, Ukraine, Vatican."

[53]Digital filtration mechanisms have helped to correct problems with one of the biggest annoyances and growing trends of the mobile user. Mobile users are often rightfully viewed as inconsiderate, careless and sometimes reckless. Almost everyone has come across the individual more concerned with their phone conversation than the two-ton vehicle they are careening down the expressway at 80 mph. With the advent of second-generation digital technologies cellular headsets and speakerphones have become a more effective means in counterattacking this annoyance and offering other drivers somewhat more tolerance. It can be amusing to see an individual talking to himself and using communicative hand gestures while alone in his vehicle, although less so at higher speeds.

[54]Harrell, Thomas J., III, "Radio Shack Scanner Modification Page," http://www3. sympatico.ca/len.c/rsmods.html, Accessed July 4, 2001.

[55]Op. cit., Dorothy E. Denning, p. 167.

[56]Ibid.

[57]Ibid.

[58]Harte, Lawrence, Tom Schaffnit, and Steven Kellogg, Op cit., *The Comprehensive Guide to Wireless Technologies: Cellular, PCS, Paging, SMR and Satellite*, APDG Publishing, Fuquay-Varina, North Carolina, August 1999, p. 51.

[59]Horak, Ray, Op cit., *Communications Systems and Networks*, IDG Books Worldwide, 2/E, 2001, p. 453.

[60]Ibid.

[61]Qualcomm acquired the rights to this technology initially found in IS-95 in the early 1980s.

[62]Technical Glossary," http://www.qualcomm.com/cda/tech/aboutcdma/0,1704,35,00. html, as defined by Qualcomm, Accessed July 4, 2001.

[63]Vitaliano, Franco, "TDMA vs. CDMA: How the Feds Blew It, Once Again", http://www. vxm.com/21R.62.html, July 4, 2001.

[64]Op. cit., Lawrence Harte, p. 51.

[65]Op. cit., Lawrence Harte, p. 50.

[66]Vitaliano, Franco, Op cit., "TDMA vs. CDMA: How the Feds Blew It, Once Again," http://www.vxm.com/21R.62.html, Accessed July 4, 2001.

[67]"GSM MOBILES REACH HALF BILLION LANDMARK—1 in 12 people on the planet now have a GSM phone," http://www.gsmworld.com/news/press_2001/press_releases_18. html, July 4, 2001.

[68]Op. cit., Ray Horak, p. 451.

[69]Ibid.

[70]"GSM Frequencies," http://www.gsmworld.com/technology/spectrum_gsm.html, July 4, 2001.

[71]Op. cit., Lawrence Harte, pp. 84–85.

[72]Op. cit., Ray Horak, p. 468.

[73]"GSM Security Features," http://www.cellular.co.za/gsmsecurity.htm, July 4, 2001. The GSM SIM can be removed or swapped to add a prepaid anonymous SIM or to update firmware and feature sets. Though it sounds very appealing and convenient for the user, in 1998 the Hamburg Computer Chaos Club posted the source code and a Windows/DOS executable for a SIM card emulator. The files that were released contained only the source code and executable not the more valuable user unique International Mobile Subscriber Identity (IMSI) or the Individual Subscriber authentication key (Ki). These sensitive credentials are analogous to the *Electronic Serial Number* (ESN) found in analog systems such as AMPS and TACS. The Ki (subscriber authentication key) can be extracted from the SIM modules that were using the standard A3/A8 algorithms in 1995 within somewhere between 8 and 16 hours. Ki extraction is easier to accomplish today, however it remains an unlikely threat. More likely, yet very difficult, would be an over-the-air attack. This attack is difficult because the card's validity is challenged six times a second over an eight-hour period. Vodafone, a major supplier of these technologies, has been using 3DES and has identified vendors who had used the much weaker data encryption algorithms in that of A3/A8. Once the encryption was cracked the sensitive SIM information could be extracted and programmed into a new SIM to clone the original phone. With this software and a corresponding SIM card reader it allows any interested user to pry at the personal information and data contents of a poorly encrypted SIM. The SIM was mostly acquired by very low-tech means such as stealing the actual handset. The victim would find international or adult phone calls on their bill. SIM card readers and software are readily available today and they obviously have their good and malicious intentions; for the most part they are used to add features such as ring tones, pictures, and to update and backup the caller's address book.

[74]The GSM cryptography standards were a huge blunder in that their most inner secrets were withheld from public scrutiny and analysis. Firstly we identify that communications can be encrypted either from end-to-end or between links. Electronic Mail using PGP encryption is a typical example of end-to-end encryption no matter how many mail servers, routers and switches the message traverses. The message is secure throughout is entire end-to-end path. Link encryption provides only for protection across single channels and not the entire path. GSM uses this idea over the airwaves between the transceiver and the base station since they are the most likely to be exploited. Researchers at the *Internet Security Applications Authentication and Cryptography* (ISAAC) group found a fatal flaw in COMP128, the algo-

rithm used to protect the identity on the SIM. This detected compromise left nearly all GSM network operators vulnerable from this breach. There are replacements for COMP128 permitted in the GSM system, but so far the *Smart Card Developers Association* (SDA) has not found a network, which does not use COMP128. Many U.S. networks that use GSM standards such as the digital PCS service could also be victimized from this threat. Upon investigation the A5 cryptographic algorithm was determined to use a 64-bit key upon which only 54-bits were in use.

[75]One of the most recent GSM cryptographic product adaptations from Siemens included the introduction of the *Top Security* (TopSec) phone. TopSec employs various strong cryptographic measures that work along with and atop whatever GSM cryptographic standard a service provider uses. The multitiered cryptographic approach offers strong speech encryption with a Diffie Hellman and RSA combined asymmetric key agreement of 1,024 bits and also offering a symmetric key of 128 bits. The phone functions similarly to that of the popular wire line based STU III phones, wherein to use encryption it requires both communicating parties to be have the same TopSec phone and it requires manual intervention to add the additional cryptographic measures. Siemens' offers the identical phone without the added security for relatively less in cost. With a very hefty price tag of nearly three thousand dollars Siemens' can be sure that their product will be popular only among government entities, corporations, and likely drug traffickers.

[76]AT&T Takes Wireless to the EDGE, by Stuart J. Johnston, *PC World*, July 18, 2000, http://www.pcworld.com/news/article.asp?aid=17701, July 12, 2001. *Enhanced Data rates for Global Evolution* (EDGE) is a new technology designed to provide operators a way to provide 3G wireless services using their existing hardware and spectrum. This is done by using a modulation scheme that is more efficient than that currently used in the GSM Standard, which is the Gaussian prefiltered minimum shift keying. For every 1-bit-per pulse rate that the GSM Standard provides, Edge's *8-phase shift key* (8-PSK) will carry 3 bits of information. Therefore, Edge has the potential to increase the efficiency of GSM three-fold. EDGE is implemented over existing TDMA and GSM networks. Its design allows an operator to provide 3G services without purchasing 3G licenses and obtaining additional spectrum.[1] This may be especially appealing in the United States where additional spectrum availability is in question. The primary two companies who will be selling EDGE technology are Ericsson, who developed EDGE, and Nokia. Both companies should have products ready for distribution beginning in 2001 through 2002. However, the development schedule will depend a lot on operators and their desire to implement EDGE either by itself or in combination with *Wideband Code Division Multiple Access* (WCDMA). Another potential challenge for EDGE may lie in security issues similar to other wireless techniques. Since this technology is designed to work over existing TDMA/GSM infrastructures there is the possibility that a wireless device could be configured to use more timeslots than it is allotted or to intercept information destined for another device. Since one of the goals of EDGE is to provide additional bandwidth there is every indication that wireless devices will be used for different types of applications, which may even include checking mail, including attachments, or accessing corporate intranets. Protection of entire packets, or at least the data within, therefore becomes a large issue since it is being broadcast over the airwaves for anyone within a cell to receive. At this time few details about the inner workings of EDGE are publicly available so it remains to be seen what kind of data protection will be used. The future for EDGE is anything but certain.

[77]http://www.ericsson.com/3g/how/wcdma.shtml, July 4, 2001. *Wideband Code Division Multiple Access* (WCDMA) is a wideband radio interface technology that provides far higher data rates than other 2G and even 3G wireless bearers available today. WCDMA technology supplies up to 2Mbps, and a highly efficient use of the total available radio spectrum. Compared to other technologies, WCDMA networks also may enable a faster and more cost-

efficient rollout. Base station deployment needs can be reduced by up to 30 percent and are available in a multitude of environments. Nokia describes that deploying WCDMA hardware with an existing GSM/EDGE base is relatively easy. Ericsson is another prominent developer of WCDMA based technologies since research began in the 1980s. The company delivered the world's first experimental WCDMA system to NTT DoCoMo in Japan in 1997. WCDMA offers the concept of "capacity borrowing" from less-loaded adjacent cells to increase the instantaneous traffic handling capacity of an overloaded cell.

[78]Sicap USSD Gateway, Product Description, Sicap Ltd., http://www.sicap.com/mobile_ussdgateway.cfm, July 4, 2001. "Unstructured Supplementary Service Data, instead of the store and forward functionality, as with SMS, USSD is session-oriented, which indicates that when a user accesses a USSD service, the radio connection stays open until it is released by the user, application, or time-out. This provides faster response times for interactive applications." Due to that nature of USSD, the user can access these services while roaming; assuming the network they are currently using has the right infrastructure to support USSD messages. As with SMS, security could be a problem depending on what services are provided with USSD. As a security mechanism it is suggested that users supply a PIN along with the USSD communication, however this is not necessarily a good thing because, as with SMS the transmission medium is easily accessible by any who have the right tools, and decoding of the data potentially could be easy. If used for mobile banking applications or other financial services then, as with SMS, there are enough rewards to make compromise attractive. Sufficient encryption will need to be utilized to protect transactions and detect spoofing of transactions. Also similar to SMS, USSD can support the use of a SIM Toolkit and Smart Card for operators to develop and manage applications, which can uniquely identify subscribers and encrypt data using such algorithms as triple DES.

[79]Huovinen, Lasse, *Authentication and Security in GPRS Environment: An Overview, by, Department of Computer Science and Engineering*, Helsinki University of Technology, http://www.hut.fi/~lhouvine/netsec98/gprs_access.html, June 21, 2001. General Packet Radio Service or GPRS is a new wireless technology being introduced as an intermediate step between 2G and 3G wireless networks. GPRS is expected to allow data transfer rates many times this rate with a theoretical limit of 171 Kbps. Security of information with GPRS is probably one of the most challenging issues facing GPRS. Since GPRS, by design, connects the wireless GPRS backbone to external packet networks, and most often this is the Internet, GPRS data can now be subject to many of the attacks seen against traditional network assets connected to the Internet. Data for applications such as user names and passwords are a potential target as is denial of service attacks. Use of GPRS potentially allows the use of FTP or Telnet, user names and passwords could be sent in clear text from the GGSN to the destination server. The use of IPSec or VPNs can help provide security by encrypting information that is sent over the Internet. During the course of a GPRS transaction authentication is encrypted using the A3 encryption algorithm. When authenticated the subscriber can choose to have data encrypted as well. If this is chosen then encryption between the SGSN and the mobile device is performed "using the *GPRS encryption algorithm* (GEA), which is a stream cipher similar to A5." However, as the GEA is kept secret, evaluation of the algorithm is difficult if not impossible. With a maximum key length of 64 bits there is also cause for concern since this is far shorter than most generally used key lengths. Even if the encryption is not compromised, theft of a subscriber's private key from the SIM card (smartcard) can be a problem. This type of attack requires physical access to the SIM card for some time as well as the technical skills to do it. However, once stolen, the thief can use the GPRS network as if they were the targeted user and incur large bills on their behalf, or potentially worse, use the stolen access as a stepping stone to attacks on other networks. The practices of mail bombing or spamming are also a significant threat to the GPRS user. If while using GPRS they are charged based on the num-

ber of bytes transmitted and received, then the consequences of large volumes of electronic mail could pose a significant threat, delaying the arrival of important mail and increasing the subscriber's bill significantly.

[80]Haĉ, Anna, *Multimedia Applications Support for Wireless ATM Networks*, Prentice-Hall, New Jersey, 2000, p. 26. *Wireless Asynchronous Transfer Mode* (WATM or Wireless ATM) is being investigated by a number of universities and research labs with the goal of using Wireless ATM and developing a standard specification to govern its implementation and use. "*Wireless ATM (Asynchronous Transfer Mode)* ATM is an emerging technology for high-speed networking. ATM is designed to support both real-time and on-real-time traffic with different delay, loss, and throughput requirements. In addition, ATM has the major advantage of being scaling." ATM has been used for many years in traditional wired networks. The technology is flexible in that it can provide large amounts of bandwidth for multimedia presentations when needed while experiencing minimal collisions and supporting high *quality of service* (QoS). At the same time it can also be used for video conferencing, which tends to be more variable in the pattern of data that is sent, and for normal network data, which tends to be less bandwidth intensive and does not necessarily mind minor delays or some retransmitted packets. At this writing, there are still many issues to be worked out with Wireless ATM. Although it seems to be in the sights of the wireless industry, it appears that WATM has a long way to go before it is commercially viable, not the least of which is formal specification, and adoption by the industry and international standards bodies.

[81]"GSM MOBILES REACH HALF BILLION LANDMARK—1 in 12 people on the planet now have a GSM phone," http://www.gsmworld.com/news/press_2001/press_releases_18.html, July 4, 2001.

[82]Buckingham, Simon, "An Introduction to the Short Message Service," Mobile Lifestreams Limited—Issued July 2000, http://www.gsmworld.com/technology/sms_success.html, July 4, 2001.

[83]Developers Zone, MobileSMS, Mobile Lifestreams Ltd., http://www.dataonsms.com/developers.asp, Accessed July 4, 2001.

[84]Developers Zone, MobileSMS, Mobile Lifestreams Ltd., http://www.dataonsms.com/developers.asp, Accessed July 4, 2001.

[85]Guide to SMS support on different networks, http://www.sms101.com/guide.htm.

[86]Rohde, Laura, "Messages can freeze popular Nokia phones," CNN.com, September 1, 2000, http://www.cnn.com/2000/TECH/computing/09/01/nokia.freeze.idg/, Accessed July 4, 2001.

[87]"F-Secure Virus Descriptions," www-f-secure.com.

[88]"New bug floods German cell networks," ZDNet Germany, August 4, 2000, http://www.zdnet.com/zdnn/stories/newsbursts/0,7407,2612018,00.html, Accessed July 4, 2001.

[89]Legard, David, "Citibank, M1 bring mobile banking to Asia," IDG New Service, Singapore Bureau, ComputerWorld Hong Kong, January 14, 1999, http://www.cw.com.hk/News/n990114002.htm, Accessed July 4, 2001.

[90]"Schlumberger Delivers Full-featured, Secure Wireless Mobile Banking Solution to Microcell," Schlumberger Press Release, November 7, 2000, http://www.1.slb.com/smartcards/news/00/sct_microcell0811.html, Accessed July 4, 2001.

[91]Wexler, Joanie, "Goals of the Wireless Multimedia Forum," Network World Fusion Newsletter, August 21, 2000, http://www.nwfusion.com/newsletters/wireless/2000/0821wire1.html, July 4, 2001.

[92]"Reasons to Have 4G," http://users.ece.gatech.edu/~jxie/4G/, last accessed July 4, 2001.

[93]"Looking ahead, researchers contemplate 4G tech," http://www.3gweekly.org/3g_article/article_0042.shtml, Accessed July 4, 2001.

[94]http://www.carucel.com/Market.htm, Accessed July 4, 2001.

2

Wireless Information Warfare

Several questions become apparent relative to the security of wireless communications systems.

What computer security threats apply to wireless systems?

Do these threats extend beyond normal CIA (confidentiality, data integrity, and availability)?

What are the predominate theories that we can examine to help us characterize a wireless system as information or risk to information *over the air* (OTA)?

If we are defending against an attack, what are the offensive operations to be considered?

The *information warfare* (IW) model helps us to define the relationships relative to the security of a wireless communications system; however, it is necessary to integrate these concepts with specific measures—such as cryptographic; *anti-jamming* (A/J), and *low probability of detection* (LPD)—and apply them to commercial and military operations to define the competing design concerns for the problem. In addition, we can apply Shannon's information concepts and Ryan's risk relationships to help define the context of information security and the value of its compromise or loss.

Wireless Is Information Warfare (IW)

The first point to be made is that wireless security measures fall under the broad category of *information warfare* (IW). Martin Libicki proposed seven categories of IW, two of which are *electronic warfare* (EW) and *hacker warfare*.[1] The former category includes communications combat in the realms of physical transfer of information (radioelectric) and the abstract formats of information (crypto-graphic). The latter category includes combat at all levels of the global information infrastructure.

Edward Waltz, a brilliant writer on IW, suggests that information warfare and information operations are integrally linked.[2] A formal U.S. Department of Defense definition of IW covers the three central aspects to this form of conflict at the national level: information dominance, information attack and information protection. Waltz presents a table of taxonomy of domains of information aggression.[3] The representative examples in Table 2-1, we see that wireless forms of information cross all the lines. Security of wireless equipment in the military, corporate and private sectors is required.

The U.S. Joint Chiefs of Staff have defined IW as "actions taken to preserve the integrity of one's own information system from exploitation, corruption, or disruption, while at the same time exploiting, corrupting, or destroying an adversary's information system and in the process achieving an information advantage in the application of force."

Waltz points out that the *information-based warfare* (IBW) component refers to "the acquisition, processing, and dissemination of information or the exploitation of information to achieve dominant awareness in the battlespace."[4] It is the authors' opinion, that the battlespace can be military or commercial and to a lesser extent private. Furthermore, the authors contend that the information transferred in that battlespace is predominantly via wireless mode.

So the question arises, how is the wireless battlespace to be addressed or limited? Limits can be put on the wireless battlespace by defining various taxonomies of classification such as IW, mobility, information theoretic, and decision/risk management. Consider each of these as intersecting sets of coordinating information that explain some of the requirements of wireless security design.

A Functional Taxonomy Based on Information Warfare

Wireless communications, by their very *mobile* nature and conservative use of the electromagnetic spectrum are subject to potentially effective Information Warfare attacks and defenses. This is true whether the target is military, commercial, or private. Taxonomy may be constructed on the basis of *INFOWAR* objectives, functions, countermeasures, and effects on targeted information infrastructures.[5] Figure 2-1 shows the *confidentiality, integrity, availability* (CIA) requirements and the objective of the countermeasures for each security property.

- Availability of information services (processes) or information may be attacked to achieve disruption or *denial of services* (DoS).
- Integrity of information services or content may be attacked to achieve corruption objectives: deception, manipulation of data, selective enhancement, or disinformation.
- Confidentiality or privacy of services or information may be attacked to achieve exploitation objectives.

Table 2-1 Taxonomy of Domains of Information Aggression

Domains of Conflict	Representative Examples
1. National (global, public sector)	Network-based information espionage, sabotage, and source Intelligence inside-agent espionage or sabotage
3. Personal (personal sector)	
	Precision physical attack on information systems (EMP, and so on.)
	Destruction of magnetic media
	Notebook computer theft
	Exploitation of former employees and competitor product, analysis Competitor trash capture, and analysis
	Arson, other nonprecision attacks on information systems
	e-commerce fraud
	Net impersonation, spoofing, email harassment, spamming
	Wiretapping and cell phone intercept
	Bank card impersonation, bank card and credit card theft
	Telephone harassment, "shoulder surfing," and PIN capture
	Credit card and database theft
	Computer destruction
	Network warfare
	Economic warfare
	Political warfare
	Command-and-control warfare

(Reprinted with permission from Waltz, Edward, *Information Warfare: Principles and Operations*, Artech House, Norwood MA, 1998.)

Sources: Cellular Carriers Association of California, (CTIA) California Highway Patrol, New York State Police, and other state officials and wireless carriers.

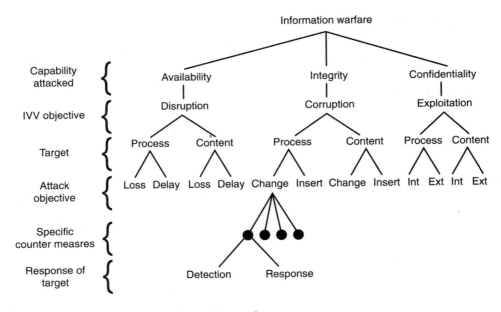

2-1 A functional taxonomy of information warfare.

[Reprinted with permission from Waltz, Edward, *Information Warfare: Principles and Operations,* Artech House, 1998.]

Any given IW operation on a wireless infrastructure or vehicle may be single, multiple, or complex combinations of specific tactical elements to achieve the basic objectives of loss, delay, insertion, disinformation, jamming, detection, or disclosure. The tactics may target the passing of messages to infer the state of information process or, more likely the content itself, for interception and exploitation, as well as to confuse the senders/receivers. For example, you might recall the 1999 embarrassing interception of a U.S. senator's conversation in Washington, D.C., executed not so perfectly from a Florida amateur's home interception station.

The functional IW actions that are applied to achieve each objective are:

- *Disruption or denial of services* (DoS) or information may be achieved by causing a loss or temporary delay in the information content or services. Jamming, overloading, *Electromagnetic pulse interference* (EMP), or physical destruction of wireless links or processors are examples of countermeasures in this category.
- *Corruption* may include replacing, inserting, or removing information and services to achieve many unexpected effects (including deception, disruption, or denial). Examples of specific countermeasures in this category include viruses with corruption engines and payloads, database worms, *man-in-the-middle* (MIM) attacks on cryptographic protocols, and sensor spoofers.
- *Exploitation* may be accomplished at external levels (passive observation) or internal levels (gaining access to internal sensitive information or services by breaching security services) to gain information intended to remain confidential.

As seen in Figure 2-1, the degree of effect of each countermeasure may be categorized by the response of the targeted information system: detection, response, and recovery.

Detection includes: undetected by the target, detected on occurrence, or detected at some time after the occurrence.

Response includes: no response (unprepared), initiate audit activities, mitigate further damage, initiate protective actions.

Recovery includes: action/passive, backup, and regroup.[6]

From the standpoint of a wireless system and infrastructure, this taxonomy includes only the first effects. One attack even undetected may have minor or political consequences, while another may bring immediate and cascading consequences. Figure 2-2 shows the interrelationships between the major wireless services, transmitting media and network layers. It is conceivable that an attack at the lower intersecting layers can devastate the communication defenses of any country because

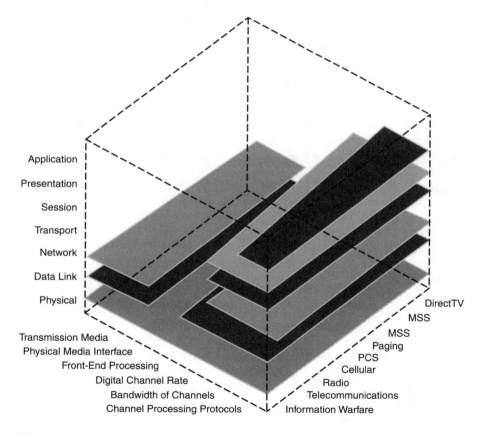

2-2 Interrelationships between the major wireless services, transmitting media and network layers.

[Reprinted with permission from Nichols, Randall K., Daniel J. Ryan, and Julie J.C.H. Ryan, *Defending Your Digital Assets Against Hackers, Crackers, Spies and Thieves*, McGraw-Hill, 2000.]

their services are not protected at the lower levels and multiple services are available (not separated) on the same computer systems.

For any given attack or defense plan, the IW taxonomy may be used to develop and categorize the countermeasures, their respective counter-countermeasures and the effects on target systems. Attacks on wireless systems have an added impact—degradation of performance. Blocking or jamming a wireless system degrades system information performance (technical degradation or destruction) and effectiveness (utility or impact on downstream users of the information system under attack).[7] Simple overloading can cause collisions in the delivery system. For example, pick a snowy day and go to the Boston's Logan Airport. See how long you can talk on your cell phone before you are transferred and then maybe again to another confused party. The chances are that you never will get back to your original conversation.

From an IW point of view, there are two operational objectives that can be applied to wireless systems: exploit information and attack-and-defend information. Information exploitation operations are defined as the acquisition, transmission, storage, or transformation of information that enhances the employment of military forces. This objective is the same for commercial and private forces to a lesser degree or scope. Two actions are possible: direct, such as interception of adversary communications to locate or extract other information; or indirect, such as surveillance and reconnaissance sensors with intelligence analysis (from eyes in the sky to private eyes).

Deception is misleading the enemy about actual capabilities and intentions. It is indirectly accomplished by conducting misleading (military, commercial, and/or illegal) operations that infer incorrect future plans or intentions. For example, think of the millions of wireless messages sent out *over-the-air* (OTA) before the Normandy Invasion or the month-long electronic warfare prior to the coalition of troops in the ground engagement during the Gulf War.

Security measures are fundamental to keeping the enemy from learning our capabilities or intentions. They may be applied directly as defensive countermeasures such as INFOSEC countermeasures designed to deny direct access to wireless (or wired) networks. They may be applied indirectly such as *communications security* (COMSEC) and *counter-intelligence* (CI).

Electronic warfare is the denial of accurate information to the enemy (or target) using the electromagnetic spectrum. It is accomplished by using electromagnetic energy to directly couple deceptive information into an information system. It can also be accomplished indirectly by jamming or deceiving a radar or RF sensor by transmitting spurious waveforms to affect the receiver. Another method is to knock out the synchronization of a cryptographic transmission through wireless media. EW can assume many forms depending on the target and desired responses.

Information corruption can be a devastating attack because it is normally done without visibly changing the physical entity within which it resides. This is a direct attack using malicious logic by penetrating security boundaries of an associated wireless (or wired) network to gain unauthorized access. The effect is a force multiplier if the target relies on the corrupted information.[8]

Commercial firms have had an impact on the development of IW and its weapons. Only a few commercial information technologies are export controlled. Information security technologies include survivable networks, multilevel security, network and communications security, digital signatures, *public key infrastructure* (PKI), authentication technologies, and wireless security.

Information technologies, again from the public sector, include network computing, intelligent mobile agents to autonomously operate across networks, multimedia data presentation and storage, and push-pull information dissemination. Information creation technologies are capable of creating synthetic and deceptive virtual information such as morphed video, fake imagery, and duplicate virtual realities.[9]

Taxonomies of Wireless Communications Networks

Typical wireless communications equipment (commercial and military) includes:

- Cellular phones. These can be analog or digital. Mobile users are supported by a fixed (or in special cases transportable) infrastructure of base stations interconnected by high-speed trunk lines. Base stations support handovers so that users can move from one *cell* (region supported by a given base station) to another cell.
- Cordless phones. For most types of cordless phones, each mobile user is supported by a single base station. A user cannot move from one base station to another while a call is in progress.
- Line-of-sight radios. Connections are limited to line of sight because of operation at frequencies above HF, the need for high data rates, lack of hardware and protocol support for multihop transmission, or some combination of these factors. There are two types:
  - Fixed or transportable, high-capacity systems for point-to-point trunking (multiple streams of data and digital voice are multiplexed together over a single connection).
  - Mobile, semimobile (stop to transmit or receive), or transportable low-capacity radios that are designed primarily for handling single two-way (typically push-to-talk) voice connections.
- Packet radio networks. The radios in these networks are digital and exchange information in a store-and-forward fashion, so that a source and destination that are not able to communicate directly may nevertheless be able to exchange information. Packets are routed through the network and may take one or more hops (between router points in network junctions) to reach the intended destination.
- Pagers. These include conventional pagers, alphanumeric pagers, and two-way pagers.
- Satellite terminals.
- Wireless local area networks (WLANs).
- Wireless modems.

Wireless communications hardware is often a separate piece of equipment used either in a stand-alone methodology (for example, cellular telephones, cordless phones, and pagers) or connected to a computer for the purpose of data communications (for example, wireless modems).[10]

The primary *raison d'être* for wireless communications is to enable mobility. *Mobility* means different things in the commercial and military worlds. Within the Internet community, the current notion of supporting host (user) mobility in the commercial world is via mobile IP. In the near term, this is a technology that will support host roaming, where a roaming host may be connected through various means to the Internet. However, at no time is a host more than one hop (that is, a wireless link, dial-up line, or so on) from the fixed network. Supporting host mobility requires address management, protocol interoperability enhancements, and the like, but core network functions such as routing still occur within the fixed network.

A military vision of mobile IP is to support host mobility in wireless networks consisting of mobile routers. Such networks are envisioned to have dynamic, often rapidly changing, mesh topologies consisting of bandwidth-constrained wireless links. These characteristics create a set of underlying assumptions for protocol design that differ from those used for the higher-speed, fixed topology Internet. These assumptions lead to somewhat different solutions for implementing core network functionality, such as routing, resource reservation, and—most importantly—security.[11]

Two alternative classification schemes for the mobility aspect of communications systems/networks are network architecture and mobility factors only.

A Classification Scheme Based on Network Architecture

Communications networks can be divided into four categories based on characteristics of the supporting infrastructure, as described in the following sections.

Wireless Systems With a Fixed Supporting Infrastructure

Most existing wireless systems fall into this category. A mobile user connects to a base station, access point, or satellite gateway; the remainder of the communications path (assuming mobile-to-fixed communications) passes over wired networks. Wired connections refer to anything that is not wireless, including the twisted-pair wiring in telephone local loops, coaxial cable, and optical fibers. Some digital cellular phones have data ports and thus can be used either stand-alone for voice or connected to a computer for data. Examples include cellular phone systems, cordless phones, and some satellite networks. In the case of the cellular and cordless phones, the path from a mobile user to the public switched network (or vice versa) involves one wireless hop (transmission/reception pair).

Cellular telephony requires a fixed supporting infrastructure that includes base stations and landlines that interconnect the base stations with each other as well as to the rest of the *public switched network* (PSN). For a small satellite terminal, such as the mobile phones used with the geostationary *American Mobile Satellite* (AMSAT), a mobile user connects to a gateway in two hops—one hop up to the satellite repeater and a second hop down to the gateway terminal (Earth station). The gateway provides a connection into the PSN.

Wireless Systems in Which Users Communicate Directly Through a Satellite or Satellites

Military satellite networks such as the *Defense Satellite Communications System* (DSCS) use fairly large satellite terminals. Mobile terminals having sufficient *Effective Isotropic Radiated Power* (EIRP) and G/T (ratio of antenna gain to effective system noise temperature) and lying within the same satellite antenna footprint can communicate directly to one another through the satellite repeater via two hops. Until relatively recently, communications between small mobile satellite terminals required four hops—two hops to reach a satellite hub and another two hops (again using the satellite as a repeater) to reach the destination terminal. Access to a gateway is required when a connection is being established to verify that users are known to the system and have paid their bills.

Wireless Data Networks That Are Fully Mobile

These would include any supporting infrastructure that is also mobile. No such commercial wireless data networks currently exist. The U.S. military is currently investigating wireless network concepts involving repeaters on UAVs (unmanned aerial vehicles). A major advantage of the UAV-based relays over satellites is that they can be moved to any location where communications are needed. Furthermore, UAV relays would probably be under the control of the theater commander, whereas satellites are not. Geostationary satellites can be moved to support a local surge in demand (or to fill a void caused by the failure of another satellite), but this requires a large expenditure of station-keeping fuel and a concomitant reduction in the useful life of the satellite. Furthermore, commercial operators of a satellite on which the DoD has leased transponders would almost certainly not move the satellite to accommodate needs of the DoD users at the expense of other users of that satellite. Thus, although geostationary satellites have sometimes been relocated as an emergency measure, this is not standard practice and should not be counted on as a remedy for capacity shortfalls.[12]

Another concept involves cellular base stations on mobile vehicles; each vehicle would carry an antenna on a tall mast (for example, 10 meters high), and would provide connectivity to users in its vicinity. High-capacity microwave trunks could be used to interconnect the mobile base stations, which would be necessary in order to provide connectivity to users served by different base stations. The high-capacity trunks would form a mobile network backbone; mobile-to-mobile connections would involve a single hop into or out of the backbone at each end. The base station vehicles would move with their forces, but might have to stop moving in order to operate.

Wireless Sytems with No Supporting Infrastructure Other Than the Mobile Nodes Themselves

Such fully mobile networks are called either mobile peer-to-peer networks or mobile mesh networks.[13]

A Taxonomy Based on Mobility Only

Consider the general problem of providing connectivity to mobile users through a supporting infrastructure of base stations. One could use a single base station capable of covering the entire area, or a number of base stations, each covering a smaller area. To make a network with multiple base stations perform like a network with only a single base station, one must interconnect the base stations and design the network so that connections are maintained when users move across the boundaries of base station coverage regions (cells). The transfer of a user connection from one base station to another is called a *handover*. Base stations must track the locations of mobile users even when they are not connected so that connections can be established to them at any time. All of this implies considerable complexity. The cellular telephone networks best exemplify untethered mobility with an infrastructure of fixed base stations.

Various alternatives are possible that achieve lower complexity by sacrificing some functionality. One of these low-complexity alternatives is *tethered mobility*. It requires that a mobile node remain within the coverage area of the same base station for the duration of a connection. *Cordless telephones* represent an extreme form of tethered mobility in which the handset can only be used in the vicinity of a specific base station; that is, it cannot communicate with other base stations. Using a single base station to cover the entire area of interest offers significant advantages in terms of reduced protocol complexity (no need for handovers) and reduced computational load. However, several major drawbacks outweigh these benefits:

- As the size of the area to be covered increases, the required base station antenna height increases (to achieve line-of-sight to the mobile users). If the area to be covered is sufficiently large, then it might be necessary to put the base station on a satellite.
- As the size of the area to be covered grows, the EIRP requirements of the base station and of the mobile users increase.
- When a large number of base stations are used, base stations that are not in close proximity can use the same frequency spectrum without interfering with one another. This frequency sharing allows for increased system capacity.
- In a military network, a single base station that covers a large area becomes a critical node, as well as a high-value (and highly visible) asset that can be an attractive target for the enemy.

Table 2-2 from Feldman, presents an alternative two-dimensional classification of mobile wireless systems in which one axis indicates the level of mobility of the supporting network infrastructure (if there is a supporting infrastructure) and the second axis indicates the level of mobility of the users with respect to any infrastructure.[14]

Table 2-2 A Scheme for Classifying the Mobility Aspect of Wireless Communications Networks[15]

	A Wired connections	B Tethered wireless	C Fully mobile
Mobility of the in-theater network ground infrastructure			
0-Fixed	Wired telephone	Cordless telephones	Cellular telephones
1-Transportable	MSE users with wired connections radio	MSE users with mobile subscriber terminals	cellular system with military base station
2-Fully mobile	network with packet or no in-theater	ground infrastructure X UAV relay	work LEO radio net-Satellites

MSE = mobile subscriber equipment.

LEO = low earth orbit

Tethered Mobility with Fixed Base Stations

In a tethered mobile communications network, users are constrained to operate within range of a single base station or access point for the duration of a connection; the base station is typically fixed. Cordless phones represent a form of tethered mobility. Conventional *wireless LANs* (WLANs) is another example. WLANs typically operate over very limited ranges—for example, a single large room or adjacent smaller rooms. Although tethered mobility might seem unattractive, there are useful military applications—for example, for voice communications and computer connectivity within and around command posts. Tethered mobility is in general much easier to implement and therefore cheaper than full mobility because a fully mobile network with base stations must be able to perform handovers. Tethered wireless systems have a substantial commercial market, and are already the subject of intense research and development activity.[16]

Fully Mobile Networks ("Comm on The Move")

These networks do not depend on user proximity to fixed ground infrastructure. Examples include packet radio network networks, which have no fixed ground infrastructure, and satellite communications, which could make use of either military satellite systems. *Comm. on the move* permits continuous and unlimited motion, which in turn reduces the risks of detection and direction finding, which are significant risks for units operating close to the *forward line of troops* (FLOT) or within range of enemy artillery.[17]

Circuit-Switched Networks and Packet-Switched Networks

There are two basic approaches to the management of resources in communications networks: *circuit-switched networks* and *packet-switched networks.*

In circuit-switched networks, a path is established from point A to point B, and a fixed data rate is reserved on each link of that path. The reserved data rate, whether used or not, is dedicated to that connection until the connection is terminated.

In a packet-switched network, information is broken into segments called packets or cells that travel through the network in an independent fashion and are eventually reassembled at the destination. Packet-switching (also known as *store and forward*) does not involve the reservation of resources for any connection.

In the *public switched network* (PSN), voice connections are handled via circuit-switching with a dedicated data rate of 64 Kbps (or 32 Kbps) in each direction. The exchange of status and call control information among switches in the PSN is handled via packet switching. Some switched data services (ISBN) are handled via circuit switching while others (for example, frame-relay and ATM) are handled via packet switching. The PSN is thus a hybrid circuit/packet-switched network. The Internet is an entirely packet-switched network.

Circuit-switching tends to be inefficient for "bursty" traffic such as messages and short data transmissions. If you establish a circuit and then terminate the circuit each time a message is sent, the overhead associated with setup and termination may be much longer than the actual time to transmit the message. If you open a circuit from A to B, and leave the circuit open so that messages can be sent immediately whenever they are generated, then the circuit will almost certainly be unused most of the time, resulting in even greater inefficiency.

One of the major benefits of circuit-switching over packet-switching for wired networks is consistent and low end-to-end delay once a connection has been established. Circuit-switched networks are well suited for connection-oriented traffic such as interactive voice and video that have real-time delivery requirements. In traditional packet-switched networks, different packets of a given stream may take different paths through the network. Delay varies from packet to packet since transmission speeds of links can vary. This is because different paths may involve different numbers of hops and queuing delays can vary for successive packets, even if they follow the same path. The delay variability of the traditional packet-switched network is acceptable for such nonreal-time traffic as email and file transfers, and even for most Web browsing. Because there is no reservation of bandwidth for connections, information transfer tends to be efficient in traditional packet-switched networks. Such networks are, however, not well suited for traffic with real-time requirements. For connection-oriented traffic with no real-time requirements—such as file transfers—missing packets can be retransmitted, and packets that are received in the wrong order can be re-sequenced. The TCP protocol uses a "sliding window" to keep track of missing packets, and it holds packets that are received out of proper order until missing packets are retransmitted, so that all packets can be delivered in order. For voice, however, the maximum acceptable delay (if the interactive quality is not to be compromised) is about 100 ms, so that you cannot afford to wait for retransmission of missing packets. Furthermore, the packet error rate must be controlled, since packets containing errors must be discarded, and gaps of more than about 50 milliseconds (ms) are noticeable to the listener and result in poor intelligibility if occurring frequently.

In recent years, packet-switched network protocols have been developed that support not only nonreal-time traffic, but also (like circuit-switched networks) real-time connection-oriented traffic. The best known of these protocols is *asynchronous transfer mode* (ATM). ATM moves data in fixed-length cells, each containing 48 bytes of user data. Although ATM is essentially packet-switched at a low level, it is able to support a variety of types of traffic— including connection-oriented traffic with real-time requirements—and can provide quality-of-service (QoS) guarantees in wired networks. ATM achieves this by requiring that successive cells in a given connection follow the same path (a *virtual circuit*) through the network by reserving resources, by regulating cell flow rates associated with different types of connections, and by *admission control* (rejecting new connections whose service requirements cannot be satisfied because of the existing network load). Current Internet protocols provide no guarantees other than TCP's guarantee of eventual delivery under reasonable conditions.

Information Theory

Wireless communications may also be considered in terms of engineering science of information theory. Based on the seminal research of Claude Shannon, communications theory provides a statistical method for quantifying information for the purpose of analyzing transmission, formatting, storage, and processing of information over channels.[18] Wireless communications are limited by maximum capacity (transmission rate) of communication channels, methods for measuring the redundant information in communicated messages both spoken and data, and the means of determining the most efficient compression rates for messages. Shannon gave us the concept of entropy, which we use to measure the chaotic value of cryptographic keys, and a method to determine spectral efficiency, which is a primary design factor for commercial wireless systems.[19]

Shannon suggested that information is defined in terms of messages about the state of a system or event. Information may be quantified by the uniqueness of the message relative to all possible messages that occur. This *uniqueness* concept (the likelihood that a message would occur in a group of messages) is used to define and quantify information content. The likelihood of each message relative to all possible message occurrences is inversely related to the information content of the individual message.

Entropy

Shannon defined the important concept of *entropy* (not to be confused with the chemical engineering thermodynamic entropy term) to relate information to its carrier message. Let M= (x1, x2, x3, . . .) be the set of all possible messages from the system X, which can take on n states, and define the information content of any message m_i about the state of X as a function m_i. Shannon defined entropy as the primary information relationship measure of each message, H as:

$$H = \sum_{i=1,n} p_i \log_2 p_i \qquad (2.1)$$

Where:

H = Entropy in bits

p_i = Probability that the random variable is in state i

n = Number of possible states of the system X

Entropy is a measure of the chaotic value of the message. It is a measure of the disorder or uncertainty about X, the state of the system. Decreases in entropy of received messages may be used to measure information gain and efficiency.[20] Waltz suggests that the goal of sensing, communicating, and processing is to decrease uncertainty and increase information.[21] However, from a cryptographic point-of-view, the goal is to increase the uncertainty or chaos in applied cryptographic keys. When all messages are equally likely, there is no prior statistical knowledge about which message may be received at any time, and the entropy is at a maximum and each message conveys the maximum potential of revealing the unknown. If the messages are not equally likely, it follows that there is prior knowledge about the state of the system, and the entropy of the system is less than the equally likely case.[22]

Figure 2-3 illustrates the principal information theoretic measures, based on entropy in a typical wireless (or wired) sensing, communication, and processing system.[23]

Mutual information is a quantitative measure of the information performance of a transmission channel as a function the entropy attributable to the *noise* contributed *by* the channel:

$$H(X;Y) = \sum_i p_i \left[\sum_j p\,(j \mid i) \log_2 \left[p\,(j \mid i) p_j \right] \right] \qquad (2.2)$$

Where:

H(X;Y) = Mutual information between output state Y and input state X

p_i = Probability that the random variable is in state i

p_j = Probability that the random variable is in state j

p (j|i) = Conditional probability relating input state i to output state j

Entropy change, or information increase, is the measure of reduction in uncertainty about state of X determined by the change in entropy H due to a message or succession of messages.

Discipline and Approach	Basis of Definition of Information	Information Metrics	Application to Information Exploitation
Philosophy— classical logic	Information is defined as "true" or "false" assertions whose validity is determined by logical calulations; relative value of information is not defined.	Deductive logic provides conclusions that are either true or false. Inductive logic provides conclusions that only have a degree of validity.	Predicate logic is applied to reasoning systems to make true/false assertions based on source inputs. Bayesian or fuzzy logic approaches provide algebraic means to perform deduction with uncertain data. Statistical inference techniques provide means of performing limited induction and learning.
Computer science semiotic logic		Abductive logic provides the "best explanation" for a given set of data.	Abduction is applied to explaining particular sets of data as a limited form of induction.
Information theory.	Information value is defined by "entropy" a measure of uniqueness of an essertion, which is a function of the probability that the assertion will occur out of all possible assertions.	Entropy A measure of the uncertainty about the state of a system. Information gain The arithmetic change in entropy due to a message. Cross-entropy The change in statistical distribution of state due to a message.	Information theoretic measures provide a means of measuring the performance of components (sensors, communication channels, and processing systems) in terms of the reduction in uncertainly about the state of a system being observed.
Decision theory	Information is measured by its application benefit to the user of information.	Utility The value of the application of the information, as measured by the user, in terms of achievement of an application objective.	Utility measures provide a means of measuring the military effectiveness of information-processing systems.
Business knowledge management	Information is measured by its economic return to the user, relative to capital investment.	Capital The economic value of information measured as utility added for interest paid to secure the information.	Capital measures provide a means of measuring the economic effectiveness of information-processing systems.

2-3   Alternative methods to define and measure information.

[Reprinted with permission from Waltz, Edward, *Information Warfare: Principles and Operations*, Artech House, 1998 page 70.]

$$I_j = \Delta H \qquad\qquad (2.3)$$

Where:

I_j = H before message – H after message

Cross-entropy is a measure of the *discrimination or* degree of similarity between two probability distributions of Ij representing the probabilities of each possible state of X:

$$D = (p,q) = \sum_{i=1,\,n} p_i \log_2 (p_i \,/\, q_i) \qquad\qquad (2.4)$$

Where:

D(p, q) = Cross-entropy between distribution [p] and [q]

p_i = Probability of element i in distribution [p]

q_i = Probability of element i in distribution [q]

These measures provide both a theoretical and practical means of quantifying information gains, using the statistical knowledge of the communication system being measured, the messages, and their information content.[24]

Mobile Capacity

In mobile communications networking, the question is: How do we assess the capacity or maximum throughput of the network? There are at least three ways to answer this question and the answers are different based on:

- Whether we consider *per user throughput* or *total network throughput*. Total network throughput is the at most the sum of all user transmit data rates at any given time.
- The *maximum tolerable bit error rate* (BER) or *message error rate* (MER). For systems in which users or nets generate mutual interference, the maximum number of simultaneous transmissions increases with the maximum (acceptable) error rate.
- The geographical dispersion of the transmitters and receivers. Where mutual interference can occur, some geometries are favorable and some are not. For cellular and related types of networks, we think in terms of maximum average number of transmitters per square kilometer or throughput per square kilometer, rather than per user throughput or total network throughput.[25]

We have different design philosophies and importance given to capacity measures depending on whether the designer is commercial or military. The design and sizing of a mobile network should reflect the type of traffic that will flow over the network. In the military, communications in a radio net involves short-range broadcasts to all participants of the net for single hop communications. Military traffic is often broadcast in nature, transmitted to all users, and favors full mesh architectures to be efficient. Tactical communications are different because a large fraction of the messages or voice calls are among small groups of nearby users. The distance between these groups may be small in comparison to the extent of the entire network. In the previous case, shared radio nets and point-to-point links or combination of both are used. These generally require more than one hop. These nets tend to be *spectrally efficient,* use less power, and offer high real capacities.[26]

We contend that capacity is an important concept but meaningless by itself. You must consider both capacity and error rate together when evaluating a given system. A secondary factor to be considered is whether there is *forward error coding* (FEC) turned on. FEC may reduce capacity ratings by one-half to one-fourth, depending on pulse mode. A 1-Mbps link with an error rate of 10^{-8} may be preferable to a 10-Mbps link with an error rate of 10^{-5} because highly compressed images cannot be transmitted over the noisier link. To use the noisier link, the images must be uncompressed which offsets the higher speed, or perform additional FEC coding which may not be feasible.

This tradeoff relates once again to Shannon's work. Shannon defined an information theoretic definition of capacity as the maximum information rate or maximum error-free user rate that can be achieved with ideal FEC coding. Capacity is generally incorrectly discussed in the open literature as only the maximum user data rate.[27]

Spectral Efficiency

There is a growing demand by both military and commercial customers for access to communications. A growing number of users who desire access want more *bandwidth* (higher data rates) per user. The military has been the loser in the recent sales of frequency spectrum to commercial service providers. There is no indication that the encroachment will be stopped in future sales. Higher capacities can be achieved by a combination of more efficient use of the frequency spectrum and greater exploitation of frequencies at X-band (8 to 12 GHz) and above. The real solution is more efficient spectral use by both military and commercial organizations.

Spectral efficiencies of military communications systems have tended to be relatively poor; efficiencies below 0.1 bps/*Hertz* (Hz) are typical, and efficiencies below 0.01 bps/Hz are not uncommon. One RAND study by Feldman showed that the *Joint Tactical Information Distribution System* (JTIDS), a military radio for broadcast messaging and voice, has a nominal spectral efficiency of 0.02 bps/Hz when 30 nets operate simultaneously, but operation of more than about five simultaneous nets will result in excessive message error rates. With five nets operating simultaneously, the maximum spectral efficiency of JTIDS is roughly 0.003 bps/Hz.

Compare this with spectral efficiencies, not counting cell-to-cell frequency reuse, on the order of 0.1 to 0.5 bps/Hz for commercial cellular systems with efficiencies toward the upper end of that range for the newer digital cellular systems.

As we discuss later, part of the explanation for this is the military need for waveforms, with *anti-jam* (A/J) and *low probability of detection* (LPD) characteristics, which are easiest to achieve by sacrificing spectral efficiency. However, this does not explain the spectacularly low spectral efficiency of many military systems. Spectral efficiency is irrelevant from the perspective of the individual system user, and it is of concern to the military system designer only to the extent of supporting a required number of users within the allocated and available spectrum. If the allocated spectrum permits a spectrally wasteful design that allows for minor economies in terms of reduced power consumption and system complexity, the military wireless system designer will select a spectrally wasteful design. For the long-range planner, who views the frequency spectrum as a scarce resource that must be carefully parceled out to competing users and groups, spectral efficiency carries a higher priority.[28] We also propose that the futurerequirements of mobile commercial and military systems —as yet undefined—will put spectral efficiency as a top priority. This is clearly evident from the jam-packed current allocation of spectrum. It looks more like a quilt than an effective distribution of frequencies (which are no longer free). And you thought space was free or private!

The commercial wireless hardware designer is concerned about profitability, not A/J or LPD. Spectral efficiency determines the capacity limit of the system, which in turn determines the maximum user base that the system can support, which determines the amount of hardware that can be sold (profitably) to service providers and users. Designers of military systems regard spectral efficiency as a nuisance. The only cost issue they concern themselves with is start-up. They are not interested in life-cycle costs or per-user costs because they do not pay for the communications hardware and services.[29]

Shannon supplied a formula for the capacity of a bandwidth channel with *additive white Gaussian noise* (AWGN). There are a variety of channel models in use. In a strict sense channel model, propagation effects are included and interference is excluded.[30] Gaussian noise is pure in that it does not include multipath, narrowband interference or other effects. The Shannon channel model is considered the baseline for many capacity calculations. Consider an ideal band-limited channel of bandwidth W Hz in which the signal is corrupted only by AWGN having a one-sided power spectral density level of N_0 watts/Hz.

In systems with channels of unequal widths, one must balance the spectral power densities (watts per Hz). This simple model does not apply to channels that corrupt signals in more complex ways such as multipath or mutual interference. Let E_b denote the energy per information bit at the receiver and let C denote the channel capacity—that is, the maximum average rate at which information can be transferred over this channel.

An important and practical relationship can be derived directly from Claude Shannon's capacity formula relating the maximum achievable spectral efficiency C/W to the signal-to-noise (SNR) E_b/N_0. The starting point is the standard form of Claude Shannon's formula for the capacity of a band-limited channel with AWGN:

$$C = W \log_2 (1 + P/N) \cdot 1\text{bit}, \tag{2.5}$$

Where:

C = Capacity or maximum average rate at which information can be transmitted over the channel, bits/sec

W = Bandwidth of the channel in Hz.

P/N = The ratio of the signal power divided by the noise power passed by the receiver front-end filtering (a dimensionless quantity).

To get the capacity equation in terms of spectral efficiency E_b/N_0, we make the substitution of $N = W \times N_0$. Noise in the power spectrum is measured as density level in watts/Hz. So the total channel noise N is equal to channel bandwidth times the power density over that channel. E_b is the energy per information bit at the receiver; N_0 is the AWGN one-sided power density level noise in watts/Hz. From this is derived:

$$P/N_0 = W\,[2^{C/W} - 1] \tag{2.6}$$

Dividing both sides by C, the channel capacity in bits/sec (the maximum average rate of information transferred over the channel):

$$P/CN_0 = W/C\,[2^{C/W} - 1] \tag{2.7}$$

To introduce the term spectral efficiency E_b/N_0 in energy per information bit, operating at capacity, the average energy per information bit equals the average signal power divided by the average information rate in bps, that is:

$$E_b = P/C \tag{2.8}$$

By substituting and rearranging, a practical formula relates the *achievable spectral efficiency C/W* to the E_b/N_0, *signal to noise ratio* (SNR):

$$E_b/N_0 = W/C\,[2^{C/W} - 1] \tag{2.9}$$

For example, suppose we want the minimum E_b/N_0 required to achieve a spectral efficiency C/W of 6 bps/Hz. We find $E_b/N_0 = 10.5 = 10.2$ dB. To obtain the maximum achievable C/W for a given SNR, we solve numerically. Although spectral efficiency can be measured in various ways, bps per Hz is probably the most common.[31]

Techniques for increasing spectral efficiency include the following:

- You can use modulation formats, such as binary Gaussian minimum shift keying, that are spectrally compact. With spectrally compact modulations, channels in an FDMA system can be packed more closely together because there is less power spillover into adjacent channels. Quadrature phase shift keying, a modulation widely used in military communications systems, is spectrally inefficient.
- It may be possible to use power control to balance power, so that amplitudes of signals arriving at a given receiver are matched as closely as possible. In systems with channels of unequal widths, you must balance the spectral

power densities (watts per Hz). Power balancing also permits closer packing of channels. For some types of wireless systems, power balancing is impractical. Systems designed to cope with jamming, for example, may require that each terminal operate at its maximum output power—clearly precluding power balancing.

- Many FDMA systems use fixed-width channels that are sized to support the highest user data rate. Dynamic adjustment of channel width, which can be accomplished using digital filtering, permits maintaining roughly constant per-channel spectral efficiency.

- In satellite systems and in other networks with repeaters, dedicated assignment of channels to specific users or pairs of users for broadcast can lead to underutilization. *Demand assignment multiple access* (DAMA) techniques can be used to assign channels dynamically as needed, permitting a population of users to share the resources.

- Even with DAMA, it is common practice to fence off pools of channels, with each pool dedicated to a specific group of users. This may lead to situations where one pool is over-loaded while another is largely unused, since demand cannot be shifted between them. Merging pools of channels together prevents this problem.

- In satellite and other repeater-based systems that use TDMA, a portion of each time slot must be reserved for guard time. This part of the slot is left empty to account for uncorrected time delay differences between transmissions arriving from different sources, so that a transmission in slot k will not overlap and interfere with a transmission in slot 41. With accurate knowledge of position and time, transmit times can be adjusted to correct for range differences to the repeater, allowing for guard times to be virtually eliminated.

- In systems with multiple repeaters (base stations), base stations that are distant from one another can use the same frequencies (or codes, for code-division multiple access systems). Such frequency reuse allows for potentially large increases in system capacity.

The military is impeded from transitioning to more efficient use of the frequency spectrum by the problem of legacy systems. In particular, radios and satellite terminals that use older modulation formats cannot interoperate with those that use newer modulations. Worse than this, it may not be possible to use this equipment in the same theater of operations because of mutual interference. Commercial systems tend to get by the legacy problem but have serious interoperability issues. Security for these systems has been largely proprietary and a general failure.[32]

Decision Theory

Information by its very nature implies that there is a measure of its value. A subset of the information model presented previously deals with decisions. Decisions (dealing with wireless design and threats) are made in the presence of uncertainty and risk by choosing among alternatives. The basis for a particular choice is determined by quantifying the relative consequences of each alternative and choosing the best alternative to optimize some objective function. The concept of utility function has been introduced to model uncertainty of decisions and its associated risk. Two utility functions provide decision preferences on the basis of the value of risk:

Value   The utility function where no uncertainty is present
Risk   The function to determine a preferred decision, which considers uncertainty

Consider a common form of utility function, a summation of weighted attributes, each of which characterizes an alternative (performance, efficiency, reliability, and so forth) The function allows us to calculate a utility value for each alternative:

$$U(x) = \sum_{i=1}^{n} v_i (x_i) \tag{2.10}$$

Where:

$U(x)$ = the utility of an alternative (x) considering n differences between attributes

v_i = the conditioning variable weighting the relative importance of attribute I

x_i = the Value of attribute i

The value of $U(x)$ is calculated for each alternative and the highest utility value is obtained. This is not a direct means of measuring information, but it does provide a measure of the effectiveness of an information system.[33]

Risk Management and Architecture of Information Security (INFOSEC)

Risk is inherent in life. As it is the antithesis of security, we naturally strive to eliminate risk. As worthy as that goal is, however, we learn through experience that complete elimination is never possible. Even if it were possible to eliminate all risk, the cost of achieving that total risk avoidance would have to be compared against the cost of the possible losses resulting from having accepted rather than having eliminated risk. The results of such an analysis could include pragmatic decisions as to whether achieving risk avoidance at such cost was reasonable. Applying reason in choosing how much risk we can accept and, hence, how much security we can afford is risk management.

Thinking About Risk

It is useful in thinking about risk management to pose a tentative relationship. This is not a mathematical equation for use in making quantitative determinations of risk level. It is an algorithm for use in thinking about the factors that enter into risk management and in assessing the qualitative level of danger posed in a given situation. Professor Daniel J. Ryan at George Washington University developed a relationship for evaluating the consequences of adverse attacks on a wireless (or wired) communication system. Risk is described as a notional relationship.[34]

Consider the following statement:

$$\text{Level of Risk} = \frac{(\text{Threat} \times \text{Vulnerability})}{\text{Countermeasures}} \times \text{Impact} \qquad (2.11)$$

Natural disasters represent real dangers to people, facilities, equipment, inventory, and other assets, including information and information systems, and have to be considered by managers as part of the larger issue of disaster planning. Reliability and the steps necessary to allow for and deal with reliability failures are also risk management issues. In information systems security and Infowar, however, we use the word *threat* in describing a more limited component of risk. Threats are posed by organizations or individuals who intend harm and have the capability to accomplish their objectives. These types of threats, and measures that may be taken to reduce or eliminate the risks they create, comprise one of the principal themes of this book. They may take the form of computer hackers, criminals, industrial or state-sponsored spies, enemy armed forces, terrorists, psychotic persons, drug lords, or saboteurs. Their organizations may be formal, as are foreign armies or intelligence services, or informal, like the terrorist group that attacked the World Trade Center, hacker groups like the Legion of Doom or Chaos, or the FBI spy Hanssen.[35]

Threats to our information or computer processing and communications systems may be from outsiders seeking access to our information assets, but more often they are from insiders—white-collar criminals, disgruntled employees harboring real or imagined grievances, or traitors who turn over their country's secrets for money or ideological incentives. Unfortunately, in real-world security situations, threats do not occur one at a time, or even independently.

Vulnerability

Vulnerabilities are characteristics of our situations, systems, or facilities that can be exploited by a threat to do us harm. A vulnerability for which there is no credible threat does not require a response by security processes. Examples of vulnerabilities include structural weaknesses of buildings located near earthquake fault zones, weak passwords on our computers and networks, easily penetrated facilities, non-vetted personnel, or operations carried out in such a way that outsiders can detect their existence and analyze their objectives. Careful attention to the design of facilities and systems can reduce or eliminate vulnerabilities. Locks and barriers can be strengthened, fences raised, alarms and monitors installed, computer systems and networks upgraded to incorporate security features, sprinkler systems installed, and a wealth of other features, devices, and procedures implemented to reduce vulnerabilities.

Threats

Managers must consider the possible consequences of attacks from a wide variety of threats. Each attack may act on a tangential vulnerability. Many exploitation attempts go unrecognized. Often threats to information and information systems are paired with a specific line of attack or set of vulnerabilities. A threat that has no vulnerability creates no risk. It is useful to deal with threat-vulnerability pairings in the risk management process. We need to recognize that there is no one-to-one correspondence, so we cannot depend upon elimination of a vulnerability to neutralize a threat, or elimination of a threat to mean that vulnerability can be tolerated safely. The numerator of our equation is, therefore, a sum of threat-vulnerability products where any given threat or vulnerability may occur in more than one product. Any threat with no associated vulnerability, or vulnerability with no threat, results in a zero addition to risk, simplifying the analysis.

Countermeasures

Countermeasures may abate the danger even if there are malevolent and capable threats, as well as vulnerabilities, which can be exploited by those threats. All else being equal, more countermeasures mean less risk, so countermeasures appear in the denominator in our algorithm. Guards can be hired, personnel subjected to background investigations or polygraph examinations, badges may be used to identify authorized personnel, procedures implemented in our computer systems, and networks to backup data bases and to enforce sound password practices, and so forth. Such countermeasures reduce the likelihood of a successful attack and so lessen risk. To distinguish between vulnerability and a countermeasure, consider the former a consequence of system design and the latter as what is available to overcome or mask the vulnerability.[36]

Impact

The impact of a successful attack depends upon the value of the target. If the impact of a security failure is small, allocation of scarce and expensive resources to security systems and processes can also be small. For example, the loss of some routine office correspondence might occasion little concern or cost. Conversely, the consequences of some security failures can be exceptionally dire. Failure of the public switched network that carries our telephone and computer communications could be devastating to the nation's economy. The use of nuclear, chemical, or biological weapons by terrorists, penetration of our cryptographic systems by foreign intelligence services, or foreknowledge of our strategic and tactical war plans by our enemies could have consequences for our country too severe to permit the smallest relaxation of security, even if such threats are relatively unlikely and the cost of protection is high. Obviously, as the value of the target rises, the impact of a successful attack goes up as well, and so our sense of risk increases. Consequently, impact is a force multiplier in our algorithm.

It is not always possible to evaluate in any quantitative sense the factors in the risk management algorithm. The cost of some countermeasures—like alarm systems or insurance—may be easily determined, although acquiring information about the true cost of countermeasures and allocating those costs among various security functions turns out to be surprisingly difficult using current methods of accounting. What portion of the cost of a wall is attributable to security rather than structural necessity? If guards were not needed to protect information and information systems, would they still be needed to protect employees from criminal intruders? If computers that are shielded against emission of potentially compromising radiation are an option, are both cases (with and without shielding) costed independently and compared, and would the shielding still be needed to protect the system against incoming radiation from the environment (nearby airport radars can cause problems in unshielded wireless receivers, for example) or deliberate attacks by info-terrorists using high energy laser beams or *electromagnetic pulse* (EMP) weapons? Even if it were easy to determine the cost of potential countermeasures, the likelihood of the threat being successful, the extent of vulnerabilities, and the impact of a possible loss are at best uncertain. As with most management problems, insufficient information makes security decisions more of an art form and less of a science.

This uncertainty is a contributing cause of our tendency to rely on risk avoidance. By assuming the threat to be capable, intense, and competent, by valuing our potential targets highly, and by conservatively estimating uncertainties, we reduce risk management to the question, "What are our vulnerabilities and how much do countermeasures cost to eliminate them?" The management problem is "How much money must I spend and where can I spend it most wisely?" In most cases, fortunately, it is possible to do better. It is often sufficient to bind the problem, even when exact figures are not available. Through careful analysis an estimate of the value of each factor in Professor Ryan's equation, balancing the risk of loss or damage against the costs of countermeasures, reveal a mix that provides adequate protection without excessive cost.

Ultimately, the risk management process is about making decisions. The impact of a successful attack and the level of risk that is acceptable in any given situation are fundamental policy decisions.

The threat is whatever it is and while it may be abated, controlled, or subdued by appropriate countermeasures, it is beyond the direct control of the security process. The process must focus, accordingly, on vulnerabilities and countermeasures. Vulnerabilities are design issues and must be addressed during the design, development, fabrication, and implementation of facilities, equipment, systems, and networks. Although the distinction is not always certain, countermeasures are less needed due to the characteristics of our systems than of their environments and the ways in which we use them. Typically, to make any asset less vulnerable raises its cost, not just in the design and development phase but also due to more extensive validation and testing to ensure the functionality and utility of security features, and in the application of countermeasures during the operation and maintenance phase as well.[37]

A Model for Cost-Effective Risk Management

A fundamental problem of risk management, then, is to link the choice of design characteristics and of countermeasures to threat and impact, in order to create a cost-effective balance that achieves an acceptable level of risk. Such a process might work as follows:

1. Assess the impact of loss of or damage to the potential target. While the impact of the loss of a family member as a parent is beyond measure, the economic value of the member as a wage earner can be estimated as part of the process of deciding the amount of life insurance to purchase. The economic impact of crime or destruction by fires in a city can be determined as part of the process of sizing police and fire departments. The impact of loss of a technological lead on battlefield effectiveness can be specified.

   Not all impacts are economic, of course. Loss of sovereignty through war or destruction of civilization in a strategic nuclear exchange is beyond calculation. On a lesser scale, the political and diplomatic impact of damage or destruction of some assets must be considered, as, for example, when an embassy is overrun (as happened in Tehran). Such considerations are often of necessity subjective and qualitative rather than quantitative in nature.

2. Specify the level of risk of damage or destruction that is acceptable. This may well be the most difficult part of the process. No one contemplates easily the loss of loved ones or of one's own life. At the other end of the scale, the destruction resulting from nuclear war is unthinkable. In between, addressing loss or destruction in terms of acceptability seems cold-hearted and unfeeling.

3. Identify and characterize the threat. The leaders of our country, diplomats, military commanders, and intelligence and counterintelligence officers who constantly seek to understand the capabilities, intentions, and activities of our enemies perform this function. The damage that can be caused by accident, disease, or such natural forces as earthquakes, hurricanes, tornadoes, fires, or floods is known. Criminal behavior can be described and predicted. Terrorist groups have been studied and their activities have been cataloged.

4. Analyze vulnerabilities. For individuals, dietary and exercise regimens can reduce vulnerability to some health threats. Fire and intrusion alarms can detect problems and alert response teams. Computer systems and networks can be designed to be less vulnerable to hacker attacks. In military and intelligence situations, both offensive and defensive specialists need to be consulted to understand how attacks might be initiated. Where potential improvements that may reduce vulnerabilities are identified, the cost of their implementation must be estimated.

5. Specify countermeasures. Where vulnerabilities are inherent or cost too much to eliminate during the design and development of facilities or systems, countermeasures must be selected to reduce risk to an acceptable level. Access to facilities can be controlled. Use of computers and networks can be monitored or audited. Personnel can be vetted to various degrees. Not all countermeasures need be used if some lesser mix will reduce risk to an acceptable level. Costs of each type of countermeasure must be estimated to determine the most cost-effective mix.

6. Allow for uncertainties. None of the factors in the risk management equation is absolute. No threat is infinitely capable and always lucky. No system is without vulnerability. No countermeasure is completely effective, and, short of complete destruction, the impact of damage to an asset is problematic. Risk management requires the realistic assessment of uncertainties, erring on neither conservative nor optimistic sides.[38]

In practice, the estimates needed for such a risk management process are accomplished in gross terms. Threat level or uncertainty may be assessed as high or low. Impact may be designated as severe or moderate. This gross quantification of factors in the risk management equation allows the design attributes used to reduce vulnerabilities and the countermeasures to be grouped so that they can be applied consistently throughout large organizations. The previous analysis of impact, threat, and acceptable risk ultimately leads the manager to appropriate decisions regarding reducing vulnerability and application of effective countermeasures.

Historical Threats to Wireless Services OTA

Traditionally threats to wireless communications have come in three areas:

- Interception of radio path
- Access to mobile services
- Interference in wireless networks

Attacks on the radio path include interception of data on the air interface, loss of confidentiality of user data, loss of confidentiality of signaling information, and loss of confidentiality of user identity information. Illegal access to mobile services generally revolves around some scheme to masquerade or impersonate a subscriber while using system services. GSM model response has to include auditable units such as mobile stations, SIM cards, subscriber identity module, home location register, visitor location register, and authentication center.

Wireless networks have vulnerabilities everywhere including user's workstation, server, router/gateway, communications path, and protocol structure.[39]

A sample listing of the wireless security considerations that designers face would have to include cellular phones and modems, roaming, packet radio, van Eck freaking (a.k.a. van Eck emissions or unintentional RF emissions from CRT display), *mobile satellite services* (MSS), cable and direct TV security policy and schemes, station authentication/management, and coexistence with wired products at a location.

Since the 1940s wireless security responses have included several developed concealment technologies such as spread-spectrum, direct sequence, frequency hopping, and multiple encryption options. These options have been applied to a growing variety of wireless data services including banking, account inquiries, transfers, bill payments, order fulfillment, investment accounts, loan/mortgage applications, securities trading, trading equities, mutual funds, options and other derivatives, quotes and alert notification, e-commerce *Business-to-Business* (B2B), health care, physician-oriented patient management systems, ambulatory, pharmacy and laboratory services, emergency alerts and remote medical telemetry, life style, positional/navigational and GPS, news, weather, and so forth.

Why Is Wireless Security Different?

There are four fundamental differences for wireless services:

- Bandwidth
- Allowable error rates
- Latency and Variability
- Power constraints

Many of these differences are seen at the network levels. Wireless networks are generally based on mobile devices communicating via some kind of an electromagnetic transmission and reception method such as:

- **Radio Frequency (RF) networks**   HF, VHF, UHF (3 MHz to 3 GHz)
- **Satellite Communications (SAT)**   SHF, EHF (3 GHz to 300 GHz)
- **Infrared (IR)**   IrDA

Wireless networks are characterized by generally low *quality of service* (QoS). Many times they employ small size devices with low power and low bandwidth options. Wireless networks compared to their wired sisters are relatively unreliable, as packet losses occur more frequently than in wired networks. They exhibit high latency and variability due to retransmissions. Network limitations necessitate efficient communications and security protocols. Wireless designers consider a whole battery of variables in their designs: user expectations, error rates, throughput, protocol overhead, compression, latency, battery life and energy-saving protocols, unknown network connectivity, out of coverage, one-way coverage, chatty applications/protocols, and keep-alive messages. The Internet has made the problem more complex. Wired Internet protocols (IPSec, SSL, or SSH) are typically not optimal for wireless networks. They are too chatty, carry too much overhead, and the timeouts are too tight.[40]

We must recognize that secure mobile devices will have:

- Relatively low computing power (compared to desktop PCs).
- Limits to the type of cryptographic algorithms a device can support.
- Limited storage capabilities.
- Power conservation imposed by functionality limitations.
- Fundamental restrictions on bandwidth, error rate, latency, and variability.
- Small footprint and compact I/O.
- Limited display capabilities; GUI becomes more challenging with different display form factors.
- Usability and user experience issues.
- Throughput sensitivities to protocol overhead and compression.

Most existing security technologies, protocols, and standards have been designed for the wired/high bandwidth environment. In many cases they are not well suited for the wireless mobile environment because they have too much overhead and exhibit tight timeouts. So we redefine implementing wireless security to mean:

- Adaptation and integration of existing solutions and infrastructure.
- Promoting consistency and interoperability among a diverse spectrum of mobile and wireless devices.
- Providing a high level of security without detrimental impact on the user experience.

In a wireless network, security features greatly differ between each of the protocol stacks, and security policy implementation and enforcement is dependent on the carrier. For example, listed are some representative differences and features in the logical OSI layers.[41]

Physical Layer Security

- Provides signal scrambling for *over-the-air* (OTA) eavesdropping protection.
- Current technologies based on splitting the bitstream into small fragments called radio frames and then applying some form of frequency based scrambling technique.
- Radio frames travel on a spread spectrum of frequencies where each fragment is identified by a digital code known only to the device and the base station.
- No other device can receive the transmissions.
- For each connection, there are billions of code combinations available.
- Example: CDMA network security.

Data Link and Network Layers

- Some protocols, such as CDPD and GSM, provide data confidentiality in these layers.
- CDPD applies encryption to each segmented datagram(s) prior to transmission.
- GSM uses a *subscriber identity module* (SIM) card to store a symmetric key known only to the mobile and the *authentication center* (AuC) at the carrier site.
- Key is used in both authentication and ciphering TDMA frames prior to transmission.

Transport Layer Security

- *Secure Socket Layer* (SSL) used extensively in Web applications to secure TCP/IP connections.
- Public keys (RSA) to exchange a session key (RC4 and other algorithms) for bulk encryption.
- Elaborate session/connection management protocol for session establishment, resumption, and termination.
- Designed for high-bandwidth connections; it is not optimized for high-latency networks.

- Client and server authentication via X.509 certificates.
- X.509 certificates have a large footprint and require significant computing power to process.
- SSL is not well suited for wireless applications.

Application Layer Security

- Application specific user authentication.
- User ID and password.
- Challenge-response authentication protocols.
- Biometrics.
- Message integrity.
- Hashing of a shared secret and some message specific data to produce a unique MAC (SHA-1, MD5).
- Application level encryption: RC5, Triple 3DES, Rijndael, and so on.
- Application level digital signatures for non-repudiation and authentication. (PKI), RSA, ECDSA (ECC).

The bearer layers are used to secure the OTA link to prevent eavesdropping threats. The transport layer incorporates security for goals of confidentiality and authentication. But the implementation is discontinuous due to the numerous transition points between wireless and wired protocols. Application level security provides for access control, authentication, confidentiality, and non-repudiation.

Designing security into wireless services means that we require wireless communications and transactions to exhibit high levels of authentication, confidentiality, data integrity, and non-repudiation. Companies offering wireless services infrastructure must provide customers high levels of assurances that their communications and transactions are secure. This becomes a non-trivial challenge when dealing with an assortment of networks, protocols, and devices.

Translating into mobile end-to-end security requirements must be confidentiality between mobile device and organization/user; organizations must be able to authenticate sensitive transactions that have been signed by the user of the mobile device and vice versa, and no intermediate entity (such as a mobile operator/carrier or middle-tier service provider) should be able to view, intelligently hear, alter, or store any of the confidential data/voice elements that make up the message or transaction. End-to-end security entails protecting voice/data with minimal cost, delay, complexity, and bandwidth overhead. Mobile and base stations must authenticate each other and allow distinct keys in a variety of environments. Two-way authentication is more effective using end-to-end encryption. Since no one organization can control the entire infrastructure, end-to-end connectivity needs to be independent of the underlying infrastructure. More and more functionality needs to be moved from the core and the perimeters of the networks to the edge devices. This needs to be done within a spectrum of emerging standards (IEEE 802.1b, wireless application protocol, WEP, Bluetooth, Future narrowband digital terminal, and so on).

Performance Measures and Key Design Tradeoffs

Commercial and military wireless communication system designers generally make different design tradeoffs. The performance of a communications system depends on design parameters whose values can be selected by the system designer and environmental parameters over which the designer has no control. The relationship between these parameters and performance metrics of interest is usually complex. Changing any single design parameter tends to impact all performance metrics, and simultaneously changing multiple designs parameters typically affects performance metrics in ways that cannot be predicted from knowledge of the single parameter effects alone.

The goal of the design process is to select the design parameters to achieve specific performance levels (or the best performance possible) subject to constraints on system cost. Cost can be viewed as another performance metric. Some of the choices the designer must make are essentially discrete or integer valued, that is, a selection among a small (or at least finite) set of alternatives. The three-way divide among narrowband, direct sequence spread spectrum, and frequency hop spread spectrum is an example of a situation wherein such a choice must be made. Other design parameters are essentially real valued. For example, antenna size and transmitter output power can take on values from a continuum. Feldman shows why the wireless system design problem is difficult for several reasons:[42]

- The designer is faced with a huge design space (each design parameter can be thought of as one dimension in a multidimensional space). Exhaustive exploration of this space is typically impractical. Thus, the designer must rule out many alternatives early in the design process on the basis of experience (his or her own or others') in order to consider a smaller, more manageable set of alternatives that can be evaluated via simulation.
- Current simulation tools at best tend to accurately model either the ISO physical layer (layer 1) on a single-link basis, or the middle ISO layers (2 to 4) for networks involving multiple nodes, but not both at the same time.
- Even without detailed modeling of the physical layer, high-fidelity simulations of large networks tend to require large amounts of computation. One cannot scale down networks for purposes of performance evaluation because the behavior of networks involving small numbers of nodes may be very different.
- The external environment in which a system must operate is often highly uncertain. Terrain type, presence of interfering equipments, jamming, and other external factors can all affect performance, but are difficult to accurately characterize and model. In the case of jamming, uncertainty about the threat is a major issue.

Military and commercial communications systems designers tend to take different approaches and reach different results primarily because the expected operating environments are different, the business practices and economics (including economies of scale) are different, and two performance attributes—robustness against jamming and low probability of detection (LPD)—are of concern only for the military.

Let's expand the criteria for comparing mobile wireless systems. Performance requirements of communications networks depend on a variety of factors, including the types and quantities of traffic to be carried, the required availability and responsiveness of the system, the operating environment, and acceptable costs for the infrastructure and user equipment segments of the network. Some performance measures are specific to certain types of networks, or to certain types of traffic, and are inappropriate in other contexts.[43] Feldman differentiates high and low performance measures.

High-Level Performance Measures

These high-level performance measures (user visible) are specific to circuit-switched networks and to connection-oriented traffic on some packet-switched networks (ATM):

- **Blocking probability**   This is the probability that a request for a circuit or connection fails because the system cannot accommodate additional circuits/connections. Note that in the current Internet, a connection can fail because a host is unreachable, but it cannot be blocked because of excessive congestion (it can, however, time out).
- **Circuit/connection setup time**   This is the time to set up a circuit or connection when blocking does not occur.

For connectionless traffic on packet-switched networks, the high-performance measures of interest are:

- Probability of (successful) delivery.
- End-to-end delay (for packets that are delivered).
- For any networks where data is transmitted without retransmissions, error rates are critically important. Error rates are typically low for wired connections, but vary enormously for wireless links.

For connection-oriented traffic with real-time requirements (on packet-switched networks), the packet delay and the *delay jitter* (variation in delay from one packet or cell to the next).

For connection-oriented traffic without real-time requirements, the user is probably most sensitive tothe connection throughput or total delivery time.[44]

Low-Level Performance Measures

Low-level (Physical Layer) performance measures are not so much a function of the network protocols, quantities of traffic, the operating environment, and hardware performance as they are dependent on the physical layer performance, such as:

- Average link throughput (user data bps).
- Average terminal power consumption (watts) and antenna size. Average

power consumption is important because it determines the operating time per charge for a given battery type and weight.

- Link error rates: bit error rate (BER), symbol error rate, and packet error rate.
- Maximum user density (number of active users per km^2).
- Spectral efficiency (bps per Hz).[45]

Military-Unique System Requirements

The military has unique requirements that tend to drive the design of military communications systems toward solutions that are markedly different from commercial systems. The most important of these involve low probability of detection, resistance to jamming, precedence and perishability, electromagnetic compatibility, interoperability with legacy systems, and security.

Low probability of detection (LPD) is critical for activities such as reconnaissance because it reduces the risks to forward battlefield spotters, and it is important in any situation where direction-finding equipment might be employed to advantage by the enemy.

Military networks must be able to offer different grades of service to traffic on the basis of *precedence* level (priority), which indicates importance, and *perishability*, which indicates when the information must be received to be of value. Optimal handling of precedence and perishability information is especially important when a network becomes congested. In packet-switched networks (Internet) network status and control information are not privileged. The commercial world has rejected the idea of different grades of service that do not provide for either precedence or perishability.

Guaranteed QoS makes sense for wired networks with stable topologies and constant link capacities but is almost certainly unrealistic for fully mobile wireless networks, even without the added factor of hostile enemy actions such as destruction of nodes and jamming of links. Furthermore, guaranteed QoS requires admission control, which is unacceptable on the battlefield except as a last resort. In critical situations, the ability to get something intelligible through in a timely fashion is probably the most important tactical user "comm." requirement.

For some military platforms, for command posts and vehicles moving in formation, *electromagnetic compatibility* (EMC) can be a problem because of interference among multiple equipments operating in close proximity (possibly on the same platform); this is the so-called "co-site interference problem."

Security is often cited as an additional military-unique performance requirement. This is not accurate, however, because the business world is becoming increasingly concerned about the protection of information, and widespread commercial use of strong encryption and authentication (digital signatures) is increasing. There are however, requirements unique to the military. Even if all user data is encrypted, *TRANSEC* is needed to protect traffic. Without this, an eavesdropper could perform traffic analysis. The commercial world rarely worries about this, even if data is protected by encryption (COMSEC). Secure multicast with frequent changes of multicast group membership may require more complex mechanisms for key generation, distribution, and authentication. The commercial world also needs to solve the problem of authenticating users who join a multicast; otherwise it would be impossible to have private conferences, pay-per-view events, and the like. However, the military authentication requirements are more complex. Military wireless networks must be capable of surviving the capture of radios by the enemy.[46]

Capacity and Spectral Efficiency were discussed in a previous section. From the graph, equation (2.9) in Figure 2-4 we see a tradeoff between power efficiency and spectral efficiency. As one can see from the graph, waveforms that achieve very high spectral efficiency require SNR, while the most power-efficient waveforms are wasteful of spectrum. Using the above equation, it is apparent that to achieve a spectral efficiency of 6 bps/Hz, the minimum required signal-to-noise ratio $Eb/N_0 = 10.5 = 10.2$ dB.

Note that although this value of SNR is a practical operating point for many wireless systems, most existing wireless systems that operate at SNRs in this neighborhood actually achieve spectral efficiencies less than 1.0, and many military wireless systems and satellite systems have spectral efficiencies less than 0.1. Thus, there is clearly substantial room for improvement.[47]

The simplest way to achieve higher spectral efficiency is by increasing Eb/No, which in turn implies increasing the transmitted signal EIRP in the direction of the receiver (recall that EIRP is the product of transmitted power antenna gain), increasing the receiving antenna gain, decreasing the receiving noise figure, or a combination of these measures. The price of simultaneous power and spectral efficiency is a substantial increase in complexity. Nevertheless, combined modulation/coding techniques that achieve fairly high power and spectral efficiency simultaneously

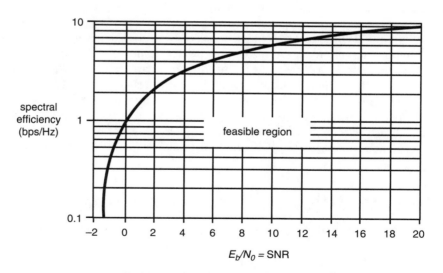

2-4 The theoretical limit for spectral efficiency C/W as a function of the signal-to-noise ratio (SNR) *Eb/No*.

[Reprinted with permission from Feldman, Phillip M. *Emerging Commercial Mobile Wireless Technology and Standards: Suitable for the Army?* Rand, 1998.]

have been developed in recent years, and commercial ASICs that implement some of these techniques are now available. Adding requirements for resistance to jamming requires some sacrifice of power efficiency, and some additional complexity as well, for example, to implement error control decoders that use jammer-side information. However, as device counts of VLSI chips and MIPS ratings of microprocessors continue to increase, higher levels of complexity are becoming available.[48]

The military tends to retain computer and communications equipment in the inventory for relatively long periods. In the commercial world, users are expected to upgrade or replace equipment every two to four years. Because volumes of military systems tend to be much smaller than those of commercial systems, the costs of R&D, software, and testing have a much greater impact on the final per-unit cost of military systems than they do for commercial products. These higher costs in turn force the military to try to retain the systems for as long as possible. Also spectral efficiency is much more important to the commercial designer because of the cost factor. Higher spectral efficiencies tend to reduce the cost of equipment.[49]

Differences in frequencies of operation, waveforms, modulation, error control coding protocols, and message formats prevent the different military radios from interoperating. Interoperability represents largely separate-service efforts that do not address the need for communications interoperation between services and with our allies for joint and combined operations. The opposite is true with commercial radios and upgrades.

Because cryptographic and ECCM algorithms in tactical radios have been implemented in hardware, and since the relevant devices and specifications are generally not made available to our allies, encrypted and jam-resistant tactical communications are problematic for combined operations.

Part of the solution for this problem may be software-based encryption; this permits one to change not only the keys, but also the underlying algorithms. Software-based encryption is practical except perhaps at the highest data rates. Secrecy with respect to the encryption algorithms used in tactical radios is almost certainly a mistake. If we trust the algorithms, then there can be no harm in making them public. If we do not trust them, then scrutiny by academic researchers is one of the best ways to find flaws. This same basic reasoning about the secrecy of encryption algorithms can be applied to the pseudorandom sequence generators used in frequency hopping and direct sequence spread spectrum, but it does *not* apply to ECCM algorithms in general. The ECCM algorithms are not available to allies and enemies alike.[50]

Offensive Information Operations

Offensive information operations target human perception, information that influences perception, and the physical world that is perceived. The avenues of these operations are via perceptual, information, and physical means.

Offensive information operations are malevolent acts conducted to meet the strategic, operational, or tactical objectives of authorized government bodies; legal, criminal, or terrorist organizations; corporations; or individuals. The operations may be legal or illegal, ethical or unethical, and may be conducted by authorized or unauthorized individuals. The operations may be performed covertly, without notice to the target, or they may be intrusive, disruptive, and even destructive. The effects on information may bring physical results that are lethal to humans.

Waltz defines Offensive operations as uninvited, unwelcome, unauthorized, and detrimental to the target; therefore, we use the term *attack* to refer to all such operations.[51]

For these reasons, this section must be considered within the context of understanding offense to prepare for defense. Security design must be preceded by an understanding of the attacks it must face. This section precedes the final section on defensive operations, developing the spectrum of attacks, while the next provides the complementary elements of protection and reaction.

Offensive information attacks have two basic functions: to *capture* or to *affect* information. (Information may refer to processes or to data, information, or knowledge content.) These functions are performed together to achieve the higher-level operational and perceptual objectives. Functions, measures, tactics, and techniques of offensive operations relating to the wireless component of IW are of immediate interest.

The fundamental functions (capture and affect) are used to effectively gain a desired degree of control of the target's information resources. Capturing information is an act of theft of a resource if captured illegally, or technical exploitation if the means is not illicit. Affecting information is an act of intrusion with intent to cause unauthorized effects, usually harmful to the information owner. The functional processes that capture and affect information are called offensive measures, designed to penetrate operational and defensive security measures of the targeted information system.[52]

Tactics are the operational processes employed to plan, sequence, and control the countermeasures of an attack. These tactics consider factors, such as attack objectives, desired effects (for example, covertness, denial or disruption of service; destruction, modification, or theft of information), degree of effects, and target vulnerabilities.

Techniques are the technical means of capturing and affecting information of humans—their computers, communications, and supporting infrastructures—are described as techniques.

In addition to these dimensions, other aspects, depending upon their application, may characterize the information attack.

The attacker's motive may be varied (for example, ideological, revenge, greed, hatred, malice, challenge, theft). Though not a technical characteristic, motive is an essential dimension to consider in forensic analysis of attacks.

Invasiveness characterizes attacks as passive or active. Active attacks invade and penetrate the information target, while passive attacks are noninvasive, often observing behaviors, information flows, timing, or other characteristics. Most cryptographic attacks may be considered passive relative to the sender and receiver processes, but active and invasive to the information message itself.

The effects of attacks may vary from harassment to theft, from narrow, surgical modification of information to large-scale cascading of destructive information that brings down critical societal infrastructure.

The means and the effects may be legal or illegal, depending upon current laws. The emerging opportunities opened by information technology have outpaced international and U.S. federal laws to define and characterize illegal attacks. Unlike real property, information is a property that may be shared, abused, or stolen without evidence or the knowledge of the legitimate owner.[53] There are two issues of concern in the wireless arena. These are the network (computer) attacks and attacks on protective cryptography. QuestTech describes the former and Waltz enumerates other payloads that encompass the entire spectrum of IW.[54]

A Taxonomy of Attack Operations

The following may be considered malevolent at the functional level (see Figure 2-5).[55]

- **Target level of the IW model**   Perceptual, information, or physical
- **Attack category**   Capture or affect

The attack matrix (Figure 2-5) is divided into the two avenues of approach available to the attacker:

- **Direct, or internal, penetration attacks**   The attacker penetrates a communication link, computer, or database to capture and exploit internal information, or to modify information (add, insert, delete) or install a malicious process.
- **Indirect, or external, sensor attacks**   The attacker presents open phenomena to the system's sensors or information to sources (for example, media, Internet, or third parties) to achieve counter-information objectives. These attacks include insertion of information into sensors or observation of the behavior of sensors or links interconnecting fusion nodes.

The object of attack defines two categories of attacks that affect information:

- **Content attacks**   The content of the information in the system may be attacked to disrupt, deny, or deceive the user (a decision maker or process). Content attacks are focused on the real-time data and the derived information.
- **Temporal attacks**   The information process may be affected such that the timeliness of information is attacked. Either a delay in the receipt of data or insertion of false data and passed on as legitimate.

Figure 4-6 shows the whole gamut of IW threats applied to computer security. It shows category of threat-malicious, unintentional, and physical and the OSI layer that it operates against, typical behaviors, vulnerabilities, protections, detection, and countermeasures. These are direct attacks seeking to penetrate security to achieve their objective.

Another way to look at the general approach of network attack vulnerabilities was developed by J. D. Howard.[56] He presented a basic taxonomy of computer and network attacks for analyzing security incidents on the network. The taxonomy structure is based on characterizing the process by five basic components that are present in any attack shown in either Figure 2-6 or 2-7.[57]

2-5 Attach Matrix categorizes information countermeasures by affect and JW attack level.

Objective Effect:	CAPTURE		AFFECT					
Security Property Attacked:	Privacy is breached		Integrity of data is invalidated. Availability of services is degraded.					
Avenue:	Indirect *Observe, Model, Infer*	Direct *Panorama and Observe*	Indirect *Cause affects through the sensors or over the open network without penetration at the target*			Direct *Penetrate and affect targeted infrastructures and affect*		
Offensive Act: Level of Attack (IW Model)	*Capture Information Resource*		Deceive	Disrupt, Deny	Destroy	Deceive	Disrupt, Deny	Destroy
Perceptual	Observe open behaviors, statements, cultural influences, and biases to alter decision processes and perception.	Observe closed-conversations, decisions, and actions by HJMINT access.	PSYOPS activities provide information to manage human perception (messages may be delivered by direct human discourse, or via the information infrastructure, such as the broadcast media or Internet).			Counterintelligence and covert operations manage perception by penetration of target audience with human agencies to convey perception themes—and to implement lower-level countermeasures (e.g., subhomed systems administrator with access).		
Information Infrastructure	Passive intercept of message traffic. Non-intrusive mapping of network topology. Cryptographic analysis.	Network about and penetrate to secure unauthorized access to data. Trojan horse prog ram. Initial summer.	Issue decaphys e-mail message. Conduct deceptive network behavior.	Deny network data collection service by flood attack max disrupts access to public sources. Insert open message traffic and alerts that diverts attention and processing resources. Insert sensor data that upsets guidance or control process.		Insert Trojan horse with deception action. Modify corrupt data by oral agent.	Insert malicious code (e.g., virus or worm) to deny or disrupt service in single host computer or access an entire network.	
Physical	Intercept van Eck radiation from CAT monitor. Inductive wiretap. Search open hash.	Capture (theft) of equipment, cryptographic keys, physical keys, storage and media. Wiretap		Theft or capture of critical components. Make available erroneous data. Masquerade or spool user to induce disruptive actions.		Penetrate physical security in capture security relevant data.	Physical bombing of facilities or supporting infrastructure. Electronic adapt (EA) or system components.	

[Reprinted with permission from Waltz, Edward, *Information Warfare: Principles and Operations*, Artech House, 1998.]

73

Threat	OSI Layer	Definition	Typical Behaviors	Vulnerabilities
Virus	Application	Malicious software which attaches itself to other software. For example, a patched software application, in which the patch's algorithm is designed to implement the same patch on other applications, thereby replicating.	Replicates within computer system, polarically attaching itself to every software application. Behavior Categories: Innocuous, Humorous, Data Altering, and Catastrophic.	All computers. Common categories: boat sector, Terminals and Stay Resident (TSR), Application Software Sleuth (for Chairman), Multitier: Engine, Network, and Mainframe.
Worm	Application Network	Malicious software which is a stand-alone application.	Often designed to propagate through a network, rather than just a single computer.	Multitasking computers, especially those employing open network standards.
Trojan Horse	Application	A Worm which pretends to be a useful program, or a virus which is purposely attached to a useful program prior to distribution.	Same as Virus or Worm, but also sometimes used to send information back to or make information available to perpetrator.	Unlike Worms, which self-propagate, Trojan Horses require user cooperation. Untrained users are vulnerable.
Time Bomb	Application	A Virus or Worm designed to activate at a certain date/time.	Same as Virus or Worm, but widespread throughout organization upon trigger date. Time Bombs are usually found before the trigger date.	Same as virus and Worm.
Logic Bomb	Application	A Virus or Worm designed to activate under certain conditions.	Same as Virus or Worm.	Same as virus and Worm.
Rabbit	Application Network	A Worm designed to replicate to the point of exhausting computer resources.	Rabbit consumes al CPU cycles, disk space, or network resources, and so on.	Multitasking computers, especially those on a network.
Bacterium	Application	A Virus designed to attach itself to the OS in particular (rather than any application in general) and exhaust computer resources, especially CPU cycles.	Operating System consumes more and more CPU cycles, resulting eventually in noticeable delay in user transactions.	Older versions of operating systems are more vulnerable than newer versions, since hackers have had more time to write Bacterium.

2-6a Network Attacks.
[Reprinted with permission from QuestTech, Inc. Falls Church, VA.]

Threat	OSI Layer	Definition	Typical Behaviors	Vulnerabilities
Spoofing	Network Data Link	Getting one computer on a network to pretend to have the identity of another computer, usually one with special access privileges, so as to obtain access to the other computers on the network.	Spoofing computer often doesn't have access to user-level commands, so attempts to use automation-level services, such as email or message handlers, are employed.	Automation services designed for network interoperability are especially vulnerable, especially those adhering to open standards
Masquerade	Network	Accessing a computer by pretending to have an authorized user identity.	Masquerading user often employs network or administrator command functions to access even more of the system, e.g., by attempting to download password or routing tables.	Placing false or modified login prompts on a computer is a common way to obtain user IDs, as are Snooping, Scanning, and Scavenging.
Sequential Scanning	Transport Network	Sequentially testing passwords/ authentication codes until one is successful.	Multiple users attempting network or administrator command functions, indicating multiple Masquerades.	Since new login prompts have a time-delay built in to loll automatic scarring, accessing the encoded password table and testing it off-line is a common technique.
Dictionary Scanning	Application	Scanning through a dictionary of commonly used passwords/ authentication codes until one is successful.	Multiple users attempting network or administrator command functions, indicating multiple Masquerades.	Use of common words and names as passwords or authentication codes. (So-called, "Joe Accounts")
Digital snooping	Network	Electronic monitoring of digital networks to uncover passwords or other data. Changes in behavior or network transport layer.	Users or even system administrators found on-line at unusual or off-shift hours. Links can be more vulnerable to snooping than nodes.	Example of the COMSEC affects COMPUSEC.

2-6a Network Attacks. (*continued*)
[Reprinted with permission from QuestTech, Inc. Falls Church, VA.]

Threat	OSI Layer	Definition	Typical Behaviors	Vulnerabilities
Shoulder Surfing	Physical	Direct visual observation of monitor displays to obtain access.	Authorized user found on-line at unusual or off-shift hours, indicating a possible Masquerade. Password entry screens that do not mask typed text. "Loitering" opportunities.	"Sticky" notes used to record account and password information.
Dumpster Diving	As	Accessing discarded trash to obtain passwords and other data.	Multiple users attempting network or administrator command functions, indicating multiple Masquerades. System administrator printouts of user logs.	"Sticky" notes used to record account and password information.
Browsing	Application Network	Usually-automated scanning of large quantities of unprotected data (discarded media, or on-line "Anger"-type commands) to obtain clues as to how to achieve access. Authorized user attempting administrator command functions.	Authorized user found on-line at unusual or off-shift hours, indicating a possible Masquerade. The information is usually assumed safe, but can give clues to passwords (e.g., spouse's name).	"Finger"-type services provide information to any and all users.
Spamming	Application Network	Overloading a system with incoming message or other traffic to cause system crashes.	Repeated system crashes, eventually traced to overfull buffer or dump space.	Open source networks are especially vulnerable.
Tunneling	Network	Any digital attack which attempts to get "under" a security system, by accessing very low-level system functions (e.g., device drivers or OS tunnels).	Bizarre system behaviors, such as unexpected disk accesses, unexplained device failures, halted security software, etc.	Tunneling attacks often occur by creating system emergencies to cause system reloading or initialization.

2-6a Network Attacks. *(continued)*
[Reprinted with permission from QuestTech, Inc. Falls Church, VA.]

Prevention	Detection	
Limit connectivity. Limit downloads. Use only authorized media for loading data and software.	Changes in the sizes of date/time stamps. Computer is slow starting, or slow running. Unexpected or frequent system failures.	Contain, identify, and recover. Anti-virus scanners: look for known viruses.
Enforce mandatory access controls. Viruses generally cannot run unless host application is running.	Change of system date/time.	Anti-virus monitors: look for virus-related application behaviors.
Low computer memory, or increased bad blocks on disks.	Attempt to determine source of infection and issue an alert.	Contain, identify, and recover. Attempt to determine source of infection and issue an alert.
Limit connectivity, employ firewalls. Worms can run even without a host application.	Computer is slow starting, or slow running. Unexpected or frequent system failures.	Same as virus and Worm.
User cooperation allows Trojan Horses to bypass automated controls.	Same as Virus and Worm.	Alerts must be issued not only to other
User training is best prevention. system administrators, but to all network users.		
Run associated anti-virus software immediately as available.	Complete user problem reports to find patterns indicating possible Time Bomb. Attempt to determine source of infection and issue an alert.	Contain, identify, and recover.
Same as Virus and Worm.	Correlate user problem reports indicating possible Logic Bomb. Determine source and issue an alert.	Contain, identify, and recover.
Limit connectivity, employ Firewalls. Frequent system failures.	Computer is slow starting or running. Determine source and issue an alert.	Contain, identify, and recover.
Limit write-privileges and opportunities to OS files.	Changes in OS file sizes, OS file date/time stamps.	Anti-virus scanners: look for known viruses

2-6b Network Attacks.

[Reprinted with permission from QuestTech, Inc., Falls Church, VA.]

Prevention	Detection	
System administrators should work from nonadmin. accounts whenever possible.	Computer is slow in running.	Anti-virus monitors: look for virus-related system behaviors.
Unexpected or frequent system failures.		
Limit system privileges of automation services to minimum necessary.	Monitor transaction logs of automation services, scanning for unusual behaviors.	Disconnect automation services until patched, or monitor automation access points, such as network sockets, scanning for next spoof, in an attempt to trace back to perpetrator.
Upgrade via security patches as they become available.	If automating this process, do so off-line to avoid "tunneling" attacks (see below).	
Limit user access to network or administrator command functions.	Correlate user identification with shift times or increased frequency of access.	Change user password, or use standard administrator functions to determine access point, then trace back to perpetrator.
Implement multiple levels of administrators, with different privileges for each.	Correlate user command logs with administrator command functions.	
Enforce organizational password policies.	Correlate user identification with shift times.	Change entire password file, or use baiting tactics to trace back to perpetrator.
Correlate user problem reports relevant to possible Masquerades.		
Employ data encryption.	Correlate user identification with shift times.	Change encryption schemes, or employ network monitoring tools to attempt trace back to perpetrator.
Limit physical access to network nodes and links.	Correlate user problem reports. Monitor network performance.	
Limit physical access to computer areas.	Correlate user identification with shift times or increased frequency of access.	Change user password, or use standard administrator functions to determine access point, then trace back to perpetrator.
Require frequent password changes by users.	Correlate user command logs with administrator command functions.	

2-6b Network Attacks. (*continued*)
[Reprinted with permission from QuestTech, Inc., Falls Church, VA.]

2-6b Network Attacks. (*continued*)
[Reprinted with permission from QuestTech, Inc., Falls Church, VA.]

Prevention	Detection	
Destroy discarded hardcopy.	Correlate user identification with shift times.	Change entire password file, or use baiting tactics to trace back to perpetrator.
Enforce organizational shredding policies.	Correlate user problem reports relevant to possible Masquerades.	
Destroy discarded media.	Correlate user identification with shift times or increased frequency of access.	Change user password, or use standard administrator functions to determine access point, then trace back to perpetrator.
When on open source networks especially, disable "linger"-type services.	Correlate user command logs with administrator command functions.	
Require authentication fields in message traffic.	Monitor disk partitions, network sockets, and so on. for overfull conditions.	Analyze message headers to attempt track back to perpetrator.
Design security and audit capabilities into even the lowest level software, such as device drivers, shared libraries, and so on.	Changes in date/time stamps for low-level system files, or changes in sector/block counts for device drivers.	Patch or replace compromised drivers to prevent access. Monitor suspected access points to attempt trace back to perpetrator.

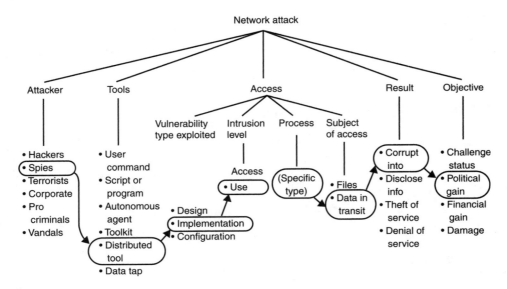

2-7 Process-based taxonomy (developed by Howard).

[Compiled from several Tables in Waltz, Edward, *Information Warfare: Principles and Operations*, Artech House, 1998.]

Components of Howard's process-based taxonomy are:

1. **Attackers**   Six categories of attackers are identified: hackers, spies, terrorists, corporate, criminal, and vandals.
2. **Tools**   The levels of sophistication of use of tools to conduct the attack are identified.
3. **Access**   The access to the system is further categorized by four branches, as follows:

- **Vulnerability exploited**   Design, configuration (of the system), and implementation bugs are all means of access that may be used.
- **Level of intrusion**   The intruder may obtain unauthorized access, but may also proceed to unauthorized use, which has two possible subcategories.

  - **Use of processes**   The specific process or service used by the unauthorized user is identified as this branch of the taxonomy.
  - **Use of information**   Static files in storage or data in transit may be the targets of unauthorized use.

4. **Results**   Four results are considered: denial of service, theft of service, corruption of information, or theft (disclosure) of information.
5. **Objectives**   The objective of the attack (often closely correlated to the attacker type).

Howard constructed the taxonomy such that any simple attack can be categorized as a process, composed of the flow through the elements in the taxonomy. Illustrated is the process thread of a network attack (state-supported agents are attackers) in which distributed (multiple-site) tools are used to exploit implementation vulnerabilities to gain use of the system. A specific system process is used to corrupt information in data packets in transit through the targeted computer to achieve a political objective of the supporting nation state.

This taxonomy clearly distinguishes the source (who), the objective (why), and the result (what) from the means (how). Each of these components is required to effectively detect, understand, and respond to attacks. The taxonomy is useful for real-time detection systems and is necessary for investigation and prosecution of attackers.

Network attacks take two forms: mapping of the Internet access and a telecommunications access mapping.[58] The goals of the network attack are to affect user access, to gain root access, to exploit system resources, or to affect system resources adversely. Figure 2-7 illustrates the general path for these tactics in increasing levels of access, giving greater potential for damage as the depth is increased.[59]

Cryptographic Attacks

The most devastating attacks on a wireless system are those that involve the cryptographic security of the system or network.[60] The analysis and breaking of encryption is performed to penetrate cryptographic information security to:

- Gain one-time access to information that has been encrypted. This information may represent knowledge, electronic funds, certification, or many other information representations.
- Commit one-time security forgery (for example, to create a secure authentication).
- Spoof a user by presenting a valid authentication intercepted and copied from a valid user.
- Fully understand an encryption and keying process to permit repeated and full access to traffic on the targeted system.

Cryptanalysis attacks seek to locate access vulnerabilities of the general cryptographic system (see Figure 2-8). A fundamental tenet of cryptographic algorithm design is that a strong algorithm's security rests entirely in the key and not the design details of the algorithm. A general rule of encryption security, known as Kerchoff's principle, is to assume that the encryption/decryption algorithms may be known by the attacker, but the system must remain secure by the strength of the method and security of the key. Cryptographic attacks against strong, known cryptosystems therefore seek to acquire or guess keys and understand the algorithms of unknown cryptosystems as follows:

- Key management systems are attacked to acquire keys or reduce the search space for brute force key searches.

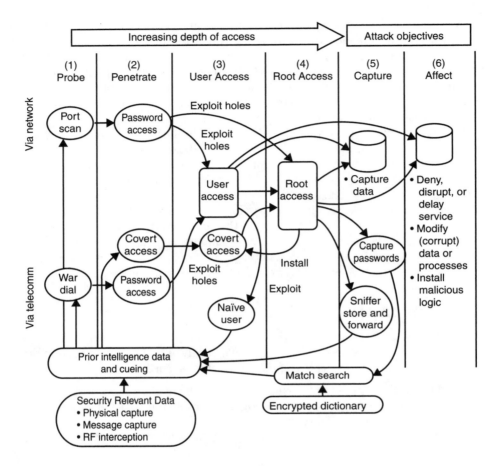

2-8 Typical access sequences for network attacks.

[Reprinted with permission from Waltz, Edward, *Information Warfare: Principles and Operations*, Artech House, 1998.]

- Key generators that format key variables and the distribution systems may be exploited if weaknesses occur in their design, implementation, or security.
- Random number generators that randomly select seed numbers to generate keys may be exploitable if they are pseudorandom and a repetitive (deterministic) characteristic can be identified. If deterministic sequences can be identified, key sequences can be predicted.
- Encryption system may be attacked if any portion of the path (plaintext or ciphertext) can be intercepted to perform an analysis.

Table 2-3 provides a simple taxonomy of the most basic cryptographic attack techniques, which include cryptanalysis and deception methods. The methods for attacking symmetric and asymmetric encryption approaches differ somewhat, and

Table 2-3 Basic Cryptographic Attack Methods

Attack Approach	Data Used to Perform Attack	Attack Technique
Cryptanalysis	Ciphertext only	Brute force Using a string of ciphertext and assumptions about the encryption method, decrypt all possible keys in the key space until plaintext is revealed.
		Guessed plaintext Guess at plaintext message, encrypt, and compare to known ciphertext to search for matches.
	Known plaintext	Brute force Search key space for encryption of corresponding known text that produced known ciphertext; even if Ciphertext not known, portions of plaintext may be guessed.
	Chosen plaintext	Brute force Obtain access to encryption process and encrypt a chosen plaintext using the keyed encryption device and analyze (symmetric system) or encrypt all possible private keys in key space (asymmetric system).
		Differential cryptanalysis Obtain access to encryption process and encrypt chosen plaintext from a specially selected subset of the key space, then analyze.
	Chosen ciphertext	Obtain access to decryption process and insert Chosen ciphertext string, obtain and analyze the decrypted plaintext.
	Partial-key	Brute force In asymmetric (public key) cryptosystems, the public key must be factored into its prime number components to derive the secret (private) key.
Deception	Ciphertext only	Replay Replay unknown but valid recorded ciphertext within key-interval for deceptive purposes.
	Key	Key theft Steal key via attack-on key management.
	Spoof key	False key insertion Impersonate key distributor to target and present a key for use by target.
	Known secure party pair	Man-in-middle Secure a position between two secure parties (A and B) and provide keys (by spoofing both to believe that attacker is A or B); intercept and decrypt traffic in-transit and maintain masqueraded key distribution.

details of these methods may be found in Table 2-3 does not include more complex timing analyses that estimate key information given the timing (number of clock cycles) of a legitimate decryption unit and destructive methods that are applied to captured equipment.[61]

Defensive Information Operations

Defensive information measures are referred to as information assurance. Information operations protect and defend information and information systems by ensuring their availability, integrity, authentication, confidentiality, and nonrepudiation. This includes providing for the restoration of information systems by incorporating protection, detection, and reaction capabilities.

This definition distinguishes protection of the infrastructure by prevention of unauthorized access or attack (proactive measures), and defense of the infrastructure by detecting, surviving, and responding to attacks (reactive measures). The assurance includes the following component properties and capabilities (collectively known as CIA):

- Availability provides assurance that information, services, and resources will be accessible and usable when needed by the user.
- Integrity assures that information and processes are secure from unauthorized tampering (for example, insertion, deletion, destruction, or replay of data) via methods such as encryption, digital signatures, and intrusion detection.
- Authentication assures that only authorized users have access to information and services on the basis of the following controls: authorization (granting and revoking access rights), delegation (extending a portion of one entity's rights to another), and user authentication (reliable corroboration of a user), and data origin. (This is a mutual property when each of two parties authenticates the other.)
- Confidentiality protects the existence of a connection, traffic flow, and information content from disclosure to unauthorized parties.
- Nonrepudiation assures that transactions are immune from false denial of sending or receiving information by providing reliable evidence that can be independently verified to establish proof of origin and delivery.
- Restoration assures information and systems can survive an attack and that availability can be resumed after the impact of an attack.

Information assurance includes the traditional functions of information security (INFOSEC), which is defined at two levels. At the policy level, INFOSEC is the system of policies, procedures, and requirements to protect information that, if subjected to unauthorized disclosure, could reasonably be expected to cause damage. At the technical level, INFOSEC includes measures and controls that protect the information infrastructure against:

- *Denial of service* (DoS)
- Unauthorized (accidental or intentional) disclosure
- Modification or destruction of information infrastructure components and data

INFOSEC includes consideration of hardware and software functions, characteristics, features, operational procedures, accountability procedures, access controls at the central computer facility, remote computer, and terminal facilities;

management constraints; physical structures and devices; and personnel and communication controls needed to provide an acceptable level of risk for the infrastructure and for the data and information contained in the infrastructure.

INFOSEC includes the totality of security safeguards needed to provide an acceptable protection level for an infrastructure and for data handled by an infrastructure. INFOSEC includes four components within communications security (COMSEC):

- ***Emanations security* (EMSEC)**   The control of emanations that may compromise internal information.
- **Electronics security**   The protection resulting from all measures designed to deny unauthorized persons information of value that might be derived from their interception and study of noncommunication electromagnetic radiations (for example, radar).
- ***Transmission security* (TRANSEC)**   The protection of transmissions ("externals") from traffic analysis, disruption, and imitative deception.
- ***Cryptographic security* (COMSEC)**   The use of encryption to protect communication content ("internals").

More recently, the aspect of survivability (the capacity to withstand attacks and functionally endure at some defined level of performance) has been recognized as a critical component of defenses included under the umbrella of INFOSEC and information assurance.

Cryptographic Measures

Cryptography provides the mathematical processes for transforming data (by encryption and decryption) between an open, or plaintext, format and a secure ciphertext format to provide the privacy property. The strength of the encryption algorithm (the cipher) is a measure of the degree to which the ciphertext endures cryptanalysis attacks that seek to break the cipher and discover the plaintext, eliminating privacy. Because of the inherent security of the processes, cryptographic techniques provide privacy for messages, authentication of users, and assurance of delivery and receipt of messages (non-repudiation).

The ultimate strength and generality of cryptographic processes lies in the mathematical formulation of the underlying transform algorithms. This introduction provides a functional introduction, but mathematical treatments in a number of texts are necessary for further understanding of the cryptosystems described. The general cryptosystem (Figure 2-8) includes the cryptographic message path that delineates the encryption, transmission, and decryption process, and a supporting method of distributing a numerical variable, or key, that controls the encryption transformation. The following subsections describe each of these processes for data encryption and the use of encryption to create digital signatures for authentication and nonrepudiation.[62]

Encryption processes apply substitution, permutation, or number theoretic methods (or combinations of these) to transform plaintext to ciphertext. The key variables that control the transformation algorithms provide the capability to change

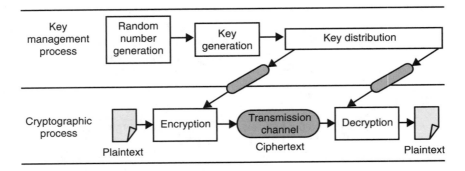

2-9 Basic elements of a cryptographic system.

the transformation, and therefore the number of possible keys (the key space) directly influences the strength of the algorithm against attack. Keying is the process of changing the key variable: as a function of a time schedule (for example, hourly, daily), each communication session, each individual message, or continuously, synchronized throughout the encryption process (key streaming). (See Figure 2-9 for the basic elements of a cryptosystem and Figure 2-10 for a simple taxonomy of common cryptosystems.) [63]

In addition to providing privacy, the encryption process provides a means of authentication of a message by an encrypted data item called a digital signature. The digital signature permits proof of identity of the sender, and proof that an attacker has not modified the message. Public-key encryption concepts provide a convenient basis to create digital signatures. Figure 2-11 compares the basics of private- and public-key encryption systems. Many implementations of cryptosystems, both secret key and public key variants, are available to the general public.

Key Management

The generation, storage, distribution, and overall protection of keys are *critical* to the security of all cryptosystems—public or private algorithms. Compromised keys provide the most direct means of unauthorized access. For this reason, physical, information, and perceptual layers of security must protect the key management functions, including those summarized as follows:

- **Key security policy**   A specific security policy must define the controls for the full life cycle of keys (generation. distribution, activation, destruction, or lifetime escrow storage) and controls for usage.
- **Key-layering hierarchy**   Keys may be defined in layers in which higher-level keys are used to encrypt lower level keys for distribution.
- **Key separation**   Keys may be separated into components for distribution on separate channels or for retention by separate parties (for added security), with provisions for construction of the complete key by the computing function of the individual components.

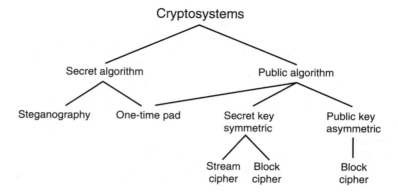

2-10 Taxonomy of common cryptosystems.

[Reprinted with permission from Waltz, Edward, *Information Warfare: Principles and Operations*, Artech House, 1998.]

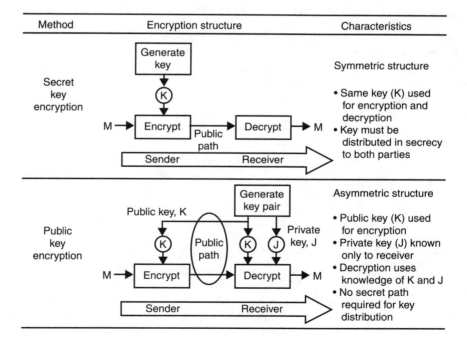

2-11 Comparison of private- and public-key cryptosystems.

[Reprinted with permission from Waltz, Edward, *Information Warfare: Principles and Operations*, Artech House, 1998.]

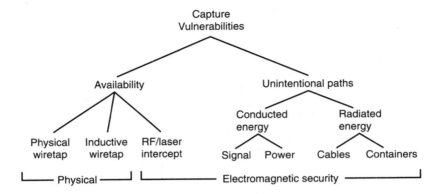

2-12 Taxonomy of capture vulnerabilities.

[Reprinted with permission from Waltz, Edward, *Information Warfare: Principles and Operations*, Artech House, 1998.]

- **Keying period control**   The validity period of keys (the "cryptoperiod") is defined as a function of time, system state, or other variable, and must be distributed with the keys to users.[64]

Electromagnetic Capture Threats

To prevent the capture of information via physical or electromagnetic intercept, the defender must protect against vulnerabilities along both intentional and unintentional paths of access available to the attacker (see Table 2-4). Offensive measures take the form of wiretapping network signal paths and intercepting unintentional signal emanations. These threats can be denied by physical security to stop access to pathways and on-site detection methods. Electromagnetic hardening (costly passive defense) and active jamming may be employed to reduce emanations to more secure levels.

Electromagnetic security is required to protect from the potential for external intercept of compromising signals on unintended signal paths conducted along signal or power lines, or radiated from equipment or interconnecting lines. The U.S. TEMPEST activities, conducted by the National Security Agency, have developed emission standards, design, control, and testing procedures for securing information systems from compromising emanations.[65]

Cryptographers use the principle of RED/BLACK separation to categorize and separate internal/plaintext (RED) and external/ciphertext (BLACK) areas of equipment, and the coupled signals (leakage) that cross the Red/Black interfaces and compromise encryption. RED/BLACK isolation is required to prevent cryptographic attacks that access both plain and ciphertext for a common message. Designers must be concerned with emanation spectra levels. Narrowband and broadband signal spectra levels are specified and radiated emanation suppression should be employed if necessary to achieve security. Security designers conduct testing of equipment

Table 2-4 Electromagnetic Emanation Protection Measures.

Unintentional Emanation Category	Target	No.	Electromagnetic Protection Controls
Radiated energy		1	Establishment of physical "zones" of susceptible signal levels and secure denied access perimeter around facility at the range of acceptable signal levels
		2	RF shielded glass, screens, and wall materials
		3	RF shielded glass, screens, and wall materials
		4	RF seals, screens, and baffles for utility penetration (e.g. power, telephone, water, air conditioning into shielded areas
		5	
		6	Active broadband jammers for external areas
	Equipment (racks, units, and cards)	7	RF shielded equipment (Faraday cage)
		8	Leakage control for equipment apertures (e.g., slits, slots, cooling filters)
		9	Conductive seals: gaskets, cauld, and epoxies
		10	Grounding for RF shields
			Prevention of control degradation via corrosion
			RED/BLACK physical separation
			RED/BLACK interface filters (electronic)
		11	RED/BLACK electro-optical coupling
		12	Fiberoptic cabling and interfaces
			Electrical cable shielding
Conducted energy	Signal lines		RED/BLACK interface filters (electronic)
			RED/BLACK electro-optical coupling
			Fiber-optic cabling and interfaces
			Ferrite sleeves ("split beads," torroids) around cables
			Spurious signal introduction
	Power lines		Power supply filtering
			AC line filtering

[Reprinted with permission from Waltz, Edward, *Information Warfare: Principles and Operations*, Artech House, Norwood MA, 1998.]

(antennas, sensors, receivers, tuners, spectrum analyzers, correlators, displays, and others) for emanations. They apply control techniques to the level of signals and monitor for compliance. Table 2-4 summarizes the major categories of emanation controls required to suppress RED/BLACK radiated and conducted emanations. Commercial firms all too seldom budget for this type of expense—and that is why they are easy targets![66]

The unintentional RF emanations from the CRT on computers are a valuable RED emanation that may be detected at ranges up to two miles. Keyboard, RS-232, and internal PC mikes also pose the risk of unintentional radiation (that is, van Eck emanations). Combinations of shielding, filtering, and sealing methods (Table 2-4) provide levels of suppression from 50 to 100 dB over frequencies ranging from KHz to GHz. These methods must be combined with physical security to prohibit hostile monitoring. The US Military has established standards for analysis, measurement, and control of EMC (electromagnetic compatibility) and EMI (electromagnetic interference). Commercial and military EMI deal with the design controls required to mitigate interference due to radio noise, cointerfering sources, man-made noise from generators plus EMC compatibility of receivers and RF transmitters.[67]

Summary

Consideration of the security of wireless communication systems, evoked discussion of what computer security threats apply to wireless systems and how they relate to the goals of CIA (confidentiality, data integrity, and availability). Applying wireless security concepts to networks and equipment is a complex process. Several different taxonomies have been presented to broaden what designers must consider to provide security for wireless networks, equipment, and information operations. Of particular interest are Waltz's IW model and Shannon's contributions to information theory. They provide a framework to evaluate the effectiveness of different designs. The IW model helps define the relationships in considering the security of a wireless communications system. However, it is necessary to integrate these concepts with specific measures, such as cryptographic, anti-jamming (A/J), and low probaility of detection (LPD), and apply them to commercial and military operations to define the competing design concerns for a specific problem. In addition, Shannon's information concepts and Ryan's risk relationships were reviewed more completely to define the context of information security and the relative value of its compromise or loss. Finally, commercial and military priorities have been differentiated in wireless security designs.

Endnotes

[1]Waltz, Edward, *Information Warfare: Principles and Operations*, London: Artech House, 1998, p. 18. (Some authors use the pseudonyms, INFOWAR and IW, interchangeably).

[2]Ibid., pp. 19–21.

[3]Ibid., p. 22.

[4]Ibid., p. 20.

[5]Ibid., p. 22.

[6]Ibid., pp. 23 ff

[7]Ibid., pp. 24–25.

[8]From INFOSEC Lecture by Professor Daniel J. Ryan, George Washington University, Washington, D.C., 2000.

[9]Compiled from notes from INFOSEC Lecture by Randall K. Nichols, George Washington University, Washington, D.C., 2001.

[10]Feldman, Phillip M., *Emerging Commercial Mobile Wireless Technology and Standards: Suitable for the Army?* Rand, 1998. p. 3. This is an excellent information source. Feldman writes with intelligence and style.

[11]Ibid., p. 4.

[12]Ibid., pp. 5 ff.

[13]Ibid., p. 6.

[14]Ibid., p. 7.

[15]Ibid., p. 7. See Table 2-2, "A Scheme For Classifying the Mobility Aspect of Wireless Communication Networks."

[16]Ibid., p. 8.

[17]Ibid., p. 8.

[18]Shannon, C. E. and W. Weaver, *The Mathematical Theory of Communication*, University of Illinois Pres, 1949.

[19]Nichols, Randall K., *ICSA Guide To Cryptography*, McGraw-Hill, 1999, pp. 158 ff.

[20]Waltz, op cit., p. 58.

[21]Ibid., p. 60.

[22]Nichols, op cit., pp. 174–174.

[23]Waltz, op cit., p. 71.

[24]Ibid., p. 62.

[25]Feldman, op cit., p. 20.

[26]Ibid., p. 21.

[27]Ibid., p. 21.

[28]Ibid., p. 22.

[29]Ibid., pp. 77–78.

[30]Ibid., p. 21.

[31]Ibid., p. 75, Appendix D.

[32]Ibid., p. 24 ff.

[33]Waltz, op cit., pp. 64 ff.

[34]Nichols, Randall K., Daniel J. Ryan, and Julie J.C. H. Ryan, *Defending Your Digital Assets Against Hackers, Crackers, Spies and Thieves,* McGraw-Hill, 2000, p 70.

[35]For an interesting read on Hanssen, see *Robert Philip Hanssen: Alleged KGB "Mole" Within the FBI*, Aegean Park Press, 2001.

[36]Nichols, Ryan, and Ryan, op cit., p. 71.

[37]Ibid., pp. 72–73.

[38]Ibid., pp. 74–75.

[39]Notes Compiled from EMSE 298IN Lectures Fall/Spring 2001 on INFOSEC and Wireless Security by Professor Randall K. Nichols, George Washington University, Washington, D.C., 2001.

[40]Ibid.

[41]Ibid.

[42]Feldman, op cit., p. 23 ff.

[43]Ibid., pp. 12–13.

[44]Ibid., p. 12.

[45]Ibid., p. 13.

[46]Ibid., pp. 14–19. Feldman presents a brilliant discussion on the interdependency and competition of design goals.

[47]Ibid., p. 24.

[48]Ibid., pp. 14, 24–25.

[49]Ibid., p. 22.

[50]Ibid., p. 25.

[51]Waltz, op cit., p. 160.

[52]Ibid., p. 252.

[53]Nichols, Ryan, and Ryan, op cit., p. 46.

[54]A rather detailed view of Information Warfare and the cyberspace environment was published by QuestTech, Inc. of Falls Church, VA. 1996. Waltz, op cit., presents a more global view in his book on pp. 254 ff.

[55]Condensed from Waltz, op cit., Figure 8.1, p. 255.

[56]Howard, J.D., "An Analysis of Security Incidents on the Internet (1989–1995)," Pittsburgh, PA, Dissertation Carnegie Mellon University, April 7, 1997.

[57]Condensed from Waltz, op cit., Figure 8.2, p. 255.

[58]Ibid., p. 200 ff.

[59]Ibid., p. 277, Figure 8.7.

[60]Ibid., pp. 278–281.

[61]Ibid., p. 280, condensed from Table 8.9.

[62]Ibid., p. 323, Figure 9.5.

[63]Ibid., p. 323, Figure 9.6.

[64]Ibid., p. 328 ff.

[65]Ibid., pp. 340–346.

[66]Ibid., p. 342, condensed from Table 9.9.

[67]Ibid., p 346, condensed from Table 9.10.

3

Telephone System Vulnerabilities

Wireless communication is changing how, what, and by whom information can be readily exchanged. Countries without a wired infrastructure are now able to establish communication with substantially fewer resources; countries with outdated wired infrastructures have an option to allow wireless markets to expand into the area. In addition, the industry is developing new uses for voice, wireless interaction with other technologies, wireless Web interaction, and e-commerce.

Users need to be concerned about the security of the information being transferred. Not only can information be intercepted by other individuals for their own use, but information about the communication vehicle and path can also be captured by intercept, resulting in unauthorized communications constituting fraud. With wireless transmission interception, no electrical impedance is affected so the interception is physically undetectable. Small communication devices also allow easy concealment of electronic eavesdropping units that are all but undetectable. A wireless device user must depend upon both information safeguards and transmission safeguards for an acceptable level of security.

As the world is increasingly connected, legal jurisdiction becomes a changing concept. If privacy or fraud is committed, which jurisdiction's law defines the crime? How can the criminal be identified, and if the criminal is identified, will prosecution be successful? Regarding privacy, what jurisdictional laws prevent message interception? Whose definition of privacy has jurisdiction? Is wired and wireless privacy the same, or are new laws or interpretations needed to address the new technology? Should additional privacy issues be addressed to protect privacy or anonymity? How will the wireless market react to perceived threats of privacy intrusion?

These are the basic questions to be asked with respect to wireless telephone system vulnerabilities. Also demanding investigation are air-to-ground interception, interruption at switch, cable, and fiber optics nodes; legalities; arenas of interception; and devices.

Interception/Ease of Interception

For as long as wireless signals have been used to carry information, individuals other than the intended recipient have made illicit efforts to obtain it. While governments and the military have gone to great lengths to protect the integrity of transmitted data, individuals and corporations have often regarded wireless intercept as unlikely to affect them directly.

The principal wireless technologies in use today are infrared and *radio frequency* (RF). While it is illegal to actively intercept wire or electronic communications,[1] anyone with a basic understanding of electronics, a soldering iron, and access to the Internet can build devices capable of intercepting wireless communications. There are generally simple countermeasures that can be taken to greatly reduce the risk of data interception, but by and large these are not used until after a hard lesson has been learned.

Equipment to listen in on private communications is a burgeoning industry in the United States. Sale of this equipment to individuals is often just as illegal as its use, but the resources of state and federal law enforcement are stretched too thin, such that illicit operations can operate openly—sometimes for years—before being shut down.

Illegal Eavesdropping Industry Within the United States (per year)

$496 million	Sale of Equipment—Imported
$392 million	Sale of Equipment—Built within the U.S.
$888 million	**Estimated Value of Eavesdropping Devices Sold in the United States**
$434 million	Services—Entry and Initial Installation
$891 million	Services—Ongoing Maintenance and Listening Post Operations
$1,325 million	**Estimated Value of Services within the United States**
$2,213 million	Estimated Total of U.S. Revenues (Goods and Services)
$512 million	Value of Eavesdropping Equipment Used Against Private Individuals
$734	Median Cost of Typical Noncorporate Eavesdropping Device (Installed)
$376 million	Value of Eavesdropping Equipment Used Against U.S. Corporate Targets
$57,500	Median Cost of Typical Corporate Eavesdropping Activity
$8,160 million	Impact (Loss) to U.S. Corporate Targets
6,550	Number of Corporate "Eavesdropping Incidents" each Year
$1.25 million	Average Impact (Loss) to Each U.S. Corporate Target
$1,247	Median Price of Typical Illegal Eavesdropping Device
$15–2,895	Price Range of Typical Illegal Eavesdropping Device
712,000	Estimated Number of Illegal Devices Sold each Year
2,720	Estimated Number of U.S. "Spy-Firms" Selling Eavesdropping Devices
278	Estimated Average Number of Devices Sold by Each Firm, Each Year

Source: U.S. State Department/INR (Bureau of Intelligence and Research), March 1997

The reason that they can operate so openly is that there are legitimate customers for their products. The military has on ongoing need for intercept and jamming equipment and special operations forces often have to rely on off-the-shelf equipment because standard military equipment is frequently too bulky, or does not operate in the RF range required for a particular mission. Law enforcement also has a legitimate need for intercept equipment to use during court-authorized wiretaps.

Interruption of Service

As wireless technology advances, there may be unexpected consequences from increasing vulnerabilities of the system. Just as a single fiber optic strand is capable of carrying thousands of conversations that only a few years ago required thousands of separate copper wires, the results have been greater efficiency, better service and lower costs. But, there is a downside to this progress. The unintended result of this infrastructure efficiency is a reduction in redundancy and an increase in the overall vulnerability of the system. The increased capacity provided by fiber optic technology has resulted in fewer cable routes necessary to meet capacity requirements. The result of having fewer cable routes is reduction in route diversity. In other words, fewer cable routes with a larger concentration of capacity results in increased vulnerability. Increase in capacity concentration has also resulted in fewer switches. Many of these switches are now collocated with other critical equipment. The lack of overall diversity in cabling, switching, and other common facilities results in an increase in vulnerability to attack in the telecommunications infrastructure.

In years past, when the majority of our cable infrastructure was composed of copper wires in cables, a *backhoe* interruption impacted only a small area. Today, a farmer burying a dead cow could cause a communication *blackout* for an entire region of the country.

Nearly everything that supports our daily lives is in some way connected to this infrastructure. Local banks are connected to the international banking community through computer links. Local power companies depend on the national electrical grid to balance electrical load requirements. The federal government and *Department of Defense* (DOD) rely heavily on this communications infrastructure. The impact of an unintentional interruption can be devastating.

Unintentional Interruptions

Unintentional interruptions are occurrences over which control was neglected or over which no control was possible under the circumstances. We have touched upon backhoe incidents, but there are more severe unintentional events possible that can affect the entire communications infrastructure. On a Monday afternoon in January 1990, the AT&T long-distance network, compromised of some 114 switching centers, each equipped with a main and backup computer—a system that should have been able to handle every conceivable problem—began to falter. In minutes, more than half of the callers using the AT&T long-distance network were greeted with a recorded message informing them that, "All circuits are busy. Please try your call again later." It took nearly nine hours for the network to be restored.[2]

When technology fails, the economic impact can be devastating. The effects can be just as devastating, or worse, when that technology falls victim to nature.

Natural Hazards

Natural hazards can and often times do bring about more of an impact to the infra-structure than any man-made event. Natural threats comprise the largest single cat-egory of repetitive threats to communities in the United States. These disasters are the result of climatic, geological/seismic, or oceanic-triggered events. They can affect any area of the country and may be localized or regional in scope, depending on the type of disaster. Severe damage resulting from a natural disaster can cause long-term damage to an infrastructure, including telecommunications systems.

Hurricanes

Hurricanes can present potentially significant impact to the entire infrastructure. Typically, hurricanes present five threats: high winds, thunderstorms and lightning strikes, floods, tornadoes, and torrential rains. Any type of aerial communications structure can be damaged by the accompanying traits of a hurricane. Damage to switches and cell sites can be the result of thunderstorms and lightning strikes. Flooding and torrential rains can affect buried cables.

Table 3-1 Hurricane Threats and Vulnerabilities

Threat	Vulnerability
Wind	Coaxial cables; telephone poles; telephone distribution systems; microwave system reliability
Thunderstorms and lightning strikes	Terrestrial equipment; switches and cell sites; site components; electrical equipment; coaxial cables; circuit boards
Floods	Flooded streams; coastal erosion
Tornado	Fixed telecommunications facilities
Torrential rains	Exposed telecommunications equipment; microwave systems

Table 3-2 Tornado Threats and Vulnerabilities

Threat	Vulnerability
High wind velocity	Coaxial cables; telephone poles and lines; telephone distribution systems; microwave system reliability
Thunderstorms and lightning strikes	Terrestrial equipment; switches and cell sites; site components; electrical equipment; coaxial cables; circuit boards

Tornadoes

A tornado strikes with such violence that it can quickly leave a path of destruction that seriously degrades or entirely wipes out the communications infrastructure in the area it hits. Again, aerial towers, like those used for cellular systems, are highly susceptible to damage from the violent winds that normally accompany tornadoes.

Winter storms

Winter storms can include heavy snowfalls, ice storms, and extremely cold temperatures. These conditions can threaten telecommunications facilities primarily by impacting electrical power sources. Heavy precipitation in the form of snow, sleet or ice, can lead to collapse of suspended (overhead) cable systems, affecting communication systems and electrical equipment.

Flooding

Flooding is the most common natural hazard. The communications infrastructure has two primary vulnerabilities to flooding: the saturation or dislodging of cables and the damage to facilities structure.

Earthquakes

Earthquakes can cause any form of communications structure, such as aerial/cellular structures and fixed facilities, to collapse. Collateral damage to electrical and underground cable facilities can result. Earthquakes can produce fires and explosions that can cause substantial damage to infrastructure.

Table 3-3 Winter Storm Threats and Vulnerabilities

Threat	Vulnerability
Power failure	Telecommunications systems; switches; repeaters
Heavy precipitation (snow, sleet, or ice)	Suspended telephone lines; traffic congestion
High wind	Physical damage to aerial structures
Ice storms	Suspended telephone lines
Extreme cold	Extreme cold may affect circuit breakers and other electrical equipment

Table 3-4 Flooding Threats and Vulnerabilities

Threat	Vulnerability
Standing flood	Coaxial cable and open wire lines; fiber optic cable; telecommunications buildings
Flash flood	Potential cable damage

Table 3-5 Earthquake Threats and Vulnerabilities

Threat	Vulnerability
Ground Motion	Central offices and buried transmission facilities; Switch Failures; Cellular
Fires	Any telecommunications structure
Explosions	Any telecommunications structure

Fire

Fire can occur close to or within telecommunications facilities. The 1988 fire at the Hinsdale (Illinois) switching office is the most recent example of a catastrophic fire affecting telecommunications infrastructure. Depending upon the type of switching equipment affected, a fire can have impacts on both local and regional telecommunications. Wildfires can burn cables servicing both communications and electrical facilities with devastating effects.

Power outages

Power outages can be caused by any of the previously described natural disasters, affecting both fixed and cellular systems.

Software failures

The telecommunications infrastructure relies on computer systems to operate. Software failure accounts for only a small portion of the outages that occur in the telecommunications structure, but when it occurs it produces an impact on the reliability of the system. As technology advances, the possibility of a catastrophic failure should be considered a real threat.

Intentional Interruptions

The interconnection and interdependence of the national communications infrastructure presents a valuable and vulnerable target to terrorists. Our complex national infrastructures are vulnerable because of their increasing interdependence. This creates critical nodes and choke points that can be attacked, which would result in major disruptions or destruction. Major power failures, problems with the air traffic control system, and breaks in gas and oil pipelines are covered in detail by the news media. Terrorists are made aware of these vulnerabilities through these same information channels.

Cell phone towers are fairly recognizable. These towers are usually placed in easily accessible areas, which, because of their necessary proximity to highways are located in areas that in general are easily approached without detection. If some type of security system is in use, it may not be enough to stop a terrorist with a pipe bomb.

The recognition of these vulnerabilities to the national infrastructure has resulted in significant actions at the highest levels. On July 15, 1996, President

Table 3-6 Fire Threats and Vulnerabilities

Threat	Vulnerability
Fire	Fixed telecommunications facilities; switching systems, cable; disruption in customer service, facilities without fire detection systems, facilities without smoke management systems

Table 3-7 Power Outages Threats and Vulnerabilities

Threat	Vulnerability
Loss of primary power to telecommunications facilities	Central offices; switch power systems
Downed power lines	Downed overhead telephone lines

Table 3-8 Software Failures Threats and Vulnerabilities

Threat	Vulnerability
Coding errors	Signaling, switching software
Operator error	
Late or erroneous patches	

Table 3-9 Primary Vulnerabilities

System Effect Hazard	Coax/Fiber Optic Cables	Central Office	Switches	Cell Sites	Electrical Equipment	Microwave Systems
Hurricanes	X	X	X	X	X	X
Tornadoes	X	X	X	X	X	X
Winter Storms	X		X			X
Floods	X	X	X		X	
Earthquakes		X	X	X	X	X
Fires	X	X	X		X	
Power Outages		X	X	X	X	X
Software Failures		X	X	X		

Clinton signed Executive Order 13010, which carried two major objectives. First, it established the President's Commission on Critical Infrastructure Protection. The Commission mandated the federal government and the private sector to cooperatively develop a plan to promote national security. Secondly, the order established the formation of the *Infrastructure Protection Task Force* (IPTF), tasked with coordinating multi-agency action within the government in responding to infrastructure crises. The IPTF's function is to identify and coordinate existing expertise, inside and outside of the Federal government, in efforts to provide expert guidance to critical infrastructures on detecting, halting, and confining an attack and to recover and restore service.

Phone Phreaking

The *Public Switched Telephone Network* (PSTN), like any other computer network, is the target of hackers and vulnerable to hacking. Hackers who target telephone networks are called *phreakers* and their version of hacking is called *phreaking*, which is basically hacking with a telephone instead of a computer. Phreakers use different boxes and tricks to manipulate the phone companies and their phone lines to gain knowledge about the phone systems and gain unbilled and unpaid access to long distance lines.

Phone phreaking hit its peak in the 1970s and 1980s. Due to technological changes and upgrades, the impact of this activity on the PSTN has been on the decline, but a new technology, cellular, has stepped in to fill the void. Phone phreaking has evolved onto cellular phone.

Legal Aspects

The FCC and the government have enacted various laws pertaining to cordless phones and listening to the conversations of others. However, just because a law exists does not ensure that it will be obeyed or is enforceable. This is a problem not just in the United States, but also in other countries.

3-1 Legal Aspects. (Courtesy of Donna Ebling, Dennis Suzanne Kimball, Jay Wilson, EMSE 298, Spring 2001, George Washington University, SEAS, Washington, D.C.)

Laws in the United States

Many laws in the United States concerning cordless phones focus on monitoring conversations without consent. Under our laws, only national security and law enforcement agents have the authority to conduct electronic eavesdropping under strict legal restrictions. This has lead to laws concerning privacy. In the United States, some of those laws include those shown in Table 3-10.

Other countries also have initiated restrictions on interception and safeguards for privacy as shown in Table 3-11.

Privacy

The Communications Assistance for Law Enforcement Act permits law enforcement access to any digital communication. Where police once had to tap telephone lines, now they can request phone companies to make digital communications available to them. Therefore, law enforcement has access to all communications. If this is true, how does a citizen protect his or her privacy? Does a citizen no longer have a right to privacy?

Law enforcement must reimburse the phone companies for the cost of adjusting any phone lines. Phone companies do not have to decrypt encrypted communication unless the phone company provides the encryption service.

New Zealanders are also worried about their privacy. Clause 19 could require that they give their keys to encrypted data to government agencies. How can they have privacy when they must hand over their keys? What if these same keys were used as a means of securing telephone conversations? Why bother to encrypt anything at all? The citizens must give any assistance in the case of the crime of unauthorized access to a computer. Any assistance could involve giving decryption keys to the government. Access to the decryption keys would allow government agencies to read encrypted data without requiring expensive technology that would break codes using time-consuming algorithms.[8]

Cryptography

Only cryptography provides end-to-end security. The distance from one end to another does not affect the cost. However, there are some concerns. If strong cryptography is available, some national and security law enforcement wiretaps will become useless. For this reason, the United States has tried to prevent strong cryptography in electronic communications. Some government agencies are concerned that if they obtain a wiretapped conversation, they won't have a key to decrypt the coded message. Citizens are concerned the government is not letting them have their privacy. If the government does not allow the cryptography, citizens will merely buy it somewhere else, and those concerns will become actualities.[9]

How is appropriate cryptography strength determined for public use? An encryption system consists of an algorithm and a key. The security of the system is determined by the complexity of the algorithm and key length. If someone cannot break into the system in a reasonable amount of time, the system is secure. Systems are becoming faster and can hold more memory. Algorithms must be very complex

Table 3-10 U.S. Laws and Their Descriptions

United States Law	Description
Communications Act of 1934 (Section 705/Privacy Act)	It is unlawful to disclose the content of radio transmissions overheard unless they are amateur radio traffic, broadcasts to the public, or distress calls. It is unlawful to use traffic monitored for personal gain.[3]
Foreign Intelligence Surveillance Act—1978	Established grounds for national security wiretaps and electronic bugs. Included surveillance of fax and computer communications.
National Security Decision Directive 145—1984	Established a policy safeguarding "sensitive but unclassified" information in communications and computer systems.
Electronic Communications Privacy Act of 1986	Illegal to eavesdrop on private digital, cellular, or PCS communications. Written to protect other types of mobile telephone calls in addition to satellite, microwave point-to-point, broadcast remote, paging, and other radio services besides cellular phones. Prohibits the manufacturing and use of scanners specifically for the interception of private wireless calls.[4]
	Illegal to *intentionally* intercept, disclose, or use the contents of any wire or electronic communication. Includes any radio transmissions except for communications to pagers or tracking devices. Cordless telephones were not included. It is legal to listen to all radio transmissions readily accessible to the general public.
Telecommunications Disclosure and Dispute Resolution Act—October 8, 1992	Concerns anti-scanner provisions and anti-cellular receiver provisions. Denies certification to cellular-capable scanners, and bans the importation and manufacture of such scanners.
Public Law 103-414, 1994	Amended the ECPA to provide equal treatment to cordless phone conversations as cellular ones. Readily accessible to the general public became to exclude all electronic communications. Electronic communications include almost all radio communications. As the law now exists, there is virtually no radio communication that is "readily accessible to the general public."[5]
	To prove interception, must prove beyond a shadow of a doubt that the interception was *intentional*.
Computer Security Act (Public Law 100-235)	National Institute of Standards and Technology is in charge of all civilian computer standards, including cryptography.
Communications Assistance for Law Enforcement Act, June 2000.	Ensures law officers will be able to access any communications using new digital technology. Requires phone companies to make digital communications accessible to law officers.[6]

Table 3-11 Foreign Laws and Their Descriptions

Foreign Law	Description
British Law	Permits interception in national security and law enforcement cases including those necessary to safeguard the country's economic well being.
Danish Information Technology Security Council—June 1996	Recommends placing no limits on cryptography use.
Nordic Postal Security Service (Denmark, Finland, Norway, and Sweden)	Provide a 1024-bit RSA-based secure email service with the postal authority handling key management.
Clause 19 in Crimes Amendment Bill—New Zealand	May force computer system owners to provide keys to encrypted data. Exempts Security Intelligence Service personnel with interception warrants from prosecution under the proposed crime of unauthorized access to a computer.[7]

and keys quite long. Phones do not have a lot of memory for long keys; yet without keys of sufficient length, the encryption will not be strong. There are private and public keys. In both, the sender of the message stores his or her key. However, some members of the public are concerned that the government might want their keys.

Jamming

Jamming of cellular phones may seem to be appealing and devices that accomplish this are available. Libraries, theaters, restaurants, airlines, and even hospitals may have a desire to use just such a device to enforce etiquette or the safety of their own equipment. But if they attempt to use this technology, they will find a serious legal roadblock. The use of jamming devices in the United States is illegal. The Communications Act of 1934, as amended, and *Federal Communications Commission* (FCC) rules do not permit these devices to be manufactured, imported, marketed, or operated within the United States. The operation of transmitters designed to jam cellular communications is a violation of 47 USC 301, 302(b), and 333. The manufacture, importation, sale, or offer for sale, including advertising, of such transmitters is a violation of 47 USC 302(b). Parties in violation of these provisions may be subject to the penalties contained within 47 USC 501–510. Fines for a first offense can range as high as $11,000 for each violation or imprisonment for up to one year. The equipment can also be seized and forfeited to the U.S. government. These regulations apply to all transmitters that are designed to cause interference to, or prevent the operation of, other radio communication systems.

Right to Free Speech and Privacy Expectations When Using Cell Phones

Do the laws against wiretapping violate the First Amendment rights of reporters with regard to publicizing information received from anonymous eavesdroppers? This was the premise of an issue brought to court. It was hoped that an agreement would be reached on the issue of the right to free speech and privacy expectations using cell phones and other wireless communication. In Bartnicki v. Vopper and the United States v. Vopper, a federal law that protected the privacy of wire, oral, and electronic communications was challenged.[10] The issue was the constitutionality of allowing lawsuits and imposing prison sentences on those who distribute illegally obtained information even if they do not know who did the wiretapping and played no part in the illegal act. Bartnicki's newsworthy cell phone conversation was intercepted. The unknown eavesdropper taped the recorded conversation and mailed it to Person A. Person A then gave it to Vopper, a radio talk show host, who played the tape on his show. Scripts of the conversation were shown on newscasts and in the newspapers. Bartnicki sued Vopper, and won in trial, but Vopper won in appeals court. They took the case to the federal government. The federal government sided with Bartnicki to prevent the laws from being overturned. Person A's involvement was not discussed.

In 1997, the FBI opened an investigation into the taping and leaking of a telephone conference call between Gingrich and his top lieutenants. The probe came after a Florida couple said they delivered a tape of the cellular phone conversation to the senior Democrat on the House Ethics Committee. The couple that intercepted that call pleaded guilty to wiretapping and paid fines. In another case, Sen. Charles Robb, a Virginia Democrat, got into hot water in 1991 over an illegal tape recording of a cellular call made by a political rival, Virginia Gov. Douglas Wilder. Robb was spared indictment. Four associates pleaded guilty in the case.

Who Is Doing The Intercepting?

Gathering intelligence through communication for political or personal gain has been a trait of successful societies since early history. The Roman Empire, Mongol Empire, and early China (Shih Huang rein, 247–210 BC) all realized that effective communication systems were vital to the success of their Empires. Important messages provided various types of intelligence reflecting their own interest/state of the Empire, and information on the societies (tribes) outside the Empire. The time element has always been important, only today the relative term *fast* is greatly more accelerated than in early empires. Today, there is voluminous information available, and the problem is to identify what information is important, and how it can be useful. Depending on who is gathering the information, sometimes the source can often be restricted to the knowledge of your competitor and/or adversary. Who is attempting wireless interception, and what countermeasures may be appropriate?

Eavesdropping is not something new. It has been practiced throughout history. During the U.S. Civil War, Confederate General Jeb Stuart traveled with a wiretapper so that he could discover the enemy's plans. During World War I, England severed Germany's transatlantic cables, forcing the Germans to communicate by radio or cables that crossed enemy lines. The Allies were then able to read these messages. This concept was also used in World War II.[11]

Joe Q. Public

An average, law-abiding citizen uses wireless communication commercial products to accomplish daily activities. As more products become available, dependence on the technology will become more common. Mr. Public could possibly be affected by two problems in the wireless communication world: invasion of privacy and fraud. Depending on the technology used, wireless communication may be intercepted.

Mobile Telephones

Older wireless telephones from the mid-1980s were tethered systems that transmitted to a base, were designed to use low radio frequency (RF) 17 MHz, and produced a signal that could be picked up a distance of one mile. The handheld unit could access several telephone bases, dependent on the unit proximity. The result could be fraudulent access of a unit for someone else's communication, with the owner of the base being charged for the usage. Regarding privacy, the signal strength and RF easily allowed scanners to eavesdrop on the conversations. Newer telephones have lowered there signal strength, which prevents a channel from being "borrowed" by a different handset, and have the capability to switch to alternative frequencies to decrease the likelihood of being picked-up via a digital scanner. Analog cellular phones, common in the mid-1990s, allowed conversations to be intercepted by scanning microwave receiver. Although the scanning equipment with this capability has not legally sold in the United States since 1994, the needed components are available at Radio Shack and can be constructed in little time.

Cellular Telephones

Technologies for digital cellular telephones include frequency hopping, and some have cryptography to prevent scanning interception. This could present a false security. In 1997, digital cell phones using *Cellular Message Encryption Algorithm* (CMEA) were identified as allowing digits dialed on the keypads—such as *Personal Identification Number* (PIN) access, credit cards, passwords, and so forth—to be picked up with a digital scanner. In 1998, reports of *Global System for Mobile communication* (GSM) simcard cloning revealed that a PC used the GSM telephone identification to have access to subscriber services. This requires physical access to the phone and does not present a problem, unless a phone is stolen. But another threat surfaced in December 1999: a flawed design of the GSM A1/A5 algorithm allowed the descrambling of conversations in real-time and a 15-millisecond attack against A5/A2, both by a typical PC with 128MB RAM. This allowed conversations to be captured, which could prove costly. At the time of that announcement, there were over 215 million GSM subscribers worldwide.

Friends and Neighbors: The Unintentional Intercept

It is quite possible to inadvertently intercept communications with devices you have in your home. In fact it has been happening since cordless phones first came out, or even before. Such accidental intercept can occur with voice devices such as phones and intercoms, or with data devices such as home networks.

Voice Systems

One well-known electronics distributor makes an instant home intercom system. You simply plug two or more of these devices into your home electrical wiring system and they provide a low-quality voice intercom throughout the house. In the event you do not have an appropriate filter on your home wiring, the signal can easily travel beyond the bounds of the house. In fact it can travel through the power grid for hundreds of feet. It is possible to sit in your home and listen in on the intercom conversations of neighbors on the next block.

A more recent, wireless version of this is the increasingly popular nursery intercom. These operate on a very narrow range of frequencies, have ranges in the hundreds of feet, and rarely offer any encryption capability. They have the additional hazard of always being on. Where the intercom only transmitted when you actively pushed the talk button, the nursery unit will happily transmit anything it hears on a 24/7 basis.

Cordless phones also used to be a significant source of grist for the inadvertent eavesdropper, but the older models had extremely limited range and frequently barely made it around the house. Later models have greatly increased range, but also normally have at least low-level encryption in place, which usually prevents accidental eavesdropping; however, as noted previously, this is not a real hurdle for a determined effort to tap your cordless lines.

Data Systems

A recent and as yet uncommon phenomenon involves wireless networking. At the current time most middle-class households have at least one computer. The rapid advances in computer capabilities over the past few years along with rapidly declining prices have resulted in millions of homes with more than one computer. Coupled with a regular exposure at work to computer networks and the ease of installing home network systems, the home networking industry is blossoming.

While corporate America has little problem getting network cable installed with drop ceilings and now pre-wired buildings, most homeowners cringe at the thought of ripping up their walls just to run some CAT 5 cable to connect little Debbie's computer to Mom and Dad's. This makes a competitively priced wireless system extremely attractive. The least expensive and also easiest to install offer no encryption capability and all network security is provided by the individual computer OS. These systems also operate at 2 Mbps, a rate quite slow when compared to even the slowest Ethernet network. On the plus side the range for the transmitter is only 150 feet at most and is not likely to be accidentally picked up by anyone further away than a next-door neighbor. These systems also do not operate on any industry standard protocols for the physical layer of communication.

Next up in price and speeds are the systems that conform to the *IEEE* 802.11b wireless transmission protocol. These systems transfer data at 11 Mbps and operate at ranges up to 300 feet indoors and 900 feet outdoors. While the cost of these systems is roughly double the previous ones, range and data transfer benefits are also greatly increased. Also the primary vendors offer an encryption system. This is normally the 40-bit WEP standard. This is a great improvement over no encryption at all, but from the perspective of accidental eavesdropping, the encryption is normally disabled at installation for performance gains and must be manually activated. This type of product is also more difficult to set up and will probably require visits from a professional to be properly configured.

There are additional wireless networking products that offer improved encryption or data rates, but these are generally far too expensive for the average home user.

With the advent of always-on broadband Internet access there is an additional consideration for the home networker. Not only is it possible to eavesdrop on a wireless home network, it is also possible to piggyback onto the Internet connection for free Internet access.

An accurate assessment of technology reveals that products claiming to be secure can change with further research and technology developments. When products are developed and tested against attacks with current advanced market technology, you must recognize that Moore's Law[12]—that technology will double its capabilities in 18 to 24 months—can present limits to secure technical assessments. The countermeasure to prevent yourself from being a victim of fraud and privacy intrusion involves being an aware consumer. Be cognizant of the risk, and decide if it is worth the efficiencies gained. As a consumer you should remain current of security claims of products used and be cautious about what subjects are discussed and what identifying information is revealed (credit cards, PIN codes, and so on). Select your third-party agents based on liability policies and review billing statements for accuracy. And a last point: Know legally what state and federal laws apply to the circumstances, and lobby your legislative representatives for consumer support.

Criminal Arena

Discussion in the criminal arena builds on the information presented for Joe Q. Public but provides explanation of how ignoring or exploiting existing laws can create profit. Several pieces of equipment exist, or can be created by modifying existing equipment, to capture electronic information and exploit the way wireless communication operates. To correct these exploitations, some of the existing laws have had to be interpreted to include wireless communication, and other laws had to be created.

Fraud

In the mid-1990s cellular telephone providers were losing a large percentage of income—in 1996 around 1 billion dollars[13]—because of fraud. Cell phones were being cloned. For analog cell phones, an ESN/MIN scanner could pick up intercepted *electronic serial numbers* (ESNs) and the *mobile identification numbers* (MIN). The ESN/MIN scanner could be poised at a highly congested area and intercept the identification codes for later use. The identifying numbers intercepted from the owners would be programmed into another cellular telephone. The calls made on the cloned telephone would be billed to the valid owner of the codes. Owners would identify the inaccurate costs on their billings, removing their financial responsibility, but the carriers would have to absorb the loss, which eventually came back to the legitimate users. Cell phone identification numbers are easy to intercept. The codes are transmitted to establish the call connections in the beginning of the session. Although the sale of the scanners that pick up the signal is illegal, minor adjustments to a conventional scanner make it possible to cover cellular bands.

Another circumstance of fraud referred to in the section "Joe Q. Public" involved digital cellular GSM phones. News accounts have not reported this as a major crime; only that the signal may he picked up on a PC for future use. The high incidence of phone cloning and economic loss to carriers have increased the use of signal encryption in recent years. There are two reasons criminals want a phone that could be identified as legally being owned by another individual: one is not being billed for the usage, and the other is anonymity. Fraudulent billing has been discussed, but the anonymity provided could prove more valuable.

In August 1999, the *Federal Communications Commission* (FCC) ruled that carriers of wireless services would have to assist law enforcement agencies in identifying the location of callers. Wired telephones have a static location, but cellular phones do not. No legal provision existed for revealing the location of a call, or if this should be considered as private and not for release to legal authorities. Carriers are now required to assist law enforcement agencies who have legal authorization to identify the cell where the call is being picked up at the beginning of the call and at the end. (Part of the Communications Assistance for Law Enforcement Act [CALEA]). If this is a cloned cell phone and not registered as belonging to the individual identified for being monitored, so much the better from the criminal's point of view.

Once technological effort is made to prevent crime by encrypting identifying codes to support customers and reduce their loses, the criminals respond by stealing cell phones outright. Encryption has made the interception of codes much more difficult. Thieves now target the cell phone itself. As noted in an article in the Globe-News in Amarillo, Texas, thieves are not breaking into a car to ransack for valuables. They can see the cell phone in plain sight and pop the window to take the phone. Most cell phones are not covered by insurance unless they are permanently part of the automobile. Resale value of the phone can run between $110 and $150[14] on the black market. Drug dealers who prefer the mobility of pagers and cell phones are creating the demand.

Pagers

Messages for pagers may be intercepted with few pieces of equipment: a pager interceptor device, a computer with special software, or a scanner that can be purchased for $300 to $1,000.[15] Message interception requires a cloned pager to capture the message, one with an identification number that matches the legitimate receiver of a message. The technique to intercept a message is usually completed and announced by hackers to see if they can do it or to get publicity showing it can be done. In New York City, sensitive government communications are sent by pager to prevent interception by radio scanners. One arrest of three workers with the *Breaking News Network* (BNN) entailed a cloned pager intercepting New York official messages. The messages were then released to the media for follow-up stories. The arrest of the BBN personnel was successful because of a disgruntled previous BBN employee providing a cloned pager and the lead to the U.S. Attorney's Office in New York. But what would the value of the news leads be worth to news companies?

Drugs Cartels

As previously mentioned, drug dealers prefer pagers and cell phones for communication. The owners may have a sense of security, being able to move yet have contact or be contacted, if needed. The cloned phone cannot be traced to the caller and the only inconvenience is the phone service being turned off after unusual billing is reviewed. In one case involving the drug cartel, officials of the Drug Enforcement Agency discovered a number of calls to Colombia on their phone bills. Cartel operatives had cloned DEA's own number[16].

The DEA is vocal about the sophistication of the electronic communication equipment the leaders of drug organizations use and make the point that the U.S. government is unable to capture evidence. The drug cartels have the necessary funds to establish their own surveillance vans and encrypt their cell phone calls so law enforcement authorities cannot decode them. During other drug captures it was found that Colombian jets had sophisticated air-to-air signal interceptors to reveal the location of U.S. military jets protecting borders. Testimony before the Senate Select Committee on Intelligence about the disadvantage the law enforcement agencies experience and the current technology available to criminals, resulted in legislation increasing the ability of law enforcement agencies to receive more funding and legislative support to curtail the organized drug operations.

Military—United States

Today communication intelligence is not only concerned with the political and military aspect, but business espionage and technological secrets can also be vital to a nation's security. The military joins other government organizations in completing *Communication Intelligence* (COMINT). Communication signals can be picked up at various locations around the world, based on their frequency and type of signals. Since the electromagnetic spectrum is organized though international cooperation, it is easy to know which frequencies are used for types of traffic to be intercepted. Various methods of disguising these intercepts have been necessary.

The Soviets had fishing trawlers with huge antennas positioned throughout specific areas in the sea. Little fishing activity was observed, but the ships would persistently stay in the areas for a prolonged period. In the mid-to-late 1960s, two U.S. "research" ships were discovered in areas by foreign services that proved to be their demise. The Liberty was nearly sunk in the Mediterranean by the Israelis in 1967, and the Pueblo was captured by the North Koreans. It was reported the Liberty was intercepting messages from the Egyptians during the six-day war. Since then, the United States has abandoned message intercept by ship and now concentrates on airborne intercept.

High-altitude satellites are the mainstay of the U.S. communication intercept in synchronous orbits, 22,500 miles high. Lower-altitude satellites have recently been included, but the high speed of travel demands numerous satellites sequenced so message traffic may be continually picked up as the transmitter and satellite work together. The intelligence involved is selecting what communication should be captured for interpretation and future analysis. Usually, if in a telephone conversation, only half a message is received, the objective is to select key phrases, or languages, and if it is data, the format may be the feature that reveals its importance. As late as 1998, it was reported that if an intercepted message was encrypted, it was automatically recorded.[17] This was only possible because of the then low amount of encrypted communication traffic.

As the amount of encrypted traffic increases, the selection criteria may change. Besides the actual message intercepted, an important part of the interception is the traffic analysis and the overall characteristics (length, timing, addressing, frequencies, and modulation).[18] This analysis involves creating databases that track the communications relationships, patterns, and signals. And lastly, once the information is available for use and the period of retention has expired, the material must be sanitized before it is released so the source is not revealed.

While the military has extensive capabilities of performing wireless intercept and analysis, they are proscribed from such activities whenever a U.S. citizen would be one of the intercepted parties. This restriction is spelled out in *United States Signals Intelligence Directive* (USSID) 18 (see Figure 3-2). During peacetime all military COMINT activity is conducted under the auspices of the *National Security Agency* (NSA). As such they operate under the same constraints as the rest of the intelligence community.[19] This being the case, there is little documentary evidence of the United States military conducting wireless intercept that could involve U.S. citizens, which effectively rules out the United States and its territories.

Other Countries

While the U.S. military may be extremely limited in its intercept activities on American citizens, Russia and other countries are not. During a 1996 hearing before the Senate Select Committee on Intelligence, this is what the Defense Intelligence Agency had to say about the Russian Signals Intelligence (SIGINT) facility at Lourdes, Cuba (shown in Figure 3-3):

> The Lourdes signals intelligence (SIGINT) facility near Havana, Cuba, is the largest Russian SIGINT site abroad. The strategic location of Lourdes makes it ideal for gathering intelligence on the United States.
>
> Russia's SIGINT effort at Lourdes is carried out by Russian military intelligence (GRU) and the *Federal Agency for Government Communications* (FAPSI). The FAPSI evolved in the early 1990s from the former KGB's SIGINT service. According to Russian press sources, the Russian Foreign Intelligence Service (SVR) also has a communications center at the facility for its agent network in North and South America.
>
> From this key facility, first the Soviet Union and now Russia have historically monitored U.S. commercial satellites and sensitive communications dealing with U.S. military, merchant shipping, and Florida-based NASA space programs. According to a 1993 statement by Cuban Defense Minister Raul Castro, Russia is said to obtain 75 percent of its military strategic information from Lourdes.
>
> The Lourdes facility enables Russia to eavesdrop on U.S. telephone communications. U.S. voice and data telephone transmissions relayed by satellites visible to the

NATIONAL SECURITY AGENCY
CENTRAL SECURITY SERVICE
Fort George G. Meade, Maryland

27 July 1993

UNITED STATES SIGNALS INTELLIGENCE DIRECTIVE
(USSID)
18
LEGAL COMPLIANCE AND
MINIMIZATION PROCEDURES

LETTER OF PROMULGATION

(U) This USSID prescribes policies and procedures and assigns responsibilities to ensure that the missions and functions of the United States SIGINT System (USSS) are conducted in a manner that safeguards the constitutional rights of U.S. persons.

(U) this USSID has been completely rewritten to make it shorter and easier to understand. It constitutes a summary of the laws and regulations directly affecting USSS operations. All USSS personnel who collect, process, retain, or disseminate information to, from, or about U.S. persons or persons in the United States must be familiar with its contents.

This USSID supersedes USSID 18 and USSIO 18, Annex A (distributed separaaately to selected recipients), both of which are dated 20 October 1980, and must now be destroyed. Notify DIRNSA/CHCSS (USSIO Manager) if this edition of USSID 18 is destroyed because of an emergency action; otherwise, request approval from DIRNSA/CHCSS before destroying this USSID.

Release or exposure of this document to contractors and consultants without approval from the USSID Manager is prohibited. Instructions applicable to release or exposure of USSID to contractors and consultatnts may be found in USSID 19.

Questions and comments concerning this USID should be addressed to the Office of the General Counsel, NSA/CSS, NST5 963-3121 or STU III 688-5015.

[signature]

J.M. McCONNELL
Vice Admiral, U.S. Navy
Director

3-2 Title page from USSID 18 obtained through Freedom of Information Act.

facility are vulnerable to Russian intercept. Although sensitive U.S. government communications are encrypted to prevent this intercept, most other unprotected telephone communications in the United States are systematically intercepted.

In addition to its military strategic value, Lourdes will increasingly be used to support the Russian economy, a current FAPSI priority. In addition to unprotected commercial information, personal information about U.S. citizens in the private and

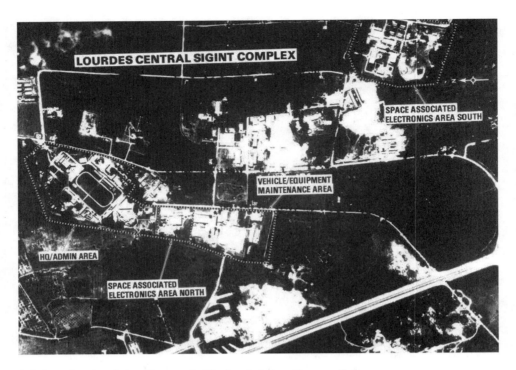

3-3 Lourdes signals intelligence facility located near Havana, Cuba.

government sectors also can be snatched from the airwaves and used by Russian intelligence to identify promising espionage recruits in these sectors.

In October 1995, Cuba and Russia produced an agreement on the continued functioning of the site until the year 2000. Although the amount of Russian compensation for the site is unclear, a 1994 agreement called for Russia to provide Cuba approximately $200 million worth of fuel, timber, and spare parts for various equipment, including military, for the operation of the facility during that year.[20]

ECHELON

ECHELON is potentially the largest wireless intercept operation ever undertaken. While still not publicly acknowledged by the U.S. government, apparently some allied countries (so called Second Parties) have made varying disclosures and announcements on the program.

The first public exposure came in 1997. Nicky Hager, a reporter from the *Covert Action Quarterly* published an extensive article detailing an elaborate data intercept and analysis network bound together under the secret UKUAS signals intelligence agreement. His contention is that ECHELON is tracking a significant portion of the world's email, fax, telex, and telephone communications. Some sources have claimed that up to 90 percent of all Internet traffic is screened by ECHELON.[21] The tracking is done through the use of intercept stations in the allied countries that compare all traffic they can intercept against different sets of keywords. Each of the various intelligence agencies from the allied countries keeps a separate dictionary on the system, and when a message is encountered containing a keyword, it is forwarded to the headquarters of the agency concerned. However, the exact capabilities and goals of ECHELON remain unclear. For example, it is unknown whether ECHELON actually targets domestic communications. Also, it is apparently difficult for ECHELON to intercept certain types of transmissions, particularly fiber communications.[22]

ECHELON Ground Stations

The first component of ECHELON is ground stations that are targeted at the ring of *International Telecommunication Satellites* (INTELSATS). This group of more than 40 satellites operates in geosynchronous orbits and are used by the telephone companies of most countries. Each is capable of serving as a relay station for thousands of simultaneous phone calls, faxes, and emails.

ECHELON's next component intercepts satellite communications not carried on the INTELSAT system. This would include satellites used for diplomatic and military communications. In large part this is done at the same stations that are working the INTELSAT problem, but there would be several other stations also working this since the group of satellites working diplomatic and military communications are often *Low Earth Orbit* (LOE) and collection stations require different positioning from those covering geostationary satellites.

The final collection component is ground-based microwave communications. Whereas the first two components require large, fixed bases where they can set up the satellite intercept dishes, microwave intercept only requires a building or antenna situated along the microwave route. It is also believed that ECHELON uses numerous satellites to catch spillover data from transmissions between cities. These satellites then beam the information down to processing centers on the ground. The main centers are supposed to be in the United States (near Denver) and England (Menwith Hill, Figure 3-4).

Each of the dictionary computer stations is linked by highly encrypted communications back to the five agency headquarters of the allied countries. A highly organized and controlled system is in place to control search initiation and who will have access to it.

In several places in Hager's article it was pointed out that certain aspects of ECHELON could not be accurately reported on because the author did not have sources relevant to that area. It was also pointed out that the ability to do the same dictionary keyword recognition on telephone conversations may not be anywhere near the same level of the ability to do it on text-based communications.

Future Research

For wireless interception, various components are needed to support different types of interception devices. Power for the units is a constant, as well as an antenna and a method to place the item where it may complete its function without being observed. Examining where the development of these components is heading gives

3-4 NSA Ground Station at Menwith Hill, England. (See Note 20 for attribution)

a view to the future development of systems to be used. In the U.S., the *Defense Advanced Research Projects Agency* (DARPA) provides funding for research in areas that could have significance for defense/military systems, as well as commercial business. Usually, if the product development can be market-driven, there is no need for government contracts to support the development. If the market seems to dictate terms that are not in line with the military and government needs, however, DARPA will provide research funds to speed the development.

Portable items present a difficult technology dilemma. The more diverse the capabilities of the wireless unit, the more power they require; the more power, the heavier the load, which removes some of the mobility. An article in Jane's International Defense Review states that current batteries only can provide up to one-tenth the power needed for military missions.[23] This is a challenge to the industry. Three grades of battery are to be created: one to last 3 hours, one to last 3 days, and one to last 10 days, with each to generate an average power level of 20 watts/12 volts, with a size restriction that can be carried by a soldier or transported in a small robot plane.

Another item that has keen appeal and is needed to support ground-to-air message transfer is *Unmanned Aerial Vehicles* (UAV). The military communications systems are mobile *Local Area Networks* (LAN), which are not designed for message intercept, but to support military deployments. The RQ-4, being built by Northrop Grumman, will have communications (Airborne Communication Node or ACN) developed by Raytheon and BA[24] that will provide a link for digital radio exchange—from soldiers in the field to fighter pilots in the air. Within years of fielding, the modular communication node will then expand into wideband communication and provide SIGNINT reconnaissance. A UAV performing this mission will have more control than a satellite and serve a larger area than a manned flight because of higher altitude capability.

New concepts of space and information transmission are also being explored through DARPA funding for systems, which on a small scale can mimic data capture in a wider area. WEBDUST is a network of micro network sensors, relaying information in a method that describes conceptual space and physical description. It is an information infrastructure that obtains, maintains, manages, and delivers spatially constrained data.[25] There are four components: the *SPatial ObjecT* (SPOT) would provide a way to tag the spatial attribute into human readable code; DataSpaces are databases that shift locations of database searches to a sub-network; Infodispensors, which would act as the relay between the SPOT and the databases; and the Spatial WEB, an interface between the User and the Infodispensor continually organizing the data for users as they pass by.

The development of this type of system would allow queries on the Web, based on a physical location, for example, such as "Where is the closest coffee shop within two miles?" The responding answer would be determined by the location where the query was issued. If this type of system works and is expanded in a larger scale, wireless intercept would include geographic data.

Law Enforcement

Criminals, military, government, and the public listen in on conversations. Law enforcement agencies also listen, but they do it legally. The Electronic Communications Privacy Act grants law enforcement agencies the right to tap phones if they can prove they have probable cause. If they can prove to a judge that they need to eavesdrop due to an illegal activity, a matter of life or death, in order to enforce a law, or to gain evidence on a criminal element, they will be permitted to do so. A felony must be involved. A court order will usually limit the monitoring to thirty days.

3-5 Law enforcement. (Courtesy of Donna Ebling, Dennis Suzanne Kimball, Jay Wilson, EMSE 298, Spring 2001, George Washington University, SEAS, Washington, D.C.)

The FCC requires that any recording of telephone conversations must be made known to those involved. However, this does not apply to law enforcement. Law enforcement agencies are also permitted to listen in on phone conversations and record them without consent. This is known as one-party-consent-provision. If one of the parties involved in the conversation gives permission to the police, monitoring is also permitted.[26]

If law enforcement agencies are monitoring your telephone conversations and the court authorized it, you will not be told until the wiretap has been terminated—usually within ninety days.

British law enforcement agencies also have problems. Government, law enforcement, and industry got together to discuss how to make Britain both a good place for e-commerce as well as a safe one. One of the technical issues important to law enforcement was encryption. Law enforcement needs a strong understanding of advances in technology, and industry must understand the needs of law enforcement. It was suggested that industry must find a way to help law enforcement conduct legal interceptions.[27]

Law enforcement is not immune to interception. Isn't it possible that the criminals are listening in on police conversations? Police digital data transmissions are binary coded. "A person knowledgeable in the area of digital technology may be able to listen to the transmissions, and if two people are using a digital radio at the same frequency, they could indeed hear the police conversation."[28] Police can avoid this by using encryption.

The police use various products to prevent others from listening to their conversations.

- CopyTele Cryptele USS-900 provides voice, data, and fax encryption for use with narcotics trafficking, corruption cases, and other high-level crimes.
- CCS International is designed to encrypt digital voices transmitted over analog phones. Users on both ends must know the algorithm and the key to decrypt the message. Transcrypt International's products prevent interception of voice and data communication from third parties using portable radios and other devices.

Various products on the market for audio surveillance are limited to law enforcement agencies. If criminals can obtain digital voice scanners, encryption will be an important countermeasure.

Applications

The various wireless applications each have their own vulnerabilities and countermeasures. This section discusses the following applications:

- Cell phones
- Handsets
- Microphones
- RF Transmitters

Cell Phone Vulnerabilities

Restaurant and theater customers are familiar with the sound. You are sitting there, enjoying a quiet dinner with your spouse, or you're watching the latest action flick, when you hear the sound of a ringing cell phone. The owner answers the call and begins a "private" conversation with a roomful of strangers listening. Maybe it's just a call from the babysitter or an important call from the office. Unfortunately, etiquette rules don't always keep up with technology. Some restaurants ask customers to turn off their cell phones before being seated. Others provide a place for patrons to take their calls without disturbing others. But technology can be used to enforce high-tech etiquette.

What about that important business meeting? The one where the CEO is going to discuss the new business plan—the plan that will rock your competitors on their heels. Wouldn't they love to be listening in on the meeting? A cellular telephone can be turned into a microphone and transmitter for the purpose of listening to conversations in the vicinity of the phone. Transmitting to the cell phone a maintenance command on the control channel does this. This command places the cellular telephone in the diagnostic mode. When this is done, conversations in the immediate area of the telephone can be monitored over the voice channel.[29]

Jamming

A cell phone jammer or call blocker, as they are commonly called, is a device that transmits low-power radio signals that cut off communications between cellular handsets and cellular base stations. The jamming effect can be digitally controlled to form quiet zones in confined places. Most jammers use a transmission method that confuses the decoding circuits of cellular handsets as if no cellular base station is within the service area. Consequently, all cellular phone calls already in progress within the defined area will be cut off and the radio link will be lost. *No service* appears on the phone's LCD display. When activated, incoming calls are handled as if the cellular handset is OFF. There are devices used for the detection of cell phone operation also. These devices can be used in conjunction with jammers. These units allow for the selective use of jamming devices.

These devices are available from several offshore manufactures along with domestic distributors. A quick search on the Internet will turn up many sources. The two primary types or models are low- and high-power. The low-power units are used in confined areas such as theatres, libraries, and hospitals. The high-power units are capable of covering areas between 20 and 200 meters.

Owning a cell phone jammer or call blocker is one thing; putting it in operation is another (see Figure 3-6). Their use in the United States is strictly illegal. The Communications Act of 1934, as amended, and FCC rules do not permit these devices to be manufactured, imported, marketed, or operated within the United States. Parties in violation of these provisions may be subject to fines as high as $11,000 for each violation or imprisonment for up to one year. The equipment can

3-6 C-Guard Cellular FireWall Manufactured by NetLine Communications Technologies. (Used by Permission of NetLine Communications Technologies [NCT], LTD, Tel-Aviv, Israel)

also be seized and forfeited to the U.S. government. These regulations apply to all transmitters that are designed to cause interference to, or prevent the operation of, other radio communication systems.

All cellular systems used today in all countries employ simultaneously two different groups of frequencies. This is to enable the user to communicate in full duplex—that is, to speak and listen simultaneously (unlike a standard walkie-talkie). The first group of frequencies is used for the *downlink* communication between the cellular towers and the mobile phones themselves. The second group is used for the *uplink* between the phone and the tower. When employing a jamming device, you have the choice of either jamming the tower or selected mobile phones. Normally, jammers are used to block cell phones and not the towers of cellular companies. Jamming of cellular towers can have wide-ranging effects, possibly rendering an entire city's cellular system unavailable.[30]

Interception

All cellular telephones are basically radio transceivers. Your voice is transmitted through the air on radio waves. Radio waves are not directional—they disperse in all directions so that anyone with the right kind of radio receiver can listen in.

Cellular phones send radio signals to low-power transmitters located within cells of five to twelve miles in radius. As your automobile travels from cell to cell, the signal carrying your voice is transferred to the nearest transmitter. Cellular phone calls usually are not picked up by electronic devices such as radios and baby monitors. But radio scanners can receive them. The FCC has ruled that as of April 1994, no scanners may be manufactured or imported that tune into frequencies used by cellular telephones or that can be readily altered to receive such frequencies.

An estimated 5 million Americans use cellular telephones. The cellular phone is a low-power radio that broadcasts over the FM band, but at a higher frequency than that used by commercial radio stations. Cellular communications rely on an array of ground antennae to pick up the signal and resend, or relay, it toward its final destination. A single antenna that is linked in a network with other antennas to blanket a local calling area covers each cell in a cellular service area.

An easily modified radio scanner available in electronics stores can intercept the cellular telephone signal for a few hundred dollars. For interception of both sides of a conversation, two scanners are needed because each party transmits its signal on a different channel. Sophisticated monitoring equipment is available that allows the interception of both sides of a cellular telephone call. This can be purchased in electronics stores for between $1,000 and $6,000.[31]

Countermeasures to Jamming and Interception

Countermeasures to jamming have challenged engineers for many years. A development during World War II—from an unlikely source—laid the groundwork for today's cellular systems.

Following the outbreak of World War II, Hedy Lamarr, as a passionate opponent of the Nazis, wanted to contribute more than just propaganda to the Allied effort. As Mrs. Fritz Mandl, the wife of a leading arms manufacturer, she had been able to observe close-up the planning that went into the design of remote-controlled torpedoes. These torpedoes had never gone into production, however, because the radio-controlled guidance system had proved to be too susceptible to disruption. She then got the idea of distributing the torpedo guidance signal over several frequencies to protect it from enemy jamming.

In the mid-1930s, Hedy Lamarr must have acquired detailed and comprehensive knowledge about military technology. Since her husband forbade her to pursue her acting career, she accompanied him to meetings with his technicians and business associates, and thus gained insight into the difficult problem of remote-controlled torpedoes. For Mandl's weapons production business, though, the torpedoes' low hit rate was not necessarily a disadvantage—the more torpedoes had to be fired, the more he was able to sell. Nevertheless, for Great Britain—confronted in 1940 by the threat of a German invasion—torpedoes that could be steered with pinpoint accuracy might be an advantage, spelling the difference between victory and defeat. This was the fundamental consideration behind Hedy Lamarr's invention. Her revolutionary technical approach was set to not transmit the torpedo's guidance signal on a single frequency, which the enemy could easily detect and jam, but rather to distribute it over numerous frequencies. The jumping back and forth between the individual frequencies occurs in fractions of a second and thus can be neither detected nor disrupted by the enemy.[32]

Over the last 50 years, a class of modulation techniques, usually called Spread Spectrum, has been developed. This group of modulation techniques is characterized by its wide frequency spectrum. The modulated output signals occupy a much greater bandwidth than the signal's baseband information.[33]

Spread Spectrum signals are more difficult to jam than narrowband signals. These *Low Probability of Detection* (LPD) and *anti-jamming* (A/J) features are why the military has used Spread Spectrum for so many years. Spread signals are intentionally made to be much wider band than the information they are carrying to make them more noise-like.

Direct sequence spread spectrum systems are so-called because they employ a high-speed code sequence, along with the basic information being sent, to modulate their RF carrier (see Figure 3-7).

In frequency hopping systems, the wideband frequency spectrum desired is generated in a different manner. It does just what its name implies. That is, it hops from frequency to frequency over a wide band. The specific order in which frequencies are occupied is a function of a code sequence, and the rate of hopping from one frequency to another is a function of the information rate (see Figure 3-8).

Code Division Multiple Access (CDMA)

Code Division Multiple Access (CDMA) is a digital air interface standard, claiming 8 to 15 times the capacity of traditional analog cellular systems. CDMA employs a commercial adaptation of a military Spread Spectrum technology. Based on Spread Spectrum theory, it gives essentially the same services and qualities as wireline service.

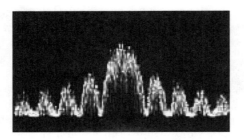

3-7 A spectrum analyzer photo of a *Direct Sequence* (DS) Spread Spectrum signal.

3-8 A spectrum analyzer photo of a *Frequency Hop* (FH) Spread Spectrum signal.

Who's Listening to Cell Phone Conversations?

In most cases, there is no way to know whether an individual communication is being monitored. Because it is so easy to monitor communications and happens so often, it is best to assume that any communication that contains information of great potential value to another person, organization, or country may be monitored. There are only two ways to counter interception of telephone and fax communications:

- Do not discuss or even allude indirectly to sensitive subjects over the telephone or fax.
- If you must use telephone or fax, encrypt all sensitive communications.

Sensitive information should not be discussed by phone or sent by fax on any unencrypted line.

Long distance communications and cellular phone calls are especially vulnerable to monitoring as they go through the airwaves. Many people think they are being secure by using double-talk, or talking around a sensitive subject, when using the phone. This may fool a casual eavesdropper who hears only that one conversation, but it is generally ineffective when someone is monitoring all your calls.

Fraud

Cellular phone fraud is defined as the use of cellular services by deceptive means to avoid paying for the benefit of the services. Often, this theft occurs when the identifying codes of a legitimate cellular phone are intercepted and then programmed into another phone using computer equipment. Reprogramming a new phone with these stolen codes results in a cloned phone. Those who engage in this illegal activity are referred to as *cloners*. The illegal interception usually results in the legitimate customer being billed for phone calls made from the duplicate phone.

The incidence of cellular phone fraud has decreased significantly in recent years primarily because wireless carriers use electronic authentication and digital encryption to recognize legitimate phone users and block unauthorized ones. Cellular phone carriers use a technology that creates a RF fingerprint of legitimate cellular phones. The use of radio frequency fingerprinting means that, even if a thief intercepts the electronic identification code transmitted during a wireless call by an authorized user, he or she can no longer use that code to make another phone. That's because the cloned phone will broadcast a pattern different from the legitimate phone, and there's no way to reliably duplicate the pattern.

Countermeasures to Fraud

There are a few things that the cellular phone user can do to help reduce the incidence of fraud. Turn the phone off. Cell phones poll the cellular base station with the strongest signal every few seconds. This is how the system knows which base station to route calls through. Limit your use of roaming features. Roaming usually defeats the use of *Personal Identification Numbers* (PINs). Cloners prefer roaming phones for this reason and they target airport parking lots, airport access roads, and rural interstates. Roaming also makes it more difficult for some cellular carriers to use fraud-detection programs to monitor an account and shut it down when fraud is detected.

History of Cordless Telephones

When cordless phones first came into existence, about 1980, they were limited in range, quality, and security. Over time, interference was reduced, quality was better, but security was still a concern. When cordless phones went digital using Digital Spread Spectrum, security improved. Information could be spread out among different frequencies, making it extremely hard to listen in to a conversation. Cell phones using digital technology also have good quality and improved security. However, the area of security could stand some improvement.

The handset is composed of different sections. Some of the most basic parts are shown in Table 3-12.

The handset receives radio signals and converts them into electrical signals that are then converted into sound. When a person talks, his or her voice is carried via another radio signal; it too is converted into an electrical signal. The person on the other end of the phone receives this signal as a voice. To accomplish the feat, the handset contains a speaker, microphone, keypad, and antenna.

Handset Features

Handset features vary from one manufacturer to another. Some handsets have only calling features, while others can help you run everyday activities such as allowing you to buy or sell stock, remember a birthday, email your co-worker, or just call your spouse as a reminder to pick up milk. Some of the features you may find on a handset include those shown in Table 3-13.[34]

Consumers can purchase many accessories for their handsets, including battery chargers via cigarette lighters, charging stands (for desk and car), headsets, mobile holders, and antenna couplers (provides access to external antenna). For example, you can buy an accessory that will allow you to switch from speaker mode to mute mode. Handsets come in basic telephone colors as well as neon colors, sports logos, and college emblems; some even have cartoon characters on them. You can buy handsets specifically for Internet use, home or office use, or both.

3-9 Handset. (Courtesy of Donna Ebling, Dennis Suzanne Kimball, Jay Wilson, EMSE 298, Spring 2001, George Washington University, SEAS, Washington, D.C.)

Table 3-12 Handset Components

Handset Section	Function
Speaker	Converts electrical signals into sounds.
Microphone	Picks up sound waves and converts them to electrical signals.
Keypad	Allows input for dialing number and accessing other phone options.
Ringer	Lets you know that you have an incoming call.
Radio Parts	Magnifies electrical signals for microphone and speakers. Transmits and receives FM radio frequencies.
LCD Displays	Indicator lights.
Battery	Provides power; can be re-charged.

Table 3-13 Handset Features

Handset Feature	Function
Scroll Keys	Allow you to move up and down through screen display.
Voice privacy	Provided by the service; encrypts the voice channel to prevent eavesdropping of your conversation.
Voice Mailbox	Collects and saves voice messages from missed calls.
Special Character Keys	Allows you to change letter case, among other characteristics.
Microphone	Changes voice to electrical signals.
Power Key	Allows you to turn your phone on and off.
Earpiece	Changes electrical signals to voice..
Selection Keys	Allows you to navigate through and select available options..
Talk and End Keys	Allows you to make a call, end a call, or silence the ringing.
Number Keys	Allows you to enter numbers and letters, or blank space in text.
Indicator Keys	Indicates strength, battery power, volume level.
Emergency Key 9	Allows you to press and hold the key to contact the emergency number programmed into your phone.
Battery	Power source for the handset.
Internal antenna	Commonly found on the back of the phone; sends or receives radio signals.

To help consumers with mounting their handsets, a company called ProFit International sells only wireless phone mounts. They do however sell tools to help you install their mounts. This company designs and produces *vehicle specific mounts* (VSMs)[35] for installing in cars, trucks, and vans.

Handsets are popular because they are mobile, operate in temperatures from –4° F to 104° F, are reasonably priced, and of convenient size. Some people might even think of them as technological marvels. However, there are some drawbacks.

Handset Vulnerabilities

Unlike computer systems, handsets are limited as to security features. They do not have the power or memory capacity of a computer system to support the same security functions. These are two requirements of good encryption. *Wireless Application Protocol* (WAP) instruments have their own security protocol, *Wireless Transport Layer Security* (WTLS). This is the equal to *Secure Socket Layer* (SSL) but has weaker encryption algorithms. WTLS is not compatible with SSL, the industry standard. Therefore, WTLS must be converted to SSL. This conversion causes a security problem. Wireless messages travel through the air to the carrier's transmitter. There they are received and passed to a gateway that channels them into the conventional wired network for transmission to the end of their journey. At the gateway, the WTLS message is converted to SSL. For a few seconds, the message is unencrypted inside the gateway. This gap in encryption could present a serious threat, such that anyone could have access to your information—be it neighborhood gossip, weekend plans, or credit card information.[36]

Encryption is not without its problems. Some GSM phones have a design flaw in their protocol. Confusing the mobile phone so it does not know its true location causes the flaw. GSM has a capacity to encrypt data traveling across the network. However, Western Europe cannot export encryption products to certain countries, and the default version of the GSM protocol does not use encryption. It also does not authenticate its base stations (hardware that communicates with the handset). It is possible to build an authorized base station that jams the signal from the real station and forces the phone to connect to it. The station is saying, this call is taking place in a foreign country; do not use encryption. The call continues on, unprotected. The false station is relaying information between the real one and the handset. This is often called a man-in-the-middle-attack.[37]

A little known vulnerability concerns pacemakers.[38] Most manufacturers recommend a minimum separation of six inches between a handset and a pacemaker. The concern is the wireless handset may interfere with the pacemaker. In addition to the six-inch separation, those persons with pacemakers who use wireless handsets should abide by the following:

- Do not carry the phone in your breast pocket.
- Use the ear opposite the pacemaker.
- If you think there is any interference, turn the handset off.

Countermeasures

Some handsets have security features that prevent unauthorized persons from using your phone. These features may require you to enter a security code to activate the phone. The handsets come with a default code that you should immediately change. For instance, the Nokia 8260[39] will not accept any entries for five minutes if someone has tried and failed five times to enter the correct security code. The lock code allows you to activate and deactivate your handset. When the lock feature is on, you cannot access most of the memory or menu features, nor can you make calls without first entering the lock code. This too comes with a default code that you should change immediately. Another feature allows you to lock your keypad. This prevents accidental key presses when the handset is resting against something in a purse or when someone is trying to use your phone without your permission. You can also restrict incoming and outgoing calls.

A new WAP feature is a standard to allow companies to run their gateway servers for secure connections between the handset and server. This standard, Proxy Navigation Model, will allow network service operators temporarily to stop giving up control of their WAP gateways to a WAP gateway located behind a company's firewall. The WAP standards specifications are at least a year ahead of handset manufacturers and software developers. However, the fact that this know-how is being suggested means those developers have a guideline to follow for future use of their applications.[40]

Microphones

> The most basic piece of equipment for all electronic gathering operations is the *microphone*.[41]

An electronic microphone is a dangerous surveillance tool. It is easy to disguise, effective, and, if correctly installed, difficult to detect. If you include the ability of being wireless and transmit to a remote location, great damage may be accomplished with little effort. U.S. laws prevent the surveillance-type microphones from being sold to non-government agencies or anyone other than a law enforcement organization. But products are available.

A microphone is a transducer, changing sound energy to electrical energy. There are two types of microphones: velocity mikes (a ribbon mike) that react to changes in velocity of particles hitting a surface, and pressure mikes (all other mikes) that react to sound waves moving a diaphragm, enabling the motion to be detected.

Types of Microphones

A microphone may be either voltage producing or regulating, depending upon whether the sensing device produces or regulates the electrical pulses to correspond to the movement received. The distinction is important. Voltage regulating microphones require electrical power from an outside source, which could become depleted, while voltage producing sensing devices have there own source of electrical power, either a crystal (as in a crystal watch) or the use of magnets. Five types of microphones exist: a *ribbon microphone* has a thin ribbon suspended in a magnetic field. Movement of the ribbon changes the magnetic flux. Wind and vibrations can easily distort the movement; it is not reliable for surveillance work. The *carbon microphone*, one of the older designs of microphone and used in telephones, employs a small amount of carbon granules and a dry cell, with a diaphragm driver on one side. As sound waves move the diaphragm the carbon dust compresses, changing the electrical resistance and thus the current flow, to reflect the sound received. In a *dynamic microphone*, as a diaphragm moves, an attached coil of wire surrounding the magnet creates a current. The current change reflects the modulation of the sound wave. A *condenser microphone* is a capacitor of two plates, one capable of movement, wherein the moveable plate reacts to the sound wave; a voltage across the two plates changes as the sound wave moves the variable plate, which, when amplified, creates a signal. A small battery is required as the voltage source. An *electret* is a variation in design of a condenser microphone, providing for a static charge in its materials and thus not requiring a dry cell voltage source. Their resistance to shock, working capacity under extreme temperatures and miniature size makes them very useful for surveillance work. And last, there's the *crystal* or *piezoelectric microphone*. With every sound moving the diaphragm, the crystal changes shape, thereby changing its electrical properties. The resulting voltage variation can be amplified and converted to sound.

The previous descriptions provide *simple* principles that may be developed into a microphone system with simple components. The speaker of an audio system not in operation may be converted to a microphone that will transmit conversations to a remote location. A contact or spike mike is a crystal microphone built from a crystal, spike (nail), and diaphragm (wall) as pictured in Figure 3-10.[42] The requisite pressure on the crystal is achieved with a rubber band held with thumbtacks. In this instance, the vibrations on the wall are detected by the spike and directed through its shaft to the crystal.

The design of the housing containing the microphone may change the sound received. Parabolic microphones house the microphone in a parabolic dish shape that concentrates the sound received from a general area to the microphone. The shape

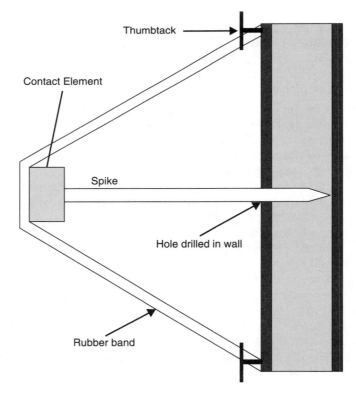

3-10 Example of a spike microphone.
[Reprinted by permission of Berkel and Rapaport, *Covert Audio Interception*, Volume 1, p. 373.]

of the dish and the placement of the microphone create the ability to easily intercept the sound. The open shape of the parabola does capture ambient noise that can limit its usability. Another design, the Shotgun microphone, places the microphone at the end of a bundle of tubes of different lengths. The direction the unit is aimed determines the azimuth from which sounds are captured by the tubes and sent to the microphone, while the length of each tube forms a limited-bandwidth resonant response.

Use of Microphones

Commercially available microphones designed for surveillance work can be very small, measuring as little as 10 cm, small enough to be hidden or disguised as a common personal or room effect. The microphones are connected to a radio transmitter to send the electronic current of sound waves to a radio receiver for real-time review or recording. This station is usually referred to as the listening post. Knowing if you have been a victim of message intercept by microphone can be difficult to determine. A review of businesses that conduct electronic surveillance prompts several questions towards making an assessment:

- Competitors seem to be just one step ahead all the time.
- Your home or premises have been broken into and very little or nothing was taken.
- Sockets or switches show signs of being moved slightly, that is, the wallpaper may be disturbed.
- Various apparently empty vehicles parked near to your premises.
- Your telephone rings but no one speaks or you just hear a short tone.
- You hear unusual sounds (crackling, clicks, volume changes) on your telephone handset.
- Indications that your handset may have been exchanged, that is, numbers in memory may be lost.
- Repairers or utility companies turn up to carry out work when they have not been called.
- Furniture or items appear to have been disturbed.
- You notice interference on your radio or television.
- An odd texture on small parts of wall, floor, or skirting boards may indicate the use of conductive paint from a hidden microphone.
- Unexplained brick or plaster dust on floor or a small discoloration showing on the wall may indicate drilling from the other side of the wall or plaster, paper being lifted to plant a microphone.[43]

Placing a microphone for successful eavesdropping can take some practice. The microphone must be placed where suspected conversations would likely take place, while avoiding any expected mechanical interference. The point of placing a microphone is to avoid detection. Good placement, less conspicuous, is at the knee or floor level since this is not easily inspected. Ceilings also provide a good location, with few items to interfere with conversation reception.

Countermeasures

Once you suspect a listening device is in your area, you must decide whether you will let the item remain to monitor your conversation, which may include misinformation, or have the item removed, alerting the eavesdropper of your discovery. Removal might not be the best answer, since other choices made by the owner might be more difficult to identify. The primary method to detect listening devices is a visual search, a sweep, of the area, along with a RF detector with a range of up to 2 GHz.[44] Using the correct unit, the RF detector can reveal the transmission frequency and the signal strength. The detection of the transmission will not be known by the owners of the microphone, since a radio receiver has no effect on the impedance of the source or destination antenna systems.[45] The visual search must be so thorough as to include areas of walls, ceilings, the underside and hidden areas of furniture, inside telephones, and so forth. The sweep could turn up suspect items that are part of required systems, such as smoke and fire alarms. Other countermeasures may include providing background ambient noise, either a water, *heating, ventilation and air conditioning* (HVAC) system, or music to be recorded making the inception of your conversations more difficult to hear. Noise units or CDs that generate white noise are available for purchase to fulfill this objective.

RF Data Communications

A large portion of wireless communication today is concerned with the transmission of data rather than voice. Some is intended to be of extremely short range, such as the *Infra-red Data Association* (IrDA) standard (3 feet) and Bluetooth[46] (30 feet), others such as the IEEE 802.11b wireless networking protocol operates in the hundreds of feet and work continues to increase that range. Additionally, we are beginning to see the availability of wireless Internet connectivity from Internet Service Providers (ISP), offering coverage across metropolitan regions. One of the pioneers in this field is Metricom with their Ricochet modem.[47]

Short Range: < 100 Feet

While not designated RF, a discussion of IrDA is appropriate here. The Infrared Data Association has established a set of standards that operate primarily at the Physical layer of the OSI model and as such leaves the handling of security to the layers above it. While nearly all laptop and handheld computers come with IrDA ports, the average user has little awareness of them and often does nothing to secure them. This was amply demonstrated when, in September 2000, the *Government Accounting Office* (GAO) investigators were able to break into *Internal Revenue Service* (IRS) computers and access taxpayer data using a handheld computer.[48] Not only were they able to access the IRS computers, but the penetration went undetected. As in most cases it was not the technology that failed, but the implementation. Among the problems the GAO noted in its report were:

- Inadequate password management. "We were able to guess many passwords based on our knowledge of commonly used passwords," the report says.
- Too many people with access to files within the IRS and in the private firms authorized to transmit returns.

- Transmission over telephone lines of tax data from private companies that was not in encrypted form. IRS officials strongly defend that practice, saying confidential transactions—whether by voice or data transmission—move by telephone every day.
- Improperly configured operating systems.

Bluetooth has attempted to address security concerns from the ground up. Being a relatively new standard (1998),[49] the Bluetooth *Special Interest Group* (SIG) noted the increasing need for security in new technology products. The hardware incorporates a frequency-hopping scheme with 1600 hops/sec, together with an automatic output power adaptation to reduce the range exactly to requirement. This would mean having to get fairly close to the unit with a rather sophisticated receiver to eavesdrop. Bluetooth also supports an encryption scheme with up to 128-bit private keys. Unfortunately the way this has been designed, the average user will probably opt for a shorter key length to simplify activation. At this point Bluetooth is still too new and lacking a broad user base to determine how vulnerable it will actually be too hostile intercept.

Medium Range: 150 feet to 300 yards

This area is primarily occupied by wireless implementation *Local Area Networks* (LANs). Several different standards have been used in the past few years for wireless networking, but the two, which currently have the largest market share, are the AnyPoint™ Wireless Home Network from Intel and the IEEE 802.11b standard which has been largely adopted as the current wireless solution for corporate networks.

As stated earlier, the Intel system is an inexpensive, entry-level system for basic home network use. It does not provide any more security features than you would get by putting network cards into your computers and connecting them with CAT 5 cable. But CAT 5 does not send out a radio broadcast of all activity happening on the network. The only protection on this system from intercept is its limited range (150 feet) and proper operating system configuration of the connected computers. In other words, it's a nice setup for the suburbs, but not recommended for an apartment building.

The 802.11b specification is becoming the de facto standard for corporate wireless networking. As implemented by most vendors it supports *Wired Equivalent Privacy* (WEP), MAC address control, and user authentication to ensure a secure network connection. None of these security capabilities are in place out of the box. Each has to be activated, and potentially, each has security holes.

Issue of Privacy

Cordless telephones are capable of accessing others' conversations, especially if the phones are tuned to the same channel. A recurring theme throughout this discussion was the lack of privacy. The laws are not effective. People are able to use scanners or legitimately and accidentally listen in without fear of consequences. If it cannot be proven that the individual intended to eavesdrop, he or she suffers no consequences; no action can be taken against him. An individual can issue his or her credit card number while using a cell phone, however, he or she is not without fear that someone will listen in and steal the number. As of now, there is no immediate solution. Some companies offer scrambling devices on their phones but if someone really wants to obtain your private information, that won't deter them. Thousands of cell phones are sold each year. Society likes the convenience. What if phone companies found a way to ensure calling privacy? Would society be willing to pay more if there were a way to ensure the privacy of the their phone calls?

Various types of encryption have been suggested as a means to secure privacy, yet phone companies are not taking advantage of encryption. The public expects privacy, but they have yet to demand it of wireless telephones. Perhaps the time is at hand. All that's needed is a way to ensure that privacy. Encryption offers the best solution to date.

Summary

Addressing basic wireless telephone system vulnerabilities and a brief introduction to the topic of wireless telephones, the concepts of air-to-ground interception and interruptions occurring at switch, cable, and fiber optics were discussed. Legalities with respect to these and their effectiveness were also presented. A person's true motive or intent hinders drafting of wireless communication laws and privacy laws. Many laws are not effective because intent is so hard to prove. Those doing most of the intercepting are from the criminal arena such as drug cartels and fraud. Hoping not to be out-listened to by the criminals, military, government, political, and law enforcement personnel are also doing lots of listening. Nor is the public innocent of listening as opportunities arise, such as listening in on neighbors, business conversations, or a cheating spouse. Is all this listening legal? Probably not, but unless it can be proven that the listening was intentional, they will remain innocent. The key to convicting anyone of eavesdropping is intent.

While privacy is a drawback to cellular phone use, there are also other vulnerabilities. Wireless applications such as cell phone, handset, microphone, and RF transmitters included a discussion on technology, vulnerabilities, and countermeasures. Although the wireless telephone is becoming more advanced technologically, the issues of security and privacy remain in need of improvement.

Endnotes

[1]United States Code Title 18—Crimes and Criminal Procedure Part I—Crimes Chapter 119—Wire And Electronic Communications Interception And Interception Of Oral Communications.

[2]Nichols, Randall K., Daniel J. Ryan, Julie J.C.H. Ryan, *Defending Your Digital Assets Against Hackers, Crackers, Spies and Thieves*, McGraw-Hill, 2000, p. 51.

[3]Laws Governing Radio Monitoring in the United States," http://www.nf2g.com/scannist/us_laws.html.

[4]Heidi Kriz, February 25, 1999 "*House OKs Wireless Privacy Bill*," Wired News, http://www.wired.com/news/politics.

[5]Terrajella, Frank, *Monitoring Times*, "U.S. Monitoring Laws," 1995, http://grove-ent.comLLawbook.html.

[6]Privacy Rights Clearinghouse, Fact Sheet #9, *Wiretapping/Eavesdropping on Telephone Conversations: Is There Cause For Concern?*" August 2000, http://www.privacyrights.org.

[7]Foreman, Michael, New Zealand—Technology News, "Government Able to Demand Keys to Encrypted Data." 5/12 /2000.

[8]Ibid.

[9]Landau, Susan, "Eavesdropping and Encryption: U.S. Policy in an International Perspective," http://www.ksg.harvard.edu/iip/iicompol/Papers/Landau.html.

[10]Raju, Chebium. "U.S. Supreme Court Hears Arguments in Cellular-wiretapping case," Dec. 5, 2000, www.CNN.com.

[11]Landau, Susan, "Eavesdropping and Encryption: U.S. Policy in an International Perspective http://www.ksg.harvard.edu/iip/iicompol/Papers/Landau.html.

[12]Moore, Gordon, 1965.

[13]Denning, Dorothy E., *Information Warfare and Security*, Addison-Wesley, 1999, p. 182.

[14]Parker, Holly, "Auto Thieves Targeting Cellular Phones," Globe-News, July 19, 1999, http://www.amarillonet.com/stories/071999/new_147-3335-001.shtml.

[15]Denning, p. 168.

[16]Ibid., p.. 183.

[17]Diffie, Whitfield, and Susan Landau, *Privacy on the Line: The Politics of Wiretapping and Encryption,* The MIT Press, 1999, p. 91.

[18]Ibid., p. 92.

[19]Extensive legal clarification on this issue can be found at http://www.fas.org/irp/nsa/standards.html#1.

[20]NSA Report to Congress on Legal Standards for Electronic Surveillance, February 2000, http://www.FAS.org/jrp/nsa/standards.html. (Very accuracy and on-target report).

[21]Lindsay, Greg, *The Government Is Reading Your E-Mail,* Time Digital Daily, June 24, 1999 (http://www.onmagazine.com/on-mag/reviews/article/0,9985,27293,00.html).

[22]"Secret Power" by Nicky Hager, http://www.fas.org/isp/eprint/sp/sp-c2.htm. [Contains 35 additional interesting references on subject.]

[23]Brief, "DARPA Leads Assault on Batteries," *Jane's International Review*, Vol. 34, February 2001, p. 27.

[24]Sweetman, Bill, "HALE Storms to New Heights," *Jane's International Review*, Vol. 34, February 2001, p. 50.

[25]WEBDUST, "Automated Construction and Maintenance of Spatially Constrained Information in Pervasive Microsensor Networks," http://www.cs.rutgers.edu/dataman/webdust.

[26]Landau, Susan, "Eavesdropping and Encryption: U.S. Policy in an International Perspective, http://www.ksg.harvard.edu/iip/iicompol/Papers/Landau.html.

[27]"Government-Industry Forum on Encryption and Law Enforcement: A Partnership with Industry," http://www.homeoffice.gov.uk.

[28]Rogers, Donna, "The ? Of Encryption," *Law Enforcement Technology,* March 2000, Vol. 27, No. 3, p. 62.

[29](Information on modifying most available cellular phones is easily found on the Internet. If you are curious, check http://www.crossbar.demon.co.uk/cell.htm.)[29]Jessica Lee, "Focus Shifts from Gingrich to Taped Call," *USA Today*, January 14, 1997, p 5A.

[30]SESP (UK) Ltd, "Cellular Phone Jammers—Principles of Operation," http://www.sesp.co.uk/3.htm.

[31]Arts & Farces LLC., Cellular Phone Privacy, Revised: December 22, 2000, http://www.farces.com/farces/info-eclipse/chap_00/chap-07/cellular-privacy.

[32]"Her Invention: Frequency Hopping," http://www.hedylamarr.at/freqHopping1e.html.

[33]"The ABCs of Spread Spectrum—A Tutorial," http://sss-mag.com/ss.html#tutorial.

[34]Nokia 8260 User's Guide: http://www.nokia.com.

[35]"ProFit International Has the Answer for Mounting Your Wireless Phone," http://www.pro-fit-intl.com.

[36]Radding, Alan. "Crossing the Wireless Security Gap," ComputerWorld, Jan. 1, 2001.

[37]Robinson, Sara. "Design Flaws in Mobile Phone Protocol Opens Security Hole," *IT Week Analysis,* Sept. 25, 2000. http://www.zdnet.co.uk/itweek/analysis/2000/36 /client/gsm/.

[38]"Get to Know Your Phone," Nokia 8260 User's Guide: http://www.nokia.com.

[39]Ibid., Reference Information.

[40]Levitt, Jason. "Wireless Devices Present New Security Challenges," *Information Week,* October 23, 2000, p. 120.

[41]Berkel, Bob, and Lowell Rapaport, *Covert Audio Interception,* Vol. 1, CCS SecuritySource Library, CCS Security Publishing, Ltd., 1994, p. 355.

[42]Ibid., p. 373.

[43]Eyetek Surveillance, The Spy Shop, http://ourworld.compuserve.com/homepages/eyetech/bugged.htm.

[44]Ibid.

[45]Gibilisco, Stan, *Handbook of Radio and Wireless Technology,* McGraw-Hill, 1999, p. 483.

[46]Bluetooth takes its name from Harald Bluetooth who was a fierce Viking king in 10th century Denmark.

[47]Metricom was founded in 1985 and offers wireless modems operating at speeds up to 128 Kbps in several metropolitan areas. At the physical layer, it operates similarly to cell phones.

[48]Story carried in the *Los Angeles Times,* March 15, 2001.

[49]Five companies started the Bluetooth *Special Interest Group* (SIG) in May 1998. They were Ericsson, IBM Corporation, Intel Corporation, Nokia, and Toshiba Corporation.

4

Satellite Communications

Ever since the invention of line-of-sight radios, people have sought to extend the range from transmitter to receiver. Television is a familiar example of the limited range for signal transmission; we are all used to regional broadcasting. For more pressing applications, regional coverage is not sufficient. Military units on land have obstructions and terrain to overcome, while naval forces have to contend with the curvature of the Earth. Aboard ship, UHF radio antennas and blinker lights on a mast can only communicate with another ship that's within approximately 20 miles of it, even if they have good line of sight.

In both cases the road to improvement is finding a way to extend the antennas by raising them higher. Companies began to try new methods—such as remotely piloted planes—to extend the range of their new mobile communication devices. Among these tactics, one system that has proved highly beneficial is the use of satellites.

History

After World War II, several projects experimented with using the moon as an extended antenna. The U.S. Army Signal Corps transmitted radar signals to the moon and bounced them back to Earth in 1948 for proof of concept. The idea was to transmit low-power microwave signals into space and then detect their echo back on Earth. The U.S. Navy followed up 1954, successfully transmitting voice messages on microwave carriers to the moon and retrieving them. These early efforts laid the groundwork for the launch of the U.S.S.R.'s Sputnik 1 on October 4, 1957, soon followed by the U.S. launch of Explorer 1 in January 1958[1] (see Figure 4-1).

NASA was formed in 1958 to assist development of space-based technology. It launched the SCORE satellite into *low earth orbit* (LEO), receiving messages at 150 MHz, storing them on tape, and retransmitting them back to Earth. Using this infant technology, President Eisenhower broadcast the first message from space—a Christmas greeting on December 19, 1958—to demonstrate its potential.[3]

4-1 U.S.S.R. Sputnik 1.[2] (Courtesy of NASA Photo Gallery. See Note 2)

With the 1960 launch of Tiros, a weather reconnaissance satellite, space became a medium for regional and global Earth monitoring of the weather, the atmosphere, agricultural crop rotation, rainforests, and other environmental issues. They were also viewed as a means to extend the coverage of broadcast television. On July 10, 1962, the voice of Elvis Presley was broadcast live to both Europe and North America via AT&T's Telstar 1, pioneering satellite transponder technology. Then in 1964, Telstar 2 and Syncom 2 were used to broadcast the Olympics from Tokyo to the United States.[4]

As LEO satellites increased in usefulness, new orbits were developed, expanding from low Earth orbit to geosynchronous orbits, where a satellite seems to hang indefinitely over the same location on the Earth's surface. The Soviets developed their Molnya orbit, a 12-hour, highly elliptical path.[5] In nontechnical terms, the Molnya orbit moves very close to the Earth at the South Pole where it is sling-shot into high orbit over the Northern Hemisphere. There it provides coverage for several hours before being coaxed back towards Earth by gravity. This engineering feat extended communications to the northern latitudes where geostationary satellites couldn't.

All of these early initiatives came together in 1965 with the launch of Intelsat 1. Intelsat was the first global communication service owned by its member countries for the purpose of developing geo-communications that would not be affordable by any one nation at the time.[6] The organization is still active today.

Satellite Orbits

An Earth satellite has many possible orbits. Because each satellite is designed for a certain function, its orbit is chosen to enhance that function. Regional and continental communications rely on a satellite positioned in stationary orbit over the equator. Earth monitoring satellites tend to use LEOs for desirable proximity to the target, and to create as a path that brings satellite sensors well into the target area. The majority of orbits are geostationary, low Earth orbit, medium Earth orbit, or specialized orbits such as polar and highly elliptical.

Geostationary Orbit

Geostationary or *geosynchronous orbits* (GEOs) are circular orbits directly above the equator. In orbital mechanics, if a satellite is positioned above the equator, it will achieve a speed at a certain point above the Earth that will keep it in a fixed position. At roughly 36,000 km or about 22,300 miles, a signal from the satellite will be accessible to more than one-third of the Earth's surface. Three geostationary satellites placed 120 degrees apart will cover the majority of the Earth's surface except for extreme northern and southern latitudes[7] (see Figure 4-2).

The geostationary orbit is a subset of the geosynchronous orbit, and in position above the equator, exhibits diminishing signal strength coverage from maximum at the equator to minimum at the poles. GEO communication satellites employ two major links with Earth: an uplink (from Earth to satellite) and a downlink. Uplinks generally emanate from major Earth ground stations with large dish antennas, although newer systems can accept signals from *very small aperture terminals* (VSATs) the size of briefcases. To avoid interference with return signals, the satellite converts the uplink signal to another frequency and retransmits it to the Earth as a downlink. That conversion takes place in the satellite with equipment called a *transponder*.[8] GEOs have become a major communication node, providing large volumes of traffic within and between hemispheres, making them the majority of all orbiting satellites today. There are approximately 200 commercial geostationary satellites in orbit[9] (see Figure 4-3).

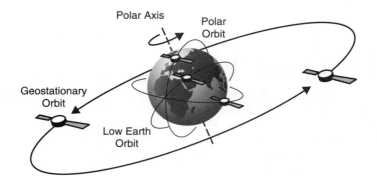

4-2 Satellite orbits. (Courtesy of Ricardo's Geo Orbit Quick-Look)

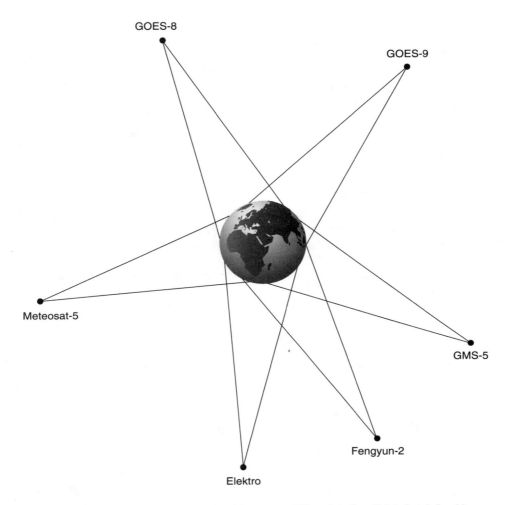

4-3 Example of geostationary coverage. (Courtesy of Ricardo's Geo Orbit Quick-Look)

Highly Elliptical Orbit

Highly Elliptical Orbits (HEOs) were developed by the Soviets to provide communication coverage of their northern territories. At 70+ degrees north and south, you can no longer see a geostationary satellite due to the curvature of the Earth. HEO orbits are inclined at approximately 63 degrees to the equator in order to avoid rotation of the *perigee* (closest point to the Earth) and *apogee* (furthest point from the Earth), thus placing the orbit above the same area on each revolution. Because of the eccentricity of the orbit, a satellite will spend about two-thirds of its time near apogee and therefore will seem almost stationary.

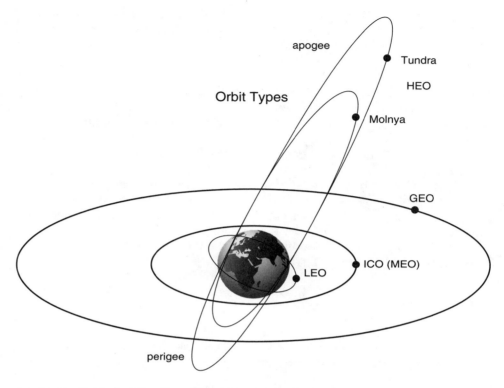

4-4 Highly elliptical orbits. (Courtesy of Ricardo's Geo Orbit Quick-Look)

If the apogee and perigee for each satellite are synchronized, a three-satellite constellation can provide 24 hours of continuous coverage (see Figure 4-4).

Low Earth Orbit/Medium Earth Orbit

Low Earth orbit/medium Earth orbit (LEO/MEO) satellites have orbits between 200km and 35,589km. Until recently, they were differentiated by altitude, a LEO being roughly 200 to 2400 km and a MEO roughly 2,400 to 10,000 km. Both are now referred to as LEOs.[10]

LEO satellites occupy either circular or elliptical orbits, with orbit periods running between 90 minutes and two hours. A satellite at an altitude lower than geostationary orbit travels faster than the Earth's orbit. Although the satellite might take 90 minutes to circle the Earth, it is only visible to certain areas for a period of about 20 minutes,[11] and it can be many revolutions later before that particular satellite has access to the same spot on Earth—a problem if the satellite needs line-of-sight to a particular ground station. The remedy is to equip the satellite with a store-and-forward capability, recording the data until it passes into view of the ground station again. LEOs have historically been used for ecological, Earth monitoring, and intelligence applications, although new ones are deployed primarily for personal communication devices such as cell phones. A LEO global communication system needs a large number of satellites to provide continuous coverage (see Figure 4-5).

Polar Orbit satellites are positioned in a low Earth orbit oriented from North Pole to South Pole. At about 850 km, an orbit period of 100 minutes is achievable. These orbits bring a satellite into view of the same spot on the Earth at the same time every 24 hours. They're generally used to measure temperature and humidity and monitor cloud cover. Some can receive, store, and retransmit data from balloons, buoys, and remote automatic stations. Others are equipped to carry search and rescue transponders to locate downed aircraft and ships in distress[12] (see Figure 4-6).

Medium Earth Orbits (MEOs) are circular orbits at altitudes around 10,000 km with a period of about six hours. Thus an MEO satellite can be observed on the ground for a few hours, as compared to 20 minutes for a LEO. A global communications system using this type of orbit requires a modest number of satellites in just two or three orbital planes.[13] A prime example is the Navistar *Global Positioning System* (GPS) (see Figure 4-7).

Typical LEO scheme for latitude specific coverage

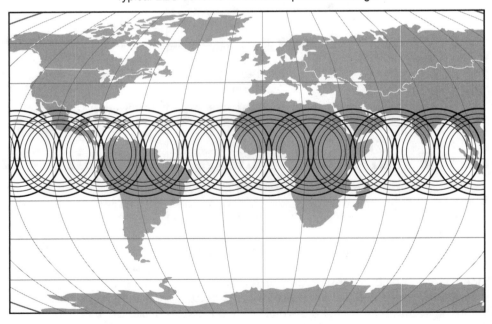

4-5 Example of LEO coverage. (Courtesy of *American Distance Learning Consortium*)

4-6 Polar Orbit. (Courtesy of *American Distance Learning Consortium*)

4-7 LEO/MEO. (Courtesy of *American Distance Learning Consortium*)

Navigation and Tracking

Although several navigation systems were deployed over the years using satellites, only the GPS has achieved general usage. The decision to open the system to civilian as well as military users has revolutionized navigation and tracking in aviation, the maritime, and on land.

Global Positioning System

GPS uses satellites and computers to determine positions anywhere on the Earth with space-based triangulation. It provides three-dimensional position, velocity, and time information 24 hours a day in all weather conditions. The GPS constellation consists of 21 satellites and 3 spares operating in MEO orbit in six orbit planes with four satellites per plane operating at an altitude of 20,000 km. Each orbital plane completes two revolutions per 24-hour period, resulting in a trace on the Earth's surface that repeats itself regularly. The satellites transmit on two L-Band frequencies, L1 at 1575.42 MHz and L2 at 1227.6 MHz. A handheld or other GPS receiver is synchronized with each satellite, so that distance to that satellite can be computed by measuring the time variation between signal transmission and receipt. Once distance from four satellites is determined, a location is calculated by triangulation, and velocity is computed from the Doppler shift in the received signal. As of May 2000, all users have accuracy to 16 meters and a time measurement accuracy of 200 nanoseconds.[14]

Wide Area Augmentation System

The *Wide Area Augmentation System* (WAAS) was developed for aviation. GPS falls short of the stringent requirements of the *Federal Aviation Administration* (FAA) for their National Airspace System. WAAS augments basic GPS requirements with greater accuracy and the capability to notify users when the system should not be used for navigation. Basically, it gathers data from GPS satellites, determines the error in the calculated position, and sends error correction to one of two geostationary satellites that then retransmits the corrections to the GPS receiver sets.[15] On September 14, 2000, the FAA declared WAAS approved for some aviation and all nonaviation uses.[16] Raytheon has a combination GPS/WAAS receiver on the market, said to be accurate to within 5 meters for better than 95 percent of the time, and within 2.5 meters for a less significant percentage.[17]

Satellite Search and Rescue

To transmit emergency signals, ships, aircraft, and individuals carry beacons called *Emergency Position Indicating Radio Beacons* (EPIRBs), *Emergency Locator transmitters* (ELTs), and *Personal Locator Beacons* (PLBs), respectively. Three frequencies are used for international distress: 121.5 MHz (a VHF signal for commercial and private aviation and some marine users), 243 MHz (a UHF signal for the military/NATO), and 406 MHz (for most maritime applications). The United States and Russia have cooperated on deploying several satellite systems to detect these signals. Cospas-Sarsat is a sun-synchronous search-and-rescue system that uses near polar orbiting satellites to detect emergency beacons.

This international system uses two Russian Cospas satellites at altitudes of 1000km with receivers at 121.5 MHz and 406 MHz. The U.S. provides two Sarsat satellites at about 850km with receivers supplied by Canada and France that cover 121.5 MHz, 243 MHz, and 406 MHz. In addition, Sarsat instrumentation packages are flown aboard NOAA environmental satellites and several NOAA *Geosynchronous Operational Environmental Satellites* (GOES) have the capability to detect the 406 MHz signal. The overall system consists of satellites, ground stations, mission control centers, and rescue coordination centers[18] (refer to Figure 4-8).

Communications: Voice, Video, and Data

In the early days of commercial satellites, their primary purpose was to create global connection for voice communications. Global commercial satellite communications officially began when COMSAT's first satellite, Early Bird, was launched from Cape Canaveral on April 6, 1965.[19]

Voice

As Early Bird was launched, large Earth ground stations were built in the United Kingdom, France, Germany, Italy, Brazil, and Japan. Global presence necessitated an

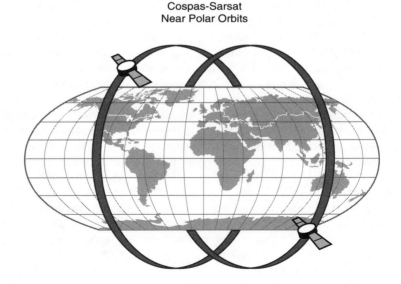

4-8 Cospas-Sarsat orbits. (Courtesy of *Satellite Today*)

international organization to assume ownership and management of the infrastructure. Agreements were signed in 1964 for the formation of the International Telecommunications Satellite Organization, INTELSAT. Over the next 30-plus years, INTELSAT grew from a few hundred telephone circuits and a handful of members to a system capable of hundreds of thousands of telephone circuits and more members than the United Nations.[20]

The importance of providing service to mobile users, specifically maritime customers, was recognized in 1979, when the *International Maritime Satellite Organization* (INMARSAT) was established in a form similar to INTELSAT. Conceived as a method of providing telephone service and traffic-monitoring services on ships at sea, it has evolved into a means for journalists with a briefcase phone to report events in real-time from all around the world.[21]

However, competition from Trans-Atlantic and other underwater cables cut into the competitiveness of communications for point-to-point communications. From 1965 until the first fiber optic cable was laid across the Atlantic in the late 1980s, satellites provided nearly 10 times the capacity for almost one-tenth the price.[22] But point-to-point voice via satellite is again becoming popular, due in part to the surge in cell phone use. As businesspersons and consumers become reliant on personal communication devices, they find that many locations lack the physical infrastructure for ubiquitous, worldwide use. Just as INMARSAT provided the answer to mobile communications at sea, new ventures were developed in the 1990s to provide cellular voice and data communications to individuals anywhere on the Earth. Although many proposed ventures have failed or have been restructured, several current and future providers include Iridium, Globalstar, and possibly a new start-up, One Stop Satellite Solutions.

Video, Audio, and Data

When underwater cable companies with fiber optic technology challenged satellites for global voice circuits, a new venture by PanAmSat created a commercial international satellite services industry, opening markets around the world. PAS-1 was launched in June of 1988. This catalyst for new services included international cable television distribution, satellite news gathering, and digital video compression to deliver information and entertainment to the world.[23]

The geostationary satellite industry realized the potential for delivering video and data to consumers, and the 1990s saw an appreciable increase in deploying multimedia satellite networks. These communication systems provide interconnections between users exchanging real time applications based on several data types such as text, voice, images, and video. One area is the direct-to-home satellite delivery of broadcast television and radio, which has seen phenomenal growth since its introduction. At the new millennium, there were over 10 million subscribers in the United States alone.[24] These providers are now looking at new applications to expand their market share and services such as pay-per-view, home shopping, electronic commerce, online and data delivery, and coast-to-coast radio. Consumers can purchase the XM radios at Radio Shack, Best Buy, and Circuit City stores. In the past, small towns had limited access to radio stations; XM will provide up to 100 new radio channels in the U.S. alone.[25]

Satellite Internet

Fiber optic cables provide high-speed Internet access but lack the essential element for end-to-end access—"last mile" capability. The prime route for bypassing the last mile is wireless connection.

For satellites to work as multimedia providers instead of being limited to broadcast, they need two transmission paths—a forward channel from a service provider to the end user and a return channel from the user terminal back to the provider. Until recently, the return channel to select programs or to order a product used a low data path, usually a phone line. That changes with the adoption of an *Interactive Channel for Multimedia Satellite Networks* (ICMSN), a standard proposed by the *European Telecommunications Standards Institute* (ETSI) in early 2000, and the advent of Ka-band satellites that can use small low-cost user terminals.[26] This return channel will provide dynamically scheduled, multifrequency *Time Division Multiple Access* (TDMA) bandwidth via a satellite link to a hub station. Multifrequency TDMA was selected over CDMA because of its high efficiency and relatively low implementation complexity. In the future, CDMA may be combined with TDMA for operations in interference-limited environments.[27]

To further Internet access to individual homes around the world, high bandwidth will be required. Providing it would represent a substantial investment by local hard-wire companies and cable TV networks. With a space-based solution, once a spacecraft is successfully placed in orbit, the customer base is enormous. One satellite can serve the entire United States; no other investment is needed to offer service to 100 million households.[28]

Earth Sensing: Commercial Imaging

Man must rise above the Earth to the top of the atmosphere and beyond, for then will he fully understand the world in which he lives.
Socrates, 450 B.C.

Collecting data about anything by means of an instrument not in physical contact with it is called remote sensing. Experiences with remote sensing during World War I encouraged work in non-military areas such as forestry, agriculture, and geology. During World War II, aerial reconnaissance expanded from direct visual to photographic efforts and into infrared detection and radar systems.

One hundred years after the beginning of remote sensing, it moved into outer space on the U.S. Explorer 6 spacecraft. For most of the next 30 years, remote sensing from space was considered to be classified intelligence data unavailable to non-government users.[29] Exceptions to this were the Landsat program in which NASA launched Landsat-1 in 1972 and the Spot Imaging Satellite, which the French launched in 1986.

Landsat

When NASA launched its first remote sensing satellite in 1972 operating at an altitude of 900 km, it was called the Earth Resources Technology Satellite. Later renamed Landsat, the first three satellites gathered *Multispectral Scanner* (MSS) data. With the 1982 launch of Landsa 4 the system began gathering both MSS and Thematic Mapper™ data. Landsat 5 (1984) and Landsat 7 (1999) are still operational. Resolution for MSS data is about 70 meters and approximately 30 meters for TM data.[30]

SPOT

In 1986, France in cooperation with Sweden and Belgium launched the SPOT-1 satellite to provide commercially available images from space with 10-meter resolution. SPOT-1 is still in service and has provided over 2.7 million images over the past 15 years. SPOT-5 is scheduled for launch in late 2001 with a new imaging instrument called the *High Resolution Geometry* (HRG) payload. It will enter a circular, quasipolar orbit at an altitude of 830 km and will pass over the equator at 10:30 A.M. The payload is an improvement on SPOT-4, resulting in a ground resolution of 5 meters and multispectral resolution of 10 meters, instead of 20 meters.[31]

European Remote Sensing

European Remote Sensing (ERS) launched in July 1991, carrying two specialized radars plus an *Along Track Scanning Radiometer* (ATSR) package capable of infrared images of Earth at one-kilometer resolution. It is used for scientific studies of land surfaces, atmosphere, clouds, and oceans. ATSR-2 was launched on ERS-2 in April 1995 carrying the same payload with one difference: it also carried an instrument called Global Ozone Monitoring Equipment. GOME is used to monitor and track icebergs, typhoons, forest fires, and sea surface temperatures as well as stratospheric and tropospheric ozone. An *Advanced ATSR* (AATSR) is under development and scheduled to be launched on the ENVISAT spacecraft in the summer of 2001.[32]

IKONOS

Space Imaging, a company in Denver, Colorado, was founded in 1994 with a vision to capture the rapidly growing digital information market. Five years later, it launched the world's first and only one-meter resolution commercial Earth imaging satellite into a 423-mile, North to South circular, sun-synchronous, near polar orbit. It can revisit any area on the Earth every 2.9 days for one-meter resolution and needs only 1.5 days for data resolution of 1.5 meters. It carries an on-board recorder for acquiring data over areas not in view of ground receiving stations located in India, UAE, Germany, Taiwan, and Oklahoma.

IKONOS is just the beginning of high-resolution remote sensing satellites. Estimates are that 43 commercial imaging satellites will be built during the period 2001 to 2010. The average number of commercial imaging satellites launched annually will jump from 1.8 in the last 10 years to 4.3 launches in the next decade. In the next five years, they expect there will be at least six additional commercial operators with a diverse range of capabilities and architectures. The near term demand for high-resolution imagery is estimated to be worth in excess of 1 billion dollars per year.[33]

Satellite Spectrum Issues

When you're walking down the street, or shooting hoops in the nearby park, or sailing on the lake, you are oblivious to the invisible waves of electromagnetic energy that bring us TV, radio, and cellular phone calls. The waves aren't relevant until one furnishes the right antenna and receiver to tune in their signals.[34]

Radio waves can be as long as a football field and as short as the size of molecules, having in common that they both travel at light speed and obey the laws of physics. Wireless, in this case satellite links, are transmissions through air rather than plasticor fibers.[35] The relationship between the wavelength in fiber and that of satellite RF links is key to end-to-end broadband for the mobile user.

The frequency of any communication signal is the number of cycles per second at which the radio wave vibrates or cycles. The distance a wave travels during a single cycle is called its wavelength. There is an inverse relationship between frequency and wavelength: the higher the former, the shorter the latter. A cycle of a very low frequency signal is measured in *hertz* (Hz), and a frequency of one thousand cycles per second is known as a kilohertz. One million cycles per second is a *megahertz* (MHz) and one billion is a *gigahertz* (GHz). We refer generally to frequencies from 3 KHz to 300 GHz as the electromagnetic spectrum, although the spectrum continues into lightwave frequencies and beyond (see Table 4-1).

When commercial communication satellites were launched in the 1960s, they did not need long radio waves that could bounce around the ionosphere for thousands of miles. They needed a direct line-of-sight RF link that would travel in a directed path from the Earth station antenna to the satellite's antenna. The International Telecommunication Union, an agency of the United Nations, allocated frequencies in the *Super High Frequency* (SHF) range from 2.5 to 22 GHz for satellite communications. These very short frequencies are called microwaves, with the same characteristics of visible light.[36] Although most communication satellites operate in the SHF range, military and navigation satellites operate at lower frequencies that yield a larger footprint for signal reception and require less precision for acquiring the uplink.

In the late 1970s and early 1980s, the first commercial Ku-band satellites were launched. Because few terrestrial microwave systems used these frequencies, the Ku-band satellites could use higher power transmitters without causing interference. In addition to the higher power, the beam of a Ku-band signal is significantly

Table 4.1 Radio Frequency Chart[37]

Bandwidth Description	Abbreviation	Frequency Range
Extremely Low Frequency	ELF	0 to 3 KHz
Very Low Frequency	VLF	3 KHz to 30 KHz
Low Frequency	LF	30 KHz to 300 KHz
Medium Frequency	MF	300 KHz to 3000 KHz
AM Radio Broadcast	AM	540 KHz to 1630 KHz
High Frequency	HF	3 MHz to 30 MHz
Short-wave Broadcast Radio		5.95 MHz to 26.1 MHz
Very High Frequency	VHF	30 MHz to 300 MHz
TV Band 1		54 MHz to 88 MHz
FM Radio Broadcast	FM	88 MHz to 174 MHz
TV Band 2		174 MHz to 216 MHz
Ultra High Frequency	UHF	300 MHz to 3000 MHz
TV Channels 14-70		470 MHz to 806 MHz
L-band	L-band	500 MHz to 1500 MHz
Personal Communication Services	PCS	1850 MHz to 1990 MHz
Unlicensed PCS Devices		1910 MHz to 1930 MHz
Super High Frequencies	SHF	3 GHz to 30.0 GHz
C-band	C-band	3.6 GHz to 7.025 GHz
X-band	X-band	7.25 GHz to 8.4 GHz
Ku-band	Ku-band	10.7 GHz to 14.5 GHz
Ka-band	Ka-band	17.3 GHz to 31.0 GHz
Extremely High Frequencies	EHF	30.0 GHz to 300 GHz
Additional Fixed Satellite		38.6 GHz to 275 GHz
Infrared Radiation	IR	300 GHz to 810 THz
Visible Light		810 THz to 1620 THz
Ultraviolet Radiation	UV	1.62 PHz to 30 PHz

narrower than a comparable C-band parabolic dish antenna,[38] correcting the tendency of one satellite's uplink signals to interfere with another's as the geostationary band crowded up. In orbit locations for North America, satellites are normally separated by 2 degrees so narrower beamwidths significantly reduces interference.[39]

One drawback with using frequencies above 10 GHz is that the wavelength is so short that rain and snow can reduce the strength of the signal.[40] Larger antennas are used to overcome the loss to rain. As frequencies expand into the Ka-band from 17 to 31 GHz, the rain fade issue will become more pronounced. Ka-band satellites, however, will play a major role in the future. Ku-band satellites are major players today, demonstrating their potential with increased bandwidth, on-board processing, and multiple-spot beams. These attributes equate to more throughput, which provides the critical link to end-to-end solutions.

Instruments and Goals of Current U.S. Satellite Encryption Policy

The satellite encryption policy under current United States law is a morass of confusing and sometimes conflicting viewpoints and laws. There is no one all-encompassing policy initiative at this time. Both the *Communications Assistance for Law Enforcement* (CALEA) and the *Federal Information Processing Standards* (FIPS) are relatively new standards that the government is using as a policy baseline for some elements of satellite encryption. The recently developed Common Criteria for information security standards also has a role in U.S. policy. Finally, as with every encryption algorithm, the United States maintains export controls over what kinds of technology are allowed to leave the country.

Export controls on satellite encryption have ramifications from the standpoint of economy and technology. We have not determined the most viable ways to implement satellite encryption, but they must be sensitive to legal issues. These issues range from the heightened use of satellite encryption in crimes or acts of terrorism, to the need to preserve the kind of privacy citizens expect.

Two methods being considered for the future direction of satellite security are public-key encryption and escrowed encryption. They must be balanced against the importance to the United States of space-based surveillance in the context of both national and global security.

Issues Associated With Current U.S. Policy

The CALEA was originally known as the digital telephony bill before it enacted in 1994. CALEA is not specifically related to the United States current policy on satellite encryption, but does provide a framework for understanding the direction of U.S. policy in the future. The law further defines the existing statutory obligation of telecommunications carriers to assist law enforcement in electronic surveillance pursuant to court order or other lawful authorization.[41]

CALEA was enacted to ensure that law enforcement would retain the ability to intercept communications regardless of the rapidly changing ways data is transmitted. The growing use of cell phones has hamstrung the ability of law enforcement officials to do so. Communications, especially satellite-based, can now be routed through so many different channels as to make them impossible for a telecom provider to track. When encryption is added to the equation, the legally sanctioned ability of law enforcement to monitor suspicious transmissions gets increasingly problematic.

CALEA attempts to provide a solution for some of these problems by giving law enforcement access to the newer forms of communication that had not been codified in the past. While CALEA doesn't deal directly with the problems of encryption or in regulating providers that carry encrypted messages, it does make clear that if the message is encrypted with a provider's own encryption, the provider must provide that traffic to law enforcement in a decrypted state.

CALEA is about access, not authority. CALEA does not expand law enforcement's fundamental statutory authority to conduct electronic surveillance. It simply seeks to ensure that after law enforcement obtains the appropriate legal authority, carriers will have the necessary capability and sufficient capacity to assist law enforcement regardless of their specific telecommunications systems or services.[42]

Federal Information Processing Standards

Federal Information Processing Standards (FIPS) provide another building block in U.S. policy towards cryptography. A number of FIPS deal specifically with satellite encryption policy[43] (see Table 4-2).

FIPS provide a framework for government procurement agents to ensure the confidentiality, integrity, and availability of satellite communication, so long as they adopt the recommended requirements. While policy models of this sort have been ineffective in the past, especially in the realm of private industry, the FIPS model is written specifically for the business world. FIP Standards attempt to align government and private sector policies much more aggressively than previous models through specific examples, such as digital signatures, which are becoming standard in the private sector.

Among the most vexing questions for official satellite encryption policies is the ongoing debate about how to implement policies. For many years, while satellite technology was viewed as an integral part of national defense, the actual U.S. policy on satellite encryption was itself classified. Since then the proliferation of far less expensive technology for satellites and encryption capabilities has created private sector confusion about which technology is considered safe and reliable for govern-

Table 4.2 FIPS and Satellite Encryption Table[44]

FIPS	Description
FIPS 46-3: Data Encryption Standard	This publication specifies two cryptographic algorithms; the *Data Encryption Standard* (DES) and the *Triple Data Encryption Algorithm* (TDEA), which may be used by Federal organizations to protect sensitive data. Protection of data during transmission or while in storage may be necessary to maintain the confidentiality and integrity of the information represented by the data.
FIPS 180-1: Secure Hash Standard	Specify the secure hash algorithm required for use with the Digital Signature Standard (FIPS 186) in the generation and verification of digital signatures.
	Specify the secure hash algorithm to be used whenever a secure hash algorithm is required for Federal applications.
	Encourage the adoption and use of the specified secure hash algorithm by private and commercial organizations.
FIPS 186-2: Digital Signature Standard	This standard specifies algorithms appropriate for applications requiring a digital, rather than written, signature. An algorithm provides the capability to generate and verify signatures.
FIPS 140-1: Security Requirements for Cryptographic Models	Provides the security requirements that are to be satisfied by a cryptographic module implemented within a security system and provides four increasing, qualitative levels of security intended to cover a wide range of potential applications and environments.

ment certification. As John Vacca puts the problem: Uncertainty over whether or not the federal government would recertify DES as a FIPS has plagued the marketplace in recent years, because withdrawal of the DES as a FIPS would cause considerable consternation among some potential buyers who might suddenly be using products based on a decertified standard.[45]

Governmental policy implementation has been glacial at best. Response time has been so slow, in fact, that some have construed the delay as intentional. But despite consternation that the United States could decertify an important authentication technology such as DES, decertification is unlikely to occur. The U.S. seems to have settled on the satellite encryption policies outlined in the FIPS as appropriate for both the public and private sectors for now.

Although there have been many policy initiatives over the years to certify new products, none have been successful. Initiatives such as the Orange Book and the Common Criteria suffer from a lack of flexibility in the networked environment. The FIPS program actually mandates a vendor who can supply some independent assurance that a product functions as it is supposed to. Governmental assistance with implementation of effective security policy has also created useful programs such as the *Computer Emergency Response Team* (CERT).[46]

International Policy Concerns

U.S. satellite encryption policy is becoming increasingly important, especially on an economic level, in the international arena. Today, safeguarding communication has become just as important for economic reasons as for national security reasons. The problem for satellite encryption export control is much the same as the problems posed by other export restrictions on top-grade encryption schemes. Other governments place far fewer export restrictions on encryption technology than the United States does, so American companies can't sell technology with robust encryption programs overseas. Add to the damaging economic constraints the fact that without some kind of agreement on how satellite encryption policies should work across national boundaries, there will continue to be major policy-gap problems between the United States and other governments. While controls on encryption have been relaxed in the last year or two, American business already lags its competitors in terms of the latest and greatest in cryptographic algorithms.

Export Controls On Satellite Encryption: U.S. Objectives

There are two major reasons that the United States has maintained such a restrictive policy. First, U.S. intelligence has always been wary of letting state-of-the art satellite encryption technology out of the country where it is may fall into the wrong hands. U.S. intelligence gathering capabilities would be compromised if an unfriendly government acquired an ability to use top-level encryption in its communications. Second, export restrictions allow the government to control and monitor what leaves the country, allowing for evaluation of any new satellite encryption capabilities for strengths and weaknesses before they leave the country. In practice, the United States uses two channels of export control: licensing and the *United States Munitions List* (USML).

Licensing and the U.S. Munitions List (USML)

When a satellite encryption technology is brought up for export review, it can be judged under either the USML or the much more lenient *Commodity Control List* (CCL) regulated by the Commerce Department. The two organizations have different requirements for determining a product to be licensable. If a product is deemed an exception under the USML, it can still be verified for export under the CCL. Table 4.3 provides comparison of some of the main differences.

As can be seen from Table 4.3, there are many reasons why a company would prefer CCL review. However, the USML is specific about what can be shifted to the CCL. Generally, a product validated by the CCL must not exceed 40-bit encryption level—completely substandard by today's reckoning. Hence satellite-grade technology will always undergo the rigorous review of the USML.

Impact of Export Controls

It's widely acknowledged that tight export restrictions have had adverse economic and technological fallout in domestic companies. The United States has a global reputation for developing robust products, many of which have built-in cryptography.

Table 4.3 Comparing the USML and the CCL[47]

U.S. Munitions List	Commodity Control List
Department of State has broad leeway to take national security into account when determining licensing.	Department of Commerce may limit exports only if they would make a significant contribution to the military potential of any other country, which would prove detrimental to the national security of the United States.
Items included if the item is inherently military in character regardless of the end use of the product Broad categories are used.	Performance parameter rather than broad categories define items.
Decisions about export can take as long as necessary.	Decisions about export must be completed within 120 days.
Export license can be denied on very general or spurious grounds.	Export license can be denied only on very specific grounds.
Every product must be licensed individually, but distribution and bulk licenses are possible.	General licenses are often issued (does not necessarily give authority for mass export).
Licensing decisions are not subject to judicial review—government has the last word.	Decisions are subject to judicial review.
Foreign availability may or may not be a consideration.	Foreign availability of products that are equivalent is a consideration.
A shipper's export declaration is required in all instances.	An SED may be required, but the exemptions can be granted.
Prior government approval is needed for export of a product.	Prior government approval is generally not needed.

Export limitations determine not just what can be exported to other countries, but also what users in the United States can use. For instance, any program with advanced cryptographic capabilities that can be downloaded from the Internet is proscribed, since it is also freely available outside the United States.

Software to be marketed overseas also costs a great deal more than those distributed domestically. Moving a product through the layers of export control takes more time and money than is feasible to get a competitive product to market within a reasonable period after development. For U.S. companies with close working partners outside U.S. jurisdiction, communications is also an obstacle; current export rules make it doubtful that they can use cryptographic satellite communications software to do business because, more than likely, the software has not been licensed for export.

Are tight export constraints preventing encryption technology from falling into hostile hands? In nearly every technological field today, a company's edge over its competitors comes from keeping proprietary information secret. Trade secrets and economic espionage are becoming a growth industry for spies in the aftermath of the cold war. Since many companies operate overseas, and increasing levels of information are being transmitted through satellite connections, appropriate satellite encryption is essential to doing business. Unfortunately, with the foreign partnerships that most companies routinely cultivate, they are virtually prohibited from using an encryption system that is both convenient and robust. If this vulnerability is not shored up soon, U.S. business concerns overseas will continue to erode in the wake of economic espionage on unsecured systems.

Are Export Controls Effective?

Despite the fear that freely exporting high-grade satellite encryption technology would cause a major blow to the country's intelligence gathering apparatus, this does not actually seem to be the case. Current controls are an attempt to strike a careful balance among U.S. national security interests, the ability of U.S. companies to enjoy effective satellite data encryption overseas, and the ability of U.S. companies to remain competitive with emerging foreign encryption technology. While export controls have certainly been effective in slowing the growth of satellite encryption technology, they have cost U.S. business a leadership position worldwide. Recent shifts in government export policy have tended toward relaxation of export restrictions over the last twenty years in acknowledgment of this fact.

Legal Issues for Satellite Encryption: Privacy

Privacy has become a de facto right of U.S. citizens through passage of various privacy acts and the expectations of society. The FBI views encryption as a roadblock to its ability to counter domestic threats, and has been quite vocal about the "threat of encryption" to Congress.[48] These two viewpoints are at odds. The government has tried to achieve an encryption policy that would allow law enforcement a good deal of access to private communications, but these measures come mostly at the expense of the privacy of its citizens.

The most notable recent attempt was the Clipper Chip initiative, a *remarkable failure as a policy measure.* Clipper is a key-escrow system. In theory, two government agencies hold the keys unique to each chip in escrow in a kind of data vault. Any time the FBI—or your local sheriff—wants to tap a phone, they ask a judge to order both agencies to relinquish the keys to your Clipper chip. With keys in hand, the FBI can unscramble any of your conversations at will. That policy raised a huge firestorm of controversy and the Clipper sank from sight, where it remains down but not out. The White House, acting as a front for the NSA and other intelligence agencies, wants to have Americans adopt Clipper voluntarily.

The FBI took it on faith that criminals, too, would buy Clipper-equipped phones. Why would criminals knowingly use a device the government could easily tap? Because criminals are stupid, was the FBI's party line.[49] In any case, it is the citizens who object. So far, whenever there has been a push to introduce technology that would affect the privacy of encrypted satellite communications, privacy advocates have created enough controversy to block it.

Export regulations have raised additional questions about privacy versus satellite encryption. As we've suggested, export controls on encryption policy has made it difficult for business to protect information with secure methods—especially satellite-based communications. In 1998, Congress introduced the E-Privacy Act with provisions to strengthen satellite-based encryption and provide the private sector with more robust security. Main points included:

1. Protecting the domestic use of strong encryption without "key recovery" back doors for government eavesdropping.
2. Easing export controls to allow U.S. companies to sell their encryption products overseas.
3. Strengthening protections from government access to decryption keys.
4. Creating unprecedented new protections for data stored in networks and cell phone location information.[50]

Unfortunately, the E-Privacy Act died at the end of the 105th Congress in 1998. Privacy advocates have kept up the fight to bring fair legislation and rules to bear. On January 13, 2000, the White House finally loosened export regulations to allow multinational corporations to begin using robust encryption techniques for satellite communication.

Law enforcement and national security officials warned that widespread use of strong encryption products would cripple their ability to track criminals and terrorists, and worked to restrict the dissemination of so-called crypto products. Industry and its supporters, however, said there already were excellent encryption products available from companies around the globe; the restrictions, they contend, merely hindered the American high-tech industry and prevented the use of products that could enhance computer security and privacy. Previous attempts to control encryption exports generally focused on *key length,* a measure of the strength of the software. The new regulations do away with restrictions on key length and requirements of a license; U.S. companies will be able to export encryption products after review by the government. Retail products can be exported to any user, even foreign governments, except those regarded by the United States as supporters of terrorism.[51]

Computer crime

Up to this point, criminal use of satellite encryption hasn't been a big problem for law enforcement. As a general rule, criminals are most likely to use what is available to the general public, and the satellite encryption available to and usable by the public has to date been minimal.[52] However, the relaxation of encryption controls does pose a threat we have yet to assess. Some criminals, such as the Cali drug cartels, already use sophisticated satellite encryption techniques, and law enforcement worries that greater public availability means greater criminal access to encryption devices.[53] FBI Director Freeh and his colleagues obviously have a point with this kind of argument, but by the same token the argument seems to circumvent conventional wisdom about the freedoms granted under the U.S. Constitution. The problem is a tough one of weighing Constitutional rights against the greater good of the citizenry, and it is one that law enforcement will have to address in the near future. After September 11, 2001, the new FBI Director, Robert S. Mueller III, has the problem of terrorism at the top of his priority list. And Congress has a host of anti-terrorism bills that will change this focus.

Surveillance

Satellite surveillance is a complex subject from a legal standpoint. It has been well documented that certain surveillance, such as tracking the movement of ICBM in Russia, falls within national security guidelines. Determining what types of tracking capabilities meet the greater good criterion is much harder. How, for instance, do we evaluate the new technology that permits satellite tracking of individual persons?

Military satellites designed to guide nuclear missiles are being used to monitor prison parolees and probationers in a technological advance designed to reduce the nation's skyrocketing prison population. But critics say it also raises the specter of an Orwellian future. The ComTrak monitoring system uses 24 DoD satellites orbiting 12,500 miles above the Earth to track 100 people in nine states. Paul Rothstein, a law professor at Georgetown University, says the system has the potential "to change the face of law enforcement and incarceration." He also sees the potential for "creating a monster." Rothstein is concerned that the ability to track parolees will be extended to more and more people being subjected to electronic monitoring under various pretexts. Jack King, spokesman for the National Association of Criminal Defense Lawyers, says, "If it's to track someone who has done his full term, like a registered sex offender or a formerly dangerous felon, then the use of this technology becomes Orwellian with all the dangers to all our freedoms that suggests. Who would they be tracking next?"[54]

Our aversion to government surveillance of citizens aside, we have to ask what is to prevent foreign governments, terrorists, or criminals from acquiring satellite tracking capability now that it is not controlled by the federal government, but by local agencies and even corporations? Unauthorized access to such capability is as pressing a security issue as is the abuse of authorized access.

Patents

Developers of satellite encryption technology must guard against the potential for patent infringement. Many of the encryption standards that developers wish to use are either covered by patents or based on patented public-key systems. The RC2, RC4, and RC5 ciphers are either patented or trade secrets, as is the IDEA cipher used in the Pretty Good Privacy application. The Digital Signature Standard issued in FIPS 186 is supposedly open to use without license, but there is confusion as to whether DSS might infringe on patents held under public-key encryption, like Diffie-Hellman.

FIPS 186 is fine for government applications since its algorithms were developed with government funding, but we have yet to see a test case of viable commercial programs using these same technologies; therefore, developers in the public sector must be skeptical of any new satellite encryption standard based on available algorithms.

Public-Key Encryption for Satellite Communication

Public-key satellite encryption technology is a good way to get shorter communications to a recipient securely and confidentially. It was originally developed in the 1970s as a new technology-based cryptographic method. Older methods relied on the sender and the receiver both knowing the decryption key. Public key cryptography made this unnecessary by using both a public and a private key. The receiver now only has to hold the senders' public-key half to decode a message. This system has many advantages: It allows authentication of the sender by verifying a digital signature, it keeps the integrity of the data intact, and it preserves the confidentiality of the data. Public-key encryption can help to eliminate the significant expense of having to exchange decoding keys physically, where a business communication needs to get halfway around the world securely.

Through authentication, public-key encryption can facilitate trust among businesses that have never communicated before. The main drawbacks of public-key encryption are:

- It does rely on a certain amount of trust the first time a public key is received.
- It takes longer to decode messages than a system where both sender and receiver know the decryption key.

Considering the time lag a public-key encryption system undergoes when handling large amounts of data, the option is best used in commercial satellite applications where real time information is not imperative.

The designer of an encrypted satellite system must always decide how much speed he or she is willing to sacrifice in the name of security. If the satellite transmission is carrying small bits of data, then public-key cryptography is more than likely appropriate. However, if the satellite transmission is carrying data that needs a lot of bandwidth or is quite time-sensitive, then a cryptographic system where both parties know the decode key is probably a better solution.

Escrowed Encryption for Satellite Communications

Escrowed encryption uses some elements of public-key encryption, but it adds in verification and key storage facility. The idea of escrowed satellite encryption got off to a bad start with the Clipper program we discussed earlier. The program envisioned a chip in every encrypt-capable satellite communication device that permits certain people to decrypt messages under certain circumstances.

The concept of escrowed encryption nonetheless is not entirely unattractive. For instance, a trusted third party holding the keys would be able to retrieve a key if the owner's was damaged, lost, or destroyed. If a critical piece of data is encrypted and sent across the world by satellite, but the receiver at the other end has damaged the decrypt key, key escrow is the only remedy.

Of course one of the main drawbacks to key escrowing is that you must identify a third party that is trusted. Furthermore, for this third party to be truly effective, he or she must be trusted by both sender and receiver. In multi-national partnerships, where would this third party be located? More than likely, an American company would want it located in the United States while a European company would prefer it be located there. In terms of communiqués between governments, it is almost certain that a foreign government would not want its keys in the hands of an escrow authority on foreign soil.

What about the varying laws between countries governing encryption technology and what can be used as a trusted product? Clearly, there are problems with the concept of escrowed encryption, especially for satellite communications that regularly travels across the globe. The value of an escrowed key system for designing and implementing secure satellite communication can only be determined case by case.

Impact on Information Security (INFOSEC) and Law Enforcement

It is obvious from the Clipper initiative and other such key escrowing schemes that U.S. law enforcement has strong objections to satellite encryption. The information security community also has serious concerns about escrowing schemes and how they affect the confidentiality of information. By its very nature, any escrowing scheme threatens the confidentiality of information by allowing third-party access. Granted this third party is ostensibly trusted, but logically it creates vulnerability.

Nonetheless, escrow must be weighed against the present method of secure satellite encryption, which is none. While escrowed encryption may not advance the cause of confidentiality, it has practical purpose. John Vacca summarizes the problem issues succinctly: Escrowed satellite encryption weakens the confidentiality provided by an encryption system by providing an access path that can be compromised. Yet escrowed satellite encryption also provides a hedge against the loss of access to encrypted data by those authorized for access.[55]

Government argues that with appropriate safeguards an escrowing system is worthwhile security against malicious attack. However, the very existence of an escrowing system paves the way for security leaks and potential abuse. Along with these risks comes a real possibility that risk will have no associated reward. Many have argued that criminals won't use technology known to be vulnerable, but will simply go outside the country for secure satellite communication technology. If so, then why tolerate the security holes that accompany escrowing technology?

Importance to the U.S. of Space Exploitation and Control

Deterrence

The space-based forces of the United States, especially the surveillance satellites, provide a deterrent to potential threats and also an early warning system when threats begin to develop. The three main U.S. objectives for space in the future are as follows:

- Promote the peaceful use of space.
- Use the nation's potential in space to support domestic, economic, diplomatic, and national security objectives.
- Develop and deploy the means to deter and defend against hostile acts directed at U.S. space assets and against uses of space that are hostile to U.S. interests.[56]

Space-based military forces rely heavily on satellite encryption technology for every role satellites play including deterrence. Space forces provide commanders both at home and in the field with an unmatched aerial perspective of the fluid nature of troop movements and especially the hostile build-up of forces. In addition to intelligence, satellites also provide a global presence permitting the withdrawal of American troops from many areas of the world where they were once necessary for deterrence purposes. Without a secure encrypted link to satellites, U.S. intelligence becomes counterproductive in that it is subject to interception. An intercepted signal is an unreliable strategically neutralized signal.

National and International Defense

More and more nations are gaining access to space and reaping the associated boost in intelligence-gathering capability. Without robust satellite encryption technology that is immune to interception or jamming, a country forfeits a significant edge on the battlefield of tomorrow. With much of the intelligence and communication capabilities of the U.S. military invested in satellites, encryption of information traveling to and from those satellites serves not just the U.S. national security interests, but security around the globe.

Surveillance

For satellite surveillance capabilities, the United States must be able to put new and more advanced satellites in orbit. Doing so entails control and exploitation of space. The United States is also careful about the regulation of satellite images being sold by American companies. Since some commercially operated satellites are licensed to sell encrypted satellite bitstreams (real-time images) that could potentially convey damaging intelligence related to U.S. national security, the government stipulates its right to prevent the capture of encrypted bitstreams in the event of an emergency.

However, since satellites are proliferating so rapidly, the United States can no longer use licensing to control availability of encrypted bitstreams. U.S. licensing has no province over satellite technology operating out of another country. It's hard to imagine what would prevent satellite surveillance and securely encrypted bitstreams from becoming more widely available to anyone who wants them, and the United States will have to adapt its policies to a world in which it's no longer the only country with this technological capability.[56]

Development, Implementation, and Management of Advanced Satellite Encryption Options and Strategies

Planning, Details, and Implementation

Encrypting services available on the Internet now are primarily designed for financial transactions, secure email, digital signatures, and certificates. Encrypting services on the Internet tomorrow must secure intellectual property that uses broadband streaming on high-bandwidth networks. When planning any new security system, there is a set of issues to resolve, and the foremost concern in developing an advanced satellite encryption system is trustworthiness. Users of the system must be convinced that the data being transmitted will be adequately protected by the system. Bases for trust in distributed systems are multiple and variable. An additional consideration, not generally found in host-centric systems, is that the degree of trust in the system will change dynamically over time. System architecture will determine the level of security provided by an encryption algorithm.

The architecture of advanced wireless communication devices presents a number of challenges to implementations of high-grade security. These challenges represent departures from more traditional means of achieving high security systems.

Figure 4-9 shows a traditional secure communication environment characterized by discrete boxes performing discrete functions. Security is achieved primarily by:

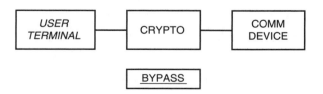

4-9 Traditional secure communication environment.

- Physical access control to user terminal
- Hard-wired connections for each channel
- High-grade hardware cryptography in a discrete box
- Very limited bypass capability within communicator channel or manual ancillary device
- System high application

In other words, the traditional basis for security is physical separation and hardware-based cryptographic protection of information and transmission.[58]

With the advent of embedded cryptography, the cryptographic function began to merge with the transmission function to achieve economies of size, weight, and power. Figure 4-10 shows embedded cryptographic equipment introducing a cryptographic chip into the equation.

The characteristics of this solution are not radically different from the previous box level scenario, with the exception that no RED/BLACK boundary is drawn inside of the equipment. The characteristics of this type of system were:

- Physical access control to user terminal
- Hard-wired internal connections for each channel
- High-grade hardware cryptography within the box
- Very limited bypass capability typically within communicator channel or manual ancillary device
- System High application
- Limited RED user applications processing[59]

Networking increases the need for communication devices that can extend packet protocols over wireless channels for improved interconnectivity. A single communicator, or a wired network of communicators, could then be placed into a remote network or networks. Figure 4-11 shows a LAN connected to a secure radio device for remote interconnection to other LANs, thus creating wide area networks in a wireless domain. The wireless device becomes the network extension in the packet-based system for both the local communicator and remote network sides. This configuration creates changes in the security implementation affecting both computer and network security measures.

The characteristics of this system are:

- Access control to network and radio services governed by software, not physical, methods

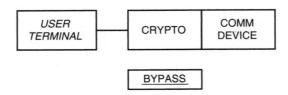

4-10 Embedded cryptographic equipment.

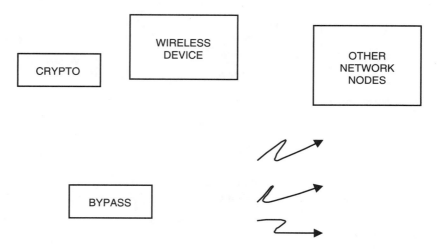

4-11 Wide area networks in a wireless domain.

- Hard-wired internal connections or computer bus for the single wireless channel configuration
- High-grade hardware cryptography within the communication device
- Bypass requirement increased to handle protocols and network information
- Separation of data classification and types performed by network; wireless System High
- Multiple access methods for the communicator networks
- Interconnection of networks at multiple communicator sites

The enhanced connectivity provided by the networked radios introduces new vulnerabilities to such attacks as virus dissemination, password theft, and malicious use. A security price is paid for connectivity, just as with terrestrial networks. Little communicator data processing is performed within the wireless device.[60]

Today's emerging wireless devices combine embedded cryptography capabilities with better RED side radio functions (that is, networking capability), multiple simultaneous channel operation within a single system, and several new characteristics that are critical from a security point of view. The security relevant characteristics in this system are:

- Multichannel/multicommunicator wireless operation
- Access control to network and wireless services governed by software that allows multiple communicators to share a single physical connection
- Virtual internal connections for each wireless communicator port and radio channel
- Single RED bus architecture
- High-grade programmable cryptography embedded within the wireless device
- Bypass requirement further increased to handle internal radio control

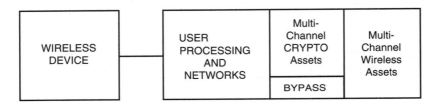

4-12 Wireless devices, embedded cryptography, and radio functions.

- Radio functions programmable for all processes
- Use of commercial software products [*Operating System* (OS) and *Object Request Broker* (ORB)]

In summary, many of the characteristics associated with computer security are now part of the wireless system.[61]

Options for Serving Data Consumers

Your system should be able to provide security for a wide range of users, from the small and discrete to the large intra- and inter-enterprise ones. For larger users, your system should be able to base access controls on the privilege attributes of users such as roles or groups (rather than individual identities) to reduce administrative costs. The system should allow a number of security domains, subject to policy, that enforce different policies but support interworking between them. Public-key technology helps large-scale interoperability. Finally, the system should manage the distribution of cryptographic keys across large networks, securely and without undue administrative overheads.[62]

Let's look at some details from one solution for high-use data customers. Communicado Data Ltd., a pioneer in satellite data networks, developed it. Transmission speeds of 2 Mbps per channel are ideally suited for high bandwidth for downloading or streaming content. Coupled with an encryption engine (Secure Media's RPK Encryptonite Engine), encryption and decryption speeds support an entire stream at satellite speeds, using a PC processor at 266 MHz, without degrading performance for the user. The RPK Engine provides strong public key encryption with a key size of up to 2281 bits, and supports authentication, digital signatures/certificates, and key management.[63] It leverages a core Mixture Generator to perform an initialization and synchronization phase followed by a combining data encryption phase, thus combining the features of a symmetric algorithm (for example DES or RC4) with an asymmetric algorithm (for example RSA, Diffie-Hellman key exchange).

Framework for Dealing With Policy Issues

The ability to deliver broadband audio and video securely over wireless communications devices demands encryption technology with high performance. Encryption and decryption speeds must be fast enough for uninterrupted delivery of high-quality media such as DVD quality music, movies, and live events—without sacrificing high levels of security. Today 5Mbs is the minimum encryption and encryption speed required to support high quality delivery of audio or video. Real-time on-the-fly encryption is necessary for live streaming delivery. This requirement will grow to 1.6 Gbps for HDTV.[64]

The mathematical foundation of a media encryption system is critical, but insufficient. The way in which the mathematics is applied, and the way the entire system is designed, also influences the level of security provided. Here are the critical components of a secure media encryption system:

- **Trusted Encryption Algorithm**   The encryption method used must be based on a trusted and well-studied area of encryption mathematics. This ensures that an appropriate level of scrutiny has been applied to the underlying mathematics by respected cryptographers and mathematicians, over an extended period of time, to uncover possible vulnerabilities. Encryption techniques that have not received sufficient scrutiny are risky—there may be hidden vulnerabilities in the algorithms that hackers can use to pirate the content.

- **Pre-Encryption of Streaming Media**   Digital media content is often replicated, redistributed and stored on edge servers in content delivery networks in order to serve larger audiences and to improve system response time. This approach requires the media to be securely pre-encrypted prior to being stored on distributed edge storage devices and then delivered to users in an encrypted state. It is important that all of the media data is encrypted when it is distributed.
Media files not encrypted prior to being placed on distributed edge storage devices are in the clear and vulnerable to hacker theft.

- **Adequate Key Lengths**   The encryption system must support key lengths that are appropriate for today's available computer systems. Generally, 126 bits is a minimum key length requirement.

- **Variable Key Lengths**   The encryption technology must support variable key lengths. This allows companies to set the level of security to what they believe is needed for the application. The ability to increase key lengths also allows companies to raise the level of security at any point in time, if required.

- **Media Keys and Content Stored in Separate Locations**   Good security practices mandate that media keys be stored separately from the encrypted content, preferably under the control of the content owner. The encryption system must support this.

- **Decryption Occurs in the Media Player**   It is vital that the media content and the decryption key are never in the clear on the client's equipment prior to the media being played. As a minimum, the decryption process must occur within the media player itself. It must be possible to extend content protection on all accessible data busses if needed, for example, within the sound card.

- **Uniquely Encrypt Each Packet** When digital media is streamed, each data packet or block of the stream should be encrypted uniquely. This provides maximum protection against systematic or coordinated hacking across a data stream. Systems that do not encrypt each packet uniquely, or use techniques where the encryption of each packet is based on the encryption of the packets before it, are susceptible to analytical attacks.
- **A Public-Key Exchange System** A public-key system, wherein different keys are used to encrypt and decrypt the data, is a more secure mechanism for key exchange than secret key systems where the same key is used to encrypt and decrypt the media. Secret key systems assume the recipients are trusted parties who will protect and not misuse the sender's secret key. If the key is compromised all security is lost.[65]

Protection of Personal Data and Privacy

In the summer of 2000, the United States joined the European Union's Safe Harbor program after more than two years of high-level discussion of the principles that could provide adequate privacy protection and ensure that data transfers from the European Union continue. Safe harbor covers all industry sectors and virtually all personal data. Without it, corporations would find it difficult to run multinational operations. Basic information about their employees would not be transferable to the United States. Accountants would not be able to perform consolidated audits for multinational firms with offices.

The decision by U.S. organizations to enter the safe harbor is entirely voluntary. Participating organizations must comply with the safe harbor's requirements and publicly declare that they do. To be assured of safe harbor benefits, an organization needs to self-certify annually to the Department of Commerce, in writing, that it agrees to adhere to requirements including notice, choice, access, and enforcement. The Department of Commerce will maintain a list of all organizations that file self-certification letters and make both the list and the letters publicly available.

The seven safe harbor principles are:

- Organizations must notify individuals about the purposes for which they collect and use information about them. They must provide information about how individuals can contact the organization with any inquiries or complaints, the types of third parties to which it discloses the information, and the choices and means the organization offers for limiting its use and disclosure.
- Organizations must give individuals the opportunity to choose (opt out) whether their personal information will be disclosed to a third party or used for a purpose incompatible with the purpose for which it was originally collected or subsequently authorized by the individual. For sensitive information, affirmative or explicit (opt in) choice must be given if the information is to be disclosed to a third party or used for a purpose other than its original purpose or the purpose authorized subsequently by the individual.

- To disclose information to a third party, organizations must apply the notice and choice principles. Where an organization wishes to transfer information to a third party that is acting as an agent, it may do so if it makes sure that the third party subscribes to the safe harbor principles or is subject to the Directive or another adequacy finding. As an alternative, the organization can enter into a written agreement with such third party requiring that the third party provide at least the same level of privacy protection as is required by the relevant principles.
- Individuals must have access to personal information about them that an organization holds and be able to correct, amend, or delete that information where it is inaccurate, except where the burden or expense of providing access would be disproportionate to the risks to the individual's privacy in the case in question, or where the rights of persons other than the individual would be violated.
- Organizations must take reasonable precautions to protect personal information from loss, misuse and unauthorized access, disclosure, alteration, and destruction.
- Personal information must be relevant for the purposes for which it is to be used. An organization should take reasonable steps to ensure that data is reliable for its intended use, accurate, complete, and current.
- There must be readily available and affordable independent recourse mechanisms so that each individual's complaints and disputes can be investigated and resolved and damages awarded where the applicable law or private sector initiatives so provide; procedures for verifying that the commitments companies make to adhere to the safe harbor principles have been implemented; and obligations to remedy problems arising out of a failure to comply with the principles. Sanctions must be sufficiently rigorous to ensure compliance by the organization. Organizations that fail to provide annual self-certification letters will no longer appear in the list of participants and safe harbor benefits will no longer be assured.

In general, enforcement of the safe harbor will take place in the United States in accordance with U.S. law and will be carried out primarily by the private sector. Private sector self-regulation and enforcement will be backed up as needed by government enforcement of the federal and state unfair and deceptive statutes. The effect of these statutes is to give an organization's safe harbor commitments the force of law as regards that organization.

Security of Information Systems

The cryptographic subsystem boundary encapsulates a set of security-critical functions that provide RED/BLACK separation within the system high operation. The cryptographic subsystem performs multiple functions for RED/BLACK separation including encryption/decryption, controlled bypass of communicator and control information, and electrical isolation. The encrypt/decrypt functions also incorporate supporting functions to include key and algorithm management, cryptographic channel instantiation, and cryptographic control. Cryptographic subsystem requirements can vary according to user functional specification, but the security architecture provides the capability to satisfy a broad range of functional security requirements.

Requirements for the cryptographic elements of a security architecture define a self-contained cryptographic subsystem that is instantiated independently from the operating environment, and has restricted interfaces to the rest of the architectural elements. The cryptographic subsystem defined here applies for Type 1 cryptography for the protection of DoD classified information.

The cryptographic functions are composed of the following elements:

- Initialization, Operation, and Termination
- Boot, Instantiation, Run-Time, normal Termination, Abnormal Termination
- RED/BLACK Isolation
- Keystream Functions
- Encrypt, Decrypt, TRANSEC, Identification and Authentication, Integrity
- Security Management Functions
- Key Management Functions, Algorithm Management Functions, Security Policy, and Enforcement
- Cryptographic Bypass
- Communicator Data, Radio Control/Status
- Cryptographic Control and Status
- Cryptographic Interfaces

The primary functions within the cryptographic subsystem are:

- Cryptographic Keystream generation capability
- Encryption and decryption of communicator information, TRANSEC Functions, Generation and validation of high grade signatures, and high-grade integrity checks
- Controlled bypass of communicator and radio information

All other mechanisms within the boundary are used to service and protect the keystream generation capability and enforce security policies for data separation and access. For proper operation, the cryptographic subsystem is placed into a known good operation state prior to running cryptographic functions. The initialization, instantiation, and teardown of cryptographic functions are critical to the security provided by the cryptographic subsystem.[66]

Identification and authentication functions for high-grade access control use cryptographic mechanisms as part of the protection function. Several additional requirements are introduced. First is the requirement for a security policy that determines approval for access (including a protected access control list and enforcement mechanism). Second, access control can be required for control of three different sources:

- Radio channel input for BLACK side remote access
- Communicator port input for RED side access
- Control interface for communicator/operator/administrator functions.

The differing sources and controls required dictate that a cryptographic function will be able to perform an I&A operation on either the RED or BLACK side of the radio, and return a result to the same side of the radio depending on the required enforcement mechanism.[67]

The integrity function verifies the accuracy of information. In this context, integrity is applied to assure that software and keys to be loaded into and used by the system are not modified in transport or during storage within the radio. In certain circumstances, integrity checks can also be applicable to communicator data.

Integrity can be verified cryptographically or non-cryptographically depending on the criticality of information to be protected, or the degree of access that outside entities might have to the information. For security-critical software that may be transported for delivery through unprotected channels, a cryptographically-based integrity technique is preferred.[68]

The traditional key management role performed within cryptographic systems is expanded to include handling of software algorithms, and security policies for multi-channel systems where functions can be changed.

The key management functions are the most security-critical set of functions in the system since the compromise of keys can compromise the information on a full network of communicator systems. Primary key management functions are:

- Key receipt and identification
- Key storage
- Key allocation and use
- Key Zeroization
- Key accounting
- Rekey

The goal of effective key management and utilization is to keep all keys BLACK to the maximum extent possible. Primary storage of keys is in BLACK form, encrypted by a key encryption key. BLACK keys can be stored in any available memory or storage, volatile or nonvolatile, as long as the tagging information is protected and bound to the keys. That is, each tag is tightly coupled to the key that it identifies. When keys are in use in RED form, they should exist only in the working registers of the cryptographic function.

The only assured method for zeroization of keys is a manual, operator/communicator activated function that eliminates all RED keys. Software methods for zeroization can provide back-up capability if properly authenticated and verified, as would be the case on a remote zeroization scenario or an OTA zeroization scenario. BLACK keys in non-volatile storage should be erased if power is available in a zeroization, but in cases of power failure, such a function may not be possible. In all cases, the key encryption key that decrypts the BLACK keys is zeroized. There are also numerous cases in which keys can be selectively zeroized or erased. Chief among such cases is the need to destroy keys that have been superceded on a net, or updated. Given the different types of keys that could be present (for example key encryption, algorithm encryption, communications, certificates, vectors) system engineering efforts will be required to determine the actual sequence of events for zeroization and erasure.[69]

Cryptographic algorithms in software form represent state-of-the-art cryptographic implementation within the cryptographic boundary. The layers of the algorithm management process are similar to those exercised for key management. One item to be emphasized: In the event that an algorithm is replaced under a mandatory modification, the holders of the algorithm will be tracked so that the modification can reach all users. This tracking can actually be applied to a broader set of software applications where a method of tracking and assured replacement of software may be necessary.[70]

An effective security policy must be in effect that establishes a set of rules that are tested for compliance and then enforced by a given security function. In aggregate, the security policy is the overall set of security rules that are observed for proper secure operation of an effective system. Elements exist both inside the cryptographic subsystem and within the INFOSEC boundary. The security policy originates from multiple sources, for example, waveform software profiles, administrator/security officer entry, mission load instructions, and embedded in boot function. Ultimately, an allocation of security policy enforcement based on criticality will be required since all aspects of security enforcement cannot be centralized. For example, a communicator access control function could not be reasonably executed within a cryptographic boundary if cryptographically based authentication is not used. Elements of the policy execution are relegated to lower levels of security implementation included individual functions for items such as access controllers, guards, and monitors.[71]

The security architecture includes an embedded cryptographic subsystem that provides functionality required for RED/BLACK bypass of communicator and radio control/status information. Two types of bypass are available, communicator information bypass and radio control/status bypass.

As we've already stated, the wireless device needs different types of bypass. Bypasses are required for initial start-up so that the system can orchestrate the complete power-up sequence. After a software load is complete, various waveform traffic control messages will be required to proceed between the RED/BLACK processors. Some of these messages are considered time-critical to the waveform. In these cases, the implementation considers the latency of the bypass control process and attempts to find mechanisms that minimize the amount of control/status information to be examined.

The communicator information bypass is typically of restricted size and fixed format. The information bypassed can be considered to be in-band with the user information itself. The communicator information bypass functions are unique to specific waveforms to be implemented in the wireless system. Each waveform is programmed and profiled in such manner that the required bypass functions are defined as to bit rate and content to permit monitoring of the correctness of the bypass function. Bypass characteristics that are monitored include length of bypass message, content of message, and format of message to be bypassed.

In the example that follows, the different types of bypass functions A, B, and C represent communicator information, and D represents radio control information bypass, which also includes inter-process communications for waveform installation and instantiation. The references to B, C, and D system high requirements at the bottom apply to a multichannel/multicommunicator environment. A is a violation of system high operation if another classified channel is operating concurrently.

Communicator Information Bypass and Radio Control/Status Bypass

A = Non Protocol Communicator Stream Data (E.G., Digital Voice)

B = Protocol Sensitive (for example, Ip) Communicator Data With Clear (Pt) Addressing

C = Path Similar To "A" Above With One-Time Clear Header For Id/Address

D = Internal Radio Control Channel Or External Network Information (for example, Router Tables)

For proper operation, internal control type messages have to pass through the cryptographic subsystem from the RED processing (for example, a RED GPP) to the BLACK processing area (for example, a BLACK GPP). These pass-thorough messages require the cryptographic subsystem to provide a bypass mode. This bypass mode allows the message to proceed from the RED GPP to the BLACK GPP unaltered. The message will be examined by a bypass mechanism. The bypass control mechanism is required to check content and length in the bypassed information. If the lower protocol layers are removed, the bypass control is only required to validate the bypassed message itself. If the lower layers of the transport mechanism are present, the algorithm has to check the protocol bits that are included with that layer. As a result, the lower the algorithm is in the stack, the harder the bypass control mechanism is to implement if the bypass policy to be loaded becomes implementation dependent. Therefore, the bypass mechanism can architecturally exist at the application layer. All transport encapsulations are thus removed.[72]

Cryptographic control and status functions provide the means for the cryptographic subsystem to communicate with the rest of the radio functions for channel establishment and operation. Although the cryptographic function set is highly isolated from the rest of the radio functions, the cryptographic subsystem will communicate with the RED and BLACK sides via Application Program Interfaces or adapters for control and status information. Commands for the cryptographic subsystem can be generated via the Human Machine Interface, application program, system program, and/or core operating system. The cryptographic subsystem security critical commands are executed internal to the cryptographic subsystem. Status reporting and cryptographic subsystem internal holdings (for example, key holdings, algorithm holdings) are restricted to administrators or internal radio entities with need to know authentication. The security policy determines which control and status information, originating from the cryptographic subsystem, is privileged.

Intellectual Property Protection

The prerequisite of information security for electronic commerce has encouraged the development of a number of useful technologies, each with its own strength and weakness. The three technologies that act as information control mechanisms for e-commerce are:

- **Digital Rights Management (DRM) systems**   These are object-centric access control systems that primarily wrap content in protective layers of cryptographic shielding.
- **Public Key Infrastructure (PKI) schemes**   These are, broadly put, user-centric access mechanisms to authenticate the identity of networks users and ascribe each privileges appropriate to his user profile.
- **Digital Watermarking**   This system invisibly buries the identity of the copyright holder into the intellectual property object, such as a song or an image. As well, watermarking systems are being used as copy control and playback control schemes being standardized by the consumer electronics and media industries.

Of these three, only digital watermarking does not default toward restricting access as its core functionality. In the context of delivering various kinds of information and content, DRM and PKI proffer keying systems to assure that payment or end-user privileges are in place before releasing content or software for consumer use. Each of these systems have their own relative strengths in particular domains, although DRM and PKI, given the sophistication required to use and manage them, are most relevant in the commercial sector. In consumer markets, however, the simplicity and technical elegance of digital watermarking qualifies it as the most appropriate technology for the domain.

DRM schemes, if properly deployed, can be powerful access control mechanisms for creators and distributors, requiring absolute certainty of information security and highly particularized control of their intellectual property. PKI can provide reliable delivery of information to individual users and a highly secure transfer medium. Yet PKI systems were envisioned primarily as network access control systems. They can mediate the transfer of information by way of the cryptographic systems that are organized by the PKI.

The logistics of key-based systems works against its use in the business world. Forcing consumers to negotiate payment and usage rights before discovering and enjoying them eliminates opportunities for impulsively purchasing the product. A trusted system is inherently command-based; increasing the likelihood for systemic failure since media content requires open and accessible means for recognition in order for markets to work correctly. Lastly, and most importantly, these kinds of schemes do nothing to stop unlawful making and distribution of unlicensed copies. Thus, they are exposed to copying, either by acoustic pick-up device or through direct recording of the music at the twisted pair.

Rather than attempting to hide information, signals, and intellectual property objects, watermarking technologies establish title and responsibility for them by embedding concealed digital watermarks into the fabric of the object containing the consumers' or distributors' identifying information. They are entwined in such that the carrier itself, a song for example, is destroyed when the watermark is removed—a feat achieved, in part, by incorporating the signal itself into the watermark.

Practically speaking, this gives artists and distributors hooks for locating and claiming title to their works that have been stolen and posted on the Web. For music that is distributed in wholly digital formats online, digital watermarks can contain title data and personal information about the consumer, providing a powerful deterrent from casually copying and sharing music files with unknown parties. Watermarking covertly also can provide a powerful disincentive to would-be pirates and their accomplices among resellers and distribution agents.

Demand for Hardware-Based Data Security

Motorola's new satellite series 9505 portable phone is currently available. The phone is encryption-capable with the attachment of a U.S. government class encryption cassette. Two modules are available, the KGV-135 and the KG-207. The KGV-135 is a high-speed general-purpose encryptor/decryptor. Production quantities have been delivered to tactical and potential space users who need wide-band data encryption for embedding into high-performance systems. The KGV-135 is an upgrade of the certified KG-135, offering increased bandwidth and COMSEC operating modes in a compact 2.31 square by .0125 thick Multi-Chip Module. Boasting wideband operation from 2 Kbps to 500 Mbps, the KGV-135 is specified to dissipate a low 13W of DC power, and nominally dissipates only 10 watts, allowing for easy heat removal. Standard interface logic levels and key protocols, as well as NSA certified cryptography and compatibility with several NSA certified COMSEC units, make the KGV-135 usable in a wide variety of systems.[73]

The KG-207 equipment is a new COMSEC high-speed digital, low power, wide band system under final development. The KG-207 equipment uses the latest Complementary Gallium Arsenide technology to achieve its high-speed and low-power performance, with operating data rates of 5 to 900 Mbps. The system consists of an *Aerospace Vehicle Equipment* (AVE) encryptor unit and a *Ground Operational Equipment* (GOE) decryptor unit. The AVE is a Hi-Rel space based unit; employed to encrypt downlink data while the GOE, a fixed site unit, is used to decrypt the received downlink data. The mechanical design, heat removal techniques, EMI/EMC, TEMPEST design techniques, and environmental capabilities are consistent with military space and ground fixed requirements. The high-speed digital interfaces are balanced differential line pairs, having a maximum VSWR level of 1.5:1 across the operational data rates. The KGT-207 AVE is a two channel, wideband digital encryption system composed of an encoder and a DC-to-DC power converter. The equipment encrypts two independent serial data streams clocked by a common clock. The key variable can be changed on each channel from a block of preassigned variables.

The operational status of the equipment can be continually monitored via telemetry signals. The KGR-207 GOE is a two-channel, wideband digital encryption/decryption system. The GOE is composed of two high-speed logic modules, a low speed controller module, two keying modules (one electronic module and one PROM module), a front panel, and a power converter. Each high-speed logic channel is capable of encrypting externally generated test data, and decrypting date or encrypted test data. The input data is clocked into each module with its own input clock. The two high-speed modules operate independently of each other. Key variables can be loaded into the high-speed logic modules from either keying module. The keying modules can be filled with new keys (either electronically for the electronic key module, or using proms for the prom rekey module). Operational commands and status are available locally at the front panel, or remotely through a GPIB interface. The high-speed modules can be configured based upon local or remote commands, with return status to the front panel and remote interface indicating the operational status of GOE.[74]

Balancing Information Technology, National Security, and Personal Privacy

Gentlemen do not read each other's mail.
Henry L. Stimson, Secretary of State

State of the Revolution

An electronic network carrying news and data, good and bad, true or false, with the speed of light anywhere on this planet, now ties the world together. This surfeit of information is changing the relationship between the government and its citizens, between one government and another; and between corporations and regulators.[75] The technology that carries the news of freedom is creating a situation which might be described as the twilight of sovereignty, since the absolute power of the state to act alone both internally against its own citizens and externally against other nations' affairs, is rapidly being attenuated. The information revolution is usually conceived of as a set of changes brought on by modern communication technologies for transiting information, and modern computer systems for processing it. It is now impossible to determine where communication stops and where computing begins.[76]

As a wide range of new IT-enabled devices and services becomes available, advances are likely to follow because cost will decrease at the same time that demand is increasing.[77] Local-to-global net access holds the prospect of affordable universal wireless connectivity via hand-held devices and large numbers of low-cost, low-altitude satellites.[78]

The Pitfalls and the Potential

The boom in satellite construction and launch in the next few years—there are estimates that more than 2000 satellites will be in orbit by the year 2003—will change the way governments and organizations around the world conduct business. Availability will change the way people live. As it does, usage will create a security nightmare for anyone whose survival depends on the protection of intellectual property, electronic commerce, electronic battlefields, and national security.

The new satellites, LEOs, Sub-LEOs, MEOs, and GEOs, described earlier in this chapter, will carry high-speed voice calls from handheld phones and, depending on the system, low and high-speed digital data. The challenge is to ensure a secure exchange of information across the globe and security will prove vital to the continued growth and usefulness of satellite communications as well as to the Internet and intranets.[79] Once achieved, the boom will prove revolutionary for those who previously did not have access to secure data in remote locations around the world.

The United States has spent years building an information infrastructure that is interoperable, easy to access, and easy to use. This structure—as complex as any in the world—is also built on an insecure foundation, one which has ignored the need to build trust into our systems. Attributes like openness and ease of connectivity that promote efficiency and expeditious customer service are the same ones that make systems vulnerable to attacks against automated information systems.

Computer breaches are on the rise and the most popular route in is through the Net, adding up to bigger losses than ever before. We are extremely vulnerable as an information-based society to the phenomenon of information warfare. Vulnerability to this type of attack will arise as a function of the increasing dependence on such technological developments as the Internet; the use of dual-use information technologies, such as satellite imaging and navigational-quality positioning data that are difficult to bring under government control; and the growing dependence of the U.S. military on nonsecure information systems.[80]

In the last century, the government-controlled national defense abilities and laws protected the commercial sector. The lines were clean and neat. Today, the cyber aspects of national defense depend as much or more upon the commercial sector as they do the government. The technologies at issue here no longer support the defense establishment alone—instead they form the nervous system of our economy and of society itself. Why is this threat so insidious and different? The answer is reasonably straightforward. Cyber-weapons allow the engineers of the attacks to use technology as a shield against law enforcement as these tools have generally escaped regulation. It is virtually impossible to apply existing international law principles to cyber-attacks against a nation's information systems.[81]

Information Vulnerability

In the Information Age, many vital interests require effective protection of information. Because digital representations of large volumes of data are increasingly pervasive, both the benefits and the risks of digital representation have increased. Larger amounts of information used more effectively and acquired more quickly can increase the efficiency with which businesses operate, open up entirely new business opportunities, and play an important role in the quality of life for individuals.[82] The risks are less obvious.

One of the most significant is the potential vulnerability of important information as it is communicated and stored. When information is transmitted via satellite in computer readable form, it is highly vulnerable to unauthorized disclosure or alteration. Many communications are carried over channels (satellites, cellular phones, and local area networks). Tapping wireless channels is almost impossible to detect or to stop. The consequences of these large-scale information vulnerabilities are potentially very serious. U.S. business, government, and individual satellite communications are targets or potential targets of intelligence organizations of foreign governments, competitors, vandals, suppliers, customers, and organized criminals. International exposure increases the vulnerability to compromise of sensitive information. The ability of individual citizens to function in an information economy is therefore at risk.[83]

Information is not zero-sum. It can be given away or stolen, and still be retained. And it can be impossible to determine that it has been stolen. With the global networks now in place, information can be distributed almost instantaneously worldwide at very little cost. Unlike something that is tangible and can be measured, some information (photographs, for example) increasingly resists characterization as real or not.[84] Mechanisms to protect information and to reduce vulnerabilities include encryption for safeguarding the transmission of sensitive data to and from satellites; authentication by requiring passwords, and access controls (permission to access data).

Importance of Information

Elements of the U.S. civil infrastructure such as the banking system, the electric power grid, the public switched telecommunications network, and the air traffic control system are central to so many dimensions of modern life that protecting these elements must have a high priority. Defending these assets against information warfare and crimes of theft, misappropriation, and misuse potentially conducted by hostile nations, terrorists, criminals, and electronic vandals is a matter of national security and will require high levels of information protection and strong security safeguards.[85]

Information has become as much of an asset to a business or government agency as buildings, equipment, and people. The problem is that managers and accountants often fail to recognize electronic information as an asset because of its less tangible nature, its relatively recent prominence, and the lack of documentation associated with monetary losses arising from loss or theft of information. In fact, there are several existing parallels. Agencies and organizations must come to recognize that accounting practices and institutions exist to protect traditional assets just as information safeguards and institutions protect information assets. There are parallels as well as differences summarized in Table 4.4 that emphasize the need for additional emphasis on information as a key resource.[86]

Table 4.4 Comparison of Information Assets with Traditional Assets

	Information Assets	**Traditional Assets**
Typical Treats	Human Error, insiders, natural disasters	Human Error, insiders, natural disasters
Management Responsibility	Chief Information Officer & Chief Executive Officer	Chief Financial Officer and Chief Executive Officer
Education	Computer Science Departments	Business Schools
Principles	Generally Accepted System Security Principles	Generally Accepted Accounting Principles
Certification	International Information Systems Security	
	Certification Consortium & Institute for Certification of Computer Professionals certifications	Certified Public Accountants

Source: OTA, 1994, and National Research Council[87]

At Risk

Only the private sector has the knowledge, expertise, and access to identify and address its vulnerabilities to cyber crime and cyber terrorism. Only the federal government has the legal authority, law enforcement tools, and defense and intelligence means to detect and deter the most serious cyber threats. Unless both groups find common ground, businesses will be picked off individually and the nation as a whole will suffer.[88]

Processing large amounts of information in a readily useable form during intense, crisis situations can be particularly difficult. We obviously are far from reaching full understanding of the impact of information warfare on doctrine, tactics, and strategy. However, the circumstances in which we find ourselves dictate that we find a way to measure the impact. One area of concern is our propensity to stovepipe activities within our structures, and the negative influences this can have on military operations. In what is probably only the beginning for nations in conflict, the Internet has already provided a medium for information warfare between two belligerent nations. During a border dispute between Ecuador and Peru, Ecuador used the Internet to publish government bulletins and excerpts from local media to tell its side of the conflict. In retaliation, Peru Internet used a gopher site in an attempt to neutralize Ecuadorian propaganda. (A gopher is an information system residing on the Internet that knows where everything is and, through an arrangement of nested menus, allows a user to continue choosing menu items until the sought-after subject is located.) The resulting verbal skirmish left both nations working to set up their own gophers.[89]

Information Warfare

Information has always been society's great equalizer. The drive to obtain information and the desire to keep it hidden form the history of cryptography.[90] But that situation is changing.

The phenomenon of Information Warfare merges modern technology with the ancient strategy of victory without violence. In these circumstances, information is a weapon and a target unto itself—not just a magnifier for physical forces engaged in traditional legal wars. The targets are the opponents' political, economic, and social infrastructures, thus raising legal, ethical, and moral issues that have not been previously confronted.[91]

The commercial world also has an interest in information warfare. A group or individual can pose an information warfare threat by setting up an entry-level operation with little more than a PC, a modem, and some readily available software. IW will be a potentially significant growth industry in the near future.[92]

Summary

Encryption can be viewed as an enabling technology that provides companies, their business partners, customers, and end users with the ability to get the information and service they need much faster and more securely. Ubiquitous digital communications will result in either a secure environment in which to conduct personal affairs and commerce or a world marked by digital fingerprints indicating our every transaction and thought. New and important issues imposed on us by our technology already include protection of privacy, infrastructure protection, law enforcement, national security, and economic competitiveness.[93]

Satellite encryption is a product as well as a technology. It's no silver bullet; many other factors, human and technical, can improve or detract from satellite communications security. Additionally, any large-scale use of satellite encryption, with or without key escrow, will depend on the existence of a substantial supporting infrastructure—deployment of which raises a different set of issues and problems.[94]

Endnotes

[1]Ricardo's Geo Orbit Quick-look, "History," http://www.geo-orbit.org/sizepgs/geodef.html.

[2]NASA Photo Gallery, http:/hq.nasa.gov/office/pao/history/sputnik/gallerysput.html.

[3]Ricardo's Geo Orbit Quick-look, p. 5.

[4]Ibid.

[5]Ibid.

[6]Ibid.

[7]Ibid., p. 2.

[8]Ibid.

[9]Satellite Today, 18 March 2001, http://www.satellitetoday.com/satcount.htm.

[10]American Distance Learning Consortium, January 23, 2001, http://www.adec.edu/tag/glossary.html.

[11]Ibid.

[12]Ibid.

[13]Ibid., pp. 15–16.

[14]American Distance Learning Consortium, p. 14.

[15]Innovative Solutions International, http://www.isicns.com/gpswsls.htm.

[16]IN Sportsman, September 14, 2000, http://www.insportsman.com/infishing/news/raytheonwaas.html.

[17]Concord Marine Electronics, http://www.concordelectronics.com/waas-gps-sail.html.

[18]Ricardo's Geo Orbit Quick-look, "Definitions," http://www.geo-orbit.org/sizepgs/geodef.html.

[19]Whalen, David J., "Communication Satellites: Making the Global Village Possible," http://www.hq.nasa.gov/office/pao/History/satcomhistory.html.

[20]Ibid., p. 3.

[21]Ibid., p. 5.

[22]Ibid.

[23]"PanAmSat's New PAS-1R Satellite in Position to Power Top Video, Internet and Data Customers."

[24]February 2000, http://biz.yahoo.com/bw/010220/ct_panamsat.html.

[25]Neale, Jason, Rod Green, and John Landovskis. 2001. Interactive Channel for Multimedia Satellite Networks, *IEEE Communications* Magazine, March, p. 192.

[25]Satellite Today, "Radio Shack Franchises to Feature XM Satellite Radios; Satellite Prepared for Launch," http://www.satellitetoday.com/premium/pubs/st/current.html.

[26]Neale, p. 192.

[27]Ibid., pp. 192–194.

[28]Ibid., p. 193.

[29]"History of Remote Sensing," http://www.aerial.evsc.virginia.edu/~jlm8h/class/USGS1.html.

[30]"American Landsat Satellite History," http://www.csrsr.ncu.edu.tw/english.ver/service/resource/landsat/landsat.html.

[31]"Spot System," http://www.spotimage.fr/home/system/system.htm.

[32]European Space Agency, "Observation of the Earth and Its Environment," http://www.esa.int/esa/p;rogs/eo_over.html.

[33]"Teal Forecasts 43 New Commercial Imaging Satellites Valued at $3.62 Billion to Be Built and Launched During 2001–2010," Logan, Utah, August 23, 2000, http://www.fas.org/eye/000823-teal.htm.

[34]Long, Mark, "Frequencies for Satellite Communications," 1997, http://www.mlesat.com/Article9.html.

[35]Gilder, George, 2001. "Out of the Copper Cage." *Glider Technology Report,* March, p. 4.

[36]Long, pp. 2–4.

[37]Ricardo's Spectrum Chart, http://www.geo-orbit.org/sizepgs/spectrumchartp.html.

[38]Long, pp. 5–6.

[39]Ibid., p. 6.

[40]Ibid., p. 9.

[41]http://www.askcalea.net/congressional.

[42]http://www.askcalea.net/about/overview.html.

[43]Vacca, John R., *Satellite Encryption,* Academic Press, 1999, p. 411.

[44]http://www.itl.nist.gov/fipspubs/by-num.htm.

[45]Vacca, p. 415.

[46]For up-to-date information, see www.cert.org.

[47]Vacca, Op. cit., p. 183.

[48]Meeks, Brock N., "Jacking in From the Narco-Terrorist Encryption Port," Cyberwire Dispatch, 1995, http://www.epic.org/crypto/ban/cyberwire.html.

[49]Ibid.

[50]Davidson, Alan, "Senators Introduce Pro-Privacy Encryption Bill, in Stark Contrast to Administration Position," Center for Democracy and Technology, Washington, D.C., May 11, 1998, http://www.cdt.org/press/051298press.html.

[51]Schwartz, John, U.S. Eases Encryption Export Rules, *Washington Post,* January 13, 2000, p. E1.

[52]Vacca, p. 151.

[53]http://www.epic.org/crypto/ban/freeh.txt.

[54]Field, Gary, Satellite "Big Brother" Eyes Parolees Technology is Same as that Used to Guide Nuclear Missiles. *USA TODAY*, April 8, 1999, A10.

[55]Vacca, p. 361.

[56]"Report of the Commission to Assess United States National Security Space Management and Organization," January 11, 2001, http://www.fas.org/spp/military/commission/report.htm.

[57]Vacca, p. 334.

[58]Security Supplement, Software Communication Architecture, para 1.2.1.1.

[59]Ibid., Para 1.2.1.2.

[60]Ibid., Para 1.2.1.3.

[61]Ibid., Para 1.3.

[62]CORBA services: Common Object Services Specification, Security Revision 1.2, para 15.8.10.4.

[63]Secure Media White Paper, Communicado (Satlink).

[64]Secure Media White Paper, Requirements for an Effective Encryption System, p. 2.

[65]Ibid., p. 3.

[66]Security Supplement, para 4.2.

[67]Ibid., Para 4.2.4.

[68]Ibid., Para 4.2.5.

[69]Ibid., Para 4.2.6.1.1.

[70]Ibid., Para 4.2.6.2.

[71]Ibid.,, Para 4.2.6.3.

[72]Ibid,. Para 4.2.7.

[73]http/www.mot.com/GSS/SSTG/ISSPD/spaceavionics/kgv135.html.

[74]Ibid.

[75]Wriston, Walter B., *The Twilight of Sovereignty, How the Information Revolution Is Transforming Our World,* Charles Scribner's Sons, 1992, p. xi.

[76]Ibid. pp. 2–3.

[77]National Intelligence Council (NIC). Office of the Director of Central Intelligence. *Global Trends 2015: A Dialogue About the Future with Non-government Experts."* Washington, D.C., NIC 2000-02, December 2000, p. E-7.

[78]Ibid. E-22.

[79]Vacca, John R., *Satellite Encryption*, Academic Press, 1999, p. 3.

[80]Institute of Foreign Policy Analysis, *War In the Information Age,* April 1996, IV.

[81]Denning, Dorothy, "Thinking About Cyberweapons Controls" (Unpublished Paper presented to the Defense Science Board, Draft of February 1, 2000), pp. 1–2.

[82]Vacca, p. 893.

[83]Ibid., pp. 894–895.

[84]Petersen, John L., "Information Warfare: The Future." *Cyberwar: Security, Strategy and Conflict in the Information Age*, ed. Alan D. Campen, Douglas H. DEarth, R. Thomas Gooden, AFCEA International Press, 1996, pp. 221–222.

[85]Vacca, p. 896.

[86]U.S. Congress. Office of Technology Assessment. *Information Security and Privacy In Network Environments.* OTA-TCT-606, U.S. Government Printing Office, September 1994, p. 43.

[87]Ibid.

[88]Lake, Anthony, "eTerror, eCrime," *6 Nightmares,* Little, Brown and Company, 2000, p. 63.

[89]Ibid. pp. 12–13.

[90]Wriston, p. 153.

[91]Ibid, p. 254.

[92]Petersen, p. 222.

[93]McNulty, F. Lynn, "Encryption's Importance to Economic and Infrastructure Security," www.law.duke.edu/journals/djcil/articles/djcil9p427.htm.

[94]Ibid., p. 133.

5

Cryptographic Security

The key to securing all communications application of cryptography with due diligence.

Cryptography is the science of keeping oral and written and other forms of communications secret as well as providing a means of authentication of the communicating parties. This chapter is devoted to principles and topics in cryptography that are germane to understanding wireless security applications. Our treatment is to foster management level understanding of cryptographic principles without undue mathematical reverence. First, we introduce the concepts of substitution, transposition, randomness, entropy, and speech universality. These are important lessons derived from historical cryptography and cryptanalysis. Second, we explore the related topic of attacks on cryptosystems. Third, we visit stream and block ciphers and their characteristics. Fourth, we explore the essential topics of key management, secret key, and public-key cryptography. Fifth, we explain the foundations for strong cryptography and the observed trade-offs. Sixth, we explore three crypto-solutions to the wireless security question: a stream cipher with a unique SHA-1 key-generation mechanism known as HORNET™, the use of ECC and its relation to bandwidth and key size, and finally Rijndael, the AES winner and how it may be applied in the wireless arena in hardware such as FPGAs and ASICs. Cryptography is based on some interesting mathematical and difficult constructs. The reader is directed to the References for historical and modern material on cryptography, its supporting mathematics, and published standards for use in commercial and government organizations.

Concealment

Among the earliest technological answers to the need for confidentiality and integrity of information was cryptography, or secret writing. David Kahn, in his monumental history of cryptography, *The Codebreakers*, traces the history of secret writing to an inscription carved about 1900 B.C. on the tomb of the nobleman

Khnumhotep II. The earliest applications were merely transformations of hieroglyphs probably used to indicate emphasis or, occasionally, for calligraphic, decorative, or other reasons. The use of such transformations for secrecy reasons—possibly originally as sort of a game or puzzle—by the Egyptians may have been the true birth of cryptography.[1]

One of the surest ways to preserve the secrecy of information is to hide it so effectively that those who seek to obtain it do not recognize its presence. Hiding a message to avoid awareness of its existence creates a *concealment cipher* or *null cipher*. Since messages can be reduced to a sequence of 1's and 0's, any patterned situation in which two different values are present can be the vehicle for hiding information. Different colored bricks or rocks in a wall or tiles in a mosaic could represent 1's and 0's. Broken or whole pickets in a fence or large/fat/tall versus small/thin/short books on a shelf would do. The possibilities are legion.

The general term for the art and science of concealment ciphers is *steganography* and computer programs implementing steganographic algorithms have begun to appear. One such routine replaces the least significant bit of the bit strings defining the pixels of a graphic image with a sequence of 1's and 0's that compose the hidden message to be sent. Since most graphics encodings provide more gradations of color than the human eye can see, coopting the least significant bits for use in hiding a message will not noticeably change the picture. A 64KB message can be easily concealed within a 1024×1024 pixel graphic in this fashion, using software available for free or downloadable as shareware in many locations across cyberspace. Figure 5-1 shows a representation of a string of 1's and 0's, concealing the entire text of the Gettysburg Address.

Were the image to be intercepted, it is highly unlikely that the intercepting party would realize that there was a hidden message at all, absent inside information that steganography might have been employed. It is a defining characteristic of concealment or null ciphers that the message is there to be more or less easily read once the trick of its concealment is known.[2]

5-1 Steganography example—the entire Gettsyburg Address is hidden in this picture.[3]

First Principles

Cryptology is the study of codes and ciphers for use in secret transmission of messages from a sender to a recipient, either or both of which may be people, processes on a computer system or network, or a file stored on a computer disc or other storage device. Ciphers are methods or systems of secreting messages, and may be concealment ciphers as discussed above or may be the transposition and substitution ciphers we explore next. Codes are special forms of ciphers in which symbols or groups of symbols replace groups of bits or characters in the original message according to a table or codebook. Creating the codebook requires identifying words, phrases, sentences or even entire messages and assigning for each a specific symbol or group of symbols. Thus, "Meet me at dawn" might be represented as "QQRST" in the codebook (see Figure 5-2). In either ciphers or codes, the original message to be sent and received is called the plaintext or cleartext and the scrambled or hidden message that is actually transmitted is called the ciphertext. The process or algorithm used in converting the plaintext to ciphertext is called variously encryption or encipherment. Recovering the original message is accomplished by using a decryption or decipherment algorithm.

Cryptology is composed of cryptography—the art and science of keeping messages secure—and cryptanalysis—the art and science of breaking messages (that is, recovering the messages without fore-knowledge of all the details of the system used to secure the message). Successful cryptography that is not readily susceptible to cryptanalysis provides privacy. It may also provide authentication and non-repudiation, and ensures the integrity of the information comprising the plaintext.

It must be noted, however, that *cryptography alone cannot solve all the problems of protecting information assets and systems*. It does not ensure availability, so denial-of-service attacks are still a danger. Nor will it, in general, protect against viruses, although it can help do so if used as part of a well-developed operation. There are two types of cryptographic algorithms (or methods for transforming plaintext messages into ciphertext): secret key cryptography (or symmetrical) which uses one key and public-key cryptography (or asymmetrical) that uses two mathematically related keys like a lock box at the bank.[4]

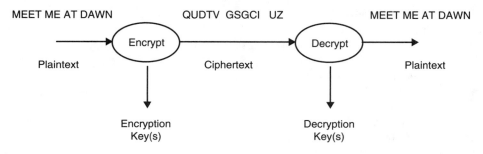

5-2 Simple encryption system.[5]

Dr. J.C.H. Ryan suggests that of the six states of information processing—input, output, display, storage, communications, and processing—that cryptography can protect only two: storage and communications.[6]

From the wireless standpoint, we can protect much of the *over-the-air* (OTA) communications via end-to-end encryption, so processing of the signals can be added to the list.

Lock-and-Key Analogy

Electronically transmitted data is vulnerable to attack and compromise. Cryptography is both the lock and the combination (or keys) that helps us protect our data. There are varieties of cryptographic methods and keys (and management of these keys). Together the method and the key determine the extent and depth of cryptographic security.

Imagine that a master locksmith has designed a combination lock and has published the entire inner workings—the nuts and bolts—of every mechanism in the lock. "Alice" buys one of these locks and changes its combination. The design is so secure that no one, not even the locksmith, can figure out the new combination. If Alice forgets the combination, no one can open the lock without trying every possible combination or by physically breaking the lock.

Further imagine that this one lock design is used to make many locks. Suppose "Bob" also buys one of these locks and changes its combination. Neither the locksmith who designed the lock nor Alice has any clue as to how to defeat the combination on Bob's or anyone else's lock, so Alice cannot open Bob's lock, and Bob can not open Alice's lock.

Alice checks that her lock is secure against the force she believes an opponent might use to open it and checks that the lock cannot be opened by merely pulling on it. She also wants to have confidence that it would take an intruder an appreciably long time to try all the possible combinations. How long Alice wants someone to have to try different combinations before hitting upon the correct one by chance determines the kind of lock she buys.

Let's use the lock and key analogy to see how Alice could protect her electronic possessions. Imagine that Alice has an envelope containing a secret message and that her lock seals the envelope to keep others from opening it. The message inside the envelope is readable if the correct combination opens the lock. The lock secures the envelope in a manner designed to destroy the envelope contents if it is opened by brute force, thus denying an intruder use of a hammer or crowbar.

Cryptography is both the lock and the combination (or key). Just as there are varieties of locks, there are varieties of cryptographic methods and keys. The joining of the method and the key determines how secure Alice's secret message is from an opponent who is not privy to the combination.

Bob can use a lock with the same design as Alice's lock; many people know that the method is to turn right to number 1, left to number 2, and finally right again to number 3. But it's Bob's individual lock combination, his *personal identification numbers* (PIN), that enables his lock to secure his personal belongings and keeps

Alice, or anyone else without the lock combination, out. What matters most in securing Bob's personal belongings is the strength of the lock and the number of possible combinations or keys.

In the same way, the lock strength and the number of possible keys are critical to securing Bob and Alice's electronic communications. Alice and Bob can use a cryptographic method or lock with the same design (as long as it's a strong method) and still securely hide their personal messages from a savvy opponent, or each other, because their individual cryptographic keys are different. As long as there are enough possible keys to keep an opponent busy trying them for a long time, Bob and Alice can feel somewhat secure that the secrets in their messages won't fall into the wrong hands. While it is obvious that a physical lock with 100,000 possible combinations is much more secure than a lock with only 1,000 possible combinations, this has not always been true, in cryptography. *The characteristics of keys play a decisive role in electronic cryptography that is not directly analogous to physical locks and keys.*[7]

Transposition Ciphers

Despite nearly 4,000 years of use, cryptography today still relies basically on only two methodologies beyond concealment, both familiar to most schoolchildren. In *transposition* ciphers, the letters of the message to be secretly transmitted are scrambled, that is, rewritten in a patterned way, and is then sent in a different order from its original form. For example, transpositions write messages horizontally into rectangular arrays, reading out the transposed text vertically. The recipient reverses the process to recover the original text:

N	O	W	—	I	S	—	T	H	E	—	T	I	M	E
F	O	R	—	A	L	L	—	G	O	O	D	—	M	E
N	—	T	O	—	C	O	M	E	—	T	O	—	T	H
E	—	A	I	D	—	O	F	—	T	H	E	I	R	—
P	A	R	T	I	E	S	—	S	T	O	P	Z	Z	Z

would be transmitted as

NFNEP OO—A WRTAR —OIT IA-DI SLC-E -LOOS T-MF- HGE-S
EO-TT -OTHO TDOEP I—IZ MMTRZ EEH-Z

The shaped patterns to be used, characters to demark words, sentences, paragraphs or to be used as fillers, and so forth have to be agreed upon in advance, comprising what modern cryptologists call encryption and decryption algorithms. Obviously, very complex algorithms are possible.

Keywords may also play a role in transposition ciphers. For example, if the eight-letter keyword computer is agreed-upon, the plaintext message is written horizontally into an array of eight-by-eight squares. The natural order of the letters of the keyword as they occur in the alphabet specifies the order in which the columns of the array are removed to compose the transposition.

Key Word	C	O	M	P	U	T	E	R
Letter Order	1	4	3	5	8	7	2	6
	M	E	E	T	M	E	A	T
	T	H	E	F	R	O	N	T
	D	O	O	R	O	F	T	H
	H	I	L	T	O	N	H	O
	T	E	L	A	T	9	P	M

Thus the plaintext "Meet me at the front door of the Hilton Hotel at 9 PM" becomes:

MTDHT ANTHP EEOLL EHOIE TFRTA TTHOM EOFN9 MROOT

The use of keywords in such a cipher vastly simplifies its operational use. The senders and recipients mutually agree upon all of the methodology, so only the keywords need to be exchanged to permit relatively secure communication using the cipher. Of course, it is vital that the preliminary exchange of keywords be conducted securely, since anyone having the key can decipher the message. *The problem of secure exchange of keys*, or *key management*, is *of paramount importance.*

Transposition ciphers can be looked upon as a set of computer instructions, one instruction per letter. Instead of building a transposition table with rows and columns, it is faster to get or move each letter to its new, transposed position. Computers do this relocation super fast—at rates of millions per second. Even the most complex transposition cipher has an easy set of instructions known as the *transportation map.*

Substitution Ciphers

In the second methodology, *substitution ciphers* are created by replacing one symbol, such as a letter of a message, with another symbol or letter in some patterned way. We might, for example, place the alphabet side by side with another alphabet that has been displaced by a few letters to the right:

A	B	C	D	E	F	G	H	I	J	K	L	M
D	E	F	G	H	I	J	K	L	M	N	O	P

N	O	P	Q	R	S	T	U	V	W	X	Y	Z
Q	R	S	T	U	V	W	X	Y	Z	A	B	C

Then we replace the first letter of the message "Meet me at dawn," the letter M—with its counterpart P, and so forth, to obtain the enciphered message "PHHW PH DW GDZQ." The recipient, knowing the key, in this case how many places to displace the second alphabet, can use the scheme in reverse to recreate the original message. Again, using a displacement of three letters to the left, we obtain the following substitution:

Plaintext: NOW IS THE TIME FOR ALL GOOD PEOPLE TO COME TO THE
Ciphertext: KLT FP QEB QFJB CLO XII DLLA MBLMIB QL ZLJB QL QEB

Any number from 1 to 25 can be used as a displacement, becoming the key for this Caesar's cipher type of substitution, after Julius Caesar who was supposed to have first used it.

More complex algorithms use an agreed upon word, or key to determine the scheme. For example, if magnetic was chosen as the key, the paired alphabets became:

A	B	C	D	E	F	G	H	I	J	K	L	M
M	A	G	N	E	T	I	C	B	D	F	H	J

N	O	P	Q	R	S	T	U	V	W	X	Y	Z
K	L	O	P	Q	R	S	U	V	W	X	Y	Z

Since each letter can occur only once in each alphabet, repetitions are ignored, so SECURE used as a key becomes SECUR. Two keywords may be used to further complicate the substitution:

S	E	C	U	R	A	B	D	F	G	H	I	J
M	A	G	N	E	T	I	C	B	D	F	H	J

K	L	M	N	O	P	Q	T	V	W	X	Y	Z
K	L	O	P	Q	R	S	U	V	W	X	Y	Z

Displacements may also be used to prevent same-letter combinations from occurring.

M	A	G	N	E	T	I	C	B	D	F	H	J
A	C	D	F	G	H	J	K	M	N	O	P	Q

K	L	O	P	Q	R	S	U	V	W	X	Y	Z
S	U	V	W	X	Z	L	I	B	E	R	T	Y

The combination of one or more words and one or more displacements constitutes the keys. As was true for transposition ciphers, the use of keys simplifies the operational application of substitution ciphers, but requires secure key management.

Neither transposition nor substitution ciphers in the simple forms presented here represent much of a challenge to an adversary who desires to recover the original message, especially if a computer is handy to aid in trying to break the codes used. However, complex variations of these two schemes can be used, often in combination, to achieve impressive levels of security.[8]

Kerckhoff's Principles

Kerckhoff (whose full name is Jean-Guillaume-Hubert-Victor-Francois-Alexandre-Auguste Kerckhoff von Nieuwenhof) was not French or Dutch but Flemish. Kerckhoff was the first to separate the general system from the specific key. The important concept is that anyone can have the cryptographic method to protect a communication. Later, as we address public-key cryptography, we can see that this is the appropriate design. Secrets are only as safe as your secret key(s). Even though the adversary may know the encryption method, it is the joining of the encryption method with the unique key that confuses messages for anyone who does not have the secret key.

In 1883, Kerckhoff wrote that wartime cryptography needed to be efficient, portable, and easy to understand. It should also have a key that was easy to change and should lend itself to telegraphic transmission. Stepping back in time a few years to the American Civil War, the Confederacy didn't know of these maxims because they trusted the fabled Vigenere cipher using only three secret keys. Mistakes were frequent and telegraphic transmission took up to 10 days, so Confederate soldiers would gallop over to the sender to get the message firsthand. The Union exploited all of these problems.[9]

Product Ciphers

By combining the methodologies of substitution and transposition, cryptographers found that using the two types together created a significantly stronger concealment cipher (called a *product cipher*) than either method alone could produce. Using both methods repeatedly does a good job of disguising plaintext patterns, making the enciphered message harder to decipher, unless the adversary has external clues. The modern day Data Encryption Standard (as 3DES) and Rijndael (the Advanced Encryption Standard winner) use multiple combinations of transposition and substitution in complex formats to achieve superior cryptosecurity.

Although substitution and transposition ciphers became more complex, they could be attacked using statistical methods. Ideally, ciphertext should present itself as a random string of letters or bits or be data key-stroked by a monkey. The cryptographer wants to eliminate any clues that might help the cryptanalyst to reclaim plaintext. This means eliminating statistical relationships between ciphertext and the underlying plaintext. Diffusion is defined as the dispersion or distribution of plaintext in a statistically random manner over the ciphertext. It frequently involves the iterated combination of substitution and transposition in some form of a product cipher. Diffusion disperses the plaintext throughout the ciphertext; it essentially hides the inevitable relationship between the ciphertext and plaintext. It frustrates the cryptanalyst's attempt to use ciphertext patterns to reveal the secret encryption key that will unravel or bypass the encryption algorithm.

The cryptographer uses Kerckhoff's principle, assuming that the cryptographer knowsthe method, language, location, and so forth, but not the secret key. The principle of confusion prevents the cryptanalyst from using the ciphertext to deduce the secret key. It may take the form of a complex substitution method. Confusion hides the relationship between ciphertext and the secret key.

Ciphers that use confusion and diffusion together are called product ciphers. Each application of confusion and diffusion is known as a round. The repeated application of rounds is called iteration. Product ciphers that use many rounds, like DES, are iterated product ciphers. A well-designed iterated product cipher encrypts a message so that no one—including the cryptosystem designer—can easily decrypt the message without knowing the secret key. With an iterated product cipher, statistical analysis of the ciphertext letters is no longer a practical option to crack the ciphertext message to yield the true message. Now the cryptanalyst's best attack is to try every possible key—a brute force attack. Just like a bully, a cryptographic method requiring a brute force attack that also has so many keys that a brute force attack is not feasible (within the available resources) is referred to as a strong method. (Psychologists will have fun with the previous definition. We are defining the strength of the bullies by how many victims attack them and how well they can resist their attacks by their resources, the key moves.)

Modern secure cryptosystems are strong but they are subject to advances in technology. Strong methods are made more secure by being published because they can be scrutinized and tested by cryptanalysts. The *Data Encryption Standard* (DES) has about 70 quadrillion potential keys and was, for nearly three decades, secure against traditional cryptanalysis. It is no longer secure (strong) because using today's computers to test the 70 quadrillion keys is a snap! Cryptosystem designers must consider performance, work factor, and technological resources that can be mounted against the cryptosystem as well as implementation issues in the networking environment, ease of use, and cost.[10] Wireless systems present additional challenges because they have additional points of attack available and potentially more leakage of information to the cryptanalyst.[11]

Classical Cryptanalysis

Classical cryptography had a weakness that was security-fatal—linguistic patterns or repetitions. Linguistic patterns hold true for every language and follow through from plaintext to ciphertext. Unique attributes of letter and word usage in languages have helped cryptanalysts decrypt secret messages for more than 3,000 years. An attempted cryptanalysis is called an attack. Cryptologists always assume that enemies know the encipherment and decipherment algorithms, so security resides entirely in the key or keys used by the cipher. This is, of course, a conservative assumption—the enemy won't always have all the details of the algorithm and its implementation, but it is wise to assume so and to design ciphers that cannot be broken even if the assumption is true.

By knowing the frequencies with which English letters in occur, it is possible to determine almost immediately if a cipher is a transposition or a substitution. For example, if E is not the most frequent letter in an English ciphertext, the cipher almost certainly involves substitution. By successively replacing letters according to the frequencies of their occurrence in the ciphertext, simple substitutions can often be broken by trial and error. Breaking simple ciphers is a hobby enjoyed today by many enthusiasts. Newspapers regularly print a variety of different cryptograms and cryptoquotes, created according to a variety of pre-agreed protocols. The popular TV game "Wheel of Fortune" is really an exercise in applied classical cryptanalysis.

Ciphers are broken by analysis relying on certain underlying regularities in the English language. All languages have such regularities, and so statistics can be used to determine which language is being used, even if the source of a message is not known (see Figures 5-3 and 5-4).[12]

Digital Cryptography

Modern cryptography is almost exclusively concerned with protecting information that is in digital form, a set or sequence of 1's and 0's. One or a combination of the two distinct processes—transposition and substitution—may be combined into a complex algorithm and applied with a key, which is also a sequence of 1's and 0's, to the plaintexts to create the enciphered message.

In Table 5-1, consider a situation in which a text message is to be protected. The message, "Meet me at dawn," may be encoded in ASCII.

English	German	French	Italian	Spanish	Portugese
		Vowels:			
40%	40%	45%	48%	47%	48%
		LNRST:			
33%	34%	34%	30%	31%	29%

5-3 Statistical regularities in European languages.[13]

E	1231	L	403	B	162
T	959	D	365	G	161
A	805	C	320	V	93
O	794	U	310	K	52
N	719	P	229	Q	20
I	718	F	228	X	20
S	659	M	225	J	10
R	603	W	203	Z	9
H	514	Y	188		

5-4 Frequencies of occurrence of letters in English.[14]

Table 5-1

M	E	E	T	NUL	M
01010101	01001101	01001101	01011100	00000000	01010101
E	NUL	A	T	NUL	D
01001101	00000000	01001001	01011100	00000000	01001100
A	W	N			
01001001	01011111	01010110	00110110		

Read in the usual way, this becomes the bitstream:

0101010101001101010011010101110000000000010101010100110100000000
1001001010111000000000000100110001001001010111110101011000110110.

But if we rearrange or transpose the bits, say by reading each byte from right to left instead of from left to right, so that 01010101 becomes 10101010, we obtain the stream

1010101010110010010011010101011100000000000010101011011001000000001
0010010001110100000000000110010100100101111101001101010011011100.

If we know the starting point of the bitstream and the length of the byte used to encode a character, it is easy to reverse each byte in order to reconstruct the original stream.

Still another transposition could be obtained by starting with the last bit and creating the transposed bitstream by taking the last bit of each byte working backwards to the first byte, and then the next-to-last bit of each byte, and so forth, producing

0011000101100111111000000000000011101010110111100111011010100111011
1000100010100110000000000000001111011011101111000000000000000.

This stream is also easy to convert to the original stream if we know that there are 16 bytes of 8 bits each.

A wraparound transposition can be obtained by starting at a pre-agreed spot in the sequence—usually not the beginning of any byte—and reading out the bits in the usual manner. For example, if the third bit is chosen as the starting point, we obtain

0101010100110101001101010111000000000000101010101001101000000000010
0100101011100000000000100110001001001010111110101011000110011001

where the first two bits of the original sequence have been placed at the end of the derived sequence.

Substitution ciphers use a key and an algorithm to replace the characters of the message with other characters that appear meaningless to the recipient. In modern communication systems, circuits to accomplish substitution rely on devices called gates which take in two or more bits and output a bit that depends on the type of gate. Pictorially, the encryption and decryption processes are as follows (see Figure 5-5).

Taking the plaintext as a stream of bits and the key as a stream of bits, the encryption key and the decryption key are identical, and the encryption and decryption algorithms are also identical—are, in fact, merely the XOR operation that is easily implemented in circuits.

To create the key bitstream, we can use any sufficiently robust pseudo-random number generator. Pseudo-random number generators are mathematical functions that produce a sequence of numbers that are apparently random numbers even though they are deterministically produced (see Figure 5-6). That is, the sequence of numbers produced by the pseudo-random number generator passes some tests designed to detect the presence of patterns that could be used, in turn, to duplicate the stream of numbers and thus crack the encryption system.

A pseudo-random number generator is like a little machine that cranks out an apparently random, but in fact deterministic, sequence of numbers that is combined by the encryption algorithm with the sequence of 1's and 0's comprising the plaintext one bit at a time to create the ciphertext. If the encryption algorithm is XOR, the process is simply that of binary addition (see Figure 5-7).

Because it is truly deterministic, if we know the *seed key* we can duplicate at the receiver the bitstream being created and used at the transmitter to encrypt the stream of bits that comprise the plaintext. This same stream, if the decryption

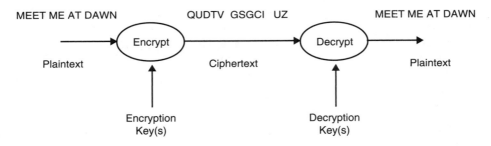

5-5 Deterministec Key.

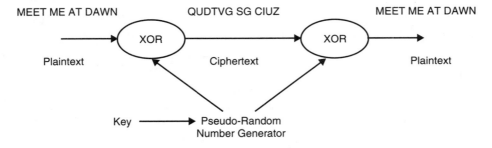

5-6 Example of Binary Addition Encryption.

algorithm is XOR, is simply added to the ciphertext to recreate the plaintext (see Figure 5-8).

The sequence of bits produced by the pseudo-random number generator is taken in blocks equivalent in length to the blocks of plaintext being processed (see Figure 5-9). The decryption process is again just the reverse of the encryption process.

In practice, pseudo-random number generators eventually repeat themselves, so we have, as a practical matter, to choose a function that does not repeat itself after only a short sequence of apparently random numbers is produced. To complete the picture of a practical encryption/decryption system, we need only point out that the pseudo-random number generator we use needs to be primed with a seed key for each random number sequence to ensure that the sequence it produces is not always the same. Seed keys may be short relative to the length of the nonrepeating

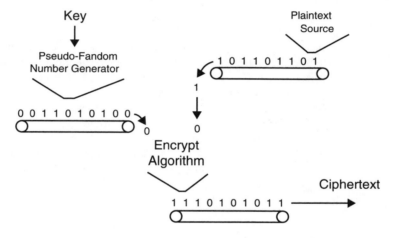

5-7 Using a pseudo-random number generator to encrypt.

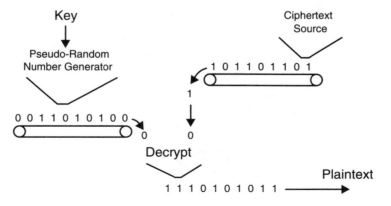

5-8 Using the pseudo-random number generator todecrypt.

pseudo-random number stream—a few dozen rather than hundreds of thousands to millions of numbers. This greatly simplifies the key management problem we discuss later. With this basis for understanding encryption and decryption keys, seed keys, and encryption and decryption algorithms, we are ready to look at a real, widely used cryptographic system, the Data Encryption Standard.[15]

Pseudo-Random Number Generation

Nothing is random. We live in perfect order. Our lives may be a little out of whack but the Universe is not. Random numbers play an integral part in cryptography.

When it comes time to generate cryptographic keys, we need some random numbers. How do we get these? If we have a 128-bit key, we need at least 128-bits of random material. Typing them in from the keyboard is not random. Suppose you typed in

jeodivnfu348refj

A little research might show that people tend not to type numbers and to use only lowercase letters and letters toward the middle of the keyboard, and that the pairs of characters are usually in left-hand or right-hand combinations. Maybe people seldom enter the same character twice in a row, and perhaps there are 4, 5, or 10 or 20 other prevalent patterns. A *brute-force* attack in such a situation would begin looking at keys that follow the tendencies of human typing. The attacker would not have to try, on average, one-half of the possible keys before stumbling onto the correct one. A search might look at, on average, only one-tenth or one-one hundredth or maybe even one-one millionths of the possible keys before success.

We can see that keys chosen this way are not actually random. What we'd like is a program that picks keys at random.[16]

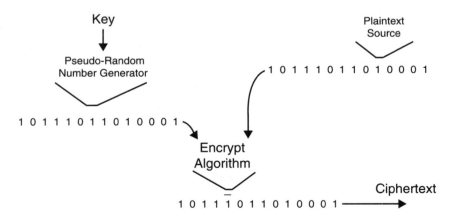

Figure 5-9 Block encryption using a pseudo-random generator.

What Is Random?

This is really a tough question. Everyone has an intuitive idea of what random is. But, as you can imagine, cryptography relies on more than intuition. Given a series of numbers, a cryptographer will apply tests to those numbers to determine if they are random. Since we're talking about computers, all numbers are represented in binary (1's and 0's), so the first test might determine whether the probability is 50 percent that the next number is 1 and 50 percent that it is 0. This is not the same thing as the probability is about 50 percent that a number is 1 and about 50 percent that it is 0. Look at the following series of 1's and 0's.

10101010101010101010101010101010101010101010101010101010

Half are 1s and half are 0s but it not a random pattern. In this example, if a number is 1, it appears the next number will be 0.

Another test might try to see if some patterns appear too often or too seldom. For example, if there are three 1's in a row are they always followed by three 0's? On the other hand, is there a pattern that will never appear? If you have a source of random 1's and 0's, look at every group of three. There are eight possible combinations of 1's and 0's as groups of three: 000, 001, 010, 011, 100, 101, 110, and 111. Each has a probability of occurrence one-eighth of the time. So we would expect to see 111 sooner or later. If you never see that pattern, the numbers might not be random. There are many tests like these. The *National Institute of Science and Technology* (NIST) has a whole battery of tests available.[17]

We perform statistical and other mathematical tests on a *random number generator* (RNG). If the RNG passes all the tests, use it to generate your keys. An attacker trying to break one of your messages will not be able to devise a method that tries more likely keys first because no key is more likely than any other key. Attackers will therefore have to try every possible key before stumbling onto the correct value. This is the definition of a brute force attack. Unfortunately, computers are deterministic machines that will always produce the same result given the same input. It's not random. So you can't get random numbers out of a computer. A software package could never produce truly random numbers.

On the other hand, there are indeed machines that generate random numbers, perhaps by examining radioactive decay, or counting ions in the atmosphere, or examining heat variations in the vicinity. Although such machines are not computers, a computer can communicate with them and receive their random numbers. Unfortunately, such RNGs tend to be expensive and slow. The average user will not have access to one. This leads us to the next best thing, a *pseudo-random number Generator* (PRNG), and it may not be good enough, as many successful attacks on cryptosystems have been mounted against the PNRG.

Pseudo-Random Number Generator (PRNG)

A PRNG is an algorithm in software that produces numbers that look random, but are reproducible. Because they are reproducible, we can't say they are truly random. But the output of a PRNG may pass all the tests of randomness. Hence, pseudo-random.

Here's how it works. Feed a seed to a PRNG and it will use that seed to generate numbers that look random. If you feed a different seed, you will get different results. Using the same seed will always get you the same numbers. A seed is a merely series of numbers or characters.

Most PRNGs work by using a message digest (a mathematically reduced unique form of the message). Here's a typical example.

Digest the seed to create an initial state. When it comes time to generate random bytes, digest the state. The result of that digest is the first part of the output. If you need more random bytes than one digesting will give you, update the state, as by adding a constant. Now digest this new state to get the next block of data. For example:

Let seed = 3707446542388966625321 . . .
Process with message digest algorithm → state:17263987143002349672491 . . .
Iteration with message digest algorithm yields pseudo-random numbers →
    5423709821369792645233 . . .

People who know some of the random bytes still won't know what the next bytes are going to be. To know what the next bytes are, one needs to know the state, but that's kept secret. To figure out the state, one needs either to know the seed used to create the state, or to reverse the digest. We saw in the section on message digests that reversing a digest is currently not possible. Therefore, if you choose a seed an attacker can't analyze successfully and if you keep it secret (or destroy it after use), an attacker can't determine what the next (or previous) bytes will be.

Why bother with the state? You could just digest the seed to get random output, and if you need more bytes, digest the output. If we did that, then knowing some of the random bytes means knowing the next ones. If we digest output to generate the next output, then so could an attacker.

The numbers look random. You know they aren't. After all, if you use the same seed again, you'll get the same results. So they're pseudo-random. But to an attacker they might as well be truly random because there's no way of knowing what the next bytes will be.

Why use a digest? The result of a message digest looks random; it passes all the tests of randomness. Furthermore, we can use as much seed as we want and still get output. Also, when we change the state, even just a little, the output is radically different. Each block of output looks nothing like the previous block.[18]

The Seed and Entropy

A pseudo-random number generator takes a huge amount of input, digests it to a smaller amount, which looks random. But the seed needs to come from a random source too. Keystrokes and system clocks are not good sources. They have patterns that can be reengineered. Cryptographers use the term *entropy* for sufficient seed. It's a term concerning the measurement of movement from order to chaos. Something totally chaotic has high entropy. Something ordered has low entropy. In cryptography, entropy is usually measured in bits. How many bits of entropy are there in this technique? A true RNG would have 1 bit of entropy for each 1 bit of output. It's totally chaotic. Totally random.

A coin flip, for instance, has 1 bit of entropy. There are two possible outcomes. Let's call heads 0 and tails 1. One flip produces either a 0 or 1. That's what 1 bit is, a 0 or 1. So one flip produces 1 bit, that bit being random, so there is 1 bit of entropy in a coin flip.

Another way to look at it is how many brute-force iterations must we execute to guarantee finding the answer? If we have complete entropy, the total number of brute-force iterations necessary to guarantee finding a 128-bit key would be 2^{128}. But if we have low entropy, say 2 bits of entropy for every 8 bits of key, the brute-force attack would simply not try those keys that are definitely not possibilities. We could find the answer after only 2^{32} iterations.

We want a 128-bit key. It would be great if we had 128 bits of entropy, a totally random key. If we don't have an RNG, we'll use a PRNG. Will we be able to get 128 bits of entropy from a PRNG? The output will look random, so the attacker won't try a brute-force attack on the output. Rather, it would be faster to find the seed unless the seed has enough entropy.

Keystrokes and time of day have order, so they have low entropy. It's not that they have no entropy; it's just low. To come up with a good seed, we need a source that has high entropy. Or we need something with low entropy, but lots of it. Suppose we did research and discovered that the keystroke seed has one-tenth of 1 bit of entropy of each 1 character (8 bits) of input. We want a 128-bit key, so we could ask for 1,280 keystrokes.

To find the key, an attacker would have to find the 1,280 keystrokes, in the proper order. Since each keystroke adds 8 bits of seed, this would seem to require $2^{1280 \times 8}$ iterations of a brute-force attack. But of course, the attacker won't try every possible combination of bits. Some combinations will never be possible and others are highly unlikely.

The measure of entropy indicates that this is equivalent to a 2^{128} brute-force attack. *That's the same amount of work it would take to do a brute-force attack on the key itself.* So cracking the message by cracking the seed is equivalent to cracking the message by cracking the key. Good programmers use several methods to gather the seed and take a percentage of the source to a seed pool. This increases the entropy and reduces the risks of failure from any one seed source.[19]

Seed as Key?

Why do we have to convert the seed into a pseudo-random number? If the seed has all the entropy we want, why not use it as the key? The answer is size. The seed may have 128 bits of entropy, but we needed 10,240 bits (or more) of seed to get it. Do you want to use a 10,240-bit key? Is it possible? Maybe the algorithm has a limit on key size. A PRNG will convert 128 bits of entropy spread out over a large number of actual bits, into about 128 bits of entropy spread out over 128 bits.[20]

The One-Time Pad

One of the most remarkable of all ciphers is the *one-time-pad* where the plaintext message is added bit by bit (or in general character by character) to a nonrepeating random sequence of the same length. The one-time-pad is also referred to as the Vernam cipher in honor of G. Vernam who developed the principle in 1917 for telegraphic communications. In the Vernam cipher the ciphertext is the bit-by-bit modulo-2 sum of the plaintext message and a nonrepeating random sequence of the same length. Since addition and subtraction are the same in GF (2), the deciphering is accomplished by applying the enciphering for a second time. The remarkable fact about the one-time-pad is *its perfect security*; assuming a ciphertext-only attack. Claude Shannon proved that even with infinite computing resources the cryptanalyst could never separate the true plaintext from all other meaningful plaintexts. The primary disadvantage, of course, is the unlimited amount of key needed. Another problem is the initial difficulty of making duplicate pads and arrangements.[21]

The appealing features of the one-time-pad suggested building synchronous stream ciphers, which encipher the plaintext by use of a *pseudo-random sequence*, thereby removing the requirement of unlimited key. A deterministic algorithm called the key stream generator under control of a secret key generates this pseudo-random sequence. With a synchronous stream cipher, the known plaintext assumption is equivalent to giving the cryptanalyst access to the key stream. For the system to be secure, it must not be possible to predict any portion of the key stream with higher reliability than just random guessing, regardless of the number of key stream characters already observed. Linear systems produce sequences, which are readily predicted and thus are cryptographically weak. They must be combined with nonlinear transformations in order to obtain desired highly complex pseudo-random sequences.

The basic principle of the one-time-pad is to statistically decouple ciphertext and plaintext by use of a truly random key sequence. The device, which emits such a random sequence, i.e. a sequence where each bit is equally likely to be 0 or 1 independently of the preceding bits, is called a *binary symmetric source* (BSS). In short, a BSS outputs a fair coin tossing sequence.

A cryptographic system is said to offer *perfect secrecy* (or is said to be unconditionally secure), if the mutual information between the plaintext message and the associated ciphertext is zero, independently of the length of the message. Then intercepting the ciphertext does not convey to the cryptanalyst any information whatsoever about the plaintext. He is confronted only with the *a priori* probability distribution over the set of possible messages.

Perfect secrecy may only be obtained; as long there are available as many random key bits as there are information bits in the plaintext stream. The operational disadvantages of the one-time-pad have led to the development of synchronous stream ciphers, which encipher the plaintext in much the same way as the one-time-pad, but with a deterministically generated random sequence.

Thus the running key generator in Figures 5-6 to 5-9 has, controlled by the true key K, the task to simulate a random sequence, which then is used to encipher the plaintext. The security of such a synchronous stream cipher now depends on the randomness of the key stream. Assuming a known plaintext attack, the cryptanalyst has full access to the running key. For the system to be secure the key stream must be unpredictable; regardless of the number of key stream digits observed, the subsequent key stream digits must be no more predictable than by random guess. This implies that it is not feasible for the cryptanalyst to determine the true key, as he would have to be able to reliably predict the key stream. A necessary requirement for unpredictability is a long period of the key stream. The period defines a linear recursion. Knowing the value of the period and the first period of the key stream determines completely the remainder of the key stream.[22]

The Data Encryption Standard

There are two innovations in computer cryptography that changed 3,000 years of message disguise engineering. The introduction of the Data Encryption Standard is one of these changes; the invention of public-key cryptography was the other. Both occurred in 1977.

The *Data Encryption Standard* (DES) is an encryption and decryption algorithm based on a routine called Lucifer that had been developed by IBM during the early 1970's. DES was adopted as a Federal standard on Nov. 23, 1976. Its official description was published as FIPS PUB 46 on Jan. 15, 1977 and became effective six months later. DES is a block cipher that encrypts and decrypts blocks of 64 bits. The encryption and decryption algorithms are identical. A key of 56 bits is used for encryption and decryption of a plaintext. An additional 8 bits are used for parity checking. Any 56-bit number can be used as a key, but a few keys are weak and must be avoided. The security of the cipher rests, of course, entirely with the key since the algorithm is known to all. Upon being given a plaintext block of 64 bits, DES performs an initial transposition, scrambling the 64 bits in a patterned way. The resulting 64-bit block is then split into two 32-bit halves, 16 rounds each consisting of a substitution and a transposition, based upon the key. After the 16 rounds are completed, the resulting two halves are rejoined and a final transposition, which is the inverse of the initial transposition, completes the enciphering operation (see Figure 5-10).

In each round, the bits of the key are shifted and 48 of the 56 bits of the shifted key are selected. The right 32-bit half of the transposed plaintext resulting from the initial transposition is expanded in a patterned way to 48 bits and is then combined using an XOR function with the 48 bits selected from the shifted key. The next eight simultaneous substitutions convert each 6-bit sub-block to a 4-bit output. The resulting eight 4-bit blocks are recombined to a single 32-bit block, which is then transposed in a patterned way and combined with the left half using the XOR function. The resulting 32 bits becomes the new right half, while the old right half becomes the new left half, completing the round. The transpositions in the round are linear and would succumb to cryptanalysis were it not for the nonlinearity introduced by the substitutions.

The initial key value is split by the algorithm into two halves, which are then shifted independently. Consequently, if all of the bits in each half are either 0 or 1, the same key insert will be used for every round. The four weak keys that must be

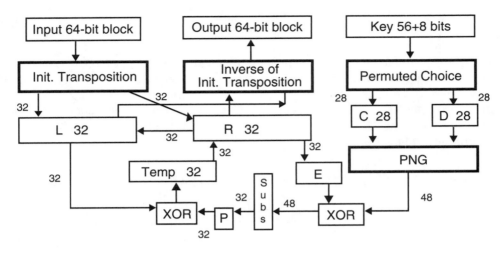

5-10 Flow details of the data encryption standard.

avoided are 0000000 0000000, 0000000 FFFFFFF, FFFFFFF 0000000, and FFFFFFF FFFFFFF. These weak keys are given in hexadecimal format. Remember that every eighth bit is a parity bit in the format that must be supplied to initialize the algorithm.

A few pairs of keys deliver a ciphertext that is identical to the plaintext, so that one of the keys can decrypt messages encrypted with the other. There are six such key pairs:

> 01FE01FE01FE01FE and FE01FE01FE01FE01, 1FE01FE00EF10EF1 and
> E01FE01FF10EF10E, 01E001E001F101F1 and E001E001F101F101,
> 1FFE1FFE0EFE0EFE and FE1FFE1FFE0EFE0E, 011F011F010E010E and
> 1F011F010E010E01, E0FEE0FEF1FEF1FE and FEE0FEE0FEF1FEF1.

Another 48 keys produce only 4 subkeys, which are each used four times. This means that 64 of the 72,057,594,037,927,936 possible keys must be avoided, which is not an overwhelming problem!

There were several good reasons for choosing the Data Encryption Standard for encrypting messages requiring privacy and authentication. DES is widely available in both hardware and software versions, so it is easy to obtain and is often already used by an intended recipient. Moreover, it has been in use for years by many users and is not known to be susceptible to a cryptanalytic attack that significantly threatens its utility. Because it is the Federal standard, its choice means that its users have *prima facie* used due diligence in selecting it and will not have to prove its effectiveness in a negligence suit as they will almost certainly have to do if another, less-well-known cipher is chosen. DES uses its 16 rounds of confusion and diffusion (iterated product cipher) on each group of eight plaintext letters. Statistical analysis of letter frequencies—the mainstay of cryptanalysis for thousands of years—is no real help in attacking a well-designed method such as DES.

On the other hand, there are reasons not to use DES. As we have seen, 56-bit keys are not considered to be long enough by many cryptographers today. As a consequence, triple DES, in which a message is enciphered three times using two or three different keys, is widely used in the financial community. Even more important, however, are the difficulties in using DES caused by the need for an expensive and cumbersome key-management system. 3DES (the most secure form of DES) will remain a standard until the new AES standard, Rijndael, is fully implemented and replaces DES/3DES in government, financial and commercial circles.[23]

Avalanche Effect

DES and other secret key block ciphers exhibit a very effective cryptographic property called the *avalanche effect*. Essentially, this means that for each bit change in plaintext, the cryptographic algorithm produces change in more than one-half of all the ciphertext bits. Ideally, all of the ciphertext changes with a change in plaintext input to the algorithm. This makes it very difficult to walk back the cat given only the ciphertext for analysis. The avalanche effect assures that DES is a very good randomizer in its own right. An example of the avalanche effect might be as follows:

Plaintext message 1: 100000000001 000101010001
Plaintext message 2: 100001000001 000101010001
DES Ciphertext message 1: 100100001111 010111000001
DES Ciphertext message 2: 101001111001 011111011000

The plaintext messages differ only by one bit (a single binary 0 or 1). The ciphertext produced is very different.[24]

A Standard Under Fire—DES Isn't Strong Anymore

In July 1998 the roof caved in on the financial and other industries using DES based cryptography products. The *Electronic Frontier Foundation* (EFF) announced their DES Cracker project. EFF organized and funded a project to build a specialized DES cracker for less than $250,000. Lead by the brilliant cryptographer Paul Kocher, President of Cryptography Research, the DES cracker broke a DES-cracking speed contest sponsored by RSA laboratories, beating out the combined efforts of massively parallel software from **www.distributed.net**. It found a 56-bit key in 56 hours by searching about 24.8 percent of the key space, or 88 billion keys tested per second! This is impressive evidence that developers of cryptographic products should not design anything else that depends on single DES. The exciting story of the DES cracker can be found in the EFF's book: *Cracking DES: Secrets of Encryption Research, Wiretap Politics and Chip Design*. A team of about a dozen computer researchers using 27 circuit boards built the machine, each holding 64 custom chips. A cable links the boards to a PC, which controls the entire process. Each custom chip, called Deep Crack, has 24 search engines, each capable of testing 2.5 million keys per second at 40 MHz. The EFF DES Cracker took less than a year to build and cost less than $250,000. It is almost 100 times faster than a Cray T3D supercomputer but at less than one hundredth of the cost.[25]

Modern Cipher Breaking

Modern cipher breaking is the process of determining the plaintext of a ciphertext without knowing the secret key or possibly even the method of encipherment. It plays a crucial role in the development of secure ciphers. It is not possible to design a secure cryptosystem (or any other security mechanism) without a thorough understanding of how it might be attacked and without testing it for vulnerabilities.

Cipher breaking can involve a combination of cryptanalysis and simple trial and error. The first step is to determine the *method of encryption and length of the key*, which typically runs from 40 bits to 128 but may be even longer (as with 3DES). Often, these are readily determined from information attached to the ciphertext or by knowing which product was used to encrypt the data. Another name for this step is *system identification*. Once the method and key size are known, the next step is to *determine the key*. Another name for this step is *key clustering*. Over an extended period of time, finding the key can mean access to considerable information. However, if each message or file is encrypted with a different key, the code breaker must get each and every key.[26]

Key Processing Rate

For a given processing rate **R** expressed as keys per second, the length **L** of key that can be broken in **T** seconds is expressed by the formula $L = \log_2 (R \times T)$. Conversely, the time **T** to crack a key of length **L** for a given rate is $T = (2^L) / R$. If 1 billion processors or computers, each capable of processing 100 million keys per second, were put to the task of cracking a 128-bit key, it would take 10^{20} years, or about 100,000 times the estimated age of the universe. That is not imminent, however, and Moore's law could hold for another 20 years or longer.

Because every row in Table 5-4 corresponds to a factor of 10 improvement, we can expect the code-breaking capabilities of a single machine to move down a row every 3.3 years. If during this same time period there is an additional factor of 10 in parallelism, then a cooperative or parallel code-breaking effort might move down two rows during that time period. At that rate, it will still be at least 35 to 70 years before one could conceive of cracking a 128-bit key within a year's time—unless, of course, there is a revolutionary change in computing that sidesteps Moore.[27]

Brute Force Attacks

Complex modern ciphers that are combinations of transpositions and substitutions, like the DES or which use powerful mathematics like *Pretty Good Privacy* (PGP), do not succumb easily to statistical cryptanalysis. They are designed to make such cryptanalysis fail. If, as is true with DES, the keys are fixed in length, attacks may take the form of a brute force attack that simply tries all possible keys, one after another. The time that such an attack will take to recover a plaintext depends directly on the number of bits in the keys.

Consider, for example, keys of 2-bit length. Only four keys are possible: 00, 01, 10, and 11. Trying all four will not take very long, and, on average, we will only have to try half of them to find the key being used. But if 3 bits are used, there are eight keys: 000,001,010,011,100,101,110, and 111. Trying them all will take twice as long, even if only half, on average, must be tested. Four bits yields 16 keys, again doubling the length of time required to recover a key, by brute force, which was used to encipher a specific plaintext. And *in general, each additional bit doubles the length of time required for a brute force attack.* If 40-bit keys are used, there are 109,951,162,776 keys to be tested. For 56-bit keys, as used by DES, there are 72,057,594,037,927,936 keys in the key space. For 100-bit keys, there are 1,267,650,600,228,229,401,496,703,205,376 keys, one-half of which, on average, will have to be tried.

Obviously, for cryptographic algorithms not susceptible to other cryptanalytic attacks, longer keys are safer than shorter keys. This assumes that the *entropy* of a key or the chaotic value of the key is maximized. Longer keys with limited random information in the key are susceptible to attacks because of the pattern in the key itself. But how long is long enough? Hackers, attacking an enciphered message, usually have tiny budgets and must use one or a small number of computers, often scavenging time for their cracking programs. Such an approach could exhaust a 40-bit key space in a few days or perhaps a week, but would be more difficult for a 56-bit key such as is used by the DES.

Anyone with the technological competence of many undergraduate computer scientists or electrical engineers could use field-programmable gate arrays, a commercially readily available technology, to construct a special purpose computer that could exhaust a 40-bit key space in a few minutes, but which would require more than a year of continuous operation to exhaust a 56-bit key space. The cost of such a special purpose computer in 1996 was on the order of U.S. $10,000, an amount that might be available to many small businesses.

A larger corporation or a government, which could budget a few hundred thousand dollars to build a larger field-programmable gate array device, or even design and build or have built a special purpose integrated circuit, might be able to exhaust a 40-bit key space in a few seconds and a 56-bit key space in a few days.

For a U.S. $10 million investment, the 40-bit key space could be exhausted in less than a second and the 56-bit key space in a few minutes. A large government-sized investment of a few hundred million dollars in special purpose integrated circuits would permit development of a device that could exhaust a 56-bit key space in a few seconds and wouldn't even notice a 40-bit key space (see Table 5-2).[28]

In 1970, Gordon Moore, cofounder of Intel, observed that computer power (in the form of transistors on a chip) doubles approximately every eighteen months without a corresponding increase of the cost of the chip; so the cost to mount a brute force attack on a key space will decrease by a factor of 10 every five years or so.

Table 5-2 Key Strength[29]

			Time to Break	
Threat	Budget	Technology	40 Bits	56 Bits
Hacker	Tiny	Scavenged time	1 week	infeasible
Small Business	$10K	FPGA	12 min.	556 days
Corporation	$300K	FPGA or ASIC	24 sec.	19 days
Big Corp.	$10M	FPGA or ASIC	7 sec.	13 hours
Government	$300M	ASIC	.0002 sec. 1	2 sec.

FPGA = Field Programmable Gate Array

ASIC = Application Specific Integrated Circuits

Today his observation is known as Moore's Law. Consequently, while today a key size of eighty bits could not be exhausted in less than several years even with an investment of hundreds of millions of dollars, 80-bit keys cannot be expected to protect information assets for more than a few years. The effect has been a corresponding doubling of processing speed in instructions per second and memory capacity in bytes per chip, with a factor of 10 improvement about every 3.3 years and a factor of 100 improvement every decade. Using computers, longer keys can be stored and used nearly as cheaply and easily as short keys, so wise managers will opt for *key lengths of well over 128 bits*.[30]

Standard Attacks

If some of the plaintext is known, this information can be exploited in what is called a *known-plaintext* attack. Even better, if ciphertext can be acquired for plaintext supplied by the cryptanalyst and enciphered under the sought-after key, an even more powerful *chosen-plaintext* attack can be employed. In the absence of any plaintext, the cryptanalyst must resort to a *ciphertext-only* attack. The *strongest ciphers* are designed on the assumption that the adversary has known plaintext and can acquire the ciphertext for chosen plaintext. The known-plaintext assumption is not unrealistic: messages often follow standard formats, for example, beginning with certain keywords such as login. A *chosen-plaintext* attack is much harder to conduct, as it generally requires access to the encryption product so that the cryptanalyst can submit plaintext and get back the encrypted ciphertext. Further, the product must be keyed with the key of interest. A smart card with a built-in key, for example, might satisfy this property.

As previously mentioned, one way to get the key is by *brute force*, that is, trying all possible keys until the right one is found. In general, if the key length is no more than about 33 bits (about 8 billion possibilities), one can expect to find it within a day on an ordinary PC. At 56 bits (about 70 thousand trillion possibilities), one needs either a supercomputer or a large network of workstations. With the latter approach, a central machine divides up the key space and assigns small chunks to other computers on the network, for example, all keys ending in 20 0's, all keys ending in 19 0's followed by a 1, and so forth. As each machine reports back with its results, the central computer either halts the search (if the key is found) or else assigns the subordinate another part of the key space.

Dr. Dorothy Denning in her *Information Warfare and Security* textbook gives a clear look at recent public codebreaking efforts against the RSA challenges since 1998 and computerized advances against the modern cryptosystems. Table 5-3 summarizes the Public Code breaking efforts as of July 1998.[31]

In all of the above challenges, the cipher breakers were given a block of plaintext and its encrypted ciphertext. This facilitated the task, as they had to test only whether a particular key actually decrypted the given ciphertext block into the known plaintext. Outside the laboratory, cipher breakers are not always so lucky, in which case they must conduct a ciphertext-only attack. To recognize the correct key during testing, the search program must analyze the decrypted plaintext to see if it is plausible for the given context. In some cases, this is not hard. For example, if the plaintext is known to be a text file or email message, then certain bit combinations will never occur; if decrypting with a trial key generates one of these patterns, the key can be ruled out. The task is more difficult, however, if the format of the plaintext is unknown or if digital compression methods are used before encryption. It can be all but impossible if the method of encryption is unknown as well.[32]

Because the search effort doubles with each additional key bit, it is not feasible to use brute force to crack a key that is substantially longer than 56 bits. Table 5-3 shows the number of key bits that can be broken in a second, hour, day, week, month, or year for a given search rate. The rate is expressed as the $\log_{10}$ of the number of keys that can be tested per second; that is, the actual rate for a row is a 1 followed by that many 0's. For example, the first row corresponds to a search rate of 100,000 (10^5) keys per second, which could be achieved on an inexpensive PC. The entries in the table were calculated on the worst-case assumption that it was necessary to try each possible bit combination before finding the correct key. Adding 1 bit to these values gives the key lengths that can be cracked on an average-case assumption, where the key is found halfway through the key space (see Table 5-4).[33]

The EFF DES Cracker supercomputer attack, which got the rate up to almost 10^{11} keys per second, falls in the seventh row.

Table 5-3 Public Code-breaking Efforts.
All but the First were RSA Challenge Ciphers.

Date	Key Length	Time	Number of Computers	Max Rate (Keys/sec)
8/95	40	8 days	120 + 2 supercomp	0.5 million/sec
1/97	40	3.5 hours	250	27 million/sec
2/97	48	13 days	3,500	440 million/sec
6/97	56	4 months	78,000	7 billion/sec
2/98	56	39 days	~22,000	34 billion/sec
7/98	56	56 hours	1 with 1,728 ASICs	90 billion/sec

Source: Dorothy E. Denning, Information Warfare and Security, Addison Wesley, 1999.

Table 5-4 Length of Keys (bits) that Can be Broken at a Given Rate and in a Given Period of Time, Where Rate is $\log_{10}$ of the Number of Keys n that Can be Tested Per Second.

Rate (10^n)	Second	Hour	Day	Week	Month	Year
5	17	28	33	36	38	42
6	20	32	36	39	41	45
7	23	35	40	42	45	48
8	27	38	43	46	48	51
9	30	42	46	49	51	55
10	33	45	50	52	55	58
11	37	48	53	56	58	61
17	56	68	73	76	78	81
23	76	88	93	96	98	101
31	103	115	119	122	124	128

Source: Dorothy E. Denning, Information Warfare and Security, Addison Wesley, 1999.

To crack the 64-bit RSA challenge key within a year, the EFF DES Cracker would have to run 10 times faster than at present. That could be done, say, using 270 boards instead of 27. To crack it within a week, however, would require a 1,000-fold speedup. That would take 27,000 boards. To crack a 90-bit key within a year would require a total horsepower of 1020 keys per second. That would correspond to 1 billion computers each testing 100 billion keys per second, that is, 1 billion DES Crackers. Cracking a 128-bit key in a year is even worse, demanding, say, 1 trillion computers (more than 100 computers for every person on the globe), each with a speed of 1 billion trillion keys per second.

That 128-bit keys are totally impossible to crack is not surprising. After all, there are more than 3×10^{38} keys to try. That's more keys than any human can possibly contemplate. If they were all written down on sheets of paper, say 30 keys per page, there would be a stack of paper going to the moon and back more than a trillion trillion times![34]

Advanced Attacks

Although key length is significant to the strength of an encryption system, it is not the only factor; *entropy* is a consideration. Also, weaknesses in design can allow key cracking that would be impossible by brute force. Two types of attack that have received considerable attention in the research community are *differential* and *linear cryptanalysis*. Differential cryptanalysis takes pairs of plaintext whose XORs (differences) have certain characteristics. These differences are exploited in such a manner that the key can be teased out without trying all combinations. Getting the key is not easy, however, and the method works only against certain ciphers. It has been used successfully to break several other ciphers in laboratory experiments.

Linear cryptanalysis works by finding simple approximations of the complex function in each round of a cipher such as DES. It was invented in 1993 by Mitsuru

Matsui, who recovered a DES key in 50 days using 12 Hewlett-Packard HP9735 workstations. The attack requires about 10 trillion blocks of known plaintext, however, so it does not pose a practical threat to DES.

Paul Kocher has investigated unconventional attacks that could exploit vulnerabilities in the implementations of ciphers. In 1995, he showed that under suitable conditions, a key could be cracked by observing the time it took to decrypt messages with that key. Then in 1998, he announced a new class of attacks, called *differential power analysis,* which could be deployed against hardware devices. By monitoring the power consumption of a cryptographic device, he could obtain information that was correlated with the key. He said he had implemented the attack against a large number of smart cards and found them all vulnerable.

Researchers at Bellcore showed that cryptosystems implemented on smart cards and other tamperproof tokens were potentially vulnerable to *hardware fault attacks* if the attacker could get access to the token and induce certain types of errors. These hardware attacks show that even if an encryption algorithm is essentially unbreakable, the environment in which it is used may have weaknesses. *Many commercial software products have encryption systems that are readily cracked, not because the math is bad or the keys short, but because of other vulnerabilities.*[35]

Two Limits of Encryption

Encryption is a powerful method for protecting data in transit or stored on media that are vulnerable to snooping or seizure. Nevertheless, it has two fundamental limitations. *First, it cannot protect data while they are being processed on a computer.* This is because data must be in the clear in order to be manipulated. Although it is possible to design cryptosystems that allow operations to be performed on ciphertext, such systems will either be weak or have limited functionality. The consequence of processing data in the clear is that if an intruder can gain access to the computer, the intruder may be able to pick up sensitive data, as it is being typed in or processed. One way this might be done is with a keyboard sniffer program, such as demonstrated by First Virtual Holdings in January 1996. Their program monitored keystrokes for credit card numbers. When the program detected that a complete number had been typed, it played sinister music and popped up a window showing the card number and type. In principle, the program could have harvested the numbers and sent them over the Internet to some unknown party. Fraud, however, was not First Virtual's objective. They wanted to show that sending card numbers in encrypted form over the network was not enough. Security must begin at the keyboard. If the encryption itself is carried out on the computer instead of on a separate smart card or other device, the intruder may even be able to pick up encryption keys while they are being used.

A second limitation of encryption is that it can be no better than the weakest link. Even if the mathematics is excellent, the implementation could be flawed or the key management system weak. In January 1998, Peter Gutmann, a security expert in New Zealand, circulated a paper on the Internet explaining how, under certain conditions, private encryption keys could be stolen from the hard disks of machines running Microsoft's Internet software, including Internet Explorer and the Internet Information Service. The attacks exploited weaknesses in the file formats used to store keys in encrypted form on disk and in a function CryptExportKey, which basically hands over the key to any program asking for it. Some of the attacks depended on badly chosen passwords or unsafe configuration settings, which users can control. Key length was less of a factor, though the 40-bit keys frequently used could be cracked by brute force. An adversary may successfully get keys and other cryptographic materials using non-technical means such as social engineering. Humans are generally the weakest link.[36]

Block versus Stream Ciphers

Transposition ciphers act, by their very nature, on *block*s of characters or bits, scrambling the natural order in which the characters or bits occur in some patterned way to produce the ciphertext. Substitution ciphers, at least in the simple form, act on the plaintext one character or bit at a time. When enciphering or deciphering messages was essentially a pen-and-paper drill, the distinction was not very important. However, the ability to encipher character-by-character turned out to be extremely useful for encipherment of communications when teletype machines automated telegraphy. To make such machines work, the Morse code, which had served so well when telegraph operators provided long-distance communications, was replaced by a coding scheme that used a fixed sequence of bits to represent each letter or number, because machines handled bits with ease. Using a *stream cipher*, the characters could be enciphered as they were typed into the teletype and transmitted immediately. At the receiving end, the arriving ciphertext could be deciphered character-by-character as they came in without waiting for a block or the entire message to arrive.

With the advent of computer-based communications systems, some of the advantages of stream ciphers disappeared. Computers work easily with blocks of bits, especially if the blocks are multiples of the byte size or word length used by the computer. Hence, today most widely used ciphers are block ciphers. Much of the modern research has been on improving block ciphers for use in commercial systems. However, in wireless systems, stream ciphers have been used to enhance speed and permit synchronization of both data and voice of broadband channels. Later in this chapter, we introduce the HORNET™ cipher used in wireless embedded security chips for telephones. Although relatively a new entry into the cryptographic playground, it has excellent characteristics for secure communication.

Cryptographic systems provide secrecy by use of transformations. At the sending site the plaintext message, under control of the enciphering key, is transformed into the ciphertext that is supposed to be unintelligible to any opponent without the secret deciphering key. At the legitimate receiver the ciphertext, under control of the secret deciphering key, is retransformed into the original plaintext. Cryptographic systems are commonly classified into block and stream ciphers.

Block ciphers divide the plaintext into blocks, usually of fixed size, and the cryptosystem operates on each block independently. Block ciphers are therefore simple substitution ciphers and must have large alphabets to prevent successful cryptanalysis by exhaustive search.

Professor Rainer A. Rueppel distinguished himself by elucidating many of the important design principles of stream ciphers.[37] His principles are applicable to wireless crypto-security designs. Stream ciphers divide the plaintext into characters and encipher each character with a *time-varying function* whose time-dependency is governed by the *internal state* of the stream cipher. After each character that is enciphered, the device changes state according to some rule. Therefore two occurrences of the same plaintext-character will usually not result in the same ciphertext character.

In this way, block and stream ciphers may be identified as cryptographic systems having one or more than one internal state, respectively. This classification may be seen in analogy to error correcting codes, which are subdivided into block, and convolutional codes.

Stream Cipher Design Considerations

For practical reasons (such as delay and ease of processing which are characteristics in the wireless arena) the semiinfinite message stream is usually subdivided into fixed size entities which are enciphered serially. There are two fundamentally different approaches to how sensible enciphering could be accomplished. When the enciphering transformation operates on each such message entity independently, then one speaks of a *block cipher*. Thus block ciphers are simple substitution ciphers and must have necessarily large alphabets to prevent cryptanalysis by brute force. This is why the suggestive name block is used to designate the size of a message entity. *Stream ciphers*, in contrast, encipher each message entity with a time-varying function whose time dependency is governed by the internal state of the stream cipher. Since, for this enciphering principle, the message entities are not required to be large, one speaks of character to designate the size of a message entity. After each character is enciphered the stream cipher changes state according to some rule. Therefore two occurrences of the same plaintext character usually do not result in the same ciphertext character. To obtain a clear distinction between block and stream ciphers, the criterion of memory can be used (see Figure 5-11).

A block cipher then specifies a memoryless device which transforms a message block $m = [m_1, --, m_J]$ under control of a key K into a ciphertext block $c = [c_1, \ldots, c_n]$ where the message text alphabet and the ciphertext alphabet usually are identical. A stream cipher specifies a device with internal memory that transforms the ith digit m_i of the message stream into the ith digit c_i of the ciphertext stream by means of a function which depends on both the secret key K and the internal state of the stream cipher at time j.

For a fixed key K, the block cipher will transform identical message blocks into identical ciphertext blocks. This allows the active wiretapper to insert, delete or

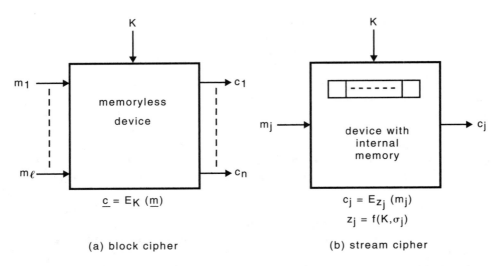

$$\underline{c} = E_K(\underline{m})$$

(a) block cipher

$$c_j = E_{z_j}(m_j)$$
$$z_j = f(K, \sigma_j)$$

(b) stream cipher

5-11 Two effects of memory on encipherment. (Source: Rainer A. Rueppel, Analysis and Design of Stream Ciphers, Springer-Verlag, 1986.)

replay previously recorded ciphertext blocks unless some additional protocol is employed that controls the sequence of message blocks. Likewise, block enciphering allows the passive wiretapper to search through the ciphertext for matches. This is a serious threat when fixed information entities (such as salary records) are treated as plaintext blocks.

Since the stream cipher encrypts each character under a time varying function of the key, it prevents deletion, insertion or replay of ciphertext, as well as ciphertext searching, one may say that a stream cipher is inherently more secure than a block cipher because of the additional dimension offered by the use of memory. But note that a block cipher may always be augmented into a stream cipher by associating memory to it. Then the block cipher is used as a nonlinear function.

Stream ciphers come in two brands: *synchronous* and *self-synchronizing*. In *synchronous stream ciphers*, the next state depends only on the previous state and not on the input, so that the progression of states is independent of the sequence of characters received. Such an enciphering is memoryless, but time varying. The output corresponding to a particular input depends only on the characters before it or after it. Consequently, the enciphering transformation is *memory less, but time varying*. The device itself is not without memory, it needs internal memory to generate the necessary state sequence. It is natural therefore, in a synchronous stream cipher, to separate the enciphering transformation from the generating process of the time-varying parameter controlling the enciphering transformation.

The sequence $z' = z_0, z_1, \ldots,$ which controls the enciphering, is called the key stream or running key. The deterministic machine, which produces the key stream from the actual key K and the internal state is called the running key generator. Whenever the key K and the internal state are identical at the sender and receiver, the running keys are also identical, and deciphering is performed. This means that the running key generators at the sending and receiving sites are *synchronized*. Whenever the running key generators lose synchronism, deciphering becomes impossible and *means must be provided to reestablish synchronization.*

In the *self-synchronizing* stream cipher, the deciphering transformation has finite memory with respect to the influence of past characters or bits so that an erroneous or lost ciphertext character causes only a fixed number of errors in the deciphered plaintext, after which the correct plaintext is produced.[38]

The Stream Cipher Synchronization Problem

Synchronous stream ciphers require perfect synchronism between the encrypting and the decrypting device. When digits are lost, added, or replayed during transmission, the keystream produced at the receiving site will be added with some offset to the cipher-stream, which effectively encrypts the cipher-stream a second time. To reestablish synchronism at the receiver usually involves searching over all possible offsets that the keystream could have experienced, or notifying the sender that the cryptosystem should be reinitialized. In both cases, large portions of the transmitted data may be lost. This difficulty of reestablishing synchronization is considered to be major disadvantage of synchronous stream ciphers.

But this apparently weak point is simultaneously responsible for the frustration of almost all active attacks. Injection, deletion or replay of ciphertext cause immediate loss of synchronization. The only active attack left to the wiretapper is selectively to alter digits in the ciphertext, which corresponds to simulating worse channel conditions than there actually are. Infrequent active wiretapping of this sort will be corrected by the error control system, and frequent changes of ciphertext digits will cause the error control system to reject the received message, and to notify the receiver. Consequently, the synchronization problem of synchronous stream ciphers is one reason for their cryptographically appealing properties. There is a possibility of tradeoff between security and synchronization difficulty. When each key stream digit is derived from a fixed number of preceding ciphertext digits, then the stream cipher becomes self-synchronizing.

The deciphering transformation has finite memory with respect to the influence of past digits so that an erroneous or lost ciphertext digit only propagates forward for M digits. The receiver resynchronizes automatically after M consecutive correct ciphertext digits have been received. Each key digit is functionally dependent on the initial state of the running key generator and on all the preceding ciphertext digits. This recursive procedure of generating the key stream diffuses the statistical properties of the plaintext over the ciphertext.

As a consequence, self-synchronizing stream ciphers are nonperiodic if the message stream is nonperiodic. Self-synchronizing stream ciphers protect against ciphertext searcher, but because of their self-synchronizing property they do not protect against injections, deletions, and replay of ciphertext. In general, self-synchronizing stream ciphers offer a lower level of security since arguments and function values of the key stream generating process are known to the cryptanalyst.

The real disadvantage of self-synchronizing stream ciphers, however, is their limited analyzability because of the dependence of the key stream on the message stream.

When a communications link employs some means for packet or frame synchronization (as is often the case in wireless digital communications), then the synchronous stream cipher may be supplied with some sort of self-synchronizing property without decreasing the security level. Let $\delta_0(i)$ be the initial state of the stream cipher at the beginning of frame i. When the initial state $\delta_0(i + 1)$ of the stream cipher at the beginning of frame i + 1 is computed by some deterministic function g from $\delta_0(i)$, that is, $\delta_0(i + 1) = G(\delta_0(i + 1))$ then one may say that the stream cipher has the frame-self-synchronizing feature.[39]

Non-Keyed Message Digests

Public-key encryption and decryption methods are in general an order of magnitude or more slower compared to secret key encryption methods like DES or Rijndael. Message digests were invented to make private key signing and hence authentication more efficient.

A message digest is used as a proxy for a message; it is a shorter, redundant representation of the message. Redundant refers to the repetition of a message to identify whether the message was modified during transmission. Communication redundancies verify that the sent message was correctly received. Message digests add redundant assurances to digital data communications. And because a message digest is usually much smaller than the underlying message, it's faster to sign (private-key encrypt) and verify (public-key decrypt) a message digest than a lengthy message.[40]

A message digest is also analogous to a fingerprint. You can authenticate a person's identity by verifying facial characteristics, name, height, weight, age, knowledge of the mother's maiden name, and so on. Similarly, a fingerprint is also a small piece of data that authenticates identity. Because fingerprints and message digests are used as unique proxies for a much larger whole, message digests are also known as digital fingerprints, or message fingerprints, or cryptographic hashes, or cryptographic checksums. Cryptographic hashes are not the same as the hashes used in computer programming. Cryptographic hashes, although similar, add important security features. We use these terms interchangeably as well as using the more abbreviated terms digest and hash.

Message digest methods super-compress messages so that encryption and decryption operate on less data and, therefore, take less time. *Secure Hash Algorithm* (SHA-1), the message digest algorithm currently recommended by government and private cryptographers, will compress all of the program Microsoft Office to about the same amount of disk space occupied by 20 x's: XXXXXXXXXXXXXXXXXXXX. SHA-1 is such an important algorithm that we have devoted an Appendix to it. SHA-1 has some important features and is very well studied. Suffice it to say that it is possibly the best cryptographic hash algorithm in the world.[41]

Although message digests are similar to popular file compression programs such as PKZip, WinZip, and gzip, a major difference is that popular compression programs are made to compress and restore files. Message digest programs can't and don't restore their compressed messages; they only compress messages. Just as a person (holistically) can't be reduced to a fingerprint, the original file cannot be reconstructed from the message digest.

Message digests come in two forms: keyed and non-keyed. Non-keyed message digests are made without a secret key and are called *message integrity codes* (MICs) or *modification detection codes* (MDCs). MIC is more commonly used, but MDC seems to be a more straightforward description of how a non-keyed message digest works. Most public-key digital signatures use non-keyed message digests.

Keyed message digests, known as *message authentication codes* (MACs), combine a message and a secret key. MACs require the sender and receiver to share a secret key. The term hash function is usually reserved for non-keyed message digests; it is sometimes used to refer to both keyed and non-keyed digest functions. Keyed does not mean that the message digest is signed (private-key encrypted). Instead, it means that the digest is made with a secret key.[42]

SHA

NIST, along with NSA, designed the *Secure Hash Algorithm* (SHA) for use with the *Digital Signature Standard* (DSS). The standard is the *Secure Hash Standard* (SHS); SHA is the algorithm used in the standard.[43] SHA produces a 160-bit hash, longer than MD5 (which principles it was based on but produces a 128-bit digest), a design by Professor Ronald L. Rivest of MIT. When a message of any length, 2^{64} bits is input, SHA produces a 160-bit output called a message digest. The message digest is fed to the DSA that computes a unique signature for the message. Signing the message digest is more efficient signing the entire message. SHA is considered secure because it is designed to be computationally infeasible to recover a message corresponding to a given message digest or to find two different messages that hash to the same message digest value. Any change to a message in transit, will with a high probability result in a different message digest, and the signature will fail to verify.[44]

There are no known cryptographic attacks against SHA. Because it produces a 160-bit hash, it is more resistant to brute force attacks (including birthday attacks).[45] SHA has survived cryptanalysis and comes highly recommended by the cryptographic community.[46] On May 30, 2001, NIST released for public comment Draft FIPS 180-2 for SHA producing 256-bit, 384-bit, and 512-bit digests.[47]

SHA-1 in the Encryption Mode

SHA was not designed to be used for encryption. However, the compression function can be used for encryption. Each of the 80 steps of SHA-1 (the improved version of SHA), divided into four rounds each of 20 steps, are invertible in the five variables— A, B, C, D, and E—used for compression. If one inserts a secret key in the message and a plaintext as the initial value, one gets an invertible function from the compression function by simply skipping the last forward addition with the input. This encryption mode was considered in a paper presented at RSA 2001 by Helena Handschuh, Lars R. Knudsen (designer of the AES runner-up candidate Serpent) and Matthew J. Robshaw.[48] It was tested on a *block cipher* known as SHACAL by Helena Handschuh.

The two best-known attacks on systems similar to SHA are linear cryptanalysis and differential cryptanalysis. A wide range of variants of the two attacks have been proposed in the literature but the basic principles are the same. Linear cryptanalysis attempts to identify a series of linear approximations Ai to the different operational components in a block cipher, be they the S-boxes, integer addition, Boolean operations, or whatever. The linear approximations are then combined to provide the approximation for the greater proportion of the encryption routine.[49]

Differential cryptanalysis is a powerful chosen plaintext attack that can often be converted into a known plaintext attack. The basic tool of the attack is the ciphertext pair, which is a pair of ciphertexts whose plaintexts have particular differences. The two plaintexts can be chosen at random, as long as they satisfy a certain difference condition, and the cryptanalyst does not have to know these values.[50] What makes differential cryptanalysis difficult on SHA is first, the use of both exclusiveors and modular additions, and second, the compression functions.[51]

It was concluded that neither differential nor linear cryptanalysis could be applied successfully in practice to SHA-1. Breaking SHA-1 in the encryption mode required either an unrealistic amount of computational time and known/chosen texts or a major breakthrough in cryptanalysis. The linear cryptanalytic attack on SHA-1 as an encryption function would require at least 2^{80} known plaintexts and that a differential attack would require at least 2^{116} chosen plaintexts.[52]

This was not the only proof of SHA-1 being used effectively in the encryption mode. On April 9, 2001, the same day that the Handschuh paper was presented at RSA 2001 in San Francisco, California, a provisional patent was filed with the U.S. Patent Office by the Wireless Encryption Division of TeleHubLink, Corporation [OTC BB:THLC] to protect its HORNET™ *stream cipher* invention for cryptosecurity in wireless and telecommunications devices.[53] HORNET™ is also based on SHA-1 in the encryption mode for a lean and mean stream cipher designed by both the authors of this book over a two-year period, in conjunction with the retired Chief Cryptographer and Cryptanalyst for NSA and the Systems Security Architect-Missile Division for Mitre Corporation.[54] HORNET™ was presented at RSA 2001 in a paper reporting on advances in wireless encryption technology.[55]

HORNET™

Many stream ciphers are secure and used in commercial and military service. And then again some are not secure or some are not used in either commercial or military applications or both. Only a few seem to have found their way into wireless applications and this is because of speed, cost, and memory limitations. Part of the reason for failure in the wireless arena was the secrecy by obscurity principle that did not provide an avenue of review by cryptographic professionals. The successful cryptanalysis of the GSM encryption system A5 is a case in point.[56] The recent AES discovery efforts were successful because of disclosure and peer review. It is not easy to make a secure cipher. It takes a long time to perform the due diligence studies required. The work doesn't stop when it appears to be secure. Just because the design team can't break it, doesn't mean some smarter mind(s) can't. This is why ciphers are investigated for years before they are accepted by the cryptographic community. Rather than present material that is fully[57] covered in many of the popular cryptography textbooks, we choose to address a new cipher based on a tested cryptographic algorithm, SHA-1, the secure hashing algorithm (revised) used in an encryption mode (supra). SHA-1 is clearly the most widely accepted and field-tested hashing algorithm in the world.

In the spirit of full disclosure and open peer review, we present details of the patented, technically reviewed (and continuing to be reviewed by independent parties), but relatively untested HORNET™ stream cipher that is being deployed in ASICs for wireless telephones to provide unclassified but low-cost security for users. HORNET™ has several unique features, not the least of which is the key generation mechanism using SHA-1 as a fundamental core. SHA-1, the de facto hash standard, is used in some new ways cryptographically:

- SHA fed by linear feedback shift register that preserves key entropy
- Initial state of shift register filled with TRNG with entropy accumulation
- Robust protection if TRNG degrades over time
- Unknown fill in initial contents of LFSR dynamically changes for each use of SHA
- Output of SHA is fed back as part of next input to increase degree of mathematical complexity
- Feed forward feature adds unknown SHA input to SHA output after feedback, but prior to use as additive key
- Both unknown key from LFSR as well as SHA output are hidden even if additive key is totally recovered from ciphertext, thus attacker never sees either the input or the output of SHA, let alone matched inputs and outputs using a constant key.
- Additive key stream is guaranteed to be on a long cycle (2^{160-1})

Refer to Figures 5-12 through 5-14 for a more detailed description of the HORNET™ stream cipher for wireless telecommunications ASICs. There are six fundamental units in HORNET™. They are:

- True random number generator on the chip
- 160-bit entropy accumulator
- Initializing key scheduler
- Sync generator
- Random pad generator
- DEK generator, key scheduler
- Encrypted data structure

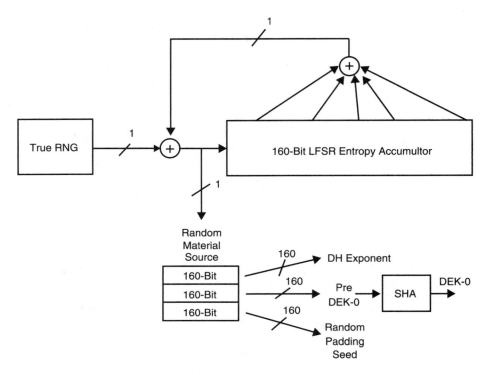

5-12 160-Bit entropy accumulator for HORNET™ cipher.

Entropy Accumulator Description

Random bits are collected from a *system on a chip* (SOC) *True Random Number Generator* (TRNG). The number of bits to be collected is at least 320 bits to start. The primitive for the 160-bit LFSR will be as previously specified $x^{160} + x^5 + x^3 + x^2 + 1 = 0$.

- Once a sufficient number of bits are collected from the TRNG, 160 bits are generated by the LFSR to be used as the *Diffie-Hellman* (DH) exponent.
- A second set of 160 bits is obtained by generating one additional LFSR bit and right-shift appending at the MSB of the first 160 bits, to be used as the preDEK-0. This is then SHA'd to obtain DEK-0. (DEK is the *Data Encryption Key*.)
- A third set of 160 bits is similarly obtained by generating one more LFSR bit, and right-shift appending at the MSB of the second 160-bit set, to be used as the random padding seed.

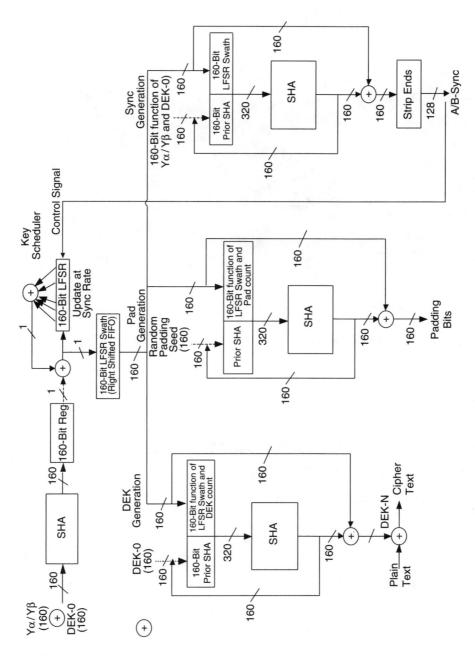

5-13 Sync, Pad, and DEK Generation for HORNET™ cipher.

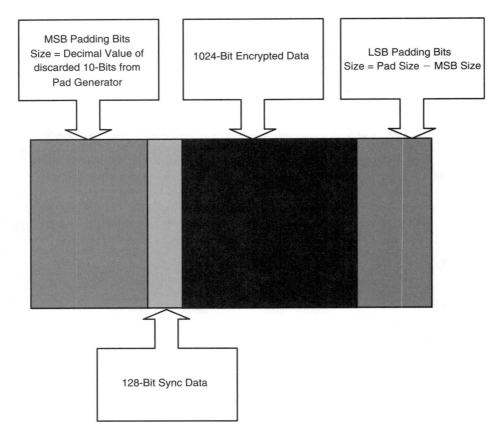

5-14 Encrypted data block from HORNET™ Chip.

Sync, Pad, and Data Encryption Key (DEK) Generation

Generation of these three components are tentatively integrated into a common framework with three congruent components.

Initializing Key Scheduler DEK-0 is XOR'ed with a 160-bit function of $Y\alpha$ (User A) or $Y\beta$ (User B) and SHA'd before inputting (one bit at a time) to a 160 bit LFSR. The entire 160-bit output of the SHA is input to the LFSR as a random forcing function to both initialize the state of the LFSR and to produce the initial 160-bit key from the key scheduler, which is stored in the right-shifting FIFO register. The reason for SHA'ing the DEK-0 function is to mitigate correlation attacks between the use of DEK-0 as the time varying key and as an initialization vector for the DEK engine. Note also DEK-0 is XOR'ed with $Y\alpha$ or $Y\beta$ to ensure that the transmit and receive channels will operate with different key streams.

Sync Generator   The left 160-bit register of the Sync generator is initiated (first time only) with a 160 bit function of Yα (or Yβ and DEK-0 [Note that Yα is for User A; likewise Yβ for User B]. The right 160-bit register of the Sync Generator reads in the contents of the 160-bit LFSR swath from the right-shifted FIFO register. The left and right 160-bit registers are then concatenated to form a 320-bit vector that is operated on by the SHA function. The output of the SHA is stored as the next entry for the left 160-bit register, and is also XOR'ed with the contents of the right 160-bit register, which is stripped (16 bits at each end) to form the 128 bit A-Sync. A new Sync is generated in anticipation of each new Sync cycle. Separate Sync generators are required for the Transmit and Receive Engines.

Random Pad Generator   The left 160-bit register of the Pad generator is initiated (first time only) with the Random Pad Seed (160 bits). The right 160-bit register of the Pad Generator reads in the contents of the 160-bit LFSR swath from the right-shifted FIFO register once per Sync cycle. The left and right 160-bit registers are then concatenated to form a 320-bit vector that is operated on by the SHA function. The output of the SHA is stored as the next entry for the left 160-bit register, and is also XOR'ed with the contents of the right 160-bit register to produce naked padding bits. Additional padding bits needed within the Sync cycle are generated by repeating the process, but modifying the right 160-bit register as a function of the pad iteration count. The Pad generator is only required for the Transmit Engine.

DEK Generator   The left 160-bit register of the DEK generator is initiated (first time only) with DEK-0 (160 bit). The right 160-bit register of the Pad Generator reads in the contents of the 160-bit LFSR swath from the right-shifted FIFO register once per Sync cycle. The left and right 160-bit registers are then concatenated to form a 320-bit vector that is operated on by the SHA function. The output of the SHA is stored as the next entry for the left 160-bit register, and is also XOR'ed with the contents of the right 160-bit register to produce new DEK bits (160 at a time). Additional DEK bits needed within the Sync cycle are generated by repeating the process, but modifying the right 160-bit register as a function of the DEK iteration count. Separate Sync generators are required for the Transmit and Receive Engines.

Key Scheduler   A new LFSR bit is generated at the Sync rate using the Sync Engine as a control source. (Note: This is done so that subsequent Sync sequences can be generated and anticipated by both Users regardless of the number of Pad or DEK iterations per cycle) The new bit is right shift appended to the MSB of the 160-bit FIFO, and the full contents of the 160-bit FIFO is copied to each of the right 160-bit Sync, Pad, and DEK generators. This way we get a new 160-bit secret/clock value on each Sync cycle while only having to generate one LFSR bit at a time. Note that the Random Pad generator and DEK generators may use the same right 160-bit basis more than once, although it's generally modified as a function of the respective iteration count. This is done to mitigate SHA attacks based on the use of a stationary key. However, if the number of DEK or Pad iterations per Sync cycle is small, then varying the right 160-bit registers between Sync cycles may not be necessary.

Encrypted Data Structure   The encrypted data structure appears as shown in Figure 5-3 for a single Sync cycle. Each Sync cycle is characterized by the same number of bits—namely a predetermined (by Host) number of Padding bits, which envelope 128-Sync bits that are immediately followed by 1024 Cipher text bits. The only variation in bit length from cycle to cycle is in the allocation of Fore (MSB) and Aft (LSB) Padding bits; however, the total cycle length is nominally maintained constant so as to operate at a constant data rate.

Pad Bits   For each cycle, a sufficient number of Padding bits are generated (in chunks of 160 bits) to provide the required number of random Pad bits per Sync cycle, along with additional Pad bits that are discarded, but whose decimal value is used to randomly determine the length of the MSB Pad sequence at each Sync cycle. Nominally the first several Pad Generator bits are used for this purpose. By varying the length of the MSB-LSB bit sequences at each Sync cycle, we are able to mitigate substitution attacks, which are a known vulnerability of conventional stream ciphers. Note that the Pad bits carry no information and do not need to be known by the receiver.

Pad Bits   For each cycle a sufficient number of Padding bits are generated (in chunks of 160 bits) to provide the required number of random Pad bits per Sync cycle, along with additional Pad bits that are discarded, but whose decimal value is used to randomly determine the length of the MSB Pad sequence at each Sync cycle. Nominally the first several Pad Generator bits are used for this purpose. By varying the length of the MSB-LSB bit sequences at each Sync cycle, we are able to mitigate substitution attacks, which are a known vulnerability of conventional stream ciphers. Note that the Pad bits carry no information and do not need to be known by the receiver.

Sync Bits   A new Sync sequence is generated for each Sync cycle by both transmitter and receiver (in each direction for full duplex operation). Detection of the Sync sequence by the intended receiver serves to signal the presence of follow-on cipher text, and lets the receiver know that it is still in cipher synchronous communication when combined with a watchdog timer function. The Sync changes in a predictable, pseudo-random manner from cycle to cycle based on a secret key that is only known by sender and intended recipient.

DEK Bits: Up to seven *Data Encryption Key* (DEK) 160-bit sequences (1120 bits) are generated at each Sync cycle (by Transmitter and Receiver) to provide the 1024 bits of key material required for encrypting plain text in chunks of 1024 bits. The last 96 bits are routinely discarded, although they can also be buffered and used so long as there is agreement between sender and receiver as to which DEK bits shall be used. Note that agreement by both parties as to the structure of the additive key sequence is necessary to ensure proper decryption.[58]

HORNET™ sports some interesting features for wireless security:

- Embedded Cryptography independent of host CPU
- A *true RNG* (TRNG) for generation of keys used in a session
- An *Entropy Accumulator* (EA) protecting against failures in TRNG
- A *Key Exchange Algorithm* (KEA) establishing a common shared secret
- A *Key Digest Algorithm* (KED) to encrypt/send the initial DEK
- A meta-crypto logic for generating a sequence of DEK's (DEKG)
- A similar meta-crypto logic for generating *periodic sync patterns (*PSP)
- A *stream cipher mode* (SCM) of operation to expand the DEK into running additive key
- An *additive encrypting rule* (AER) combining key and plaintext using the XOR operation to produce running cipher
- A method for periodically inserting a synchronization pattern and looking for it at the receiving end
- A method for *padding* (PAD) and randomly inserting the padding within the cipher and synchronization frames
- A method to vary the position of the underlying plaintext within the frame[59]

A fundamental issue with in every cryptosystem is the source of random numbers, the TRNG. HORNET™ TRNG on the ASIC chip has two nice features:

- Op-amp based chaotic processor that behaves in an unstable manner
- Resistance and capacitance values extracted from manufacturing technology specifics (interlayer distances, Interlayer capacitive loads, threshold voltage values, and so on)[60]

HORNET™ is actually a *family* of cryptographic primitives for FPGA's and ASICs used in wireless applications. HORNET™ options include an ECC option with 521-bit key and Rijndael at 128, 192 and 256 key lengths. Later in this chapter, ECC is covered and Rijndael is reviewed in the context of the AES finalist's published performance tests at two CHES2000 and RSA2001. *Only time will tell whether HORNET™ survives in Internet minutes, hours, or even years and is accepted by the global cryptographic community as a viable wireless security solution.* At the very least, it sports some interesting "clean and mean" principles—most important of which is using SHA-1 in an encryption mode.

Advanced Encryption Standard

In 1998, researchers from 12 different countries submitted 15 candidates for the *Advanced Encryption Standard* (AES)—the new enciphering method (and successor to DES/3DES) that was adopted by the federal government. Since 1998, cryptographers have tried to find ways to attack the different AES enciphering methods, looking for weaknesses that would compromise the encrypted information. On August 9, 1999, NIST narrowed the field of contenders from 15 candidates to 5.

The AES is a public algorithm designed to protect sensitive government information well into the next century. It will replace the aging Data Encryption Standard, which NIST adopted in 1977 as a Federal Information Processing Standard used by federal agencies to encrypt information. DES and 3DES are used widely in the private sector as well, especially in the financial services industry.

NIST's Information Technology Laboratory chose the following five contenders as finalists for the AES:

- **MARS** Developed by International Business Machines Corp. of Armonk, N.Y.
- **RC6** Developed by RSA Laboratories of Bedford, Mass.
- **Rijndael** Developed by Joan Daemen and Vincent Rijmen of Belgium
- **Serpent** Developed by Ross Anderson, Eli Biham,, and Lars Knudsen of the United Kingdom, Israel, and Norway respectively
- **Twofish** Developed by Bruce Schneier, John Kelsey, Doug Whiting, David Wagner, Chris Hall, and Niels Ferguson

No significant security vulnerabilities were found for the five finalists during the initial analysis of the algorithms, and each candidate offered technology that is potentially superior for the protection of sensitive information well into the 21st century.

NIST requested proposals for the AES on September 12, 1997. Each of the candidate algorithms supports cryptographic key sizes of 128, 192 and 256 bits. At a 128-bit key size, there are approximately 340,000,000,000,000,000,000,000,000,000,000,000,000 (340 followed by 36 0's) possible keys.

The global cryptographic community has been helping NIST in the AES development process by studying the candidates. NIST used feedback from these analyses and its own assessments to select the finalists. The studies evaluated security and how fast the algorithms could encrypt and decrypt information. The algorithms were tested on everything from large computers to smart cards.

During the evaluation process NIST considered all comments, papers, verbal comments at conferences, reports and proposed modifications, and its own test data. Each candidate algorithm was discussed relative to the announced evaluation criteria and other pertinent criteria suggested during the public analysis. In the author's opinion, the NIST evaluation process was not only fair but also extremely thorough. The winner was announced October 2, 2000: the *Rijndael Algorithm*.

Rijndael is a block cipher, designed by Joan Daemen and Vincent Rijman. The cipher has a variable block length and key length. It is currently specified how to use keys with a length of 128, 192, or 256 bits to encrypt blocks with a length of 128, 192, or 256 bits (all nine combinations are possible). Both key length and block length can be extended in multiples of 32 bits. As was demonstrated at CHES 2000 in Worchester, MA, Rijndael can be implemented efficiently on a wide range of processors and platforms. The design of Rijndael was influenced by the design of the block cipher Square. Detailed reports on the process and winner—*Rijndael* are available on the AES Web site;[61] at the Rijndael authors' Web site with various optimized code implementations[62] and with substantial details and pictures from cryptographer John Savard's site.[63]

Key Management-Generation and Distribution of Keys

The Data Encryption Standard is an example of a symmetric cipher. That is, both the sender and the recipient of enciphered messages must have the same key to make the cipher work. Since the security of the cipher depends entirely, as covered above on the key, it is vital that the key to be used is known only to the two parties using the cipher. If a third party can discover the key, either by stealing it or by crypt-analysis, the cipher can no longer guarantee privacy and authenticity.

The processes used to generate symmetric keys in a way that they cannot be stolen at their source to transmit them securely to all intended users of the cipher and to store them securely until they are needed to encipher or decipher messages are together called key management. Such schema may be as simple as using the telephone to exchange keys for e-mail messages that have been encrypted using a symmetric cipher and transmitted via the Internet, or as complex as highly secure key generation facilities coupled with trusted couriers to distribute the keys to secure storage facilities available to the users.

Various steps in the key management processes may be automated. If large numbers of keys are needed, as will certainly be the case when there are large numbers of users, computers may be used to generate the keys. Obviously, the security of the keys depends upon the security of the facility and computer system being used for key generation. Transfer of the keys to secure storage facilities available to the users may be made by specially designed portable computers carried by trusted couriers. And, of course, the computer systems used to encrypt and decrypt messages and the facilities in which they are operated must be secure.

The real key distribution problem for a large group of communicating parties is a function of the number of users: $1/2 \ (n^{2-n})$ keys are required for a group of n users. Table 5-5 illustrates examples of n users and corresponding $1/2 \ (n^{2-n})$ required keys. For example, to secure a large corporation, the post office, or the U.S. Army represents a significant secret key distribution problem.

Table 5-5 Examples of n and Corresponding $1/2 \ (n^{2-n})$ Values[64]

n	$1/2 \ (n^{2-n})$
2	1
3	3
10	45
100	4,950
1,000	499,500
10,000	49,995,000

Key distribution and management can be simplified by requiring all users to communicate via a central node. Then, instead of each potential pair of users needing a common key, requiring each of n users to have access to and securely retain n − 1 keys, each user needs only the key for communicating securely with the central node. Bob, desiring to send a message securely to Alice, sends the message securely to the central node using their pre-agreed key. The central node deciphers the message and reenciphers it using the key it shares securely with Alice, sending the message safely then to Alice. Of course, the central node still must know n − 1 keys, but each user is only responsible for the security of its own key and cannot compromise the keys that belong to other users.

It may be possible in some cases to use a key server to distribute keys to pairs of users for their use during specified periods or for specific exchanges of one or a few related messages (called sessions). In such systems, all users of the cipher are provided with keys, properly protected, with which they can communicate securely with the key server online. When Alice needs to communicate securely with Bob, she requests a session key from the key server. The key server uses its secure communications paths with Alice and Bob to provide each of them with the same session key, which is used only for that exchange of messages between Alice and Bob, and then is securely discarded. This approach has the advantage that the central server does not get involved in the decipherment and re-encipherment of messages between users.

In any case, the keys for communication with the central node or key server must be created securely and distributed and stored using trusted processes. Such processes are at best expensive and may be slow and inflexible as well. Symmetric cryptography cannot, however, be used without them.

Recapping our discussion, designing a strong cipher is not the only step toward security. Key management is an equal challenge. Key management includes the generation, distribution, storage, and recovery of secret keys.

Programs that generate keys typically use some pseudo-random process that includes readings of system state information, for example, clock time. Unless these values are cryptographically unpredictable and have sufficient variability, an adversary may be able to determine a key by observing the system. For example, shortly after a French programmer cracked the 40-bit Netscape key in eight days, Ian Goldberg and another Berkeley student, David Wagner, found that Netscape's keys could often be hacked regardless of whether they were 40 bits or 128. The problem was that the keys were generated from values that could be determined or guessed by anyone with an account on the machine, in some cases within 25 seconds. It was as though they were only 20-bits long. Netscape corrected the problem.

For some applications, users generate their own keys or participate in the key generation process. For example, they might provide a password, which is used as the key or to derive the key, or they might type random characters on the keyboard, which are used with clock time and other system state information to generate a random key. Passwords suffer the same weaknesses in this context as they do in environments where they are used to control access to computing resources.

When encryption is used to protect communications, some method is needed whereby the sender and receiver can agree on a secret key. Yet for obvious reasons, the sender cannot just send a key in the clear to the receiver. If the channel were secure there would be no need to encrypt in the first place.

One approach is to agree on a key off line by meeting in person. Often, however, this is not practical. The parties may be on opposite sides of the continent or the world.

A second approach is to ship the key via some other channel that is secure, for example, a trusted courier, with corresponding delay disadvantage. For many applications such as electronic commerce, users and programs running on their behalf need a way to establish a key immediately.

A third approach is to use a trusted key center, which shares a long-term secret key with each individual. These keys might be generated and distributed offline. Then, when one party, Alice, wants to send a message to another, Bob, Alice requests a message key from the key center, naming herself and Bob. The center generates a random message key and returns one copy encrypted under Alice's private key and one under Bob's. After decrypting her copy of the message key, Alice encrypts the message with the key and sends it to Bob along with his copy of the encrypted message key. Bob decrypts the message key with his private key and then decrypts the message.

All of the steps can be automated, so that neither party needs to be explicitly aware of the key center. Alice would just compose a message to Bob and instruct her mailer to send it encrypted. Bob's mailer might automatically decrypt the message for him or ask him if he wants it decrypted. A drawback to this approach is that it requires a trusted third party, which is a potential bottleneck and source of vulnerability. Nevertheless, the method has been used successfully in numerous application environments, including banking. The Kerberos system developed at the Massachusetts Institute of Technology under Project Athena uses this approach to provide a secure campus-wide computer network. Message traffic is encrypted with DES. A fourth approach, described next, uses public keys.[65]

Public-Key Systems—The Second Revolution

In 1976, two cryptographers at Stanford University, Whitfield Diffie and Professor Martin Hellman, invented a method whereby two parties could agree on a secret message key without the need for a third party, an offline exchange, or transmission of any secret values; independently, Ralph Merkle also came up with a solution, but his method involved substantial overhead both in computation and in transmissions. Diffie and Hellman called their scheme a public-key distribution system. This breakthrough in cryptography was announced that offering privacy and authentication without the need for cumbersome and expensive key management processes. In this new scheme, two keys were produced that were mathematically related in a way that each could be used to encipher messages that the other could decipher, a situation reminiscent of some of the weak keys for DES described above. Unlike the situation for weak DES keys, however, knowing one of the key pairs for this new scheme provided no advantage in discovering the other member of the pair.

This system provided a means whereby, if the key pair was generated securely and one of the keys was kept private, the other could be safely published for anyone to know. Then, anyone desiring to send the holder of the private member of the key pair could use the public member of the key pair to encipher a message that could only be deciphered by the holder of the private key. If Bob and Alice want to communicate privately, Bob uses Alice's public key to encipher messages to her, which Alice reads with her private key. Then Alice enciphers her replies using Bob's public key, which he deciphers with his own private key. Such schemas are called public-key encryption systems.[66]

Public-Key Distribution and Diffie-Hellman

The Diffie-Hellman method is based on the concept of a public-private key pair. The protocol begins with each party independently generating a private key. Next, they each compute a public key as a mathematical function of their respective private keys. They exchange public keys. Finally, they each compute a function of their own private key and the other person's public key. The mathematics is such that they both arrive at the same value, which is derived from both of their private keys. They use this value as the message key. For this to be secure, the public key must be computed as a one-way (irreversible) function of the private key, otherwise an eavesdropper listening in on the communications could intercept the public keys, compute one of the private keys, and then compute the message key. However, not just any one-way function can be used, as it must be suitable for generating a common message key. Diffie and Hellman's invention uses exponentiations in modular arithmetic to compute the public keys and message key.

Modular arithmetic is like standard arithmetic, except that it uses numbers only in the range 0 up to some number N called the modulus. Whenever an operation produces a result that is greater than or equal to N, N is repeatedly subtracted from the result until the value falls within the range 0 to $N - 1$ (this is the same as dividing by N and taking the remainder). For example, $5 + 4 \bmod 7 = 2$. If a result goes negative, N is added to it until it is within range. Again, for example, $2 - 5 \bmod 7 = -3 \bmod 7 = 4$. Whereas ordinary integer arithmetic can be viewed as operations over numbers placed along a straight line that stretches to infinitely large positive numbers in one direction and infinitely large negative numbers in the other, modular arithmetic can be viewed as operations that take place over a finite ring with N notches around the circumference labeled 0 through $N - 1$, with 0 following $N - 1$.

In modular arithmetic, exponentiation is a one-way function. That is, whereas it is easy to compute a number: $y = g^x \bmod N$ for some secret value x; it is much harder to compute x from y if the numbers are large enough, say several hundred digits long (we assume g and N are known). This is referred to as the discrete logarithm problem because **x** is the logarithm of **y** base **g** (mod **N**) and the numbers are finite and whole (no fractions or decimal points).

With the Diffie-Hellman method of public-key exchange, Alice and Bob establish a secret message key as follows.[67]

1. Alice generates a secret key **xa** and Bob a secret key **xb**.
2. Alice then computes a public key **ya**, which is **g** raised to the exponent **xa** modulo **p**, where **p** is a prime number (that is, it cannot be decomposed into the product of other numbers).
3. Bob computes a public key **yb** by raising **g** to the exponent **yb** modulo p.
4. They exchange their public values.
5. Alice then raises Bob's public key to her exponent modulo **p**, while Bob raises Alice's public key to his exponent modulo **p**.
6. They both get the same result, namely **g** raised to both exponent's **xa** and **xb**, which they use as the message key **K**.
7. Mathematically, $\mathbf{ya} = \mathbf{g^{xa}} \bmod \mathbf{p}$; $\mathbf{yb} = \mathbf{g^{xb}} \bmod \mathbf{p}$; $\mathbf{K} = \mathbf{ya^{xb}} \bmod \mathbf{p} = \mathbf{yb^{xa}} \bmod \mathbf{p} = \mathbf{g^{xa[xb]}} \bmod \mathbf{p}$.

To illustrate using small numbers (in practice the numbers would be several hundred digits long), suppose that $\mathbf{p} = 11$, $\mathbf{g} = 5$, Alice's private key is $\mathbf{xa} = 2$, and Bob's is $\mathbf{xb} = 3$. So:

1. Alice computes her public key from generator and private key: $ya = g^{xa} \bmod p = 5^2 \bmod 11 = (25 - 2 \times 11) = 3$
2. Bob computes his public key from generator and private key: $yb = g^{xb} \bmod p = 5^3 \bmod 11 = (125 - 11 \times 11) = 4$
3. Alice computes their shared key from Bob's public key and her private key: $K = yb^{xa} \bmod p = 4^2 \bmod 11 = (16 - 1 \times 11) = 5$
4. Bob computes their shared key from Alices's public key and his private key: $K = ya^{xb} \bmod p = 3^3 \bmod 11 = (27 - 2 \times 11) = 5$
5. We check generator property: $p = g^{xaxb} \bmod p = 5^{[2 \times 3]} \bmod 11 = 5^6 \bmod 11 = (15625 - 1420 \times 11) = 5!$

The Diffie-Hellman method and variants of it are used in several network protocols and commercial products, including the AT&T 3600 Telephone Security Device. One attractive feature is that the protocol can be used without long-term keys. All keys can be generated on the fly and discarded at the end of a conversation. Long-term public-private keys can be used but have the disadvantage of always producing the same message key between any two parties. An alternative is for the sending party to generate a key on-the-fly but use the permanent public key of the receiver. With this approach, the sender can compute the message key, encrypt the data, and transmit a single message containing the public key and ciphertext data.[68,69]

Digital Signatures

In some implementations of public-key cryptography, when the private key is used to encipher a message the public key can then be used to decipher the message. Such a scheme does not protect privacy since everyone has access to the public key and can therefore read the message. But only the holder of the private key could have written the message, provided that the private key has been securely kept.

This strong form of authentication that the message received could only have been sent by the holder of the private key corresponding to the public key used to decipher the message is sufficient to prove—in court if necessary, at least in states which have recognized such authentication as valid—that the message did indeed come from the purported sender. The sender cannot repudiate the message, making this scheme of encryption as valid as an inked signature on a paper document, and it is accordingly called a digital signature.

Note that this is not a digital representation or image of a pen and ink signature, but a message that has been encrypted using a private key and decrypted using a corresponding public key. It authenticates the document because the document could only have been so enciphered using the private key, which is deemed to have been held securely by its owner, because it assures everyone that the message could only have come from the holder of the private key. Digital Signatures are exactly the type of authentication needed to facilitate electronic commerce.[70]

Certificate Authorities

This by no means implies that public-key cryptosystems are without problems in either implementation or use. Since a cryptanalyst will have, like everyone else, access to the public key used to encipher a message, if the message is small it might be possible to use a brute force attack and try all possible messages until that one is found which produces the ciphertext observed. Of course, this disadvantage can be easily avoided by padding the message with random bits or characters unrelated to the basic message to be conveyed. Even so, public-key ciphers are particularly susceptible to attack when the cryptanalyst can choose different ciphertexts for decipherment and knows what the plaintext is for each such ciphertext. If a digital signature produced by such a cipher is the result of the inverse application of the encipherment algorithm, it is vital that different keys be used for encipherment and digital signing, if such an attack is to be avoided.

A more fundamental problem lies in the method used to authenticate the public key. If you retrieve a public key from someone's Web page, or receive it in an e-mail, how do you know that it really belongs to the person to whom you think it belongs? What has prevented Bob from sending you a public key using Alice's name so that you think it is hers? When you think you are sending a message that can only be read by Alice, you will then actually be sending a message that can only be read by Bob. You should never use a public key unless you are positive that it belongs to the person with whom you are trying to communicate.

To avoid such a problem, you must be sure that the public key you are using truly belongs to the recipient you intend to receive and read your messages. If you get the key directly from the person, you can be sure it is his or hers. If you get it from a third party, that third party must be one whom you can trust to not deceive you and to not be negligent in forwarding a public key that has not been validated as belonging to the party to whom it purports to belong. For widespread use of public keys among strangers, as will be necessary in electronic commerce, we will need on-line access to trusted third parties who will maintain databases of public keys in a form called certificates which have been placed into the database only after carefully authenticating their owners. Such trusted third parties are called *Certificate Authorities* (CAs). Of course it will be vital that the CA store the databases securely and that the certificates with their private keys be communicated securely to those who need to use them.

To see how the scheme works, assume that Alice wants to send Bob, her stock-broker, an order. She composes her message: "Buy 100 shares of Trigraph, Inc. at U.S. $5.00 per share." She uses her private key to encipher the message so that Bob can be assured that it comes, in fact, from her. She then asks her CA to send her Bob's public-key certificate. If Bob uses the same CA, his public-key certificate is taken from the database, digitally signed with the private key of the CA, and returned to Alice. Alice knows it came from the CA because it is digitally signed and she can decipher it using the public key of the Certificate Authority. Moreover, she trusts the CA to have authenticated the key when Bob delivered it to the CA, so she knows it truly belongs to Bob. Alice uses Bob's public key to encipher the buy message she has digitally signed with her private key and sends the ciphertext to Bob. If Bob uses a different CA, then cross certification between CAs would be a requirement.

Bob deciphers the message with his private key. Then Bob asks the CA for Alice's public-key certificate and uses it to decipher her digitally signed plaintext, which he now knows only she could have sent. He knows he can rely on the message and make the buy for her. If he sends her a receipt for her message, digitally signed with his own private key, she knows—and can prove—that he got the message. Dates and times can be included on both messages, if desired, or the messages can be passed through the CA who can add a time stamp digitally signed by the CA using its own private key.[71]

Using Public-Key Cryptography for Key Management

Public-key cryptography seems to solve the key management problem. Keys must still be created using secure processes because the private keys must be kept private. However, there is no need for expensive and cumbersome processes for distributing and storing keys, since the public keys do not have to be kept private for the scheme to ensure confidentiality and authentication. So why doesn't everyone just use public-key cryptography when they need cryptography?

One answer lies in the relative efficiency of the algorithms. Symmetric encryption is generally much faster than public-key encryption. The speed difference doesn't amount to much if only small messages are involved, but can be significant when messages are large. Thus, if bulk encryption is needed, to send securely large amounts of information, symmetric encryption is much to be preferred.

But the keys for symmetric encryption are relatively small. Even when the keys are chosen conservatively to prevent cryptanalytic attacks by exhausting the entire key space they are only a few hundreds or thousands of bits long. They can be enciphered easily and quickly, then, using at least some forms of public-key cryptography and, having been exchanged safely with those parties who need them, they can be used for bulk encryption using the faster symmetric routines. Technologically, this solves the problem of key management. Table 5-6 summarizes the similarities and differences between secret key and public-key cryptography.[72]

Algorithms

When we peruse the literature of cryptography, we find many pages devoted to the practical and theoretical algorithms that are the part and parcel of this science. Most of the public-key ciphers available today depend upon a special class of mathematical problems that are theoretically possible to solve but the solution of which would take so long, even using computers that finding the solution for any given message is impractical. The security of such ciphers rests on the fact that even given the public key, it is infeasible to determine the private key, and given the ciphertext it is infeasible to determine the plaintext.

Among some good texts on cryptography, cryptographic mathematics is explained thoroughly in Bruce Schneier's book *Applied Cryptography*. Elliptic curve cryptography is covered expertly in Alfred J. Menezes, Paul C. van Oorschot, and Scott A. Vanstone's *Handbook of Applied Cryptography*. Cryptographic security and implementation issues are fully covered in Randall K. Nichols' *The ICSA Guide to Cryptography*. H. X Mel and Doris Baker provide a very readable text in *Cryptography Decrypted*. Richard A. Mollin's *An Introduction to Cryptography* is for the mathematically inclined. Finally, William Stalling' *Cryptography and Network Security: Principles and Practice* is thoroughly enjoyable. The reader is directed to the Reference section for other fine texts on the subject. Our coverage in this chapter will be limited to classification and difficulty of software based cryptographic systems. We then discuss the hardware implementations in FPGAs and ASICs, which may be cost-effective in securing wireless devices.

Algorithms are the ***raison-d'etre*** for cryptography. What is needed is a scheme to put the mathematics into simple focus. The author suggests that there are two practical ways to classify cryptographic algorithms. First, we can classify algorithms by their underlying difficulty of mathematical system and second,[73] we can classify them by their cryptographic purpose. Cryptography algorithms span the mathematical gambit of number theory, complexity theory, elliptic curves, vector calculus, tensors, and set theory.[74]

**Table 5-6 Summary of Similarities and Differences
Between Secret Key and Public-Key Cryptography**

Attribute	Secret Key	Public/Private Key
Years in Use	Thousands	Less than 50
Current main use	Bulk data encryption	Key exchange, digital signatures
Current standard	DES, Triple DES, Rijndael	RSA, Diffie-Hellman, DSA, Elliptic curves
Encryption/decryption	Fast	Slow speed
Keys	Shared secret between at least two people	Private: kept concealed by one Public: widely distributed
Key exchange	Difficult and risky to transfer a secret key	Easy and less risky to deliver a public key Private key never shared
Key length	56-bit obsolete 128-bit considered safe	1,024 bits suggested (RSA) Many users demand 2,048 bits ~ 172 elliptic curve
Confidentiality, Authentication, Message integrity	Yes	Yes
Non-repudiation	No Don't need trusted third party to act as witness	Yes Digital signatures: need trusted third party
Attacks	Yes	Yes

Difficulty of Mathematical Systems

In the first classification scheme, there are three types of mathematical problems considered both secure and efficient, that is, not crackable, found easier than postulated or impractical to calculate. The three mathematical problems on which practical cryptosystem security is based:

- **Integer factorization problem (IFP)**   RSA is the principal and best-known cryptosystem in this category.
- **Discrete logarithm problem (DLP)**   Examples include the U. S. Government's *Digital Signature Algorithm* (DSA), the Diffie-Hellman key agreement scheme, the ElGamal encryption and signature schemes, and the Schnorr signature scheme.

- **Elliptic curve discrete logarithm problem (ECDLP)** Examples of this type include the *elliptic curve analog of the DSA* (ECDSA), and the elliptic curve analogs of the Diffie-Hellman key agreement scheme (ECDH), the ElGamal *encryption and signature schemes* (ECEG), and the Schnorr signature scheme (ECSS).

A second classification method separates cryptographic algorithms by cryptographic purpose or functionality:

- Symmetric
- Asymmetric
- Authentication systems
- Digital signatures

There is overlap among the proposed schemes of classification.[75] We will consider the first classification method in this chapter.

Integer Factorization Systems

Diffie and Hellman discovered the concept of public-key cryptography in 1976. Ron Rivest, Adi Shamir, and Len Adleman developed the first practical public-key cryptographic system at MIT. The system was named RSA in honor of its inventors.

Security

RSA is the best known of a family of systems whose security relies on the difficulty of *the integer factorization problem* (IFP). The integer factorization problem is defined as follows: Given an integer, a whole number, **p** is *prime* if it is divisible only by 1 and **p** itself. Now, given an integer **n** which is the product of two large primes, determine those factors, that is, find primes **p** and **q** such that

$$p \times q = n \tag{5.1}$$

An RSA public key consists of a pair (n, e), where e is a number between 1 and $n - 1$, and n is the product of two large primes p and q. It is widely believed that to break RSA in general, the integer factorization problem must be solved (hence factored) for the integer n. The factorization problem has been studied for over 300 years and no super-efficient method of computation has been discovered. Since there is no efficient algorithm for the integer factorization problem, **n** can be chosen to be large enough to ensure that the system is secure. To provide even short-term security, given today's computing power, **n** should be at least 300 decimal digits long (300 decimal digits is approximately 1024 bits.)[76]

In order to break the RSA algorithm the integer factorization problem must be solved for the integer n. The security of the RSA algorithm can be increased greatly by ensuring the integer n is a large number. The larger the number the more secure the system is. In order to use RSA, or any other system that utilizes the integer factorization problem, modular arithmetic must be used. The speed and efficiency of RSA or any other system that uses IFP relies heavily on the speed of performing exponential modulo n.[77]

There are a few different types of factoring attacks on the integer factorization problem. The main two types of factoring algorithms are general-purpose and special purpose. General-purpose factoring algorithms depend on the size of n, while special-purpose algorithms attempt to exploit the different ways that n can be factored.[78] The record for factoring with either of these methods (as of December 2000) is 512 bits. It took a team using 292 off-the-shelf computers a little more than five month to do the job. With a brute force attack, each time you add a bit to the key size, you double the time it takes to break. For each added bit, factoring programs require an additional 1.035 to 1.036 times longer to run. This scales to 3 to 30 million years for a 1,024-bit key.[79]

Implementation

RSA, and other members of the integer factorization family, can be used both for encryption and for digital signatures (the digital equivalent of real signatures). To describe the operations used to perform these processes, modular arithmetic must first be defined. Modular addition and modular multiplication modulo n work just like ordinary addition and multiplication, except that the answer to the calculation is reduced to its remainder on division by n, so that the result always lies between 0 and $n - 1$. The phrase mod n is written after each calculation to denote modular arithmetic. Modular arithmetic plays a central role in the implementation of all three types of public-key cryptosystems.

When RSA is used either as an encryption scheme or as a digital signature scheme, exponentiation modulo n must be performed. Suppose m, a number between 0 and $n - 1$, represents a message. Then the modular exponentiation

$$m^x \ (\mathrm{mod}\ n) \tag{5.2}$$

must be calculated for some number x when m is transformed. This *modular exponentiation dominates the time taken to perform the transformations* involved in the RSA system, so that the time required to calculate modular exponentiation modulo n essentially determines the time required to perform RSA.

In short, the *security* of RSA, and the other members of the integer factorization family, rests on the difficulty of the integer factorization problem, and its efficiency rests on the speed of performing exponentiation modulo n.

Discrete Logarithm Systems

Security

Another mathematical problem defined in terms of modular arithmetic is the discrete logarithm problem modulo a prime p. Fix a prime number p. Then given an integer g between 0 and $p - 1$, and y which is the result of exponentiating g, we define the following relation between g and y:

$$y = g^x(\text{mod } p) \tag{5.3}$$

for some x.

The discrete logarithm problem modulo p is to determine the integer x for a given pair g and y. The prime p used in discrete logarithm systems should also be at least 150 decimal digits (500 bits) in length to provide short-term security.

Like the integer factorization problem, no efficient algorithm is generally known to solve the discrete logarithm problem modulo p. Taher ElGamal was the first to propose a public-key cryptosystem based on this problem. In fact, ElGamal proposed two distinct systems: one to provide encryption, and one to perform digital signatures. In 1991, Claus Schnorr discovered a variant of the ElGamal digital signature system, which offers added efficiency compared to the original system. The U.S. government's Digital Signature Algorithm (DSA) is also based on ElGamal's work. The aforementioned systems are the best known of a large number of systems whose security is based on the discrete logarithm problem modulo p.

As with IFP, there are both special-purpose and general-purpose algorithms that are used to solve the discrete logarithm problem. The fastest general-purpose algorithms known for solving the discrete logarithm problem are based on a method called the index-calculus. The index-calculus method uses a database consisting of small prime numbers and their associated logarithms. This method may also be applied on a distributed computer network and run in parallel.[80]

Implementation

As was the case with RSA, modular exponentiation must be performed to operate discrete logarithm systems. In every case, the dominant calculation in each of the transformations is

$$g^x(\text{mod } p) \tag{5.4}$$

for some integer x, and a fixed number g between 0 and $p - 1$.

Therefore, discrete logarithm systems rely on the discrete logarithm problem modulo p, and the efficiency of the speed of performing modular exponentiation modulo p.

The Elliptic Curve Cryptosystem (ECC)

The mathematical theories surrounding elliptic curves date back to the 17th Century, when mathematicians researched the various structures and shapes of geometric formulas. The basis for *Elliptic Curve Cryptography* (ECC) is rooted in the properties of an elliptic curve. Even though elliptic curve theorems were originally developed around 1650, it was not until 1955, when a Japanese mathematician named Yutaka Taniyama applied elliptic curves to Fermat's Theorem, that they were widely recognized. Taniyama used an elliptic curve to help solve Fermat's Last Theorem ($x^n + y^n = z^n$).[81]

Contemporary ECC is an effort that started on two separate fronts in 1985. Working independently, two mathematicians proposed a public-key system that used groups of points on an elliptic curve. These mathematicians were Victor Miller at IBM and Neil Koblitz from the University of Washington. Their work utilized the discrete logarithm problem over the points on an elliptic curve. Applying their theory to elliptic curves meant that ECC could be efficiently used to provide both digital signatures and an encryption system to applications. In the process, these two mathematicians introduced to the cryptographic world an alternative to traditional public-key cryptography.[82]

Elliptic curve systems use a variant of the *Discrete Logarithm Problem* (DLP). But, instead of straight integer algebra, elliptic curve systems use an algebraic formula to determine the relationship between public and private keys within the universe created by an elliptic curve.

The discrete logarithm problem modulo p was described in terms of modular arithmetic on the remainders of division by p. This is not the only mathematical structure that forms the basis for discrete logarithm problems. ECC security rests on the discrete logarithm problem applied to the points on an elliptic curve and has some powerful and unique features available for use in cryptographic systems. ECC can be used to provide both a digital signature scheme and an encryption scheme.

An elliptic curve (see Figure 5-15 and Equation 5.5), defined modulo a prime p, is the set of solutions (x,y) to an equation of the form:

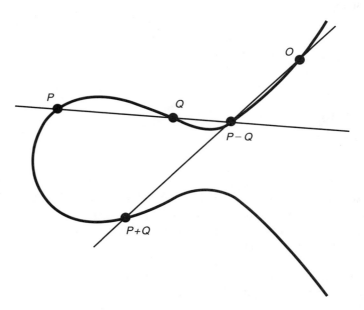

5-15 Example of elliptic curve.[83]

$$y^2 = x^3 + ax + b \pmod{p} \tag{5.5}$$

for two numbers a and b. If (x,y) satisfies the above equation then $P = (x,y)$ is a point on the elliptic curve. An elliptic curve can also be defined over the finite field consisting of 2^m elements. Such a representation offers extra efficiency in the operation of the ECC.

It is possible to define the addition of two points on the elliptic curve. Suppose P and Q are both points on the curve, then $P + Q$ will always be another point on the curve.

The elliptic curve discrete logarithm problem can be stated as follows. Fix a prime p and an elliptic curve. xP represents the point P added to itself x times. Suppose Q is a multiple of P, so that

$$Q = xP \tag{5.6}$$

for some x. Then the elliptic curve discrete logarithm problem is to determine x given P and Q.

Security

The security of the ECC rests on the difficulty of the elliptic curve discrete logarithm problem. As was the case with the integer factorization problem and the discrete logarithm problem modulo p, no efficient algorithm is known at this time to solve the elliptic curve discrete logarithm problem.

One of the advantages of ECC is that the *elliptic curve discrete logarithm problem* (ECDLP) is believed to be harder than both the integer factorization problem and the discrete logarithm problem modulo p. This extra difficulty implies that ECC may be one of the strongest public-key cryptographic systems known today. Moderate security can be achieved with ECC using an elliptic curve defined modulo a prime p that is several times shorter than 150 decimal digits. This is a real advantage from a computer hardware and software implementation viewpoint.

Implementation

Just as modular exponentiation determined the efficiency of integer factorization and discrete logarithm systems, so the calculation of equation 5.6 for a point P on the elliptic curve and some integer x that dominates the calculations involved in the operation of an ECC cryptosystem. The process of adding elliptic curve points requires a few modular calculations, so in the case of integer factorization, discrete logarithm systems, and elliptical curve cryptosystems the operation of a public-key cryptographic system is dependent upon efficient modular arithmetic. What is very interesting is that the prime p used in an ECC system can be *smaller* than the numbers required in the other types of systems, so another advantage of ECC is that the modular calculations required in its operation are carried out over a smaller modulus. This may lead to a significant improvement in efficiency in the operation of ECC over both integer factorization and discrete logarithm systems.

In summary, ECC security rests on the elliptic curve discrete logarithm problem, while efficiency is dependent on the fast calculation of xP for some number x and a point P on the curve.

Comparison of Public-Key Cryptographic Systems

Security and efficiency are two important issues for comparing IFP, DLP, and ECDLP public-key cryptographic systems.

The longer it takes to compute the best algorithm for the problem, the more secure a public-key cryptosystem based on that problem will be.

It must be emphasized that none of the aforementioned problems—IFP, DLP, or ECDLP have been proven to be *intractable* (that is, difficult to solve in an efficient manner). Rather, they are believed to be intractable because years of intensive study by leading mathematicians and computer scientists have failed to yield efficient algorithms for solving them.

Formally the running time for the best general algorithm (sub-exponential running time) for both the IFP and DLP problems is of the form of algorithm A, whose inputs are elements of a finite field Fn or an integer n; the form of A is:

$$L_q \{\alpha, c\} = \Theta(\exp((c + o(1)))(\ln n)^\alpha (\ln \ln n)^{1-\alpha}) \tag{5.7}$$

for a positive constant c, $0 \leq \alpha \leq 1$. a is usually of the order of $1/3$, so $(1 - \alpha)$ is $2/3$.

When a satisfies the constraint $0 \leq \alpha \leq 1$, then A is a subexponential time algorithm. When $\alpha = 0$, $L_q\{0, c\}$ is a polynomial in ln n, while for $\alpha = 1$, $L_q\{1, c\}$ is a polynomial in n, and thus fully exponential in ln n.

The best general algorithm for the ECDLP is fully exponential time—its running time is

$$\Theta(\sqrt{p}) \tag{5.8}$$

In simple terms, this means that the ECDLP may be considered harder with respect to time than either the integer factorization problem or the discrete logarithm problem modulo p.

The best algorithm known to date for the ECDLP in general is the Pollard rho-method, which takes about $\sqrt{\pi n/2}$ steps where a step is an elliptic curve point addition. In 1993, Paul van Oorschot and Michael Wiener showed how the Pollard rho-method can be paralleled so that if r processors are used, then the expected number of steps by each processor before a single discrete logarithm is obtained is $\sqrt{\pi n/2}/r$. Most significantly, no index-calculus-type algorithms are known for the ECDLP as for the DLP. No subexponential-time general-purpose algorithm is known for the ECDLP problem.

Menezes and Jurisic compared the time required to break the ECC with the time required to break RSA or DSA for various modulus sizes using the best general algorithm known. Values were computed in MIPS years that represent a computing time of one year on a machine capable of performing 1 million instructions per second. As a benchmark, it is generally accepted that 10^{12} MIPS years represents reasonable security at this time, since this would require most of the computing power on the planet to work for a considerable amount of time or a major break-through in cryptanalysis.

Menezes and Jurisic found that to achieve reasonable security, RSA and DSA would need to employ a 1024-bit modulus, while a 160-bit modulus should be sufficient for the ECC. They found that ECC required a smaller modulus than RSA or DSA and that the security gap between the systems grew as the key size increased. For example, 300-bit ECC is significantly more secure than 2000 bit RSA or DSA.

Another way to look at this security issue is to compare the equivalent strength of RSA/DSA keys and ECC keys for smartcard applications. Table 5-7 shows that in smart card applications requiring higher levels of security, ECC is able to offer security without a great deal of additional system resources.

Efficiency

When talking about the efficiency of a public-key cryptographic system, there are, in general, three distinct factors to take into account:

- **Computational overheads** How much computation is required to perform the public key and private key transformations
- **Key size** How many bits are required to store the key pairs and associated system parameters
- **Bandwidth** How many bits must be communicated to transfer an encrypted message or a signature

Clearly the comparisons should be made between systems offering similar levels of security, so in order to make the comparisons as concrete as possible, 160-bit ECC is compared with 1024-bit RSA and DSA. These parameter sizes are believed to offer comparable levels of security.

Table 5-7 Key Size: Equivalent Strength Comparison[84]

Time to Break MIPS/Year	RSA/DSA Key Size	ECC Key Size	RSA/ECC Key Size Ratio
10^4	512	106	5:1
10^8	768	132	6:1
10^{11}	1,024	160	7:1
10^{20}	2,048	210	10:1
10^{78}	21,000	600	35:1

Computational overheads

In each of the three systems, considerable computational savings can be made. In RSA, a short public exponent can be employed (although this represents a trade-off and does incur some security risks) to speed up signature verification and encryption. In both DSA and ECC, a large proportion of the signature generation and encrypting transformations can be pre-computed. Also, various special bases for the finite field $F_2{}^m$ can be employed to perform more quickly the modular arithmetic involved in ECC operation. State-of-the-art implementations of the systems show that with all of these efficiencies in place, ECC is an order of magnitude (roughly 10 times) faster than either RSA or DSA. The use of a short public exponent in RSA can make RSA encryption and signature verification timings (but not RSA decryption and signature generation timings) comparable with timings for these processes using the ECC.

Key Size Comparison

Table 5-8 compares the size of the system parameters and selected key pairs for the different systems.

Table 5-8 presents evidence that the system parameters and key pairs are shorter for the ECC than for either RSA or DSA.

Bandwidth

All three types of systems have similar bandwidth requirements when they are used to encrypt or sign long messages. However, the case when short messages are being transformed deserves particular attention because public-key cryptographic systems are often employed to transmit short messages (that is, to transport session keys for use in a symmetric-key cryptographic system). For comparison, suppose that each is being used to sign a 2000-bit message, or to encrypt a 100-bit message. Tables 5-9 and 5-10 compare the lengths of the signatures and encrypted messages respectively. These tables suggest that ECC offers bandwidth savings over the other types of public-key cryptographic systems when being used to transform short messages.

ECDLP and Wireless Devices

ECDLP may be a good choice for many wireless devices, which have limitations on power, space, memory, and cost because of its smaller key sizes offering high levels of security. The ultimate goal of a secure infrastructure is to have a complete end-to-end solution that will provide unbreakable absolute security while not out-stripping the current resources and processing power available. Advocates of ECC are focused on creating more efficient uses of current resource allocations in cryptography. Since any networked system can benefit from algorithms that reduce bandwidth and processing time, the ability to decrease the size of the key without diminishing the

Table 5-8 Size of System Parameters and Key Pairs (Approx.)[85]

	System Parameters (Bits)	Public Key (Bits)	Private key (Bits)
RSA	n/a	1088	2048
DSA	2208	1024	160
ECC	481	161	160

Table 5-9 Signature Sizes on Long Messages (e.g., 2000-Bit)[86]

	Signature size (Bits)
RSA	1024
DSA	320
ECC	320

Table 5-10 Size of Encrypted 100-bit Messages[87]

	Encrypted Message (Bits)
RSA	1024
ElGamal	2048
ECC	321

effectiveness of the key strength has far-reaching implications. ECC offers an ideal use for small, low-memory, low-processing applications such as cellular phones, smart cards, and numerous other devices.

For many wireless devices or any other device that do not have the capability to incorporate large amounts of memory, processor power, or high production costs implementing ECC may be ideal. Because of the smaller key sizes required, much less memory space is required in the components that make up the security systems. Each year the number of transistors that can fit on one integrated circuit is increasing at an almost exponential rate; also, Moore's Law states that processing power doubles every 18 months. This has led to enormous technological breakthroughs that could have only happened using more powerful processors. These breakthroughs have increased the power of wireless communication devices by incorporating more and more circuits into their designs. ECC can be used to secure the communications of these devices more efficiently than any other algorithm. ECC's smaller memory requirements mean that less space on the circuit board of a communication device is taken up by the cryptographic systems memory requirements. These small keys sizes also do not require as much processing power as other cryptographic algorithms use. The mathematics involved in processing, generating key pairs, and performing the actual encryption and decryption functions of ECC are complicated but do not require nearly the same amount of processing power as other algorithms that use IFP and DLP.

Key Generation in Wireless Devices for IFP, DLP, and ECDLP

Generating key pairs using cryptographic algorithms can be a difficult and complex task. In order to generate an RSA key pair, a high-quality random number generator must be used in order to produce the two prime numbers. Then, these prime number candidates must be tested to ensure that they are not susceptible to specific types of attacks. Lastly, the modular equation must be solved to determine the private exponent. This is a complex process made more difficult because it must be performed in a secure environment without any error. This need for security and lack of errors is extremely crucial. If any errors occur, or if the security of the process has been compromised in any way, the actual private key will be disclosed. In order to successfully perform this key generation process a great deal of software code is required to create a secure environment as well as provide error checking.[88]

In order to generate an ECC key pair, two operations are needed. The first operation is the generation of a valid domain parameter. This domain parameter is open to the public in order to ensure that the domain parameter confirms to the appropriate specifications. After a domain parameter is created, a high-quality random number generator is used to create a private key.[89]

Both RSA and ECC require a high quality random number generator in the key generation process. ECC is more efficient than RSA due to the lack of additional code that is required for RSA to provide additional security and error checking.

Bandwidth in Wireless Devices

Another main concern of implementing cryptographic functions into small wireless devices is the bandwidth requirement. *Bandwidth* is the volume of encrypted bits required to be sent in order to transfer a message—in this case an encrypted message. Sizes of signatures and actual encrypted messages used by ECC are also much smaller than those used by other algorithms. As shown previously, it is clear that when ECC is used to encrypt and send shorter messages it requires a great deal less bandwidth. This information can be directly related to the current push to migrate almost all communication systems from switched systems to packet-based systems. For wireless communication devices using a packet-based system, the implementation of ECC would require less bandwidth than any other cryptographic algorithm. Today, the demand for more bandwidth is apparent in every market. It is critical to engineer techniques that will allocate more bandwidth to smaller, wireless communications devices. When more bandwidth is essential, securing the data through encrypting the packets or messages should not absorb a great deal of that bandwidth. This is where ECC may be the appropriate solution due to the small amounts of associated overhead required to encrypt packets.

Scalability

When dealing with memory or processing power the key question today is: How does it scale? Processor power and memory speeds are increasing everyday. When relating this to cryptographic systems that will reside on tightly constrained systems, such as small devices or wireless devices, scalability is sometimes not possible. For algorithms such as RSA, the key sizes and processing power requirements are fairly high. If a manufacturer were to base a cryptographic system that is incorporated into a small device on an RSA key length of 2048 bits, it might be difficult to make this more secure using larger key sizes. As discussed previously, this is due to the fact that RSA key lengths need to increase almost exponentially in order to provide a more secure algorithm. This could be made impossible due to the space, memory, and processing power of these small devices. These devices have integrated circuits, which perform the memory and processing functions, and these integrated circuits may not be capable of dealing with memory and processing requirements that increase exponentially. ECC is more efficient and scales much better than other algorithms. This is a result of the small increases in key lengths required to provide greater levels of security. In addition, ECC does not require a great deal of processing power and the processing power requirements will not increase as dramatically in comparison to other algorithms.

Processing Overhead

For many algorithms, the processing requirements are very demanding. When implementing these algorithms into electronic designs, it is common to require a crypto processor. These processors are pre-programmed to perform very specific calculations that are required for some of these algorithms. The crypto processors not only take up precious space, but they add about 20 to 30 percent to the cost of the chips. This increase in cost is a very significant amount because these devices are commonly produced by the thousands. ECC does not require additional crypto processors in order to function most efficiently. This enables ECC to be integrated into systems that have very tight limitations on space and cost.[90]

When additional steps need to be taken to encrypt, decrypt, sign, and verify data, performance can be a major factor. The addition of public-key cryptographic systems and algorithms add a substantial amount of processing overhead to the normal operations of a system. When adding these systems to smaller devices that have processing power constraints, the selection of the most efficient cryptographic algorithm is crucial. If the processor overhead that is required to perform these encryption, decryption, and verification functions is too great, this may negatively affect the functionality of the system itself. This is important when this is applied to small wireless devices. If a wireless telephone is used to communicate using voice, and the encryption functions take a long time, then conversations can become almost unbearable due to the latency added by the processing time. The computational overhead required by ECC is much less than that required by RSA. This is due to the different types of calculations required in conjunction with the small key sizes used by ECC. As a result ECC is appropriate for use in devices, which have processing and power limitations, such as wireless devices.

Certicom is one of the industry leaders in testing and utilizing ECC for public-key encryption systems. The following table displays the results of performance tests using Certicom enhanced ECC and the RSA cryptosystem. The University of California Berkeley posted Table 5-11, which displays the results of performance testing ECC on an Intel Pentium III 850 MHz workstation.

Additional to the discussion of strengths and weakness inherent in the algorithm, the provision, implementation, administration, and maintenance of ECC in the commercial industry requires that, in an effort to attain desired results, at least the following considerations should be analyzed:

- Ease of use
- Return on investment
- Interoperability
- Flexibility
- Association with standards.

Below is a list of some of the products that are already commercially available, including a brief definition of the functionality of each, that incorporate ECC. The role that ECC plays in each product is particularly emphasized. Deploying a secure cryptosystem that requires fewer resources and less computational power is especially important in the wireless arena where the devices, network, and system infrastructure are inherently more constrained and sensitive to size and bandwidth. The advantage of reduced memory and processing time makes the ECC solution even more feasible. ECC provides greater efficiency than either integer factorization systems or discrete logarithm systems, in terms of computational overheads, key sizes, and bandwidth. In implementations, these savings mean higher speeds, lower power consumption, and code size reductions.[91]

This is true in software applications but may not be true in hardware-based applications because of the modular exponentiation operations and small memory usually available on embedded devices. The implementation of ECC would be beneficial in many forms because of the reduced key sizes in many modern portable devices: smart cards, cellular phones, and handheld computers/*personal digital assistants* (PDAs).

Smart cards

Smart Cards have proven useful as a transaction and/or authorization scheme, especially in European countries. Current Smart Cards are developed to be small with a limited amount of processing power and storage. The typical Smart Card that is used

Table 5-11[92] ECC In Commercial Industry

Function	Certicom Security Builder 1.2 163-Bit ECC (ms)	RSA BSAFE 3.0 1024-Bit RSA (ms)
Key Pair Generation	3.8	4708.3
Sign	2.1 (ECNRA) 3.0 (ECDSA)	228.4
Verify	9.9 (ECNRA) 10.7 (ECDSA)	12.7
Diffie-Hellman Key Exchange	7.3	1654.0

ECC/RSA Performance Benchmarks

	Strength (MIPS years)	Public Key Size	Private Key Size	Signature Size	Initialization Time	Key Generation Time	Sign Time	Verify Time
DSA 512	+1E+04	1900	1600	368	0	34	21	33
DSA	+1E+11	3500	2680	368	0	18	68	1024122
ECC 431	+1E+11	170	163	336	1162	103	91	160
RSA	+1E+11	1080	2624	1024	40	4100	67	10243
ECC 594	+1E+20	240	232	464	2040	100	102	224
RSA	+1E+20	2104	5184	2048	0	68000	460	204816

ECC Performance

as a storage/processing card usually has a 5-MHz processor with 256 bytes to 1KB of RAM. This is usually enough power to carry out a single-function transaction but would be unstable or unusable if the there were multiple tasks to perform. Such complications could arise if the card tried to perform an encryption routine while also processing Access Control verification routines. The fact that current Smart Cards have no methods in place to communicate and verify with the owners is a major risk for corporations to undertake. In order to get around the authentication problem, Smart Cards often require the owner to enter a password through a reader.[93]

Smart Cards have many standards in place for manufacturers to use and develop. The physical size (ISO 7810) and the placement of the microprocessor (ISO 7816-2) are just a few. Other benefits of Smart Cards are that many of them already have some form of encryption system built into them. This security allows for Digital Cash to be stored, processed, and transferred in a relatively safe manner. Smart Cards for driver's license, military, and medical identification are just a few possibilities where ECC could be applied. Other possibilities would include monetary Smart Cards for Public Transportation and possibly even Credit/Cash Cards that could be used instead of having to carry cash. ECC could improve the encryption key strength found in some of these cards because the key size is so much smaller than with other encryption routines. The possibility of deploying Smart Cards that use ECC would also make a good match because the cards possess a small processor and are capable of storing data in memory.[94]

Cellular Phone Networks

Considering what the cellular manufacturers have been promising with wireless Internet, data transfer, and the ability to send and receive emails, the current state of cellular networks is quite primitive. This is especially true about the older CDMA network infrastructure that is found in the United States. Other reasons for the poor performance that are multiplied because of the design of the original network usually consist of adding new features onto cell phone networks that were originally built for analog and digital voice.[95]

Table 5-12 shows the current *Code Division Multiple Access* (CDMA, which the prevailing cellular network designed around), and how channel bandwidth and data transfer capacity are shared.

The older design offers low bit rates and poor interoperability, and these are just some of the downsides of the original network design. Dornan states, The only CDMA system in use so far is cdmaOne, developed by Qualcomm but now supervised by an independent organization called the *CDMA Development Group* (CDG). It has been standardized by the *Telecommunications Industry Association* (TIA) as IS-95a, and is popular among cellular operators in America and Asia.[96]

The moves to improve the cellular network are gradually gaining ground. There have been recent improvements; however, it is unsure whether they can be implemented effectively with the number of manufacturers using older technologies. The FCC's inability to license any new portion of the RF spectrum could further slow the

Table 5-12[97] CDMA Channel Bandwidth and Data Transfer Shaved Capacity

Code Division Mulitple Access (CDMA) System	Channel Bandwidth	Chip Rate	Maximum Capacity	Real Capacity
cdma One IS-950	1.25 MHz	1.2288 MHz	11.5 Kbps	64 Kbps
cdma 2000 1XMC	1.25 MHz	1.2288 MHz	384 Kbps	144 Kbps
cdma 2000 1Xtreme	1.25 MHz	1.2288 MHz	5.2 Mbps	1.2 Mbps
cdma 2000 HDR	1.25 MHz	1.2288 MHz	2.4 Mbps	621 Kbps
cdma 2000 3XMC	3.75 MHz	3.6865 MHz	4 Mbps	1,117 Mbps
Wideband CDMA (W-CDMA)	5 MHz	4.096 MHz	4 Mbps	1,126 Mbps

upgrades that are needed in the United States. Zeglis recounts a recent discussion with Japan's leading wireless maker, NTT DoCoMo, which showed optimism about the limitations here in the United States, W-CDMA will allow us to support business customers seamlessly between the United States and Japan. But according to NTT DoCoMo, having the same network technology is not enough. AT&T's global roaming ambitions are limited by the lack of available spectrum in the United States. There is still no clear spectrum allocated for 3G services, and the 2-GHz band adopted elsewhere around the world is already allocated for other services in the United States.[98]

Secure cellular transmission, if implemented on the current network, could further disrupt the service and cause more problems. With only slow progress as the network infrastructure is continually upgraded instead of being replaced, ECC could improve the efficiency of the current system dramatically. ECC could efficiently provide strong encryption without sacrificing processing capabilities or data size.

Handheld Computers/Personal Digital Assistant (PDAs)

Personal Digital Assistants (PDAs) are increasingly becoming the middle ground between desktop computers and mobile applications such as Smart Cards and cellular phones. There are even PDAs currently on the market that can replace a user's cellular phone or even a Smart Card by simply attaching an external module befitting the desired application or installing software for beaming tokens to participate in an electronic transaction. However, unlike the Smart Cards, the PDAs on the market today are not equipped with any real method of authentication or an encryption system. The access control that they usually have is very weak or nonexistent. Both of these shortcomings are no doubt the result of the limited storage capacity and small processing power that were originally built into these devices.

The security vulnerabilities that surrounded the older PDAs a few years ago were created by the obvious lack of performance and storage capacity at the time they were designed. Typical older model PDAs had a processing power of around 16 MHz with about 2MB of RAM.[99]

This was simply not enough power or storage space to run applications that use any encryption routines that could generate keys or digital certificates. The good news is that the technology over the past few years has steadily increased. Now, newer PDAs are available with processing power of up to 206 MHz with 32MB of RAM, with the option to attach modules with even more memory in relatively the same size.[100]

With the improvements in this area it may not be long until a PDA will comfortably handle additional roles of voice communication and/or electronic commerce. The need for securely beaming to an automated teller machine to download Electronic Cash will not be far off once a fast and efficient way to secure the transactions is implemented. Because of these performance advances, the PDA market is clearly ready for cryptographic systems.

ECC can be most beneficial in areas that need to optimize storage and processing power without overloading system capacities. The next section will examine how far ECC has matured as measured by the acceptance of various organizations responsible for cryptographic standards.

BSAFE Crypto-C

RSA's BSAFE Crypto-C product is a toolkit that allows privacy and authentication features to be customized and built into applications. BSAFE Crypto-C includes support for PKCS#11 (*Public-key Cryptography Standard*) and BHAPI (*BSAFE Hardware API*) that will allow the application to communicate with hardware such as smart cards (for secure key storage) and cryptographic accelerator cards (for performance improvements) (see Figure 5-16).[101]

BSAFE Crypto-C includes cryptography support for

- The RC4® stream cipher
- The high performance RC5™ block cipher
- The next-generation RC6™ block cipher
- The RSA Public-key Cryptosystem
- MD5
- SHA-1
- ECC algorithms for key agreement, encryption, and digital signatures[102]

BSAFE Crypto-C supports the following standards: ANSI X9.30, X9.31, X9.32, X9.42, X9.56, X9.62, and X9.63 financial standards. BSAFE Crypto-C can be run on the following platforms: Windows 95, 98, NT, and 2000, Sun, Solaris, HP-UX, Linux, and AIX (IBM's UNIX Operating System).[103]

Cryptography in Embedded Hardware: FPGA and ASICs

Some of the most interesting cryptography work is being done on the hardware side of the security house. In 2000, two papers were instrumental in defining the AES candidates' roles with FPGAs and ASICs. Andreas Dandalis, Victor K. Prasanna and Jose D.P. Rolim presented "A Comparative Study of Performance of AES Final Candidates Using FPGAs"[104] and from NSA by Bryan Weeks, Mark Bean, Tom

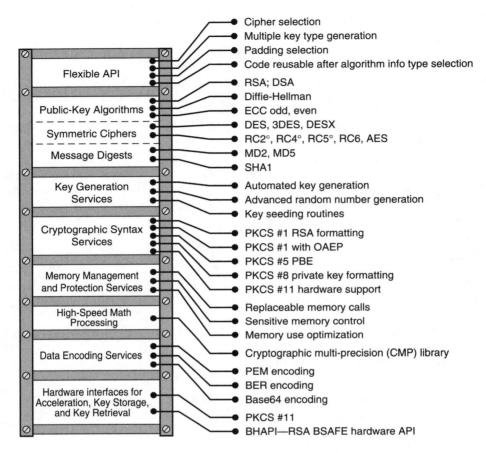

5-16 RSA BSAFE Crypto-C functional layers.[105]

Rozylowicz, and Chris Ficke wrote "Hardware Performance Simulations of Round 2 Advanced Encryption Standard Algorithms."[106] Both of these papers reported AES candidate performance characteristics in hardware.

On top of this was a stunning paper by Kris Gaj and Pawel Chodowiec at RSA2001 entitled "Fast Implementation and Fair Comparison of the Final Candidates for Advanced Encryption Standard Using Field Programmable Gate Arrays."[107]

Dandalis, et al., implemented the AES final candidates using *Field Programmable Gate Arrays* (FPGAs). The goal of their study was to evaluate the performance of the AES final candidates using FPGAs and to make performance comparisons. The time performance metrics were throughput and key-setup latency. Throughput corresponds to the amount of data processed per time unit while key-setup latency is the minimum time required to commence encryption after providing the input key. Key latency is the key measure for applications where a small amount of data is processed per key and key context switching occurs repeatedly, like wireless.

FPGA technology is a growing area that has the potential to provide the performance benefits of ASICs and the flexibility of processors. This technology allows application-specific hardware circuits to be created on demand to meet the computing and interconnect requirements of an application. Moreover, these hardware circuits can be dynamically modified partially or completely in time and in space based on the requirements of the operations under execution

Private-key cryptographic algorithms seem to fit extremely well with the characteristics of the FPGAs. This is especially true for wireless applications. The fine-granularity of FPGAs matches extremely well the operations required by private-key cryptographic algorithms such as bit- permutations, bit-substitutions, look-up table reads, and Boolean functions. On the other hand, the constant bit-width required alleviates accuracy-related implementation problems and facilitates efficient designs. Moreover, the inherent parallelism of the algorithms can be efficiently exploited in FPGAs. Multiple operations can be executed concurrently resulting in higher throughput compared with software-based implementations. Finally, the key-setup circuit can run concurrently with the cryptographic core circuit resulting in low key-setup latency time and agile key-context switching.[108]

FPGA Overview

Processors and ASICs are the cores of the two major computing paradigms of our days. Processors are general purpose and virtually can execute any operation. However, their performance is limited by the restricted interconnect, data path, and instruction set provided by the architecture. ASICs are application-specific and can achieve superior performance compared with processors. However, the functionality of ASIC design is restricted by the designed parameters provided during fabrication. Updates to ASIC based platforms incur high cost. As a result, ASIC-based approaches lack flexibility.

FPGA technology is a growing area of research that has the potential to provide the performance benefits of ASICs and the flexibility of processors. Application specific hardware circuits can be created on demand to meet the computing and interconnect requirements of an application. Hardware circuits can be dynamically modified partially or completely in time and in space based on the requirements of the operations under execution. As a result, you can expect superior performance to the equivalent software implementation executed on a processor.

FPGAs initially were an offshoot of the quest for ASIC prototyping with lower design cycle time. The evolution of the configurable system technology led to the development of configurable devices and architectures with great computational power. As a result, new application domains become suitable for FPGAs beyond the initial applications of rapid prototyping and circuit emulation. FPGA-based solutions have shown significant speedups compared with software and DSP based approaches for several application domains such as telephony, signal and image processing, graph algorithms, genetic algorithms, and cryptography among others.

The basic feature underlying FPGAs is the programmable logic element, which is realized by either using anti-fuse technology or SRAM-controlled transistors. FPGAs have a matrix of logic cells overlaid with a network of wires. Both the computation performed by the cells and the connections between the wires can be configured. Current devices mainly use SRAM to control the configurations of the cells and the wires. Loading a stream of bits onto the SRAM on the device can modify its configuration. Furthermore, current FPGAs can be reconfigured quickly, allowing their functionality to be altered at runtime according to the requirements of the computation.[109]

FPGA-Based Cryptography

FPGA devices are a highly promising alternative for implementing private-key cryptographic algorithms. Compared with software-based implementations, FPGA implementations can achieve superior performance. The fine-granularity of FPGAs matches well the operations required by private-key cryptographic algorithms (for example, bit-permutations, bit-substitutions, look-up table reads, and Boolean functions). As a result, such operations can be executed more efficiently in FPGAs than in a general-purpose computer.

Furthermore, the inherent parallelism of the algorithms can be efficiently exploited in FPGAs as opposed to the serial fashion of computing in a uni-processor environment. At the cryptographic-round level, multiple operations can be executed concurrently. On the other hand, at the block-cipher level, certain operation modes allow concurrent processing of multiple blocks of data.

For example, in the ECB mode of operation, multiple blocks of data can be processed concurrently since each data block is encrypted independently. Consequently, if p rounds are implemented, a throughput speed-up of $\Theta(p)$ can be achieved compared with a single-round based implementation (one round is implemented and is reused repeatedly). By adopting deep-pipelined designs, the throughput can be increased proportionally with the clock speed. On the contrary, in feedback modes of operation (for example, CBC, CFB), where the encryption results of each block are fed back into the encryption of the current block, encryption cannot be paralleled among consecutive blocks of data. As a result, the maximum throughput that can be achieved depends mainly on the encryption time required by a single cryptographic round and the efficiency of the implementation of the key-setup component of an algorithm.

Besides throughput, FPGA implementations can also achieve agile key-context switching. Key-context switching includes the generation of the required key-dependent data for each cryptographic round (for example, subkeys, key-dependent S-boxes). A cryptographic round can commence as soon as its key-dependent data is available. In software implementations, the cryptographic process cannot commence before the key-setup process for all the rounds is completed. As a result, excessive latency is introduced making key-context switching inefficient. On the contrary, in FPGAs, each cryptographic round can commence earlier since the key-setup process can run concurrently with the cryptographic process. As a result, minimal latency can be achieved.

Security issues also make FPGA implementations more advantageous than software-based solutions. An encryption algorithm running on a generalized computer has no physical protection. Hardware cryptographic devices can be securely encapsulated to prevent any modification of the implemented algorithm. In general, hardware-based solutions are the embodiment of choice for military and serious commercial applications (for example, NSA authorizes encryption only in hardware). Finally, even if ASICs can achieve superior performance compared with FPGAs, their flexibility is restricted. Thus, the replacement of such application-specific chips becomes costly while FPGA-based implementations can be adapted to new algorithms and standards. If performance is essential, ASICs solutions are superior.[110]

Results

The results of Dandalis (et. al) suggest that Rijndael and Serpent favor FPGA implementations *the most* due to the ideal match of their algorithmic characteristics with the characteristics of FPGAs. The Rijndael implementation achieves the lowest key-setup latency time, the highest throughput, and the highest hardware use. The results suggest that Rijndael achieves the best performance across different platforms (that is, ASIC, FPGA, and software). The results of Dandalis (et. al) also compared favorably with the results of ASIC-based implementations reported by the NSA team above (refer to Tables 5-13 to 5-15).[111]

Kris Gaj and Pawel Chodowiec tested all five AES candidates using a Virtex Xilinx FPGA. They focused on one architecture optimum from the point of view of throughput to area ratio for two of the block cipher modes for each candidate. For feedback cipher modes, all the AES candidates' implementations used the basic iterative architecture, and achieved speeds ranging from 61 Mbps for MARS to 431 Mbps for Serpent. For non-feedback cipher modes, four AES candidates were implemented using a high-throughput architecture with pipelining inside and outside of cipher rounds, and achieved speeds ranging from 12.2 Gbits/s for Rijndael to 16.8 Bits/s for Serpent. Serpent and Rijndael outperformed the other three AES candidates by a factor two in both throughput and latency and their results support the AES choice of Rijndael.[112]

Summary

The purpose of this chapter was to introduce cryptographic countermeasures and their applicability in the commercial and wireless theaters. The science is no longer arcane and has wide use in protecting public and private communications. We chose to provide a helicopter view and have differentiated only some of the technical solutions affecting wireless devices such as stream ciphers, ECC, and embedded hardware. We elaborated on a new stream cipher, HORNET™. It incorporates a novel use of SHA-1 as an encryption engine in a stream cipher and reportedly provides a mechanism to solve the stream cipher synchronization problem. We expanded on ECC and discussed several constrained but positive tradeoffs that may be realized in wireless applications. There are many cryptographic options available for securing end-to-end and IP based wireless applications. Performance criteria of the system will dictate the appropriate measures. Of particular interest is the AES finalist Rijndael, as current reports of its testing in FPGAs and ASICs are yielding remarkable throughputs and latency. The reader is directed to the References to investigate the many aspects of cryptography.

Table 5-13 Three Performance Comparisons for Throughput

AES Algorithm Source	Elbert	Throughput Mbps Dandalis	GAJ
MARS	—	101.88	39.80
RC6	126.50	112.87	103.90
Rijndael	300.10	353.00	331.50
Serpent	444.20	148.95	339.40
Twofish	119.60	173.06	177.30

Source (see notes)[113, 114, 115]

Table 5-14 Performance Comparisons with FPGA Implementations

AES Algorithm Source	Mbps AOKI, Bassham	Throughput Dandalis	Speed-up	Key µs Bassham	Setup Dandalis	Latency Speed-up
MARS	188.00	101.88	1/1.84	8.22	1.96	4.19
RC6	258.00	112.87	1/2.28	3.79	0.17	22.29
Rijndael	243.00	353.00	1.45	2.15	0.07	30.71
Serpent	60.90	148.95	2.44	11.57	0.08	144.62
Twofish	204.00	173.06	1/1.17	15.44	0.18	85.78

Source (see notes)[116, 117, 118, 119, 120]

Table 5-15 Performance Comparisons with ASIC Implementations

AES Algorithm Source	Mbps NSA ASIC Weeks	Throughput Dandalis	Speed-up	Key µs NAS ASIC Weeks	Setup Dandalis	Latency Speed-up
MARS	56.71	101.88	1.79	9.55	1.96	4.87
RC6	102.83	112.87	1.09	5.74	0.17	33.76
Rijndael	605.77	353.00	1/ 1.171	0.00	0.07	—
Serpent	202.33	148.95	1/ 1.35	0.02	0.08	—
Twofish	105.14	173.06	1.64	0.06	0.18	1/3

Source: NSA ASIC[121, 122], NSA ASIC[123, 124]

Endnotes

[1]Kahn, David, *The Codebreakers: The Story of Secret Writing*, Weidenfield and Nicholson, 1967, pp. 157ff.

[2]Katzenbeisser, Stefan, and Fabien A.P. Petitcolas, *Information Hiding: Techniques for Steganography and Digital Watermarking*, Artech House, 2000.

[3]Nichols, Randall K., Daniel J. Ryan, and Julie J.C.H. Ryan, *Defending Your Digital Assets Against Hackers, Crackers, Spies and Thieves*, McGraw Hill Professional Books, 2000, p. 167.

[4]Nichols, Randall K., Daniel J. Ryan, and Julie J.C.H. Ryan, *Defending Your Digital Assets Against Hackers, Crackers, Spies and Thieves*, McGraw Hill Professional Books, 2000, p. 168.

[5]Nichols, Ryan, and Ryan, op. cit., p. 168.

[6]From slides and lecture at George Washington University, Washington D.C., GWU EMSE 256 by J.C.H.Ryan, 2/19/01.

[7]Mel, H.X., and Doris Baker, *Cryptography Decrypted*, Addison Wesley, Boston, 2001, p. 33ff.

[8]Nichols, Ryan, and Ryan, Defending, op. cit., pp. 169–172.

[9]Nichols, Randall K., *Classical Cryptography Course, Volumes I and II*, Laguna Hills, CA: Aegean Park Press, 1996 and 1997, pp. 140, 147.

[10]Nichols, Ryan, and Ryan, Defending, op. cit., pp. 183–186.

[11]From slides and lecture at George Washington University, Washington DC, GWU EMSE 298IN, 4/16/01.

[12]Nichols, Classical Cryptography Course, p. 9 & 93 ff.

[13]Nichols, Ryan, and Ryan, Defending, op. cit., p. 175.

[14]Ibid.

[15]Nichols, Ryan, and Ryan, Defending, op. cit., pp. 183–186.

[16]Mel, op. cit., p. 314.

[17]See http://www.nist.gov.

[18]Mel, op. cit. pp. 315–316.

[19]Ibid., p. 318.

[20]Ibid., p. 319.

[21]Kahn, op. cit., pp. 394ff.

[22]Rueppel, Rainer A., *Analysis and Design of Stream Ciphers*, Springer-Verlag, 1986, pp. 8–10.

[23]Nichols, Ryan, and Ryan, Defending, op. cit., p. 184.

[24]Mel, op. cit., p. 42.

[25]Electronic Frontier Foundation, *Cracking DES: Secrets of Encryption Research, Wiretap Politics, and Chip Design*, O'Reilly Press, 1998.

[26]Kumar, I. J., Cryptology: *System Identification and Key Clustering*, Aegean Park Press, 1997, pp. 3ff.

[27]Denning, Dorothy E., *Information Warfare and Security*, Addison Wesley, 1999, p. 294.

[28]Nichols, Ryan, and Ryan, Defending, op. cit., p. 177.

[29]Ibid.

[30]Ibid.

[31]Denning, op. cit., Table 11.1, p. 292.

[32]Ibid.

[33]Ibid., Table 11.2, p. 293.

[34]Ibid., p. 294.

[35]Ibid., p. 296.

[36]Ibid., p. 309.

[37]Rueppel, op. cit., pp. 5ff.

[38]Ibid., pp. 5–7.

[39]Ibid., pp. 14–16.

[40]Mel, op. cit., pp. 127ff

[41]Ibid., p. 128.

[42]Ibid., pp. 142, 151.

[43]National Institute of Standards and Technology, NIST FIPS PUB 186, Digital Signature Standard, U.S. Department of Commerce, 1994.

[44]Schneier, Bruce, *Applied Cryptography*, 2nd ed., John Wiley & Sons, 1996, pp. 442–446.

[45]Ibid., p. 445.

[46]Burnett, Steve, and Stephen Paine, *RSA's Security's Official Guide to Cryptography*, Osborne, 2001, p. 149.

[47]http://CSRC.NIST.gov/encryption/TKHASH.html.

[48]Hanschuh, Helena, Lars R. Knudsen, and Matthew J. Robshaw, "Analysis of SHA-1 in Encryption Mode," Topics in Cryptology, CT-RSA 2001, Springer, 2001, pp. 70ff.

[49]Matui, M., "Linear Cryptanalysis Method for DES Cipher," In Advances In Cryptology, EUROCRYPT 93, LNCS 765, pp. 386–397, Springer-Verlag, 1997.

[50]Biham, Eli, and Adi Shamir, *Differential Analysis of the Data Encryption Standard*, Springer-Verlag, 1993, Chapter 3.

[51]Handschuh, et. al, op. cit., p. 78.

[52]Ibid., p. 82.

[53]Lapat, Ronald H., Randall K. Nichols, Edward J. Giorgio, and Panos C. Lekkas, Provisional Patent Application, Attorney Docket No. 21558-019, A Method and System For Securing Information Communicated Between a Plurality of Communication Devices, USPO, Attorneys: Mintz, Levin, et. al, April 9, 2001.

[54]Ibid.

[55]Nichols, Randall K., *Advances in Wireless Security For Telecommunications Systems using FPGA's and ASICs*, RSA 2001 paper, April 10, 2001.

[56]Biryukov, Alex, Adi Shamir, and David Wagner, Real Time Cryptanalysis of A5/1 on a PC, Fast Software Encryption Workshop 2000, April 10–12, New York City. Available at: www.ccc.de/mirrors/cryptome.org/a51-bsw.htm.

[57]Schneier, op. cit., Authoritative and comprehensive coverage of most systems.

[58]Lapat, Ronald H., Randall K. Nichols, Edward J. Giorgio, and Panos C. Lekkas, Description of Invention: HORNET™ Technology from *Wireless Encryption Division* (WETD) of TeleHubLink Corporation, submitted with HORNET™ Provisional Patent Application, USPO, April 9, 2001.

[59]Compiled from slides from Nichols' RSA 2001 presentation. op. cit.

[60]Ibid.

[61]www.nist.gov/aes.

[62]www.esat.kuleuven.ac.be/~rijmen/rijndael/.

[63]http://fn2.freenet.Edmonton.ab.ca/~jsavard/.

[64]Graff, John C., Cryptography and E-Commerce, John Wiley & Sons, 2001, pp. 35–45.

[65]Ibid., p. 46ff.

[66]Denning, op. cit., pp. 298–299.

[67]Ibid., p. 300.

[68]Ibid., pp. 299–300.

[69]Graff, op. cit., Table 10.5 and modular arithmetic discussion, pp. 114ff.

[70]Nichols, Ryan, and Ryan, op. cit., p. 204.

[71]Ibid., pp. 204–205.

[72]Mel, op. cit., Table 15.2, p. 161.

[73]The first classification system condensed, with permission, from material from public white papers from Certicom's Web site, "Current Public-key Cryptographic Systems," April 1997, http://www.certicom.com/research/download/eccwhite1-3.zip.

[74]Nichols, Ryan, and Ryan, op. cit., p.188.

[75]Nichols, Guide, op. cit., Chapter 8.

[76]Burnett, Steveand Stephen Paine, op. cit., author's conclusion based on discussion on pp. 102–104, re 512-bit factoring and RSA experience. The author agrees and suggested the same result in 1999 in his book Defending, op. cit., p. 192.

[77]Certicom, "Current Public-key Cryptographic Systems," April 1997, http://www.certicom.com/research/download/eccwhite3.zip, p. 3.

[78]Certicom, "Remarks on the Security of the Elliptical Curve Cryptosystem," September 1997, http://www.certicom.com/research/download/eccwhite3.zip, p. 3.

[79]Burnett, Steveand Stephen Paine, op. cit., p. 102.

[80]Certicom, September 1997, p. 5.

[81]http://www.ort.edu.uy/REDOC/fermats.htm.

[82]Nichols, Guide, p. 240.

[83]http://www.dice.ucl.ac.be/crypto/joye/biblio_ell.html.

[84]Nichols, Ryan, and Ryan, Defending, op cit and original citation, "Current Public-Key Crypotgraphic Systems, " Certicom White Paper, April 1997, http://www.certicom.com.

[85]Ibid.

[86]Ibid.

[87]Ibid.

[88]Johnson, Don B., "ECC, Future Resiliency and High Security Systems," Certicom, March 30, 1999, http://www.certicom.com/research/download/eccfut.zip, p. 2.

[89]Ibid., p. 3.

[90]Certicom, May 1998, p. 6.

[91]Ibid, p. 251.

[92]Ibid, p. 7.

[93]Certicom, "The Elliptic Curve Cryptosystem for Smart Cards," May 1998, http://www.certicom.com/research/wecc4.html.

[94]Ibid.

[95]Dornan, Andy, "CDMA and 3G Cellular Networks," *Network*, Sept 5, 2000, http://www.networkmagazine.com/article/NMG20000831S0006.

[96]Dornan, 2000.

[97]http://img.cmpnet.com/networkmag2000/content/200009/tut.gif.

[88]Staff, "Short Circuits," *Network* Magazine, January 8, 2001, http://www.teledotcom.com/article/TEL20010105S0025.

[99]http://www.palmos.com/dev/tech/hardware/compare.html.

[100]http://athome.compaq.com/showroom/static/iPAQ/handheld.asp.

[101]http://www.rsasecurity.com/products/bsafe/cryptoc.html.

[102]Ibid.

[103]http://www.rsasecurity.com/products/bsafe/cryptoc.html.

[104]Dandalis, Andreas, Victor K. Prasanna, and Jose D.P. Rolim, *A Comparative Study of Performance of AES Final Candidates Using FPGAs*, in Cryptographic Hardware and Embedded Systems—CHES 2000, Cetin K Koc, ed, Springer, 2000, pp. 125–140.

[105]http://www.rsasecurity.com/products/bsafe/cryptoc.html.

[106]Weeks, Bryan, Mark Bean, Tom Rozylowicz, Chris Ficke, "Hardware Performance Simulations of Round 2 Advanced Encryption Standard Algorithms," Third AES Candidate Conference, April 2000.

[107]Gaj, Kris, and Pawel Chodowiec, "Fast Implementation and Fair Comparison of the Final Candidates for Advanced Encryption Standard Using Field Programmable Gate Arrays," RSA 2001, in Topics in Cryptology—CT RSA2001, LNCS 2020, Springer, 2001, pp. 85–89.

[108]Dandalis, op. cit., p. 125

[109]Ibid., p. 126.

[110]Ibid., p. 128.

[111]Ibid., pp. 137–139.

[112]Gaj, Kris, and Pawel Chodowiec, *Fast Implementation and Fair Comparison of the Final Candidates for Advanced Encryption Standard Using Field Programmable Gate Arrays*, op. cit., pp. 84, 99.

[113]Elbert, A. J., W Yip, B. Chetwynd, and C. Paar, "An FPGA Implementation and Performance Evaluation of the AES Block Cipher Candidate Algorithm Finalists," Third AES Candidate Conference, April 2000.

[114]Dandalis, op. cit.

[115]Gaj, Kris, and Pawel Chodowiec, "Comparison of Hardware performance of the AES Candidates using Reconfigurable Hardware," Third AES Candidate Conference, April 2000.

[116]Aoki, K., and H. Lipmaa, "Fast Implementations of AES Candidates," Third AES Candidate Conference, April 2000.

[117]Bassham, L.E., III, "Efficiency Testing of ANSI C Implementation of Round 2 Candidate Algorithm For the Advanced Encryption Standard," Third AES Candidate Conference, April 2000.

[118]Dandalis, op. cit., p. 136.

[119]Bassham, op. cit.

[120]Dandalis, op. cit., p. 136.

[121]Weeks, op. cit.

[122]Dandalis, op. cit., p. 137.

[123]Weeks, op. cit.

[124]Dandalis, op. cit., p .137.

6

Speech Cryptology

We think of digital technology as the backbone of our entire information industry. Today digital communication techniques are ubiquitous. The explosive growth of the semiconductor and microelectronics industries, coupled with the invention of the transistor in 1947, made modern digital communications possible at its present day scale. A key driver, the transformation of audio information into digital signals, is now a routine process incorporated into our telephone, television, and music equipment. Many of these capabilities were pioneered during World War II in a successful effort to provide secure voice communications for high-level government officials. This chapter explores cryptographic principles required to secure and exploit *over-the-air* (OTA) speech transmissions.

It Started with SIGSALY

Before the United States entered WWII, the United States and the United Kingdom were using transatlantic *high-frequency radio* (HF) for voice communications between senior leaders. The *analog* voice privacy system in use, called the *A-3*, provided reasonable protection against the casual eavesdropper, but it was vulnerable to anyone with sophisticated unscrambling capability. This system continued to be used during the early part of the war, and government officials were warned that they could be overheard (just as we have warned politicians who ignore the advice). Germany set up a listening station in the Netherlands (because of excellent reception and LPD) that broke the U.S.-U.K. link conversations in real time. This situation was intolerable, but neither the United States nor the United Kingdom had a ready solution.[1] The story of the German listening post given to us by the master cryptological historian David Kahn, suggests that the Germans were ahead of us in the secure voice contest until about July 1943.[2]

In a converted youth hostel on the Dutch coast, 200 yards from the sea, engineers tended the electronic equipment that produced one of Germany's most sensational World War II intelligence coups. It snared the voices of Franklin D. Roosevelt and Winston Churchill flashing in scrambled form through the ether and restored them automatically and instantaneously to their pristine form. Translations of its tape recordings of these intimate talks then went to the Fuhrer himself.

This apparatus belonged to the Research Institute of the Deutsche Reichspost. During the 1930s, the Research Institute had been studying voice privacy methods for the German post office, which, like most European post offices, ran the nation's telephone system. At the start of the war, the head of the Reichspost decided that descrambling enemy conversations would be of more help to Germany, so he shifted Kurt E. Vetterlein, a 29-year-old engineer, from scrambling research to descrambling. Vetterlein felt that the transatlantic radiotelephone connection between Great Britain and the United States was the most interesting, and he concentrated on that.

To prevent anyone with a short-wave receiver from listening to the conversations that passed over this circuit, the *American Telephone & Telegraph* (AT&T) Company and the British post office mangled the voices upon transmission and restored them upon reception with an electronic mechanism called the A-3. AT&T housed its A-3 in a locked room at 47 Walker Street, New York, and all radiotelephone transmissions passed through it before being propelled into the ether for the long leap across the Atlantic.

Since the Deutsche Reichspost also had an A-3 for radiotelephone communications with America, Vetterlein knew the principles of its operation. But he did not know the variables that enshrouded the American messages in secrecy. Using transmissions from America intercepted near Bordeaux in occupied France, Vetterlein and his assistants, working in the Deutsche Reichspost building on the Ringstrasse in Berlin, attacked the problem with oscilloscopes and spectrographs, filters and patience. By the end of 1940, they had reconstructed the A-3's secret parameters—the widths of the sub-bands, their division points, their inversions, and their intersubstitutions, which changed 36 times every 12 minutes. For the day-to-day solution of the conversations, Vetterlein wanted to construct a mechanism that would descramble them as they were being spoken. This demanded an extremely exact time standard because the A-3 shifted its enciphering pattern every 20 seconds in the 36-step cycle, but it was the only way to cope with the volume of communications.[3]

Vetterlein's Forschungsstelle

In looking for a place to set up his intercept post, Vetterlein found that near Noordwijk on the coast of the Netherlands gave the best reception. It could pick up both the ground wave of the transmitter in England and the back lobe of its beam toward America. Vetterlein took over the youth hostel and began installing his equipment—enough to fill a couple of living rooms: three or four single-sideband receivers, filters, modulators, switching equipment, tape recorders, and the timers. Based on a quartz-stabilized watch, these held his descrambler so close to the A-3 that even if no messages passed for an entire day, the equipment would lose only a fraction of a syllable when communication started up again.

By the fall of 1941, Vetterlein's unit, called the Forschungsstelle (Research Post), was intercepting and descrambling messages. Engineers under Vetterlein monitored the Allied conversations 24 hours a day. The calls were intercepted in scrambled form by two rhombic antennas, instantaneously disentangled by the apparatus, and tape-recorded in the clear. Often as many as 60 calls a day came in, and never fewer than 30. A half-dozen highly qualified interpreters listened to them and selected those of intelligence value. At first they translated them on the spot and teleprinted the German in cipher to Berlin. But scrambling degrades the quality of speech, and this, plus static and the occasional imprecision of translation, led to the messages being sent on in English.[4]

The operation was not cut and dried. Once the AT&T engineers changed the subband widths, compelling Vetterlein to repeat some of his analyses. In 1943, after commandos captured some coastal radars, the Germans feared that this might happen to the Forschungsstelle as well so it was moved to Valkenswaard, a small town in the southeast Netherlands. Here a compact brick-and-concrete bunker in the shape of an L was built for it in woods at the intersection of Nieuwe Waalreseweg and De Hazelaar streets at the north of the town. The men worked in areas guarded by inch-thick steel doors, cooked in their own kitchen, slept in rooms with dormer windows, and relaxed in a living room with a fireplace. A fence topped by barbed wire surrounded the bunker. In the fall of 1944, the unit retreated to Bavaria. But here the distance from the transmitter considerably impaired its results.

Most of the intercepts revealed middle-level bureaucrats discussing middle-level problems. Many dealt with requests for reinforcements, aircraft, and other supplies. The lack of substance in the talks came from the general recognition that the scrambler was insecure. The circuit's operators constantly warned the speakers of this. The speakers mostly used it despite this insecurity when they needed a quick answer to a question or had to rapidly settle a matter that required some discussion but would not give anything away, or sometimes when they just wanted to hear one another's voices.

Nevertheless, Churchill and Roosevelt were not always as careful as they should have been. Churchill was practically addicted to the telephone, picking it up at all hours of the day and night to call Roosevelt, who in his turn surprised the Germans with his indiscretions. He, Churchill, and a few other high officials were not given the warnings about insecurity that the lower officials were—an indication to the Germans, when this was omitted, that an important person was coming on the line. Partly because of this, partly because of their rank, some of the Roosevelt-Churchill conversations disclosed matters of more import than the other intercepts. Many of Churchill's indiscretions dealt with Italy. By July 1943, the intercepts "takes" were marginal at best. The spectacular technical feat of tapping into the top-level Allied radiotelephone conversations produced no great results and they probably did not give the Germans any real insight into U.S. intentions, but the United States was certainly kept guessing.[5]

Fortunately, the technical groundwork for a solution was already in place. About 1936, *Bell Telephone Laboratories* (BTL) began exploring a technique to transform voice signals into digital data that could then be reconstructed (or synthesized) into intelligible voice. It was called a vocoder, short for voice coder. An early demonstration of the voice synthesizer portion of the vocoder was even a part of the 1939 World's Fair in New York. The approaching war forced the investigation of true voice security. The vocoder was selected by BTL as the basis of a new high-tech voice security system. BTL proceeded on its own to develop this much-needed capability and was soon able to demonstrate it to the satisfaction of the Army. The U.S. Army awarded a contract to BTL in 1942 for the production of the first two systems. This system eventually came to be called *SIGSALY* and was first deployed in 1943.[6]

The BTL development group worked under the direction of A. B. Clark (who later led the Research and Development activities of the new National Security Agency from 1954 to 1955) and developed a vocoder-based system, which emphasized the preservation of voice quality. They chose a 12-channel system. Ten of the channels each measured the power of the voice signal in a portion of the total voice frequency spectrum (generally 250 to 3000 Hz), and two channels were devoted to pitch information of the speech as well as whether or not unvoiced (hiss) energy was present. This work was essentially completed in 1942, and patents were filed. BTL invented the fundamentals of digital, encrypted voice, and the means to transmit it.

A 1983 review of this remarkable system for the Institute of *Electrical and Electronic Engineers* (IEEE) attributes no fewer than eight firsts to SIGSALY:

1. The first realization of enciphered telephony
2. The first quantized speech transmission (Quantization is when an analog signal is made digital, it is made discrete in both time and amplitude. Discretization in time is called *sampling* and amplitude discretization is called *quantization*.)
3. The first transmission of speech by *Pulse Code Modulation* (PCM)
4. The first use of companded PCM (Companding is the analganation of a discrete signal from its parts).
5. The first examples of multilevel *Frequency Shift Keying* (FSK)
6. The first useful realization of speech bandwidth compression
7. The first use of *Frequency Shift Keying-Frequency Division Multiplex* (FSK—FDM) as a viable transmission method over a fading medium
8. The first use of a multilevel "eye pattern" to adjust the sampling intervals (a new, and important, instrumentation technique)

The IEEE article also points out that the system can be thought of as being one of the first successful applications of Spread-Spectrum technology.[7]

Digitizing Voice Information via SIGSALY

An overview of the general scheme for digitizing voice information is shown in Figure 6-1 and encrypting it is shown in Figure 6-2.[8]

It is a rare thing indeed to produce a new system with so many unique features. These were not simply improvements; they were fundamentally new and absolutely necessary for the system to work. The concepts were proven in the lab, but before the system was ready for final development and deployment, there were several important system features that needed refinement.

Key generation was a major problem. The basic requirements for the key (one essential part of the total encryption system) was that it should be completely random, and must not repeat, but could still be replicated at both the sending and receiving ends of the system. This was accomplished for SIGSALY by using the out-

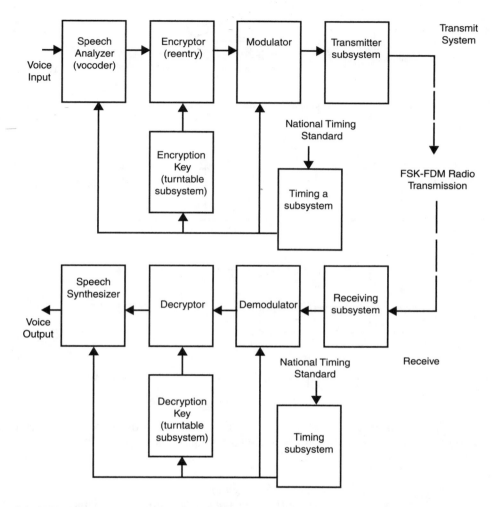

6-1 SIGSALY. (Courtesy of NSA National Cryptology Museum, Laurel, MD)

put of large (4-inch diameter, 14-inch high) mercury-vapor rectifier vacuum tubes to generate wideband thermal noise. This noise power was sampled every 20 ms and the samples then quantized into *six levels of equal probability*. The level information was converted into channels of a *frequency-shift-keyed* (FSK) audio tone signal that could then be recorded on the hard vinyl phonograph records of the time.

The FSK signal was recorded on 16-inch diameter wax platters, which were then transformed into "masters." The masters, which in commercial use would have been used to make thousands of records each, were used to produce only three records of a particular key generation segment. Key distribution, a problem, was accomplished by means of transporting and distributing the phonograph records. These records were taken to Arlington Hall Station in Virginia, and the masters were destroyed.

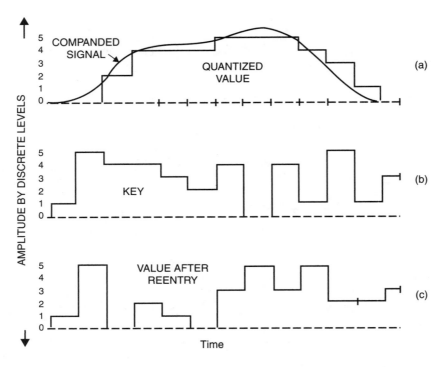

6-2 Early Vocoder. (Courtesy of NSA National Cryptology Museum, Laurel, MD)

Once the systems were deployed, the key-pair was distributed by courier from Arlington Hall to the sending and receiving stations. Each recording provided only twelve minutes of key plus several other functional signals, which were necessary for seamless key output.

Later advances in recording technology permitted the simultaneous direct recording of the key on two acetate disks backed by aluminum. This technique reduced drastically the time required to make each record and also reduced cost. Since the keys were changed for every conference and on a regular schedule, there were a large number of recordings made and distributed under strict controls. The key recordings were destroyed after use.

The system required that the key be used in 20 ms segments. Therefore, it was necessary for each record to be kept in synchronism within a few milliseconds for fairly long periods of time (one hour or so). This was accomplished by the use of precisely driven turntables. The turntables themselves were remarkable machines. Each was driven by a large (about 30-pound) synchronous electric motor with hundreds of poles. The motor was kept in constant operation, and the power for it was derived directly from dividing down the terminal's 100-KHz crystal oscillator frequency standard. The accuracy of the standard was maintained within one part in 10 million to keep the system in synchronism for long periods of time.

Since one record held only about 12 minutes of key, it was necessary to have two transmit and two receive turntable subsystems at each terminal. In this way, a transition could be made from one key-pair to another. However, there was another problem: How did the system get started in synchronism?

Each terminal was a standalone operation that depended on its own internal clock referenced to a national time standard. Systems were started at prearranged times, generally 1200 GMT for U.S.-U.K. exchanges. No synchronizing signals passed from one terminal to another.

Prior to starting, the phonograph pickup was indexed to the first record groove. This process consisted of listening to the pickup output click as it was slid along the edge of the record in order to determine when it fell into the first groove. This was easier with the original hard records than with the softer acetate records. Once the pickup position was established and the time came to start the session, a clever mechanical device was used to obtain a simultaneous start at both ends of the link. The turntables were attached to the shaft of the synchronous motor by means of a clutch and spring arrangement. At the startup time, the clutch was automatically energized and a pinball type plunger was activated, which provided the initial starting motion to the turntable by releasing a spring that then pulled the turntable from its starting position to the same speed and in lock with the rotation of the synchronous motor. All of this enabled the motor to keep its synchronized position. At the end of the process, each turntable would be running at a definite and precise rate, and the key-pair would be synchronized to the accuracy required for operation.

Of course, fine adjustments in relative timing were required. These were made by the use of 50-*Hertz* (Hz) phase shifters (Helmholz coils) in the basic power/timing circuitry that drove the turntables. The operator could adjust a separate phase shifter to control the timing within the receiving system to account for the transmission time, which was on the order of 16 ms for a transatlantic circuit. Operators initially established the synchronization by carefully adjusting the phase of the synchronous motor and listening to the quieting in the audio output when the key-pairs were in synchronism. Operators often monitored the quality of the conversations and adjusted the system in a similar manner. The entire synchronization process was complex, but it worked. The turntable-based key-record system was called SIGGRUV when the vinyl records were used and SIGJINGS when the acetate records were used.

A mechanical alternative to the recorded key was called *Alternate Key* (AK). The AK subsystem consisted of a large number of stepping switches, relays, and other devices. It started the key derivation process with a rotor device normally associated with teletype encryption systems. It was a complex and relatively unreliable system that required constant maintenance attention. There was a difference in system operating characteristics between using the recorded key and the AK subsystem.

When the system was using a recorded key and lost synchronization, there was almost always an abrupt and total loss of system capability. When the AK system began to deteriorate, it usually did so in small increments, which resulted in a sound like a horse galloping. In just a few seconds, a small gallop developed into a full gallop as the first small error (caused, for example, by a faulty relay contact) was multiplied and propagated throughout the system. AK was used by the system operators mainly for daily maintenance purposes. This subsystem was called SIGBUSE.

A simplified overview of the total system is shown in Figure 6-1 representing a one-way transmission. Return transmissions used the same key setup. SIGSALY took up a huge amount of room by today's standards. Pictures of the system can be seen at the Cryptological National Museum at NSA, which is a treasure to visit and is open to the public.[9]

SIGSALY terminals were established in Washington, D.C., London, Paris, North Africa, Hawaii, Guam, Manila, and Australia, among others. In London, the bulk of the SIGSALY equipment was housed in the basement of an annex to Selfridge's Department Store while the actual instrument used by Churchill and his staff was about a mile away in the War Rooms under the Admiralty Building and near the prime minister's residence at 10 Downing Street. The Washington, D.C., end of the system was installed in the recently completed Pentagon in the summer of 1943. The original installation schedule called for a system to be in the White House itself, but the Pentagon location was chosen to permit the system to be more easily used by senior members of the military (and possibly to give President Roosevelt better control over his own schedule since he would not be interrupted at all hours by callers).[10]

Members of the Army 805th Signal Service Corps were sent to staff all SIGSALY locations. In addition to the requirements for special security, they dealt with the complexities of the technology. Western Electric Company specifications were used, and immaculate daily records were kept. The equipment was normally operated for about eight hours a day, and the remaining sixteen were used for maintenance! The large number of vacuum tubes required constant checking. In some cases they were removed and checked so often that the sockets started to go bad. Maintenance schedules were adapted with experience to avoid such problems, but maintenance remained a challenging job. Power supplies were critical elements in the system and were adjusted using a standard cell and galvanometer system to a probable accuracy of one-tenth of a volt in 150 volts. Tens of power supplies were adjusted daily. Ninety-six stepper circuits also needed daily adjustment. Despite all the complexity, the efforts of the 805th, coupled with the fundamentally sound design, made the SIGSALY system operationally effective. There was surprisingly little operational downtime.

The ability to use truly secure voice communications at high organizational levels was a great advantage to the Allies in the conduct of the war and in the critical activities, which followed it. Not only was SIGSALY a highly successful secure voice system, but also it provided a springboard into the digital communications world. It encouraged the BTL staff and their government counterparts to think more about communications in digital terms rather than in the traditional analog processes. The rapid development and deployment activities also offer a challenge for present-day members of the cryptologic community.[11]

SIGSALY was a truly remarkable beginning for speech security systems and the "digital revolution." Here are some remarks by then president, Dr. O. E. Buckley of Bell Telephone Laboratories at the formal opening of SIGSALY Service, 15 July 1943:[12]

We are assembled today in Washington and London to open a new service, secret telephony. It is an event of importance in the conduct of the war that others here can appraise better than I. As a technical achievement, I should like to point out that it must be counted among the major advances in the art of telephony. Not only does it represent the achievement of a goal long sought—complete secrecy in radio-telephone transmission—but it represents the first practical application of new methods of telephone transmission that promise to have far-reaching effects.

To achieve the result represented by this system, there have been done several very remarkable things. Speech has been converted into low frequency signals that are not speech but contain a specification or description of it. Those signals have been coded by a system that defies decoding by any but the intended recipient. The coded signals have been transmitted over a radio circuit in such a way that an interceptor cannot even distinguish the presence or absence of the signals. At the receiving end, the signals have been decoded and restored and then used to regenerate speech nearly enough like that which gave them birth that it may be clearly understood. To do these things called for a degree of precision and a refinement of techniques that scarcely seemed possible when the researches that led to this result were undertaken. That speech transmitted in this manner sounds somewhat unnatural and that voices are not always recognizable should not be surprising. The remarkable thing is that it can be done at all.[13]

Overview of SIGSALY Encryption Process for Single Vocoder Channel

The general concept of the encryption process for a single vocoder channel is presented in Figure 6-2. In each of the lines of this figure, the vertical axis segment represents levels of quantization, and the segments of the horizontal lines represent time in the 20-ms increments used in the SIGSALY system.

Line (a) in the figure represents the six-level quantization of the output of the vocoder channel. Although difficult to show in this diagram, the individual signal quantization steps do not represent equal power changes in the actual input signal. The steps were logarithmetic and a part of the companding process. This process had been shown to produce improved intelligibility in the reconstructed voice output.

The random key is illustrated by line (b) in the figure. This is the information produced from the recordings played on the turntable subsystem. The key was combined with the quantized signal information in a process, which was then called reentry. The reentry combination process is mathematically described as adding the two quantized values mod 6.

Line (c) represents the encrypted data stream, which would then be transmitted by the FSK-FDM radio equipment. The essentials of the receiving and decryption process are the reverse of the encryption process. First, the transmitted multichannel signals are demodulated. Then each channel is decrypted by subtracting the key mod 6 from the signal. It is obvious that the 20-ms segments of the quantized signal information and the key information must be synchronized in exactly the same manner at both the transmitting and receiving ends of the system. It remains to recombine the vocoder channel outputs, incorporate the pitch information and then reconstruct the audio signal and transform it into intelligible speech. This entire new process was extremely difficult to implement in the technology of the 1940s. Once the encrypted signal was produced, a means to transmit it in a reliable manner was needed. The BTL staff solved the problem by inventing multilevel frequency shift keying.[14]

Cryptology of Speech Signals

The problem of secure speech may be expanded to encompass many languages. Speech is the most common means of communication. Apart from linguistic information (that is, the meaning the speech sound conveys) a lot of nonlinguistic or personal information about the speaker is also conveyed with the spoken message. As in the case of text, the need arises to make the speech communication secure, the security level varying from a simple form of privacy to high levels of security for strategic messages of great importance. Before we discuss the techniques and principles of providing security to spoken messages, it is important to understand the anatomy of speech and the various methods available for its analysis.

The properties of speech and general techniques of signal analysis are required for speech processing, following by the cryptography of speech and a description of a range of security techniques, starting from simple analog scramblers to the most complex digital ciphers and vocoders. With this background we embark on the cryptanalysis of speech, describing the tools and techniques available for cryptanalysis and the methods used for cryptanalysis of specific scramblers.

Speech: Production and Nonlinguistic Properties

The human voice can be represented as a series of sounds called phonemes. A *phoneme* is the smallest element of speech that makes a difference in the meaning of the spoken word. All the different speech sounds derive power from the respiratory system as air is pushed out of the lungs. Air is forced through the vocal folds, known as the vocal cords. The opening between the vocal folds is known as the *glottis*. The air passage above the vocal cords and up to the lips is called the vocal tract, the shape of which can be changed by changing the position of the articulators (that is, the lips, jaws, tongue, velum, and so forth, as seen in Figure 6-3).

The vocal tract and the nasal cavity act as tubes of nonuniform cross sectional area that produce varying resonances when excited by air pushed up by the glottal excitation source. The resonance frequencies are called the formant frequencies or *formants*. The formant frequencies for any particular phoneme vary slightly from individual to individual as these also depend on the shape and dimensions of the vocal tract. This basic apparatus of speech production can produce different sounds depending on the shape of the vocal tract and the source of excitation. The 40 different phonemes of the English language can be classified into three distinct classes namely: voiced, unvoiced (or fricative), and plosives.

When we breathe outward, the vocal cords are held apart allowing free passage of air, but if they are held closer leaving only a narrow passage between them, the air

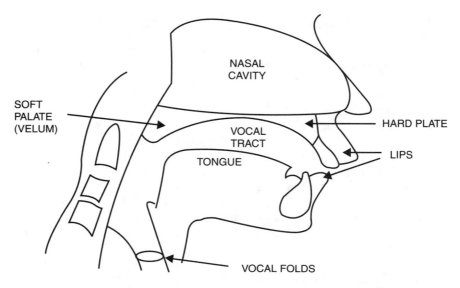

6-3 A view of the vocal organs. (Courtesy of I. J. Kumar and Aegean Park Press)

stream flow equilibrium instability forces them together momentarily resulting in no flow of air. If the air pressure persists or increases below the vocal cords they are blown apart, the pressure lessons, then is reapplied. This vibratory cycle continues and the flapping action of the vocal cords converts the stream of air into a series of pulses that excite the vocal tract cavities (as in *a, e,* and so forth). Such sounds are called voiced sounds and the frequency at which the vocal cords vibrate is called the pitch frequency. Changing the length, thickness, and tension of the vocal cords varies this frequency. In general, the pitch is higher for females and children as compared to males, the normal adult male range being 100 to 400 Hz, the female and child upward to 3000 Hz or more. The unvoiced sounds are produced by voluntarily holding the vocal cords apart slightly, yet forcing air through them and then partially shutting off the air stream to produce turbulence, using the articulators. This creates a broad-spectrum noise to excite the vocal tract as in *sh, ss,* and so forth. Plosive sounds are similar to voiced sounds, but in such cases the air stream is momentarily completely shut off using the articulators and then abruptly released as in *p, V,* and so forth.[15]

The Structure of Language

Linguistic anthropologists have used cryptography to reconstruct ancient languages by comparing contemporary descendants and in so doing have made discoveries relative to human history. Others have made inferences about universal features of language, linking them to uniformities in the brain. While yet others study linguistic differences to discover varied worldviews and patterns of thought in a multitude of cultures.

The Rosetta Stone, found by the Egyptian Dhautpol and the French officer Pierre-Francois Bouchard near the town of Rosetta in the Nile Delta, gave us a look at Syriac, Greek, and Egyptian hieroglyphs all of the same text. Andrew Robinson covers the fascinating story of its decipherment.[16] Of special interest was the final decipherment of the Egyptian writing containing *homophones*—different signs standing for the same sound.

Until the late 1950s, linguists thought that the study of language should proceed through a sequence of stages of analysis. The first stage was phonology, the study of sounds used in speech. Phones are speech sounds present and significant in each language. They were recorded using the International Phonetic Alphabet, a series of symbols devised to describe dozens of sounds that occur in different languages.

The next stage was morphology, the study of forms in which sounds combine to form morphemes—words and their meaningful constituents. The word *cats* has two morphemes, /cat/ and /s/, indicating the animal and plurality. A lexicon is a dictionary of all morphemes. A morpheme is the smallest meaningful unit of speech. Isolating or analytic languages are those in which words are morphologically benign, like Chinese or Vietnamese. Agglutinative languages string together successive morphemes. Turkish is a good example of this. Inflection languages change the form of a word to mark kinds of grammar distinctions, such as tense or gender. Indo-European languages tend to be highly inflectional. The next step was to study syntax, the arrangement and order of words in phrases and sentences.

Phonemes and Phones

No language contains all the sounds in the International Phonetic Alphabet. *Phonemes* lack meaning in themselves, but through sound contrasts they distinguish meaning. We find them in minimal pairs, words that resemble each other in all but one sound, an example being the minimal pair pit/bit. The /p/ and /b/ are phonemes in English. Another example is bit and beat that separates the phonemes /I/ and /i/ in English. Friedman describes similar phenomena called homophones and uses them to solve a variety of cryptograms.[17]

Standard (American) English (SE), the region-free dialect of TV network newscasters, has about 35 phonemes of at least 11 vowels and 24 consonants. The number of phonemes varies from language to language—from 15 to 60, averaging between 30 and 40. The number of phonemes varies among dialects. In American English, vowel phonemes vary noticeably from dialect to dialect. You might wish to pronounce the words in Figure 6-4, paying attention to whether they distinguish each of the vowel sounds. North Americans do not generally pronounce them at all.

Phonetics studies sounds in general—what people actually say in various languages.

Phonemics is concerned with sound contrasts of a particular language. In English /b/ and /v/ are phonemes, occurring in minimal pairs such as *bat* and *vat*. In Spanish, the contrast between [b] and [v] doesn't distinguish meaning and therefore these are not phonemes. The [b] sound is used in Spanish to pronounce words spelled with either b or v. However, in Spanish, the [b] and [v] may be given a slight f

```
┌─────────────────────────────────────────────────────────┐
│              Vowel Phonemes                              │
│           Standard American English                      │
│   According to Height of Tongue and Tongue Position      │
│        in Front, Center, and Back of Mouth               │
│                                                          │
│                                      Tongue High         │
│        i              u                                  │
│        I              U                                  │
│        ea    ua    o                                     │
│         e          ou               Mid                  │
│          ae    a                                         │
│                                                          │
│                                     Tongue Low           │
│                                                          │
│     Tongue          Central       Tongue                 │
│     Front            Back                                │
└─────────────────────────────────────────────────────────┘
```

6-4 Phonemes. (Courtesy of R. K. Nichols, The ICSA Guide to Cryptography, McGraw-Hill, 1999)

in English sound, however, meaning must be clear to be technically considered as a phoneme. (Nonphonemic phones are enclosed in brackets.)

Phonetic symbols are identified by English words that include them; note that most are minimal pairs.

high front (spread)	[i] as in beat
lower high front (spread)	[i] as in bit
mid front (spread)	[ea] as in bait
lower mid front (spread)	[e] as in bet
low front	[ae] as in bat
central	[ua] as in butt
low back	[a] as in pot
lower mid back (rounded)	[ou] as in bought
mid back (rounded)	[o] as in boat
lower high back (rounded)	[U] as in put
high back (rounded)	[u] as in boot

In any language, a given phoneme extends over a phonetic range. In English the phoneme /p/ ignores the phonetic contrast between the [pH] in pin and the [p] in spin. How many of you noticed the difference? [pH] is aspirated, so that a puff of air follows the [p]. Not true with [p] in spin. To see the difference, light a match and watch the flame as you say the two words. In Chinese the contrast between [p] and [pH] is distinguished only by the contrast between an aspirated and unaspirated [p].[18]

Historical Linguistics

Knowledge of linguistic relationships is often valuable to determine the events of the past 5,000 years. By studying contemporary daughter languages, past language features can be reconstructed. Daughter languages descend from the same parent language that has been changing for thousands of years. The original language from which they diverge is called a *protolanguage*. French and Spanish are daughter languages of Latin. Language evolves over time into subgroups (closely related taxonomy) but with distinct cultural differences.

The Chomsky Model (see Figure 6-5) for cultural influences defines the rules for message transfer from speaker to hearer or writer based on sounds and phonological content. Figure 6-6 highlights the main languages and subgroups of the Indo-European language stock.

All these daughter languages have developed out of the protolanguage spoken in Northern Europe about 5,000 years ago. English, a member of the Germanic branch, is more closely related to German and Dutch than it is to Italic or Romance languages, such as French and Spanish. However, English shares many linguistic features with French through borrowing and diffusion.

The doctrine of linguistic relativity is central to cryptographic treatment of language ciphers. It states that all known languages and dialects are effective means of communication. *Nichols' Theorem* states that if they are linguistically related, they can be codified, enciphered, deciphered, and treated as cryptographic units for analysis and statistical treatment.[19]

Figure 6-6 pertains to live languages. Professor Cyrus H. Gordon in his fascinating book *Forgotten Scripts,* shows how cryptography is used to recover ancient writings. He tells the story of the unraveling of each of these ancient languages:

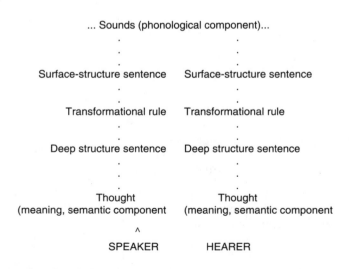

6-5 Chomsky Model for cultural influences. (Courtesy of Nichols, ICSA Guide To Cryptography, 1999)

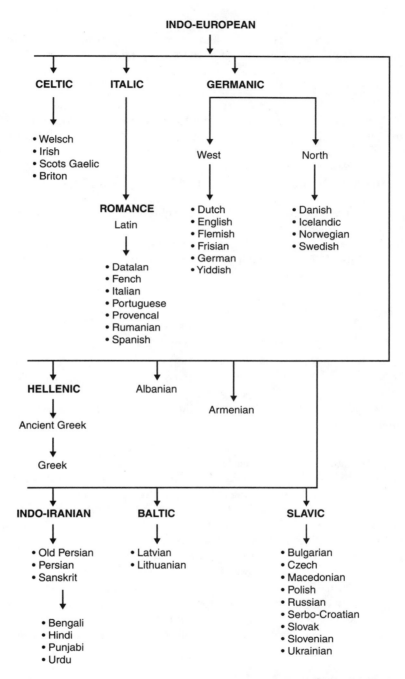

6-6 Main languages of Indo-European stock. (Courtesy of Nichols, ICSA Guide To Cryptography, 1999)

Egyptian, Old Persian, Sumer-Akkadian, Hittite, Ugaritic, Eteocretan, Minoan, and Eblaite. He specializes in cuneiform and hieroglyphic inscriptions and gives us a glimpse into the ancient societies that gave birth to the Western world.[20]

Threads

There is a common cryptographic thread for most languages. All known writing systems are partly or wholly phonetic and express the sounds of a particular language. Writing is speech put in visible form in such a way that any reader instructed in its conventions can reconstruct the vocal message. The Sumerians and, almost simultaneously, the ancient Egyptians invented writing as "visible speech" about 5,000 years.[21]

The ancient Mayan knew that it was 12 cycles, 18 katuns, 16 tuns, 0 uinals, and 16 kins since the beginning of the Great Cycle. The day was 12 Cib 14 Uo and was ruled by the seventh Lord of the Night. The moon was nine days old. Precisely 5,101 of our years and 235 days had passed. So said the ancient Mayan scribes. We remember the day as 14 May 1989.

Writing Systems

Three kinds of writing systems have been identified:

- *Rebus*, which is a combination of logograms and phonetic signs
- *Syllabic* consonant vowel, combinations, examples of which are Cherokee or Inuit
- *Alphabetic*, which is phonemic, the individual consonants and vowels making up the sounds of the language

Writing systems can also be classified by their signs. Table 6-1 differentiates writing systems by the number of signs used.[22]

The numbers of sounds that may be communicated as a function of these signs are immense. The problem of encrypting those sounds to ciphertext and reconstructing them as understandable plaintext represents a complex security process. An excellent description of the production mechanism and properties of speech is given in Goldberg and Riek, 2000.[23]

Most *voice coders* (vocoders) model the vocal tract to simplify analysis of the speech signal. A source-filter model can represent the complete mechanism of speech production. The effect of the resonating cavities can be modeled as a frequency selective filter, which operates on the excitation source. The frequency spectrum of the glottal excitation source is multiplied by the frequency characteristics of the filter to give the overall spectrum. Figure 6-7 shows the classic source-filter model of speech.

Classic Source-Filter Model

During encoding, the model parameters are determined to represent accurately the input speech. For decoding, the structure of the model, along with the encoded parameters, provides guidelines for reconstructing the output speech.

Table 6-1   Signs in Writing Systems

Writing System	Number of Signs
Logographic	
Sumerian	600+
Egyptian	2,500
Hittite Hieroglyphic	497
Chinese	5,000+
"Pure" Syllabic	
Persian	40
Linear B	87
Cypriote	56
Cherokee	85
Alphabetic or Consonantal	
English	26
Anglo-Saxon	31
Sanskrit	35
Etruscan	20
Russian	36
Hebrew	22
Arabic	28

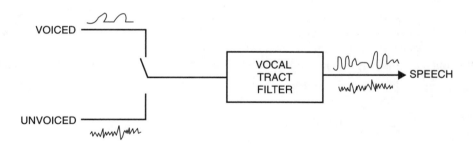

6-7 Source-filter model (Classic). (Courtesy of Goldberg, CRC Press, 2000)

The source-filter model is a widely used speech production model. The source-filter model patterns the vocal tract as a (usually linear) time-varying filter. The source energy for this filter is the excitation signal. The different ways of coding this excitation signal are generally what separates these source-filter speech coders from one another. The source-filter model results from considering the excitation and vocal tract as separable components in the production of speech. The excitation is produced at some point in the vocal tract, and then the excitation is spectrally shaped (or filtered) by the rest of the vocal tract.

The throat, nose, tongue, and mouth form a resonating air-filled cavity that predominantly dictates the sound produced by the human vocal system. The resonant frequencies of this tube are called formant frequencies. Different configurations of the vocal tract result in different formant frequencies. The formant frequencies are one of the two major factors that dictate which phoneme the vocal tract will produce. The other major factor is excitation of the vocal tract.

For voiced speech, a periodic waveform provides the excitation to the vocal tract. The periodic waveform results from the glottal pulses created by the rapid opening and closing of vocal cords. White noise is a simple model for unvoiced speech. White noise is random and has a flat spectral shape wherein all frequencies have equal power. The white noise is assumed to be generated when air passes through a constriction. Some sounds like /z/ are produced by both exciting the vocal tract with a periodic excitation and by forcing air through a constriction in the vocal tract. This is known as mixed excitation. One of the challenges in coding speech is to accurately represent sounds as voiced, unvoiced, or mixed.[24]

General Source-Filter Model

Figure 6-9 illustrates the flow of signals and information for a generalized source-filter model. The pitch information is usually contained in a pitch-period value with values changing over time. Based on the pitch period, the periodic excitation block produces a pulse waveform that represents the glottal pulses. The noise excitation block outputs a noisy sequence with a flat spectral response. The two excitations are input to the mixing decision. Time-varying information about the voicing of speech is the other input. Based on the level of voicing in the original speech, the mixing decision block combines the periodic and noisy excitations in appropriate amounts to produce the excitation signal.[25]

A classic version (see Figure 6-8) of the two-state, source-filter model incorporates a hard voiced/unvoiced decision for each segment of speech. In that case, the "Mixing Decision" functions as a switch, and the excitation is entirely voiced or unvoiced, depending on the classification. The vocal tract information is fed into the

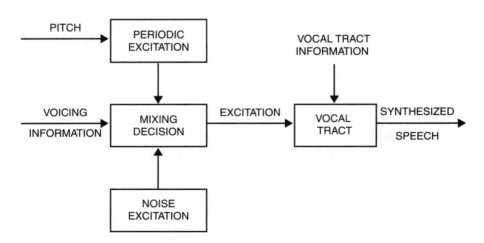

6-8 Generalized source-filter model. (Courtesy of Goldberg, CRC Press, 2000)

vocal tract box to produce a vocal tract filter. The filter shapes the spectrum of the excitation to that of the original speech.

In practice, the vocal tract information can be represented by several methods, including a linear predictor and Fourier magnitudes. The vocal tract model to produce the synthesized speech filters the excitation. The goal is to have the synthesized speech sound, perceptually, to the human ear as close to the original as possible.[26]

The excitation source for voiced speech has an overall spectrum that decays at about 12 db/octave. This is passed through the vocal tract filter, which has nearly flat frequency response leading to output speech with -12 db/octave response. Speech is then radiated from the lips, which act as a differentiator giving a 6 dB/octave boost to the whole spectrum, resulting in overall 6 db/octave decaying spectrum of speech. As the actual production of speech involves mechanical movement of the articulators in finite time, the speech signal changes relatively slowly with time. Speech is termed as quasi-periodic or quasi-stationary, being periodic only for a short duration but varying randomly over a long interval.

The speech signal can be displayed through the use of a device called the sound spectrograph, producing a spectrogram (Figure 6-9), which is a three dimensional representation of speech with time on the horizontal axis, frequency on the vertical axis, and the darkness of the pattern being proportional to the signal energy. The spectrograph is an important tool for understanding and analyzing speech.[27]

Continuous Speech Spectrogram

The spectrogram displayed in Figure 6-9 along with its corresponding time waveform presents an example of continuous speech spectra. The phrase is "jump the lines." An affricate is a "plosive" followed by a "fricative." The word "chip" is an affricature of the initial sound /G/ and /SH/. The affricate *j* begins the utterance from 50 to 100 ms. The following vowel extends from 50 to 100 ms. The lower energy nasal /m/ ranges from 230 to 280 ms. The plosive /p/ is centered at 300 ms. The voiced fricative /TH/ is brief and located at 360 ms. The vowel /e/ lies between 370 and 450 ms. The lower energy consonant /l/ is between the vowels 450 and 510 ms. The diphthong /aI/ of the word *lines* covers the time from 510 to 810 ms. The nasal /n/ extends from 810 to 900 ms. The final voiced fricative /z/ lasts from 920 to 100 ms. Discontinuities in coded speech formants and pitch information due to coding errors result in degrading artifacts that are easily noticed in the reconstructed speech.[28]

The invention of the sound spectrograph was motivated towards improvement of communications for the deaf by opening the avenue of visual hearing. Spectrogram reading has helped a great deal in our understanding of normal speech by providing a means of automatically displaying the changing content of the speech for the eyes to see.

The spectrogram is a three-dimensional plot of the variations of the speech energy spectrum with time. The spectrograph records the speech signal so that it can be repeated over and over for analysis. A finite duration of the signal is considered and the magnitude squared of its Fourier transform (to obtain the energy present at a given instant in a particular band) is computed. This is repeated at various time instants to obtain a time-dependent estimate of the energy spectral density.

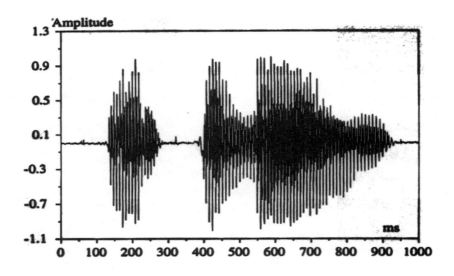

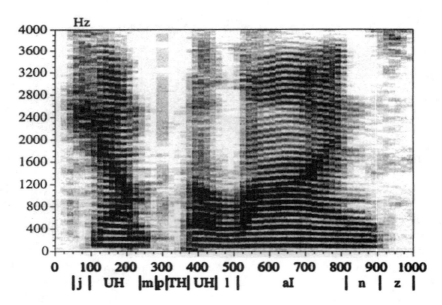

6-9 Spectrogram and Time Waveform. (Reprinted with permission from Goldberg and Riek, 2000, p. 28, Figure 2.13.)

The band of frequencies chosen for analysis at a particular instant can be varied. So, we can have a narrowband spectrogram where the band chosen for analysis is as small as 29Hz (Figure 6-10a) or a wideband spectrogram (Figure 6-10b) where analysis is done for about 300 Hz at a time. A wideband spectrogram gives a poor frequency resolution but a good time resolution, whereas, a narrowband spectrogram

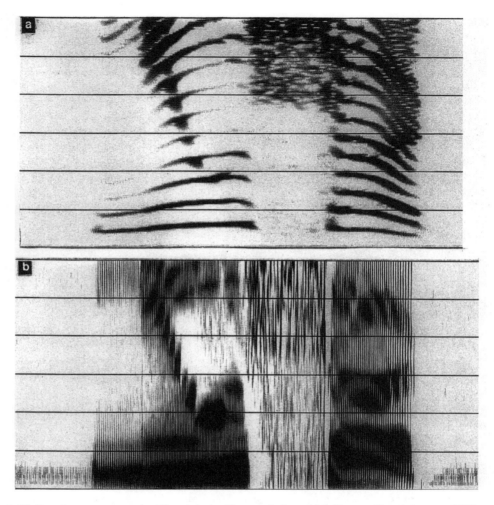

6-10 Spectrogram example. (Reprinted with permission of I.J. Kumar, *Cryptology*, p. 313)

illustrates the finer frequency variations at the cost of the time resolution. This is because, when the duration we consider is too long, the assumption that speech is stationary for the duration of analysis is no longer valid and the details of the energy variations in time are lost, although it results in a finer frequency resolution as the number of points on which FFT has been performed increases. (If N is the number of samples and f_s is the sampling frequency, the frequency resolution is f_s / N.) On the other hand, if the duration is too small, the frequency resolution is degraded.

The wideband spectrogram of Figure 6-10b illustrates a number of characteristics of speech. The few broad dark regions correspond to the formant frequencies. The dark regions vary with time, thereby displaying variations of the formants with time.

Another feature, which can be clearly observed in the wideband spectrogram, are the vertical striations that appear in the region of the voiced speech. These correspond to the pitch period of the speech and are absent in the unvoiced regions (as in /sh/ in the spectrograms). Now compare these with the spectrograms of Figure 6-10a, which is the narrowband version of the same speech. Here, the pitch harmonics are clearly visible along the frequency axis but the vertical striations are completely missing, as the time resolution is poor and is of the order of a number of pitch periods. Here, the unvoiced regions are differentiated by the lack of harmonic structure.

Using these spectrograms one can get a great deal of information about the parameters of speech. The pitch of the speaker of the speech in Figure 6-10a can be measured to be about 250 Hz. The formant frequencies at different instants can be measured from Figure 6-10b. It can also be observed that the energy is higher in the lower bands of speech.[29]

To obtain the spectrogram, a recording medium is required. With advances in signal processing and digital technology, the present day spectrograph uses a unique combination of the special digital signal processing chips and general-purpose microprocessors. Speech is digitized and stored in memory for the digital signal processor to perform *fast Fourier transforms* (FFT) and analyze it. The microprocessor controls the total data acquisition and analysis and displays the spectrograph on the video terminal. Software for such spectrograms based on FFT is also available.

The spectrograph can be integrated with any standard personal computer with sufficient memory as specified by the software. The acoustical signal so produced is converted to an electrical signal using a microphone and is characterized by amplitude, time, and frequency components. The simplest form of a signal is the sine wave represented as $A \sin(\omega t + \Phi)$ where A is the amplitude of the wave, t represents the time and Φ is the phase angle. The number of cycles of a period of sine wave that occurs in one second is called the frequency. If the period of the waveform is T, the frequency f is given by $1/T$. For the sinusoid, this is equal to $\omega/2$ where ω is the angular frequency; Φ determines the initial height of the wave at $t=0$ and is called the phase of the sinusoid.

Speech or, in general, any signal or periodic function can be represented as the sum of sinusoids. The sinusoids, which actually occur in the signal, are called the frequency components of the signals and the range of the frequency components is termed the bandwidth of the signal. Typically, bandwidth of the speech signal is 300 to 3300 Hz (that is, 3 kHz).

The communication system can handle only a range of frequencies for which it is designed. This range is termed as the system bandwidth and for accurate communication; the system bandwidth should be greater than or equal to the signal bandwidth. If the system bandwidth is large, it will unnecessarily add noise to the signal. For example, an amplifier having bandwidth of 10 kHz amplifies all the signals up to 10 kHz and if such an amplifier is used for speech, some of the noise components from 3.3 to 10 kHz are also amplified. Hence, ideally, the bandwidth of the system and message should be the same.[30]

Sampling of the Speech Waveform

Speech signals are analog in nature because they originate as sound pressure waves. In a simple telecommunications system, consisting of input (human voice and speech), transmitter, transmission channel, receiver, and output, the microphone acts as an input transducer that converts the speech pressure waves into electrical energy. Similarly, the loudspeaker in the receiver acts to convert the received electrical signal into sound. The transmission channel is the medium in which the electrical signal is conveyed from transmitter to receiver. In practice the transmitter would include an amplifier so small sound inputs will reach the receiver. After transduction by the microphone into an electrical signal, the speech signal is still analog. All speech-coding algorithms rely on computer processing of discretely sampled versions of the speech. To accurately represent the original speech with discrete samples requires a few guidelines.

First, electrical signals are merely varying voltages and currents. However, it is convenient to consider the power of a signal rather than either voltage or current. Power, in watts, is defined as the rate of doing work or the rate of change of energy. Power defined is P = vi or it equals one watt of work done in one second when current of one amp passes through a resistive network with a voltage of one volt across it. If power is varying, then the power at any one instant is the instantaneous power. Instantaneous power rate of energy transferred at a particular instant is independent of waveforms of the voltage or current. For a purely resistive network, from Ohm's Law, v = ir, then Power is proportional to v^2 or $P = v^2/r = i^2/r$.[31]

Guidelines for voice transmission include identifying the transmission channel between the terminals by its bandwidth and the impairments that might occur to the signals that it carries. Five principal causes of impairments are:

- Attenuation and its variation with frequency
- Noise
- Non-linearity of the channel
- Changes in propagation time with frequency
- Echoes

Radio propagation in the form signal strength, gains, and losses are often stated in dB form. Any number expressed in dB is logarithmic, which makes it convenient to compare values that may differ by many orders of magnitude. DB values are ratios and are governed by:

$$N(dB) = 10 \log_{10} (N) \tag{6.1}$$

$$N = 10^{(dB)/10} \tag{6.2}$$

In general, when they are measured in decibels, the power loss or gain of a telecommunications system, which has components connected in cascade, is the sum of the power gains or losses of the individual components. We balance (envelope) the electrical requirements between transmitter and the receiver and factor in the losses due to the transmission channel.

Toward further discussion of the system we need to know the capabilities of the microphone and the loudspeaker. We need to know the sensitivity of the microphone, that is, the electrical power output from the microphone for the minimum required speech input signal level. We must be able to specify the loudspeaker electrical input power required to produce an adequately audible output for the minimum required output signal load. Finally, we need to know the power loss attributed to the transmission channel.

Assume, for example, that the minimum power output of the microphone is 0.015 mW and that the power that must be delivered to the loudspeaker for minimum signal level is 15 mW. Suppose that half the power is lost in the cable; that is, there is a power loss of 3 dB. (A power ratio of 1:2 is a loss of 3 dB by equation 6.1.) To produce a sound at the loudspeaker that corresponds to that at the microphone, the amplifier must recover the loss in the cable and implement gain of 15:0.015, representings the power ratio of loudspeaker to microphone. Thus we must provide an amplifier with a gain (capacity) of [10 log (15/0.015) + 3] dB = 33dB.

Wherever we place the amplifier, it will contribute both ambient and internal noise and, of course, the noise will be amplified. Noise may take many forms and, illustrating some of them, we discuss what happens to the signal as it passes through the channel.[32]

Some of the signal power may be lost during transmission. As the signal passes through a telecommunications system it suffers attenuation in the passive parts of the system, for example, lines and radio paths. In addition a certain amount of noise and interference is likely to affect the signal. Although the attenuation can be compensated for by subsequent amplification, in practice the amplifier itself will add further random noise to the signal. Thus each time the signal is boosted it is more heavily contaminated by noise. Clearly, if a system is to be assessed, we must have some meaningful way of measuring the noise in a channel and of comparing the levels of noise at different points in the system. Common practice is to refer to the *signal-to-noise ratio* (S/N) at each point. By convention this is a power ratio and is equal to the signal power divided by the noise power.

When a signal enters the transmission channel it already contains a certain amount of contaminating noise. During transmission—whether down a line or over a radio path—both the signal and noise are attenuated. However, while this attenuation is taking place, extra noise is also being added to the signal. (In the case of a cable system, this addition might be thermal noise from its resistive parts while for a radio path it might be atmospheric noise.) Thus the S/N at the output of the transmission channel is likely to be considerably lower than at the input. Similarly, when an amplifier is used, although the signal and noise that are present at its input are amplified by the same factor, the S/N is lowered still further because the amplifier adds extra noise from both the passive and active components within it. In fact just about every part of a telecommunications system will contribute to the deterioration of the S/N of the signal passing through it.

Another important factor to be considered is the ratio of the acoustic power produced by the loudest compared to the quietest inputs to the input terminal. This is normally referred to as the dynamic range of the message source. A reasonable quality system should, typically, be able to cope with a dynamic range of about 70 dB. But to achieve this, the entire system must be able to handle such a range of signals. If any part of the system cannot cope with the highest input then considerable distortion of the signal will result.[33]

Yet another consideration for a telecommunications system is the bandwidth it can manage. These involve linear circuits. Linear circuits have two interesting properties: Suppose we have a circuit with a set of input signals $X = [x_1, x_2, \ldots)$ which produces outputs $Y = [y_1, y_2, \ldots]$ where, for each i, y_i is the output corresponding to the input x_i. The circuit is said to satisfy the principle of homogeneity, if, whenever any x_i is multiplied by a constant and input to the circuit, the output signal is y_i multiplied by the same constant. The circuit satisfies the principles of superposition if when the input signal is the superposition (or sum) of x_i and x_j (for any two input signals x_i and x_j) and the output signal is the sum of y_i and y_j. Any circuit that satisfies both principles is called a linear circuit.[34]

Many of the components and circuits of a telecommunications systems are either linear or, when restricted to a limited range of values for the input and output, may be considered as such. This range is also usually referred to as the dynamic range of the appropriate component or circuit. If our telecommunications system includes components that are not actually linear, but we wish it to act as a linear circuit for all messages, then we must ensure that the dynamic range of the entire system is at least as large as that of the message source. Failure to do this may lead to distortion of the signal output from the receiver. This causes a particular problem for circuits involving scramblers. The scrambling technique must not lead to transmitted signals whose dynamic range goes beyond that of the channel, the receiver terminal or, indeed, any part of the transmitter terminal through which it must pass.

Linear circuits can be advantageous. Any circuit modifies the electrical signal at its input to produce an electrical signal at its output. Clearly we would like to be able to analyze the circuit's response to every possible input signal (the *input space*). However, it is almost certainly not practicable to generate every possible input signal to determine the corresponding output. If the circuit under consideration is linear, then knowledge of the output corresponding to two input signals gives the response to all input signals that are obtained from the original two by either superposition or multiplying by constants.

By determining the actual outputs corresponding to a few input signals, one can use the principles of homogeneity and superposition to deduce and predict the outputs from a much larger number of inputs. A subset of the input space is called a *generating set* if every possible input signal can be obtained by multiplying its elements by suitable constants and/or adding together appropriate combinations of them. Also, as we know the output corresponding to each of the generating signals, we can use the principles of homogeneity and superposition to deduce the output of any possible input signal.

Most telecommunications channels may be regarded as linear circuits, at least for signals within their dynamic range. It is possible to find a generating set for the input signals and the most practical one is the set of sinusoids.

A sinusoid is a waveform represented by an equation of one of the following two forms:[35]

$$A \cos (\omega t + \Phi) \text{ or} \tag{6.3}$$

$$A \sin (\omega t + \Phi) \tag{6.4}$$

where A, ω, and Φ are constants and t represents time. The constant A is called the amplitude of the wave. Since both cosine and sine functions have a maximum value of 1, it is the height of the peaks of the waveform, above its average value. By convention, A is assumed to be positive. Since the functions sin x and cos x both have period 2π, the sinusoids A cos ($\omega t + \Phi$) and A sin ($\omega t + \Phi$) are periodic, but have period $2\pi/\omega$. However, it is not the usual practice to talk about the period of a sinusoid. Instead it is customary to quote its frequency f.

The frequency is the number of periods, which occur in 1 second. For any periodic waveform, if the period is T and the frequency is f, then f = 1/T and for a sinusoid, f = $\omega/2\pi$ or $\omega = 2 \pi$ f. (The unit of frequency is the *Hertz* (Hz) and 1 Hertz is a frequency of 1 cycle/sec.) Since f is the frequency and $\omega = 2 \pi$ f. ω is called the angular frequency of the sinusoid. The constant Φ determines the initial height of the wave; that is, the height when t = 0, and is called the phase of the sinusoid. If two sinusoids have different phases then we say that they are out-of-phase and the difference in the two values of Φ is called the phase difference.

We assert that a set of sinusoids is a generating set for input signals; we claim that the waveform of any input signal can be obtained by adding together an appropriate combination of them.

If a signal, or waveform, is written as a sum of sinusoids then the sinusoids that actually occur in this sum are called the frequency components of the signal. The bandwidth of a signal is then the range of frequencies occupied by the frequency components of the signal and the bandwidth of a telecommunications system is the range of frequencies that the system can handle.

The bandwidth of an older hi-fi amplifier might be specified as 15 kHz, which means it could handle signals whose frequency components take any value from 0 to 15 KHz. One bandwidth of particular relevance is that of recognizable speech. This is about 3 KHz and extends from approximately 300 Hz to about 3.3 kHz.

If a signal is to be transmitted through a system, then, to avoid any distortion, it is clearly necessary to ensure that the range of frequencies, which the system can handle, includes all the frequency components of the signal. The system bandwidth must be at least as large as large as that of the signal. (It is also desirable that the bandwidth of the system should be no larger than that of the signal.) If the system's bandwidth is too large, then the system may accept more noise than is necessary and this, of course, will result in a decrease in the S/N. Noise and interference should be kept to a minimum.

Thus, in all telecommunications systems where noise may be significant, it is common practice to ensure that the frequency characteristics of the channel, transmitter terminal, and receiver terminal (including amplifiers, and so forth) are the same as those of the signal. In particular the bandwidth should be the same for both the system and the message. A bandpass filter may achieve this goal. The *bandpass filter* is designed so that all signals outside its selected band are attenuated to a negligible level. This careful matching of the bandwidths of the telecommunications system and the message source improves the audio quality of the system. However, it causes great problems for the scrambler designer. Many scramblers are retrofitted to existing telecommunications systems that are likely to operate in narrow bandwidths. Sophisticated scramblers increase the signal bandwidth. Since the existing bandwidth is likely to vary from system to system, the user may end up with a system in which the scrambler occupies a larger bandwidth than supported by the rest of the system. This causes degradation of the speech quality and delivered service.

Transmission channels are categorized under two general headings: bounded and radio. Bounded channels include electrical conduction in wires, cables, optical fibers, and radio channels, including all forms of electromagnetic radiation in space (for example, microwave, satellite, and so forth). Telecommunications systems include both bounded and radio communications. Such a system is provided when a telephone conversation takes place between one user in a car while the other is in an office. This is likely to entail a radio link from the car to the local exchange of the second user and then a line from this exchange to the office.

The electrical signal generated when speech is directed into a microphone is called the *base-band signal* that has a normal frequency range extending from 300 Hz to 3.3 kHz. In most telecommunications systems the shape and frequency components of this base-band signal are usually modified in some way to obtain a form more suitable for transmission. The process is called *modulation* and the process of recovering the base-band signal from the modulated signal is called *demodulation*. Two reasons for modulating the baseband signal are to make more efficient transmission possible and to make possible the simultaneous transmission of a number of signals over the same channel.

An *echo* is a delayed version of the message produced by reflections in the system. A normal telephone network is designed to ensure that only acceptable delays occur; if scramblers are introduced to the system they are likely to produce extra delays that may result in an unacceptable system. Furthermore if the echoes become scrambled, the user will be faced with the extra distraction of having unintelligible signals in his or her earphone.

Returning to the issue of sampling speech waveforms, let s-analog (t) represent the analog speech signal. The sampled signal then becomes:

$$S(n) = \text{s-analog } (nT) \qquad\qquad (6.5)$$

where n takes on integer values and T is the time between samples or sampling period.

If s-analog (t) is band-limited (no frequency components higher than a known limit), and is sampled fast enough (T small enough), s(n) provides a complete and unique representation of s(t).

Fast enough is twice the highest frequency component, termed the Nyquist rate:

$$T \leq 1/2 Fmax \qquad (6.6)$$

This is illustrated in the plots in Figure 6-11. In the first plot, s(t) is sampled more than twice as fast as the highest frequency. For simplicity, s(t) is shown to have one dominant frequency component, but the discussion holds true for any bandlimited signal. In the second plot, s(t) is sampled at two samples for each period of the major frequency component, which is just barely enough to represent the signal. In the third plot, the signal is under sampled so that an ambiguity results.

When considering only the discrete samples, the high-frequency solid line appears identical to the low-frequency dashed line due to undersampling. This misrepresentation of frequencies is known as *aliasing*. A frequency greater than half the sampling frequency in the original signal has been aliased as the lower frequency of

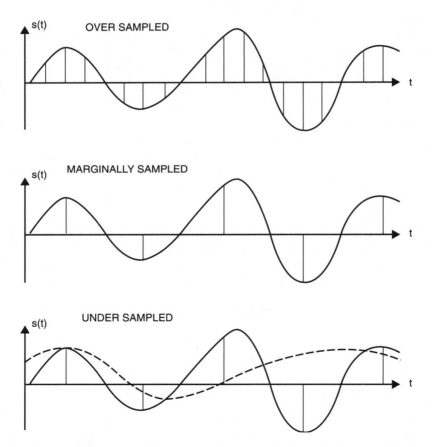

6-11 Sampling and Nyquist rate. (Reprinted with permission from Goldberg and Riek, Figure 3.1, p. 35)

the dotted, sampled waveform. The aliasing can be eliminated by bandlimiting the speech before it is sampled. Speech is naturally bandlimited to have the vast majority of its energy below 7 kHz. But, to sample speech at rates below 14 kHz, or to remove the small amount of energy above that range, a lowpass filter is applied before sampling. In practice, speech is often lowpass filtered before the sampling to slightly less than 4 kHz and then sampled at 8 kHz. This is referred to as *narrowband speech*, and is the common input for most of the coders. The 4 kHz bandwidth preserves good intelligibility, speaker identity, and naturalness. However, for higher quality sound, speech can be sampled and coded at higher sampling and coding rates.[36]

The Fourier Transform

Perhaps the most important mathematical concept that we must understand in the cryptology of speech is the Fourier transform. Joseph Fourier (1768–1830) was a bit of an enigma and his discovery was not in the science of signals but heat recovery. Fourier was the only mathematician ever to serve as Governor of Lower Egypt. He had supported the French Revolution, and was rewarded with an appointment to the Ècole Polytechnique. He had always loved the army and wanted to be an officer, a career denied him because he was the son of a tailor. When the opportunity came to accompany Napoleon on a military campaign in Egypt, Fourier resigned his position and went along, and was appointed Governor in 1798. When the British took Egypt in 1801, Fourier returned to France.

Fourier studied the flow of heat in metallic plates and rods. The theory that he developed now has applications in industry, government, intelligence, and the study of the temperature of the Earth's interior. He discovered that many functions could be expressed as infinite sums of sine and cosine terms, now called a trigonometric series or Fourier series. A paper that he submitted to the Academy of Science in Paris in 1807 was studied by several eminent mathematicians and rejected because it failed to prove his claims. (This sickness in mathematicians has carried forth to modern times but gratefully engineers have been immune to such folly.) They suggested that he reconsider and refine his paper and even made heat flow the topic for a prize to be awarded in 1812. Fourier won the price, but the Academy refused to publish his paper because of its lack of rigor. When Fourier became the secretary of the Academy in 1824, the 1812 paper was published without change.

As Fourier became older, he developed a Howard Hughes notion. Whether influenced by his stay in the heat of Egypt or by his own studies of the flow of heat in metals, he became obsessed with the idea that extreme heat was the natural condition for the human body. He was always heavily bundled in woolen clothing and kept his rooms at high temperatures. He died at age 63 "thoroughly cooked."[37]

In the application of mathematics to communication and its security, the Fourier transform represents a signal in terms of complex exponentials or sinusoids because:

$$e^{-j\omega n} = \cos(\omega n) - j\sin(\omega n) \tag{6.7}$$

The frequency representation of a signal through the *Fourier transform* (FT) facilitates processing and signal visualizations that are inherently frequency oriented.

The discrete-time Fourier transform pair is defined by the forward transform:

$$S(\omega) = \sum_{n=-\infty}^{\infty} s(n)e^{-j\omega n} \tag{6.8}$$

and the inverse transform:

$$s(n) = \tfrac{1}{2\pi} \int_{-\pi}^{\pi} S(\omega)e^{j\omega n}d\omega \tag{6.9}$$

Is a mathematical link between the frequency and time representations of a time sequence s(n). $S(\omega)$ is the *frequency response* of s(n). In all cases, $S(\omega)$ is a periodic signal with a period of 2π.

In general, $S(\omega)$ is a complex signal. For the real time-domain signal s(n) the real part and the magnitude of $S(\omega)$ are even, and the imaginary part and phase are odd. As such, the Fourier transform for a real signal is specified completely by the range $0 < \omega < \pi$. For the range $-\pi < 0 < 0$, the magnitude and real part are flipped left to right; the imaginary part and phase are flipped and inverted.[38]

Because most speech signals are not known over all time, the Fourier transform does not exist without modification of the speech signal and the transform. The discrete Fourier Transform (DFT) is a much more usable frequency transformation of a speech waveform. The DFT is a Fourier representation of a sequence of samples of limited length. Instead of being a continuous function of frequency as is the FT, the DFT is a sequence of samples. The samples of the DFT are equally spaced along the frequency axis of the FT. The DFT is defined as:

$$S(k) = \sum_{n=0}^{N-1} s(n)e^{-j\frac{2\pi}{N}kn} \tag{6.10}$$

where N is the length of the segment.

In this formulation, s(n) is considered to be periodic with a period of N; s(n) repeats the finite sequence for all of n. Also the DFT can be thought of as sampling the Fourier transform at N evenly spaced points on a frequency axis. The inverse DFT is given by:

$$s(n) = \frac{1}{N} \sum_{n=0}^{N-1} S(K)e^{j\frac{2\pi}{N}kn} \tag{6.11}$$

The inverse transform is the same as the forward transform, except for a scale factor of 1/N and a sign change of the exponential argument.

Speech is highly *non-stationary*, meaning that statistics change over time. The information-carrying nature of the signal is responsible for the changes. When the properties of a signal are invariant to a shift in the time index, the signal is *stationary*. Different phonemes can be heard with different time instances of the same spoken sentence. Different frequency components exist in different time sequences of the spoken sentence. Although a speech signal is not stationary, it can be treated as *quasi-stationary* in small segments (20 ms or less). For this the Fourier transform of small segments of speech is therefore valuable in speech signal processing. A running spectrum with time is chosen with time as the independent variable; the spectral computation is made on windowed, weighted past-values of the signal. The specified time interval (20 ms) is used for the segment and the segment is weighted accordingly. The truncated weighted segment of speech is Fourier transformed. The resulting frequency parameters are associated with the time segment of speech corresponding to the center of the analysis interval. The transform is adapted to:

$$S(k) = \sum_{n=0}^{N-1} s(n)w(n)e^{-j\frac{2\pi}{N}kn} \tag{6.12}$$

where $\omega(n)$ is the windowing function and N is the length of the window.[39]

The Fast Fourier Transform (FFT)

The *Fast Fourier Transform* (FFT) is a group of techniques to rearrange the DFT calculations to make them computationally efficient. Direct calculations of the DFT requires a number of multiples on the order of N^2. DFT reduces that number to the order of N log N. The process uses symmetry and periodicity of the exponential factor to reduce the computations. The DFT works by recursively decomposing the N-point DFT into smaller DFT's. The most common implementation is for powers of 2 because of convenience of fitting the recursive structure. The FFT method can be applied to any sequence length that is a product of smaller integer factors.[40]

Windowing Signal Segments

The window function, $\omega(n)$ serves two ways:

- To select the correct segment of speech for processing
- To weight the speech samples of s(n)

The selected speech segment is called a *frame*. The shape of the window affects the frequency representation, S(k) by the frequency response of the window itself. It can be shown using Z-transforms (a generalized Fourier method) that convolution in the time domain is multiplication in the frequency domain. Multiplication in the time domain corresponds to convolution in the frequency domain. (Filtering is a basic digital signal processing operation used in speech coding. Filtering is the mathematical operation of the convolution of a digital signal with the input sequence to produce an output sequence.) The convolution sum is defined as:

$$y(n) = s(n) \times h(n) = \sum_{k=-\infty}^{\infty} s(k)h(n-k) \tag{6.13}$$

The output sequence y(n) is the result of passing the input sequence, s(n) through the digital filter, h(n).

The multiplication of a time-domain speech sequence s(n) with a time domain window, ω(n) is the same as a convolution of S(k) and W(k) in the frequency domain. The impact of a window shape can be analyzed by examining its FFT.[41]

Window Function

The window function, ω(n), serves twofold:

- To select the correct segment of speech for processing
- To weight the speech samples of s(n)

The selected segment of speech is referred to as the *speech frame*. The shape of the window affects the frequency representation, S(k), by the frequency response of the window itself. Convolution in the time domain is multiplication in the frequency domain. Conversely, multiplication in the time domain corresponds to convolution in the frequency domain. The multiplication of a time-domain speech sequence s(n) with a time-domain window ω(n) is the same as the convolution of S(k) and W(k) in the frequency domain. So, the impact of a window shape can be analyzed by examining its DFT.

Figure 6-11 displays the time-domain shapes for two windows of length 300 samples. The Hamming window is the dotted line. The Hamming and Hanning are both raised cosine functions with similar frequency characteristics. The Hamming (raised at the edges) features good attenuation of the first few sidelobes and a nearly flat response for the higher frequency sidelobes. The first few sidelobes of the Hanning are higher in amplitude, but the higher frequency sidelobes continue to roll off to negligible low values.

The Hamming window is given by:

$$\omega(n) = 0.54 - 0.46 \cos 2n\pi/N \text{ for } 0 < n < N - 1 \tag{6.14}$$

The Hanning window is given by:

$$\omega(n) = 0.5 - 0.5 \cos 2n\pi \text{ for } 0 < n < N - 1 \tag{6.15}$$

The frequency responses of the Hamming, Hanning, and rectangular windows are shown in Figure 6-12a and 6-12b. As can be seen, the main lobe of the rectangular window is about half as wide as the Hamming or Hanning. The side lobes are much lower for the Hamming and Hanning than the rectangular. The first side lobe of the Hanning is approximately 20 dB higher than the Hamming, but the Hanning sidelobes rapidly decrease to low levels.

Selecting the window shape, and its resulting frequency response, is a tradeoff between a narrow main lobe in the frequency domain and low sidelobes. A narrow main lobe improves frequency resolution so that in the resulting DFT magnitude, closely spaced, narrow components are separated. A narrow main lobe, as in the rectangular window, comes at the expense of high side lobes. These side lobes add a

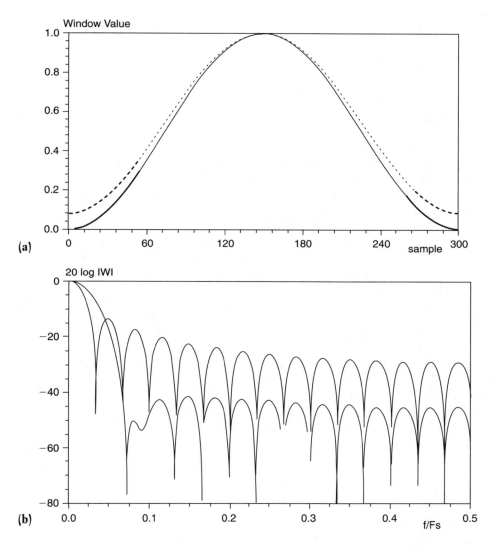

6-12(a), 6-12(b) Hamming, Hanning, and Rectangular Windows. (Reprinted with permission from Goldberg and Riek, Figures 3.5 to 3.6, p. 46)

noisy appearance to the DFT magnitude due to interference from adjacent harmonics making it more difficult to discriminate low magnitude components.

For the Hamming window, the approximate bandwidth of the main lobe is:

$$BW = 2Fs/N \qquad (6.16)$$

where N is the length of the window in number of samples.

The impact of window selection on the Fourier transform of a speech segment can be seen in Figure 6-13. It shows a Hamming window and its DFT transform. The Hamming-windowed, time-domain segment displays the influence of the center-weighted, symmetrically decaying ends of the window shape. The mid frequencies of 1500 to 2500 Hz structure appears noisy, making it difficult to distinguish the pitch harmonics. This is caused by *spectral leakage* where the energy associated with one pitch harmonic obscures neighboring harmonics.[42]

Linear Prediction Modeling

Linear prediction modeling (LP) is a widely used method that represents the frequency shaping attributes of the vocal tract in the source-filter model. LP analysis is used in speech coding and characterizes the shape of the spectrum of a short segment of speech with a small number of parameters for efficient coding. *Linear predictive coding* (LPC) predicts a time domain speech sample based on linearly weighted combinations of previous samples. LP analysis is a method to remove redundancy in a short-term correlation of adjacent samples. The LP formulation is made via the differential equations defining a lossless tube modeling the vocal tract. A complete derivation is given in Goldberg.[43]

Sound waves are pressure variations that propagate through air by the vibratory movement of air particles. Modeling these waves and their propagation through the vocal tract provides a framework for characterizing how the vocal tract shapes the frequency content of the excitation signal. Goldberg (supra) models the vocal tract as a uniform lossless tube with constant cross-sectional area. A system of partial differential equations describes the changes in pressure and volume velocity over time and position along the tube.[44]

$$- \partial p / \partial x = \rho / A \; \partial u / \partial t \qquad (6.17)$$

$$- \partial u / \partial x = A / \rho c^2 \partial p / \partial t \qquad (6.18)$$

x = location in tube
t = time
p (x, t) = sound pressure at location x and time t
u (x, t) = volume velocity flow at location x and time t
ρ = density of air inside tube
c = velocity of sound
A (x, t) = cross-sectional area of tube at location x and time t

The simple model of the vocal tract has the same properties of a simple electrical system. Comparing the wave equations of the lossless tube system to the current i (x,t) and voltage v (x,t) equation for a uniform lossless transmission line:

$$- \partial v / \partial x = L \; \partial i / \partial t \qquad (6.19)$$

$$- \partial i / \partial x = C \; \partial v / \partial t \qquad (6.20)$$

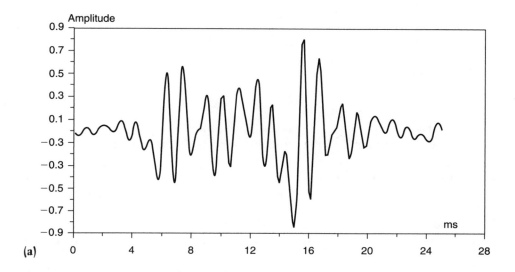

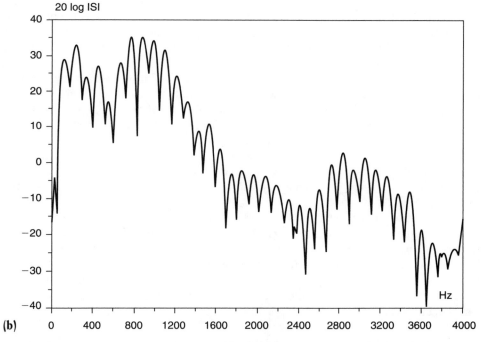

6-13(a), 6-13(b) Hamming, Hanning, and Rectangular Windows. (Reprinted with permission from Goldberg and Riek, Figures 3.5 to 3.6, p. 46)

The last four equations are equivalent with the following variable substitutions:

Electrical System	Acoustic System
L (inductance)	ρ/A
C (capacitance)	$A/\rho c^2$
V (voltage)	p
I (current)	u

To use the LP model for speech analysis, we can estimate the LP parameters for a segment of speech, such as autocorrelation, covariance, or quantization.[45]

Quantization and PCM

Goldberg and Riek present detailed information on a variety of waveform coders: PCM, nonlinear PCM, differential PCM, adaptive delta modulation, *adaptive differential pulse code modulation* (ADPCM), channel coders, formant coders, and perceptual speech coders. To view these concepts briefly, this section discusses one popular waveform coder—*pulse code modulation* (PCM).

The goal of quantization is to encode data accurately using as little information (as few bits) as possible. Efficient and accurate parameter quantization is central to speech coding because pertinent information must be represented as accurately as the coding requirements dictate using as little information as possible. Quantization can be applied directly to a sampled speech waveform or to parameter files such as the output of a vocoder analysis.

Waveform coders encode the shape of the time-domain waveform. Basic waveform coding approaches do not exploit the constraints imposed by the human vocal tract on the speech waveform. As such, waveform coders represent nonspeech sounds (such as music and background noise) accurately, but do so at a higher bit rate than that achieved by efficient speech-specific vocoders.

Vector quantization (VQ) encodes groups of data simultaneously instead of individual data values. Advances in vector quantization of *line spectral frequencies* (LSFs) is one of the primary reasons for improved speech quality in leading low bit-rate coding schemes.

When uniform quantization is applied directly to an audio waveform, the process is called *pulse code modulation (PCM)*. Pulse code modulation is the simplest method of speech coding. An analog speech signal is sent into an anti-aliasing analog lowpass filterthat eliminates all frequencies above half the sampling rate. The signal is then sent through an *analog-to-digital* (A/D) converter, converting the signal to a sequence of numbers, with the time distance between sample points equal to the sampling rate. The signal, now a sequence of numbers, can be stored or sent through a digital transmission channel.[46]

The PCM analysis process is displayed in Figure 6-14. The input signal is an analog signal, typically a varying voltage level in an analog circuit. The lower plot of the input signal represents the continuous-time frequency domain of the input speech. The second plots time domain upper, frequency domain lower, displaying the continuous-time impulse and frequency responses, respectively, of the analog low-pass filter. The input speech is bandlimited by the lowpass filter with the result displayed

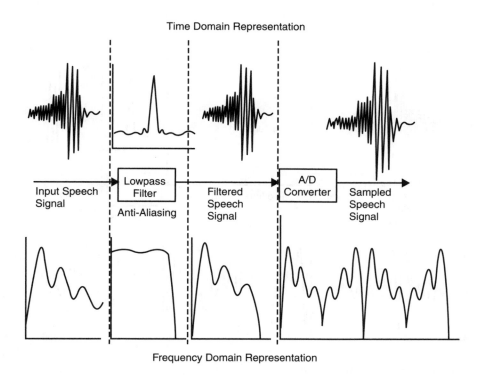

Time Domain Representation

Input Speech Signal → Lowpass Filter (Anti-Aliasing) → Filtered Speech Signal → A/D Converter → Sampled Speech Signal

Frequency Domain Representation

6-14 Time Domain Hamming and DFT. (Reprinted with permission from Goldberg and Riek, Figure 7.1 and 7.2, pp. 91–92)

in the third set of plots. The bandlimited analog signal is sampled at discrete time intervals to produce the last plots. The samples are shown as dots on the time domain waveform. The frequency domain plot indicates the cyclical nature of the Fourier representation of a discretely sampled signal.

To reconstruct the analog signal, the digital signal is passed through a *digital-to-analog* (D/A) converter and then filtered by a simple low-pass interpolating analog filter which generally has the same characteristics as the anti-aliasing pre-filter that was used to filter the original analog signal. A representation of the PCM reconstruction process can be seen in Figure 6-15. The discretely sampled signal is converted to the pulse-type waveform of the second plots. This waveform has higher harmonics not present in the original signal. The lowpass filter removes these unwanted higher frequencies.

PCM is a simple coding scheme and is often used when transmission bandwidth (or storage space) is not a limitation. PCM is susceptible to bit errors more than other speech waveform coding methods such as delta modulation, because a single bit error can change a value from the positive maximum value to the minimum value possible. Therefore, if speech quality is important in a noisy transmission environment, PCM is not desirable even if the coding bit rate is not an issue.[47]

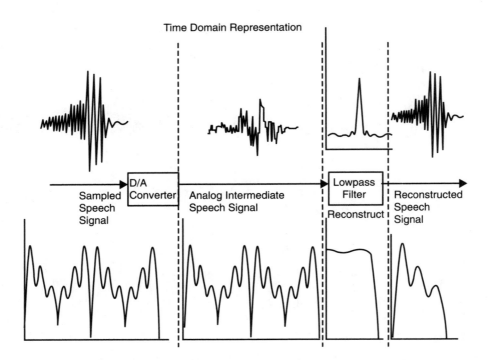

Time Domain Representation

6-15 Frequency domain representations. (Reprinted with permission from Goldberg and Riek)

The reconstruction error (the difference between the original signal and the reconstructed signal) is affected by quantization error that is introduced in the PCM coding scheme. This error is introduced during the process of analog-to-digital conversion. The signal values must be approximated to the closest possible discrete values to represent a signal digitally.

Transmission of Speech Signals

When the signal has been processed, quantized, and encoded it can be transmitted over various types of channels. In general, any signal can be transmitted in analog or digital form. In analog transmission, the message is continuously varying whereas in the digital system the message is permitted to take only one of the finite discrete values. Accordingly, there are systems that are totally analog, or systems which process the signal digitally and then use a D/A converter before transmission, and the transmission is analog (see Figure 6-16a and 16b).

Synchronization

Possibly the most important factor for proper communication of secured messages is synchronization. The receiver can descramble/decipher the message correctly only if the pseudo-random generator is started at the precise moment at which to select the proper code or to encipher the message. Usually the receiver detects

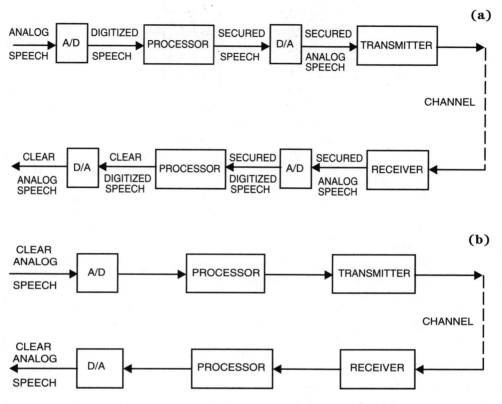

6-16(a) Analog system with digital processing; **(b)** Digital system. (Courtesy of I.J. Kumar, *Cryptology*, 1997)

some noise pulses even when there is no message transmission. To enable the authorized receiver to differentiate between the actual message and noise, a synchronization signal is sent. This synchronization signal also ensures that the sequence generators at the receiver and the transmitter are in step. At the same time it is desirable that the interceptor should not recognize the synchronization signal.

There are two types of synchronization schemes commonly used, namely, *initial synchronization* (or single shot systems) and *continuous synchronization*. As the name suggests, in initial synchronization system the synchronization information is transmitted only at the beginning of every transmission after which a clock is used to maintain the synchronization. The main disadvantage of such a system is that it prohibits late entry. If the receiver misses the synchronization signal, the whole message is lost because there is no way to know the contents of the sequence generator at a later stage. The synchronization signal has to be more robust than the signal used for continuous synchronization, as the receiver to obtain the message should receive this correctly. This makes such systems more suitable for communication over poor channels.

In continuous synchronization, the message is continuously interrupted to transmit the synchronization information. Every synchronization signal contains the new message key, which normally is a function of the previous key. So even if the receiver fails to get the synchronization signal it can generate the expected message key and continue decryption. This method is known as *fly wheeling*. The advantage of continuous synchronization is that it permits late entry. Even if the receiver misses some part of the message it can commence decrypting as soon as it receives a synchronization signal.

The synchronization signal can be as simple as a combination of two tones of different frequenciesthat switch from one to another to convey the timing information. Alternatively, the timing information can be obtained by transmitting some preset data sequence with the receiver's next synchronization update, so when this sequence is received the timing information is conveyed. Both the tones and the data sequence should be chosen to not occur in normal speech data or noise. The synchronization may be based on a key or a frame (segment of the ciphertext).

The synchronization signal can be transmitted in a number of ways. If initial synchronization is employed, it is obvious that the synchronization bits are transmitted at the beginning of the message. The complete band may be utilized to transmit the synchronization bits using any of the digital modulation techniques, *frequency shift keying* (FSK), *phase shift keying* (PSK) and so forth. In these modulating techniques, different frequencies or phase of the carrier is used to represent bit 1 and bit 0.[48]

Continuous synchronization systems either send the synchronization information on a separate channel thereby increasing the bandwidth, or the speech and the synchronization bits share the same channel by employing frequency or time multiplexing. The portion where the speech energy is very low in the speech spectrum (usually around 1800 to 2000 Hz), a small band of 100 to 200 Hz is used to transmit the synchronization information using any of the digital modulation techniques. This requires excellent notch filters for removing the speech from the small band. Secondly, such communications can be jammed easily by sending a very high power signal at that frequency. Multiplexing with speech in the time domain can also carry the synchronization information. Speech is suppressed for a small duration and the synchronization information is transmitted. Though removal of a small portion of speech may seem to be quite disturbing it certainly has an advantage as an anti jamming measure.[49]

Cryptography of Speech Signals

Only the simpler cryptographic methods of encoding and cryptanalysis of speech signals will be discussed in these final two sections of this chapter. The reader is referred to the reference section for detailed design procedures.

However quickly articulated, speech is a redundant, slow, and varying signal. Specific patterns of numerous phonemes are responsible for the different sounds we hear. To make speech secure, its structure must be disturbed such that it becomes unintelligible. Ideally, for maximum security, speech should be so transformed by the security process that the *residual intelligibility,* the extent to which the original signal can be understood when listening to the secure message, is zero. At the same time the authorized receiver, on applying the inverse transformation, should be able to recover the speech with the same or nearly the original quality. The method employed to achieve the desired level of security also should be tolerant of noise and free of channel distortions, result in a signal with approximately the same bandwidth, be compatible with the existing communication system, and introduce no excessive processing delay.[50]

Towards achieving these goals, whatever approach is selected must assure that distortion caused by the scrambler should be reversible and the descrambled speech should have almost all of the characteristics of clear speech. Depending on the mode of implementation, we can have *analog* or *digital* systems. Most modern systems are digital.

In the analog domain, there are three basic dimensions of the speech signal, upon which the processor operates to make the speech secure: time, frequency, and amplitude. Accordingly there are time domain, frequency domain and hybrid or two-dimensional scramblers. In general, the analog scrambler does not obscure or remove any information from the speech; it simply rearranges the information to create a new signal that bears one-to-one correspondence with the old signal. Analog scramblers are similar to transposition ciphers in text, where a block of values of a parameter are taken and permuted. These systems can be classified as narrowband systems and they can be used over a telephone channel.

The digital technique for making speech secure is to encipher the speech using pseudo-random sequences. The digitized bits of speech are added modulo -2 to the pseudo-random sequence in a fashion similar to stream ciphers for text. Depending on the method used for digitizating speech, the cipher system may be a wideband system (based on waveform coding) or a narrowband system (based on source coding). We consider the basics of analog scramblers and then discuss digital speech ciphers/coders. The authors draw heavily from (with permission) and the reader is directed to the brilliant work of Kumar[51].

Analog Scramblers

The two main types of analog scramblers are time and frequency domain scramblers. There are many scrambler systems from which to choose, some of which are a combination of two or more single dimensional scramblers. When more than two scrambling techniques are combined to achieve the security, sometimes the resulting scrambler is referred to as a multi-dimensional scrambler. The term *multi-dimensional* is actually a misnomer because, though the number of scrambling techniques used is more than two, the dimensions of the signal are time and frequency only.

In general the analog scrambler perturbs only three parameters that provide the required amount of security, namely, frame size, segment size, and the scrambling code used to design a system. Practical constraints serve as guidelines for deciding these parameters. The optimum values vary for different types of scramblers: what may be good for a frequency domain scrambler may be useless for a time domain scrambler.

Historically, the earliest scramblers were based on the manipulations of the signal in the frequency domain.[52] These were adequately robust for transmission through the channel but most of them are characterized by their speech like rhythm. They can be broadly classified as:

- Frequency inverters
- Band-splitters
- Transform-based scramblers[53]

Frequency Inverters

As the name suggests, the frequency inverter simply inverts the spectrum so that the lower frequencies are moved to the upper part of the band while the higher frequencies are moved to the lower band. If we consider the full speech band of 3000 to 3300 Hz to be inverted around a carrier ωc of say, 3400 Hz, each individual sinusoidal component will be modulated by the carrier and the spectrum would be divided into bands. (See Figure 6-17.)

The two bands above and below the carrier frequency are called the upper and lower sidebands respectively. The sidebands are merely mirror images of each other with the upper and lower frequencies interchanged. The fixed frequency inverter, which has just been described, is actually of no use from the security point of view, as a listener can, after some amount of hearing adjustment, understand the message directly. To avoid this, either random frequency inversion or frequency hopping inversion is employed where the carrier frequency is varied.

To ensure that only a negligible portion of speech is outside the signal band, the inverting frequency is randomly varied over a small range in the neighborhood of 3 kHz. Depending on how quickly the carrier frequency is changed, we can have slow

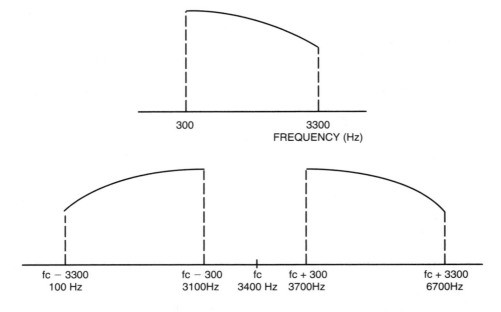

6-17 Speech Spectrum. (Courtesy of I.J. Kumar, *Cryptology*, 1997)

random inversion (less than 5 changes or hops/second) or fast random inversion of greater than 5 hops/sec. Sometimes some of the segments of a frame are inverted and at other times they are left unchanged. This is characterized as selective inversion. In both these methods the signal falling outside the band of 3 kHz is simply lost, which causes slight deterioration in the quality of speech but it can be acceptable. The main disadvantage of such systems is their speech-like rhythm and also their high residual intelligibility, the latter due to the fact that the components around 1.5 kHz remain more or less undisturbed. The Cobra Microtalk 2, a popular personal communicator, still uses this security method on its quiet subchannels.[54]

Band Splitters

The second option for scrambling speech in the frequency domain is to split the spectrum into smaller bands and either shift them to some other position, invert individual bands, or combine both the shift and invert operations. The basic concept is to disturb the structure along the frequency axis and create discontinuities.

Two-Band-Splitter

Here, a particular frequency is chosen at which the frequency band is to be split into two bands. The frequency chosen is designated the *split point,* pictorially denoted in Figure 6-18a. The speech spectrum, has larger amplitude at low frequencies as compared to the high frequencies, and may be represented by a triangle. This spectrum is split into two parts I and II. Within the two parts of the spectrum there are three options:

- Shift the spectrum to interchange the positions of the two bands that is, *band-shifter*.
- Invert one or both the parts of the spectrum that is, *band-inverter*.
- Combine shift and invert that is, *band-shift-inverter*.[55]

Band-Shifter

This involves shifting only the lower frequency band to high frequencies and vice versa. As such, it does not affect the intelligibility of speech but if the shifting is done with variable split points, it can cause some problem in listening. Though this method is rarely employed as such to provide security, it can add complexity when combined with other scrambling techniques. This method is also known as *reentrant* because it appears as if the frequencies cannot be directly accommodated in the band up to 3000 Hz reenter from the lower end of the band.

Band-Inverter

Either of the two bands can be inverted, as in Figure 6-18. This approach is not particularly effective because some portion of the speech band remains, as is, which is sufficient to cause it to reveal intelligible speech. Even when this does not occur such scramblers can provide security only of the level of random inversion.

In Figure 6-18c both the bands are inverted individually around 1.5 kHz, the equivalent to applying the band shifter to inverted speech. Using a frequency hop-

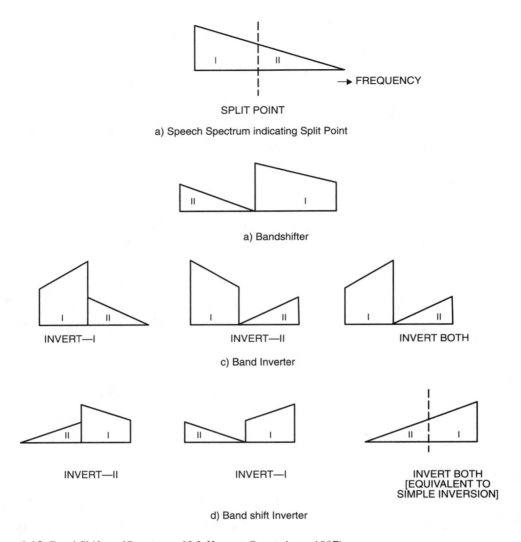

a) Speech Spectrum indicating Split Point

a) Bandshifter

c) Band Inverter

d) Band shift Inverter

6-18 Band Shifter. (Courtesy of I.J. Kumar, *Cryptology*, 1997)

ping inverter, the carrier frequency can be varied around 3 kHz to minimize the loss of signal, falling outside the band. Modulating by some carrier frequency is equivalent to shifting the frequency band. If we choose a carrier frequency of 3800 kHz to modulate the speech occupying 300 to 3000 kHz, the inverted lower band occupies 800 to 3500 kHz that cannot be directly accommodated in the band up to 3000 kHz. The signal beyond 3000 Hz is brought down to the range of 300 to 800 Hz so that the bandwidth remains within the spectrum. Here also, the residual intelligibility is not much affected, because a single band usually can provide enough information to retrieve intelligibility.[56]

Bandshift-Inverter

The bandshift-inverter system combines the operation of shifting and inversion, where inversion of either of the bands can be combined with shifting. Figure 6-19 shows the spectrogram where the lower band up to 1.5 kHz is shifted and inverted. In general, for all types of band splitters, a number of split points are chosen, selected to use an appropriate key every 10 to 20 ms. A faster rate of changing is not really helpful in reducing the residual intelligibility as, even when some of the segments are not heard properly, the human brain can fill the gap to make sense of the sound. Using a rate beyond the optimum value actually increases the distortion after descrambling and causes deterioration in the speech quality.[57]

n-Band-Splitter

This is a more general form of the two-band splitter where the total frequency band is divided into a number of subbands (more than two) that are then permuted to occupy a new position in the spectrum. Figure 6-20 outlines the scheme of scrambling and the block diagram for implementation of the scrambler. Each subband is modulated to the desired position according to the scrambling code. The most complex part of the scrambler is the filter bank, which is required to divide the spectrum into subbands. The subbands may be chosen to be equal or unequal, overlapping or non-overlapping. For nonoverlapping subbands, sharp filter cut-off rates are required (the signal outside the desired band should be highly attenuated with negligible power). These are difficult to realize. Sometimes unequal width bands, with narrow bands in the lower frequency range, and wider in the higher range are employed to ensure that the high information carrying lower portion of the speech is disturbed more by scrambling.

The permutation used to scramble the bands can be changed from frame to frame to increase security, in which case it is called a rolling code band-splitter. Figure 6-21 shows the spectrogram of the rolling code 4-band splitter where the dank bands can be seen shifted to various frequencies in different segments.

Though, theoretically, there can be 4!= 24 possible rearrangements, only few are useful, and even these have low residual intelligibility. These are referred to as *good codes*. Usually the best test for deciding whether the permutation is good or not is the listening test, and it has been observed that:

- Adjacent bands left together after scrambling enhance intelligibility.
- Bands moved as far as possible from their original position reduce intelligibility.

The shift factor, which is defined as the average absolute difference between the original position of each band and their position after scrambling, should be high. Consider the following permutation:

$$\begin{vmatrix} 1\ 2\ 3\ 4 \\ 2\ 3\ 4\ 1 \end{vmatrix}$$

The shift factor is $\{ |1 - 2| + |2 - 3| + |3 - 4| + |4 - 1| \} / 4 = 1.5$

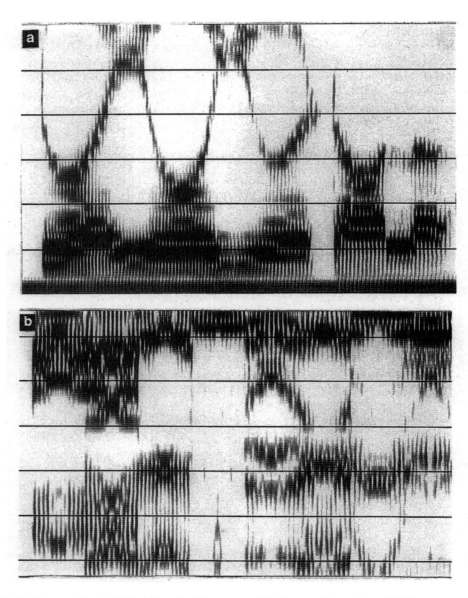

6-19 Clear vs. Band-Shifted Speech. (Courtesy of I.J. Kumar, *Cryptology*, 1997)

The descrambling code to be applied to the scrambled speech to obtain the original is as follows: After scrambling, the subband 1 occupies position 2, so in descrambling band 2 should go back to 1. Therefore the descrambling permutation is:

$$\begin{vmatrix} 1 & 2 & 3 & 4 \\ 4 & 1 & 2 & 3 \end{vmatrix}$$

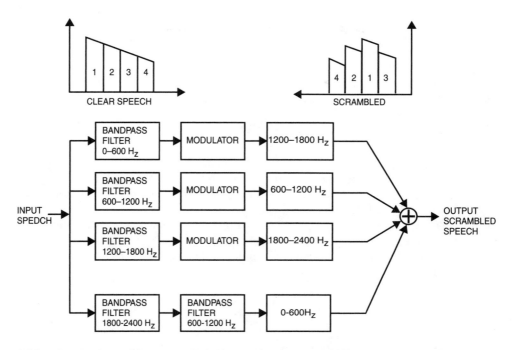

6-20 4-Band splitter. (Courtesy of I.J. Kumar, *Cryptology*, 1997)

The property of the human ear and brain, to use the redundancy of speech to advantage and make sense out of an incomplete conversation, combined with the fact that 40 percent of the energy in speech lies within first two sub-bands (that is, up to 1000 Hz) make the choice of permutations very important. A good permutation for a band-splitter should have a high shift factor because it is desirable that the bands move as far as possible from their natural position and also that the adjacent bands should not remain together after scrambling. Based on these criteria, a scoring system is devised to rank the permutations. Normally, for implementation, a look-up table of good permutations is formed and stored in memory, from whence the code is selected in a pseudo-random fashion. The permutation should be changed as quickly as possible, but by changing the code too frequently, the discontinuities and hence the distortions are increased. Synchronization between the transmitter and the receiver also becomes more critical with increased rate of change of code and hence the rate is limited to about four to five changes per second.

Another possible variation is to employ a large number of sub-bands. The greater the number of sub-bands, the more will rearrangements be possible, but, as the number of sub-bands increase, the more complicated becomes filter design. Also the problems of group delay (that is, the different delays of frequencies themselves when transmitted through the channel), becomes significant.

Sometimes the band-splitter is made more complex by randomly inverting some of the sub-bands; by so doing the criteria for selecting the good codes can be relaxed.

A code in which some of the bands do not move from their original position can be accepted if these bands are inverted. Similarly, if adjacent bands are not separated after scrambling but one of them is inverted, the resulting scrambled speech becomes unintelligible. N-band-splitter technology has become common since the advancement in digital signal processing but such systems continue to be quite expensive.[58]

Transform Based Scramblers (TBSs)

TBSs are based on linear transforms of the speech signal. Frames of N samples are transformed into an N component vector. Scrambling is achieved by permuting these transform components before applying the inverse transform to obtain the scrambled time domain signal. At the receiver end, the descrambler first transforms the received signal into the transform domain and then applies inverse permutation to bring the components into their original position before transforming the result back to the time domain, to obtain the descrambled speech.

Consider the vector S of N speech samples and an N × N transformation matrix T such that:

$$C = TS \tag{6.21}$$

Where C is the transformed vector of N components. If an N × N permutation matrix P is applied to C, to permute the transformed coefficients,

$$D = PC \tag{6.22}$$

By applying the inverse transform T we obtain scrambled speech in the time domain $S' = T^{-1}D$

At the descrambler end the clear speech vector can be obtained by applying the inverse procedure:

$$S = T^{-1}P^{-1}S' \tag{6.23}$$

The only condition on the transform is that S should be a real value for it to form the new speech signal. There are a number of transforms that can be used for this purpose. TBSs are not frequency domain scramblers in the true sense. Other than DFT no transformation leads to frequency representation of the signal. In particular the transform selected should:

- De-correlate the information in the transform domain, thus reducing the redundancy inherent in speech.
- Restrict the bandwidth of the scrambled speech to reduce distortion.
- Be easy and practical to implement.

The transforms that can be used are Discrete Fourier transform, Prolate Spheroidal transform, *Discrete Cosine transform* (DCT), and Discrete Walsh Hadamard transform. The DFT and DCT are best suited for speech scrambling because they result in low residual intelligibility of the scrambled speech and high quality speech on descrambling. In addition both can be implemented easily using standard signal processing hardware.

The system delay in such systems is dependent on the number of elements N. At the same time, higher N would mean a greater number of permutations. A compromise exists between the two and usually N is chosen to be around 256. Here, the bandwidth occupied by the signal does not remain the same as the original because of the discontinuities caused after permutation. This bandwidth expansion is compensated for by setting the coefficients (which are outside the frequency range of speech) to zero and then permuting the remaining M samples. Theoretically we can have M! permutations but not all of them are good codes, as they do not provide sufficient security. The permutations must be carefully chosen and can be changed from frame to frame to make the system more complex. Figure 6-21a and 6-21b show the spectrogram before and after application of a 256-point FFT based scrambler, and it is evident that such a scrambler is quite successful in breaking the continuity of speech.[59]

The major problem with these scramblers is their sensitivity to channel characteristics. Due to channel distortions it is difficult to preserve the individual sample integrity, that is, the individual received sample is not similar to the original sample, which affects the quality of the received sample. These scramblers are now being implemented for practical use in view of the easy availability of digital signal processing chips to perform fast DFT and channel equalization.

Channel equalization is an important technique to improve the received signal quality. It is known that the telephone channel introduces some attenuation as well as delay, each are each different for different frequencies. A channel equalizer is a device that has delay and attenuation characteristics which are the inverse of the channel.[60]

Time Domain Scramblers (TDSs)

To review the time waveform of Figure 6-23, it is seen that the speech waveform is slow-varying. Time domain scramblers try to break this continuity so the speech does not remain meaningful. To achieve this, the speech waveform is divided into a number of small segmentsthat are processed individually or in blocks. The main considerations for any TDS system is the choice of the segment size and the frame size, the audio quality deterioration acceptable, and the delay involved in processing.

The segment size is critical in TDS, as the length determines how much information is contained in the segment. It is desirable to keep the information content small in each segment but unfortunately, this means having too many discontinuities for a small duration of speech. The sudden changes produce an increase in the high frequency components. These higher frequencies cannot be accommodated properly due to the limited bandwidth of the transmission channel, leading to degradation of quality. As discontinuities occur only at the segment boundaries, smaller segment size increases the number of segments per unit time and hence more discontinuities, leading to greater distortion. The second effect governing the segment size is the group delay. Individual frequency components of the signal are delayed differently in the channel due to smearing of segment boundaries. The segment size should be large enough to ensure that these transients are not objectionable.[61]

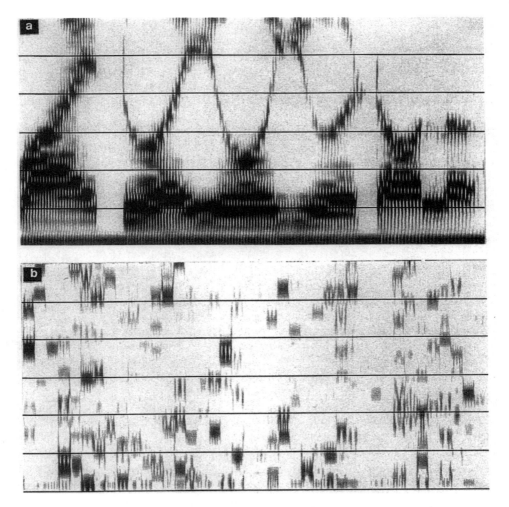

6-21 256-point FFT-based scrambler. (Courtesy of I.J. Kumar, *Cryptology,* 1997)

The segment size should be greater than the difference between maximum and minimum delay. The optimum segment size, keeping the degradation as well as the time delay within acceptable limits, is 16 to 60 ms. The number of segments per frame (the frame length) determines the delay between the times the signal is fed and clear speech is obtained. If segment size is T seconds and there are N segments per frame, the delay is 2NT seconds, as the transmitter as well as the receiver should have all the N segments to permute to obtain the scrambled or descrambled speech. It is desirable to keep this delay minimum, but having a greater number of segments creates a larger number of possible permutations, which is desirable from security point of view. Also, large frames ensure that the speech is varying within the frame; otherwise the permutation will not affect the intelligibility of the signal. Generally 8 to 10 segments per frame are chosen in practical systems. Acceptable levels of distortion and delay set a practical limit to the security that can be achieved.[62]

TDS techniques are of two kinds: time segment (also known as time element scrambling) and time sample scrambling. We will briefly look at the former; the latter has a high transmission sensitivity that restricts its use.

Time Element Scrambling

In *time element scrambling* speech is divided into frames with a number of segments per frame. These segments are permuted in a pseudo-random fashion. This method is also known as *time segment permutation* or *time division multiplexing*. The choice of segment size and frame size is a compromise between the acceptable delay, which increases with increase in the segment size and distortion and which decreases with the increasing segment size. A good compromise is a 16 to 60 ms segment with 8 to 10 segments per frame. Apart from the segment and the frame size, the other important feature of such systems is choice of the permutation. The selection of choice can have either a fixed permutation for the whole message or varied using a key from frame to frame.

Although ideally for a frame of eight segments, the total number of permutations available is 8! = 40320, not all of them can be used, as some do not provide enough security. A good permutation is also dependent on the parameter on which the scheme of scrambling operates; what may be good for a time domain scrambler may prove to be useless foe a frequency domain scrambler. The qualifying test for a permutation is that it should result in low residual intelligibility.[63]

The more strictly these rules are observed the fewer the number of permutations will be found useful out of 40320. Usually, 1024 or 512 permutations are utilized. The permutations, satisfying the conditions are subject to listening tests before confidence in their security level can be achieved. Different systems require various security levels and therefore the number of allowed permutations vary. One way to choose a permutation is to form a scoring scheme based on listening tests and select or reject a permutation according to its score. The good codes chosen according to the criteria discussed in this section usually result in a code which receives a high score. When a decision based on the agreed-upon selection criteria the permutation may be generated at the time of transmission, using the sequence generator, or then screened, or can be generated and stored in memory, from whence the sequence generator will select them randomly as required.

While with the former method, all the possible good codes can be used, the main disadvantage is that sometimes the time required to arrive at an acceptable code may become very large. In this case, with the criteria set codes in memory we have ourselves restricted the choice. We can ensure that the time delay is not large and also that codes are mutually secure; that is, when we scramble speech using one code and then test by trying to descramble with some other code, the message remains scrambled. This condition cannot be assured if the sequence generator is used to generate codes directly. Clearly, the selection and generation of permutations is an important feature of time element scramblers.[64]

There are various methods of implementing a time element scrambler. Broadly, they can be classified as *hopping window* and *sliding window* scramblers.

Hopping Window

Figure 6-22 illustrates a typical hopping window system, sometimes referred to as a *block time element scrambler*. Speech is digitized and stored in the memory frame by frame. Segments are selected, according to the permutation chosen from the set of permutations stored in ROM, converted to analog, and transmitted. With the hopping window technique, memory is filled in sequentially, and the segments of the frame are selected only when the whole frame has been stored in memory.[65]

Sliding Window

In the *sequential time element* scrambler or *sliding window* system in contrast to the hopping window scheme, the new segment fills in the location that has been vacated for example, 1 ft. of the new frame occupies the location vacated by 2, and any of the eight locations can again be selected at a given time. Effectively it means that the segments of one particular frame can be received anywhere during the message, rather than being confined to one frame. There is a possibility of some segment not being chosen for transmission for a very long time, creating a problem, as the delayed selection will incur a large and variable delay and generate an almost infinite memory requirement at the receiver. To avoid this, a maximum delay may be imposed for any segment within which that segment must be chosen. Usually this delay is chosen to be twice the frame size, which means that all segments will definitely be transmitted within two frame lengths. If a segment has overstayed, the scrambler will release this segment irrespective of the code selected by the pseudo-random generator. Actually there is no need to have a frame in this type of scheme, as the signal can be treated continuously, but the concept of frame helps to control the permutations[66] (see Figure 6-23).

Two-Dimensional Scramblers

Single dimensional scramblers leave significant residual intelligibility. To improve security, techniques in the time and frequency domains can be combined. The time domain scrambler helps destroy the speech rhythm, which is characteristic of frequency domain scramblers. The frequency domain scrambler destroys spectral characteristics of phonemesthat leave clues in the time domain system. There are several possibilities:

- **Time element scrambler with random frequency inversion**   The frequency scrambler in such systems is a single carrier for inversion purposes or a number of carriers for inversion. In the former, a single carrier of 3 kHz may be chosen, and the segments inverted or left as is depending on a code. The code changes randomly, thereby changing the segmentsthat are to be inverted in each frame. In the second case, a set of different carrier

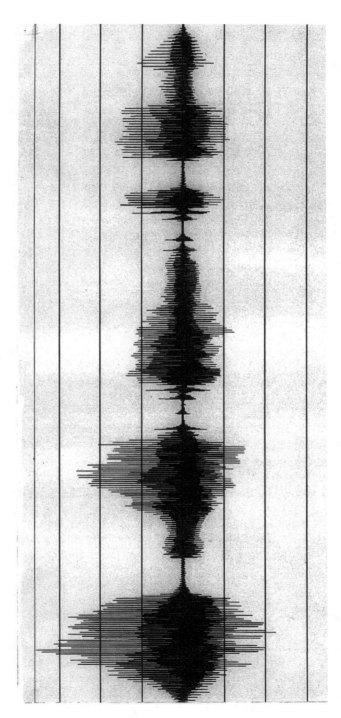

6-22   Hopping Window and Sliding Window. (Courtesy of I. J. Kumar, Cryptology, 1997)

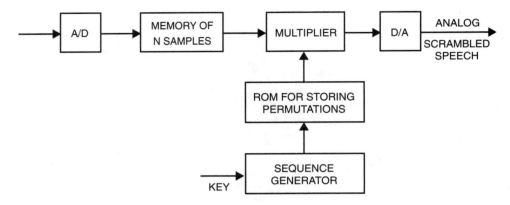

6-23 Hopping Window and Sliding Window. (Courtesy of I. J. Kumar, Cryptology, 1997)

frequencies is employed and, based on some key, various segments in a frame are inverted around different carriers. QoS may deteriorate due to restricted bandwidth.

- **Band Splitter with time element scrambling**   In this type of system the frequency reentrant technique is combined with time element scrambling, either hopping or sliding window format, to provide security. Figure 6-24 shows the characteristics of this type of system. The TDS scrambler breaks the continuity in the time domain and the 2-Band splitter disturbs the frequency structure. The split points are chosen randomly from segment to segment. Scrambling is noncommutative because the codes for descrambling will change depending on the order of operations.

- **Multband-splitter with time element scrambling**   This system combines the band-splitter with time element scrambling. Figure 6-25 presents a spectrogram of such a system. There are four subbands and four time segments per frame. The final transmission is four times as fast. Though a higher level of security is achieved, it is at the cost of memory. Channel disturbances are larger at the receiver end as the number of discontinuities increase.

- **Variable segment size, time element scrambling**   The different segments in a frame consist of a varying number of samples that add difficulties in detecting the correct segment size. The number of fixed samples in a fixed time varies. See Figure 6-26.

- **Dynamic time reverberation with frequency inversion and cyclic band shifting**   In time reverberation, multiple time echoes are added to the present signal. The speech is first inverted, band shifted, and then subjected to reverberation to obtain the scrambling effect.

- **Delayed subband with time element scrambling**   The speech subbands are delayed in different ways before applying a band-splitter.

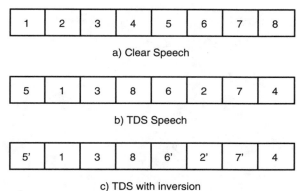

a) Clear Speech

b) TDS Speech

c) TDS with inversion

6-24 TDS with frequency Inversion.

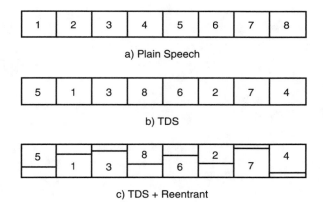

a) Plain Speech

b) TDS

c) TDS + Reentrant

6-25 2-Band-Splitter with Time element scrambler.

All two-dimensional scramblers have a residual intelligibilitythat is less than the product of the residual intelligibilities provided by the respective one-dimensional components, at a cost of increased complexity.

Scrambling schemes can be combined (*multi-dimensional scramblers*) although the main advantage is not increased security but improved QoS of the received message.[67]

Digital Scramblers

Analog scramblers have the inherent weakness that traces of the original speech are present in the scrambled version and that the transmitted signal is definitely not like white noise. Digital encryption techniques are used to achieve higher levels of security. In such systems, the A/D (analog-to-digital converter) changes speech into a sequence of bitsthat are enciphered using a PRS (pseudo-random sequence) in a manner similar to those used for data. The cryptogram has characteristics similar to

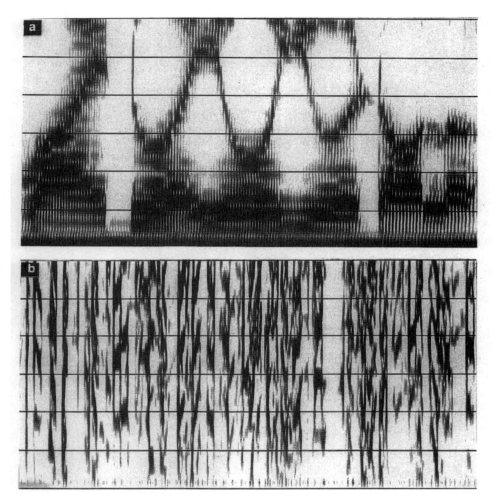

6-26 Spectrogram of (a) Clear speech; (b) Scrambled output of 4 band splitter with time domain scrambling of 16 bands.

white noise, so much so, that even the presence or absence of the signal is not apparent. These bits are then transmitted as a digital signal. The deciphering equipment recovers the clear speech by using the same pseudo-random sequence as the enciphering sequence.

The main problem with digital transmission is the bandwidth required for proper transmission. However, conventional A/D conversion techniques, that is, waveform coders, produce very high bit ratesthat cannot be transmitted using the telephone channels of 3 kHz bandwidth. There are two solutions for this problem—either to transmit over special wideband communication channels or reduce the bit rate before encryption and then transmit using a conventional telephone channel.[68]

Source Coding of Speech

One way to reduce the bit rate without much loss of information is by *source coding of speech*. Such systems are called *Vocoders*. The best source for technical detail on vocoders is Goldberg.[69] Source coding is based on the source-filter model for speech production (Figure 6-8a), where the vocal tract is represented by a time varying linear filter, which is excited by a periodic glottal pulse source for producing voiced speech, and a random noise source for unvoiced speech production. The parameters required for synthesizing speech are:

- Voiced/unvoiced decision for proper source selection
- Pitch to specify the rate of the voiced source
- Filter coefficient to specify the spectral characteristics

For most speech sounds, these parameters vary slowly as compared to actual speech, and there is no need to transmit them at the speech-sampling rate. The number of parameters, the bits required to quantize each parameter, and the rate at which the information updates are adjusted to obtain the required level of quality and intelligibility are factors to consider before using source coding. The drawback is that the reconstituted speech may sound artificial and synthetic because of the artificial glottal excitation pulse used.[70]

Formant Vocoder

The formant vocoder parameterizes speech into formant frequencies, pitch, and gain. A combination of three or four filters are required, whose center frequencies track the formant resonances of the acoustic model (formant frequencies). The vocoder achieves band saving because it represents the complete spectrum by three or four formant frequencies. These formant frequencies can be obtained from speech and used for synthesis. Formant vocoders are parallel or cascaded depending on whether the formant frequencies used for synthesis are connected in parallel, each being excited by the excitation source, or they form a chain of filters with the output of one exciting the next filter. Three to four bits are sufficient to represent each formant to result in intelligible speech. Therefore bit rates for such vocoders can be as low as 30 bps. The performance of vocoders depends on how accurately the formant frequencies have been determined. Because of the difficulties in formant frequency determination such vocoders are not commonly used.[71]

Channel Vocoder

The channel vocoder is based on the perception of speech being dependent on the preservation of the short time amplitude spectrum of speech. It consists of a bank of filters whose center frequencies and bandwidths are selected according to the perceptual characteristics of the human ear. Figures 6-27 and 6-28 present the block diagram for a channel vocoder for both input and decoded speech. The bank of filters covers the entire speech range that is, 300 to 3400 Hz. The energy of speech within each band is measured and transmitted along with the pitch values and the voiced/unvoiced decision. With proper designing usually 36 o 40 bits per frame are required

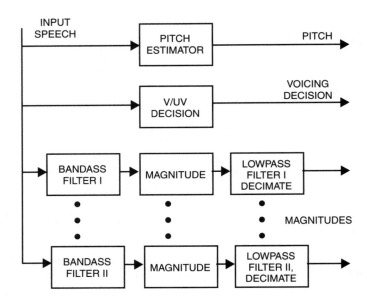

6-27 Channel Vocoder: Analysis of Input Speech. (Courtesy of Goldberg and Rieke, A Practical Handbook of Speech Coders, 2000)

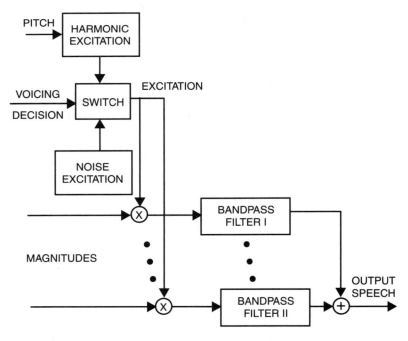

6-28 Channel Vocoder: Synthesis of Decoded Output Speech. (Courtesy of Goldberg and Rieke, A Practical Handbook of Speech Coders, 2000)

to provide intelligible speech. The quality of channel vocoder is machine like due to the errors in voiced/unvoiced determination and pitch estimation. The performance depends upon the number of filters, their spacing, and their bandwidth: the more the number of filters, the finer is the quality of speech. The number of frequency channels is a design decision of the channel vocoder that represents a trade-off between bit rate and synthesized speech. The number of channels is fixed for a given implementation. Channel spacing and bandwidth is usually non-linear with some bands being used to cover the lower frequenciesthat are perceptually significant.[72]

Linear Prediction Based Vocoder (LP)

The LP vocoder is based on the linear prediction analysis of speech. This is a time domain method and the basic idea is that the present sample value of the signal is dependent on several past sample values and thus can be expressed as a linear combination of these values:

$$\underline{X}(n) = a_1 x(n - 1) + a_2 x(n - 2) \dots a_p x(n - p) \tag{6.24}$$

where $\underline{X}(n)$ is the value predicted using the past p values of the signal x(n).

The error of prediction e (n) can be written as:

$$e(n) = x(n) - \Sigma a_k x(n - k) \text{ for } k = 1, 2, \dots p \tag{6.25}$$

The multipliers, a_k's, are called the linear prediction coefficients (LPC). They are adjusted to minimize the prediction error. The total prediction error E is given by:

$$E = [\, x(n) - \Sigma a_k x(n - k) \,]^2 \tag{6.26}$$

The number of samples should be chosen so that they correspond to a frame size of about 10 to 25 ms of speech for acceptable speech quality. Large number of samples will give a coarse representation of the speech spectrum. The error E resembles a train of impulses, spaced at pitch intervals for voiced speech, whereas, for unvoiced speech E resembles white noise. Figure 6-29 displays a block diagram for the LPC encoder and Figure 6-30 shows the LPC decoder.[73]

An important point to be noted is that the pth prediction co-efficient is dependent on all the coefficients of order less than p; the predictor coefficients are not all independent. This implies that the parameter value depends on the order of analysis. Another drawback is that a small change in these filter coefficients can effect the synthesized speech dramatically, which makes these coefficients unfit for transmission. Transforming these coefficients into some other set of numbers can solve both these problems. Two alternatives are used for transmission, reflection and log area ratio coefficients.

Reflection Coefficients

The intermediate quantities k_i's are known as *reflection coefficients*. The name is taken from transmission line theory where the reflection coefficient specifies the

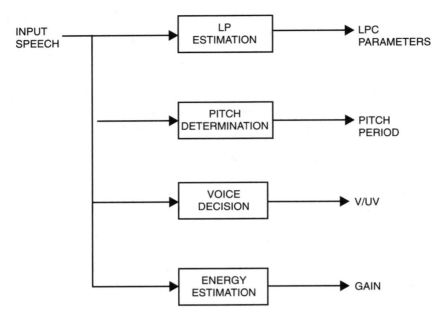

6-29 LPC encoder. (Courtesy of Golberg and Riek, 2000)

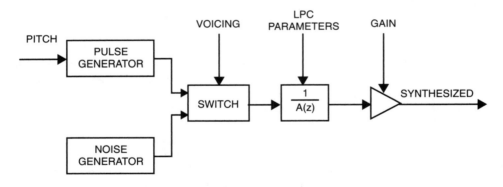

6-30 LPC decoder. (Courtesy of Golberg and Riek, 2000)

amount of powerthat will be reflected back from the boundary between two sections of different impedances. The vocal tract behaves as a transmission line of differing cross sections for the acoustic wave. As the reflection coefficients are bounded by ± 1 it is easy to quantize and transmit them. The reflection coefficients, together with the gain, give a good estimate of the spectral properties of speech. The reflection coefficients can be directly calculated using lattice filters.[74]

Log Area Ratio Coefficients

Another set of parametersthat can be derived from the reflection coefficients, is the *log area ratio* coefficients. The vocal tract can be considered to be equivalent to a lossless acoustic tube formed by joining cylindrical sections of equal length. If we consider the area of the ith section to be Ai, it can be shown that the ith coefficient is equal to the k_i^{th} reflection coefficient at the ith junction and is expressed as

$$k_i = (A_i - A_i + 1) / (A_i + A_i + 1) \qquad (6.27)$$

The log area ratios are defined as:

$$G_i \log [A_i + 1 / A_i] = \log [(1 - k_i) / (1 + k_i)] \qquad (6.28)$$

These are also appropriate for quantization. There are many variations of the basic linear prediction technique. In the standard linear prediction schemes, the pitch, gain, and voiced/unvoiced information is directly coded for each frame. Sometimes, taking into account the variations of speech can save a considerable number of bits. The coefficients and pitch are updated only when the change in them exceeds a threshold valuethat is pre-decided. There are many schemes proposed which eliminate the transmission of the pitch information explicitly.[75]

In *Residual Excited Linear Prediction* (RELP) the residual error, obtained after predicting the speech sample using the LP coefficients, is transmitted from which the pitch, gain, V/UV information is obtained at the receiver. The RELP coder can operate under noisy conditions up to 9.6 Kbps.

In *Voiced Excited LPC* (VELP) the low frequency portion of the speech signal is transmitted directly, from which the source information is extracted.

Another very effective algorithm is *Vector Excitation coding* or *Code Excited Linear Prediction* (CELP). This is also an efficient method that can achieve transmission bit rates as low as 4 Kbps. In CELP coders each speech frame, for which LPC parameters and pitch values are obtained, is subdivided into smaller segments and for each segment an excitation code book which has been formed based on large number of different speech data vector is searched, giving the minimum mean square error between the actual and the synthesized speech. The index of the vector selected, and the LPC value, are encoded and transmitted. CELP is complex but it can result in acceptable quality speech at bits rates as low as 4.8 Kbps. CELP also improves the quality at higher rates.

The parameters of any of the vocoders mentioned above are quantized and coded to obtain a sequence of bitsthat are then permuted or enciphered, to achieve security. Permuting the bits within each frame can be one method for providing security, but the permutations cannot be made variable as no additional bits for synchronization can be sent. This method of permuting the LPC parameters is only partially successful in distorting the speech.[76]

To encipher the sequence of bits obtained after digitization (waveform or source coding), they are modulo-2 added to a pseudo-random sequence generated using shift registers or other stream cipher such as HORNET™. The spectrogram of

Figure 6-26 shows the enciphered speech; observe that the characteristics of speech are not visible at all. The spectrogram is similar to the spectrogram of *random noise or white noise*.

The most important aspect of such systems is the encryption algorithm used. Earlier cipher feedback generators or self-synchronizing sequence generators were employed for enciphering speech. The major advantage of such systems is that the bit used for enciphering is a function of the previous n bits of the cipher and therefore there is no additional signal required for synchronization of the generators. On the other hand, as the present bit of the sequence is a function of the n previous bits, even a single bit in error at the receiver can result in a large error, making the resulting frame of speech totally unintelligible. A noisy channel, while moderately acceptable for clear speech, may become practically unsuitable for secure communications. For similar reasons the block ciphers that also use some combination of input bits to obtain the ciphered bit are not really suitable for speech encipherment. The most commonly used technique for enciphering speech is stream ciphering. The major advantage of stream ciphers is that they do not propagate error. Thus, the same channel can be used for communicating both the clear and enciphered speech.

Sinusoidal Model

Figure 6-31 shows the model for sinusoidal analysis and synthesis coding. The sinusoidal model assumes the source-filter model, where the source (model of the vocal cord glottal excitation) is modeled by a sum of sine waves. Within certain parameters both voiced and unvoiced excitation can be modeled effectively; in this way voiced speech can be modeled as a sum of harmonic sine waves spaced at the frequency of

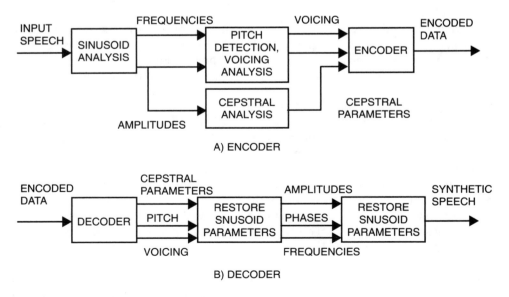

6-31 Sinusoidal Analysis and Synthesis Coding. (Courtesy of Goldberg and Riek, 2000)

the fundamental, with phases tied to the fundamental. Unvoiced speech can be represented as a sum of sinusoids with random phases. The speech waveform can be modeled by:

$$s(n) = \sum_{l=1}^{L} A_l \cos(\omega_l n + \phi_l) \tag{6.29}$$

where A_1, ω_1, φ_1 represent the amplitude, frequency, and phase of each of the L sine wave components, respectively.

Sinusoidal Parameter Analysis

In the general case of sinusoidal modeling, the frequency location of the sinusoids is not constrained to the pitch harmonics. This approach, without quantization, accurately models signals containing multiple speakers or music. However, to encode speech efficiently, the number of parameters must be reduced: Limits on parameter values are necessary. The sinusoidal speech coder is based on the knowledge that when speech is voiced purely, the frequency components of the signal correspond directly to harmonics of the pitch. As a result, the sine wave parameters correspond to harmonic samples of the short time discrete Fourier transform (DFT).

For this situation, Equation 6.25 simplifies to

$$s(n) = \sum_{l=1}^{L} A_l \cos(l\omega_0 n + \phi_l) \tag{6.30}$$

The amplitude estimates $A_1 = |Y(l\omega_0)|$ and the phase estimates $\omega_1 = \angle Y(l\omega_0)$ can be calculated from the DFT of the input speech, $Y(\omega)$. For this purely voiced case, the DFT will have peaks at multiples of ω_0, the pitch frequency. When the speech is not perfectly voiced, the DFT will still have a multitude of peaks, but at frequencies that are not necessarily harmonically related. In these cases, the sine wave frequencies are taken to be the peaks of the DFT, and the amplitudes and phases are still obtained by evaluating the DFT at the chosen frequencies. All of the above analysis is performed using a Hamming window of at least 2.5 times the average pitch period. A time window of this length is long enough to accurately resolve the individual sinusoids.

Figure 6-31 is a block diagram of the sinusoidal transform encoder and decoder. The input speech is Fourier transformed and the Sinusoidal Analysis block determines the peaks of the magnitude. The frequencies and amplitudes are analyzed for pitch harmonics to determine pitch and voicing information. The amplitudes are transformed to the *cepstral* domain for more efficient coding.

The voicing information is derived from the pitch estimator and parameterized as a cutoff frequency. Frequencies below the cutoff are voiced and harmonic. Above the cutoff, they are considered unvoiced and not harmonic, with random phase. The decoder decodes the pitch and voicing information and transforms the cepstral information inversely. This information is combined to restore the amplitudes, frequencies, and phases for the component sine waves. The sine waves are synthesized to produce the output speech. The harmonic components (those below the voicing cutoff frequency) are synthesized to be in phase with the fundamental pitch frequency. Unvoiced components (above the voicing cutoff frequency) are synthesized with a random phase.[77]

Standards

Many of the previously mentioned vocoders, in modified form, have become standards. The U.S. Department of Defense adopted a 2.4 Kbps LPC vocoder in 1982, modified it and it became Federal Standard 1015, LPC-10e. For the required 8kHz sample rate the frame length is 22.5 ms and 54 bits/frame achieve the 2.4 Kbps total rate. The *Groupe Speciale Mobile* (GSM) of the *European Telecommunications Standards Institute* (ETSI) standardize an RPE (regular pulse excitation coder which uses pulses to approximate the excitation signal but restricts pulse locations to even spacing) for mobile cellular applications. The standard uses 13 Kbps for speech coding and the remainder of the 22.8 bps channel for error control. Federal Standard 1016, CELP at 4.8 Kbps was adopted in 1991. The CELP algorithm operates at a frame rate of 30 ms with subframes of 7.5 ms. The ITU G.723.1 Algebraic CELP/Multi-pulse coder at 5.3/6.3 Kbps is designed for video conferencing and *voice over Internet* (VoIP) applications. The ETSI GSM Enhanced Full Rate Algebraic CELP at 12.2 kbits/sec encodes speech at 12.2w Kbps and is primarily for mobile cellular use. The IS-641 EFR 7.4 Kbps Algebraic CELP for IS-136 North American Digital Cellular works with TDMA systems. And the list continues to grow.

Cryptanalysis of Speech Systems

A few remarks are in order about cracking the systems discussed in previous pages. Cryptanalysis of speech signals involves either determining a code or the private key for descrambling and restoring speech by means of this key, or obtaining the parameters of speech from a secured version and synthesizing speech using these parameters. Compared to cryptanalysis of text, where only the EXACT transformation key leads to decryption, speech systems DO NOT require an exact key. The properties of speech can be used to obtain an approximately correct key to obtain sufficiently intelligible speech. Some scramblers that seem to be highly secure according to the manufacturer's specifications may turn out to be weak when tested.[78]

It is well to realize that every analog-based scrambling system is insecure. They're too many clues and far too many procedures to exploit the clues mathematically. Analog systems are at best trade-offs between security and speech synthesis.

Cryptanalysis of any incoming speech data may be carried out in two steps:

1. Identification of the scrambling/ciphering scheme.
2. Descrambling/deciphering using the various parameters of speech to obtain intelligible speech.

The former is known as *system identification* and interesting work has been done in this instance by Kumar (1997), Nichols (1999), and Kant (2001). The human ear, the brain, and the parameters of speech serve as important tools for achieving this goal.

Tools and Parameters for Cryptanalysis of Speech

The human ear and brain provide the most basic tool for cryptanalysis of speech. In spite of the best efforts of the cryptographer, it is difficult for him or her to sufficiently destroy the information contained in the speech signal. The ear can tolerate surprisingly high levels of interference in the form of noise, frequency distortions, and missing portions. The brain and the ear together make use of the redundancy of speech to decode a message even if it is not heard clearly. It has been found experimentally that even infinitely clipped speech, that is, speech where only signs of the samples are made available, retains almost full intelligibility and so does speech filtered up to 1.5 kHz. Even when we hear speech that has been low-pass-filtered up to 800 Hz, a considerable amount of intelligibility is obtained from a cryptanalyst's point of view.

Our brain has the added ability to concentrate on a particular conversation of interest while immersed in a number of parallel conversations (known as the cocktail party effect). This leads to intelligibility in some types of scramblers if all the segments of a frame are heard simultaneously. The combined effect of the capacity of the ear and the brain help us in obtaining intelligibility from a scrambled speech even if we descramble it incorrectly. But before we put our brain and ears on the job, the speech should be descrambled to some extent. The most important toolthat helps us to identify the system of scrambling is the sound spectrograph.

Application of Sound Spectrograph to Cryptanalysis

The 3-D spectrogram of clear speech is capable of giving comparison of all the details that is, pitch, voiced/unvoiced decision, formant frequencies and energy of speech for the eye to observe in graphical form. Any distortion/alteration caused by the scramblers can be detected by observing the spectrogram carefully. The ear can recognize the presence of discontinuities in the time domain and variations in the frequency domain but it cannot establish the nature of the scrambler. Using the spectrogram we can observe that the frequency band scrambler disturbs the spectrum, which is depicted as horizontal discontinuities as in Figure 6-32 and Figure 6-33, whereas systems employing time manipulations show vertical cuts or boundaries as in Figure 6-34.

A number of systems show horizontal as well as vertical boundaries indicating that they are two-dimensional scramblers. (One can actually cut the spectrogram along these boundaries and rearrange the elements to restore the speech-like pattern by trying to maintain the continuity at the boundaries.)

Apart from identifying the scrambling technique used, the spectrogram also helps in determining some of the parameters of the scrambler. The interval between the two boundaries along the time axis corresponds to the segment size in time and the interval between two discontinuities along the frequency axis corresponds to the frequency band. This can be measured directly from the spectrograph and can be helpful in exactly identifying the scrambler. Thus, apart from removing the mystery

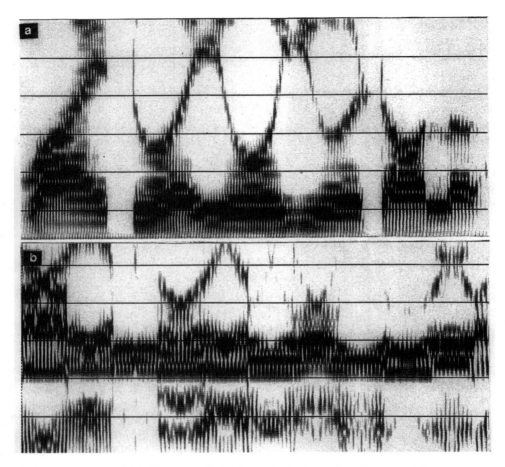

6-32 Spectrogram of (a) Clear speech, (b) band shifted speech. (Courtesy of Kumar, Cryptology, 1997)

of the scrambling method, the spectrographic studies are capable of providing useful information about the parameters of scrambling which are used for actual descrambling.

When the scrambling method has been identified using the spectrogram, the actual descrambling of the message involves either rearranging the segments based on matching of certain parameters of speech, or synthesis using the speech parameters. These parameters are obtained by processing the speech signal. Based on the time or frequency representations used for processing, these are called the time domain or frequency domain parameters. The basic assumption in most of the analysis techniques is that the signalthat is being processed changes relatively slowly with time. Sufficient data should be available to calculate the required parameter of speech without smearing it. Short segments, for which speech is assumed to have fixed properties, can be isolated and processed. Various parameters can be extracted for such segments and are used for cryptanalysis.

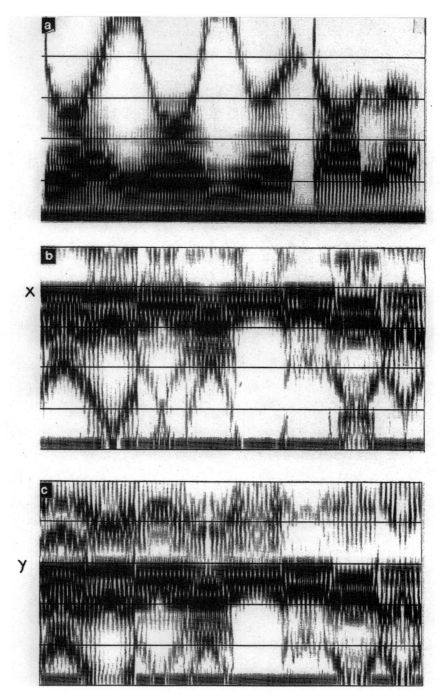

6-33 Spectrogram of (a) Clear speech; (b) speech with lower band inverted (0 to 2 kHz); (c) speech with both bands inverted (0 to 1.5 kHz and 1.5 to 2.5 kHz).

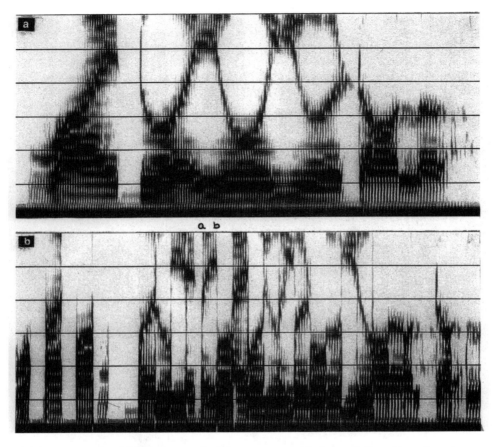

6-34 Spectrograph of (a) clear speech; (b)output scrambled speech from time elemnt hopping window scrambler. (Courtesy of Kumar, Cryptology, 1997)

Under the assumption of their being quasi-stationary all the parameters are calculated for short durations of the order of 10 to 30 ms. Kumar presents details on time domain parameters:

- Short time energy function
- Short time autocorrelation function
- Short time average magnitude difference function

And frequency domain parameters:

- FFT of spectrum estimation
- Filter bank methods
- Homophonic speech processing
- Model based techniques
- LP-based spectral estimation
- Maximum entropy spectral estimation

And frequency domain descrambling methods:

- Frequency inverters
- Random frequency inversion
- Selective inversion; reversal of the band splitter and n band splitter; pattern matching; edge approaches for time element scramblers and a host of other techniques.

All the parameters mentioned above represent the source of the vocal tract characteristics of the speech. The energy and pitch are characteristics of the glottal excitation source. The formant frequencies depend on the vocal tract characteristics. The vocal tract characteristics are speech dependent. Moving the articulatorsthat are responsible for changing the shape of the vocal tract requires finite time and varies slowly with time because of their mechanical inertia.[79]

Analog Methods

There are, in general, three methods used to descramble/decipher speech cryptograms/messages:

1. To estimate some parameters of speech for a small segment and use it as a feature to match adjacent segments. Descrambling may involve comparison of a single parameter (for example, energy for frequency inverters) or may depend on the combination of a number of parameters (as for time element scramblers).
2. Speech can be synthesized by extracting the parameters of speech from the scrambled/ciphered version.
3. A simple pattern matching technique can be employed to identify the phonemes in the ciphered/scrambled speech with the help of a codebook. This template matching technique is possible because of the fact that speech can be represented by a finite number of feature vectors.

The basic steps required to descramble or decipher speech can be thought of as an integrated computer system with A/D, D/A, and spectrographic facilities (Figure 6-35). Our main point is that all analog-based scrambling systems are insecure.[76]

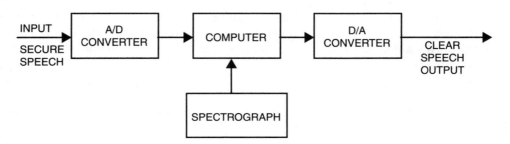

6-35 Integrated Computer System for cryptanalysis of speech. (Courtesy of Kumar, 1997)

Cryptanalysis of Digital Scramblers/Ciphers

Analog scramblers leave vital clues for cryptanalysts in the spectrogram. Repeated listening of the scrambled speech also at times leads to intelligibility (as in the case of frequency inverters). However, in case of digital speech ciphers the spectrogram appears totally noise-like. Spectrographic studies or repeated listening of the ciphered speech are usually of no help. Return to Figure 6-26 and note how few clues there are to work with when the spectrogram looks like white noise. This is a characteristic of digital encryption.

Consider a LSFR based digital cipher. This is not the most secure approach, there are many other options ECC, Rijndael [the AES winner] and so forth. One possible entry is to recover the key using the technique of shift register synthesis or algorithm reengineering. This method requires that some length of enciphered bit stream and the corresponding exact plain data bit stream should be available to the cryptanalyst for a given plain text attack. In case of speech, the data rates are of the order of 16 Kbps or much higher and to satisfy the above stated requirement, are almost impossible to achieve. Even synchronization delay of few milliseconds between the plain speech bit stream and the enciphered bit stream would make the determination of the shift register generator (for an LSFR-based solution), by trials through various shifted positions, impractical. The approach is therefore not practical for solving the digital ciphers.

Another approach to determine the generator (again for an LSFR-based system) could be based on the facts that there are a large number of silence regions in speech and the ciphered bit stream of such portion of speech is simply the shift register sequence corrupted by the noise. By locating such silence regions and then studying the bits in these regions, one might possibly identify the generator of the pseudo-random encryption sequence.

Noise Cancellation

As the aim of the cryptanalyst is to gather intelligence information and while the quality of the recovered signal is not necessarily his or her concern, it may be better to attack the problem through signal processing techniques. The ciphered speech may be treated as a signal buried in digital noise and it may be enhanced using noise cancellation techniques. Some parameters of speech, such as pitch and the first formant may be determined and speech may be synthesized for two or three pitch periods. Using this synthesized speech an estimate of noise can be obtained by modulo-2 addition of the synthesized speech and the ciphered speech. The parameters of the next frame that is, one pitch period, may be estimated using the parameters of the previous frame and the estimated noise based on previous frame. Using such an iterative approach is plausible, as speech is so redundant as a signal that the digitization and subsequent addition of noise still leaves enough information in it to allow the synthesis approach to succeed.

The above approach also leads to some very interesting problems in pattern recognition. These are:

- The problem of discrimination of pseudo-random noise and pseudo-random noise-added speech, which can help in determining the silence regions in the ciphered speech. The sequence bits obtained in the silence regions may lead to synthesis of the shift register used to generate the noise sequence.
- Recognition of voiced/unvoiced portions of enciphered speech.
- Recognition of phonemes in enciphered speech.

An entirely different approach can be based on template matching discussed in Goldburg (1993). Speech can be represented by a finite number of templates. Some features that do not change totally after enciphering can be matched with the incoming enciphered speech to obtain the nearest clear speech. The judicious mix of high speech signal processing hardware and software provide solutions to the problems (supra) in relation to cryptanalysis of uncompressed digital encrypted speech.[81]

Cryptanalysis of Linear Prediction Based Vocoders

In Linear prediction based systems speech is characterized by its parameters, namely pitch, voicing decision, gain, and reflection coefficients. In LPC based systems, these parameters are quantized, coded, and enciphered using a pseudo-random sequence before transmission. Although these systems are generally considered to be highly secure because the redundancy of speech has been removed or considerably attenuated, in practical terms, the problems involved in the cryptanalysis of these systems may not be as formidable as in the case of wide-band digital ciphers.

The basic properties of the speech and the pseudo-random sequence can be exploited to obtain some information about the message. Consider the following facts:

- Each coefficient, after linear prediction analysis, is represented by a fixed number of bits and the relative position of the coefficients in the frame remains the same.
- Runs of zeros in the pseudo-random sequence leave some of the coefficients unchanged and runs of ones in the pseudo-random sequence invert some of the coefficients (that is, replace 1's by 0's and vice versa). For example, assuming that the pseudo-random sequence for a 100-stage linear shift register generated encryption with primitive feedback polynomial runs of zero of length 1, 2^{99}; runs of zeros of length 2, 2^{98}; and so forth. The expected number of runs of zeros of length five in one frame of 54 bits will be $(2^{100 \times 54}) / (2^5 \times 2^0)$ which is 1.7 that is, approximately 2. The expected number of runs of zeros of length two in one frame will be about 14. So we can safely expect two to three coefficients per frame to remain unchanged and an equal number to be totally inverted, other coefficients being affected partially.
- Speech can be completely represented by a finite number of templates as discussed in Gray.[82]

One approach that evolved from these facts is to form templates of reflection coefficients of clear speech and match the reflection coefficients of the enciphered speech with the stored reflection coefficients of these templates. The template revealing the maximum number of coincidences and inversions is the most probable match for the ciphered speech.

Thoughts About Cryptanalysis of Public-Key Systems

The public-key systems—RSA, ECC, DLP, PGP, and especially those based on the AES standards such as Rijndael Algorithm, TwoFish, Serpent, Mars, and so on—have been based on the solution of some hard mathematical problems. These algorithms have been designed to provide cryptographically random ciphertext. Statistical analysis alone is not enough to yield enough valuable clues to decipherment of their secrets. Implementations have flaws and the cryptanalyst may search for wedges into the cryptograms so communicated. The security of these systems is closely related to developments in computer technology and the special purpose architecture that may be available to the enemy. It is a fact that that many of the strong systems have been broken, either by brute force on the keys or flaws in the structure or implementation, or through stealth on the host network. In order to maintain certainty about the security of such systems, one must ensure public disclosure, due diligence and academic/corporate investigation, and constant vigilance for any cryptanalytic technique which has some definite probably of success. The effort involved must be proof against a huge effort (computer wise) by enemy and friend alike. The history of the NSA STU-III [now STE] secure telephone, which can be viewed at the National Cryptologic Museum in Laurel, MD is one of high due diligence and preparation to provide digital security for speech communications used in national security communications and at government level. However, security by obscurity fails the test. The A5 debacle is a good example of what happens when due diligence languishes.

Cryptanalysis of A5 Algorithm

In 1994, the roof caved in on the conversation security of 100+ million GSM telephone customers in Europe. The A5 encryption algorithm was the GSM standard for digital cellular mobile telephones. A5 is a binary stream cipher where the keystream is the XOR of three clock controlled (in a stop/go manner) LFSRs of total length 64. Very short keystream sequences are generated from different initial states obtained by combining a 64-bit secret session key and a known 22-bit public key. All the feedback polynomials were sparse. In most of the following attacks the attacker is assumed to know some pseudo random bits generated by the A5 algorithm. Since GSM telephones send a new frame every 4.6 secs, the first two minutes of conversation equals approximately 2^{15} frames sent. In 1994, Ross Anderson announced a 2^{40} attack on the A5 system. At Crypto 99, David Wagner announced an attack on A5/2 that required only about 2^{16} steps using a few pseudo random bits. Briceno found that there was a 10-key bit "zeroization" which made an exhaustive search attack of 2^{54} possible. Anderson and Roe found that by guessing the 19 and 22 bit registers they could reduce the attack to about 2^{45} searches. Golic improved the attack to 2^{40}

steps and again with a time memory tradeoff concluded that an attack of 2^{22} was feasible. The coup de grace was delivered in December 1999 by Biryukov and Shamir with a real-time attack on A5/1, the strong version of the encryption algorithm, on a single PC with 128MB RAM and two 73GB hard disks which could extract the conversation key in less than a second from the output produced by the algorithm in the first two minutes. The attack requires a onetime parallelizable data preparation stage whose complexity was a trade-off between 2^{38} and 2^{48} steps.[83]

The A5 algorithm was proprietary and in silent dismay until its public destruction in 1999. It is a good example of the need for public vetting of algorithms (with the exception of ECCM, which only NSA verifies for the U.S. Government) and the fragility of weak cryptographic systems.

Summary

Speech is the most common form of communication. Both linguistic and nonlinguistic information is conveyed with the spoken message. As in the case of text, need arises to make speech communication secure, the security level varies from simple privacy to very high levels for strategic messages of great importance. Of the two types of security afforded speech systems, analog and digital, analog systems have been shredded the most severely, and are all essentially insecure. Digital systems present a much more difficult problem of computer- and signal-technology-based issues.

Endnotes

[1]Boone, J.V., and R.R. Peterson, "The Start of the Digital Revolution: SIGSALY Secure digital Voice Communications in World War II," NSA, 3/11/2001, p. 1, http://www.nsa.gov/wwii/papers/start_of_digital_revolution.htm.

[2]David Kahn, Hitler's Spies: German Military Intelligence in World War II, Macmillian, 1978, p. 172.

[3]Ibid., pp. 172–174.

[4]Ibid., pp. 172–174.

[5]Ibid., p. 175.

[6]Boone, J.V., and R.R. Peterson, Op. cit., p. 3.

[7]Bennett, William R., Fellow, IEEE, "Secret Telephony as a Historical Example of Spread-Spectrum Communications," IEEE Transactions on Communications, Vol. COM-31, No.1, January 1983, p. 99.

[8]Boone, J.V., and R.R. Peterson, Op. cit., p 4 ff.

[9]Ibid., p. 7.

[10]Ibid., p. 8.

[11]Ibid., p. 9.

[12]Ibid., p. 11.

[13]Boone, op. cit. pg. 8.

[14]Ibid., p. 12 ff.

[15]Kumar, I. J., Cryptology, Aegean Park Press, 1997, pp. 308–311.

[16]Robinson, Andrew, The Story of Writing, Thames and Hudson, 1995, pp. 24–29 & ff.

[17]Nichols, Randall K., Classical Cryptography Course, Vol. I, Aegean Park Press, 1996, pp. 84–85.

[18]Kumar, I. J., Cryptology, Ibid., pp. 66–67.

[19]Ibid., p. 67.

[20]Gordon, Cyrus H., Forgotten Scripts, Basic Books, 1982.

[21]Kumar, I. J., Cryptology, Ibid., p. 69.

[22]Nichols, ICSA Guide to Cryptography, Ibid., p. 69.

[23]Goldberg, Randy, and Lance Riek, A Practical Guide Of Speech Coders, CRC, 2000, p. 29.

[24]Ibid., p. 29.

[25]Ibid., p. 30.

[26]Ibid., p. 30.

[27]Ibid., pp. 30–31.

[28]Ibid., p. 28, Figure 2.13.

[29]Kumar, I. J., Cryptology, Ibid., pp. 313–314.

[30]Ibid., p. 313.

[31]Beker, Henry J., and Fred C. Piper, Secure Speech Communications, Academic Press, 1985, p. 34.

[32]Ibid., pp. 34–36.

[33]Ibid., p. 36.

[34]Ibid., p. 37.

[35]Tolstov, Georgi P., Fourier Series, Dover, 1962.

[36]Goldberg, Randy, and Lance Riek, Ibid., p. 35 ff.

[37]Berkey, Dennis D., Calculus, 2nd Ed, Saunders College Publishing, 1988, p. 508.

[38]Goldberg, Randy, and Lance Riek, Ibid., p. 40 ff.

[39]Ibid., pp. 42–44.

[40]Oppenheim, A., and R. Schafer, Discrete Time Signal Processing, Prentice Hall, 1989.

[41]Goldberg, Randy, and Lance Riek, Ibid., pp. 45–46.

[42]Ibid., p. 47.

[43]Goldberg op. cit. pg. 46.

[44]Ibid., pp. 50–52.

[45]Ibid., p. 54.

[46]Ibid., p. 90.

[47]Ibid., p. 92.

[48]Xiong, Fugin, Digital Modulation Techniques, Artech House, 2000.

[49]Torrieri, Don J., Principles of Secure Communications Systems, 2nd Ed, Artech House, 1992.

[50]Kumar, I. J., Cryptology, Ibid., pp. 322–324.

[51]Kumar, op cit.

[52]Kahn, David, The Codebreakers, 2nd Ed, Macmillan, 1999.

[53]Kumar, I. J., Cryptology, Op. cit., p. 323.

[54]Ibid., p. 323.

[55]Ibid., p. 327.

[56]Ibid., p. 325.

[57]Ibid., p. 337.

[58]Ibid., p. 332.

[59]Ibid., p. 332.

[60]Beker, Henry J., and Fred C. Piper, Secure Speech Communications, London: Academic Press, 1985, pp. 120–151.

[61]Kumar, I. J., Cryptology, Op. cit., pp. 333–334.

[62]Ibid., p. 326.

[63]Ibid., p. 327

[64]Ibid., p. 329.

[65]Ibid., p. 337.

[66]Ibid., p. 338.

[67]Ibid., p. 340.

[68]Ibid., p. 345.

[69]Goldberg and Riek, Op. cit.

[70]Ibid., pp. 345ff.

[71]Beker, Henry J.,and Fred C. Piper, Op. cit. pp. 63–70.

[72]Ibid., p. 70.

[73]Goldberg, Randy, and Lance Riek, Ibid, Op. cit., pp. 132 ff.

[74]Ibid., p. 133.

[75]Ibid., p. 54.

[76]Ibid., pp. 51–57.

[77]Ibid., pp. 130–132.

[78]Kumar, I. J., Cryptology, Op. cit., pp. 352 ff.

[79]Ibid., p. 352.

[80]Ibid., pp. 352–362.

[81]Goldberg, Op. cit., p. 87.

[82]Gray, op. cit.

[83]A detailed discussion is found in the fascinating paper by Alex Biryukov, Adi Shamir, and David Wagner, "Real Time Cryptanalysis of A5/1 on a PC, *Fast Software Encryption Workshop 2000*, April 10–12, 2000, NYC.

The Wireless Local Area Network (WLAN)

A *wireless local area network* (WLAN) is a flexible data communications system implemented as an extension to, or as an alternative for, a wired LAN. WLANs transmit and receive data over the air via RF technology, minimizing the need for any wired connections, and in turn, combining data connectivity with user mobility.[1] WLANs provide all the functionality of WLANs without the physical constraints, and configurations range from simple peer-to-peer topologies to complex networks offering distributed data connectivity and roaming. Besides offering end-user mobility within a networked environment, WLANs enable physical network portability, allowing LANs to move with users that make use of them.

The tradeoff for flexibility and mobility is more threats from hackers using portable computing devices or scanners to intercept data or gain access to the LAN. Unwired LANs are more susceptible to attacks by outside forces via the Internet than wired LANs are. A hacker can crack a network from the convenience of his or her car parked nearby the location of the WLAN. IEEE 802.11, the WLAN standard, provides reliable transfer of wireless data but is vulnerable to hacking or eavesdropping.[2]

In fourth quarter 1999 and first quarter 2000, a collection of reputable vendors brought to market a host of 802.11b-compliant products. The void that IT managers had been facing was finally filled with high speed, interoperable, insecure, and lower-cost wireless equipment.[3] Many IT operations justified the loss of security on the tradeoff for ways to inject mobility, flexibility, and scalability into their networks.

WLANs eliminate the physical link to the network, allowing users to connect directly to a distribution system without interconnecting wires and cables. The network backbone is no longer hidden behind walls and floors nor need it be anchored to a particular physical location. With a WLAN in place, an office infrastructure may be peripatetic, and free to grow and move to suit the needs of the organization.

To say that WLANs are completely without wires would not be strictly correct. Unless a piece of equipment is battery-powered, there must be a power cable connection, and a typical configuration has one or more fixed access points that are connected to a LAN via a traditional data cable. The access points broadcast to and receive information from wireless clients that are within the transmission range. Under ideal circumstances, assuming an environment with few obstructions, the coverage area for a single access point can reach up to several hundred feet and support a small group of users without introducing noticeable performance degradation.

In its simplest form, a WLAN comprises a single transceiver, called an *access point* (AP), that is connected to a wired network via an Ethernet cable as shown in the left frame of Figure 7-1. Access points exist at fixed locations throughout the organization and serve as communications beacons. Network clients with a wireless network adapter installed are able to facilitate data transfer from client to access point and thus from client to server. Introducing more access points near the coverage boundaries of previously deployed broadcast units can extend a wireless network's range. Functioning in a manner similar to cellular telephones, WLANs communicate within cells. Overlapping cells at their perimeters, as depicted in the right frame of Figure 7-2, enables network administrators to extend coverage areas. As clients "roam" around the office, they move from cell to cell, maintaining a connection at all times.

Wireless Transmission Media

Wireless LANs employ *radio frequency* (RF) and *infrared* (IR) electromagnetic airwaves[4] to transfer data from point to point. The *Federal Communications*

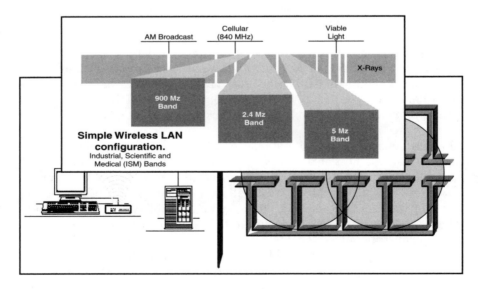

7-1 WLAN overview. (courtesy of *Wireless LAN Alliance*)

Commission (FCC) and a general world agreement set aside the radio frequencies that are available for unlicensed commercial use. These *Industrial Scientific and Medical* (ISM) bands include the 900-MHz, 2.4-GHz, and 5-GHz bands that are used by many commercial wireless communication devices. The majority of emerging WLAN devices are designed to operate in the 2.4-GHz band due to global availability and reduced interference.[5]

Several transmission mediums are capable of transferring data across airwaves. Like most technologies, they each have their own benefits and limitations. Infrared systems and narrowband radio systems are the leading technologies being used by the wireless industry.

Infrared Systems

While capable, infrared (IR) systems do not make for a practical enterprise WLAN solution and therefore are not widely employed, IR is able to transfer data by taking advantage of those frequencies located in close proximity to, but beneath visible light on the electromagnetic spectrum. These high bands face the same limitations as visible light in that they cannot penetrate nontransparent objects such as walls, floors, and ceilings. As a result, WLANs transmitting via IR are restricted to operating, at best, within the same room, and could be further limited to a short-range line-of-sight restriction.[6]

Narrowband Radio Systems

Narrowband radio systems transmit and receive data on a specific radio frequency. Different users communicate on alternative frequencies or channels to ensure some level of privacy and avoid interference. Radio receivers are constructed to listen only for their designated frequency and to filter out all others. The natural limitation to this system should be clear: If another transceiver is operating at the same frequency and within range, interference will occur and data will no doubt be lost or corrupted. Another downside of implementing narrowband technology is that, at least in the United States, a license must be obtained from the FCC for each site where it is to be implemented.

Wideband Radio Systems: Spread Spectrum

Instead of using a single frequency, the Spread-Spectrum technology, as its name suggests, traverses the frequency band to reliably transmit data. Originally employed by the military, Spread Spectrum distributes the signal over a wide range of frequencies uniformly, thus consuming more bandwidth in exchange for reliability, integrity, and security of communications. This so-called wideband usage lets devices avoid interference and other signal noise in a way not possible with narrowband transmissions. The benefits come with a price. By their nature, wideband communications are noisier and therefore easier to detect; luckily, to an improperly tuned receiver a Spread-Spectrum signal appears as nothing more than background noise.[7]

Spread Spectrum comes in two forms: *Frequency-Hopping Spread Spectrum* (FHSS) and *Direct-Sequence Spread Spectrum* (DSSS). Of the two, frequency-hopping is less costly to deploy; however, direct-sequence has the potential for more widespread use. This can be attributed to the higher data rates, greater range, and built-in error correction capabilities of DSSS.

Frequency-Hopping Spread Spectrum (FHSS)

FHSS successfully mitigates the effects of interference by attaching the data signal to a shifting carrier signal. This modulated carrier signal literally hops, as a function of time, from one frequency to the next across the band. Each transceiver is programmed with a hopping code that defines the order and range of frequencies used. To properly communicate, each device must be configured with the same hopping code to ensure that signals are sent and received at the correct time and on the proper frequency.[8] As a result, synchronized transceivers effectively create a logical communications channel with data rates reaching 2 to 3 Mbps and a range of 1,000 feet without installing repeaters.[9]

For interference to occur, the conflicting narrowband signal would need to be broadcast at the same frequency and at the same time as the hopping signal. Should errors in transmission occur on one frequency, the signal will be re-broadcast on a different frequency at the next hop, as shown in Figure 7-2. To receivers that are not programmed with the appropriate hopping code, FHSS transmissions appear to be short duration impulse noise.[10] Distinct hopping codes can be implemented on the same WLAN to prevent sub-WLANs from interfering with one another. FHSS-based WLANs are best for supporting a high number of clients when ease-of-installation is key and either outdoors or in relatively open indoor facilities.[11]

Direct-Sequence Spread Spectrum (DSSS)

DSSS infuses a redundant bit pattern into each bit being transferred. The inserted bits are referred to as a chip or a chipping code.[12] By including the chip, a receiver is able to perform data recovery routines on signals based on statistical analysis. A greater number of bits in the chipping code will result in a signal that is less likely to be negatively affected by interference. As it is increasing the signal size, DSSS requires more bandwidth to operate, generally using three non-overlapping frequen-

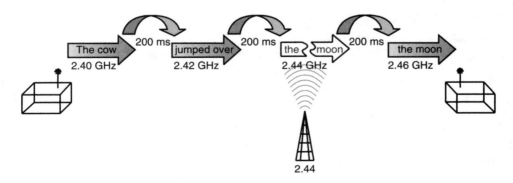

7-2 Frequency Hopping Spread Spectrum (FHSS). (Courtesy of *Anyware Network Solutions*)

cies to communicate. The error-correcting capability prevents DSSS from needing to retransmit data that may have been corrupted while en route, as shown in Figure 7-3.

Recall that FHSS systems countered interference by trying to avoid signal collisions through constant motion, essentially attempting to out-pace conflicts. While this is a successful method, it limits data throughput to relatively small packets because the modulation technique has adverse affects on larger data rates. To compensate, DSSS systems include error-correcting bits, thus removing the need to hop frequencies and to retransmit in the event of an error. As a result data rates up to 11 Mbps and ranges up to several miles can be achieved with DSSS.[13]

WLAN Products and Standards— Today's Leaders?

The majority of the products from the United States support the IEEE 802.11b standard for WLANs, while European companies are producing devices based on the HyperLan II standard. 802.11 has been in use for many years in one form or another. It has generally been regarded as, at best, moderately secure, but it has never had to face the range of threats we anticipate for WLANs. Recent cryptographic reports on its security indicate that it is seriously flawed.[14]

In the WLAN standards arena, we find security described over and over as an *option*. Although it is paid appropriate deference in all the WLAN assessments, security is understood first as an impediment to increased data transmission and second as appropriate protection. The onus of security is clearly on the user, although the refinements in more recent standards include security enhancements.

802.11 Security?

IEEE 802.11 provides for security through authentication and encryption. In the Ad Hoc or Extended Service Set network mode, authentication can be either open system or shared key. A network station that receives a request may grant authentication to

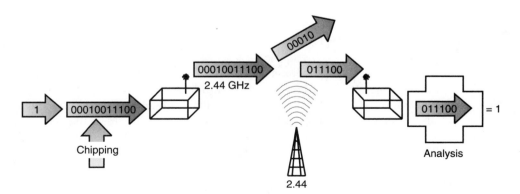

7-3 Direct-Sequence Spread Spectrum (DSSS). (Courtesy of *Anyware Network Solutions*)

any request or only to those stations on a defined list. In a shared key system, only those stations that possess an encrypted key will receive authentication.[15]

IEEE 802.11 specifies an optional encryption capability called *Wired Equivalent Privacy* (WEP). As the name indicates, the intent is to establish security commensurate to wired networks. WEP employs the RC4 algorithm from RSA Data Security. The RC4 algorithm encrypts over-the-air transmissions.

The security dilemma for 802.11 is that WEP encryption capability does not extend to end-to-end transmission. It protects only the data packet information and does not protect the physical layer header so that other stations on the network can listen to the control data needed to manage the network. (Presumably the other stations cannot decrypt the data portions of the packet.[16])

IEEE 802.11b

Like its predecessor, 802.11b works in the 2.4- to 2.48-GHz band and aims at providing users with connectivity in any country. It also addresses both Ad Hoc and Extended Service Set networks.

Unlike 802.11, though, the IEEE 802.11b removes FHSS as a data transmission mode and establishes DSSS as the standard transmission technology. It does so because DSSS handles weak signals well. With DSSS, data can be extracted from a background of interference without having to be retransmitted. With DSSS as the selected transmission technique, the 802.11b standard also establishes data rate speeds of 5.5 and 11 Mbps.

Some 802.11b-compliant equipment offers an *optional* 128-bit encryption scheme, up from its predecessor's 40- and 64-bit encryption scheme. Also, vendors are producing 802.11b equipment with *network interface cards* (NICs) that possess a unique MAC address and a unique public- and private-key pair. With these enhancements, WLAN administrators can require all hardware address and public-key combinations be entered into the access points (APs) before the network is established, or they can configure the access points to keep track of the combinations they encounter and reject any mismatches. By doing this, an administrator can prevent an attacker from breaking into a network via MAC address spoofing.[17]

Securing WLANs

A WLAN operates in the same manner as a wired LAN except that data is transported through a wireless medium—usually radio waves—rather than cables. Accordingly, a WLAN harbors many of the same vulnerabilities as a wired LAN, plus some that are specific to it. This section discusses common threats facing WLANs, some of the countermeasures that have been designed to address those threats, and the strengths and limitations of those countermeasures.

Eavesdropping

The principal threat is the potential for unauthorized parties to eavesdrop on radio signals sent between a wireless station and an AP, compromising the confidentiality of sensitive or proprietary information. Eavesdropping is a passive attack. When a radio operator sends a message over a radio path, all other users equipped with a compatible receiver within the range of the transmission can listen to the message. Furthermore, because an eavesdropper can listen to a message without altering the data, the sender and intended receiver of the message may not even be aware of the intrusion.[18]

Wired LANs are also vulnerable to eavesdropping, but not to the same extent. A wired LAN may radiate electromagnetic signals through cabling, but an eavesdropper must be close to the cabling to hear the signals with a listening device. By contrast, someone eavesdropping on a WLAN may be located some distance from the network and may even be outside the physical confines of the environment in which the network operates. This is because radio signals emitted from a WLAN can propagate beyond the area in which they originate, and can penetrate building walls and other physical obstacles, depending on the transmission technology used and the strength of the signal.

Equipment capable of intercepting WLAN traffic is available to consumers in the form of wireless adapters and other 802.11-compatible products. The difficulty for eavesdroppers is to decode a 2.4-GHz digital signal because most WLAN systems use Spread-Spectrum technology, which is resistant to eavesdropping. In addition, if encryption is used, eavesdroppers must decipher encrypted content. Despite these difficulties, eavesdropping poses a significant threat to WLAN communications.

Unauthorized Access

A second threat to WLAN security is the potential for an intruder to enter a WLAN system disguised as an authorized user. Once inside, the intruder can violate the confidentiality and integrity of network traffic by sending, receiving, altering, or forging messages.[19] This is an active attack, and may be carried out using a wireless adapter that is compatible with the targeted network, or by using a compromised (for example, stolen) device that is linked to the network.

The best protection against unauthorized access is to deploy authentication mechanisms to ensure only authorized users can access the network. Such mechanisms are regularly deployed on wired LANs, not only to prevent unauthorized access, but also to detect intrusions when they occur. Discovering intruders attempting to access a WLAN isn't easy. This is because unsuccessful attacks might be misinterpreted as unsuccessful logon attempts caused by the high *bit error rate* (BER) of radio transmissions or by stations belonging to another WLAN.[20]

A variant of unauthorized access is an attacker who deceives wireless stations by setting up a counterfeit AP. When a wireless station is first powered on or when it enters a new microcell, it chooses an AP to link to, based on signal strength and observed packet error rates. If accepted by the AP, the station tunes to the radio channel that the AP is using. By setting up a counterfeit AP with a powerful signal, an attacker might be able to lure a station onto his or her network in order to capture secret keys and logon passwords. Alternately, the attacker may reject the logon attempts but record the messages transmitted during the logon process, for the same purpose.[21]

The first type of attack described above is very difficult to implement, because the attacker must have detailed information to be able to trick the station into believing that it has accessed its home network. Otherwise, the attack may be easily detected. The second type of attack is easier to implement, because the attacker only requires a receiver and an antenna that is compatible with targeted stations. This attack also is more difficult to detect because unsuccessful logons are relatively common in WLAN communications. The best protection against both types of attacks is to use an efficient authentication mechanism that enables wireless stations to authenticate to APs without revealing secret keys or passwords.[22]

Interference and Jamming

A third threat to WLAN security is radio interference that can seriously degrade bandwidth (data throughput). In many cases interference is accidental. Because WLANs use unlicensed radio waves, other electromagnetic devices operating in the infrared or 2.4-GHz radio frequency can overlap with WLAN traffic. Potential sources of interference include high-power amateur, military, and *industrial, scientific, and military* (ISM) transmitters. Microwave ovens are a possible source, but most WLAN vendors design their products to minimize microwave interference. Another concern is the operation of two or more WLANs in the same coverage area; some WLANs are designed to operate in close proximity to other systems while others are not.[23]

Of course interference may also be intentional. If an attacker has a powerful transmitter, he or she can generate a radio signal strong enough to overwhelm weaker signals, disrupting communications. This is a condition known as jamming,[24] and is a denial-of-service attack. Two types of jammers that may be used against WLAN traffic are high-power pulsed full-band jammers that cover the entire frequency used by the targeted signal, and lower-power partial-band jammers that cover only part of the frequency used by the targeted signal.[25]

Jamming equipment is readily available to consumers or can be constructed by knowledgeable attackers. In addition, jamming attacks can be mounted from a location remote from the targeted network (for example, from a vehicle parked across the street, or an apartment in the next block). Direction-finding equipment can detect the source of jamming signals, but not necessarily in time to prevent the jamming.[26]

Physical Threats

WLANs can be brought down by damage to or destruction of the underlying physical infrastructure. Like a wired LAN, a WLAN operating in infrastructure mode relies on a variety of physical components, including APs, cables, antennas, wireless adapters,[27] and software. Damage to any of these components could reduce signal strength, limit coverage area, or reduce bandwidth, hampering the ability of users to access data and information services (for example, file servers, printers, and Internet links). If severe enough, compromise of the physical infrastructure could even shut down WLAN operations.

Infrastructure components are susceptible to the conditions of the environment in which they operate, especially if it's outdoors. APs can be obstructed by snow, ice, and distorting radio signals. Antennas mounted atop poles or buildings can be knocked askew by winds or bent by ice, changing the angle of the beam width used for transmitting signals. This can be especially problematic for antennas with narrow beam widths, such as parabolic dish antennas.[28] Antennas and APs can also be damaged by nearby lightning strikes or water intrusion into the cabling and connectors linking it to the wired network.[29] Finally, accidents and improper handling can damage wireless adapters and wireless stations.

Physical components may also be subject to attack. WLANs generally rely on a smaller physical plant than do wired LANs, making them less vulnerable to sabotage, but they are not entirely safe. For example, an attacker could cut the cabling that connects an AP to the wired network, isolating affected microcells and disrupting power to the receiver. An attacker might also be able to damage or destroy an exposed AP or the antenna connected to it. An attacker might also steal or compromise a wireless station or adapter and use it to try to intercept WLAN traffic or to gain unauthorized access to the network. Finally, an attacker could avoid the WLAN altogether and instead sabotage the wired network, disrupting the operation of all WLANs connected to it.[30]

Countermeasures

WLAN systems most commonly use Spread-Spectrum technology to transmit data. Spread Spectrum is designed to resist eavesdropping, interference, and noise. To the casual listener, the signal sounds like random background noise. Spread Spectrum consumes more bandwidth than do narrowband transmissions (which concentrate signals into a single frequency), but it produces a signal that is easy to detect if the receiver knows the parameters of the transmission. The receiver uses the same spreading code used by the transmitter to regroup the spread signal to its original form.[31]

Frequency-Hopping Spread Spectrum (FHSS)

The 2.4-GHz band is divided into 75 one-megahertz channels. A radio signal is sent (hopped) over all 75 frequencies in accordance with a pseudo-random code sequence that is known to both the transmitter and the receiver (see Figure 7-4). The FHSS physical layer has 22 hop patterns; the pattern chosen by the transmitter is taken from a predetermined set specified by the code. The receiver tracks that hopping pattern. When the transmitter and the receiver are properly synchronized, data is transmitted over what is essentially a single channel. To an eavesdropper, the signal appears to be unintelligible short duration impulse noise. In addition, because the signal is spread across multiple frequencies, the potential for interference is minimized.[32]

Direct-Sequence Spread Spectrum (DSSS)

Under the original 802.11 standard, DSSS breaks each data bit in the signal (0 or 1) into 11 sub-bits called chips, which are converted into a waveform (see Figure 7-5). The waveforms are then transmitted over a wide range of frequencies. The receiver unspreads the chip to recover the original data. If one or more bits are lost or damaged during transmission, the receiver can use installed statistical techniques to

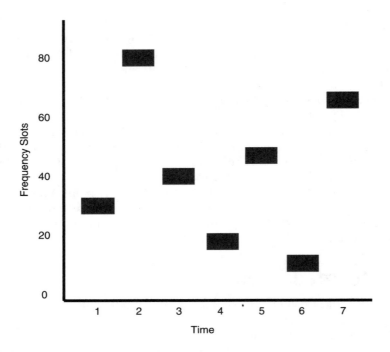

7-4 Hopping code. (Source: The Wireless LAN Alliance)[33]

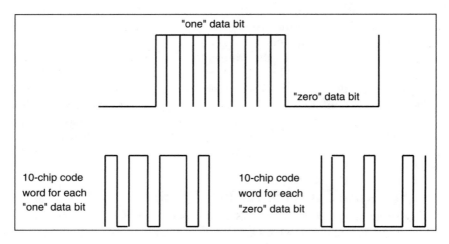

7-5 DSSS Chip Codes. (Source: The Wireless LAN Alliance)[34]

recover the original data. Under the 802.11b standard, DSSS uses 64 8-bit code words to spread the signal. To an eavesdropper or other unauthorized user, a DSSS signal appears as low-power wideband noise. Therefore, most narrowband receivers ignore it. In addition, interference is minimized because the signal is spread over a wide range of frequencies.[35]

Both FHSS and DSSS pose difficulties for outsiders attempting to intercept radio signals. In the case of FHSS, an eavesdropper must know the hopping pattern that is used in the transmission. In the case of DSSS, the eavesdropper must know the chipping code (802.11) or code words (802.11b). In both cases, the eavesdropper must also know the frequency band and modulation techniques in order to accurately read the transmitted signal. Furthermore, radio systems use a form of data scrambling that facilitates the timing and decoding of radio signals. An eavesdropper must also know this scrambling pattern if he or she is to read intercepted data.[36]

Adding to an eavesdropper's difficulties is the fact that Spread-Spectrum technologies do not interoperate with each other (that is, a WLAN using FHSS cannot communicate with WLAN using DSSS, and vice versa). Even if two different systems are using the same technique, they cannot communicate if they are using different frequency bands (for example, a system using DSSS cannot communicate with another system using DSSS if they are operating on different frequencies).[37] Consequently, an eavesdropper cannot use one Spread-Spectrum technique to intercept radio signals transmitted by the other technique. Nor can he or she intercept radio signals without knowing the frequency that is used, even if he or she has an 802.11-compatible receiver.

Despite the ability of Spread-Spectrum technology to resist eavesdropping, it is only secure if the hopping pattern or chipping code is unknown to the eavesdropper; however, these parameters are published in the 802.11 standard, and therefore are public knowledge. The modulation method is also specified. Using this information, a knowledgeable eavesdropper could build a receiver to intercept and read unprotected signals.[38] Nevertheless, the inherent strengths of Spread-Spectrum technology are sufficient to defeat most would-be eavesdroppers and therefore contribute to the security of WLAN communications.

Spread-Spectrum technology also minimizes the potential for interference from other radios and electromagnetic devices by spreading radio transmissions over a wide range of frequency bands. Nevertheless, it is vulnerable to jamming. Depending on the type of jammer used, errors are produced at the demodulator output, disrupting affected signals. In general, FHSS tends to be more effective than DSSS against narrowband jamming and partial-band noise jamming, because the jamming tends to corrupt only a fraction of the hopped code. With DSSS, all codes are corrupted to some extent by the jamming signal. In addition, FHSS spreads signals over a wider range of frequencies than DSSS does.[39]

Two other technologies used in some WLAN systems are infrared and narrowband, described in the following section. Both technologies lack the robustness of Spread Spectrum to resist eavesdropping and interference.

Infrared (IR)

IR is the third radio technology specified in the original 802.11 standard. IR transmits data at very high frequencies that are just below visible light on the electromagnetic spectrum. Like light, IR cannot penetrate walls and other solid or opaque objects; the transmitter and receiver must have direct line-of-sight or else use diffuse technology. Low-power IR systems have limited range (approximately three feet for most computers). High-power IR systems can transmit radio signals over longer ranges, but poor weather conditions and the requirement for direct line-of-sight minimize the effectiveness of these systems for mobile users. In addition, IR signals transmitted in the open are vulnerable to interception, interference, and jamming. Consequently, IR systems typically are used for high-security applications in enclosed facilities. IR systems also tend to be more expensive than FHSS and DSSS systems, and the data rate is low at one to two Mbps. The result is that IR systems are used in few commercial WLAN products.[40]

Narrowband

Some WLAN products use narrowband technology that transmits and receives radio signals on a specific frequency. The effect is to keep the radio signal as narrow as possible. Cross-talk among radio channels is prevented by coordinating different channel frequencies among different users. The receiver tunes only to those signals on its designated frequency and rejects all others. The drawback of narrowband is that eavesdroppers can easily detect transmitted signals, and it is vulnerable to interference and jamming. In addition, narrowband requires a license from the Federal Communications Commission (FCC) for each site where it is used, unlike Spread-Spectrum technologies that do not require FCC licensing.[41]

The Infamous WEP

Although WLAN systems can resist passive eavesdropping, the only way to effectively prevent third parties from compromising transmitted data is to use encryption. The purpose of WEP is to ensure that WLAN systems have a level of privacy that is equivalent to that of wired LANs by encrypting radio signals. A secondary purpose of WEP is to prevent unauthorized users from accessing WLANs (that is, provide authentication). This secondary purpose is not explicitly stated in the 802.11 standard, but it is considered an important feature of the WEP algorithm.[42]

WEP is a critical element for securing the confidentiality and integrity of data on 802.11-standard-based WLAN systems, as well as for providing access control through authentication. Consequently, most 802.11-compliant WLAN products support WEP as either a standard or an optional feature. The manner in which WEP provides encryption and authentication is described next.

Encryption

WEP uses a secret key that is shared between a wireless station and an access point (AP). All data sent and received between a wireless station and an AP may be encrypted using this shared key. The 802.11 standard does not specify how the secret key is established, but it does allow for an array that associates a unique key with each station. In general practice, however, one key is shared among all stations and APs in a given system.

WEP provides data encryption using a 40-bit (weak) [802.11] or 128-bit (strong)[802.11b] secret key and a RC4 *Pseudo Random Number Generator* (PRNG). Two processes are applied to plaintext data: one encrypts the plaintext, and the other protects it from unauthorized modification while it is in transit. The secret key is concatenated with a random *initialization vector* (IV) that adds 24 bits to the resulting key. This key is inserted into the PRNG that generates a long pseudo-random key stream. The sender XORs the key stream with the plaintext to generate encrypted text, or ciphertext, and transmits it to the receiver along with the IV. Upon receipt of the ciphertext, the receiver uses the IV and its own copy of the secret key to produce a key stream that is identical to the key stream generated by the transmitter. The receiver then XORs the key stream with the ciphertext to reveal the original plaintext.[43]

To protect the ciphertext against unauthorized modification while in transit, WEP applies an integrity check algorithm (CRC-32) to the plaintext, which produces an *Integrity Check Value* (ICV). The ICV is then concatenated to the plaintext. The ICV is in effect the fingerprint of the plaintext. The ICV is attached to the ciphertext and sent to the receiver along with the IV. The receiver combines the ciphertext with the key stream to uncover the plaintext. Applying the integrity algorithm to the plaintext and comparing the output IVC to the transmitted ICV verify the decryption. If the two ICVs are identical, the message is authenticated; that is, the fingerprints match.[44] Figures 7-6 and 7-7 illustrate WEP encryption and decryption, respectively.

Despite the potential strength of WEP for protecting the confidentiality and integrity of data, it has limitations that can only be addressed by proper management. The first problem stems from the reuse of the IV. The IV is included in the

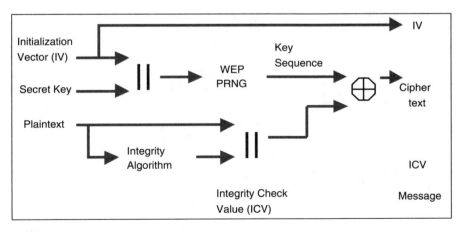

7-6 WEP encryption. (Source: Sultan Weatherspoon, "Overview of IEEE 802.11b Security," *Intel Technology* Journal, Quarter 2, 2000)

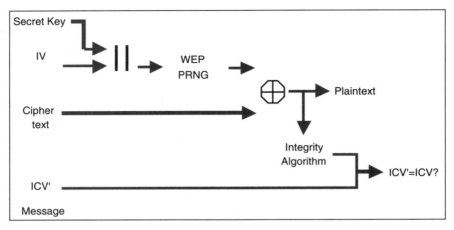

7-7 WEP decryption. (Source: Weatherspoon, "Overview of IEEE 802.11b Security")

unencrypted part of a message so the receiver knows what IV to use when generating the key stream for decryption. The 802.11 standard recommends—but does not require—that the IV be changed after each transmission. If the IV is not changed regularly, but is reused for subsequent messages, an eavesdropper may be able to cryptanalyze the key stream generated by the IV and secret key and thus decrypt messages that use that IV.[45]

The problem of IV reuse potentially leads to another. Namely, once an attacker knows the key sequence for an encrypted message, based on a reused IV, he or she can use this information to build an encrypted signal and insert it into a network. The process is to create a new message, calculate the CRC-32, and modify the original encrypted message to change the plaintext to the new message. The attacker can then transmit the message to an AP or wireless station, which would accept it as a valid message. Changing the IV after each message is a simple way to prevent both this problem and the issue described previously.[46]

Key distribution is another problem. Most WLANs share one key among all stations and APs in the network. It is unlikely that a key shared among many users will remain secret indefinitely. Some network administrators address this problem by configuring wireless stations with the secret key themselves, rather than permitting end users to perform this task. That's an imperfect solution; however, because the shared key is still stored on the users' computers where it is vulnerable. In addition, if a key on even one station is compromised, all the other stations in the system must be reconfigured with a new key. The better solution is to assign a unique key to each station and to change keys frequently.[47]

Although WEP encryption is designed to be computationally efficient, it can reduce bandwidth in use. According to one report, 40-bit encryption reduces bandwidth by 1 Mbps, and 128-bit encryption reduces bandwidth by 1 to 2 Mbps. This degree of drop is relatively small, but users may still notice it, especially if the signal is transmitted via FHSS, which transmits signals at a maximum of only 3 Mbps. In many cases, the exact impact will depend on the product that is used and number of users on the system.[48]

Authentication

WEP provides two types of authentication: a default Open System, whereby all users are permitted to access a WLAN, and shared key authentication, which controls access to the WLAN and prevents unauthorized network access. Of the two levels, shared key authentication is the secure mode. It uses a secret key that is shared among all stations and APs in a WLAN system. When a station tries to associate with an AP, the AP replies with random text by way of a challenge. The station must use its copy of the shared secret key to encrypt the challenge text and send it back to the AP in order to authenticate itself. The AP decrypts the response using the same shared key and compares it to the challenge text sent earlier. If the text is identical, the AP sends a confirmation message to the station and accepts the station into the network. If the station does not have a key, or if it sends the wrong response, the AP rejects it, preventing the station from accessing the network.[49] Shared key authentication is illustrated in Figure 7-8.

Note that shared key authentication works only if WEP encryption is enabled. If it is not enabled, the system will default to the Open System mode, permitting almost any station within range of an AP to access the network.[50] That creates a window for an intruder into the system, where he or she may send, receive, alter, or forge messages. Make sure that WEP is enabled whenever secure authentication is required.

Even when shared key authentication is enabled, all wireless stations in a WLAN system may have the same shared key, depending on how the system is installed. For such systems, individual authentication is not possible; all users—including unauthorized ones—with the shared key can access the network. This weakness can

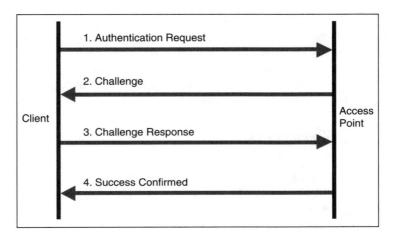

7-8 Shared key authentication. (Source: Sultan Weatherspoon, "Overview of IEEE 802.11b Security," *Intel Technology* Journal, Quarter 2, 2000)

result in unauthorized access, especially if the system includes a large numbers of users. The more users, the greater the likelihood that the shared key could fall into the wrong hands.

Finally, in many WLAN systems, the key used for authentication is the same key used for encryption. This particular weakness compounds the problems described previously. If an attacker has the shared key, he or she can use it to not only to access the network but also to decrypt messages, thus creating a dual threat. The solution is to distribute separate keys throughout the system—one for authentication and another for encryption.

Wired Equivalency Protocol Flaws Too Public

WEP has been found to be highly (albeit spectacularly) flawed, to the serious detriment of its security claims and supporters. WLANs have be successfully subjected to various forms of attack, including decryption, based upon statistical analysis. WEP has the additional vulnerability of ignoring some unauthorized traffic or an unauthorized decryption, injected by an attacker tricking the access point.[51] Because of these drawbacks, it's likely that WEP will be used in the future only in conjunction with VPNs.

Other Authentication Techniques

It's reasonable to consider authentication techniques other than shared key authentication. *Extended Service Set Identification* (ESSID) is a commonly used access control technique. ESSID is a value programmed into each AP to identify which subnet the AP is on. This value can be used for authentication to ensure that only authorized stations can access the network. If a station does not know the ESSID, it is not permitted to associate with the AP.[52]

In addition, some manufacturers provide for a table of *Media Access Control* (MAC) addresses in an *access control list* (ACL) that is included in the AP. When a station tries to associate with the AP, the router in the AP reads the unique MAC address on the station's wireless adapter and determines whether it is on the ACL. Access to the network is restricted to those stations on the list; others are rejected. This enables network administrators to include or exclude wireless stations.[53] This capability provides a valuable layer of additional security, not only to exclude outside stations but also to exclude those stations that belong to the network but have been compromised (for example, a stolen computer).

Physical Security

Precautions must be taken to protect the physical components of a WLAN from accidents, weather, and vandalism. Those precautions should be commensurate with the type of risks to which the components are exposed, the probability that these risks will occur, and the impact that an occurrence would have on WLAN operations. If the equipment cannot be adequately protected, it should be hardened to minimize the impact of these conditions. APs and antennas should be securely mounted and located in areas that minimize their exposure to potential sources of interference, including microwave ovens and other transmitters. If outdoors, APs and antennas should be situated to minimize exposure to high winds, snow, and ice, or else they should be properly sheltered. Lightning arrestors should be deployed to suppress the effect of lightning strikes. Cabling should be housed in protective covering, where possible, and nearby pipes and water tanks should be properly maintained to prevent leaks and accidental spills.[54]

In addition, unauthorized personnel should be denied access to WLAN equipment. Locate APs and antennas in securable areas, away from the public traffic and protected with appropriate barriers and access controls. Intrusion detection systems such as closed-circuit television may also be used to monitor remote or exposed assets.

Along with physical measures, employ appropriate administrative controls. Wireless stations assigned to WLAN users should be properly logged and the identity of the users recorded. ACLs should be maintained and regularly updated. WLAN equipment should be properly labeled to ensure identification if it is damaged or destroyed. Labeling may also deter theft. Response procedures should be developed in the event that WLAN equipment is compromised, damaged, or destroyed.

Finally, users should be educated on the importance of protecting their stations from theft, damage, and misuse. For example, users should never leave their stations unattended in public areas, and they should log out from the network if they are not using it. In addition, users should not eat or drink near their station, and they should avoid working near possible hazards, such as microwave ovens. They should also immediately report any occurrence of suspicious activity involving the WLAN, including all cases of compromised or stolen equipment.

Summary

Despite the advantages of wireless networking, WLANs are vulnerable to security threats. Common threats include eavesdropping, unauthorized access, interference and jamming, and physical damage. Depending on how a WLAN is designed or configured, such threats may be prevented or mitigated. For example, systems that use Spread-Spectrum technology are resistant to passive eavesdropping and interference. Systems that use the WEP encryption algorithm are resistant to active eavesdropping and provide client authentication. If WEP is employed, however, measures must be taken to ensure that encryption keys are properly managed. Finally, the physical components of a WLAN can be protected from damage by installing physical safeguards and providing training to users.

Endnotes

[1]"How will WAP work with GPRS?" http://wap.com/cgi-bin/wapfaq.cgi?chapter=9.4, 1 February 2001.

[2]"The IEEE 802.11 Standard, Wireless LAN Standard," http://www.wlana.org/learn.

[3]"Enterprise Wireless LAN Market Update," http://www.instat.com/abstracts/ln/2000/ln0011wl_abs.htm, Cahners In-Stat Group, December 2000.

[4]"What is a Wireless LAN: Introduction to Wireless LANs," www.wlana.com/learn/educate.htm, Wireless LAN Alliance (WLANA). January 1, 2001.

[5]"Wireless Networking: The Next Generation," Cisco Systems, Inc., 2000 (CD-ROM).

[6]"What is a Wireless LAN," http://www.wirelesslan.com/wireless/, WirelessLAN.com Answer Page, September 28, 1999.

[7]Ibid.

[8]Geier, Jim, "Spread Spectrum: Frequency Hopping vs. Direct Sequence," http://www.wireless-nets.com/whitepaper_spread.htm, May 1999.

[9]"Wireless LAN Technical Overview," http://www.anyware-ns.com/technical_overview.htm, Anyware Network Solutions, January 9, 2001.

[10]"What is a Wireless LAN: Introduction to Wireless LANs," www.wlana.com/learn/educate.htm, Wireless LAN Alliance (WLANA), January 1, 2001.

[11]"Wireless LAN Technical Overview," http://www.anyware-ns.com/technical_overview.htm, Anyware Network Solutions, January 9, 2001.

[12]"What is a Wireless LAN: Introduction to Wireless LANs," www.wlana.com/learn/educate.htm, Wireless LAN Alliance (WLANA), January 1, 2001.

[13]"Wireless LAN Technical Overview," http://www.anyware-ns.com/technical_overview.htm, Anyware Network Solutions, January 9, 2001.

[14]Borisov, Nikita, Ian Goldburg, and David Wagner, "Intercepting Mobile Communications: The Insecurity of 802.11 (Draft)," 3.

Borisov, Nikita, Ian Goldburg, and David Wagner, "Security of the WEP Algorithm," www.isaac.cs.berkeley.edu/isaac/wep-faq.html.

Hong Siang, Teo, "Security in Wireless LAN," July 1, 2000, http://202.85.163.46/articles/wireless/WLAN_security.pdf.

Uskela, Sami, "Security in Wireless Local Area Networks," Helsinki University of Technology, www.tml.hut.fi/Opinnot/Tik-110501/1997 /wireless_lan.html.

Weatherspoon, Sultan, "Overview of IEEE 802.11b Security," *Intel Technology Journal* (Quarter 2, 2000), p. 1.

"Wireless LAN Security White Paper," Wireless LAN Alliance (WLANA), 2000, www.wlana.com.

[15]"The IEEE 802.11 Standard, Wireless LAN Standard," http://www.wlana.org/learn.

[16]Ibid.

[17]Ibid.

[18]Borisov, Nikita, Ian Goldburg, and David Wagner, "Intercepting Mobile Communications: The Insecurity of 802.11 (Draft)," p. 3.

Borisov, Nikita, Ian Goldburg, and David Wagner, "Security of the WEP Algorithm," www.isaac.cs.berkeley.edu/isaac/wep-faq.html.

Hong Siang, Teo, "Security in Wireless LAN," July 1, 2000, http://202.85.163.46/articles/wireless/WLAN_security.pdf.

Uskela, Sami, "Security in Wireless Local Area Networks," Helsinki University of Technology, www.tml.hut.fi/Opinnot/Tik-110501/1997 /wireless_lan.html.

Weatherspoon, Sultan, "Overview of IEEE 802.11b Security," *Intel Technology Journal* (Quarter 2, 2000), p. 1.

"Wireless LAN Security White Paper," Wireless LAN Alliance (WLANA), 2000, www.wlana.com.

[19]"Wireless LAN Technology for Mobility, Performance and Security," Ericsson Enterprise, www.ericsson.com/wlan/te-security.asp.

[20]Uskela, Sami, "What's New in Wireless LANs: The IEEE 802.11b Standard," 3Com Corporation, 2000, www.3com.com/technology/tech_net/white_papers/503072a.html.

[21]Ibid.

[22]Ibid.

[23]"Which Products Should I Buy?" WirelessLAN.com Answer Page, www.wirelesslan.com/product; and "What is a Wireless LAN: Introduction to Wireless LANs," WLANA, 2000, 8, www.wlana.com.

[24]Muller, Nathan J., *Desktop Encyclopedia of Telecommunications*, 2nd ed., McGraw-Hill, 2000, p. 814.

[25]Feldman, Philip M., "Emerging Commercial Mobile Wireless Technology and Standards: Suitable for the Army?" RAND, 1998, p. 8.

[26]Uskela.

[27]End users access the WLAN through wireless adapters that are installed on their wireless stations. Adapters come in various forms, including PC cards for laptop computers, ISA or PCI adapters in desktop computers, and integrated devices in hand-held computers. *See* "Introduction to Wireless LANs," p. 3.

[28]Telex® Wireless Products Group, "WLAN Antenna: Frequently Asked Questions," www.telexwireless.com/wlanfaq.htm.

[29]Telex® Wireless Products Group.

[30]Although affected users might be able to set up an ad hoc network to continue communications, they would be isolated from the wired network, and therefore probably could not carry on effective operations for an extended period.

[31]Muller, p. 813.

[32]Muller, p. 816, and "What's New in Wireless LANs: The IEEE 802.11b Standard."

[33]www.wlana.com

[34]www.wlana.com

[35]Muller, p. 815; "What's New in Wireless LANs: The IEEE 802.11b Standard," "The IEEE 802.11 Wireless LAN Standard White Paper," WLANA, 2000, www.wlana.com; "What is a Wireless LAN: Introduction to Wireless LAN," p. 6.

[36]van der Merwe, Jacques, "Securing Air," *Infrastructure News*, June 26, 2000, www.computerweek.com, and "Wireless LAN Security White Paper."

[37]Feldman, p. 46.

[38]The Modulation Method for FHSS is 2–4 Level Gaussian FSK, and the Modulation for DSSS is Differential BPSK and DQPSK, See "The IEEE 802.11 Wireless LAN Standard White Paper" and Siang, p. 2.

[39]Feldman, pp. 14–17, 72. Feldman observes, however, that commercial spread spectrum techniques do not use secure spreading sequences, due to key distribution problems, and therefore have no advantage over nonspread (that is, narrowband) systems. In addition, the spreading gains used in commercial systems tend to be much smaller than the spreading gains used in military systems, reducing their ability to resist broadband jamming.

[40]"Wireless LAN Technical Overview," www.anyware-ns.com/technical_overview.htm; "The IEEE 802.11 Wireless LAN Standard White Paper," and "Wireless LAN Security White Paper."

[41]"What is a Wireless LAN: Introduction to Wireless LANs," p. 6.

[42]Borisov, Goldberg, and Wagner, "(In)Security of the WEP Algorithm."

[43]Weatherspoon, p. 2, Borisov, Goldburg, and Wagner, "Intercepting Mobile Communications," p. 2.

[44]Weatherspoon, p. 2;

[45]Borisov, Goldberg, and Wagner, "Intercepting Mobile Communications," pp. 3–4, 7–8; Weatherspoon, p. 3.

[46]Ibid.

[47]Borisov, Goldberg, and Wagner, "Intercepting Mobile Communications," pp. 6, 11.

[48]Brooks, Jason, and Herb Bethoney, "The LAN, PAN, WAN Plan," *eWEEK*, 14 January 2001, http://www1.zdnet.com; and Siang, p. 2.

[49]Weatherspoon, p. 3.

[50]Weatherspoon, p. 3, and Siang, p. 2.

[51]"Wireless LANs Have Serious Flaws, Berkeley Researchers Say," ComputerWorld Magazine, February 12, 2001.

[52]"What's New in Wireless LANs: The IEEE 802.11b Standard."

[53]Ibid.

[54]National Institute of Standards and Technology (NIST), *An Introduction to Computer Security: The NIST Handbook*, pp. 146, 166–167, 170–172.

NIST, SP 800-14, *Generally Accepted Principles and Practices for Securing Information Technology Systems*, September 1996, pp. 41–42.

Critical Infrastructure Assurance Office (CIAO), *Practices for Securing Critical Information Assets*, January 2000, pp. 27–29.

NIST, Guidance Federal Information Processing Standards (FIPS) Publications (PUB) 191, *Guidelines for the Analysis of Local Area Network Security*, November 9, 1994, http://www.itl.nist.gov/fipspubs/fip191.htm.

8

Wireless Application Protocol (WAP)

The *Wireless Application Protocol* (WAP) is a concerted attempt to develop and implement a standard for communicating information between wireless devices and the Internet. WAP has enjoyed fairly broad industry support, with major contributions from manufacturers Ericsson, Motorola, Nokia, and Phone.com (formerly Unwired Planet). These principal organizations created the WAP Forum in the summer of 1997.[1] Since its inception, the Forum has grown to well over 350 commercial firms. WAP is promulgated to:

- Improve productivity and service. Real-time information is available anytime, anywhere within the organization, greatly enhancing workforce flexibility and mobility.
- Improve infrastructure installation speed, simplicity, and costs. Eliminate pulling cable through conduit, walls, and ceilings.

Because wireless technology provides so many advantages (including portability, mobility, timeliness, and ease of installation), its disadvantages (including security and limited spectrum availability) are being aggressively attacked by proponents. To judge from actions, the industry agrees that the potential rewards of a robust wireless IT capability far exceed the risk of information loss and capital investment. A real question remains, however, as to whether WAP was ready for prime time when first deployed in 1999 and 2000. Wireless devices, as desirable as they are, start out with limitations that make them awkward for communications applications:

- Small display capabilities
- Limited processing capabilities
- Clumsy input devices
- Low bandwidth—only about 9600 bps

The WAP Forum aimed not at reengineering devices, but at promoting a standard specification for the technology used to develop applications, services, and platforms that operate through wireless communications networks. Such a standard is desirable to eliminate much of the struggle for device interoperability and open up the field to third-party developers. It mitigates some device limitations by greatly reducing the bandwidth needed for interoperability. Initial WAP specifications were published on April 30, 1998, for an open, global wireless protocol, based on existing Internet standards such as XML and IP, for all wireless networks.

In terms of industry acceptance, WAP initially fared much better outside North America. Growth in the use of wireless devices in both Europe and Asia has far outstripped the United States. Part of the reason is the relatively poor quality of wired services in those markets, and the daunting cost of upgrading it. In many countries a customer can wait upwards of three months to acquire a single, regular telephone installation, but can obtain a cellular telephone, complete a contract for service, and be operational in under an hour. The customer faced with such impediments to wire line services is likely to be quite tolerant of wireless limitations and quirks.

The WAP Forum *still* projects that WAP will be a best-of-class standard, although not necessarily the only standard, for wireless access to the Internet. Experts anticipate that better than 50 percent of requests for Internet connectivity will come from wireless devices and unwired users by the year 2004. WAP's ability to coexist with Bluetooth and WLANs, as the floor standard, will play a critical role in customer acceptance. How it fares with or against i-Mode by NTT DoCoMo will also be a consideration.[2] In other words, market factors are more important than architectures to establishing an open standard for wireless communications. To understand WAP in the context of established network reference models, see Figure 8-1.

Comparison of the TCP/IP, OSI, and WAP Models

The WAP protocol stack is made up of the:

- Application Layer
- Session Layer
- Transaction Layer
- Security Layer
- Transport Layer

The Application Layer, operating as the *Wireless Application Environment* (WAE):

- Provides an environment in which to develop and execute applications and services for portable and wireless devices.
- Includes a microbrowser, a markup language interface, and Push technology to transmit data to applications residing on clients, plus multimedia message capabilities and content formats.

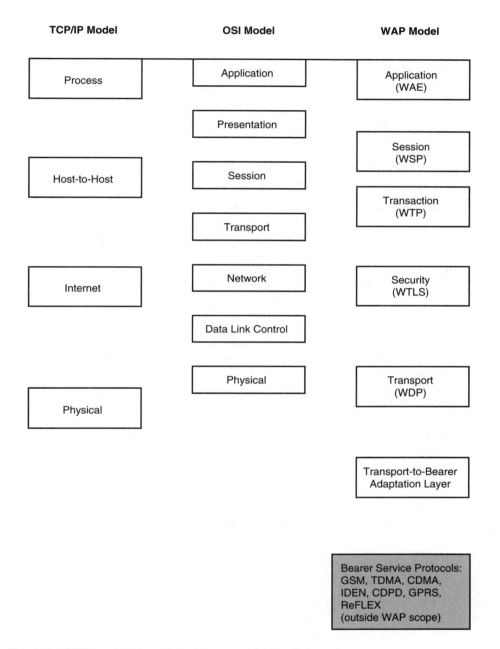

8-1 OSI, TCP/IP, and WAP models. (Courtesy of Gartner Group)

The Session Layer, operating as the WAP Session Protocol (WSP), manages the exchange of content. WSP:

- Provides shared state between network elements across multiple requests.
- Conducts a "negotiation" to ascertain client capabilities so that content can be customized.

The Transaction Layer, operating as the *WAP Transaction Protocol* (WTP), permits transaction processing, albeit of questionable reliability. WTP provides data streaming, hypermedia, and message transfer.

The Security Layer, operating from *Wireless Transport Layer Security* (WTLS):

- Currently allows for authentication, privacy, and secure connections between applications. It is sometimes considered an optional layer.
- WAP 2.0 will provide privacy facilities, authentication, integrity checks, and non-repudiation capabilities. At this point the layer is considered mandatory. Key features include: cryptographic libraries for signatures and various forms of authentication at the different layers. At the transport layer, WTLS and TLS handshakes will be supported.
- User identification and authentication through the *wireless identity module* (WIM).
- In WAP 2.0 provides PKI services enabled via supporting servers. Secure transport will be offered at the transport layer, and bearer service security can be added.

The Transport Layer, operating from the *WAP Datagram Protocol* (WDP) environment:

- Protects the upper layers from bearer services (SMS, CSD, USSD) belonging to the operator.
- Provides a set of consistent services mapped to the bearer services available.

Bearer Services Protocols are outside the WAP structure and are the services with which WAP wants to communicate. To a great degree this puts the network services, data link, and physical layers outside of WAP. However, WAP's success or failure will be determined largely by its ability to interact with the bearers, and it is expected that there will be many more bearers in the future.

How WAP Works

Because wireless bandwidth is constrained, HTTP is not feasible in WAP applications.[3] Therefore, WAP-enabled devices (clients) communicate via a WAP gateway. Gateways, built by companies such as Phone.com and Nokia, are generally located adjacent to a service provider's Mobile Telephone Exchange to translate wireless protocols into Internet protocols.

The gateway turns those requests into standard Web-based requests using protocols defined in the WAP specifications. The gateway then, acting as an Internet client, sends the request to a server providing WAP content. The gateway directly retrieves and reformats the requested information, then sends it on to the requesting client.

Currently, users tend to be tied to a particular gateway by hard-coded phone numbers in their handsets. However, the WAP Forum is working on ways to enable users to move seamlessly from gateway to gateway for broader access to WAP content.[4]

A basic WAP configuration is shown in Figure 8-2. WAP is global, open, and platform-independent. In the future, WAP is also likely to become an *International Standards Organization* (ISO) reference model, which is considerably more than an industrial standard. At this point WAP provides a standard most of the wireless industry can understand and work with.

The following wireless standards have emerged and found their own niches: Bluetooth is the 10-meter standard; WAP will be the wide standard; and WLAN will be the floor standard. However, WAP, Bluetooth, WLAN, cellular, and IP have different signaling and may not be compatible or interoperable. The three standards will need to achieve application commonalities to ensure interoperability and access to data in all applications.

The WAP Forum has formal relationships with the:

- *World Wide Web Consortium* (W3C)
- *Internet Engineering Taskforce* (IETF)

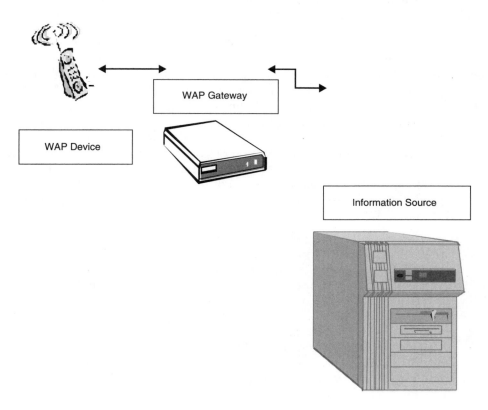

8-2 The status of WAP standards.

- *Cellular Telecommunication Industry Association* (CTIA)
- *European Telecommunication Standards Institute* (ETSI)
- *Telecommunications Industry Association* (TIA)
- *European Computer Manufacturers Association* (ECMA)

The Security Status of WAP

WAP is being asked to secure a number of famously vulnerable applications that WAP terminals are expected to provide:

- Online currency conversions
- Access to email
- Current bank account information
- Trading stocks and bonds
- Outcomes of sporting events and scores
- Breaking news stories

Despite the sensitivity of the information these applications exchange, WAP security measures are being developed piecemeal. Currently the primary guardian of WAP security is WTLS. WTLS scores reasonable marks for confidentiality, authenticity, non-repudiation, and data integrity, but falls short of providing an adequate defense against viruses, worms, denial of service attacks, Trojan horses, and so forth.

The oft-cited reason for the failure of WTLS to address these most common of information security attacks is that they are too dynamic to suppress in the wireless environment. Content protection (and specific countermeasures against specific attacks) occurs in the content-rich network environment—before the information is ever dispatched to the wireless environment. Encryption might appear to be a reasonable safeguard to add to the wireless portfolio, but most wireless devices lack the memory necessary to support it.

The wireless environment also presupposes a certain level of trust. Users must assume, or verify, that their network infrastructure is equipped with sufficient protection to insure information security in advance of dissemination.

Beyond the general issues for WTLS, there are at least two security issues of direct concern to WAP:[5]

Login security, also referred to as *calling line identification* (CLID) technology, is not yet available. This critical feature enables the server to identify the end user. Since no method of CLID currently exists for the wireless environment, users are advised to establish higher-than-normal levels of trust with networks and correspondents.

White spot is the loaded term applied to the brief period of time when an encrypted signal is decrypted and exposed (in the clear) before being re-encrypted and sent out again. White spots occur when a signal from the WAP terminal has been encrypted to the WAP gateway, but decrypted at the WAP gateway, for routing to the standard servers of the LAN/WAN environment (see Figure 8-3).

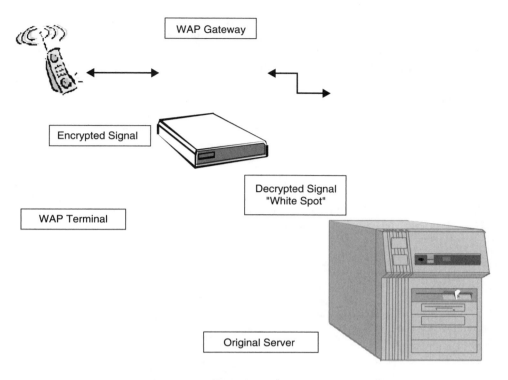

8-3 Potential WAP security solutions. (Courtesy of www.F-Secure.com 2001)

Although the number of WAP applications is limited, security products for wireless (let alone WAP) devices are even scarcer. Until the development of WAP 2.0 specifications, the security services of the stack were considered optional and no one could predict with any accuracy where they would be applied. WAP 2.0 makes security services mandatory, and the industry is still discovering where they will be applied.

A 2001 survey by the Computer Security Institute reports that less than 2 percent of wireless devices contain virus protection. In the past, carriers were able to shrug off this miniscule percentage because few viruses had yet been reported. It is perceived wisdom among wireless providers that wireless devices still lack the processing power to execute viruses—a circumstance, please note, that these same providers are expressly trying to change because several viruses have been reported to attack wireless products and PDAs.[6] Moreover, early wireless applications were limited mostly to convenience features such as organizers, contacts, and calendars, and not to critical functions such as banking and trading. Once wireless ceases to be a novelty and becomes our primary communications medium, few would disagree that WAP will have to exhibit functionality at the same level of security—if not higher—than that accepted in the wired information environment.

Figures 8-4 and 8-5 illustrate security settings for data exchange in both wired and wireless systems, followed by a suggested configuration for security services.

As these figures imply, many security services (like performance enhancing services) will be offered through supporting servers, proxy servers, and gateways. As additional components are added to the network, so goes one of the central precepts of network management: the network's inherent complexity and risk quotient rises with them. Yet in every instance, additional resources are required for the wireless network. These security concerns are being addressed aggressively in the WAP Forum.

Viruses

Established virus management vendors—F-Secure, McAfee, Norton among them— have indicated their intention to provide a workable wireless solution (with or without WAP). F-Secure has already delivered AV software for a variety of wireless devices.

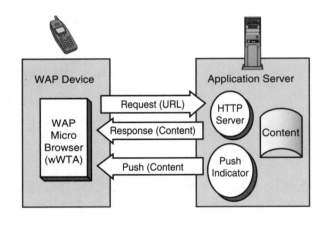

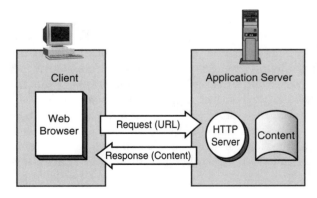

8-4 WAP 2.0 programming model vs. WWW programming model.[7]

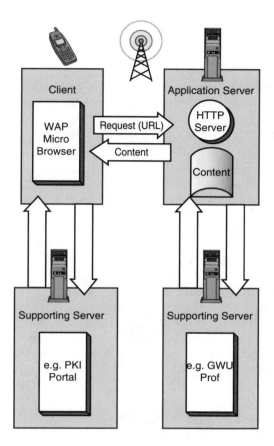

8-5 Possible configuration for security services.[8]

The current reality is that there is little virus activity reported in the wireless world. It's still unclear whether that's due to small capacity in the devices or our current inability to detect the attack. What is clear is that once applications are developed, with or without WAP, the thrill of the hunt will draw out the virus developers.

Authorization

Authorization ensures that the user may have access to requested information. The functionality depends largely upon authentication, followed by some rules of access control. For WAP devices, authorization will, at least at the outset, be left to the application.

Non-repudiation

Parties cannot safely be permitted to deny their role in a transaction. This requires some form of authentication and digital signature. Progress in this regard has come slowly from the use of smartcards and tokens, and we are likely to see more of the same.

Authentication

Initially, use of certificates with WAP devices can be characterized as awkward at best. Entrust/Xcert, RSA, and Verisign, among others, have now made certificates available specifically for wireless. RSA has developed a SecureID operation that will work with the Nokia 9210. Others in the WAP Forum will be similarly joined in the future.

Secure Sessions

The most prevalent incursion into wireless security at present appears to be in authentication and SSLs for WAP. Several organizations provide certificates, and SSLs for WAP are also available. Supporters of WAP hope for *lightweight directory application protocol* (LDAP) adaptation to WAP.[9] The greatest exposure at present seems to be the WAP gateway. While the transmission from the client to the gateway, and between the gateway and the information resource, may be protected via encryption, we are still susceptible to the white spot.

Wireless Identity Modules may be a solution on a par with *subscriber identity modules* (SIMs). They offer security functionality independent of the WAP device and are as tamper-resistant as smartcards. WIM can have its own encryption, decryption, and authentication capabilities. RSA now provides SecureID for the Nokia 9210, with plans to expand it to other WAP-enabled devices.

Security Products

Products on the market for wireless and WAP security are still evolving. Few come from the leaders in Internet security like RSA, Entrust, Verisign, and others.[10] While those companies have agreed to expend some effort on the problem, their commitment to WAP, as distinct from wireless in general, appears to be lukewarm. Consider this poll of vendors in the WAP space (Table 8-1).

Among newer products entering the market are several interesting secure applications from smaller or non-provider companies. See Table 8-2.

Figure 8-6 provides insight into how a WAP network is typically configured. In this configuration security is provided for, but not enforced. It will need to be strengthened as the customer base is increased.

Note that some applications already have built-in encryption. At the session level, SSL ensures message integrity, while PKI and certifications provide for authentication and confidentiality. Browsers will have access to certificates, and 128-bit SSL is sustainable.

Here's what industry is saying about WAP security:

> Even with 2.0, Bob Kalka, "manager of security evangelism division at Tivoli," sees many risks to WAP-based e-business—viruses and access control, among others.[11]

Is WTLS enough? Some think so. It can protect data integrity, privacy, authentication, and Denial of Service between WAP devices, WAP gateways, and Web

Table 8-1 Existing WAP Security Products

Company	Wireless Product(s)/Area of Interest
BEA	Security add-on for the gateway integrated into weblogic application server.
Jataayu	Carrier grade and enterprise version of WAP gateway, with WTLS implementation and runs on NT/98, Linux, Solaris.
Nokia	Developed in Java and Java servlets.
Silicon Automation	WAP client and gateway; full WTLS implementation.
Infinite Technologies	WAPlite gateway with WTLS built using Baltimore Tech toolkit.
Kenyon	WTLS Gateway independent of the WAP Gateway. It handles security functionality and communicates with the WAP gateway using UDP/IP.
Baltimore Technology	Broad range of products — corporate solutions, development kits, and security hardware. Telepathy Suite for wireless. Telepathy WAP Security Gateway interposed between the mobile device and the WAP gateway and provides security through WTLS. To work, need to host own WAP gateway, because WTLS uses unsecured UDP over IP. WAP CA and PKI implementations and services. Telepathy WTLS Gateway Toolkit includes an implementation and a high level API to hide encryption and signature algorithms, including RSA and 3DES, among others.
Ericsson	Not significant in either the software world or in the security arena, and now, with its announced retreat from manufacturing the cell phone, it is questionable where it will fit in the WAP arena.

servers. But Graham Cluley of Sophos Anti-Virus thinks WAP phones are not powerful enough yet to harbor viruses, and as a result, is concerned that a false sense of security will keep virus control products inactive, while Nokia fears proliferation of scripts will bring on viruses. Since there is a 6- to 12-month delay between adoption of a new WAP standard and products being brought to market, there is also enough lead-time to develop viruses, hack jobs, and other malicious code.

Eric Olden of Securant expresses concern that adding a separate security infrastructure creates a huge additional burden of management and administration. He promotes an integrated, single security system for both Web and wireless applications, which would provide:[12]

- A single point of control to set, monitor, and enforce policies
- Elimination or reduction of human intervention when a user profile changes
- Delegation of routine tasks such as adding, moving, deleting users, changing passwords, and updating profiles
- Extends e-business to m-business

Steve Gold, in his article "No strings Attached,"[13] reports the following:

- There is no real security for WAP.
- WAP 2.0 will permit downloading of Java applets for security applications running 128-bit SSL.

Table 8-2 WAP Compatible Wireless Security Products

Company	Product	Description	Positives	Negatives
Space4Rent[14]	Advanced Messaging Solutions	Virus scanning, cleaning, spam filters.		Expensive.
Infinite.com	Infinite WAP Server[15]	Provides SSL services through WTLS.	Low cost, good international distribution and support, trial version off the Web, modular. Confusing.	Difficult end-user pricing.
Site Guardian[16]	Virtual Creations	Provides a Web site monitoring service. Picked as SC Magazine's Best Buy.	Low cost, demo, good service offerings.	Compact HTML and WML developments in the future may scuttle its WAP service plans.
Brokat[17]	Mobile Wallet	Allows goods and services to be purchased securely using any wireless device, including WAP-enabled cell phones. Full range of banking services 128-bit encryption onetime PIN technology.	Allows secure purchases.	Can be compromised on most telephone company networks.
Neomar Inc[18]	Neomar	Supports research in Motion's Blackberry PDA and palm-compatible PDAs. Supports security from the ground up. Supports WTLS. HTTP authentication support. WAP stack support.	Supports authenticated, secure access to the Web. Rules out most WAP-enabled mobile phones prior to WAP 1.2.	
SmartTrust[19]	SmartTrust Personal	Allows secure financial transactions and other security-critical services across GSM channels. It plans to evolve to support WAP as well. Shrink wrapped. Relies on WAP-embedded infrastructure, WAP 3.0 outline includes Java. PKI-based. Smartcard-compatible.	Proven track Record; it may have a future WAP implication.	Mediocre support.

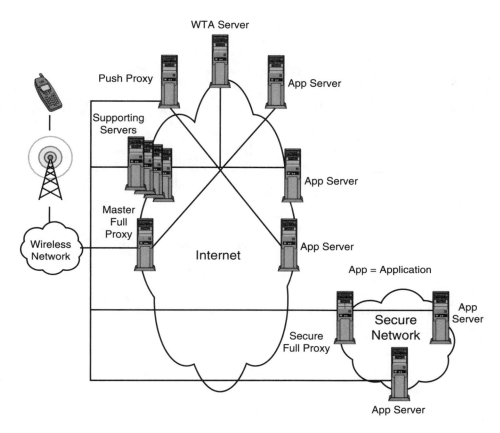

8-6 Example WAP network.[20]

- The WAP server developers bringing the first 2.0 security products to market are Symbian EPOC-based smart phones, Psion PDA, Palm, and Handspring Visor.
- Phone.com and Software.com are integrating Baltimore Technologies wireless e-security in their Openwave System, linking BT's wireless certificate service to their UP.Link Server (WAP Gateway) and Enterprise Proxy.
- Twelve vendors are collaborating on standards for security in the OASIS XML-based technical committee, among them BT, Entegrity, Entrust, HP, IBM's Tivoli Systems, iPlanet E-Commerce Solutions, Sun-Netscape Alliance, Oblix, OpenNetwork Technologies, Securant Technologies, and TransIndigo. Results are projected to be at least one year away.
- Central Command has enhanced AVX Professional to manage software across the Internet through Web or WAP phones.

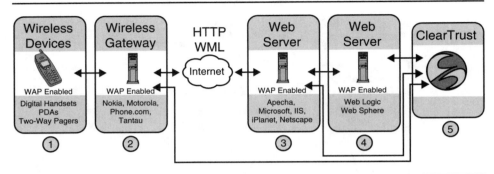

ClearTrust SecureControl Supports Wireless Internet Transactions

① User accesses the Web resource through wireless device.

② CTSC Plug-In for WAP Gateway provides coarse-grained access control.

③ CTSC Plug-In for Web Server provides coarse-grained access control.

④ CTSC Java API for App Server provides coarse-grained access control.

⑤ ClearTrust authenticates users through PIN, WTLS minicertificates, or passwords.

8-7 How ClearTrust SecureControl works. (Courtesy of Securant Technologies™)[21]

Securant Technologies™ ClearTrust Control

ClearTrust SecureControl has marketed an enterprise Web-centric access control and policy management system for eBusiness. It can be used to secure and manage Web-based transactions originating from wireless devices for any environment. SecureControl provides a single, rules-based infrastructure that dynamically manages user access permissions to Web-enabled resources, whether the access device is wired or wireless. ClearTrust claims to provide wireless with all the same security features it affords Web browsers, including support for authentication of digital certificates, token cards, and smartcards.

Securant seems convinced that WAP will link wireless and Web technology to provide users with a viable convergence. They expect WAP 2.0 to resolve many existing security issues, but only if robust security processes and adjuncts can secure end-to-end transmissions.

WAP Security Architecture

WAP Security Architecture design issues are still largely in flux. Existing models are based on either a single-tier or two-tier solution. A single-tier solution requires a WAP-to-Web link. Such a link has been investigated and abandoned as not feasible at this time. A two-tier architecture is currently the preferred approach, with the gateway sitting between the WAP device and the ISP. Security then becomes an adjunct to the gateway.

> **Three-tier architecture**   A single gateway between WAP and ISP, possibly a wireless portal with some third-party content. This would avoid redesign of content for WAP, but its complexity is undesirable, as is risk in the tunnels.
>
> **Four-tier architecture**   Two gateways—WAP-to-Web conversion outside the firewall, WAP-to-Web transcode inside. The architecture is all but unscalable, and still has security flaws.
>
> **Five-tier architecture**   Three gateways, one for security, one for protocol, one for transcode . . . becomes complex, expensive, and difficult to manage.[22]

Marginal Security

Security for WAP products is currently marginal. Proposed solutions increase WAP's reliance on gateways, proxies, and supporting servers, adding a security increment while also adding an increment of increased threat from complexity and overhead. From the designer's perspective, a better security solution will be found only in better infrastructure specifications.

Wireless Access to the Internet

Currently, most cell phones are based on PCS (CDMA or TDMA) and/or digital cellular technologies in the United States, and GSM in Europe, and a microbrowser is built into the phone. With WAP content and gateway, providers are growing in numbers, and soon the mobile Internet user will have access to a plethora of WAP-enabled sites. Nokia offers a digital cell phone that is WAP-enabled and has a built-in WAP browser. Although WAP is still in its maturing stages, it has so far proven itself worthy in supporting wireless Web access.

Wireless Middleware

Wireless middleware is a component on the WLAN network that helps connect wireless devices with a target server on a WLAN or wired network counterpart. It also performs various functions such as data compression, data security, data synchronization, database connection, information store and forward messaging, and screen scraping. As such, wireless middleware offers a partial solution to some restrictions of wireless technology. Not only does it add layers of security/encryption, but it can also accept data from HTML/XML format and deliver the reformatted content to the wireless device. Securing middleware may prove easier than securing gateways.

Two methods are used to transfer information from a Web site to a wireless device, namely Web morphing and screen scraping. The dynamics of the data on a Web site determines which solution is most effective. Morphing techniques work best when the site and/or data are constantly changing. Scraping works best if the Web site is static—in other words, expect to scrape each time a Web site changes. A company wishing to ensure secure data transfers between Web and wireless device currently has two options: Purchase third-party server applications that perform morphing, or outsource the requirement to one of hundreds of vendors in the market today.

Summary

According to Gartner's research, WAP has a transient future:

- WAP will be the dominant standard in the European Union through 2003.
- WAP is the transitory answer to a (3G) need that demands long-term solutions. Therefore, WAP applications will be short-lived. Developers that believe this to be true have little incentive to provide better security in the short term.
- WAP is not a global strategy, but Gartner believes U.S. handsets currently using HTML will evolve to WAP in the near future.[23]

Endnotes

[1]http://www.iec.org/tutorials/wap/topic01.html, March 5, 2001.

[2]Schramm, John, "Security Issues in WAP and I-Mode" [article online], (December 2, 2000, Sans Institute) available from http://www.sans.org/infosecFAQ/wireless/WAP4.htm; Internet. I-Mode is the wireless Internet product of Japan's NTT spin-off DoCoMo (do como is Japanese for *anywhere*). I-Mode is the Japanese answer to WAP. The two technologies function similarly and provide similar service to their subscribers. As of September of 2000, DoCoMo reported a subscriber base of twelve million users. DoCoMo has predicted that their subscriber base would exceed 17 million users by the first quarter of 2001. Internet content that is I-Mode compatible is distributed in a reduced version of HTML. Subscribers to the service access this reduced size Internet via their Web-enabled telephone devices. Early I-Mode enabled phones were capable of receiving text and limited graphics. In 2000, devices became available that were Java capable. These Java phones are now being promulgated throughout the I-Mode user base and allow users to access much more dynamic wireless Internet content, in full color. Users of the service are charged a small monthly fee and are then charged for each 128-bit packet that is sent or received from the user's Web phone. Most I-Mode security architecture is proprietary. The specification for this technology has not been released publicly as yet. For a security professional, this is an almost insurmountable leap of faith in the provider's technology and maintenance. What is known of I-Mode's security is that the new Java-based handsets, being offered by Ericsson and Nokia, are capable of 128-bit Secure Socket Layer (SSL) encryption. This may lead to a false sense of security in that the use of the technology, which is possible but not guaranteed, would only assure encryption of the air link. Where and how the information is transmitted once it has reached the DoCoMo Center, as all of it does, is unknown. Despite this possible security nightmare, the devices and the service are immensely popular in Japan. Japan's I-Mode commands approximately 81 percent of the world's wireless Internet users. DoCoMo has acknowledged that security on I-Mode is an important factor in their research and development, but has yet to specify exactly how they are addressing the issue. A recent press release indicates that DoCoMo has partnered with

VeriSign Japan to incorporate SSL technology at the server level. See:"Verisign Japan Adapts Encryption Technology to I-Mode," (January 23, 2001, AsiaBizTech) Available at:, http://www.nikkeibp.asiabiztech.com/wcs/leaf?CID=onair/ababt/moren/121657.

[3]Gartner Group, Wireless Application Protocol (WAP): A Perspective, November 20, 2000. WAP applications are developed using wireless markup language (WML) and WMLScript.

[4]Wexler, Joanie, "WAP Under the Hood," Network World Wireless in the Enterprise Newsletter, October 16, 2000.

[5]wap@f-secure.com, February 1, 2001.

[6]Ibid.

[7]WAP™ Architecture: WAP-210-WAPArch, Proposed Version 17-October-2000, pp. 12–13.

[8]WAP™ Architecture: WAP-210-WAPArch, Proposed Version 17-October-2000, p. 15.

[9]Professional WAP, ISBN 1-861004, WROX Press, p. 521.

[10]Ibid., pp. 584–586.

[11]Armstrong, Illena, "What's Happening with WAP," *Security,* Vol. 12, 2001 No. 2, p. 32.

[12]Ibid.

[13]ibid.

[14]Ibid., p. 63.

[15]Ibid.

[16]Ibid., p. 64.

[17]Ibid., p. 66.

[18]Ibid.

[19]bid., p. 68.

[20]WAP™ Architecture: WAP-210-WAPArch, Proposed Version, October 17, 2000, p. 16.

[21]*Support for WAP,* White Paper, January, 2001, p. 4.

[22]WatchIT.com Program 20000904, p. 22–25.

[23]Gartner Group, DPRO-90909, November 20, 2000, p. 9.

9

Wireless Transport Layer Security (WTLS)

Wireless Local Area Networks (WLANs) are expected to have a reassuring effect on e-commerce, but not until we've established that both the sender and receiver can be trusted and are who they say they are. It follows that there must also be a way to guarantee that the information has not been intercepted or modified in route. *Wireless Transport Layer Security* (WTLS) was developed for this purpose as a replacement for the flawed WEP 802.11b security. It works by performing client and server authentication to confirm the identity of the sender and his or her message. It also encrypts the data in transit to keep the information secret and checks the integrity of the data after it arrives.

WTLS is a useful wireless security standard based on the IETF's *Transport Layer Security* (TLS) protocol, which in turn was expressly developed as an Internet standard version of *Secure Socket Layer* (SSL).[1]

Secure Socket Layer

SSL enables secure data transfer between two devices over a public network, providing authentication, confidentiality, and data integrity through the use of encryption. The protocol has two primary functions: *to provide privacy between client and server*, and *to authenticate the server to the client*. Originally developed by Netscape Communications to allow secure access of a browser to a Web server, SSL became a de facto standard over the years and was licensed for use in other applications. Today, SSL is the most widely used method of securing data on the Internet. Since it is protocol- and application-independent, SSL can secure other protocols by operating above the Transport layer, yet below the Application layer, of the OSI reference model (see Figure 9-1). According to Netscape: SSL uses TCP/IP on behalf of the higher-level protocols and in the process allows an SSL-enabled server to

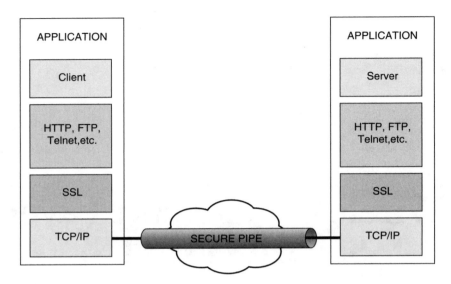

*Add trusted protocol security to your
internet applications quickly and easily*

9-1 SSL position in protocol stack. (Source: RSA Security)

authenticate itself to an SSL-enabled client; it allows the client to authenticate itself to the server, and both machines to establish an encrypted connection.[2]

SSL has two subprotocols: The SSL Record Protocol defines the format used to transmit data, and the SSL Handshake Protocol (shown in Figure 9-2) exchanges a series of messages when an SSL connection is established. The sub-protocols provide the following SSL functionality:[3]

- Authenticates the server to the client
- Lets client and server select the cryptographic algorithms that they both support
- *Optionally* authenticates the client to the server
- Uses public-key encryption techniques to generate shared secrets
- Establishes an encrypted SSL connection

TLSv1 is built on SSLv3, which has long been implemented for browser security by both Netscape and Microsoft.[4] SSL is called from the browser when the reference starts with https://, indicating a request for an SSL session. The browser then initiates a session on the servers' TCP port 443. SSL attempts to negotiate a secure session. If the negotiation is successful, it is indicated by a padlock or key appearing in or around the status bar, depending upon the browser in use. What happens behind the scenes from a security perspective is handled primarily by the Record Protocol of the SSL.

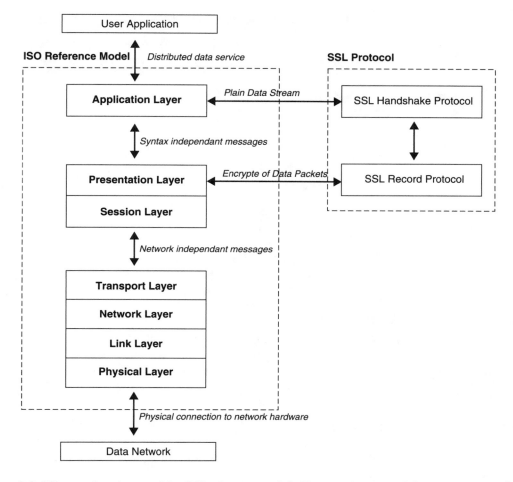

9-2 SSL at various layers of the OSI reference model. (Source: cisat.jmu.edu)

Record Protocol

The Record Protocol provides SSL confidentiality and integrity services by encryption and by appending a *Message Authentication Code* (MAC) to the application data. The Record Protocol is the base protocol used by many of the upper layer protocols (see Figure 9-3).

Here's how it works. The application data is first fragmented into 214-byte blocks, compressed if desired, and to insure that the data has not been altered in route, a MAC is computed by the sender and placed over the fragmented and compressed data. A shared secret key is also generated and used at the distant end to achieve the same calculation on the receiving end of the transmission. This MAC is computed again by the receiver and compared to the incoming MAC. If it matches

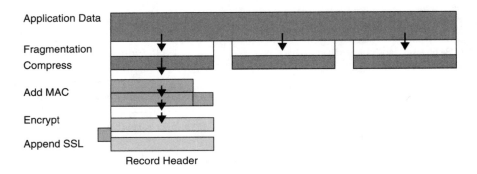

9-3 Record Protocol operation.

the original calculation confidence can be placed in the integrity of the data and a high level of assurance that it has not been altered. The message is then encrypted symmetrically by the use of a secret key, and finally a header is attached.

SSL Handshake Protocol

The purpose of the SSL handshake is threefold. First, the client and server need to agree on a set of algorithms, which will be used to protect the data. Second, they need to establish a set of cryptographic keys, which will be used by those algorithms. Third, the handshake may optionally authenticate the client. The overall process follows:

Client	**Server**

1. Supported ciphers, Random--→
2. ←--------------------------------Chosen cipher, Random, Certificate
3. Encrypted Master Secret --→
4. Compute Keys   4. Compute Keys
5. MAC of handshake messages--→
6. ←---------------------------------------MAC of handshake messages

1. The client sends the server a list of algorithms it's willing to support, along with a random number used as input to the key generation process.
2. The server chooses a cipher out of the list and sends it back along with a certificate containing the server's public key. The certificate is a binding unit and provides the servers identity for authentication and the server supplies a random number, which is used as part of the key generation process.
3. The client verifies the server's certificate and extracts the server's public key. The client then generates a random secret string call the pre_master_secret and encrypts it using the server's public key. It sends the encrypted public key to the server.

4. The client and server independently compute the encryption and MAC keys from the pre_master_secret and the client and server's random values.
5. The client sends a MAC of all the handshake messages to the server.
6. The server sends a MAC of all the handshake messages to the client.[5]

Two goals have been accomplished in this process. First, the set of algorithms is agreed upon, and second, a set of cryptographic keys is established. The server chooses the algorithm from the clients supporting algorithm set. Note that step 3 is the critical step because all the data to be protected depends on the security of the pre_master_secret. Steps 5 and 6 confirm that the handshake itself has not been tampered with. Because the client and server provide random numbers as inputs to the key generation process, the handshake is secure from replay attacks.[6]

Transport Layer Security

TLS was introduced by the IETF to provide privacy and data integrity between two applications communicating over the Internet. As a variant of SSL version 3, TLS offers several enhancements.[7] SSL opens and closes a new socket for each message, whereas TLS establishes a secure connection, and can pass numerous messages through the same socket, providing much better throughput. TLS also provides greater separation between the handshaking process and the record layer, allowing for implementation of new authentication methods in the future. As TLS was designed to minimize network activity, an optional session caching scheme was introduced to improve performance. Other differences between SSL and TLS are addressed in Table 9-1.

Advantages and Disadvantages of SSL/TLS

SSL and TLS each provide a method of securing data to ensure authentication, confidentiality, and integrity, and an effective means of encrypting data to defend against tampering and spoofing. They were designed to operate in conjunction with other protocols, allowing for future protocols or changes to encryption schemes. TLS is also backwards compatible with earlier versions of SSL.

Table 9-1 SSL vs. TLS

SSL	TLS
Minor version 0	Minor version 1
Uses a preliminary HMAC algorithm	Uses HMAC as described in RFC 2104
Does not apply MAC to version information	Applies Mac to version information
Does not specify a padding value	Initializes padding to a specific value
Limited set of alerts and warning	More alerts and warnings for detailed information and troubleshooting
Fortezza is an option for key exchange and encryption	Fortezza not available

Source: jmu.edu

The effectiveness of SSL/TLS depends on the size of the encryption key. SSL has been cracked in less than a week using relatively short keys, such as 40- or 56-bit. 128-bit cipher keys are recommended for securing e-commerce or business applications. Sometimes SSL can be fooled during the handshake process. The protocol compatibility check is unprotected, and may be tampered with to institute a weaker encryption level.

An external drawback is that U.S. law presently inhibits exportation of encryption keys by requiring a license for certain cryptographic products.[8] In the interest of national security, this law is enforced to prohibit terrorist information from being exchanged using electronic means. It can also inhibit commercial transactions that otherwise would be considered reasonable and routine.

Three common commercial implementations of TLS are Netscape, Microsoft, and Entrust.

Netscape

Netscape Corporation created SSL to secure connections between Internet browsers and Internet servers. As SSL became an accepted standard, Netscape received the usual requests to move SSL under a standards body. The new protocol was designated *Transport Layer Security* (TLS) and was submitted to the *Internet Engineering Task Force* (IETF's) TLS Working Group in early 1997. With SSL 3.0 as their starting point, the working group published TLS Protocol 1.0 into the standards track. While Netscape browsers still support SSL, the company officially supports TLS as of Netscape Version 6.0.

Microsoft

Ever since SSL has emerged as a de facto standard, Internet Explorer has supported its own various versions. Microsoft also developed its own proprietary transport layer protocol, *Private Communications Technology* (PCT), to resolve problems associated with SSL v2.0. The company supported PCT in versions of Internet Explorer through 4.x.[9] After SSL v3.0 was released, however, and the movement to make TLS an Internet standard was initiated, Microsoft dropped support for PCT in favor of joining forces with the TLS working group. Some Microsoft products such as S-channel continue to support PCT for backwards compatibility only, but the company specifically discourages use of PCT for any future development.[10]

Entrust

Entrust provides support for TLS v1.0 in its Entrust Toolkit for SSL/TLS. This toolkit lets developers incorporate SSL/TLS security into server-oriented C++ applications. Developers can also use the TLS protocol to create secure a communications channel between a server and a client. Entrust has also implemented support for wireless solutions that use WTLS with WAP.

EAP-TLS

Like all IETF protocols, TLS can combine with other protocols to provide new solutions. One such example puts TLS with the *Extensible Authentication*

Protocol (EAP) to provide authentication to point-to-point connections. Microsoft implemented the EAP-TLS protocol in its Windows 2000 operating system. EAP is an IETF proposed extension to PPP that allows the dynamic addition of authentication plug-in modules at both the client and server side of the PPP connection.[11] This extension was deemed necessary to improve the authentication provided in PPP implementations. EAP allows third-party authentication modules to interface with a PPP implementation through a generic interface.

Authentication provides a means by which network managers can authenticate the identity of those attempting to access to computer resources and they data they house. In its simplest form it consists of password protection and intelligent tokens.

Password protection is imposed to restrict individuals on a site, host, application, screen, or field level. Passwords should obviously be long, with high *entropy* (chaotic) value, alphanumeric in nature, and changed periodically.[12] There is a current trend towards the use of dedicated password servers for password management. The *Password Authentication Protocol* (PAP) is a commonly used mechanism for password protection in support of remote users. While PAP is easy to use, passwords are typically sent to the *Remote Access Server* (RAS) in *plain text* (in the clear) and *unencrypted* (see Figure 9-4).[13]

Intelligent tokens are hardware devices that generate one-time passwords to be verified by a secure server. They often work on a cumbersome challenge-response basis. The *Challenge Handshake Authentication Protocol* (CHAP) is an example of this improved approach. CHAP involves the RAS's challenging the remote user with a random number. The user responds with a digest, which is an encrypted password based on the random number challenge. The RAS then decrypts the password using the same random number key to verify the identity of the remote user.

The CHAP addresses some limitations of the PAP authentication process. More specifically in the wireless applications, CHAP furnishes challenge-response authentication using the *Message Digest 5* (MD5) one-way encryption scheme, which it applies in the response to a challenge issued by the remote access server (Figure 9-5). CHAP is more secure than PAP since the password is not sent in a CHAP implementation. Instead, the password is used to create a hash of the challenge string. The server can use its own copy of the password to create its own hash and compare the two. In that case the connection is accepted if the two hashes match and rejected if they don't.

However, CHAP does have its own vulnerabilities. For instance, it requires that passwords be stored in a reversibly encrypted form.

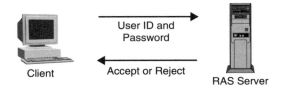

9-4 Password Authentication Protocol (PAP) communications.

9-5 Challenge Handshake Authentication Protocol (CHAP) communication.

Some experts see the *Microsoft CHAP* (MS-CHAP) as an improvement on CHAP (Figure 9-6). In CHAP, the plaintext version of the password must be available to validate the challenge response, but in MS-CHAP, the remote access server requires only the MD4 hash of the password to validate the challenge response.

In the configurations we've discussed for PPP authentication above, the remote client and remote server perform the authentication process. Another possibility is using the Remote Access Server (RAS) simply as a pass through to a backend authentication server located in the enterprise. This configuration distinguishes the *Remote Authentication Dial-in User Service* (RADIUS) protocol. RADIUS servers can provide centralized user authentication and authorization instead of having to configure each remote access server to provide this capability (Figure 9-7) and can provide authentication to their clients from anywhere on the Internet.

Alternatives to SSL/TLS

TLS is not the only protocol to provide secure data transfer. Others like IPSec, SSH, RADIUS, and LEAP can be used in various combinations to supplement or replace it.

IP Security (IPSec)

IP Security (IPSec) is a set of open standards developed by the IETF and documented in Internet general *Request-For-Comments* (RFC 2401) and related RFCs. It provides for end-to-end encryption and authentication at the network layer to protect IP packets between IPSec-compliant devices. IPSec is currently supported in IPv4 and will be mandatory in the future IPv6. Today, IPSec is most commonly found in network devices such as routers, switches, firewalls, and remote access servers (Figure 9-8).

Services offered by the IPSec protocol suite include:

- Access control
- Connectionless integrity
- Data origin authentication
- Protection against replays (a form of partial sequence integrity)
- Confidentiality (encryption)
- Limited traffic flow confidentiality[15]

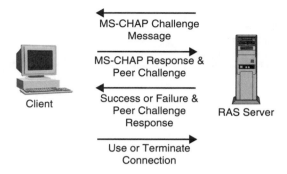

9-6 MS-CHAP V2 communications.

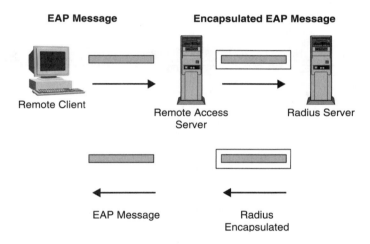

9-7 RADIUS configuration.

These services use two transmission protocols, IP *Authentication Header* (AH) and IP *Encapsulating Security Payload* (ESP), together with one of the available key management protocols.

Authentication Header Protocol (AH)

As defined by the IETF in RFC 2402, AH turns away denial-of-service attacks, but doesn't provide for confidentiality. The AH protocol calculates a message authentication code, or MAC, and inserts it in the Authentication Data field of the AH header (Figure 9-9) to be placed in the packet after the IP header. To verify data integrity, the receiving device will calculate the MAC as well and compare its results against the MAC received with the packet.

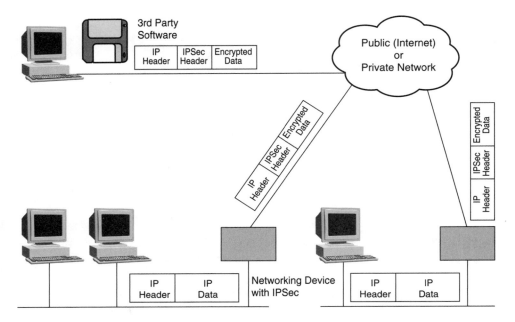

9-8 Typical IPSec usage. (Source: CyLAN Technologies, Inc.)

Bit	8	16	
Next Header	Payload Len	RESERVED	
Security Parameters Index (SPI)			
Sequence Number Field			
Authentication Data (variable)			

9-9 Authentication header format. (Source: RFC 2402)

AH also protects against a replay attack, in which the attacker obtains a copy of an authenticated packet and sometime later transmits it to the intended destination. The receipt of duplicate, authenticated packets may cause a disruption in service.[16] To prevent this, AH makes use of a counter stored in the Sequence Number Field.

Encapsulating Security Payload (ESP)

ESP (RFC2406) confers a level of authentication, integrity, and replay protection. In addition, and unlike AH, ESP provides confidentiality. However, ESP authentication is inferior to AH's in that it authenticates only the transport layer header and not parts of the IP header too. Based on your particular security requirements, you may decide to implement AH, ESP, or both. The ESP protocol will add a header to the packet and also between the IP header and the transport layer header (Figure 9-10).

Transport and Tunnel Modes

AH and ESP can both be implemented in either transport mode or tunnel mode. In *transport mode*, which is used for transmitting data between two hosts, only the data is encrypted. The header information remains in the open so packets can be routed between the hosts. *Tunnel mode* is used when transmitting data between two security gateways such as two routers. Here the sending gateway encrypts the entire IP packet and appends a new IP header entering the receiving gateways address in the destination address. When the receiving gateway receives the packet, it strips off the outer IP header, decrypts the packet, and sends the packet to the final destination. This configuration is typically referred to as a *Virtual Private Network* (VPN).[17] While tunnel mode does not provide end-to-end encryption, it does hide the sending and receiving addresses while the packet is on the public network. Notice that this scenario hinders our ability to perform traffic analysis inside the secure tunnel. The packet will take on different structures depending on the mode used.

Most implementations of IPSec are between two gateways or between a gateway and a host. Companies may implement IPSec when connecting a branch office to the home office over the Internet. With IPSec the data passing between the two routers can be encrypted and thus protected as it moves through the public network. This gateway-to-gateway usage avoids the costs of building private networks while still maintaining security of information assets. In another configuration, IPSec can be implemented to connect a remote user to the corporation network over the Internet.

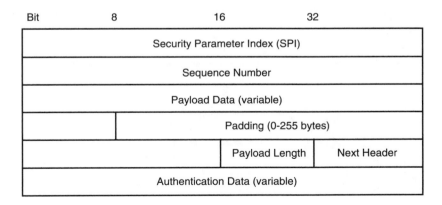

9-10 Encapsulating Security Payload (ESP) header format. (Source: RFC 2406)

Secure Shell (SSH)

Secure Shell refers to both an application and a protocol suite enabling secure connection of two computers over a public network. SSH, originally developed for the UNIX environment as a secure replacement for the following UNIX protocols: Telnet, *remote login* (rlogin), rcp, and rsh provide secured TCP tunnels.[18] SSH version 5 (released 2001) has improved cryptography and is designed for general purpose VPNs. The SSH protocol architecture as submitted to the IETF is broken down into three major components (shown in Figure 9-11):

- **Transport Layer Protocol**   Provides server authentication, confidentiality, and data integrity/
- **Authentication Protocol**   Provides user authentication.
- **TConnection Protocol**   Provides multiple data channels in a single encrypted tunnel.

SSH Transport Layer Protocol

The SSH Transport Layer Protocol provides server authentication, strong encryption, and integrity protection comparable to TLS. Authentication is based on the use of public key cryptography. A list of key formats defined in the IETF draft is presented in Table 9-1. SSH will also provide optional compression. As with TLS, SSH typically runs on top of a TCP/IP connection. During an SSH connection, a key exchange method, public key algorithm, symmetric key algorithm, message authentication algorithm, and a hash algorithm are all negotiated.

Once a server has been authenticated, host and client negotiate a symmetric key for bulk encryption, used to encrypt all transmissions between the two thereafter. Table 9-2 shows the ciphers supported in the Internet draft document.

The SSH transport layer protocol uses MACs to provide data integrity in addition to confidentiality. A MAC is a hash or unique key that represents the exact contents of the message. Each message has a different MAC, and this unique representation of the message guarantees that what the receiver received is what the sender sent. The MAC is computed from a shared secret packet sequence number, and the contents of the packet. The MAC algorithms currently defined in the IETF draft are presented in Table 9-3.

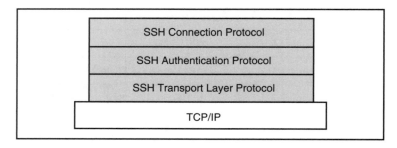

9-11 SSH Protocol Architecture. (Courtesy of F-Secure, Inc.)[19]

Table 9-1 SSH Public Key Formats

Key Format	Status		Description
Ssh-DSS	REQUIRED	Sign	Simple DSS
Ssh-rsa	RECOMMENDED	Sign	Simple RSA
x509v3-sign-rsa	RECOMMENDED	Sign	X.509 certificates (RSA key)
x509v3-sign-dss	RECOMMENDED	Sign	X.509 certificates (DSS key)
Spki-sign-rsa	OPTIONAL	Sign	SPKI certificates (RSA key)
spki-sign-dss	OPTIONAL	Sign	SPKI certificates (DSS key)
pgp-sign-rsa	OPTIONAL	Sign	OpenPGP certificates (RSA key)
pgp-sign-dss	OPTIONAL	Sign	OpenPGP certificates (DSS key)

Source: IETF draft-ietf-secsh-transport-09.txt

Table 9-2 SSH Ciphers

Ciphers	Status	Description
3des-cbc	REQUIRED	Three-key 3DES in CBC mode
Blowfish-cbc	RECOMMENDED	Blowfish in CBC mode
Twofish256-cbc	OPTIONAL	Twofish in CBC mode, with 256-bit key
Twofish-cbc	OPTIONAL	Alias for "twofish256-cbc"
Twofish192-cbc	OPTIONAL	Twofish with 192-bit key
Twofish128-cbc	RECOMMENDED	Twofish with 128-bit key
aes256-cbc	OPTIONAL	AES (Rijndael) in CBC mode, with 256-bit key
aes192-cbc	OPTIONAL	AES with 192-bit key
aes128-cbc	RECOMMENDED	AES with 128-bit key
Serpent256-cbc	OPTIONAL	Serpent in CBC mode, with 256-bit key
Serpent192-cbc	OPTIONAL	Serpent with 192-bit key
Serpent128-cbc	OPTIONAL	Serpent with 128-bit key
Arcfour	OPTIONAL	The ARCFOUR stream cipher
Idea-cbc	OPTIONAL	IDEA in CBC mode
Cast128-cbc	OPTIONAL	CAST-128 in CBC mode
None	OPTIONAL	No encryption; not recommended

Source: IETF draft-ietf-secsh-transport-09.txt

Table 9-3 SSH MAC Algorithms

Algorithm	Status	Description
hmac-sha1	REQUIRED	HMAC-SHA1 (digest length = key length = 20)
Hmac-sha1-96	RECOMMENDED	First 96 bits of HMAC-SHA1 (digest length = 12, key length = 20)
Hmac-md5	OPTIONAL	HMAC-MD5 (digest length = key length = 16)
Hmac-md5-96	OPTIONAL	First 96 bits of HMAC-MD5 (digest length = 12, key length = 16)
None	OPTIONAL	No MAC; not recommended

Source: IETF draft-ietf-secsh-transport-09.txt

SSH tolerates compression well. If compression is used, only the payload field is compressed, with encryption performed afterward. Table 9-4 lists the compression methods currently defined in the Internet draft.

SSH Versus TLS Implementations

SSH provides many of the same functions as WTLS/TLS[20] and is now supported under Windows in addition to UNIX and Linux. It has been implemented on the Palm OS by the *Internet Security, Applications, Authentication and Cryptography* (ISAAC) group, a research project in the Computer Science Division at the University of California, Berkeley. Top Gun SSH is an SSH (version 1) client for palmtops running PalmOS and having a TCP/IP stack. This includes the Palm Pilot Pro, Palm III, Palm V, and the corresponding models of Workpad and Visor.[21] In addition, Mov Software has implemented an SSH client on the Windows CE platform with its sshCE product. sshCE provides secure communication from a handheld device to a SSH enabled host.[22] SSH is now supported on two of the most popular *personal digital assistant* (PDA) operating systems.

Light Extensible Authentication Protocol (LEAP)

Cisco Systems has made use of the EAP and RADIUS protocols in *wireless LAN* (WLAN) solutions. However, instead of using the EAP-TLS standard, Cisco has developed a standard called *Light Extensible Authentication Protocol* (LEAP). LEAP provides support to a variety of operating systems that may not natively support EAP and also provides alternatives to certificate schemes such as EAP-TLS by using dynamic key derivation. By supporting a broad range of operating systems and dynamic key derivation, LEAP provides the mechanism to deploy large-scale enterprise WLAN implementations.

EAP was meant to provide methods for a PPP server to authenticate its clients, and for the client to authenticate the server. EAP also allowed for the passing of authentication information through the PPP server to a centralized authentication server that validated clients on behalf of the PPP server. In a WLAN the wireless access point does not link to its client through a PPP link, but through a WLAN. In early WLAN implementations, the access point was designed to have a single key. Programmed into each client so that traffic could be encrypted, an administratively intensive and insecure implementation. Now, using EAP, the client and RADIUS server can have a shared secret to perform centralized authentication.

It's feasible to use *Public-Key Infrastructure* (PKI) with EAP-TLS as the authentication method. However, this implementation has several drawbacks: First, PKI schemes are CPU-intensive on the client system. Second, PKI systems require

Table 9-4 SSH Compression Methods

Method	Status	Description
None	REQUIRED	No compression
Zlib	OPTIONAL	GNU ZLIB (LZ77) compression

Source: IETF draft-ietf-secsh-transport-09.txt

extra careful planning and administration. Finally, PKI systems may be costly. EAP-MD5 is not a solution, as it does not provide for mutual authentication between the client and server.

Because of these drawbacks, Cisco developed LEAP to be implemented with its EAP solutions. It calls for the client and the RADIUS server to have a shared secret, usually a username and password. Enough information can be passed between the RADIUS server and the access point to allow the client to derive an encryption key unique between the two. The LEAP implementation provides five benefits:

- CPU load on the client is reduced.
- Support can be provided to operating systems that do not natively support EAP.
- PKI infrastructure does not need to be implemented.
- Mutual authentication is supported.
- Each client connection has a unique secret key.

Wireless Transport Layer Security and WAP

WTLS is the security protocol of the Wireless Application Protocol (see Figure 9-12). Sponsored by the WAP Forum industry association, WAP is the set of protocols in the transport, session, and application layers that normalize the applications that operate over wireless communication networks. Over 350 companies to date have signed on to the development of this universal wireless standard.

At the session level, *Wireless Session Protocol* (WSP) decides whether a given session will be connection-oriented or connectionless. If the device needs to talk back and forth, it is assigned a connection-oriented session, and that information is forwarded to the *Wireless Transaction Protocol* (WTP) Layer. If on the other hand, WSP assigns a connectionless session, it forwards to the Wireless Datagram Protocol Layer, which works with the network carrier layer to adapt WAP to a variety of

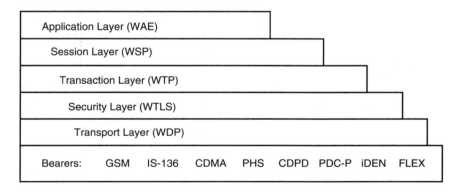

9-12 WAP protocol Stack.

bearers. WTP keeps the data flowing smoothly, and classifies the transaction request as being either reliable two-way, reliable one way, or unreliable one way. The WTLS layer provides integrity checking and encryption, and performs client and server authentication.

Understanding Wireless Transport Layer Security

WTLS is designed for securing communications and transactions over wireless networks. It is being implemented in all the major microbrowsers and WAP servers, and is expected to play a major role in e-business in the near future. WTLS works by creating a secure confidential communication pipe between two entities by the use of encryption and digital certificates exchanged between the two entities that wish to communicate (normally a mobile phone and a WAP Server).

The underlying *Record Protocol* (RP) is a layered protocol that accepts raw data to be transmitted from the upper layer protocols. RP compresses and encrypts the data to ensure data integrity and authentication. RP is also responsible for decrypting and decompressing data it receives and verifying that it hasn't been altered. The Record Protocol is subdivided into four protocol clients (see Figure 9-13).

WTLS Handshake Protocol

The handshake (see Figure 9-14) is where all the security parameters such as protocol version, cryptographic algorithms, and the method of authentication and key techniques are established between the two parties. The handshake process starts with the client initiating a "Hello" message to the server, announcing that it wishes to communicate. In a successful session, the server will respond back with an acknowledgment "Hello." During these greetings, the two parties are agreeing on the session capabilities. The client announces the encryption algorithm that it supports, and the server responds by determining the session properties to be used.

Next, the server sends its certificate key and it requests the client's in return. When the client receives the server hello-done message, it responds by authenticating itself and providing its digital certificate. The client then sends a client key exchange message containing a pre-master secret encrypted with the server's public key, or else it provides the information that both parties need to complete the

Handshake Protocol	Alert Protocol	Application Protocol	Change Cipher Spec Protocol
Record Protocol			

9-13 WTLS internal Architecture.

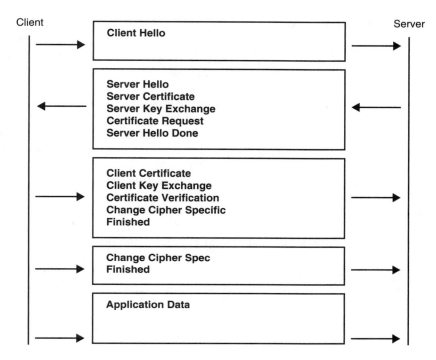

9-14 WTLS Full Handshake Flow Chart.

exchange. The client then sends a finished message reporting that the information transmitted has been verified. At this point the server sends a finished message and a change cipher spec message, which is a means for both parties to agree on the session parameters they will start their session with.

WTLS Alert Protocol

The Alert Protocol is responsible for error handling. If either party detects an error, that party will send an alert containing the error. The messages range from warning, to critical, and fatal. Depending on the message that is transmitted, the session will either be restricted in some way or possibly terminated. The Application Protocol is merely the interface with the upper layers.

WTLS Change Cipher Protocol

The Change Cipher Specific Protocol is the protocol that handles the changing of the cipher. This is established while the security parameters are being negotiated during the handshake. The change cipher notification can be sent by either the client or the server, and sets the current write state of the pending state and the receiver sends the current read state to the pending state.

Pros and Cons of WTLS

Simply put, wireless networks provide less bandwidth, stability, and reliability than their wired counterparts. *Latency,* or dropped packets, contributes to their inefficiency. In addition, wireless devices uniformly have less CPU power, memory, and battery life. Encryption techniques normally consume a great deal of CPU usage, memory, and bandwidth.[23] All these limitations make wireless hard to secure.

WTLS has been instrumental in securing wireless devices such as cellular phones, PDAs, and laptops. It compensates for device shortcomings with respect to power and memory by minimizing protocol overhead, using better compression strategies and more efficient cryptographic algorithms. Specifically, WTLS uses RSA's RC5, or *Elliptical Curve Cryptography* (ECC) to encrypt data, and transport it over wireless links.

The protocol works in conjunction with PKI and wireless cookies to provide a wireless security solution. PKI uses digital certificates to secure application platforms and browsers. Wireless cookies help maintain session management in the same manner as Internet cookies. The combination offers a fairly good wireless security solution. Although it is not the whole solution, WTLS is essential to the security of wireless communications for the following reasons: it provides data integrity, privacy, authentication, and denial-of-service protection for WAP devices; it provides protocol independence; and it allows developers to implement new technologies without compromising security functionality.

WTLS Vulnerabilities

As a reasonably secure solution, *WTLS still must be regarded as vulnerable, particularly in protocol translation.* When a packet using WTLS moves through the air and hits the WAP gateway, it can't traverse the wire until it has been converted to SSL or TLS. During conversion, there is a short period (fractions of a second) when the message is not encrypted, and therefore susceptible to eavesdropping or packet sniffing. Critics view this as a major vulnerability. Some companies outsource this service to ensure that the WAP gateway is external.

Others downplay this vulnerability by pointing out that a hacker would have to have access to the carriers gateway, have root access to that machine, and do a core dump at exactly the right millisecond. The argument for improbability is perhaps not sufficient, so long as the possibility exists unchallenged and the potential consequences are substantial.

WTLS also has some exposure in that wireless devices lack robust processing power. Methods of encryption must stay relatively low-level to accommodate the power and speed constraints imposed by devices. When cellular phones and PDA devices are able to use more advanced chip technology and increase battery and performance, the level of security will automatically increase. Today if a cellular phone has to encrypt and decrypt a 128-bit message, the user will notice a substantial degradation in performance, and may be unable to complete the transaction.

Implementations of WTLS

Several commercial firms have implemented WTLS:

3ui.com

Universal Ubiquitous Unfettered Internet has developed and is distributing a WTLS implementation for the Kennel open source WAP gateway,[24] launched in July 1999 by Wapiti Ltd. The most recent version of the Kennel gateway has been certified by the WAP Forum as the first WAP 1.1 open source gateway. This implementation supports authentication, confidentiality, and integrity using the algorithms in Table 9-5.

Note that the 3ui open source version of WTLS does not include the RC5 block cipher and the RSA key exchange algorithms as they have been patented by RSA. If users wish to implement these encryption technologies, they will have to purchase the commercial version of the software.

Motorola

Motorola, Inc., supports the WAP environment with two WAP server configurations —a Basic version and an Enhanced version. Both support Class I and Class II Security (including Certificate Key Manager). The WAP server will also support bulk cipher and Keyed MAC algorithms using Diffie-Hellman, RSA, and Elliptic Curve Key Exchange algorithms.[26]

RSA Security

RSA security has made significant contributions to the WAP architecture and currently provides a product for WTLS development called RSA BSAFE WTLS-C. RSA BSAFE WTLS-C helps developers add cryptographic and certificate management features to wireless applications, devices, and systems through easy-to-use APIs. In conjunction with RSA BSAFE SSL-C, developers can create entire WAP applications from Web server, through the WAP gateway to the WAP client. RSA BSAFE WTLS-C is compatible with the major WAP gateways and supports both X.509 and WTLS certificates.[27]

Table 9-5 Algorithms used in 3ui's Implementation

Features	Algorithms
Key Exchange Suites	- RSA_anon (RSA key exchange without authentication)
	- DH_anon (Diffie-Hellman key exchange without authentication)
Bulk Encryption Algorithms	- RC5_CBC
	- DES_CBC
Keyed MAC Algorithm	- SHA

Source: 3ui.com

Baltimore Technologies

Baltimore Technologies is also supporting the WAP environment and WTLS. Their product, Telepathy *WAP Security Toolkit* (WST), is a software development kit allowing application developers to create secure encrypted sessions between applications. Telepathy WST contains an implementation of WTLS v1.1. Using the SDK, developers will be able to develop secure communications between the WAP device and the gateway. The Telepathy WST API includes fully configurable support for:[25]

- Session caching
- Security renegotiation
- Temporary key reuse
- Dynamic reconfiguration during a session
- Integration into datagram layers defined in the WAP specification (that is, UDP/IP and WDP)

Telepathy WST supports various algorithms to provide authentication, encryption, and integrity, as listed in Table 9-6.

Telepathy WST is available as a set of ANSI C libraries with an object-oriented interface. Telepath WST provides support for the following platforms:

- Win32 (Windows 95/98, Windows NT)
- Sparc Solaris 2.5+
- HP-UX 10.2+
- Linux

Additional Sources

The official specification for the Secure Sockets Layer Protocol (Version 3.0) is available in several formats plus errata from the Netscape Web site at **www.netscape. com/eng/ssl3/**.[28] The Transport Layer Security specification is the proposed standard of the *Internet Engineering Task Force* (IETF). IETF documents may be found from the organizations Web site at **www.ietf.org**.[29] A definitive security

Table 9-6 Algorithms used in Baltimore Technologies Implementation

Features	Algorithms
Key Exchange Suites	- RSA
	- DH
Bulk Encryption Algorithms	- RC5
	- DES
	- Triple DES
	- IDEA
Keyed MAC Algorithm	- SHA-1
	- MD-5

Source: Baltimore Technologies

analysis of the Secure Sockets Layer protocol is that of David Wagner and Bruce Schneier at **www.counterpane.com/ssl.html**.[30] Three cryptographic algorithms of particular importance to the many SSL/TLS implementations are MD5 and SHA hash algorithms and the RSA public key encryption and digital signature algorithm.[29]

Endnotes

[1]Thomas, Stephen, *SSL and TLS Essentials: Securing the Web,* John Wiley & Sons, 2001. An excellent text on the directions and future of SSL and TLS.

[2]http://www.netscape.com

[3]Ibid.

[4]Rescorla, Eric, *SSL and TLS, Designing and Building Secure Systems*, Addison Wesley, 2001, Figure 2.3, p 48. Rescorla's work is perhaps the best reference in the field on the nuances of SSL and TLS. SSL has a family tree of variants. It was introduced in 1994 (SSLv1) and first released by Netscape in 1994 (SSLv2). Microsoft introduced its PCT version in 1995 that had authentication only, "rehandshake" and certificate chains. Netscape released SSLv3 in 1995 that included authentication, support for Diffie-Hellman (DH) and Digital Signature Standard (DSS), closure handshake and certificate chaining. Microsoft countered again with STLP in 1996, which added shared secret authentication, datagrams, and some performance optimizations. The IETF (Internet Engineering Task Force) changed the name to TLS for Transport Layer Security (1997–1999) The most contentious change in TLS was the decision to require DH, DSS, and 3DES (triple-DES). The offshoot of this decision is that many implementers have to implement both RSA and DH/DSS to be able to work with all browser versions. The current level is WTLS (1998), which we find in the wireless WAP forum and supports wireless security infrastructure.

[5]Ibid., pp 58–59.

[6]Ibid.

[7]Ibid., pp 50. & ff.

[8]http://www.bxa.doc.gov/. The Bureau of Export Administration has loosened its stranglehold on requiring SSL licenses.

[9]Microsoft Corporation, *Comparison of Internet Explorer 4.0 and Netscape Navigator for Windows 3.1*, March 18, 1999, http://www.microsoft.com/Windows/ie/Info/techdocs/ie4p2compguide.asp.

[10]http://msdn.microsoft.com/library/psdk/secpack/schannel_00c4.htm.

[11]Horak, Ray, *Communications Systems & Networks*, 2nd Ed., M&T Books, 2001, p. 518. There are many standard protocols to move data in the form of datagrams over the Internet. *Point-to-Point* protocol (PPP) is an extension to the *serial line interface protocol* (SLIP). SLIP remains the most basic protocol for handling *Internet Protocol* (IP) packets of information in a serial bit stream across a voice-grade telephone connection. Installed on both the users workstation and the provider's server SLIP forwards packets created by the TCP/IP (the famous Transmission Control Protocol and Internet Protocol) software, which operates at Layer 3 (Network) and Layer 4 (Transport) of the OSI standard reference model. PPP performs the same functions as SLIP. Additionally, it performs fairly sophisticated compression in order to eliminate unused or redundant data in the headers of long sequences of packets in a transmission stream. Further PPP supports multiple native machine and network protocols and supports subnet routing. PPP installed on a telecommuters home PC enables communications with the home office through a router connected to an Ethernet LAN. PPP also supports IP packet communications through the Internet. A very detailed look at PPP may be found in Chapter 10 of Thomas A. Maufer's IP *Fundamentals*, PTR PH, 1999.

[12]Nichols, Randall K., *ICSA Guide To Cryptography*, McGraw-Hill, 1999, pp. 613–616.

[13]Horak, Op. Cit., pp. 540–541.

[14]Kent, S., and R. Atkinson, *Security Architecture for the Internet Protocol RFC2401*, 11/98, http://www.ietf.org/rfc/rfc2401.txt.

[15]Nichols, Randall K., Daniel J. Ryan, and Julie J.C.H. Ryan, *Defending Your Digital Assets Against Hackers, Crackers, Spies, and Thieves,* McGraw-Hill, 2000.

[16]A good discussion of practical VPNs is found in Chapter 11 and Appendix G of Nichols, Ryan, and Ryan, Op. Cit.

[17]F-Secure Corporation, *Cryptography and Data Security Toolkit, Users and Administration Guide*, May 7, 1997, www.F-Secure.com.

[18]F-Secure Corporation, *F-Secure Releases Secure Access Solution for Windows Servers*, 1/30/01, http://news/2000/news_2001013000.shtml.

[19]See www.F-Secure.com.

[20]Goldberg, Ian, *Top Gun ssh for PalmOS*, http://www.ai/~iang/TGssh/.

[21]mov Software, *sshce*, 10/2/00, http://www.movsoftware.com/sshce.htm.

[22]Nichols, Professor Randall K., RSA 2001 Presentation, *Advances In Wireless Security with ASICs*, April 10, 2001.

[23]Information on the 3ui WTLS product was obtained from http://www.3ui.com/.

[24]Motorola, *Motorola and WAP*, http://www.motorola.com/MIMS/ISG/wap/r3tech.htm.

[25]RSA Corporation, *Wireless Transport Layer Security for C*, http://www.rsasecurity. com/products/bsafe/wtlsc.html.

[26]Baltimore Technologies plc, *Telepathy WST*™ *White paper*, 2001, http://www. baltimore.com/library/whitepapers/wsecure.htm.

[27]Freier, Alan O., Philip Karlton, and Paul C. Kocher, *The SSL Protocol Version 3*, Netscape Communications Corporation, March 4, 1996.

[28]Dierks, T., and C. Allen, *The TLS Protocol Version 1.0* [RFC 2246], The Internet Engineering Task Force, January 1999.

[29]Wagner, David, and Bruce Schneier, *Analysis of the SSL 3.0 Protocol*, The Second USENIX Workshop on the Electronic Commerce Proceedings, Usenix Press, November 1996, pp. 29–40.

[30]National Institute of Standards and Technology, Secure Hash Standard [NIST FIPS PUB 180-1] U.S. Department of Commerce, work in progress, 1994–2001; R. Rivest, *The MD5 Message-Digest Algorithm* [RFC 1321] IETF, April 1992; R. Rivest, A. Shamir, and L. Adleman, *A Method for Obtaining Digital Signatures and Public Cryptosystems*, Communications of the ACM, 21(2), pp. 120–126, February 1978.

10

Bluetooth

Bluetooth is a low-cost, low-power, short-range radio link for wireless connectivity between mobile devices and *wireless area networks and local area networks* (WAN/LAN) access points. It includes both a hardware specification and software architecture. Bluetooth operates in the unlicensed 2.4 GHz ISM band, and this fact is both a strength and liability. But because numerous other wireless devices and protocols also operate in this band, Bluetooth has been plagued by interference problems. To solve them, Bluetooth designers turned to frequency-hopping solutions where they encountered another set of problems. Some countries have a narrower ISM band than others, and Bluetooth devices developed to operate in these countries are incompatible with Bluetooth devices elsewhere.

Despite these hurdles, Bluetooth proponents still get giddy with the numerous possibilities Bluetooth offers for mobile applications. In fact, few people would contest the vision. But Bluetooth is off to a bumpy start with incomplete interoperability, high costs, and slow development cycles. That means we've yet to see the breadth of implementation that will test security measures and yield significant experience with the security model. In this chapter we'll look at security provisions based on specifications, architectures, and extrapolations from wireless communications technologies with similar provisions.

Bluetooth has three security modes, the lowest having no security mechanisms, and the highest enforcing authentication, authorization, and encryption at the link-level. The intermediate level enforces authentication and encryption selectively through a mechanism known as the *security manager*. Authentication uses the SAFER+ block cipher, and encryption of data between devices is achieved by an implementation of E_0, a stream cipher. These algorithms are both symmetric, leaving Bluetooth open to the charge of poor security implementation in light of the numerous PKI solutions on the market today. Other security issues to address include spoofing and denial of service due to intentional jamming or passive interference, especially from microwave devices as simple as microwave ovens.

Bluetooth Basic Specifications

Bluetooth supports voice and data communication and point-to-point or point-to-multipoint transmissions. The specification is ambitious. It describes a small-footprint technology that optimizes the usage model of all mobile devices, and provides for

- Global usage
- Voice and data handling
- The ability to establish ad hoc connections and networks
- The ability to withstand interference from other sources in open band
- Negligible power consumption in comparison to other devices for similar use
- An open interface standard
- Competitively low cost of all units, as compared to non-Bluetooth correspondents.[1]

Bluetooth Technology

The Bluetooth radio is built into a small microchip operating in the 2.4 GHz band. The chip has two power levels: a lower level that covers the personal area within a reasonable sized room and a higher level that can cover the medium range space in a home or shop. Software controls and identity coding built into each microchip are used to limit communication strictly to those units preset by their owners.[2] The microchip can be included in a variety of products. The Bluetooth SIG proposes currently five usage models:

- **A three-in-one phone**   The cellular phone acts as a portable phone at home, a mobile phone when traveling, and a walkie-talkie when in range of another Bluetooth-enabled phone.[3]
- **An Internet bridge**   The mobile computer can surf the Internet anywhere, regardless of whether the user is connected through a wireless modem or landline.[4]
- **A platform for interactive conferencing**   Electronically exchange documents with selected participants without any wired connections.[5]
- **The ultimate headset**   Connect your wireless headset to your mobile phone, mobile computer, or any wired connection to keep your hands free for more important tasks when at the office or in your car.[6]
- **An automatic synchronizer**   Automatically synchronize data between desktops, laptops, cellular phones, and PDAs. The user can change calendar or contact information in any one device and all communicating devices will automatically update.[7]

Beyond the Bluetooth SIG, proponents are invoking a lot of other potential uses for Bluetooth. They are practical but enticing. For example, utility meter readers might be able to drive down the street and securely register readings from each subscribed address on a Bluetooth-enabled PDA.[8]

Bluetooth Specification Development

Bluetooth takes its name from Harald the Viking, who is known for uniting Denmark and Norway.[9] The Bluetooth *Special Interest Group* (SIG) serves as the governing body of the specification, which is composed of industry leaders in communications and many other technical fields. Ericsson, Intel, Nokia, and Toshiba originally formed the SIG in 1998.[10] Currently, there are over 2100 members of the SIG.[11] In 1999, the SIG released version 1.0 of the Bluetooth specification and expects to release version 2.0 of the Bluetooth specification in late 2001 (see Figure 10-1 for milestones). The progression of information interchange has been:

Point-to-Point→LAN→Internet→Ubiquitous Connectivity.[12]

Bluetooth is one of many technologies promising ubiquitous connectivity. Once described as a connect-without-cables technology in keeping with its early design mission (1.0A and 1.0B), Bluetooth has seen its utility steadily expanded. It is now being positioned as a contender in the *Personal Area Network* (PAN) arena, alongside heavyweights like the HomeRF[13] and 802.11b (also known as Wi-Fi)[14] specifications. *Wireless LAN* (WLAN) standards are aimed at different markets and have different security goals. (See Table 10-1 for a comparison of systems.)

With speeds reaching 10 Mbps, Bluetooth is suitable for video and multimedia signals. Bluetooth specifications released in the late 1990s focused primarily on data/voice transmission for always-on digital appliances, so support for applications

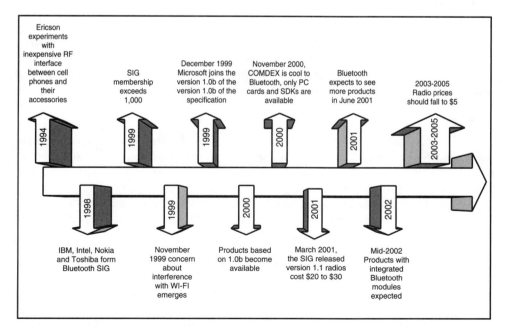

10-1 Important Timelines in the Bluetooth Evolution Process. (Source: ZDNET, eweek)

Table 10-1 Selected Wireless Standard Compared

	IEEE 802.11b	HomeRF	Bluetooth
Speed	11 Mbps	1, 2, 10 Mbps	30–400 Kbps
Use	Office or campus LAN	Home office, house, and yard	Personal area network
Types of terminals	Add-on to notebook, desktop PC, palm device, Internet gateway	Add-on to notebook, desktop PC, modem, phone, mobile device, Internet gateway	Built into notebook, cell phone, palm device, pager, appliance, car
Typical configuration	Multiple clients per access point	Point-to-point or multiple devices per access point	Point-to-point or multiple devices per access point
Range	50–300 feet	150 feet	30 feet
Frequency sharing	Direct sequence spread spectrum	Wideband frequency hopping	Narrowband frequency hopping
Backers	Cisco, Lucent, 3Com, WECA consortium	Apple, Compaq, Dell, HomeRF Working Group, Intel, Motorola, Proxim	Bluetooth Special Interest Group, Ericsson, Motorola, Nokia
Status	Shipping	In development	In development
URL	www.wirelessethernet.com	www.homerf.org	www.bluetooth.com

(Courtesy of: www.zdnet.com)

has been somewhat late in coming. This omission led the Bluetooth SIG to organize committees to build various application profiles for the next version in order to help Bluetooth devices communicate with one another and coexist with other wireless protocols.[15]

Design Decisions

One of Bluetooth's design strengths is low cost. If it's going to work as a cable replacement technology, it cannot be much more expensive than the cable it aims to replace.[16] The Bluetooth low-cost system solution consists of hardware, software, and interoperability requirements,[17] implemented in tiny, inexpensive, short-range transceivers in currently available mobile devices, either embedded directly into existing component boards or added to an adapter device (such as a PC card inserted into a notebook computer).[18]

The decision to operate Bluetooth over the ISM band was made to sidestep any need to obtain a spectrum license from each country, and to allow Bluetooth-enabled devices to operate globally. However, this objective has not been fully met. Some countries have placed limitations on the frequency range of the ISM band and have denied free unlicensed access to the full band. Bluetooth devices must now be made with a variety of frequency specifications, resulting in devices of different frequencies that can't talk to each other, and thereby delivering a serious blow to the goal of ubiquity. The Bluetooth SIG has been actively pursuing governments in dissenting countries to harmonize the usage of ISM band and prevent embarrassing incompatibilities among devices.

Piconets

The basic Bluetooth network is called a *piconet.* Piconets are arbitrary collections of Bluetooth-enabled devices physically close enough to be able to communicate and exchange information.[19] Bluetooth technology enables many types of wireless devices to communicate with one another, as well as with devices on a wired network. An example of Bluetooth's use would be the transmission of information from a *Personal Digital Assistant* (PDA) to a cellular phone. Bluetooth makes this possible by using radio waves in the 2.4-GHz spectrum to transmit the data. Using radio waves allows Bluetooth to send and receive both voice and data transmissions in real-time. This frequency is unregulated worldwide, which is particularly advantageous to a new technology. Bluetooth communications can be conducted individually (point-to-point) or en masse (point-to-multipoint). A multipoint transmission using this technology is limited to eight devices, which, as a group, are called a piconet.[20] Figure 10-2 provides an example of a Bluetooth piconet, in which multiple enabled devices connect with each other and a corporate LAN via a Bluetooth hub. Multiple piconets can be combined into *scatternets* (groups of piconets) to increase the scope of Bluetooth networks.[21]

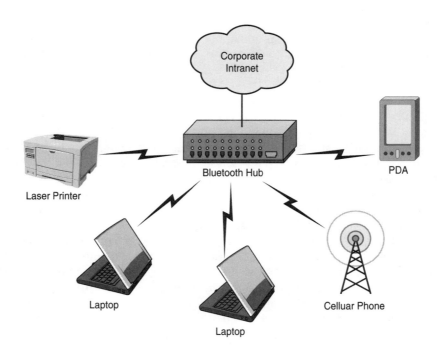

10-2 Sample Bluetooth Piconet.[25]

Bluetooth Security Architecture

The Bluetooth security architecture, as specified by its SIG, includes provisions for authentication and encryption. All security functions are performed at the link level. Four items are needed to establish the security of a Bluetooth transmission: a 48-bit unique device address, a 128-bit pseudo-random private key used for authentication, an 8-128 bit private key used for encryption, and a 128-bit pseudo random number generated by the device.[22] The Bluetooth specification also details three security modes the protocol can operate under:

Mode 1—Non-secure   No security is enforced by the protocol.

Mode 2—Service-level enforced security   Security is enforced after channel setup.

Mode 3—Link level enforced security   Security is enforced prior to channel setup.

Note that a Bluetooth device can operate in only one security mode at a time. A device operating in Mode 3 will not authenticate with other devices on a selective basis but will authenticate all devices that attempt to communicate with it.[23]

In addition to the three security modes, Bluetooth allows two levels of trust—trusted and untrusted—and three levels of service security. Trusted devices are defined as having a fixed relationship and thus, full access to all services. Untrusted devices do not maintain permanent relationships or are labeled untrusted, resulting in restricted service access[24] (see Figure 10-3).

The weaknesses in Bluetooth's security architecture affect the confidentiality, authentication, availability, non-repudiation, and privacy of a transmission. Confidentiality is always a concern with open-air transmissions and Bluetooth does not require encryption of all transmissions. In many cases this is left to the application layer.

Legacy applications that do not offer encryption capabilities require a third-party application to keep transmissions confidential. This lack of required encryption potentially leaves user transmissions in the clear. One published weakness of Bluetooth describes a situation where an attacker could obtain the encryption key between two devices. And once the key is compromised, the attacker could eavesdrop on transmissions, masquerade as one of the users, or insert false communications into the data stream.[26]

Authentication is a problem with Bluetooth because devices are authenticated, not users. A stolen device could be used in a malicious way by an attacker if the user did not configure device security (for example, use a complex PIN). As Bluetooth appears to be a candidate for communications involving payments, device theft appears to be a fundamental weakness. If the device is the only item authenticated, non-repudiation may become an issue. If a thief uses a stolen device to make a purchase from a vending machine with no surveillance equipment (for example, a video camera), the device's owner could successfully argue it was not the owner making the purchase. Without user/owner verification, communications cannot be guaranteed to be authentic.

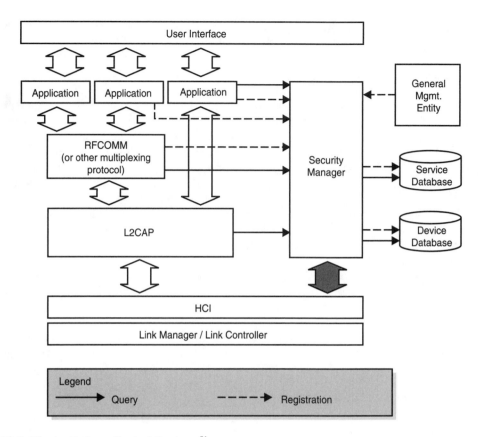

10-3 Bluetooth Security Architecture.[31]

The fact that Bluetooth operates in an unregulated air space may become an availability weakness. Bluetooth and 802.11b devices can cause each other performance degradation when operated in close proximity. Tests by Symbol Technologies Inc. and the Toshiba Corporation confirmed that while the two can coexist in a location, performance loss increases if the two are within three meters of each other.[27] *If Bluetooth and 802.11b are within a half meter, the effect can be significant.*[28] The conflict is a result of both technologies operating within the 2.4-GHz spectrum. Bluetooth uses frequency-hopping at a rate of 1600 hops/sec to reduce interference from other devices operating in the 2.4-GHz spectrum and the possibility of eavesdropping. This greatly reduces interference effects on Bluetooth devices, but does not eliminate them.

Finally, the privacy of transmissions is an issue for Bluetooth users. Every Bluetooth device has a unique identifier. When a device interacts with, or moves into the range of, a Bluetooth network, that identifier can be logged. If these log databases were merged, a record of the device's movements would be created. If someone combined that database with the warranty records for the devices, a record of the owner's movements could be logged. This idea may seem far-fetched, but the same is being done for the online and home shopping habits of computer users.

Scatternets

When two devices establish a Bluetooth link, one acts in the role of master and the other in the role of slave. The master does not enjoy special privileges or authority; instead it determines the frequency-hopping pattern for communications between devices. A master may communicate with multiple slaves—as many as 7 active slaves and up to 255 parked slaves. (Bluetooth components operate in four modes: active, sniff, hold, or park. Each mode operates at a different level of activity and power consumption, with park mode being the lowest level of each.)

Slaves communicating with a particular master constitute the piconet on the fly. The glue that binds piconets is that all its devices are synchronized. Therefore, even if additional devices are in piconet proximity, they must be communicating with a master to become part of it.[29]

If multiple piconets cover the same area, a unit can participate in two or more by applying time multiplexing, as long as channels are kept separate and phases are calibrated. A Bluetooth unit can act as a slave in several piconets, but as a master in only one piconet.

A set of Bluetooth piconets is called a scatternet, which has the interesting property of being able to form without any integration of the piconets involved (see Figure 10-4).[30]

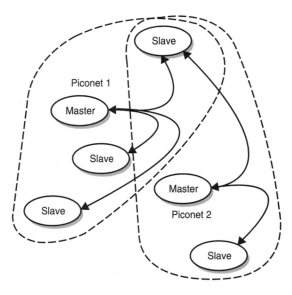

10-4 Scatternet Example. (Source: William H. Tranter, et al., *Wireless Personal Communications: Bluetooth and Other Technologies*)[33]

The Bluetooth stack

Bluetooth's uniqueness stems from its architecture. Although Bluetooth does not exactly match the *Open System Interconnection* (OSI) model, comparing the two helps highlight the division of responsibility in the Bluetooth stack[32] (see Figure 10-5).

- **Physical Layer**   Responsible for electrical interference to the communications media, including modulation and channel coding. Bluetooth carries out this function through its radio and baseband protocols.
- **Data Link Layer**   Provides transmission, framing, and error control over a particular link. In Bluetooth, this function is handled by the link controller protocol, which covers the task and control end of the baseband, including error checking and correction.
- **Network Layer**   Controls data transfer across the network, independent of the media and network topology. Under the Bluetooth protocol, the higher end of the link controller and part of the *Link Manager* (LM) handles these responsibilities—setting up and maintaining multiple links.
- **Transport Layer**   Controls multiplexing of data transferred across the network to the level provided by the application, and thus overlaps with the high end of the LM and *Host Controller Interface* (HCI), which provides the actual transport mechanisms.
- **Session Layer**   Supplies management and data flow control services, which are covered by *Logical Link Control and Adaptation Protocol* (L2CAP) and the lower ends of RFCOMM/SDP.

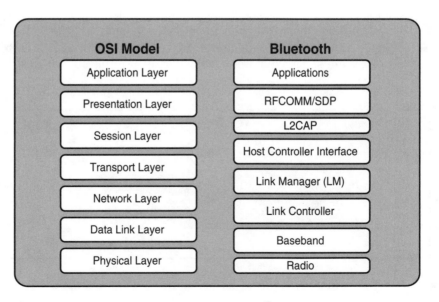

10-5 OSI Reference Model and Bluetooth Architecture.[43]

- **Presentation Layer**   Provides a common representation for Application Layer data by adding service structure to the units of data, which is the main task of the RFCOMM/SDP.
- **Application Layer**   Responsible for managing communications between host applications.[34]

Security Functions at the Baseband Layer

Baseband sits above the radio in the Bluetooth stack and governs the physical RF link between Bluetooth units in a piconet, including modulation, de-modulation, synchronization, and transmission.[35,36] Modulation is used to maximize the number of digital bits carried by one cycle of the bandwidth, thus making better economy of available bandwidth. Baseband also manages physical channels, frequency-hopping, packet creation, error encoding and correction, encryption/decryption, power control, and paging and inquiry for Bluetooth devices.[37] (Inquiry and paging procedures ensure that two different devices can synchronize their transmission-hopping frequency and clock.[38]) All baseband data packets can be provided with a level of error correction and encrypted for privacy.[39]

Of all responsibilities held by the baseband, two directly affect security: frequency-hopping and encryption. Bluetooth uses frequency hopping on a transmission to reduce interference and power consumption while providing security[40] (see Figure 10-6). Frequency-hopping was first developed to secure military communications,[41] but in the Bluetooth context it actually provides less security due to the openness of the ad hoc networking model. It is also ineffective in preventing denial-of-service attacks, which can be accomplished by flooding the ISM band with interference.[42]

Encryption is Bluetooth's way of managing interception. Since Bluetooth provides peer-to-peer communications over the air, it is possible for others to listen in on conversations or tap into the data interchange. To protect the data interchange, security measures are specified at both the link and the application layers.[44] Even

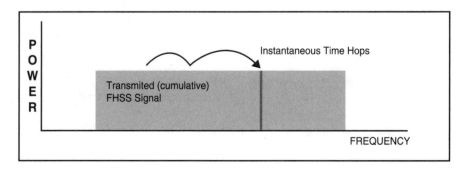

10-6 Frequency Hopping Spread Spectrum (FHSS). (Source: Virginia Polytechnic Institute)[43]

so, Bluetooth interchanges are not considered truly secure. Although Bluetooth provides for authentication of devices and encryption of data transferred between devices, its cryptographic implementations have come under criticism.

Security Functions of the Service Discovery Protocol

Service Discovery Protocol (SDP) is the mechanism whereby Bluetooth devices discover which services are available and how to access them for subscriber connection.[45] It's a simple protocol with minimal requirements on the underlying transport. SDP uses a request/response model where each transaction consists of one request PDU and one response PDU, but can't guarantee that a series of requests will return responses in the same order requests were issued.[46]

The privacy promise of SDP is that the protocol will let device owners decide just how available they want to be. Managing availability protects users from unwanted squawking and also prevents every stranger with a compatible PDA from surfing through your personal files while your own PDA sits in your pocket. Right now it looks like SDP does provide reasonable availability management, but doesn't protect vulnerable access points in enterprise environments.

Figure 10-7 shows how a WLAN can be configured to avert attacks. A Bluetooth device may well sit between laptops and servers, providing connectivity to the access point and thereby a doorway to the corporate intranet and the Internet. It is perfectly possible that a compromised wired network can provide attacker access to a Bluetooth network, and vice-versa.

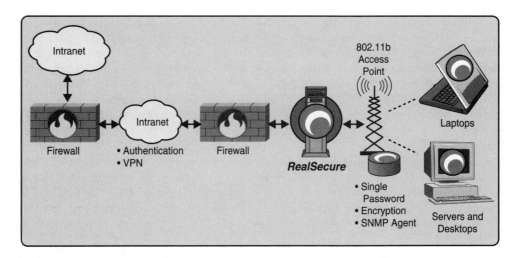

10-7 Wireless LAN Configuration. (Source: Internet Security Systems)

Table 10-2 International Bluetooth Frequency Allocations

Geography	Regulatory Range	RF Channels
U.S./Europe/Most Other Countries	2.400–2.4836 GHz	f=2.402 + k MHz, k=0 . . . 78
Spain	2.445–2.475 GHz	f=2.449 + k MHz, k=0 . . . 22
France	2.4465–2.4835 GHz	f=2.454 + k MHz, k=0 . . . 33*

*Most references show France allocating 23 channels in the ISM band for Bluetooth.

Security Functions at the Link Layer

Piconets are examples of ad hoc, publicly available networks, created spontaneously when proximate Bluetooth devices go through the process of discovering one another and mutually verifying identities. By design, Bluetooth presents a bare minimum of obstacles to ad hoc networking in order to promote widespread use of *personal area networks* (PANs). The IEEE defines PANs as wireless connectivity for fixed, portable, and moving devices that fall within a personal operating space extending 10 meters in all directions.[47] Targeted devices include the small and very portable (cellular phones, pagers, PDAs, headsets, microphones, and bar code readers) and also those that may now be linked to their environment by one or more cables (PCs, printers, speakers, and displays).

Like many forms of wireless transmission, Bluetooth's outgoing broadcasts can be intercepted. Incoming communications can be falsified or *spoofed*. The specification contains two security modes at the link level to guard against such intrusions, but because Bluetooth actively seeks to facilitate the creation of ad hoc networks, implementation of these modes must remain flexible enough to provide device security while not impeding the basic functionality of the system.

Within these considerable constraints, what forms of security can Bluetooth deliver? One previously mentioned is frequency-hopping within the 2.4GHz ISM frequency band. The initiating device, or master, determines the pseudo-random hopping scheme to be used for the duration of the piconet, enabling all participating devices to change to the same frequencies at the same instant in time. This scheme works both to prevent interference from other devices on the same frequencies—such as WLANs and microwave ovens—and to block illicit listening devices (those not part of the piconet) from obtaining any significant part of the data stream on an uninterrupted basis.

Bluetooth devices entering the network are authenticated via a series of challenge-response communications. Each device serves to verify another. This provision minimizes the possibility of spoofing, or impersonating another valid device. It discourages illicit access to data or system functions. Additionally, the highly limited range of Bluetooth devices provides some level of security against eavesdropping, because attack devices are rarely in range.

Once device identities have been established and mutually agreed upon through one or more authentications, the master unit in the piconet has the option of requiring encrypted communications. If it does, the master unit will create and issue to participating devices a temporary key then used as a current link key for all the devices on the given net.

Frequency-Hopping

To avoid interference from the other devices nearby (including other Bluetooth piconets that may be operating within the vicinity), Bluetooth alters the broadcast frequency in a pseudo-random way at a rate of 1,600 times per second, or once every 0.625 ms. Effective transmission is premised on the fact that interference is usually present in only a limited portion of the available range, making long odds against two sequential packets both being blocked. Any packets that are not successfully delivered will be retransmitted on another frequency within the range, and the number of retransmissions will be minor compared to the volume of the entire data stream.

Using its internal clock, the master unit determines the hopping scheme to be used for the duration of the piconet. Within each Bluetooth device is an always-on, always-running 28-bit clock operating at a rate of 3.2 kHz. (This is double the normal Bluetooth hop rate of 1,600 hops/sec and has an accuracy rate of [20ppm.])[48] This clock determines when a device can or cannot transmit, and when it can or cannot receive transmissions.

When the piconet is first formed or joined, slave devices determine the value of the master clock. Using the difference between that clock and their own as an offset, they can apply the algorithm in the Bluetooth *Frequency Selection Module* (FSM) to calculate the net's frequency-hopping sequence and change frequencies accordingly, always in synch with the master unit (see Figure 10-8). Depending on the country of use, the FSM within the device will be set to operate in a hopping mode for either 23 or 79 channels.

A piconet's channel hopping sequence is a function of the 28 least significant bits of the master device's address, the clock timing information, and the country mode (either a 0 or 1). All devices synch to the frequency determined. This frequency changes every two ticks of the clock, so the 3.2 kHz clock results in a 1.6 kHz, or 1,600 per second, rate of change. To further bind the units in operation on a particular piconet, each device transmitting on a selected frequency first precedes the packet with a channel access code also generated from the address of the master unit. Other member units on that same net will accept only transmissions properly identified as belonging to the piconet in use.

Channel Establishment

When two Bluetooth devices come within range of each other and want to communicate, the link manager requests establishment of a link-level connection. For devices operating in security mode 1 or 3, a *Logical Link Control and Adaptation Layer* (L2CAP) connection is created without further queries and channel establishment is complete. Devices in security mode 2, however, must undergo another set of steps. The security database is queried to see if the device is authorized for ac-

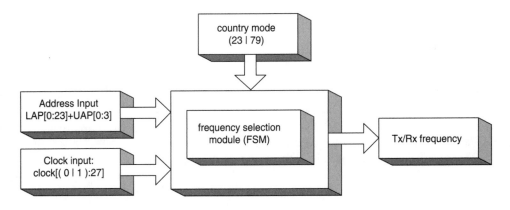

10-8 Frequency Selection Module (FSM). (Courtesy: Miller and Bisdikran)

cess. If not, the device is rejected and the process ends. If so, the device is granted access and then categorized as requiring or not requiring authentication. Where no authentication is needed, an L2CAP connection is established. Otherwise devices are authenticated, and encryption may or may not be initialized. The L2CAP connection follows completion of these two steps. Figure 10-8, shown in the next section, illustrates channel establishment procedure for all three-security modes.

Security Manager

Bluetooth Security policies are administered by exchanging queries with the security manager.

Figure 10-9 shows how the security manager interfaces with the *Host Controller Interface* (HCI), *Logical Link Control and Adaptation Layer* (L2CAP), *Radio Frequency Communication Protocol* (RFCOMM), applications, user interface, and the service and device databases.

The security manager performs the following functions:

- Stores security-related service information.
- Stores security-related device information.
- Answers access requests by protocol implementations or applications.
- Enforces authentication and/or encryption before connecting to the application.
- Initiates or processes input from *External Security Control Entities* (ECSEs), such as device users or applications, to set up trusted relationships on the device level.
- Initiates pairing and query PIN entries by the user. PIN may also be affected by an application.[50]
- Answers access requests from protocol layers.
- Answers HCI queries on whether to apply authentication and/or encryption to a connection.[51]

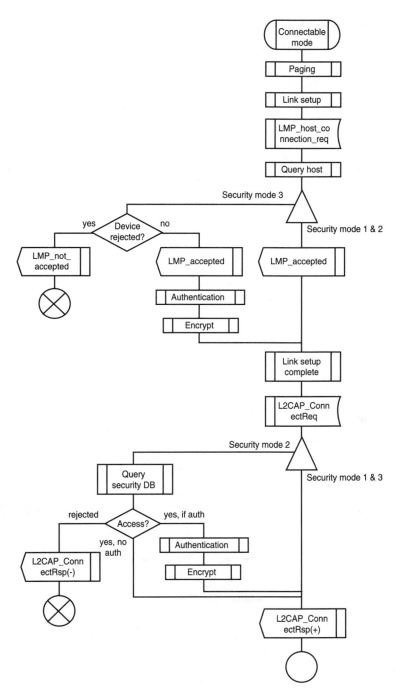

10-9 Illustration of Channel Establishment using different security modes. (Source: Bluetooth Specification 1.1—Generic Access Profile)

Bluetooth lets us set security levels for both devices and services. The security manager administers the databases that contain device and service information. Security is enforced when protocol or service access is requested. The security manager then queries the service or protocol to see whether authentication or authorization is required; if so, it performs these checks. It then checks to see if encryption is required; if so, it verifies that the necessary link key is available and starts encryption. At any point in this process (see Figures 10-10 and 10-11), if the requirements are not met, the security manager denies access.

Device classification is split into three categories and two levels of trust:

Trusted Devices   Devices that have been previously authenticated and are marked in the database as trusted. They enjoy a fixed relationship with full access to services for which the trust relationship has been set.

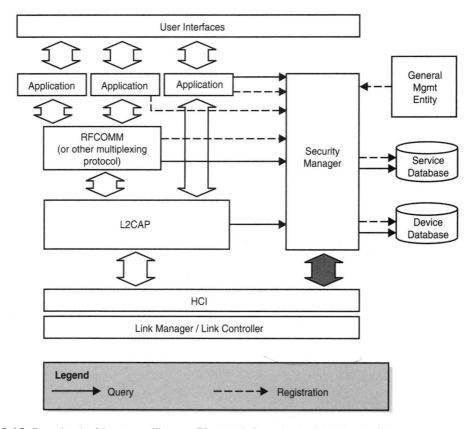

10-10 Security Architecture. (Source: Bluetooth Security Architecture 1.0)

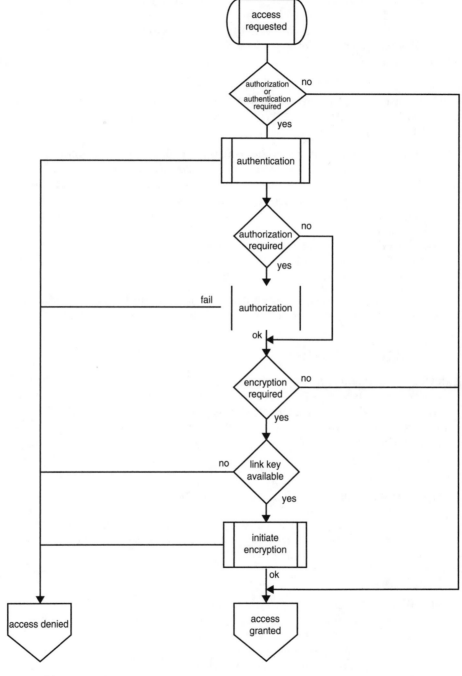

10-11 Example flow chart for access check by the security manager. (Source: Bluetooth Security Architecture 1.0)

Untrusted Devices   Devices that have been previously authenticated, but not marked as trusted in the device database. They will have restricted access to services. It is likely that these devices do not have a permanent relationship with the other device.[52]

Untrusted Unknown Devices   Devices that have no security information in the device databases.

In similar fashion, the service database holds information as to whether authentication, authorization, and/or encryption are required for access. Services are categorized three ways:

Authentication and Authorization Required   Services grant automatic access only to devices that have been previously authenticated and for which a secret key, also stored in the service database, has already been exchanged. Manual authorization is also possible with the use of a PIN.

Authentication Required   Services may be accessed by any device that can be authenticated.

Open Services   Services that require neither authentication nor authorization. An example of an open service is a *virtual business card* (vCard) or other publicly available information.

Default settings for services are authentication and authorization for an incoming connection and authentication for an outgoing connection.[53]

Authentication

All devices in a piconet must be properly identified to the other members (Figure 10-12). Slaves as well as masters may perform authentication. Four elements are used in the Bluetooth authentication process: the *device address* (BD_ADDR), two keys (a private authentication and a private encryption key), and a *random number* (RAND) (see Table 10-3).

In *Bluetooth Demystified*, Nathan J. Muller concisely describes initial contact between devices:

> When two Bluetooth devices come within range of each other, the Link Manager entity in each discovers the other. Peer-to-peer communication between Link Managers occurs through messages exchanged via the *Link Manager Protocol* (LMP). These messages perform link setup, including security mechanisms like authentication and encryption keys, and the control and negotiation of base-band packet sizes. Through this message exchange, LMP also controls the power modes and duty cycles of the Bluetooth radio devices, and the connection states of Bluetooth units in a piconet.[54]

Link Managers exchange messages in the form of *packet data units* (PDUs)—the network-level communications used between devices. PDU communication takes precedence on the network over user data, but can still be delayed by interference and the resulting retransmissions. In the case of delayed transmissions, any device that has failed to communicate with others within a 30-second timeout period is simply dropped.

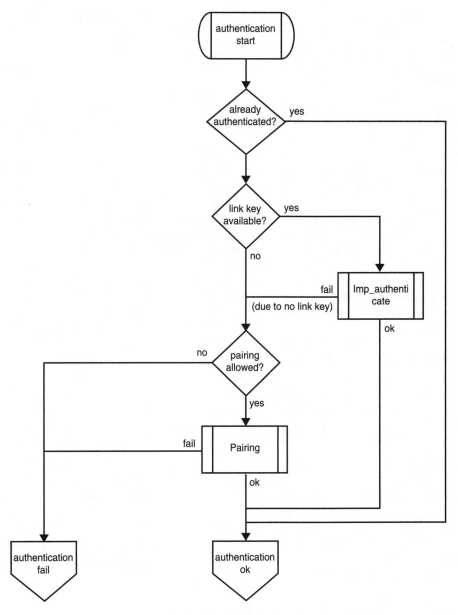

10-12 Example flow chart for authentication procedure. (Source: Bluetooth Specification 1.1)

Table 10-3 Entities Used in Authentication and Encryption Procedure

Entity	Size
BD_ADDR	48 bits
Private user key, authentication	128 bits
Private user key, encryption configurable length (byte-wise)	8–128 bits
RAND	128 bits

Source: Bluetooth specification 1.1

Authentication begins when a verifying unit sends a PDU containing a random number to the claimant (present but unidentified) unit. The claimant returns an answer containing an encrypted version of the random number, its own Bluetooth Device Address, and a secret key. If the response is as expected by the verifying device, the claimant is considered authenticated. Optionally, the devices may then switch roles and the whole process will be repeated in reverse.

When authentication fails, a certain amount of time must pass before another attempt can be made. This prevents an intruder from simply trying a large number of keys in an effort to gain entry to the network. For each failure, the requisite time period increases in length exponentially. Once the timeout period has passed, however, the interval returns to its initial length. Just how long all these intervals are depends on the particular implementation. Possible reasons for authentication failure may include the following:

- The connection has ceased to exist.
- Authentication is not supported on the device contacted.
- No key is available on the targeted device.
- Authentication has been disabled. (It is possible to turn authentication on or off, but not on a per-session basis.)

When no link key can be established between two devices, a pairing process starts where an initialization key is generated and used for authentication. The key is created by entering a common *personal identification number* (PIN) in each of the devices. (Note that the Bluetooth Generic Access Profile, which defines the term's used by a device's user interface, uses the term *Bluetooth passkey* when referring to the PIN.) This generates a temporary key from which the authentication proceeds as thought a link key were present. Certain devices without a user interface may contain a fixed PIN number for this type of process.

Authentication with the SAFER+ Block Cipher

Bluetooth uses a variant of the SAFER+ cipher to perform authentication of any devices present. Originally designed in a joint effort by the Swiss Federal Institute of Technology and Cylink Corporation as a candidate (but not accepted as the global standard) for the *Advanced Encryption Standard* (AES), it has since been released as a public domain model. Chosen as the security algorithm for the Bluetooth model in September 2000,[55] SAFER+ generates 128-bit cipher keys from a 128-bit plaintext input, although when circumstances require a user input number, this length may be shorter or the key may be generated using a seed number from the device-specific PIN contained within the instrument itself. Thorough discussions of the SAFER+ algorithm[56] are available from the *National Institute of Standards* (NIST) Web site at **www.nist.gov/aes** and at the Cylink Corporation Web site at **www.cylink.com**. James L. Massey of Cylink Corporation also provides at the NIST Web site a detailed explanation of the algorithm.[57]

Encryption

Link encryption keys used between Bluetooth devices are divided into three main types: link keys, sub-keys, and the resultant encryption keys, each generated by one of five algorithms within the SAFER+ algorithm set. Devices using encryption must first authenticate themselves to one another using the challenge-response method we've briefly described. Using a link key generated through this authentication as a basis, an encryption mode request is transmitted in one of two forms—either for point-to-point encryption between two particular devices or as an encryption of all broadcast packets for the piconet. The maximum key size used is 128 bits, but depending on country specific laws pertaining to encryption, this key size may be reduced. Once the request is accepted by all of the participating devices, a negotiation of the key size is initiated. When it successfully concludes, encryption is instituted by the broadcast of a start encryption signal.

The process continues with the master device prepared to receive encrypted data, the slave(s) prepared to send and receive encrypted data, and finally the master prepared to send encrypted data.[58] All encryption within the transmission is symmetric.

Encryption Modes

Three different encryption modes are possible if a master key is used:

- No encryption.
- Broadcast traffic is not encrypted, but individually addressed traffic is encrypted.
- Both broadcast and point-to-point traffic is encrypted.

If a unit key or combination key is used, broadcast traffic is not encrypted, but individually addressed traffic may be encrypted.[59] The master and slave must agree which mode will be used. The master sends a request to the slave, which either accepts or rejects the proposed mode. If the initial mode is rejected, then the master can try again, this time proposing a different mode. This process is illustrated in Figure 10-13.

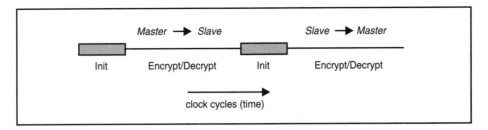

10-13 Overview of the operation of the encryption engine. Between each start of a packet (TX or RX), the LFSRs are reinitialized. (Source: Bluetooth Specification v1.1 baseband specification.)

Key Length Negotiation

Before two devices can start encrypting the traffic between them, they must negotiate an appropriate key length. The key size used to encrypt data varies from 8 to 128 bits. Two reasons are given in the Bluetooth specification for this variability:

- Country-specific regulations, both for export controls and on allowable domestic key length
- To allow for a future security upgrade without the need for a redesign

Further, the user cannot set key size within a specific unit; it must be factory-preset to preclude users from overriding the permitted key size. Each Bluetooth device contains a perimeter defining the maximum allowed key length.

Key length negotiation is similar in structure to encryption mode negotiation (see Figure 10-14). First, the master device sends a suggested key length to the slave. Initially, this value is set as large as possible. If the slave accepts, the encryption process is initiated. However, if the slave can't handle the suggested key length, it sends the master a counter-proposal. Once again, if the new key length suggested is acceptable to the master, encryption begins. Occasionally, two devices are unable to reach agreement. In this case, the negotiation is aborted and encryption cannot be initialized. Figure 10-15 illustrates a successful key length negotiation.

Encryption With the E_0 Stream Cipher

Bluetooth employs a 128-bit symmetric stream cipher called E_0 to protect the confidentiality of data during transport between two or more devices. The cipher is composed of three parts:

- **Payload Key Generator**   Generating the payload key is the first part of enciphering. This process uses four variables: the encryption key, K_C; the Bluetooth device address, *BD_ADDR*; the Clock; and a random number, *RAND*.

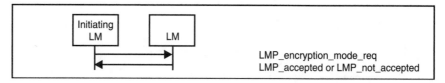

10-14 Negotiation of the encryption mode. (Source: Bluetooth Specification 1.1)

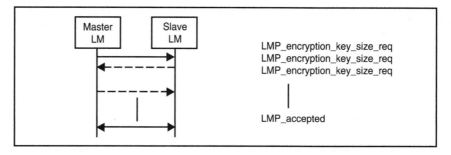

10-15 Key length negotiations with a successful outcome. (Source: Bluetooth Specification v1.1 baseband specification)

- **Key Stream Generator** After the payload key is derived, the key stream generator uses a series of four *Linear Feedback Shift Registers* (LFSRs) to generate the key stream.
- **XOR function** The plaintext is then XORed with the keystream to produce ciphertext (encryption) or the ciphertext is XORed with the keystream to produce plaintext (decryption).

E_0 cipher implementation is described in detail in section 14.3.4 of the Bluetooth specification (version 1.1). The encryption key, K_C, is normally derived from the authentication key during the authentication process using a random number issued by the master before entering the encryption mode. This random number is publicly known.[60] The Bluetooth Address, *BD_ADDR*, can also be easily obtained via an MMI interface or by an inquiry by another Bluetooth device.[61] The random number *RAND* can be derived from a random or pseudo-random process in the Bluetooth unit. It is sent from the master to the slave device during the initialization process, as shown in Figure 10-16.

Each packet payload is encrypted separately.[62] Access codes and packet headers are rarely encrypted.[63] The E_0 stream cipher is susceptible to divide-and-conquer attack in certain circumstances,[64] a vulnerability that has been addressed by the re-synchronization of the cipher after each packet is transmitted or received. (See Figure 10-17.)

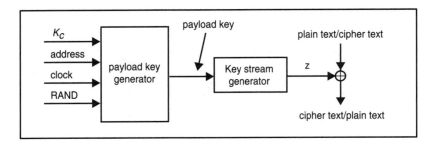

10-16 Stream ciphering for Bluetooth with E_O. (Source: Bluetooth specification v1.1 baseband specification)

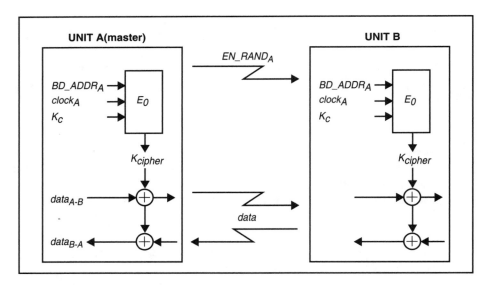

10-17 Functional description of the encryption procedure. (Source: Bluetooth Specification v1.1 baseband specification)

Despite all of these precautions, E_0 still is the subject of criticism. A research paper by Markus Jakobsson and Susanne Wetzel at Lucent Technologies describes two attacks on the cipher itself.[65] One is a reverse-engineering attack of complexity 2^{100}, less than the 2^{128} encryptions needed to brute-force the cipher. The attacker takes a guess at the contents of the three smaller LFSR registers. He or she then reverse engineers the content of the largest register and can determine whether his or her guess was right by comparing the actual output to the generated output.[66]

Another attack requires an attacker to calculate N internal states of the cipher, and sort and store the corresponding output key streams in a database. Observing a certain amount of actual key stream could result in a collision between the actual key stream and a key stream stored in the database.[66] This approach can break the cipher with time and memory complexity of 2.[67]

Other research from the Nokia Research Center in Helsinki, Finland, provides a shorter shortcut on the scale of Θ (2^{64}) steps needed to break the Bluetooth stream cipher, E_0, given an output key stream segment of length Θ (2^{64})[68]

We conclude that reliance on this type of cipher could become a liability, especially in light of the spectacular failure of a similar cipher, A5/1, used in European GSM cellular phones.[69]

Threats to Bluetooth Security

The goal of making the Bluetooth security infrastructure as transparent as possible to the user makes for a rather complex security structure. Complex structures are less secure than simple ones. For example, Bluetooth has no provision for legacy applications to make calls to the security manager; if you want this capability, you'll need an adapter application.[70] Also troubling is the fact that applications can act as *External Security Control Entities* (ECSEs) and set up trust relationships at the device level, presenting an opportunity for exploitation by malicious code.

Jamming

Jamming is intentional interference that prohibits transmission of information. Jamming a Bluetooth signal could be a form of military aggression or defense. In a nonmilitary context, jamming may be illegal, depending on the locality. Australia and Japan already allow limited jamming in establishments such as theaters through government-controlled licenses. The jury is still out in Hong Kong, Malaysia, France, and Italy. The United States and Britain are firmly against commercial jamming devices.[71] In Canada, as in most places, only law enforcement and emergency services can legally interfere with radio signals.[72]

Theoretically, it's possible to jam a Bluetooth signal by overpowering the signal. However, due to the 10-meter restriction for piconets, interfering equipment would have to be quite close to the Bluetooth transmitter/receiver or else be much more powerful than the Bluetooth device.

One place where jamming is being considered a plus is in public areas like restaurants or concert halls. The intention is to prevent the cell phones of customers and patrons from ringing at inappropriate times. Some researchers believe that Bluetooth lets restaurant owners switch customer cell phones from ring to vibrate. Products for this purpose are already on the market.

Jamming Bluetooth signals could be a means to prevent your cell phone from ringing and it could be a means to prevent your competition from advertising. The legalities are fuzzy. Since the Bluetooth signal is a radio signal, there will always be a way to jam it with the proper resources and enough determination.

Bluetooth holes

There are presently four main areas of concern with regard to Bluetooth security:

- Bluetooth device address attacks
- Key management issues
- PIN code attacks
- No support for user authentication

Applications can choose to make a device connectable or discoverable. That's a weakness because it can be exploited to track devices via the unique BD_ADDR device identifier.[73] Device identification can also be spoofed and lead to the disclosure of personal information.[74] A possible attack upon the key management structure was described by Juha Vainio (see Figure 10-18):

> There is also a problem in the unit key scheme. Authentication and encryption are based on the assumption that the link key is the participants' shared secret. All other information used in the procedures is public. Now, suppose that devices A and B use A's unit key as their link key. At the same time (or later on), device C may communicate with device A and use A's unit key as the link key. This means that device B, having obtained A's unit key earlier, can use the unit key with a faked device address to calculate the encryption key and therefore listen to the traffic. It can also authenticate itself to device A as device C and to device C as device A.[75]

Key exchange is also risky because, until a secure link is established between two devices, all exchanges between the two are sent as plaintext—including the variables used to derive keys. The only defense that can be invoked during key derivation is repeated application of PIN code, a cumbersome and weak way to provide security.[76] This problem could be fixed by using public-key cryptography for key exchange, but the required infrastructure would only introduce more complexity to an already complex architecture.

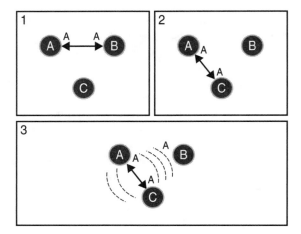

10-18 Spoofing due to Non-Secret Link Key. (Source: Palowireless.com)

Another exposure for Bluetooth is that it does not provide for authentication of users, only for devices. A stolen Bluetooth-equipped phone or PDA can serve as a stepping-stone to other types of attack or, if tied to financial services, allow for fraud. The solution, of course, is to build security in at the applications level, employing more robust symmetric ciphers such as TripleDES, Rjindael, Serpent, Blowfish, RC4, or public-key systems such as Diffie-Hellman or the RSA algorithm, now in the public domain after its patent expired in September 2000.

Unaddressed, security concerns may become Bluetooth's Achilles heel, and at present require users to exercise due diligence when implementing a Bluetooth system.

Summary and Security Assessment

The security challenges of Bluetooth are many and complex. Bluetooth is designed to enable devices to communicate with each other with little or no input from the end user. Automated connectivity combined with the wireless transmission medium all but invites vulnerabilities. The short range of most Bluetooth transmissions is not in itself a safeguard, given that the Bluetooth specification includes allowances for three classes of devices, the most powerful with a range of up to 100 meters.[77]

Markus Jakobsson and Susanne Wetzel have identified three far-reaching security problems in specification 1.0B:[78]

- Susceptibility to an eavesdropping and impersonation attack
- Susceptibility to a location attack
- Susceptibility to an attack on the cipher itself

The specifics are well detailed in their paper, and they're disturbing. The location attack the researchers describe is a scenario wherein the perpetrator exploits device discovery and inquiry to track the movement of a victim carrying a Bluetooth-enabled device.

A more daunting prospect for assessors may be the security breaches that Bluetooth could blow open in a hitherto secure environment. Companies have diligently set up almost impregnable firewalls, but wireless-networking technologies can open a window wide enough for infiltrators to penetrate. The problem is that encryption is generally effective in inverse proportion to the level of convenience in communication. Bluetooth is simply scrambled, spreading its data over numerous different spectrums, rather than encrypted in complex algorithms.[79] Furthermore, Bluetooth security authenticates only the device and not the user. For secure information flow, additional application level security must be deployed to authenticate the user.[80]

One leading expert on electronic surveillance has been quoted as saying "Bluetooth has no security. It just has an illusion of security."[81] That may be overly inflammatory, but from a business standpoint, the fact that security holes were identified prior to any significant hardware production should indicate that this means of communication is not secure. If that's your conclusion, limit application of Bluetooth-enabled devices to those devices that do not contain sensitive, proprietary, or valuable information. Be aware that from a legal standpoint, the location tracking Bluetooth permits could prove to be an invasion of privacy that incurs major liability for companies with Bluetooth-enabled devices in their organization.

Many of the problems we've examined will naturally abate with experience. Each decision to implement has to be based upon the state of the art at the time of implementation. Bluetooth proponents believe that once basic problems have been corrected, more sophisticated security methods may be implemented on the upper levels. The security specification itself only considers generic threats to wireless transmission, and more functional security has to be built above it.[82]

Endnotes

[1]Johnson Consulting, http://www.abc.se/~m10183/bluet00.htm, last accessed on June 2, 2001.

[2]Bluetooth Special Interest Group, The Official Bluetooth Web site, http://www.bluetooth.com/developer/specification/overview.asp, Accessed June 2, 2001.

[3]Bluetooth Special Interest Group, The Official Bluetooth Web site, http://www.bluetooth.com/bluetoothguide/models/two_in_one.asp, Accessed June 2, 2001.

[4]Bluetooth Special Interest Group, The Official Bluetooth Web site, http://www.bluetooth.com/bluetoothguide/models/internet.asp, Accessed June 2, 2001.

[5]Bluetooth Special Interest Group, The Official Bluetooth Web site, http://www.bluetooth.com/bluetoothguide/models/interactive.asp, Accessed June 2, 2001.

[6]Bluetooth Special Interest Group, The Official Bluetooth Web site, http://www.bluetooth.com/bluetoothguide/models/ultimate.asp, Accessed June 2, 2001.

[7]Bluetooth Special Interest Group, The Official Bluetooth Web site, http://www.bluetooth.com/bluetoothguide/models/automatic.asp, Accessed June 2, 2001.

[8]Held, Gil, *Data Over Wireless Networks: Bluetooth, WAP & Wireless LANs*, McGraw-Hill, 2001, p .212.

[9]Armstrong, Illena. "Plugging the holes in Bluetooth." *SC* Magazine, February 2001, pp. 23–40.

[10]Telefonaktiebolaget LM Ericsson. Bluetooth History, March 26, 2001, http://bluetooth.ericsson.se/companyove/history-bl/.

[11]Bluetooth SIG. Bluetooth Special Interest Group, March 26, 2001, http://www.bluetooth.com/sig/sig/sig.asp.

[12]Siep, Tom, *An IEEE Guide: How to find what you need in the Bluetooth Spec*, The Institute of Electrical and Electronics Engineers, Inc., 3 Park Avenue, New York, NY 10014-5997, p. 19.

[13]http://www.homerf.org/. HomeRF is one of the new wireless networking technologies that appears to be ideally suited to the new broadband-enabled home. With the release of HomeRF version 2.0, HomeRF can provide eight simultaneous toll-quality voice connections, eight prioritized streaming media sessions and multiple Internet and network resource connections of up to 10 Mbps. It is a single specification that allows PCs, peripherals, cordless phones, and other consumer electronic devices to communicate with each other. With its unique ability to blend toll-quality voice, data, and streaming media simultaneously, it is the only home networking solution capable of meeting the growing demand of distributing high quality digital voice, music, and video. The voice quality not only exceeds that of digital cell phones, but also is nearly identical to that of the standard telephone. This technology allows for videoconferencing, MPEG4 video distribution, and even remote Dolby Surround speakers all using the same wireless standard in the same location. Further, it provides this ability at

low cost, size and power consumption restraints, while still providing for security and interference immunity, without requiring any additional home wiring. From every angle, one can see that HomeRF was designed from the start with the consumer in mind. This could explain why HomeRF products account for 95 percent of the wireless home networking devices sold today.

Although possibly not suited for enterprise-wide or even campus-wide implementation, first generation HomeRF has a transmission range of about 150 feet and the ability to pass through walls. This not only allows for most any house-wide networking, but would also be suitable for office-wide implantation within an enterprise without adding to or even using currently available building wiring. HomeRF 2.0 adds support for low-cost roaming of HomeRF devices. Devices enabled by both HomeRF and Bluetooth, which is aimed at providing short-range cable replacement for mobile devices, would combine the unique features of both for operation outside the home. This could prove to be very useful and is expected to be widely implemented, provided Bluetooth can prove to be secure. While these two standards share many features at the physical layer, they support different markets. Providing a means to connect these markets will allow the consumer to communicate between, or possibly even combine, more of their wireless devices.

[14]Champness, Angela, *IEEE 802.11 is the path to high-speed wireless data networking,* Online document: www.parkassociates.com/events/forum99/F99papers/ieee802.11.htm, March 21, 2001. IEEE 802.11 is a WLAN standard developed by the IEEE (Institute of Electrical and Electronic Engineering) committee, specifying an *over-the-air* (OTA) interface between a wireless client and a base station or Access Point, as well as among wireless clients. Access points are the bridges between wireless and wired networks. A wireless PC card in each notebook sends packets over the 2.4-GHz wireless band to an Access Point. Each packet has a group ID and an Ethernet ID identifying the originating card. The 802.11 standard provides MAC and PHY functionality for wireless connectivity of fixed, portable and moving stations moving at pedestrian and vehicular speeds within a local area. Specific features of the 802.11 standard include the following: support of asynchronous and time-bounded delivery service; continuity of service within extended areas via a Distribution System, such as Ethernet; accommodation of transmission rates of 1 and 2 Mbps; support of most market applications; multicast (including broadcast) services; network management services; and registration and authentication services.

Target environments for use of the standard include the following inside buildings (such as offices, banks, shops, malls, hospitals, manufacturing plants, and residences) and outdoor areas, (such as parking lots, campuses, building complexes, and outdoor plants).

The 802.11 standard takes into account differences between wireless and wired LANs. Bandwidth The ISM spread spectrum bands do not offer a great deal of bandwidth, keeping data rates lower than desirable for some applications. The 802.11-working group, however, dealt with methods to compress data, making the best use of available bandwidth. Efforts are also underway to increase the data rate of 802.11 to accommodate the growing need for exchanging larger amounts of secure data.

Wireless LANs transmit signals over much larger areas than that of wired media, such as twisted-pair, coaxial cable, and optical fiber. In terms of privacy, therefore, wireless LANs have a much larger area to protect. To employ security, the 802.11working group coordinated their work with the IEEE 802.10 standards committee, responsible for developing security mechanisms for all 802 series LANs.

The topology of a wireless network is dynamic; therefore, the destination address does not always correspond to the destination's location. This raises a problem when routing packets through the network to the intended destination. Thus, a need may arise to use a TCP/IP-based protocol, such as Mobile IP, to accommodate mobile stations.

The IEEE 802.11 standard for WLANs is a significant milestone in the evolution of wireless networking technology. It is limited in scope to the *physical* (PHY) and *medium-access-control* (MAC) network layers. The PHY layer corresponds directly to the lowest layer defined by the International Standards Organization in its seven-layer *Open System Interconnect* (OSI) network model. The MAC layer corresponds to the lower half of the second layer of that same model with *Logical Link Control* (LLC) functions making up the upper half of OSI layer 2. The standard specifies a choice of three different PHY layers, any of which can underlie a single MAC layer.

The standard provides for an optical-based PHY that uses infrared light to transmit data, and two RF-based PHYs that employ different types of spread-spectrum radio communications. The infrared PHY typically will be limited in range and most practically implemented within a single room. The RF-based PHYs, meanwhile, can be used to cover significant areas and indeed entire campuses when deployed in cellular-like configurations. The RF PHYs include *Direct Sequence Spread Spectrum* (DSSS) and *Frequency Hopping Spread Spectrum* (FHSS) choices. As the names imply, both DSSS and FHSS artificially spread the transmission band so that the transmitted signal can be accurately received and decoded in the face of noise. The two RF PHYs, however, approach the spreading task in significantly different ways.

FHSS systems essentially use conventional narrow-band data transmission techniques but regularly change the frequency at which they transmit. The systems hop at a fixed time interval around a spread or wide band using different center frequencies in a predetermined sequence. The hopping phenomenon allows the FHSS system to avoid narrow-band noise in portions of the transmission band. DSSS systems, meanwhile, artificially broadening the bandwidth needed to transmit a signal by modulating the data stream with a spreading code. The receiver can detect error-free data even if noise persists in portions of the transmission band.

In 802.11, the DSSS PHY defines both 1- and 2-Mbps peak data rates. The former uses *Differential Binary Phase Shift Keying* (DBPSK) and the latter uses *Differential Quadrature Phase Shift Keying* (DQPSK). The standard defines the FHSS PHY to operate at 1 Mbps and allows for optional 2 Mbps operation. The PHY uses 2- or 4-level *Gaussian Frequency Shift Keying* (GFSK) modulation.

Both DSSS and FHSS WLANs will operate in the same frequency band and neither requires site licenses or permits throughout the United States, Europe, and Asia. The standard specifies that the WLANs operate in the 2.4-GHz band that regulatory agencies around the world have set aside for spread spectrum usage. One of the key advantages of the RF PHYs is the ability to have a number of distinct channels. The channel allows WLAN users to colocate channels in the same or adjacent areas to boost aggregate throughput or to deploy a cellular-like array of channels that support roaming clients. In the case of DSSS, different channels simply use different frequency bands. In the case of FHSS, the hopping sequence used differentiates one channel from the next, but all channels operate in the same wide frequency band.

DSSS and FHSS PHYs use the allocated RF spectrum in the 2.4-GHz band in different ways. Moreover different regions with slightly different regulations throughout the world affect exact channel schemes for both PHY types. Generally, the 802.11 specification defines 13-MHz DSSS channels that are used to carry a spread 1-MHz signal. Channels overlap with a new center frequency located at 5-MHz intervals. For deployment in the United States, the standard defines 11 independent DSSS channels in the ISM bandwidth allocated by the FCC. Throughout much of Europe and much of Asia that follows the lead of European regulatory agencies, DSSS implementations can leverage 13 channels. In Japan, however, the allocated bandwidth only supports a single channel. In the United States and Europe, the channel definition ensures that three frequency-isolated channels are available for collocation.

FHSS systems, meanwhile, are mandated to use 79 hops or center frequencies in the United States and Europe and 23 hops in Japan. Typically, FHSS systems dwell at each hop for 20 ms. The specification defines 78 different hopping sequences, and each independent hopping sequence is defined as a channel. Practically, however, only a few channels can be effectively deployed in close proximity to one another.

Regardless of the type of PHY chosen, IEEE 802.11 supports three basic topologies for WLANs—the *Independent Basic Service Set* (IBSS), the *Basic Service Set* (BSS), and the *Extended Service Set* (ESS). The MAC layer implements the support for IBSS, BSS, and ESS configurations.

IBSS configurations are also referred to as an independent configuration or an ad hoc network. Logically, an IBSS configuration is analogous to a peer-to-peer office network in which no single node is required to function as a server. IBSS WLANs include a number of nodes or wireless stations that communicate directly with one another on an ad hoc, peer-to-peer basis. Generally, IBSS implementations cover a limited area and are not connected to a larger network.

BSS configurations rely on an *Access Point* (AP) that acts as the logical server for a single WLAN cell or channel. Communications between node A and node B actually flow from node A to the AP and then from the AP to node B. At first, it may seem that the AP adds an unnecessary layer of complexity and overhead to the WLAN, but the AP enables features of 802.11 that will be described later. Moreover, an AP is necessary to perform a bridging function and connect multiple WLAN cells or channels, and to connect WLAN cells to a wired enterprise LAN.

ESS WLAN configurations consist of multiple BSS cells that can be linked by either wired or wireless backbones. IEEE 802.11 supports ESS configurations in which multiple cells use the same channel, and configurations in which multiple cells use different channels to boost aggregate throughput.

[15]Nobel, Carmen, "Still waiting for Bluetooth—Expect further delays; don't chuck your crimpers, Cat. 5 just yet; wireless technology," *eWeek*, ZDNet, Available at: http://www.zdnet.com/eweek/stories/general/0.11011.2710689.00.html, Accessed April 23, 2001.

[16]Ibid.

[17]Muller, Nathan J., *Bluetooth Demystified,* McGraw-Hill, 2000, p. 16.

[18]Ibid.

[19]Bray, Jennifer, and Charles F. Sturman, *Bluetooth, Connect Without Cables*, Prentice-Hall PTR, 2001, p. 44.

[20]Bluetooth SIG. The Bluetooth technology overview, March 26, 2001, http://www.bluetooth.com/developer/specification/overview.asp.

[21]Ibid.

[22]Vainio, Juha T. Bluetooth Security, May 25, 2000, March 26, 2001, http://www.niksula.cs. hut.fi/~jiitv/bluesec.html#chap5.

[23]Ibid.

[24]Muller, Thomas. Bluetooth Security Architecture—Version 1.0, July 15, 1999, March 26, 2001, http://www.bluetooth.com/developer/download/download.asp?doc=174.

[25]Muller, Thomas. Bluetooth Security Architecture—Version 1.0, July 15, 1999, March 26, 2001, http://www.bluetooth.com/developer/download/download.asp?doc=174.

[26]Albright, Peggy. Bluetooth Cavity? SIG says 'No', September 11, 2000, March 26, 2001, http://www.wirelessweek.com/index.asp?layout=story&articleId=CA13821&stt=001.

[27]Merritt, Rick. Conflicts between Bluetooth and wireless LANs called minor, February 21, 2001, March 26, 2001, http://www.eetimes.com/story/OEG20010220S0040.

[28]Khaira, Manpreet S., and Zehavi, Ephi. Wireless Infrastructure: Bluetooth can co-exist with 802.11, February 27, 2001, March 26, 2001, http://www.eetimes.com/story/OEG20010227S0020.

[29]Op. cit., Miller, p. 26.

[30]Op. cit., Tranter, p. 253.

[31]Op. cit., Tranter, p. 254.

[32]Ibid., p. 6.

[33]Ibid., p. 7.

[34]Ibid., pp. 6–7.

[35]Bluetooth Architecture Overview, http://filebox.vt.edu/users/sangle/bluetooth/architecture.htm, Accessed May 23, 2001.

[36]Op cit., Siep, p. 44.

[37]Palowireless.com, Bluetooth Resource Center, "Bluetooth Baseband," Available at: http://www.palowireless.com/infotooth/tutorial/baseband.asp, Accessed May 29, 2001.

[38]Op. cit., Muller.

[39]Op. cit., Muller.

[40]Interview with Ron Sperano, Program Director for the Mobile Market Development Department of IBM, http://www.itradionetwork.com/scripts/speranor.html, conducted October 18, 2000, Accessed June 18, 2001.

[41]Ibid.

[42]Schuchart, Steven J., Jr., "The Bluetooth Invasion Begins," *Network Computing*, March 19, 2001, http://www.networkcomputing.com/1206/1206ws3.html, Accessed June 18, 2001.

[43]Pearce, Jim, "Virginia Polytechnic Institute's Spread Spectrum Introduction," Spread Spectrum Scene, Available at: http://www.sss-mag.com/primer.html, Accessed June 30, 2001.

[44]Op. cit., Siep, p. 60.

[45]Ibid., p. 79.

[46]Ibid.

[47]IEEE, "IEEE 802.15 WPAN™ Task Group 1 (TG1)," IEEE Web Site, Available at: http://www.ieee802.org/15/pub/TG1.html, Accessed June 30, 2001.

[48]Op. cit., Miller and Bisdikian.

[49]Rodbell, Mike, "Standards & Protocols: Bluetooth—Baseband and RF Interfaces", *Communications Systems Design* Magazine, April 2000, Available at: http://www.csdmag.com/main/2000/04 /0004stand.htm#bluetab, Accessed June 18, 2001.

[50]Ibid.

[51]Op. cit., Bray, p. 311.

[52]Op. cit., Anand.

[53]Op. cit., Muller, p. 296.

[54]Op. cit., Muller.

[55]"Cylink Secures Bluetooth™ Wireless Networking Technology—Cylink's SAFER+ Algorithm Provides User Authentication for Emerging Wireless Networking Standard," Cylink Corporation Web site press release dated September 20, 2000, Available at: http://www.cylink.com/news/press/pressrels/92000.htm, Accessed June 18, 2001.

[56]Massey, Prof. J.L., Prof. G.H. Khachatrian, Dr. M.K. Kuregian, SAFER+ Candidate Algorithm for AES—Submission Document, Cylink Corporation, June 1998.

[57]Massey, James L., "On The Optimality of SAFER+ Diffusion;" Cylink Corporation, Sunnyvale, CA; Available at: http://csrc.nist.gov/encryption/aes/round1/conf2/papers/massey.pdf, Accessed June 18, 2001.

[58]Ibid.

[59]Vainio, J.T., "Bluetooth security," Proceedings of Helsinki University of Technology, Telecommunications Software and Multimedia Laboratory, seminar on Internetworking: Ad Hoc Networking, Spring 2000, Available at: http://www.niksula.cs.hut.fi/~jiitv/bluesec.html, May 25, 2000, Accessed June 18, 2001.

[60]Ibid., p. 161.

[61]Ibid., p. 148.

[62]Ibid., p. 161.

[63]Ibid., p. 158.

[64]Op. cit., Vainio.

[65]Jakobsson, Markus, and Susanne Wetzel, Security Weaknesses in Bluetooth, Lucent Technologies—Bell Labs, Information Sciences Research Center, Murray Hill, NJ, www.bell-labs.com/user/markusj/bluetooth.pdf, Accessed June 18, 2001.

[66]Op. cit., Jakobsson and Wetzel.

[67]Op. cit., Jakobsson and Wetzel.

[68]Hermelin, M.,and K. Nyberg, "Correlation Properties of the Bluetooth Combiner," Proceedings of the ICISC '99, Springer LNCS 1787, 1999, pp. 17–29, Available at: http://citeseer.nj.nec.com/271131.html, Accessed June 18, 2001.

[69]Biryukov, Alex, Adi Shamir, and David Wagner, "Real Time Cryptanalysis of A5/1 on a PC," Proceedings of the Fast Software Encryption Workshop 2000, April 10–12, 2000, New York City, Available at: http://cryptome.org/a51-bsw.htm, Accessed June 18, 2001.

[70]Op. cit., Muller, p. 308.

[71]"To Jam or Not to Jam? Debate Heats up on Silencing Pesky Cell Phones," News-Journal Wire Services, News-Journal online.com, April 22, 2001, Available at: http://www.news-journalonline.com/2001/Apr/22/STECH1.htm, Accessed June 30, 2001.

[72]Ibid.

[73]Op. cit., Jakobsson and Wetzel.

[74]McDaid, Cathal, Bluetooth Security, Cathal's Corner, http://www.palowireless.com/infotooth/cathalscorner.asp, Accessed June 30, 2001.

[75]Op. cit., Vainio.

[76]Ibid.

[77]Op. cit., Vainio.

[78]Op. cit., Jakobsson and Wetzel.

[79]Op. cit., Goldberg.

[80]Ringqvist, Mattias, and Will Daugherty, "Can Bluetooth Compete with WLAN?" *ZDNet News*, May 4, 2001, http://www.zdnet.com/zdnn/stories/comment/0.5859.2715556.00.html?chkpt=zdnn_rt_latest, Accessed May 30, 2001.

[81]Op. cit., Goldberg.

[82]Op. cit., Vainio.

11

Voice Over Internet Protocol

VoIP Generally Speaking

According to IPAXS Corporation, "Since the enactment of the 1996 Telecom Act, the landscape of the telecommunications service providers has forever changed and is continuing to evolve with the increased prominence of the Internet at the heart of it."[1] Most people not only freely exchange their phone number for business transactions and as contacts, but also their e-mail address. Some even require that you e-mail them before calling, compounding the likelihood of being overheard.

The transmission of *voice packets* across an Internet protocol is known as *voice over IP* or (VoIP). VoIP could change the way we communicate on the Web, as well as the way we do business. If implemented successfully, it holds out the promise of unified communications. It might well provide a low cost solution for the building and transmission of networks, and allow a number of applications to be accessible through the same media for transmission.[2] In a world where people are starting to use the Internet and cellular phones by preference to communicate, it is not surprising that the merging of the two is pushing to the forefront of technology.

VoIP technology enables computer users to establish voice conversations through the computer via connection to the Internet. Although clearly the Internet Protocol was designed to be most effective with data transmissions, voice applications are now viable and even practical because implementations of the IP architecture are already virtually ubiquitous in networks and communication systems.

The Buzz Around VoIP

The primary appeal of VoIP is its vaunted ability to save money for customers as well as service providers. VoIP is thought to be very cost effective. Desirable new applications and the bypassing of the switched telephone network and all its toll charges, is driving interest higher."[3] To alleviate monthly recurring charges for various locations or sites, service providers could reconfigure multilocations and long-distance calls using customers' existing network infrastructure. These measures reputedly add up to an almost 50-percent reduction in communications over traditional telephony. If so they will open the global marketplace to more and smaller companies.

The deployment of VoIP has its downside. VoIP is an offspring of Internet technology, and consequently inherits all the vulnerabilities of the parent network. VoIP does not provide the high-quality, uninterrupted voice transmission that businesses demand (and receive) over the telephone. Disconnections must be mitigated for VoIP to realize its full potential. The Internet is famously less reliable than the traditional telephone system for connection. Until it improves, VoIP is unlikely to gain traction as a universal standard method of networks and telephones.

Other hurdles for VoIP to overcome are packet loss and fragmentation (not uncommon in IP networks), and the delay, latency, and jitter that accompany it. These factors, though not threats per se, do affect confidentiality and reliability on VoIP systems. Latency can be a direct result of the number of routers on the network: if a packet must travel through many hops between routers, latency accumulates to an unacceptable degree. Jitters occur when unrelated packets take the same route through the network but arrive at different times, causing delay.[4] Finally, VoIP disappoints expectations of reliability, flow control, error detection, and error correction derived from circuit-switched telephony. Packet switched data, as all IP data is, can reach its destination synchronized, fragmented, or not at all.

There are no universal standards in place for implementing and maintaining VoIP. Currently as each new vendor enters the VoIP market, they vary procedures and standards in ways that further complicate the field of play. Already there are cases where a technology product from Acme can't achieve acceptable quality of service unless it communicating with another Acme product. This kind of protocol promulgation makes VoIP applications much more complex and resistant to familiar security measures.

VoIP Standards

H.323 is the most widely used VoIP standard. H.323 is used as a packet standard in *multipoint control units* (MCUs) such as internetworking systems, gateways, gatekeepers, and terminals.[5] The H.323 standard was created by the International Telecommunications Union in June 1996, as a result of variations in standards relating to videoconferencing. The first version focused on the transmission over a local area network using IP. Two years later in January of 1998 the newer version addressed the wide area network infrastructure.[6] Today, H.323 is known as the "umbrella" ITU standard for other multimedia voice related technology.[7] Some standards within the umbrella of H.323 are H.225 for call control and call signaling, H.245 for media and multimedia control, H.235 for security and encryption and H.450 for supplementary services and advanced call features.[8]

A major criticisms leveled against H.323 is the time and complexity involved in setting up a call. First, the protocol uses multiple roundtrip messages to establish signaling and control for any call between two terminals. Moreover, H.323 requires that TCP connections be used to carry the messages, requiring an additional roundtrip exchange. The recently released version 3 is an improvement and includes both a "fast connect" procedure that effectively consolidates the Q.931 messages exchanged between terminals, and a tunneling procedure that lets H.245 share a single TCP connection with Q.931."[9] Additional and emerging standards currently used in VoIP based solutions includes: SIP, RTP, RTCP, RRP, and MGCP. The standards picture is consequently too complex to say with any intelligence what development paths VoIP will take over the next five years (see Tables 11-1 to 11-6).

Table 11-1 VoIP ITU-T Standards and Recommendations—Signaling

H.323 V2	Packet-Based Multimedia Communications Systems
H.225.0	Call signaling protocols and media stream packetization for packet-based multimedia (includes Q.931 and RAS)
H.225.0 Annex G	Gatekeeper to gatekeeper (interdomain) communications
H.245	Control protocol for multimedia communications
H.235	Security and encryption for H-series multimedia terminals
H.450.x	Supplementary services for multimedia: 1. Generic functional protocol for the support of supplementary services in H.323 2. Call transfer 3. Diversion 4. Hold 5. Park & pickup 6. Call waiting 7. Message waiting indication
H.323 Annex D	Real-time fax using T.38
H.323 Annex E	Call connection over UDP
H.323 Annex F	Single-use device
T.38	Procedures for real-time group 3 facsimile communications over IP networks
T.120 series	Data protocols for multimedia conferencing

Source: http://208.240.89.129/voip/standards.htm

Table 11-2 IETF RFCs and Drafts

RFC 2543	**SIP: Session Initiation Protocol**
RFC 2327	SDP: Session Description Protocol
Internet Draft	SAP: Session Announcement Protocol

Source: http://208.240.89.129/voip/standards.htm

Table 11-3 IETF Gateway Control

Internet Draft	**MGCP: Media Gateway Control Protocol**
Internet Draft	MEGACO protocol
Draft	SGCP: Simple Gateway Control Protocol
Internet Draft	IPDC: IP Device Control

Source: http://208.240.89.129/voip/standards.htm

Table 11-4 Media Transport—IETF

RFC 1889	**RTP: Real-Time Transport Protocol**
RFC 1889	RTCP: Real-Time Transport Control Protocol
RFC 2326	RTSP: Real-Time Streaming Protocol

Source: http://208.240.89.129/voip/standards.htm

Table 11-5 Media Encoding ITU—Voice

Standard	Algorithm	Bit Rate (Kbps)	Typical end-to-end delay (ms) (excluding channel delay)	Resultant Voice Quality
G.711	PCM	48, 56, 64	<<1	Excellent
G.723.1	MPE/ACELP	5.3, 6.3	67–97	Good (6.3), Fair (5.3)
H.728	LD-CELP	16	<<2	Good
G.729	CS-ACELP	8	25–35	Good
G.729 annex A	CS-ACELP	8	25–35	Good
G.722	Sub-band ADPCM	48, 56, 64	<<2	Good

Standard	Algorithm	Bit Rate (Kbps)	Typical end-to-end delay (ms) (excluding channel delay)	Resultant Voice Quality
G.726	ADPCM	16, 24, 32, 40	60	Good (40), Fair (24)
G.727	AEDPCM	16, 24, 32, 40	60	Good (40), Fair (24)

Source: http://208.240.89.129/voip/standards.htm

Table 11-6 Video Standard Algorithm

Standard	Algorithm	Bit Rate (Kbps)	Picture Quality
H.261	Discrete cosine transform (DCT) with motion compensation	px64 (p=# of ISDN B channels)	Low
H.263	Improved version of H.261	Various	Medium

Source: http://208.240.89.129/voip/standards.htm

The Rise of VoIP Technology

Consensus is that VoIP technology has yet to live up to its potential. Industry experts appear divided between those who believe this technology is many years away from widespread application and those who believe VoIP to be the wave of the near future. Today these opposing views seem to complement each other nicely while the opponents identify flaws and obstacles; proponents race to resolve them.

Businesses see VoIP as enhancing productivity, improving customer service, and as a low-cost alternative to PSTN voice service. Investors see enormous long-term potential in VoIP as the technology that eventually replaces telephone infrastructure, as we know it. The current market trend is to integrate voice and data communications into a single network. Combining voice and data communications eliminates cost associated with operating and maintaining two separate networks. In addition, it supports new multimedia applications that typically allow users to talk and exchange data images in the same session.[10] These two points have persuaded many organizations to phase VoIP into their strategic planning. However, there is much more to this technology than meets the eye. The industry is looking hard at upwards of 20 issues that must be resolved in tandem to make VoIP future-ready. Here are a few:

Network Traffic

TCP and IP protocols were originally developed for applications that were not necessarily time- or bandwidth-sensitive (for example, e-mail, file transfers, remote access, and so forth). The goal is to engineer a low-cost way to connect many systems over a robust network. Technically this would meet basic support requirements for data communications over the network, but the approach is not as satisfactory for supporting voice and video traffic over a similar network. The variations in bandwidth requirements, style of traffic, and latency concerns for multi-service voice and data traffic makes quality of service exceedingly difficult to manage.

Table 11-7 Traffic Categories[11]

Type of Traffic	Bandwidth	Typical Style	Latency Sensitivity	Jitter Sensitivity	Loss Sensitivity
Bulk Data Transfer	10–100 Mbps	Periodic two-party	Low	None	Low
Transaction Data	<1 Mbps	Bursty, two-party	Moderate	None	None
Voice and Facsimile	8–64 Kbps	Variable, two-party multiparty	High	High	Low
Multimedia (voice plus image)	Up to 384 Kbps for video	Variable, two-party or multiparty	High	Moderate	Low
Video on Demand & Streaming	28.8 Kbps–1.5 Mbps	Variable multiparty	Low	Low	Low

Source: Techguide.com LAC, June 30, 2001.

Billing and Interoperability Dilemma

In traditional *public switched telephone network* (PSTN) systems, billing is established based on the length of a telephone call using a dedicated line. In a packet-based network, *charges are accrued in accordance with the amount of bandwidth used.* This raises a significant difference between the two because billing is continuous during silence periods of conversation using PSTN, while silence results in cost savings in a packet-based system. This difference in billing standards is just one area where *Asynchronous Transfer Mode* (ATM), *Voice over Frame Relay* (VoFR), and VoIP must interact effectively to determine proper billing in support of voice over packet networks.[12]

Interoperability

There is no problem with interoperability in transmission when using two gateways from the same vendor; however, using gateways from different vendors may not be as successful. H.323 suites usually vary from vendor to vendor and, according to work done by Network World Test Alliance, only two or three vendors provide true H.323 support; most operate with modified or extended versions that do not always work together.[13] Even more challenging is the interoperability among telephones and switches. In the world of vendors, "open systems" does not mean compliance among standards and therefore cannot be expected to be interoperable.[14]

Competitive Long Distance Rates

Over the last few years, toll charges have dropped and have become quite competitive. Prepaid calling cards and cellular telephones have greatly contributed to this reduction in costs.

Caution: Implementation Ahead

Practical problems like those just addressed naturally inhibit implementations and the invaluable experience it provides to security planners. But part of the rationale for proceeding with caution is that there are known security risks associated with VoIP. Even more troubling are the security risks that have yet to be identified. VoIP also raises possible legal problems for monitoring voice traffic. Laws for monitoring data traffic are much different than those for telephone conversations and could quite naturally have an adverse impact on confidentiality for those charged with protecting nondisclosure agreements: the military, attorneys, chaplains, doctors, and so on.[15]

Evaluating the strategic potential of VoIP technology is a glass half full, glass half empty proposition. Consumers tend to see half-full glasses, and the economic outlook for infant technologies remains positive. Developments that took place in the telecom industry during the last five years of the 20th century are projected to have a revolutionizing effect on the American way of life well into the new millennium.[16] VoIP is cradled into this projection and will undoubtedly be among those developments that change our lifestyles. After all, a positive economic forecast indicates much more than the significance of communications technologies—it underscores the prospective consumer demand for these technologies. Although starting modestly, it is possible that VoIP technology will be the sleeping giant nurtured by such demand. The rapid growth of Internet access is another factor in favor of VoIP technology. Small-scale, generally noncommercial VoIP pilot projects are everywhere on the Internet and over time will accumulate as a body of knowledge.

The Vendor Market

Caution goes by the wayside when we look at the vendor markets for VoIP. As one analyst put it, it's where the money is. Some specifics are shown in Tables 11-8 to 11-10.

Table 11-8 VoIP Gateway Vendors

Vendor	Product	Notes
3Com	Total Control 1000/2000 Media Gateway	VoIP Gateway
Cisco Systems	AS5300/Voice Gateway	VoIP Gateway
Com21	DOXphone	VoIP GR-303 Gateway
Convergent Networks	ICS2000 Broadband Switch	VoIP Softswitch and Gateway
General Bandwidth	G6	VoIP GR-303 Gateway
Lucent Technologies	PathStar Access Server	VoIP Softswitch
Lucent Technologies	IMerge NCS Gateway	VoIP GR-303 Gateway

continues

Table 11-8 VoIP Gateway Vendors *(continued)*

Vendor	Product	Notes
Netspeak	ITEL	VoIP Softswitch
Nortel Networks	Communications Server 2000	VoIP Softswitch
Nuera	ORCA	VoIP Softswitch and Gateway
Sonus Networks	PSX6000	VoIP Softswitch
Syndeo	Syion 426	VoIP Softswitch Platform
Tellabs	SALIX 7000	VoIP Softswitch and Gateway
Terayon	BandLeader AG-3000	VoIP GR-303/V5.2 Gateway
TollBridge Technologies	TB200	VoIP Softswitch and Gateway
Unisphere Networks	SMX-2100 and SRX-3000	VoIP Softswitch and Gateway
ComMatch	Duet 3000 and 6000	VoIP Gateway

Source: Cable Datacom News http://www.cabledatacomnews.com/iptel/VoIPgateway.html, last access June 15, 2001

Table 11-9 VoIP Service Providers

Service Provider	Service	Price Per Minute	Gateway Vendor	Description
AudioTalk Networks (650) 988-2040	AudioTalk available	2 cents	Cisco	Service is worldwide; no hardware or software installation required.
Equant (770) 612-4700	Equant VoIP	7 cents and 11 cents	Cisco	Service is available in 50 countries including the U.S., U.K., France, Germany, and in the Asia-Pacific; pricing represents calling form the U.K. to Germany and from the U.S. to France.
Global Crossing (310) 385-5200	WebSaver	6.5–8 cents	Sonus, Lucent	Service is planned in seven U.S. regions by April 2000 and to the entire U.S. by December 2000.
GTE Internet-working (800) 472-4565	Internat'l VoIP Direct	3 cents	Cisco	Service is working available worldwide to ISPs, Internet Telephony Service Providers and Telco's; 90 million VoIP traffic minutes sold per month.
InnoMedia (888) 251-6250	InnoSphere	2–5 cents	Inno Media	Service is accessible anywhere in more than 200 countries via InfoTalk stand-alone VoIP appliance or InfoAccel VoIP PCI card.
Ipx (201) 324-2700	Ip-Linknet	3–60 cents (U.S. and Internat'l)	Cisco, Lucent, Cirilium, Motorola, Nuera	Basic VoIP service offered worldwide; telecommunications advanced service provider and portal.

Service Provider	Service	Price Per Minute	Gateway Vendor	Description
Nexbell Communication (216) 344-2611	Multiple Exchange Transport Service (METS)	5–1.25 cents (U.S. and Internat'l)	Cisco	Service offers nationwide local access origination numbers.
Sositel Digital Voice Networks (712) 266-0836	Nationwide Communications Network	1–6 cents	Sosinc Communications	Service is offered to 105 locations in the U.S.
VOCALscape Communications (604) 878-0440	VocalVillage .Com	5–90 cents (U.S. and Internat'l)	VOCAL -scape Communications	An Internet telephone services portal; service scheduled to launch worldwide in July 2000.
VOCALscape Communications (604) 878-0440	Vocal-commerce. com	5–90 cents (U.S. and Internat'l)	VOCAL - scape Communications	An Internet phone services portal; service scheduled to launch worldwide in July 2000.
ZeroPlus.com (301) 601-8700	ZeroPlus. com	3.9 cents	e-Net	Worldwide service includes call hold, call waiting, call transfer; PC-to-PC is free.

Table 11-10 VoIP Product Comparison (Partial List)[17]

Product	Gateway Type	LAN Interface	Standards	Pricing
3Com NBX 100 Communications System 2.0	IP PBX	1 Ethernet, Fast Ethernet	H.323 Version 2	$4,000–$51,000
3Com Total Control 1000 Media Gateway	VoIP integrated Remote access Concentrator	2 Fast Ethernet	H.323 v2, Proposed; SIP; plans to support proposed Megaco/H.248	$50,000–$250,000
AltiGen Communications AltiServ with Open Edition 3.5	Software plus voice Cards; 333-MHz Pentium, Windows NT Server, 128Mb RAM	1 Fast Ethernet	H.322 Version 2	$5,620–$20,920

continues

Table 11-10 VoIP Product Comparison (Partial List)[17] *(continued)*

Product	Gateway Type	LAN Interface	Standards	Pricing
Artisoft TeleVantage 3.0	Software plus voice cards; Windows NT 4.0 Server; 200 MHz-Pentium, 64MB RAM	8 Ethernet	H.323 Version 1	$8,000–$110,000
Cabletron Smart Voice Gateway Integrated Routing	VoIP stand-alone Gateway	8 Ethernet	H.323 Version 2, proposed MGCP	$3,300–$32,800
Cirillium 2000	VoIP stand-alone Gateway	1 Ethernet	H.323 Version 2, proposed MGCP	$3,600
Cirillium 2500	VoIP stand-alone Gateway	1 Ethernet	H.323 Version 2, proposed MGCP	$6,900
Cirillium 4000	VoIP stand-alone Gateway	1 Ethernet	H.323 Version 2, proposed MGCP	$12,200
Cirillium 6000	VoIP stand-alone Gateway	1 Ethernet	H.323 Version 2, proposed MGCP	$32,300
Cisco 3660 Modular Mulitservice Access Platform	VoIP integrated router Gateway	Up to 26 Ethernet, Up to 14 Fast Ethernet, Up to 8 Token Ring, Up to 6 ATM-OC3, Up to 6 ATM-25	H.323 Version 1 and 2, SGCP	$16,700–$81,000
Cisco 3640 Modular Mulitservice Access Platform	VoIP integrated router Gateway	Up to 16 Ethernet, Up to 8 Fast Ethernet, Up to 4 Token Ring, Up to 3 ATM-OC3, Up to 3 ATM-25	H.323 Version 1 and 2, SGCP	$10,500–$44,000
Cisco 3620 Modular Mulitservice Access Platform	VoIP integrated router Gateway	Up to 8 Ethernet, Up to 4 Fast Ethernet, Up to 2 Token Ring, 1 ATM-OC3, 1 ATM-25	H.323 Version 1 and 2, SGCP	$6,900–$20,000

Product	Gateway Type	LAN Interface	Standards	Pricing
Cisco 2600 Modular Mulitservice Access Platform	VoIP integrated router Gateway	6 Ethernet, 2 Fast Ethernet, 1 Token Ring, 1 ATM-25	H.323 Version 1 and 2, SGCP	$4,495–$17,000
Clarent Gateway 100	VoIP stand-alone Gateway	1 Fast Ethernet	H.323 Version 2, RTP RFC2508	$4,000–$30,000
Clarent Gateway 400	VoIP stand-alone Gateway	1 Fast Ethernet	H.323 Version 2, RTP RFC2508	$35,000–$90,000
Clarent Carrier Gateway	VoIP stand-alone gateway	1 Fast Ethernet	H.323 Version 2, RTP RFC2508	$165,000–$235,000
E-tel FreeRide TLT	VoIP stand-alone Gateway	2 Ethernet	H.323 Version 1 and 2; proposed SIP, MGCP	$350–$450
Franklin Telecom Tempest DVG (Data Voice Gateway)	VoIP stand-alone Gateway	1 Ethernet	H.323 Version 1	$16,621
Info Systems Talkie Convergent Services IG2 Switch	VoIP stand-alone Gateway	Up to 10 Ethernet, Fast Ethernet	H.323 Version 2	$10,000–$200,000
InnoMedia InfoAccel	Software plus card; Windows 95/98; 166-MHz Pentium, 16 MB RAM	1 Ethernet	H.323 Version 2	$100
InnoMedia InfoAccel tform		Up to 26 Ethernet, Up to 14 Fast Ethernet, Up to 8 Token Ring, Up to 6 ATM-OC3, Up to 6 ATM-25		
Cisco 3640 Modular Mulitservice Access Platform	VoIP integrated router gateway	Up to 16 Ethernet, Up to 8 Fast Ethernet, Up to 4 Token Ring, Up to 3 ATM-OC3, Up to 3 ATM-25	H.323 Version 1 and 2, SGCP	$10,500–$44,000

continues

Table 11-10. VoIP Product Comparison (Partial List)[17] *(continued)*

Product	Gateway Type	LAN Interface	Standards	Pricing
Cisco 3620 Modular Mulitservice Access Platform	VoIP integrated router gateway	Up to 8 Ethernet, Up to 4 Fast Ethernet, Up to 2 Token Ring, 1 ATM-OC3, 1 ATM-25	H.323 Version 1 and 2, SGCP	$6,900–$20,000
Cisco 2600 Modular Mulitservice Access Platform	VoIP integrated router gateway	6 Ethernet, 2 Fast Ethernet, 1 Token Ring, 1 ATM-25	H.3233 Version 1 and 2, SGCP	$4,495–$17,000
Ericsson Datacom IP Telephony (IPT) 1.6	VoIP integrated switch	2 Ethernet, Fast Ethernet	H.323 Version 1 and 2 proposed SIP	$25,000–$500,000
Infosoft Technologies CallLogiX 3.0	Software plus voice card; Windows NT 4.0, 350-MHz Pentium, 128MB RAM	1 Ethernet, Fast Ethernet	H.323 Version 1	$6,400–$72,000

Technical Issues for VoIP Calling

Under H.323, a gatekeeper controls the VoIP network. Some of the more common features of a VoIP gatekeeper include the ability to:[18]

- Allocate voice, video, and data
- Manage network bandwidth
- Handle routings for multiple H.323 gateways
- Provide for charging and billing
- Support network security and subscriber authentication

With respect to security, Green indicates that gatekeepers can manage admissions into the VoIP network based on resource utilization or other criteria.[19] For example, Radvision (**www.radvision.com**), whose protocol stacks and gatekeeper software are found in many VoIP products, lets the user define IP endpoints as an identifier character string to restrict authorization. In essence, these alphanumeric identifiers act as a VoIP network password.[20]

Speech Encoding

Do not assume that VoIP encoding of speech is inherently secure. Even though H.323 identifies security features, few manufacturers currently comply. Using low bandwidth or even proprietary vocoders may improve the intrinsic security of VoIP conversations, but only for as long as the would-be eavesdroppers fail to identify your gateway vendor. If you use a higher bandwidth vocoder, a savvy network engineer can easily tap into your conversation somewhere on the IP pipe between gateways.

We've said that VoIP security relies on the features found in H.323. However, only a fully compliant gateway can provide the full range of security inherent in the protocol. Then, once the call moves from the gateway, it faces the same vulnerabilities as any IP package transmitted over the Internet. A more comprehensive discussion follows.

Voice Network Security Vulnerabilities

Vulnerabilities, defined as threats that, if exploited, could harm a system or network, will be analyzed in the following broad categories: physical, natural, hardware, software, communications, and human.[21] These vulnerabilities are not unique to VoIP but affect all networks carrying voice transmissions, regardless of transmission medium.

Physical vulnerabilities exist for equipment rooms that house gateways, switches, routers, and servers. For example, buildings that lack adequate access control mechanisms or physical guards render assets contained within the building vulnerable to theft and destruction. *Natural* vulnerabilities such as severe weather conditions could negate the availability of networks that carry voice transmissions by destroying switching centers. *Hardware* failure of equipment such as gateways, switches, and hubs, can fail and facilitate a denial of service. Unpatched *software* or hardware that contains known vulnerabilities could be exploited or used to install back doors that could negatively affect the integrity or availability of voice transmissions. *Communication* vulnerabilities could allow individuals with malicious intent to intercept, eavesdrop, or jam voice transmission signals. *Human* vulnerabilities include errors made due insufficiently trained staff.

Confidentiality, Integrity, and Availability Attributes

Confidentiality, integrity, and availability are attributes inherent in the information security process and can be applied to systems and networks to gauge their overall security state. For a system or network to possess confidentiality means that the information contained, transformed, or transported by that system or network cannot be read or retrieved by unauthorized entities. The integrity attribute provides reasonable certitude that information contained, transformed, or transported by a system has not been modified by unauthorized entities while in one of the following three states: containment, transformation, and transportation. The availability attribute provides a reasonable certitude that information contained, transformed, or transported by a system or network is at hand and provides a high rate of dependability.[22]

VoIP and the Wireless Security Environment

A VoIP implementation sends voice transmissions in a digitized format, over a network using the *Internet Protocol* (IP) for routing. The voice packet is sent from an origination point to the destination point indicated in the IP packet header. *The Real-Time Protocol* (RTP) is typically used to assist in the timely delivery of packets containing voice data. Like TCP, which works at the transport layer for data transmissions and provides connection-oriented services, RTP helps guarantee reliability in the delivery of voice-oriented packets. RTP normally runs above UDP.[23] It must be noted, however, that TCP may not be a viable solution for VoIP-based solutions due to its questionable reliability in terms of delivery.[24] The packet may continue to be routed indefinitely.

Private Networks

Because of potentially less traffic congestion, VoIP solutions typically work more efficiently on private networks managed by a corporation or a service provider. When a voice transmission enveloped in an IP packet travels from a private network to the public network (the Internet), a gateway is used to handle the conversion process between networks. It is easier to secure the private network, and then turn attention to securing the gateways out.

WEP

Recently, serious vulnerabilities were discovered in the 802.11 standard.[25] The *Wired Equivalent Privacy* (WEP) security protocol could allow unauthorized individuals to capture, monitor, and modify transmissions without the knowledge of the individual transmitting or receiving the transmission. In addition, WEP could facilitate the decryption of transmissions through passive monitoring, primarily due to the lack of randomness of the encryption key. Moreover, active attacks against transmissions can occur as a result of illicit knowledge of the encryption key and by spoofing the packets. The destination of packets can be altered and finally, a decryption table can be developed to produce a "key stream . . . to decrypt all other packets."[26]

Confidentiality, Integrity, and Availability in VoIP Implementations

Confidentiality provides a reasonable certainty that information remains private to the greatest extent possible. Voice, data, and video transmissions are examples of information that are contained, transformed, or transmitted by a system or network. Each can employ encryption to increase the level of confidentiality of a system or network. Wireless networks, which implement VoIP solutions, are highly susceptible to eavesdropping because they send packets over radio waves. Although an encrypted transmission over a radio wave can be intercepted, strong end-to-end encryption that implements a high degree of randomness could render the reading of that transmission nearly impossible.[27]

As for integrity, the ever-present possibility of airwave eavesdropping on an unencrypted or inadequately encrypted transmission is a threat. The eavesdropper could modify data in transit, thus negating the reliability of that transmission. In addition, latency or a delay in the transmission of a VoIP packet could contribute towards the corruption of data if packets are lost.[28] For example, if a caller speaks the following sentences over a VoIP solution: *I need a ride to the hospital. I am having a stroke. I have to get to the hospital across town.* However, the called party hears the following phrase because of lost voice packets: *I need a ride . . . across town.* The called party may not be able to sense the urgency or may not be able to respond appropriately to what was spoken.

The availability attribute provides a reasonable certitude that information contained, transformed, or transmitted by a system or network is at hand and provides a high rate of dependability. The PSTN has a high degree of availability.[29] Except in a case of nonpayment, it is highly unlikely that a telephone operating over the PSTN will become unavailable. Even if the lighting in your home is knocked out due to severe weather conditions, more than likely the telephone system will still be available.

IP Spoofing and VoIP

VoIP is an IP datagram packed with voiced information instead of data. As a result, it is subject to the same vulnerabilities of a data-based IP network including spoofing. According to Daemon9, Route, and Infinity of Phrack Magazine, when an IP spoofing attack is launched, typically a destination host is attacked through a trusted host (see Figure 11-1). Attackers normally disable the trusted host to monitor the packets traveling between the two systems (the destination host and the trusted host) and to impersonate the trusted system. The trusted host is impersonated by changing the source address in the IP header. Since IP is a connectionless method for routing packets, there is no error-checking mechanism. The IP protocol typically relies on higher-level protocols at the networking layer of the OSI model to provide error-checking mechanisms such as TCP, RTP, or UDP. After an IP packet has been modified to show the trusted host as its source, and if the destination machines accept address-based authentication, the destination machine can easily be fooled into thinking that the packet has been sent by the trusted host.[30] In the case of voice, conversations containing trade secrets, for example, can be routed to an unintended party.

To mitigate the risk associated with IP spoofing attacks, an authentication mechanism stronger than address-based authentication is required. Hosts internal to a destination host environment should form only trusted relationships. In addition, it is suggested that encryption is employed to protect transmissions.[31] Vendors such as Net Talk[32] and Aravox Technologies[33] have created VoIP-based firewalls to provide protection and authentication for VoIP implementations. VoIP firewalls should be considered behind a VoIP gateway for authentication purposes. A VoIP gateway provides conversion services between networks. As a result, a trusted relationship may be created.

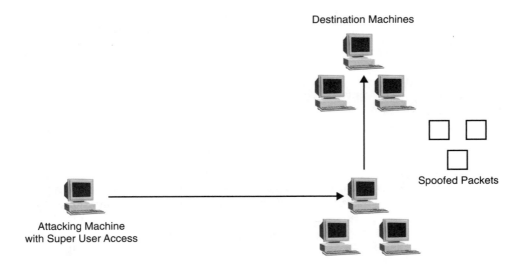

11-1 IP Spoofing.

Interception and Eavesdropping of Voice Transmission Over the Air

Signals that contain VoIP information transmitted over a wireless network are subject to interception and eavesdropping. Intercepting a signal is analogous to stealing the signal. Typically, transmissions can be intercepted with scanning equipment tuned into the appropriate frequency of the transmission[34] or sniffers strategically placed on certain parts of a network. A sniffer attached to the network in which a packet travels can actively monitor IP packets, including those that contain voice. A sniffer can read all information contained within the packet. Although a sniffer can be used for legitimate purposes, such as diagnosing traffic bottlenecks, unscrupulous individuals can illegally monitor network traffic by planting a sniffer on the network. The sniffer can be used to pick up authentication measures such as user identification codes and passwords or highly sensitive information. Routers can contain sniffing devices that are not only capable of routing a packet to a desired location but can also read the entire contents of that package.[35] In some cases, the interception and eavesdropping of transmission is illegal, and protected by the Electronic Communication Privacy Act. However, a court order requested by law enforcement officials could give concession to interception and eavesdropping.

CNN reports that the Federal Bureau of Investigations has created and deployed an electronic monitoring tool termed DCS1000 (formally known as Carnivore) that captures, filters, and stores packets of data traveling across an *Internet Service Provider's* (ISP) network. The DCS1000 tool initially captures all email or other electronic communication that could include voice information stored in IP packets traveling across an ISP network. The DCS1000 tool is used like a network sniffer. After obtaining the appropriate court orders, agents from the FBI and potentially technical personnel from the ISP attach the DCS1000 tool to the ISP network. The FBI and the ISP localizes the suspect's data on the ISP's network. The DCS1000 tool captures data (this could include data from individuals not the target of a criminal investigation) and makes a copy of the data. The suspect is unaware of this process as the original copy of the data packet(s) stays intact and continues its normal transmission. The captured copy of the suspect's data is filtered and permanently stored and filed within the DCS1000 tool. Data collected that is not included in the court order is discarded.[36]

To mitigate the risk associated with interception and eavesdropping, strong end-to-end encryption can be employed. Encryption standards such as Triple DES or the Rijndael standard, when fully implemented, should suffice in terms of providing the confidentiality of voice transmissions.

Denial of Service

A denial of service prevents a system or network from operating in the manner in which it was designed and could adversely impact the Information Security process in terms its confidentiality, integrity, and availability attributes. A denial of service cannot only impact service provided by an entity but could adversely impact an entity's reputation, and financial stability. Processing delays (latency) could give a misconceived notion that a denial of service has occurred. Neglect in adequately securing physical assets and applying appropriate patches to hardware and software components could facilitate a denial of service. In a wireless environment, jamming the signal associated with a wireless transmission can render a system or network inoperative.

Jamming is a mechanism used to override radio signals or waves by broadcasting a stronger signal to confuse the target of that signal. In a totally wired network, the risk associated with a denial of service can be mitigated in several ways. For example, network and host-based intrusion detection can be installed to monitor network patterns and signatures associated with a denial of service attack. However, this may prove a little more difficult for wireless networks due to the over the air factor. Special equipment can be employed to detect, spread, or burst hostile signals for wireless transmission. Additional mitigation remedies for VoIP-based solutions implemented over a wired and wireless network could include the installation of an uninterruptible power supply (UPS), VoIP-based firewalls, anti-virus soft-ware, Virtual Private Network, cryptography, and a contingency plan as examples.[38] In addition, physical and technical security for gateways, routers, servers, and transmitting and receiving points should be considered[39] to mitigate the risks associated with unauthorized IP spoofing, interception, and eavesdropping, or denials of service over VoIP-based solutions.

Summary

IP-based networks are widely used around the globe. VoIP allows companies, as well as households, to use leading edge technology without changing their current network infrastructure.

VoIP is presently less reliable than the traditional telephone. VoIP can suffer from delay. It can drop or lose connections. If the delays and uncertainty in establishing a connection are addressed properly, the future may be bright for VoIP. It will have to prove itself reliable before most organizations change over completely.

Competing standards and evolving technologies have led to a proliferation of non-compatible (that is, proprietary) vendor products, software applications, and service providers, resulting in a virtual "Tower of Babel" for consumers interested in acquiring and using IP telephony. Further, a point raised by Black, the untamed nature of the Internet begs the question of how, not when, VoIP will be implemented. Which protocols (Frame Relay, ATM, SONET, or other) and which standards will lead to the development of products and services for achieving full VoIP implementation? In addition to uniform standards, security vulnerabilities inherent with VoIP implementations are key issues.

Security vulnerabilities affect all infrastructures and architectures that carry voice transmissions including the *Public Switched Telephone Network* (PSTN), cellular/PCS systems, and voice. They cannot be ignored.

Endnotes

[1]"IP Telephony Opportunities," Available at: http://www.ipaxs.com/images/Iptel-opportunities.pdf, Accessed June 13, 2001.

[2]"Voice over IP Calculator," Available at: http://www.voip-calculator. com/protocols.htm, Accessed May 14, 2001.

[3]"Voice/Network Test," Available at: www.empirix.com/empirix/voice+network+test/resources/gos+testing+for+voipp.html [paper #21], Accessed June 14, 2001.

[4]www.echoplex.net/Knowledge_Base/VoIP.html.

[5]Black, Uyless D., *Voice Over IP,* Prentice Hall, 1999.

[6]Elachi, Joanna, "Standards Snapshot: The State Of The Big 3 in VoIP Signaling Protocols," 11/27/00, Available at: http://www.commweb.com/article/COM20001127S0008.

[7]Nokia, "H.323—The Standard," Available at: http://www.helike.com/nokiaip/h323.html, Accessed July 1, 2001,

[8]Ibid., p. 15.

[9]Ibid., p. 14.

[10]"Voice Over IP Service and Performance in Satellite Networks," *IEEE Communications* Magazine, March 2001, Thuan Nguyen, Ferit Yegenoglu, and Agatino Sciuto, COMSAT Laboratories, Ravi Subbarayan, Lockheed Martin Global Communications.

[11]The Technology Guide Series, "QoS in the Enterprise," Jerry Ryan, http://www.techguide.com, p. 9.

[12]Ibid.

[13]Audin, Gary, "VoIP? A question of perspective," Business Communications Review, April 2001.

[14]Ibid.

[15]Intercom, May 2001. Op. cit.

[16]Douskalis, Bill, *IP Telephony. The Integration of Robust VoIP Services*, Prentice Hall, 2000.

[17]"Voice over IP query results," Network World Fusion, Available at: http://www2.nwfusion.com/bg/voip/voipresult.jsp?_tablename=voip, Accessed June 13, 2001.

[18]Ibid.

[19]Ibid.

[20]Ibid.

[21]Russell, Deborah, and G.T. Gangemi, *Computer Security Basics*, O'Reilly & Associates, 1992, pp. 12–13.

[22]Nichols, Randall K., Daniel J Ryan, and Julie J.C.H Ryan, *Defending Your Digital Assets Against Hackers, Crackers, Spies & Thieves*, McGraw-Hill, 2000.

[23]Collins, Daniel, *Carrier Grade Voice Over IP*, McGraw-Hill, 2001, p. 52.

[24]Ibid.

[25]www.extremetech.com/print_article/0.3428.a%3D11271.00.asp. A new paper, "Weaknesses in the Key Scheduling Algorithm in RC4,"by Adi Shamir and Itsik Mantin of the Weitzmann Institute in Israel and Scott Fluhrer of Cisco Systems, argues that the underlying cipher that provides security in 802.11 wireless LAN protocol can be cracked on a standard PC in about 15 minutes. And unlike other attacks, the length of the key is not important since the complexity of the attack grows linearly and not exponentially. A related attack by AT&T Laboratories by a team headed by Aviel Rubin concluded that the 802.11 was insecure because they could violate it security using a $100 wireless network card and a Linux driver to grab the raw WEP packets.

[26]Mehta, Princy C., *Wired Equivalent Privacy Vulnerability*, SANS Information Reading Room, 2001, Available at: http://www/sans.org/infosecFAQ/wireless/equiv.htm, Accessed May 27, 2001.

[27]Nichols, Randall K., *ICSA Guide to Cryptography*, McGraw-Hill, 1999, pp. 399–406.

[28]Cravotta, Nicholas, *Voice Over Packet: Putting It All Together*, EDN, 2000, p. 112.

[29]Collins, Daniel, *Carrier Grade Voice Over IP*, McGraw-Hill, 2001, p. 2.

[30]Daemon9, Route, Infinity, "IP Spoofing Demystified: Trust Relationship Exploitation" (article on-line), *Phrack* Magazine, 1996, Available at: http://www.networkcommand. com/docs/ipspoof.txt, Accessed May 30, 2001.

[31]Ibid.

[32]http://www.nettalk.com.

[33]http://www.aravox.com.

[34]Nichols, Professor Randall, Class lecture—Wireless Security and Cryptographic Countermeasures, EMSE 298, Summer 2001.

[35]Ibid.

[36]"See How Carnivore Gathers Data for the FBI," CNN 2000, Available at: http://www. cnn.com/2000/TECH/computing/08/25/carnivore/index.html.

[37]Nichols, Professor Randall, Interviewing Notes, The George Washington University, June 11, 2001.

[38]Nichols, Randall K., Daniel J. Ryan, and Julie J.C.H Ryan, *Defending Your Digital Assets Against Hackers, Crackers, Spies & Thieves*, McGraw-Hill, 2000.

[39]McMurry, Mike, *Wireless Security* (article online), SANS Information Security Reading Room, 2001, Available at: http://www/sans.org/infosecFAQ/wireless/wireless_sec.htm.

12

Hardware Perspectives for End-to-End Security (E2E) in Wireless Applications

To establish a bulwark of security for the safety of communications, minimum requirements are

- Confidentiality
- Authentication
- Integrity
- Non-repudiation

A further item that might be added to this list is

- Secure remote access

Secure remote access implies confidential communication of specific items like passwords, challenge-response dialogs, cryptographic keys, session keys, or *initialization vectors* (IVs), also known as *seeding values*. These values must be corroborated through authentication servers, which approve or disapprove according to specific security policies, any access to the IT resources the legitimate user seeks to obtain.[1]

These aspects of communications security deal with content and usage security. There are indeed other aspects of communications security, just as there are also other types of attacks:

- Denial of service
- Jamming
- Interception

Denial of service (DoS) is a highly publicized type of attack in the packet-communications world. Damage occurs when hackers flood servers with SYN requests that ultimately bring down functionality as the server runs short of bandwidth. An example of a SYN-flood attack is the 2000 overseas-originated DoS attack that crippled e-bay and Amazon for two days at an estimated cost of $100,000 per hour to each company.

Fear of interception is always prevalent in the wireless communications world, in some networks more than in others. These days it is within almost everyone's grasp to intercept an analog modulated signal using inexpensive and rather unsophisticated off-the-shelf scanners. Things become somewhat more complicated to the average wireless user as technologies migrate to the more digital transmission. People tend to assume that because it is digital, it is more secure. This view originates in the novelty of the technology and is compounded by a nebulous marketing style on the part of vendors and carriers. The only pertinent difference between analog signaling and digital is that you need a different kind of scanner to intercept traffic. Both are equally easy to procure and both are equally efficient. They may be illegal in some countries, but legality is no premise for peace of mind.

Original digital wireless networks were based on the TDMA technique but soon evolved to FDMA for the allocation of temporary access to the precious bandwidth needed by so many subscribers. TDMA (for example, IS-136) networks use $\pi/4$-*Differential Quadrature Phase Shift Keying* (DQPSK) as modulation technique ($\pi/4$-DQPSK) that is readily demodulated and therefore by definition the signal may be intercepted going to or coming from a tower. Once intercepted, computing technology available in a simple network sniffer or packet analyzer will then display (or dump into files for subsequent analysis) frames, where the traffic may be studied at leisure and the interceptor can analyze addresses, phone and account numbers, headers, trailers, passwords, and content at will. In the case of data, the meaning of content is clear. In the case of voice, if the payload in each time slot of the TDMA example is separated, a binary file may be created containing the vocoded traffic. An inexpensive software-based vocoder implementation of the type used in the network at hand (for instance CELP for IS-136) will decode the recorded coded voice and create a decompressed file, which when run on a DAC converter (for example, through an I/O adapter) will produce audibly the intercepted traffic. The complexity of the task is comparable to an undergraduate engineering homework assignment.

From the 1990s onward, wireless communication has been based on CDMA technologies, including varieties using DS/CDMA (direct-sequence) and FH/CDMA (frequency-hopping). FH/CDMA may be further split into *Fast Frequency-Hopping* (FFH) and *Slow Frequency-Hopping* (SFH) systems. While hopping, the signal becomes less susceptible to interference, therefore acquiring inherent resistance to jamming.

Taxonomy of Communications Systems

The sheer multitude of possible applications in the wireless communications demands we organize application hierarchies and interactions into classifications that assist understanding. Computing models must be mapped into the communications fabric. With map in hand, we can start to envision what is needed for end-to-end security, and what has been proposed to address these needs.

Communicating devices are essentially computers, equipped with CPUs either of the CISC and RISC variety or DSP processors along with program memory and data memory. Their computing capabilities can range from meager to truly awesome depending on functionality needed, quality of design, and, of course, price elasticity of the targeted markets. Computing taxonomy models are therefore immediately applicable to communications devices.

Client-Server versus Peer-to-Peer

In client-server applications, high-capacity computers (*servers*) support a set of databases with the pertinent information while other computers (*clients)* access this information periodically by making formal requests. This cooperative computing model, pioneered in the 1980s, has been a devolution of the mainframe computer towards decentralizing computing resources, precipitated by the emergence of the PC.

An offspring of the client-server model has become dominant in Internet-based communications. The ubiquitous HTTP protocol is a classical example of client-server relations. When you click your browser on a hyperlink, an amazing sequence of events is launched: A request goes to the appropriate server (even to the other side of the planet) for this specific HTML page, which will be supplied by the server from its proverbial "treasure chest" and transmitted back to the client who requested it. The client computer's browser then disposes of all but the elements needed locally to interpret the HTML code it receives. It then displays the appropriate content inside the browser. Why has this model been so successful? The answer is efficiency. Sending code in ASCII form is far more efficient than sending digitized versions of the Web pages themselves. HTML enables local construction of Web page content, which otherwise would occupy precious Mbps of communications bandwidth and result in waiting periods users won't tolerate.

The communicating devices in a client-server situation have different roles to play and as such their functionality and features are in most cases different. Occasionally the devices can be physically identical (such as a client PC communicating with other PC as server). Even in this case the SW profiles are different as the two machines must behave differently, and therefore the roles cannot be confused easily. In essence a client asks for information or service and the server obliges or tells the client to try later. Occasionally the server can ask the client to receive some services or information and the client responds by accepting or postponing. The client system usually possesses the requisite intelligence and capacity to use the information received from the server to construct the local presence of the information display to benefit the user.

Client-server is the preponderate model for e-commerce and for m-commerce. The industry has taken a strong socket-based approach for its security implementation. In the classical wired world, SSL seems to be more or less the established model of SW-implemented security. It is acceptably strong (especially in conjunction with 128-bit cryptographic key schemes, like 3DES or IDEA) and it is well understood by many programmers. Carrying over the philosophy to a wireless medium, the WTLS approach has been an evolution of SSL towards wireless. The problem is that the wireless gateway that translates WWW language scripts and *Wireless Markup Language* (WML) commands obliges the encrypted data traveling from a server through an SSL tunnel to be decrypted inside the wireless gateway and then re-encrypted into a TLS tunnel over the air. This unacceptable procedure is the Achilles heel of the model, from the end-to-end point of view.

In the peer-to-peer computing model, systems have essentially the same capabilities and play more or less identical roles in the same or different contexts. There is no need for, or interest in, client-server relationships. Instead there is computing democracy where every device is on a par. Let's take the typical example of a telephone call. When you pick up the phone and call somebody, the devices entering into communication session are peers. They may be available or not, they may accept the call or not. No specific service is requested and granted as in the client-server model, where the whole application is unavailable when the server is unavailable. If the person you're calling cannot be found at one number, you can try another number. Or if the callee doesn't hear you well, the caller can shout or send a fax. SSL or WTLS can be applied to a peer-to-peer communications model, but falls far short of the functionality and performance requirements other advanced end-to-end techniques offer.

Circuit-Switched versus Packet-Switched or Frame-Switched Communications

The need to optimize bandwidth while controlling costs has been a carrot for innovators for the last 25 years throughout the packet explosion, starting with the X.25 protocol that revolutionized data communications. Data to be transmitted, previously sent in an unbroken stream, was finally broken into small manageable units known as *packets*. The revolutionary idea was that instead of a full-time active, physically present connection, called a *circuit*, between the end stations, now a communications session could be established between two ends with a virtual circuit. As long as there were alternative routes between the end stations, the intermittent X.25 switches would define the optimal route along which packets should be switched one by one. Individual packets could be sent to their destination over different routes based on traffic load-switching tables, with the liberating concept that individual packets could arrive out of order, in which case the end station would be expected to have the intelligence to rearrange them into their correct order before presenting the data to a higher layer application or to the user.

Soon the X.25 fabric started evolving under pressure of increasing application sophistication. Computer graphics and the CAD/CAM explosion in the 1980s, along with burgeoning telephony applications, engendered frame relay. The principle is again the same (a packet and a frame are essentially alike for practical purposes) with specific bit fields within a frame similar to X.25 and others specific to frame relay. Frames can now be switched over higher speed physical links and associate new concepts with the delivery of sophisticated services.

Quality of Service (QoS), wherein a carrier basically guarantees the network latency and throughput, is being instituted through a series of signaling constructs in which the frame relay network flags congestion and alerts upstream intermittent switches to reroute traffic so as to accommodate specific service requirements. It also creates capabilities for subsequent automatic requests for retransmission of specific frames when they have been badly received. These are just a few of the examples of pioneering services the frame-relay networks brought about.[2,3]

Frame relay systems are usually standalone switches that can be connected to an end-device with either RJ-11 adapters or Ethernet LANs. To some extent, frame relay switches can be considered precursors of today's routers. In some embedded cases the frame relay end device called a *frame relay assembler disassembler* (FRAD) takes the form of a PC adapter, usually on high-speed internal buses like the PCI bus. This PCI adapter is plugged inside a PC or workstation to give it physical access to a frame relay network.

The more tightly the end of the network is built into an end-device, the higher the security one expects from such a configuration. Traditional frame relay network security relied (and still does in many corporate networks such as the Swiss banking system) on X.25 and frame relay encryptors. These are usually rack-mountable devices that encrypt and decrypt transmissions on-the-fly without affecting packet (frame) headers and trailers. They process only the payload, ensuring confidentiality. Some but not all of these devices offer authentication as well, as part of a larger information security infrastructure. Some can handle up to E-3 speeds, while some can only work on T-1 speeds. They all more or less share the same underlying functional characteristics. The frame headers and trailers are not encrypted which ensures that the frames are switchable or routable by the network infrastructure independently of the context they carry. Only the corresponding encryptor at the other side of the link will be able to decrypt the payload.

The previous statement immediately strikes a chord of sensitivity regarding end-to-end security, because as the information revolution exploded, people realized that ensuring a link from a FRAD in front of my building to a FRAD in front of yours is not enough. There are still two significant portions of the link where the session is insecure. These are the spans from my end-device (telephone or PC or workstation) up to the FRAD in my premises, and then likewise in your premises from FRAD to end-device. Numerous analyses have been published as to how and why insiders cannot be trusted. Nor can the insider danger be mitigated. Vendors who capitalized on this model of security soon found themselves in a no-win situation. Customers made heavy investments for security and didn't get compensatory peace of mind. The model was even transplanted to the IP realm as we will see further on.

As an example of a Frame Relay data packet encryption approach, Figure 12-1 depicts the payload portion of the packet as encrypted using the *Data Link Connection Identifier* (DLCI) information in the Frame Relay Header, to determine what *Data Encryption Key* (DEK) to use for the operation.

Flag and header information is not encrypted. The *Data Information Field* (DIF) is extended to accommodate a special 16-byte Crypto Header. Since the DIF has changed appreciably, the polynomial-based *Frame Check Sum* (FCS) must be

(a) Plaintext Frame

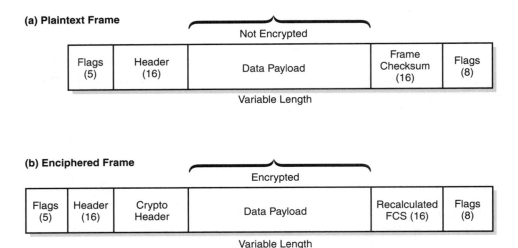

12-1 Frame-Relay Protocol Sensitive Encryption.

recalculated. This example of a frame relay encryptor shows a system that not only encrypts on-the-fly using 3DES encryption, but also contains sophisticated anti-spoofing and anti-playback mechanisms to prohibit an active middleman attack, when, for instance, an attack is mounted against a payment-clearing house, either by impersonating Bank A for Bank B or Account C for Account D. This defense relies on an encrypted embedded pre-numbering of frames (before encryption occurs), so that anyone tampering with the payload, relying only on the frame relay network's overriding packet assembly, is sure to get exposed.

The receiving encryptor will always know if someone has tampered with the data, the order of transmission, or other session parameters. Commonplace techniques for discovery originated from specific network design fostered—if not specified outright—many years ago by the government.

This implies that the techniques to be explored have been originated and tested over many years of critical applications environments, under the government's study and that government, despite its "Big Brother" tinge, has been an irreplaceable catalyst for an explosion of information security breakthroughs as part of its underlying mission to protect the nation.

In a sense these commercial frame-relay encryption products of the mid-1990s predicted what was about to permeate the IP world. Something akin to a cultural revolution began when we realized that the unique principles of Layer 2 of the OSI model were so desirable that we might want to extend them one layer higher, at the network level. The idea is straightforward: With secure sessions at the IP layer where network addresses are established, the actual routing of the traffic can be completely transparent for the user. Some parts of transmission can be routed over a frame relay network, some parts over an ATM backbone, and yet other parts over the POTS. Corporate IT managers reacted to the idea and pushed for protocols that would enable equipment vendors to write functional specifications and product definitions.

The result was IPSec, a massive protocol effort based on a series of RFC documents specifying how a Layer-3 encryptor should function and accentuated by the fact that IP had already started to overtake the corporate networks for structuring and addressing. This last development propelled an abundance of initiatives to make up for IP's shortcomings in addressing, clustering, and broadcasting capabilities. But the most significant evolution was in the security realm under the auspices of IPSec.

IPSec introduced two underlying mechanisms formulated for building packet headers and trailers: *Authentication Header* (AH) and *Extended Security Payload* (ESP). Their purpose was to allow the IPSec-compliant device to encrypt the payload of an IP packet and at the same time augment it with an associated overhead bit structure that authenticated bidirectionally the session, the device, and even the user, given an associated infrastructure of higher-level protocol suites. Classical techniques from the everyday cryptography realm (DES, Triple DES, MD5, and so forth) were sanctioned, providing a lot of detail to determine how a product should behave to be IPSec compliant. (IPSec is covered in detail in several standard textbooks.)[4,5,6] Under IPSec, devices from different vendors communicating with each other exchange information about their respective capabilities within the first few milliseconds of handshake. One might liken this to one party saying "Hi, I speak English and Dutch in both modern and medieval versions," and the other party responding "Good, I speak medieval Dutch and Sanskrit" which would push the two parties to fall back on their common denominator of capabilities to establish a secure session (in this absurd case, in medieval Dutch).

Essentially all this technology was already available four or five years earlier in the frame-relay realm, except that at that time fierce competition precluded an industry-wide interoperability compliance forum. The same idea of encrypting sessions with different keys, and monitoring networks with management software like SNMP and RMON, finally became reality in Layer-3 security.

A centralized network management function, now seconded in several cases with a centralized network security function, uses classical network management tools and techniques to set up monitoring agents inside the network devices. These agents keep track of events and report back to the network management system either by being periodically polled or by the classical SNMP method every time something significant happens. The encrypting devices must have the embedded intelligence to communicate with the network management system, reporting events, activity, and exceptions. The monitored device also must be able to either

- Communicate to the network management host the status of specific parameters of interest when interrogated about the values of specific objects (the answers will be reflected inside the dynamic object database of the network manager).
- Set the value of specific parameters as instructed by the network manager host.

The latter obviously is of significant security concern as one is always concerned that a rogue device (controlled by an adversary) might alter values on specific critical parameters. This makes clearer the need for proper device authentication and more secure communications over TCP/IP, the communication method of choice for SNMP type of network management schemes. The interested reader is referred to the extensive coverage of the subject in two excellent books by Stallings.[7,8]

A network management system affords a real-time view of the behavior and performance of the secure network, aware at every instance which node is up and which down, which thread or session or user is engaging which virtual circuit, from which location specific sessions are being initiated, and whether these events should be flagged for physical security inspection. The network manager must also ascertain what types of attacks are being staged on specific parts of the network, and where they originate. He implements a *management information base* (MIB) database of objects as a hyper-detailed logging record of network activity. INFOSEC and COMSEC vendors have even integrated such facilities with classical network management platforms like HP OpenView, NetView, and so forth, thereby making security management easier for corporate networks and organizations.

IPSec has become a consortium-wide effort to detail specifications for compliance on everything from the choice of encryption algorithms and configuration mode to secure key generation and exchange between communicating parties. IPSec techniques like ISAKMP and Oakley were meant to generate session cryptographic contexts in a fully compliant method that ensures interoperability among vendors. One should note that as late 2001, many IPSec compliant products have failed to achieve interoperability despite the noble goals of the consortium and the high expectations of the industry. There is currently a group within IPSec that verifies inter-compatibility of products. Just as the modem industry, despite its slow start, achieved interoperability after 25 years, one can be reasonably sure that in the next two to three years inter-compatibility issues for IPSec compliant products will be resolved.

IPSec products can be either stand-alone boxes attached to an end-device (PC, workstation, or server), or as adapters that fit into the I/O bus (usually PCI-bus compatible) of a router or PC. The end-to-end security scheme based on IPSec takes on the following form, slightly reminiscent of the frame relay past:

- If the IPSec security module is embedded inside a router, it only protects the link from your router (in front of your building) to my router (in front of my building). This is the same problem, described earlier, which frame relay encryptor manufacturers encountered. It is a commercially unwinnable conflict for vendors where the true end-to-end security offering will ultimately prevail. End-to-end is not meant to be router-to-router. Router manufacturers have (for obvious reasons) pushed this realm with their own (or OEM-originated) embedded offers but there are serious security and performance concerns about their model that the majority of users does not know or conveniently chooses to ignore.
- If the IPSec security is embedded inside an end-device (like a PC) with a PCI-type of adapter, then this IPSec functionality (running on it as a coprocessor to the system's host CPU) is interfacing with the host through the I/O bus potentially using standard DMA (direct memory access) techniques, and creating other security lapses.

- To address some of the security lapses alluded to in the previous point, some vendors have the IPSec security run as embedded SW on the host CPU. The security advantage this approach will suffer from a severe performance degradation that will ensue, the so-called cycle stealing on the host CPU.
- IPSec and the cryptographic algorithms it uses observe a software-based paradigm, which is ideal for the manipulation of alphanumeric data. The awesome yet inexpensive computing power available inside switches, routers, and wireless phones has pushed forward the software engineering explosion that accompanies such developments. It is straightforward to write code that reads data and structures in the IPSec AH or ESP headers and trailers. It is the way to go considering the intricacies of e-commerce and client-server communications. However, this same IPSec asset becomes a liability when real-time heavy-duty content must be transmitted with minimum latency and maximum performance predictability. In that context fast and inexpensive hardware takes over the preferred slot of choice, otherwise the sheer torrent load of data to be dealt with simply chokes the computational intelligence, overflows the limited buffering capabilities and exhausts the throughput capacity of even the most sophisticated IPSec device. The result (as a small heads-up to the reader who may be surprised, having been indoctrinated from much marketing hype and brainwashing) is that for real-time voice transmissions as well as for audio and video distribution, IPSec is *not* the solution for the implementation of end-to-end security. Other powerful techniques will have to prevail, especially in resource-constrained devices.

Unicast versus Broadcast Communications

People and systems do not communicate solely on a one-to-one basis. Multitudes of applications must communicate with many. A communication session may not necessarily be full duplex, or even duplex at all. When I am listening to my favorite FM radio station, the station does not need to receive an acknowledgment that I heard the program loud and clear. And even if it did, the transmission technique doesn't permit me to communicate this information.

For purposes of this discussion, broadcasting implies that a source transmitting simultaneously to many other stations does not require feedback. If recipients need a capability to communicate in reverse direction, terms like *teleconferencing* or *video-conferencing* or even *networking* apply. The functional requirements are unique for each of these multi-party cases, as is the functionality of the associated equipment.[9,10]

In the conference call instance, the cryptographic context to be negotiated by the end devices at session set-up must be accessible transparently to all parties involved. In a telephony case, the established *Diffie-Hellman* (DH) protocol, or the alternative ECC-DH protocol, based on elliptic curve cryptography, allows two communicating parties to calculate independently a so-called session key that obviates most known attacks even for a sophisticated eavesdropper. This is a milestone in the evolution of affordable secure communications for the masses. Until recently nothing short of multi-thousand-dollar pieces of equipment was required in order to engage in robustly secure communications. Embedded technology is decimating the cost consideration.

Where more than two parties are involved, a cryptographic protocol that addresses the needs of two parties is short of a solution. Schneier has documented a simple but workable variation of the DH protocol for multiple users.[11] Another approach modifies the protocol to accommodate a sequence of DH sessions on a pair basis between the master and each of the slaves; at the end the master communicates the overlying session key that it established and imposed to all parts. This scheme of course does not scale easily. The time required to accommodate large audiences can be prohibitively long. If in human terms, it takes two to three seconds to complete the DH handshake between two inexpensive telephones, either or both of which are wireless, one can imagine how exasperated the users should be of a conference call with from six to seven partners where the handshake has to be repeated in round-robin fashion, taking minutes of wasted (and billed) session time.

Public-key cryptography is an area of active research. The ideal solution seems to be an approach like the one *Pretty Good Privacy* (PGP) took years before on multiple-key-encrypted email. A session key is generated for all legitimate users to employ if they wish to access the corresponding encrypted information/session. The session key is encrypted by each individual user's public key and sent to him or her. Simple teleconferencing aside, the ability of companies to download content through a fundamentally insecure multimedia network like the Internet will be of critical importance in the business context of the near future.

Most Internet users already understand the basic concepts of e-commerce and m-commerce. I can sit at my desktop and with a few mouse clicks, order books, or wine, or office supplies to be delivered to my door, or speak with my broker and advise "sell company X and buy company Y for my portfolio." These are point-to-point communications that are well controlled from a security viewpoint by the engineering community (although not even close to being equally well implemented by vendors). But what happens in end-to-end communications, as when a movie is downloaded through wireless channels? If the cable TV industry, operating in a wired medium with medium access codes and network addresses, cannot police stolen signal cases and finds itself obliged to offer an 800 number for anonymous callers who wish to denounce their neighbors for cable-stealing, one wonders how on earth the HBOs, Disneys, or Time-Warners of the world will be able to broadcast over the air secure content to legitimate customers. It should be obvious that if one can co-opt cable signal and get away with it, one can intercept wireless transmission in the privacy of one's home, boat, or car and NOT get caught. Guaranteed.

What is the solution? The answer should not be a surprise: a bi-directionally authenticated scalable fast and inexpensive end-to-end encrypted wireless tunnel (also known as wireless VPN). This will be called the *Wireless End-to-end Secure Communications* (WESC) premise. An encrypted tunnel must be established dynamically every time a legitimate user requests specific content. (Keep these terms in mind, as what is required to satisfy all these criteria will be presented in subsequent text.) Each time he or she receives a request, the provider will have to go through the entire authentication process: who you are, whether you have a valid account in good standing, whether you are creditworthy, whether there is still enough credit in your account, whether you seem to be the person you say you are, and so forth. Likewise, when you dial Disney and try to download a movie, you want to be sure that you are in touch with a Disney server and not with a credit-card fraud ring that gathers information from innocent users by posing as Disney. All of this has to happen in real-time and within a time window that will not frustrate the user. Classical cryptographic session protocols are ideal for such applications because the user initiates and negotiates a transmission from the server, in a one-to-one communication.

In the secure broadcast case though, there are several varieties and some limitations. If a session is announced beforehand, a user's device might dial independently on a one-to-one basis, negotiate a secure DH-like session, log on to a menu-driven service after making some choices, and receive from the server the cryptographic key and authentication material for the broadcast. This bypasses scalability concerns to a certain extent and clearly creates a base for secure broadcasting: only users in possession of the broadcaster's cryptographic context will be able to receive and decrypt the content. If the session is not announced, and occurs unexpectedly in real-time when someone dials, then we have to revert to the model for scalable distribution of decryption keys by legitimate users. In this event, the subscriber will contact a ticket server and obtain the ticket that contains the session key. The cryptographic session is established using the SAME session key for all subscribers and only a ticket-holder can decrypt the broadcast. *Digital rights management* (DRM) is a major issue now being debated by the entertainment industry, among others, and the standards are obviously still in flux.

Note that the context of a wireless device, mostly resource-constrained, dictates specific performance speed, computing capabilities, physical size and weight, battery lifetime, and power consumption constraints directly relevant to the performance of the end devices.

Land-Based versus Wireless-Based Communications

Yet another point of view from which we can study end-to-end secure communications is the fabric of the network the communicating parties are using. Party A can be on a wireless GSM telephone in Europe or South Asia while communicating with Party B, who can be on a Japanese wireless TDMA or Korean CDMA telephone, or on a wire line phone in the USA. The latter can be a Signaling System 7 telephone or even a simple computer-based telephony package running on a lowly laptop PC. *Market expectation is that if end-to-end secure communications are to materialize, users can expect to establish secure sessions in an economically satisfactory way, without knowing or caring about what type of device the other party is using, or what types of networks have to be traversed in order to establish a connection.*

This is a bold statement. In the example of Figure 12-2 the two communicating end-users do not need to know that there is, for example, an ATM backbone, or a carrier Intranet with dedicated bandwidth or even a frame relay network between them. They should not be preoccupied as to whether there is copper or fiber optics or air-interface towers between them. It all has to be acceptably fast, reliable, and above all trustworthy.

Traditionally, wireless security solutions for telephony, as for the point-to-point radio security of walkie-talkies using scramblers or link encryption, could cover only the air portion of the communications link. We have seen what terrible repercussions this has on the perceived security it affords the users. We've also seen that for end-to-end security to be feasible and believable something has to be embedded inside the end-devices. This something, which will shortly be given shape and form, either is embedded by the device designer or else injected into the end devices by somebody else. In the latter approach somebody else can be a carrier, or the government, or even a corporate governance body. Such a scenario, despite its financial payoff, does not make sense in a free society. People do not like their security to depend on third parties, and companies like it even less. The logical inference is that end-to-end security requires designed-in capabilities.

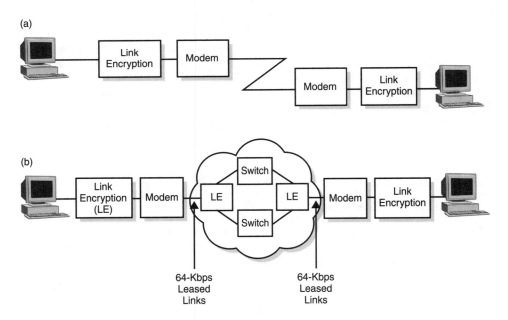

12-2 Link Encryptors.

Transmission Medium (Non-LAN Point-to-Point, LAN or WAN, or LAN-WAN-LAN)

Whether or not we're networked while communicating is an important data point for security decisions. We'll assume that if my computer is connected through an RS-232C cable to yours, we shall not call ourselves networked but merely connected. The industry has long been using specific point-to-point links where security is needed. The solution to the security riddle was, of course, encryption and this was the first level of secure communications using a link encryptor. Figure 12-2 illustrates the principle.

The link encryptor was the predecessor of the protocol-sensitive encryptor. All transmitted bits are encrypted and only the receiver knows how to decrypt them. Whether there are higher-level communications protocols with associated commands handshake-exchanged by the communicating parties is irrelevant. All traffic is encrypted. Such traffic cannot be switched or routed by a network infrastructure, as is the case in frame relay, ATM or IP networks, as the headers and trailers of potential packets/frames are also encrypted. Therefore any switches or routers between the parties will not know how to interpret the encrypted bits flying by and thus there can be no intelligent decisions. The link encryption method of securing communications is still used on specific links, usually of critical importance, either in the industry or the government, where networking is not only not available, it is plainly undesirable. A backup line to a corporate IP department disaster recovery site, or a missile launcher's communications station that must receive shooting coordinates from HQ, are typical examples.

Although technically this category satisfies our definition of end-to-end secure communications, the fact that the communicating parties can communicate only among themselves is a severe limitation. The term *end-to-end secure* communications will be used for devices that can be switched easily from a session with one user to another session with another user.

In LAN or WAN connections, and independently of the physical medium of the network, the end device is not the switch or the router, although the majority of users implement security schemes only from and to the switch or router. The end device is sitting on and is an element of the network: a PC, a workstation, a handset, an MP3 music player, a server, and so on. The end-to-end scheme we've delineated implies that every one of these systems must contain the embedded mechanisms that are needed for secure communications. Consider the scenario where a call is made from a wireless phone, and the party called works on a desktop PC that is connected on a corporate LAN, and the LAN is equipped with a VoIP gateway to the telephone realm of the outside world. Security will be end-to-end only if the telephone and the PC of the party called contains similar embedded originating COMSEC functionality.

Transmission Nature: Voice versus Data (Audio, Video, Alphanumeric)

Looking at end-to-end communications security from all angles entails due consideration of voice vs. date. Voice communication is the backbone of telephony in all its shapes, forms, and platforms. Transmission of data, audio, or video though is the transmission of compressed or encoded bit streams, and is therefore comprised of bits that must be transmitted intact if content reconstruction is going to be possible at the receiver. Note that security has yet to be mentioned in this context.

Although the average user has the impression that today everything is digital including voice, the facts are not so simple. Voice is first digitized and then companded (COMpressed and then exPANDED nonlinearly) by coding devices. The speech coding aspect is well covered in Chapter 6 and in the literature.[12,13,14,15,16] Speech coding is the work of voice coders (or vocoders). Traditionally there are two types: source and waveform coders. As waveform coding (see, for example, Sklar,[17]) is a classical sub-field of basic communications engineering, which involves numbers of symbols transmitted simultaneously, we will not expand on it here.

In industry usage today, the term vocoder connotes source coding, implying that vocoders are a model of the speech generation mechanism. Speech can be seen as a two-step process:

1. Interaction caused by air pushed upwards by the diaphragm from the lungs with the larynx (or vocal cords) behaving as a valve.
2. The ensuing acoustic emissions caused by this interaction. By controlling the vocal cords, acoustic emissions can be made periodic (voiced sounds) or turbulent (unvoiced sounds).

All mechanical interference with the air one expels by lips, tongue, teeth, and so forth, affects the spectral content of the excitation. The vocoder models speech likewise in two steps: an excitation model and a time-varying lossy resonator model.

Vocoders work by a nonlinear process that must be inversely replicated at the receiver for wired networks and at the air-interface tower for wireless communications. The vocoders of choice are different in different networks. For instance GSM uses a technique called RPE–LTP (regular-pulse excitation–longterm prediction). Choice criteria for wireless network vocoders are elaborate,[18,19,20,21,22] but GSM will serve to illustrate the nonlinear compression caused by the vocoder. A human voice is converted to an analog electric signal by the handset's microphone. This analog signal is digitized by sampling it with an ADC (analog-to-digital converter). Frequencies above 4 kHz are filtered to reduce nonproductive work by the ADC. Baseband voice signals are limited in telephony to between 300 Hz and 3.4 kHz. The GSM system samples the signal after this filtering. Every 125 microseconds a sample is taken of the signal and quantized into a 13-bit word. The number 125 ms comes from the sampling rate of 8,000 samples per second (sampling frequency 8 kHz, as Nyquist specified, which is twice the larger spectral component to be transmitted). At its output, therefore, the ADC converter delivers (see Figure 12-3) 8,000 × 13 bps = 104 Kbps.

The vocoder then engages two major processes:

- *Linear predictive coding* (LPC) and *regular pulse excitation* (RPE) analysis
- *Long-term prediction analysis* (LTP)

The reader is referred for GSM systems engineering details to the ETSI/GSM standard.[23] The speech coder now transforms the 104 Kbps into a series of blocks of 260 bits once every 20 ms, corresponding to a bit stream with net data rate of 13 Kbps. Therefore the compression effect mentioned above is exhibited. This process, also known in GSM jargon as speech transcoding, is highly computation intensive and as such is an ideal target for DSP processors. From this point the vocoded output must be channel-coded to make the bit stream robust to override channel noise, interference and losses like multipath fading. Channel coding adds redundancy to the bitstream and ultimately in the case of GSM a bitstream of 22.8 Kbps will be sent to the modulator and subsequently to the RF section for transmission. The process will be reversed at the receiver, as shown in Figure 12-3.

It's important to realize that there is no universal acceptance of one vocoder around which to standardize. As a result, a type-1 vocoder in a wireless end-device will most probably not interoperate with another end-device equipped with a type-2 vocoder. One example is the case where user A is on a GSM phone communicating with another user B on a landline. For voice transmission to be smooth and intelligible, A's vocoding process has to be inverted at the tower and adapted to a new scheme making it compatible with B's. Likewise when A calls another user C on a

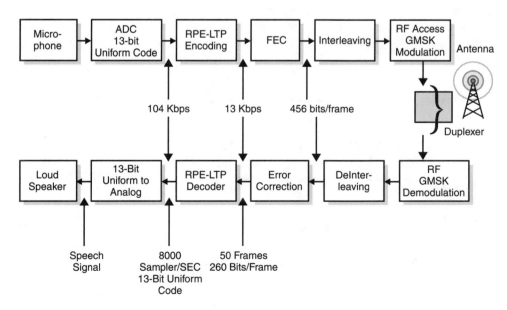

12-3 LPE RTP vocoding in a GSM wireless phone.

CDMA phone, their two vocoders are by definition and design noncompatible, which calls for the transformation to take place at the two corresponding towers. A's transmission, upon arrival at the tower keeping track of user A, will be reversed and re-encoded according to the land network's vocoder, and then fed into the land network.

When the transmission arrives at User B's tower it will be decoded from the land network's vocoding and reencoded using User C's vocoding technique, which the handset of User C can understand and decode. Even if two wireless users communicate on the same type of network, if they have to communicate through a land-sub-network and despite the fact that the end vocoders are compatible, the land-to-air-interfaces will enforce a decoding and reencoding with the appropriate vocoding techniques. In case of a GSM to GSM user communication session, the transmitted traffic will go from RPE–LTP in the handset to RPE to LTP at the tower. This is seen from Figure 12-4, which shows in the case of GSM how the voice transcoding is happening at the BTS (also known as BSS or tower). Then the signal at the tower will go from RPE to LTP to landline network vocoding from where it will be transmitted over the land network and eventually perhaps onto another tower (possibly ultimately the same one if the users are in physical proximity with each other). It will then be decoded from the landline vocoding method and revocoded using RPE to LTP before being transmitted intelligibly to the waiting correspondent party.

In the preceding discussion, tower does not designate that something is located physically at the air-to-land interface "tower", but instead it can be some intermediary infrastructure base (which usually has a different name in every type of wireless network), which we here generically termed a "tower." In the case of GSM (see Figure 12-5) we have many *Base Transceiver Stations* (BTSs), each of which manages a series of wireless stations, then BTSs controlled by one or more *Base Station Controllers* (BSCs) and then one or more *mobile switching centers*

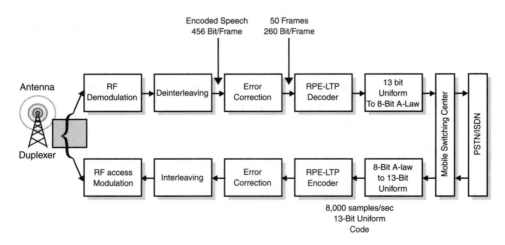

12-4 GSM Base Transceiver Station (BTS) also known as Base Substation System (BSS) showing tower vocoders and the interface with land network.

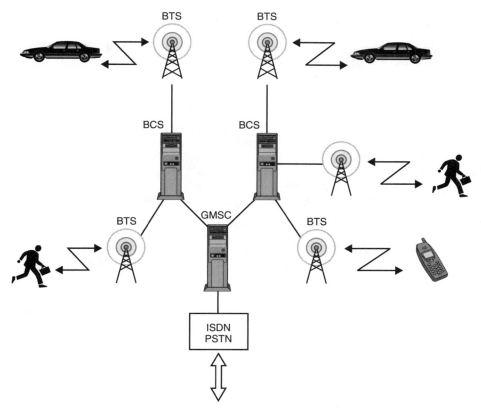

12-5 GSM network architecture.

(MSC's) that interface the network of BTS's with the classical PSTN telephony networks. Speech transcoding happens inside the BTS as shown in Figures 12-4 and 12-5.

All this would be of little interest here if not referenced to the principal point of discussion: *end-to-end security*. As vocoding is not an end-to-end scheme, if one encrypts the output of a vocoder A, having somehow established a cryptographic session with a User B, once it arrives at User B (assuming that either A or B or both are wireless users) the cipher traffic will be completely irreversible. The reason for this unfortunate situation is that the air-to-land interfaces through which it went have applied one or more nonlinear vocoding processes on the plaintext bits. This amounts to a process that cannot be reversed, therefore, the plaintext cannot be recovered mathematically.

Only two approaches are available for the solution of this problem:

- Encrypt voice before the vocoding process in the handset.
- Encrypt voice, but transmit it as data over the data channel, where no vocoding interfaces intervene in the transmission path.

The former implies encrypting before compressing. This is an irreversible process mathematically and therefore it is discarded as a design option. There is only one viable choice for end-to-end voice security: Voice must be encrypted and transmitted through the data channel by means of the wireless network infrastructure at hand. Encrypted voice is in this way treated exactly like data, independently of whether it is audio or video or alphanumeric data that must be transmitted securely over an insecure network.

Another potential avenue for exploration is combining vocoding and encryption into one process. Figures 12-6, 12-7, and 12-8 show that an end-to-end encryptor must be located in the vicinity of the channel coder inside a handset, but handset architect and designer have several options. For the equipment designer, the latest TDMA- and CDMA-type of wireless telephones pose printed-circuit board real-estate issues of major concern. Handsets have shrunk to extraordinarily small sizes and aggressive marketing has established usage models where one must be able to fit a telephone in a shirt pocket or purse.

The corresponding pressure to integrate becomes overwhelming and handsets become a two-chip system containing a host CPU (usually embedding a RISC processor for the overall application manager, screen menu, and so forth); and a DSP processor, called the baseband processor, where convolutional coding, PN spreading functions, echo cancellation, channel equalization algorithms, and so on are running in real-time using its native mathematical processing capabilities. In that case an encrypting/authenticating engine implemented as an IP core can, in principle, fit into either of the two as shown in Figures 12-9 and 12-10.

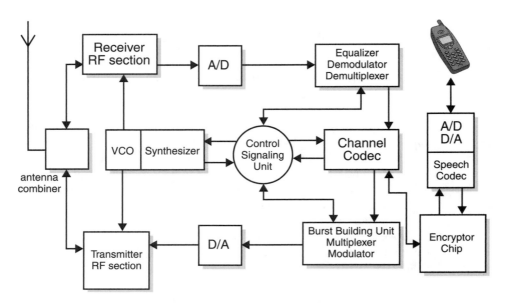

12-6 One possibility of an end-to-end encryptor/authenticator in a traditional wireless handset is as an ASIC next to the codec.

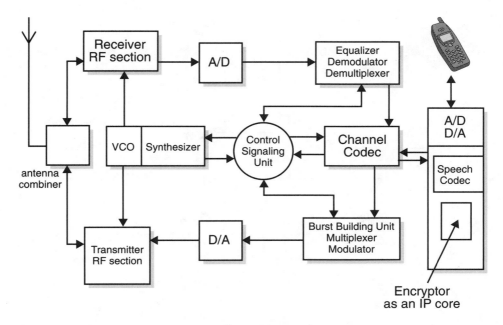

12-7 Insertion of an end-to-end encryptor/authenticator as an IP core inside a codec chip.

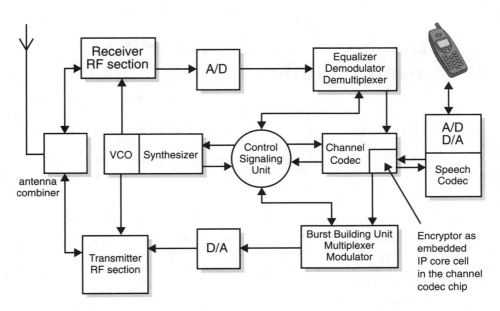

12-8 An end-to-end encryptor/authenticator can be embedded as an IP core inside a codec.

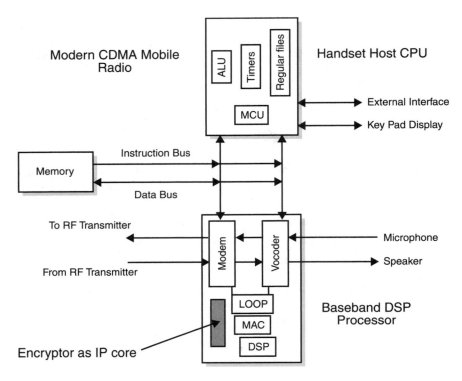

12-9 An encryptor/authenticator embedded inside the CDMA handset's baseband chip.

Quantity, Speed, and Predictability of Transmitted Information

One of the interesting techniques proposed for traffic encryption is time-smearing.[24] The technique involves nonlinear-phase FIR digital filter-based convolutional techniques, which spread the time signature of individual bit slots over adjacent bit slots of a window that rolls over the transmitted bit stream; the result is not only an unrecognizable bit stream, but one where the original information bits are now mapped to a set of output bits. This time-domain redundancy is the base for the time-smearing technique's significantly increased resilience to noise and therefore link reliability, as well as (given an appropriate multiplicative-weights code generation mathematics and degree of phase randomness) communications security. The downside is the significant increase in effective bit rate, as the original bit traffic has been multiplied by 4, 6, 8, or more depending on the FIR coefficients bit length and a signal delay imposed on the traffic equal to half the length of the smearing filters (times the bit-rate clock cycle), something that for some applications is not an issue but for some others is.

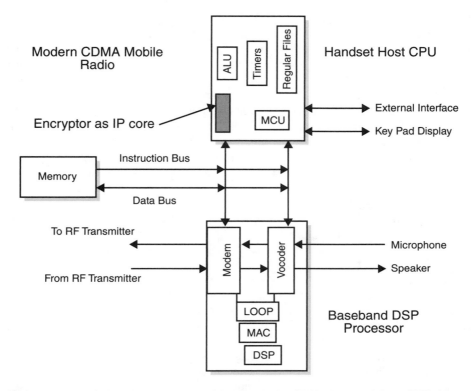

12-10 An encryptor/authenticator embedded inside the CDMA handset's host CPU chip.

Protocol Sensitive Communications Security

With the multidimensional context in mind, it is good to consider briefly from the hardware point of view, some of the compromises and trade-offs one must confront when designing a network solution to wireless security. From the day-to-day realm of wired packet communications, security approaches evolved both historically as well as functionally towards the current wireless devices. The choices, sacrifices, and options made during the last several years will not only become clear but will be shown to have been justified.

Earlier the possibility of embedding cryptography inside a switch or router was mentioned. This solution was pursued for four or five years, originally by encryption vendors who would propose their own boxes be placed next to a FRAD, switch or router. Soon the switch and router manufacturers realized that the added value of security, as requested by the market, signified an increase in overall value, so it was but a matter of time before they proposed their own embedded solutions, either developed in-house or captured by company acquisitions.

An initial look at the independent encryptor box connected before or after the router, and the tradeoffs of doing it either way, may be illuminating. Figure 12-11 shows two possible ways to connect a network speed encryptor to a router. The first case, Figure 12-11, with the encryptor is installed ahead of the router, has the advantage that the router can be protected from hacking as only valid VPNs can be established, but the network translation addresses now will not work. The VPNs use their own addressing scheme, which does not abide by IP addresses and masking; hence this solution, albeit the more secure from a network point of view, is also the least desirable, as it cuts away a significant portion of the IT department flexibility. In the second case, the encryptor is positioned behind the router. Those VPNs established for users of the corporate LAN (protected this way by the encryptor behind the router) are superbly protected, however since the router is physically exposed to the insecure network it is exposed to hacking.

Trying to find a solution that didn't oblige customers to install another box, but still let switch and router manufacturers get in on the security bonanza of the security, vendors began to embed security technology inside their own boxes. This security takes the form of either a security coprocessor or security software running on the main processor of the router.

Figure 12-12 illustrates the typical structure of a router. The routers and protocols that help us decide how to switch traffic among different avenues is the subject of a lot of good literature.[25,26,27,28,29] Our discussion here is limited as to how traffic is switched by the router hardware.

The router, a bus-based fast computer, reads input traffic from I/O ports and writes it (potentially modified) on different I/O ports. The I/O ports of course are of a different type: Ethernet 10 Base-T, 100 Base-T, X.25, frame relay, RS-232, BSC,

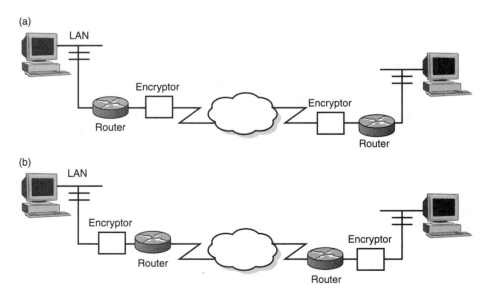

12-11 Topographical relationships between a router and a network encryptor.

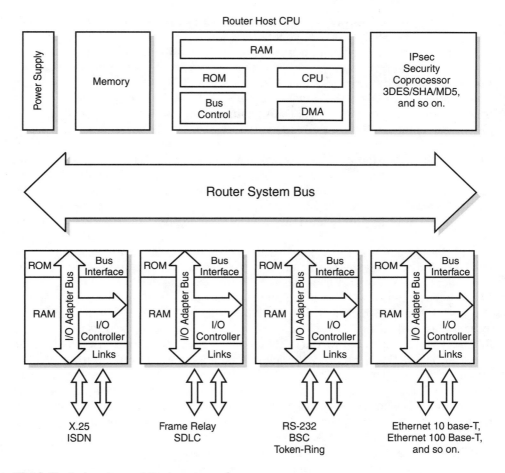

12-12 Typical router architecture example.

SDLC, ISDN, and so forth. The manufacturer or user configures the router to switch traffic among its ports in an elaborate set of possibilities of data coming from and data going to. Routers contain an operating system that manages the HW resources in real-time. A master CPU supervises the router's internal system, and also manages all the I/O resources. A broad set of protocols has been developed to build routing trees and switching paths in real-time. Routers keep dynamic sets of lookup tables in memory that must be consulted prior to making a routing decision. These tables in conjunction with the appropriate routing protocols will tell the router to switch outgoing traffic from, for instance, port X to a port Y because the latter is connected on a different sub-tree structure of the network from the connectivity efficiency point of view.

If a security coprocessor is introduced into the router as an adapter with special hardware on which cryptographic functions like 3DES or SHA or RSA are run systematically, this security coprocessor is exactly what the name implies: a coprocessor. The router's main CPU will know if and when it needs the security coprocessor's services and will usually work in the following way:

Assume that incoming data from port A must be switched to port C. As soon as the data came in from port A, the I/O controller associated with port A initiated a DMA request telling the router host CPU (master CPU) that it has data coming in. The host CPU authorizes the transfer per specified policies and continues doing its other chores. By using a classical DMA channel, the I/O controller associated with port A now transfers the data into memory using the router bus. While this transfer is in process, the system bus cannot be used by anybody else, including the main CPU. As soon as the data has been transferred, the I/O controller A will interrupt the host CPU, based on a whole interrupt request and acknowledgment ritual (among many interrupts that compete for the host CPU's attention), to let it know that the transfer has been concluded successfully. Then the I/O controller A returns to serving other needs at its port, while now at its leisure the host CPU must deal with this data. If the data must be switched to port C, the router main CPU (host) has to inform the I/O controller associated with port C that data are on their way to be transferred according to specific criteria (packaged, framed, and so on). The I/O controller C must now start planning its buffering facilities and timeout mechanisms.

In our example, the host CPU directs that the data must first be encrypted per the session setup, which has dictated that a digital signature per RSA must be attached as well as an IPSec communication session is being held using, perhaps, 3DES encryption with keys K1 and K2 and maybe SHA is to be used as the hashing function. This is the reason why the security coprocessor (or cryptographic accelerator) is available. The host CPU will then alert the security coprocessor that there is a block of data in memory, located at address X. This block of data is Y Kbytes long and the security coprocessor must "fetch" it and work on it along the following specifications. The host CPU gives a detailed context to the security coprocessor for the cryptographic context (for example, choice of 3DES algorithm mode), SHA hashing details (to pad or not to pad the appropriate private and public keys for the execution of the RSA algorithm), or the context will be part of the data in the memory. Memory first must be properly prepared by the host CPU or the I/O controller that fetched/placed it there in the first place, and structured so that the corresponding driver of the security coprocessor can tell which of the fetched bytes are context and instructions and which are actual data.

As soon as the security coprocessor finishes its previous tasks and closes the corresponding context cleanly, it will acknowledge the interrupt, and request from the bus DMA controller the right to proceed with the fetch from memory. As soon as the DMA controller gives it the right to move, the security coprocessor will initiate a Read from memory that will take control of the bus, read the data in from main memory, and write that same data into the security coprocessor adapter's buffer memory. If there is more data than buffering capability, the situation will have to be managed in repetitions of the process until the data to be encrypted is exhausted. The details go beyond the scope of this presentation but one can see the point. Plaintext data now is in the security coprocessor adapter's memory. The local hardware proceeds with the cryptographic processing until it is done. Attempts to stop it will most probably be ignored, unless higher priority interrupt vectors are acknowledged, in which case the coprocessor will have to flush the current activity to main memory, switch rapidly to follow the new instructions from the host CPU and then get back to its previous work.

When the data has been encrypted and formatted, the coprocessor may try to send it to the I/O controller C by requesting a DMA authorization from the router's host CPU. If at that point the Port C happens to be busy with another transfer, the request may be denied. Instead (as usually would be the case) the security coprocessor will have to write the processed data to main memory (again by DMA access it needs to obtain). This will mean that bus control has to be obtained and data transferred to memory, while the host CPU is alerted that Q amount of data is written to memory starting at address Z, to be used by Port C, or if the security coprocessor does not know the destination it will tell the host CPU that this data is the result of the task M it assigned earlier to the coprocessor. When the host CPU is free, it will then alert the I/O controller associated with Port C that Q quantity of data is available in main memory, starting at address Z, and then the I/O controller of port C will have to initiate another DMA request as soon as it is free of its previous work to get the data. Now the data is finally in the port C buffer and the local hardware intelligence will packetize it, frame it, and transmit it to the appropriate next stage in the network.

If there is no security coprocessor or accelerator, it is reasonable to discount the top right adapter in Figure 12-12 and imagine that security functionality runs on the router's host CPU under the router's operating system. It will run on a time-sharing basis, by stealing cycles, with all the other chores (including the operating system) that CPU must run. This approach has several weak points, as discussed in the following sections.

The plaintext data travels on the router bus at least twice, once when input is going from port A to memory and once when going from memory to the Security Coprocessor. This infers that a well-placed ill-intentioned insider has two opportunities to intercept the plaintext data, buffer it, and even channel it from another port D or F, hidden from users connected through ports A and C. Router manufacturers do not like to raise this issue and thereby exhibit paranoia, although this is the Achilles heel of the embedded security solution inside routers or switches. Incidentally, this is the same weakness exhibited by a communications security adapter based on an I/O card (like a PCI or PCMCIA adapter for instance) inside a PC or workstation. Plaintext traffic can be intercepted by several means inside the computer system while it traverses the I/O bus and before it ever hits the storage disk or the display for the legitimate and intended recipient. In fact, unless a system is heavily guarded around the clock, such an arrangement is absolutely unheard of in critical government installations.

If one runs the security function in software on the same main CPU of the router, to avoid exposing the data in plaintext twice to a hostile insider, the tremendous computing load of the cryptographic functions will simply steal so many cycles that the host CPU will barely have time to build and consult routing tables so it can make routing decisions, its raison d'être. This clearly shows how untenable that solution is in terms of security. A switch essentially follows a similar architectural structure and therefore the discussion is applicable to both realms.

Evolution Towards Wireless (HW and SW Avenues)

There are two schools of thought as to how to implement security in wireless devices, one based on *hardware* (HW) and the other on *software* (SW). SW is pervasive and the explosion in chip capabilities has fueled similarly dramatic growth in SW functionality, something which until only recently was unheard of. Using SW for building security is a legitimate and even convenient approach, probably adopted with WAP-based products that implement both stack and security in SW running on the host CPU inside wireless devices. As discussed in Chapter 8, WAP-based security techniques are not only insecure in that they create red bridges in the wireless gateway; they are also untenable from a performance point of view in streaming bit traffic. Since authentication and encryption happen in real-time for a one-pass processing of the data, the computing performance needed dictates a hardware-based solution instead.

Many HW-based solutions enable these methodologies using a *system-on-a-chip* (SOC) approach. As some of the most successful SOCs are implemented around powerful core CPUs or DSP processors, the ultimate answer for end-to-end secure communications is embedded software executed from a ROM or flash memory on-board the SOC chip. Purists may argue that this then is really a software solution. From the implementation point of view we will call it a hardware solution, because it does not permit the traditional software solution accessible to anyone with a PC, a compiler, and an editor.

Encryptor Structures in Wireless

Scramblers are one of the first methods of providing rudimentary voice security for wireless devices. Sometimes people confuse scrambling and encrypting, although they are not at all alike. Scrambling usually occurs at the analog processing stage of vice input or, more rarely, when only slightly inside the digital realm just after the voice digitization stage. It uses relatively simple techniques of rearranging formants and in some case spectrally relocating specific parts of the transmitted information. Although this affords some level of confidentiality against the average eavesdropper, it is not considered a safe method of transmission because any telecom engineer has the ability to reverse the operation and break security. Scramblers are usually deployed as proprietary techniques in specific brand products and are widely used in land-mobile systems, inexpensive portable radios, etc. By definition, they are inadequate for secure data transmission, as they corrupt the plaintext by their non-repetitive analog processing structures.

Full-fledged mathematical encryption is required to ensure a product that can be characterized as secure. Encryption techniques with different degrees of adequacy for different algorithms can be applied equally well to voice and data. An encryption system typically uses either block ciphering or stream ciphering techniques. Most block ciphers (3DES for instance) are easy to put together in software implementations and as such are readily available for baseband telephony. Typical offerings have a RISC processor (such as MIPS) running 3DES in software on low bit rate telephony (9,600 bps) along with a more or less acceptable way of establishing a secure session based on DH.

The DH protocol is well understood allowing creation of a session key, on which the two devices exchange the traffic encryption key that is to be used in real-time. Typically, the traffic encryption key is the same for both simultaneous channels of transmission and reception, is used by both parties for encryption and decryption, and it remains throughout the whole session, although each session will have a different key. The HORNET™ family of commercially available ASICs is an example that takes us a couple of steps further. Although more will be said in the next chapter about HORNET™ as an example of the direction HW-based communications security is taking, a summary of its characteristics is appropriate here:

- The HORNET™ system can change traffic encryption keys with random frequency, every few milliseconds, dynamically on-the-fly and in complete synchronization between the communicating end devices.

- The traffic encryption keys are 160 bits long and generated through the irreversible SHA function. Possibility of accidental collision for an attacker is 2^{-160}, which is essentially zero for all practical purposes. Brute force also is also commensurately much larger than the effort needed to attack a 128-bit 3DES Rijndael scheme. Even in the unlikely event that this could happen in one's lifetime; only the plaintext of a few milliseconds worth of transmission will be deciphered. One is devoid of clues as to how the next key will appear, and no actual content information is compromised, just as the milliseconds at the start of an utterance gives little clue whether a vowel or consonant is being pronounced.

- The encryption keys are not the same as the decryption keys, so the two channels of a full-duplex link, although working in full cryptographic synchronization, will not allow an attacker the luxury of a full session plaintext acquisition.

- The encrypted traffic is never positioned on the same bit boundary of frames as there is randomized padding before and after each frame of encrypted traffic payload.

- Periodically synchronization sequences (of different bit appearance every time) will be interjected along with padding bit blocks of random length inside the transmitted bit stream. Therefore, an attacker intercepting the traffic does not know whether sync sequences are being dealt with, or randomly chosen padding bits or encrypted data and, if yes, if this was encrypted with the same key as some of the previous frames, and again which ones of the previous frames. The attacker has a major problem locating ciphertext inside the transmitted (and intercepted) stream, much less to decipher it.

Interception and Vulnerability of Wireless Systems

\Wireless transmissions have been subjected to attacks of many types. The security discipline of *electronic warfare* (EW) emerged in response during WWII.[30,31,32,33] Schleher's account of EW is pertinent to this discussion and strongly recommended for further investigation by the interested reader.[34]

The authors choose to skip substantive discussion of a large subarea of EW that protects against the interception and subsequent analysis of radar signals. Although a radar system does communicate some information to its operator, it does not fit the profile of communications device in the classical sense where one individual or computer system communicates with one or more similar units. Of interest is EW in electronic weapons systems and *command, control, and communications* (C³) systems. The functional interest is to explain the vulnerabilities of these systems and how EW support measures and ECM systems function to exploit them.

The concept of EW is well understood in the military and intelligence communities. Identifying threats; analyzing, prioritizing, and classifying them; and deciding how to use one's own resources to render these threats ineffective is what it's all about. In industry EW is a relatively new concept, but one vendors and consultants are beginning to see as pretty useful for customers. Neutralizing an enemy's C³ system while maintaining one's own has obvious advantages. A defending general wants to ensure that the potential effectiveness of enemy weapons and units is assessed, so that communications with specific sensors and battlefield management posts is intercepted, analyzed, and acted upon.

EW is organized into three categories: *Electronic Support Measures* (ESM), *Electronic Countermeasures* (ECM), and *Electromagnetic Counter Countermeaures* (ECCM). In ESM the objective is to intercept, identify, analyze, and localize an enemy's transmission sources, as well as to decide what steps to take in order to deploy appropriate forces or to counter the detected threat. An associated area is gathering and collection for intelligence purposes of electromagnetic data radiated by hostile or adversary sources. Both *communications intelligence* (COMINT) and *non-communications electronic intelligence* (ELINT) electromagnetic data are categorized as *signals intelligence* (SIGINT). ELINT will not be discussed here.

ECM may be defined as the actions taken to inhibit or contain an enemy's use of the electromagnetic spectrum. Typically this activity takes the form of either deception or jamming. *Jamming* is an intentional transmission of electromagnetic energy with the objective to impair functionality of electronic devices—for example, transmitters and/or receivers—used by the opponent. *Deception* on the other side can be manipulation of the opponent, which implies simulation or alteration of friendly signal with the to spoof, and it can also be imitative, which implies introducing radiation that imitates a hostile transmission into hostile channels.

ECCM involves the actions taken to ensure friendly use of the electromagnetic spectrum despite the presence of EW. ECCM is more likely to enhance the protection of tracking and surveillance radar systems than actual communications systems and it assumes several forms:

- A higher carrier frequency can be used than otherwise expected, so the ratio of peak antenna gain to average side lobe level can be maximized.
- *Low probability of intercept* (LPI) and *low probability of detection* (LPD) design principles are engaged. This technique is based on three approaches:

  - Spreading the spectrum of transmission over the widest possible band, in addition to using a pseudo-random code, prohibits the enemy from easily constructing a matched filter to the waveform (the classical way to eavesdrop).
  - Use of ultra-low sidelobe (see Figure 12-13) antennas (greater than −40 dB sidelobes) reduces the radiation level received through the antenna's sidelobes.
    - Power management, where communications with another party close by will happen at smaller levels of transmitted radiation, effectively making the communication transmission invisible to EW sources operating from a greater distance.

Figure 12-13 illustrates the importance of sidelobes in an EW scenario. The undesired sidelobes in this case will make the antenna sensitive to radiation traveling along the oblique shown axes. If the antenna is transmitting, besides the intended central lobe it transmits along side-directions, sometimes (depending on the antenna design) along the center of more than one sidelobe per quadrant. This is very helpful for SIGINT purposes since for the interception of hostile transmission the receiver rarely has to be positioned precisely on the line of sight of the direct point-to-point transmission path. Occasionally, one can intercept signals surrepti-

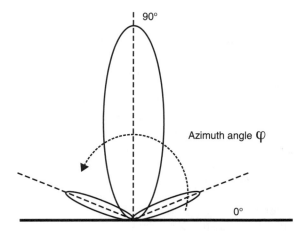

12-13 Generic sensitivity pattern (in polar coordinates) of a highly directional beam antenna shown from the top.

tiously from the sidelines. If the antenna is receiving, besides the highly directional intention along the central lobe, it will also be receiving (albeit at a lower dB level) radiation transmitted to it from side angles. This side door is in many cases an almost divine gift for a jammer.

The protection of one's own transmissions from enemy SIGINT is called *signal security* (SIGSEC) and this involves both *communications security* (COMSEC) and *transmission security* (TRANSEC). COMSEC through robust cryptography prohibits observation of the content to unintended recipients. TRANSEC protects transmissions from hostile interception and use. Changing of transmission frequencies and call signs is one of the typical TRANSEC techniques. Proper authentication of devices also falls under the TRANSEC umbrella as only authorized transmitters can communicate with their intended receivers. Other TRANSEC techniques involve site masking, dummy antenna loads when testing, highly directional antennas, and even emission control, so any nonimportant use of communications transmissions is avoided.

Spreading of the spectrum is accomplished by means of two fundamental techniques, both of which are based on the use of pseudo-random code sequences, which either (a) are injected into the transmitted stream by the direct-sequence method, where the information-bearing signal is multiplied directly by a high-chip rate spreading code, or which (b) are used to change instantaneously the transmission frequency of the signal, in which case the result is frequency-hopping. It is well to distinguish between wideband and narrowband DS spread-spectrum systems, and also between two types of FH systems. *Slow Frequency-Hopping* (SFH) where multiple symbols can be transmitted during every frequency hop and *Fast Frequency-Hopping* (FFH) systems, where multiple frequency hops occur during the transmission of one symbol, also may be considered. There is a multitude of excellent references on all aspects of spread-spectrum communications.[35,36,37,38,39,40] We will review in the following sections how vulnerable spread-spectrum communications are and CDMA more in particular to their interception.

Unlike ESM receivers used for hostile radar detection, the tactics used for interception of communications transmissions are not quite the same. Communications systems usually operate on discrete channels. They are relatively powerful, have wide-beam antennas with weak sidelobes and use modulated *continuous-wave* (CW) transmissions. A CW signal, by definition, carries neither amplitude nor phase information. Conventional radio transmissions are generally easy to intercept or jam, so recently *frequency-hopping* (FH) methods have been used to fool the jammer, the assumption being that by the time the ESM receiver of the enemy has located the transmission burst, changing the frequency randomly will create an elusive target for the enemy. For the military and intelligence communities this puts a premium on *direction-finding* (DF) techniques that allow the geographical pinpointing of the hostile transmission.[41,42] However, this may not be the case given enough resources and technical competence on behalf of the adversary.

Again ignoring scanning for hostile radars in a battlefield case, use of narrowband receivers using compressive or diffractive Bragg cell techniques is mandated.[43]

They scan the spectrum for stable high-duty cycle transmitters, which could be either CW radars, pulsed Doppler radars, or data links. This will generate a coarse sorting of hostile transmissions, which is plotted as a three-dimensional histogram showing bitstream size vs. angle of arrival (frequency agility) versus transmission frequency. A dynamic update of a database reveals the obvious and decision processes should be in place to prioritize threats with appropriate action to be taken.

Communications ESM and Interception Receivers

In the nonclassified literature, there are eight major types of DSM and COMINT receivers of interest:

- *Crystal Video Receiver* (CVR) receiver
- *Instantaneous Frequency Measurement* (IFM) receiver
- YIG tuned narrowband superheterodyne
- Wideband superheterodyne
- Spectral analyzer ESM receiver
- Channelized receiver
- Compressive receiver
- Acousto-optical Bragg cell receiver

CVR

The CVR is a physically small, lightweight, and rather inexpensive device. It was developed originally for pulsed signal detection (hence its radar applicability in EW) and it is used for wideband searches preferably in the 2- to 18-GHz range. The CVR basically consists of a(n)

- Frequency demultiplexer that decomposes the incoming signal into several wide and contiguous spectral bands each with its own detector
- RF *low-noise amplifier* (LNA) for high sensitivity
- Detector, which usually has a logarithmic characteristic as opposed to the classically prescribed square-law because the latter unfortunately yields dynamic range saturation problems when signal amplitude is to be accurately quantified on one channel or when angular measurements need to be made by comparing received signal from matched receivers over adjacent antennas
- Log-video amplifier. When such a log-video amplifier is equipped with appropriate circuits for switching or chopping the underlying carrier, the CVR can be used for the detection of continuous wave signals, while without such circuitry it is predominantly used in radar detection EW.

As the detection process removes both frequency and phase, the CVR receiver can measure neither of these two parameters. In a densely crowded environment where several signals are present simultaneously in the bandwidth under investigation, amplitude distortion is caused past the detection stage and therefore the risk is real that critical signals to be intercepted and/or monitored can be effectively masked by other undesirable signals—for example, jamming.

IFM

The *instantaneous frequency measurement* (IFM) receiver usually consists of a limiting RF amplifier and a phase detector for two components that have each incurred a varying phase shift (one goes through a delay line) with respect to the incoming signal, which is a function of the input frequency. A phase correlator and envelope detector generates a pair of signals that are proportional to the sine and the cosine respectively of the phase shift. From this point, with simple calculations, the system can display the incoming frequency and phase as functions of the delay line value and the amplitudes of the two quadrature signals.

To further improve the frequency resolution, military grade IFM interceptors are equipped with large banks of frequency discriminators (using delay lines of varying length), which operate on the signal in parallel. The IFM technique is useful for the deinterleaving of multiple transmitters in a dense signal environment. The technique is especially applicable on frequency-agile transmitters but it suffers from the drawback that only one—the strongest—signal can be locked onto and measured at one time. In the case of more or less equivalent signals, the IFM receiver will yield an answer that approximates the average frequency and phase values of the strongest signals it intercepts in a channel. The originally analog IFM receiver has evolved into a *digital IFM* (DIFM) receiver where the frequency measurement is displayed as a digital word. In the DIFM a bank of frequency discriminators or correlators is used, where the longest delay corresponds to the frequency resolution of interest and the shortest delay determines the highest frequency to be measured. As in the analog version, the two quadrature (sine and cosine components) signals are run through a binary comparator that yields outputs offset by multiples of $\pi/2$. A set of M correlators divide the scanned frequency range into 2^M frequency cells.

YIG-Tuned Narrowband Superheterodyne

The tuned or scanning narrowband superheterodyne uses a *yttrium iron garnet* (YIG) frequency pre-selector, followed by a mixer that is driven by a swept-frequency local oscillator and a narrowband *intermediate frequency* (IF) amplifier that precedes a log-video amplifier as an envelope detector. Scanning superheterodynes are sensitive receivers with strong selectivity (especially due to the YIG pre-electors), however, smart scanning techniques must be used when few and specific pulses must be intercepted (such as a burst transmission). This is done by preprogrammed search on specific threat bands of interest so acquisition time is minimized. The operation is sequential. Each resolution frequency cell is swept by tuning the narrowband YIG with the YIG local oscillator. Analysis proceeds sequentially until transmission activity is detected. Typical rates of sweeping capabilities for such a receiver is 100 MHz of spectrum swept per millisecond of elapsed time. The higher the resolution of the frequency sweeps the narrower the bandwidth of the search must be. One usually engages the technique in two types of environments:

- When the band of interest or the waveform is known. As in the case of wireless cellular communications one can tune the system in very high resolution.
- When the transmission band is unknown (as in military or intelligence interception) first a broadband search has to be initiated with a more broad resolution and the fine resolution search will follow in a more pointed way into areas of suspected activity.

This is done by computerized methods of so-called smart controllable instantaneous bandwidth schemes.

YIG-Tuned Wideband Superheterodyne

The wideband version of the YIG-tuned superheterodyne is the use of a wide band filter right after the antenna, followed by a mixer which uses a fixed tuned local oscillator for the down-conversion of various RF bands to a common IF band for subsequent processing. Usually, the mixer is supplied by one or more among several options:

- A single-fixed-frequency oscillator
- A bank of switchable oscillators
- A fast-tuned VCO (voltage-controlled oscillator)

The wideband variety of YIG-tuned superheterodynes is best engaged in detection and identification of wideband transmissions, frequency-agile, pulse-compression, and phase-encoded pseudo-noise spread-spectrum transmissions. When rapid scan through several frequencies is required within microseconds sometimes wideband switchable filters are used instead of YIG-tuned filters.

The most serious problem of superheterodyne receivers is the possible interference of base or harmonics of the *local oscillator* (LO) radiation, which can be coupled onto the IF signal during up-conversion of adjacent transmitters and hence can become detected by enemy interceptors, an utmost undesirable situation in military or intelligence missions. Excellent shielding and specialized filtering is needed to ensure the LO signal does not arrive at the mixer or even worse at the antenna itself. Using this method, *single-sideband* (SSB), AM, or FM signals can be immediately identified and *frequency-shift keying* (FSK) modulation—as one example—can easily be decoded by a simple modem in readily available inexpensive commercial equipment.

Spectral Analyzer ESM Receiver

A convenient and rather straightforward way of tracking down the frequency content of a signal or a multitude of signals is to use *Fourier-transform* (FT) techniques and generate the spectral profile of the intercepted signal in real-time. As the FT of a time varying waveform is a complex quantity with magnitude and phase dependency, in this specific context it's best to look only at the magnitude profile. The explosion of semiconductor capability and more specifically the enhanced capabilities of DSP processors today have made such real-time calculations commonplace.

Channelized Receiver

The channelized receiver is essentially a combination of a large array of contiguous filters that cover the band of interest. Besides its ELINT application, in the COMINT arena the channelized receiver is most useful for resolving multiple beam transmissions radiating from the same site but at different frequencies as well as any transmitters that are separated by more than the basic channel bandwidth in the configuration at hand. When one uses a narrowband scanning superheterodyne receiver in a channelized configuration, there is a significant time penalty that has to be paid to permit the filter to settle at each frequency resolution cell. The result is that this *dwell* time of the order of microseconds, which is obviously prohibitively slow for individual radar pulse detection and characterization, is more than adequate to ensure CW transmissions. In fact the *probability of interception* (POI) is close to 100 percent.

Compressive Receiver

For interception of short bursty transmissions in unexpected bands, one must scan very fast and the time the narrowband filter needs to settle in each position is very long. In that case a wideband filter is used whose output is sensitive to the frequency input. Such a filter is the so-called dispersive chirp filter, which is useful in pulse compression radars. Embedding such a filter in the interception receiver makes the receiver a compressive one.

The compressive receiver consists first of a mixer wherein the local oscillator signal is multiplied with a linear frequency-modulated (*chirp*) signal whose frequency is swept rapidly across the band under investigation. The mixed signal is passed through a dispersive delay line whose delay is varied with frequency. This line's delay characteristics must be matched with the linearly swept (chirped) waveform. The envelope of the compressed video waveform emerging from the dispersive filter can be shown to be the magnitude of the FT of the incoming signal. Above that, the relative position in time of the compressed output signal spectrum with respect to that of the premultiplied input signal is a direct function of the input signal frequency, and hence all the necessary data is immediately available for a computerized calculation of the carrier frequency. Locking the carrier will then trigger the mechanisms for automatic modulation recognition. It is a short step to realize that, as long as hackers have enough resources and budget, it is almost impossible to transmit without being detected most of the time.

Acousto-Optical Bragg Cell Receiver

The elements of this type of spectral analyzer are

- A laser which injects coherent light onto a Bragg cell
- The Bragg cell itself which reflects light into angles that are proportional to the light frequency
- A lens combination that steers reflected light onto a *photodiode array* (PDA).

The spatial distribution of light intensity across the surface of the PDA is correlated with the Fourier transform of the input signal across the Bragg cell aperture, while the energy distribution across the PDA output is the Fourier spectrum of the signal. The Bragg cell's acoustic attenuation and optical diffraction characteristics decide the bandwidth resolution. The basic principle of operation is an acousto-optic inter-action where a traveling sound wave injected into the bulk of the Bragg cell crystal (usually lithium niobate) causes waves of compression and decompression hence rarefaction of the crystal's lattice structure. This changes the index of refraction in different places inside the crystal, which in turn acts as a diffraction grating whose spacing is proportional to the acoustic wave's length, which again is proportional to the wavelength of the incoming RF signal. This angular deflection versus frequency effect is at the heart of acousto-optic processors and it can be implemented either in bulk crystals or in integrated optical assemblies. Dynamic range is somehow limited for Bragg cell receivers as the quantity of power one can couple to the detector array is limited and third-order inter-modulation products arising from operating components beyond their linear range can play a significant role.[44]

SAW Technology

Surface-acoustic wave (SAW) filters have revolutionized the design of interception receivers.[45,46] The fundamental idea behind SAW filters is that two transducers (input and output) are attached to a crystal substrate, which is usually quartz or more often lithium niobate. The transducers are usually finger-shaped metal layers photo-deposited by lithography mask on the substrate, much as in standard semi-conductor manufacturing practice. When an IF signal is applied to the input trans-ducer, a piezoelectric distortion occurs on the crystal, and the wave propagates from the input transducer to the output transducer. This wave has an amplitude that is material-dependent (more precisely it is proportional to the so-called piezoelectric constant of the crystal), while also a function of the input signal strength and the geometrical shape and size of the fingers. By shaping the finger's size and position along the direction of wave propagation (a design process called apodization), the filter's time characteristics and frequency-domain parameters can be controlled by fine-tuning the weight effects of each finger. One therefore can control the fre-quency response of the device by different mask layouts on the crystal substrate. SAW filters are robust, intrinsically stable and require no tuning. With modern manufacturing technology, they can be repetitively manufactured with consistent quality.

Both channelized and compressive receivers can be built using SAW technology. Modern spread-spectrum transmission technologies are representative of a series of breakthroughs in telecommunications that apparently permeates all types of ad-vanced wireless communications, from *2nd generation* (2G), through so-called 2.5G all the way to *3rd generation* (3G) networks. Spread-spectrum techniques, originally developed during World War II, were identified by radar engineers as a means of protecting radar transmitters against jamming. While attempting to improve jam-resistant communication systems, work on spread-spectrum systems yielded spectacular results in several areas, such as interference suppression, energy density reduction, high-resolution ranging (or determination of position location), and above all multiuser access to the same common transmission medium. The technology is called generically spread-spectrum as the transmission bandwidth employed is much greater than the minimum bandwidth needed to transmit the information. According to Sklar's classis coverage, a spread-spectrum system is defined by the following characteristics:[47]

- Occupies a bandwidth much in excess of the minimum bandwidth needed to transmit the information
- Spreading is accomplished by means of a spreading signal, often called a spreading code, which is independent of the transmitted data and where
- Despreading (recovery of the original data) at the receiver is accomplished by correlation of the received spread signal with a synchronized replica of the spreading signal used to spread the information

From this definition, one can see why FM or PCM transmission techniques, although they increase the transmission bandwidth beyond what is needed, do not qualify to be called spread-spectrum techniques because they don't satisfy all three legs of this definition.

Spread-spectrum systems have been exhaustively documented in several superb references.[48,49,50,51,52,53,54,55] Spread-spectrum systems are believed by many people to be reasonably secure. Unfortunately, in practice, they are insecure communication systems.

Signals with bandwidth W and time duration T will have a dimensionality of their signaling space of approximately 2WT. If one wants to increase the dimensionality, one can either increase the bandwidth W by spreading the spectrum, or one can increase the time T by time spreading (a term coined since 1988 by Sklar) also known as *time hopping* (TH). We will use the term time spreading in this book as a time hopping technique. This is different from the time smearing process (also referred to as time spreading) invented, patented and documented by Webb[56] with applications in transmission error correction or signal encryption applications, a subject that we will return to later. With TH (spreading), a message transmitted at a bit rate R is allocated a longer transmission-time duration than would be used with a conventional modulation scheme. During this longer time the data is sent in bursts according to the spreading code structure and content. Transmissions are spread in the time domain in a TH system. The advantages are obvious in terms of defense against an interceptor or jammer, as the average adversary does not readily know the signaling subspace.

There are two prevalent techniques for generating spread-spectrum transmissions: *direct sequencing* (DS) and *frequency hopping* (FH). TH is similar to FH as a defense against jamming in that the location of the actual transmission is unknown to adversaries and the defense principle is the same in the time and frequency domain, although the technical details of the implementation are different. In some systems, combinations of these fundamental techniques are used—for example,

DS/FH, FH/TH, and even DS/FH/TH. As these are extensions of fundamental methods previously discussed, we will not cover them here, but you must remember that composite techniques are easily addressable when it is necessary to intercept and the resources to do so are available.

In the early years of spread-spectrum transmission, the spread traffic was sent along with the spreading code itself by the simultaneous transmission of a modulated and an unmodulated random wideband noise through a different channel. The receiver would use the unmodulated carrier as the reference signal for despreading (correlating) the data-modulated carrier, known as the *transmitted reference* (TR) method. The basic advantage of the TR approach was the absence of a significant synchronization problem to resolve at the receiver, since the despreading code was transmitted simultaneously with the useful information. The main disadvantages of the TR technique were that: the potential adversary could listen to the despreading code being transmitted in the clear; a jammer could easily spoof the system by sending a pair of waveforms acceptable to the receiver; performance would be sharply degraded at low SNR environments when noise was present in both signals (information and reference); and twice the bandwidth and power needed was used, as the reference signal had to be transmitted as well.

Modern spread-spectrum systems employ a technique called *stored reference* (SR), where the spreading code is independently generated both at the transmitter and receiver. The advantage of the SR technique is that a well-designed spreading code signal cannot be predicted simply by monitoring the transmission. The downside is that the deterministic nature of the code generation (mandatory for both transmitter and receiver since each must be able to generate the code signals almost simultaneously and independently of each other) implies the code is not random, which of course means that it is periodic, even with long periods, Such sequences in conjunction with a couple of other criteria to be enumerated are called *pseudonoise* (PN) or pseudo-random signals.

PN sequences for *code division multiple access* (CDMA) spread-spectrum systems is a large area of ongoing research.[57,58,59,60,61,62] We'll consider some fundamental characteristics of PN sequences and their generation here. A pseudo-random sequence is deterministic and not random at all, since both the transmitter and receiver are able to generate it at the same time. It is called pseudo-random because it has some unique and rather interesting statistical properties:[63]

- **Balance property**   In each period of the sequence, the number of binary 1's differs from the number of binary 0's by at most one digit.
- **Run property**   A *run* is defined as a sequence if a single type of binary digits (for example, all 1's or all 0's). The appearance of the alternative digit in a sequence is the start of a new run. The length of a run is the number of digits in the run. Among the runs of 1's and 0's in each period, it is desirable that about one-half the runs of each type are of length 1, about one-fourth are of length 2, one-eighth are of length 3, and so on.
- **Correlation property**   If the period of a sequence term by term compares with any cyclic shift of itself, it is best if the number of agreements differ from any number of disagreements by not more than one count.

PN sequences are generated by *linear feedback shift register* (LFSR) structures, which are covered elsewhere in this book. LFSR-generated sequences can be classified as *maximal length* or *nonmaximal length*. Maximal length sequences generated by LFSR's with n stages have a period of p clock pulses, where $p = 2^n - 1$. If the sequence length generated by an n-stage LFSR is less than $2^n - 1$ the sequence is of nonmaximal length.

A useful characterization of PN sequences is by means of the autocorrelation function R(t). This concept and its massive application in today's communications is covered in detail in several statistical signal processing textbooks.[64,65,66] In the case of periodic pulse waveform representing a PN code, we use the terms *PN code symbol* or *chip,* to denote each fundamental pulse. For such a PN waveform of unit chip duration and period p chips, the normalized autocorrelation function may be expressed as R(t) = (1/p) (number of agreements less number of disagreements in a comparison of one full period of the sequence with a time position cyclic shift of the sequence).

Figure 12-14 illustrates the autocorrelation function of a typical PN sequence for a quick browse of typical characteristics. The width of the spike shows the bit duration, hence the bit rate. The distance between consecutive peaks sets the period, hence the number of stages of the generating LFSR can be deduced. The rest of the PN sequence guessing process then is a classical LFSR attack.

Note that when the PN codes are public knowledge, as they are in wireless telephony networks, such mathematical gymnastics are not required and interception work is more straightforward.

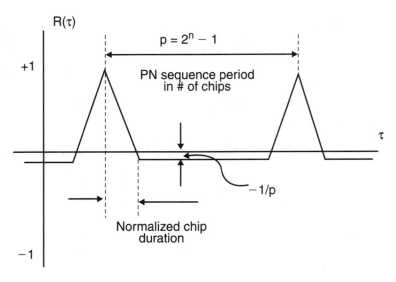

12-14 PN sequence's autocorrelation function.

Direct-Sequence Spread-Spectrum Systems Interception

Direct sequencing (DS) is the spectrum spreading technique (see Figure 12-15) when a carrier wave is first modulated with a data signal and then the modulated data signal is again modulated with a high-speed (wideband) spreading signal. This DS-and-carrier-modulated spread signal now can be despread by correlating or remodulating the received signal with a synchronized replica of the spreading signal code, delayed by a time T_{de}. This time T_{de} is the receiver's estimate of the propagation delay T_d from the transmitter to the receiver. When $T_{de} = T_d$, the code signal at the receiver is synchronized with the code generation at the transmitter.

Post despreading, a regular demodulator handles the rest of the demodulation process at the receiver. Automatic modulation recognition can be applied as a technique at this point of the interception, but it will be explored in another section. Synchronization circuits and phase-locked loops are an elaborate part of what is required in a system (see Figure 12-16) where essentially no knowledge exists up front about the PN sequences at hand.[67,68,69,70] Pilot signal identification, acquisition, tracking, and estimation are the consecutive steps required to do this in a military and/or intelligence defense environment. Where sequences are routinely documented, as in commercial wireless telephony environments, these steps are not necessary.

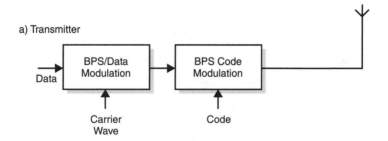

a) Transmitter

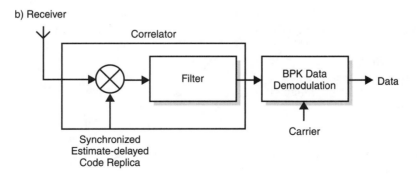

b) Receiver

12-15 Direct Sequencing (DS) spread-spectrum system.

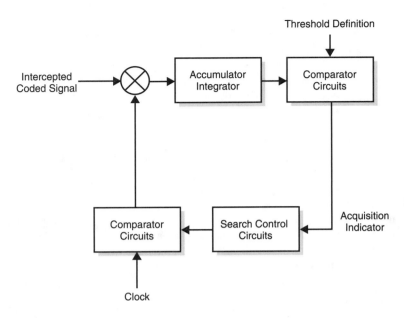

12-16 Serial search acquisition in a direct sequencing context.

For multiple access to common bandwidth, every user is allocated a specific PN code that is quasi-orthogonal with respect to the codes used by other users in the same cell. *Orthogonality* means that at despreading time, any other PN-coded signal detected by the receiver will demodulate (multiply) itself automatically away from the desired signal.

Frequency-Hopping Systems Interception

In FH systems, where the underlying modulation technique commonly is *M-ary frequency shift keying* (MFSK) with k = $\log_2$ M, k bits determine which one of M frequencies is to be transmitted. The position of the M-ary signal set is then shifted pseudo-randomly (using a PN sequence to schedule the mechanism) by a frequency synthesizer over a hopping bandwidth. Figure 12-17 shows a typical FH/MFSK system. In the case of interception and if a real-time search must be initiated to discover the PN-sequence that drives the frequency-hopping schedule, a typical solution is the serial search mechanism[71], which scans the code space rapidly. Figure 12-18 is a simple circuit that exhaustively will scan the bandwidth of interest for frequency acquisition.

The acquisition problem is defined as a blind search through a region of time or frequency uncertainty in order to detect and synchronize the received spread-spectrum signal with the locally generated spreading signal. Acquisition can be coherent or noncoherent. As the despreading process typically occurs before

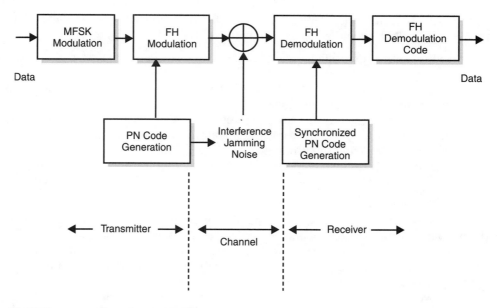

12-17 Frequency-hopping system.[72]

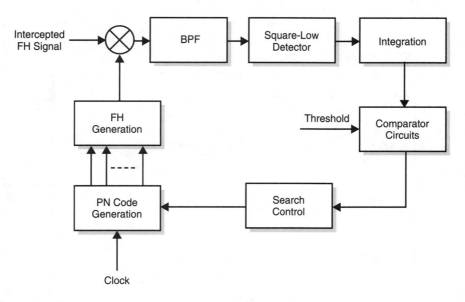

12-18 Serial search acquisition of frequency-hopping schedule.

carrier synchronization, acquisition is mostly of the noncoherent detection type. The problem difficulty is amplified by a combination of the following factors:

- Uncertainty in the calculation of propagation delay between transmitter and receiver
- Relative clock instabilities in the transmitter and receiver amounting to changing phase differences dynamically
- Uncertainty of the impact moving systems (source or destination moving, as in an airplane, ship, or in a vehicle) exhibit through the associated Doppler frequency shifts and their influence on readings stability
- Relative oscillator instabilities between the communicating systems that create frequency offsets between the two locally and remotely generated signals

Search mechanisms can be either parallel or serial. Parallel mechanisms lend themselves to large bank designs (see Figures 12-19 and 12-20 for the DS and FH cases respectively). Serial search systems are less expensive and more transportable. An interesting case is the *rapid acquisition by sequential estimation* approach (dubbed RASE) proposed by Ward[73], in Figure 12-21.

The switch starts from position nr.1. The RASE mechanism reads the first n bits for the received signal code chips and loads its best estimate for these n chips into the n stages of the local PN generator. As a PN sequence's next state depends on the previous combination of states, the RASE mechanism makes an educated guess as to the next state of the PN code. If the first n chips are correctly estimated, all the following PN code chips from the local generator will be correct. The switch is then thrown to position 2 and for a certain period of time, there is a comparison between

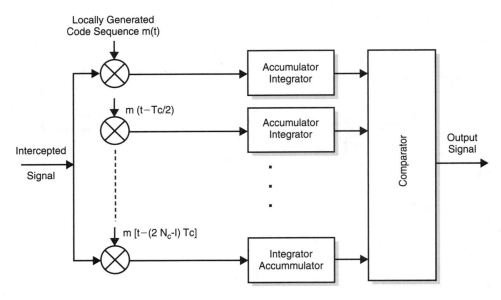

12-19 Parallel search engine for DS spreading sequence acquisition.

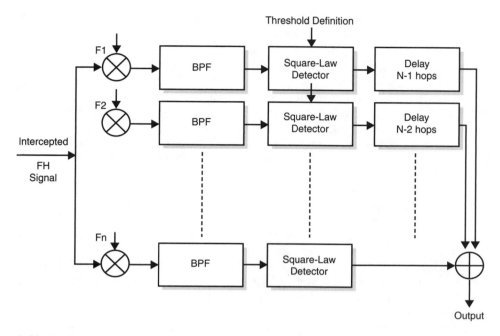

12-20 Parallel search engine for FH acquisition.

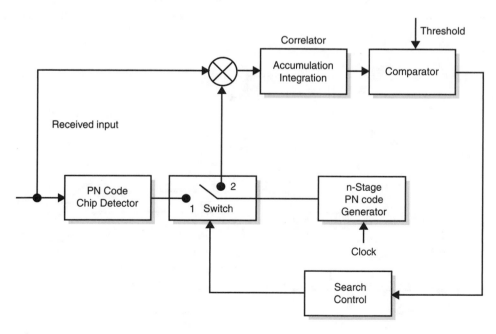

12-21 Rapid acquisition by sequential estimation (RASE) mechanism.

received and locally generated chips. If, after this passage of time there is full matching, complete acquisition of the code is assumed. If not, the switch is thrown back to position 1 and a new estimate for n chips is generated and loaded and the process is repeated. The RASE system, although fast in code acquisition speed, suffers from noise vulnerability and interference.[74] The point is not advocacy for specific techniques on their engineering merits, or their cost/performance characteristics, but rather to show you how vulnerable spread-spectrum communications can be when the adversary is properly equipped and trained.

When acquisition or coarse synchronization is accomplished, it has to be refined with fine synchronization or tracking. Tracking is done by coherent and non-coherent techniques. In practice, if neither the carrier frequency nor the phase is known beforehand, non-coherent methods are strongly favored.

The tracking loops are categorized as *delay-locked loops* (DLLs) and as time-shared early-late tracking loops commonly called *tau-dither loops* (TDLs). The DLL approach for the tracking of an already acquired spread-spectrum BPSK-modulated signal is characterized in Figure 12-22.

Two data paths produce a time-shifted replica of the PN code sequence by one chip duration, an early and a late replica. Fine synchronization with the incoming coded signal is generated as follows: The BPF filters pass the data and average the output of the two correlations, the square-law detectors remove the data and the summing amplifier drives a VCO. When the two paths combine into a positive feedback signal the VCO is instructed to increase its frequency thereby forcing the signal through further correlations to become smaller and ultimately negative. When the summation amplifier output signal is feeding back negative input into the VCO the frequency of the oscillator is decreased thereby generating positive change to the feedback value.[75,76,77]

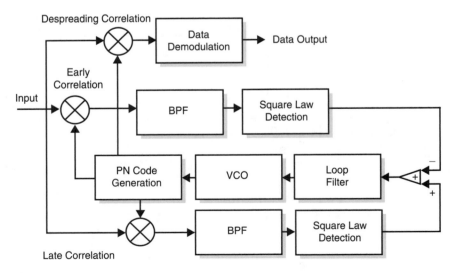

12-22 Delay-locked loop for tracking an acquired DS signal.

The TDL technique follows the same principle of an early and late correlation comparison by does so by switching the same correlator back and forth, thereby saving the cost of an extra correlation circuit. It has been shown to be slightly lower than the DLL technique in SNR-related performance of only 1.1 dB[78] and it is a frequently used technique when cost, compactness, weight, and portability of the interceptor are of major concern.[79,80,81]

Modulation Recognition and COMINT System Output Processing

All COMINT systems comprise three main stages:

- An interception receiver front-end
- A modulation recognizer
- An output processor

The first of these three has been discussed. The third will not be covered at length here because it is a conjunction of system functions requirements depending on the application at hand. Typically, when the signal content has been intercepted and acquired in a digital transmission realm, the COMINT system output processing will desegregate and decompose it logically on a per-session basis. This approach is indicated if the traffic is multiplexed, resulting in dumping of the content of intercepted *private virtual circuits* (PVCs) or *switched virtual circuits* (SVCs)—for example, for frame relay or plain number-to-number calls for ordinary cellular or land-based telephony. Perhaps the primary interest at a particular time of the COMINT operation lies in only one specific session among the many intercepted. The content will be removed from any frames, cells or packets and laid out in structured files depending on what underlying protocol is structuring them, such as GSM, IP, and so forth. In the majority of transmissions over data channels and if the content has been properly acquired, but is not immediately recognizable, one can safely assume it is encrypted, in which case it will have to be passed along to appropriate groups of experts for cryptanalysis and decipherment. This last step in the chain, although well known and understood in many cases, does not mean that the work is necessarily trivial.

After decomposing the frames of a voice channel, and stripping away the convolutional or turbo codes, reconstruction of the bit sequence will happen exactly as it is happening at the intended receiver's vocoder. This allows simultaneous and faithful voice reconstruction at the COMINT receiver's output processor. The telephony session can be recorded or not depending on the application needs or the difficulty of the intelligence-gathering task. In some cases such as a battlefield situation, a multilingual human operator will be monitoring the communication and reporting to superiors if and what is perceived as information of interest to the mission.

In many cases, links must be monitored on a more persistent basis. A speech-to-text system automates the task by generating an ASCII text file that preserves the intercepted sessions for documentation or to feed more sophisticated language analysis stages. Collection of text files in which complete telephone discussions have been recorded can be easily scanned by rudimentary software looking for matches of specific words or sentences, in which case a hit will be flagged for subsequent analysis. The last two logical stages of the flow, also in specific cases, can be replaced by real-time processing hardware that checks word matching at the speech level (independent of speaker), in which case a potential hit will flag the session as potentially of interest. The flagged session is then switched to a human operator or recorded for subsequent analysis.

Interception of an *already-known* signal domain is much easier than blind interception of traffic: not knowing what frequency is being used, what modulation scheme has been imposed, how it is internally coded and structured and whether it is encrypted or not. Within an already-known domain one knows precisely what frequency to pinpoint, how to acquire and lock into the carrier and what to do to demodulate and extract the baseband signal of interest. Everything can be done with an inexpensive and in most cases off-the-shelf system. The rest of the task is output processing, therefore, business as usual in the COMINT community.

Unknown domains are a different story in both quantitative and qualitative terms. Thus, we will elaborate on all aspects of the interception process. Modulation recognition is highly important, especially in military and intelligence environments, where the transmission characteristics of the opponent are not known *a priori*. It is of crucial importance while trying to recognize the modulation of a transmission to preserve the integrity of the signal, so content does not get lost for subsequent analysis and appropriate decisions can be made by a field commander for subsequent action (ECM and jamming, or physical attack).

Originally four techniques (all human-operated) were used for modulation recognition:

- Time studies were made of the intercepted IF waveform with an oscilloscope to determine if there was transmission of interest. The fact that somebody transmits at a known frequency does not mean there is useful or meaningful information there. A defending force can noise-modulate a series of frequency channels and occupy enemy forces and resources with needless COMINT.

- Spectral analysis at the IF frequency band, a technique with which operators would start from a wide search band and prioritize signals for subsequent analysis. The technique was used as a template builder where characterized hostile transmitters would be known to transmit at specific windows. This technique has clearly become largely obsolete since the onset of spread-spectrum transmissions.

- AM and FM demodulator displays are used for the demodulation of AM, MASK, and FM, MFSK, and MPSK signals. Regular dual-beam oscilloscopes can be used in the field for this method.

- With his or her earphones a trained human operator performs an audio analysis with earphones that would reveal by recognition that an AM or FM transmission was in use, at what pitch, and other information, and then subsequently an oscilloscope time base would be carefully tuned by hand.

With the advent of revolutionary communications techniques, more sophisticated methods had to be developed for the modulation recognition of RF transmission modulations.

A first approach was to design and build a bank of parallel demodulators. Only one would be activated and, based on some decision algorithm, the system would provide an output. In reality the system would be used as a sweep engine, a mechanism continuously scanning the problem space of alternative modulations one could expect to be present. This method is still used in some cases, but it requires awesome computing storage facilities (not easy to carry and protect at the battlefield) and it is limited by the choice of demodulators in the bank. The bank will yield a meaningful output only if one of its available demodulators happens to match in a satisfactory way the modulation method of the intercepted signal.

The human operator-controlled modulation recognition system made famous by World War II movies has been largely replaced by *automatic modulation recognition* (AMR) systems. Decision-theoretical techniques as well as *neural networks* (NN) are used, in conjunction with radiation detection and *direction finding* (DF) equipment, in the same system. *Modulation recognition* (MR) is needed for hostile transmitter classification and for the extraction of its transmitted signal features. The first thing an MR system needs is some bandwidth information, so it can fine-tune its attention. The information is provided by the energy detection parts of the COMINT receiver's front-end. When the bandwidth and carrier frequency has been identified, regular parameter estimation is then the generic technology used to identify the bit rate, the modulation type, and so forth. As the preservation of the intercepted signal integrity (for subsequent analysis) is of paramount importance, a wrong decision may inject the intercepted signal into the wrong demodulator and therefore the signal can get irrecoverably corrupted, lost, or destroyed. If one mentally classifies intercepted transmissions into analog and digital, whose modulation type is sought, then it is noteworthy that not all known modulations are referred to in the published literature.[82,83,84,85,86,87]

From a mathematical point of view, the AMR problem is a classification problem of three levels:

- Deciding where in the signal the transmitted information (instantaneous values of amplitude, frequency, phase, or any combination of the above) is hidden
- Measuring the symmetry of the intercepted signal spectrum around the carrier frequency
- Knowing the source of the modulation signal

The most comprehensive is the first of these three. The second is applicable in the recognition of digital modulations and the third is applicable when absolutely no prior knowledge exists about the nature of the signal to be intercepted, namely, even if whether or not it is analog-modulated. The fundamental coverage (see notes 87 to 95) and methods used in an AMR system are a combination of signal detection (sometimes under heavy underlying noise), parameter estimation, adaptive control, channel identification, signal reconstruction, and tracking.[88,89,90,91,92,93,94,95,96,97]

To extract a signal's critical features, one must segment its envelope. The segment's length depends on the fading length of the actual reception. Concentrate on one signal at a time, assuming that the channel-specific effects—such as multipath fading, weak signal reception, frequency instability, and interference from adjacent channels—have been adequately addressed by the COMINT receiver's front-end. Several techniques are used for this, such as spatial- and time-diversity (like RAKE receiver's fingers, a method heavily used in CDMA) for multipath component segregation, sophisticated *phase-locked loops* (PLLs) for frequency tracking and locking, and others. Of course the results are always expressed as a degree of confidence and they depend on the *signal-to-noise ratio* (SNR) at hand. In very noisy environments the AMR system may make a mistake. The higher the SNR the more confident the decision is and the better the quality of the AMR decision. Simulations have shown a strong dependency on the SNR of the decision confidence of each different method but the value of 10-dB SNR seems to be close to the limit of what has been perceived (at least in the open literature) as a threshold of operability. In the sense that either decision-theoretical or NN-based AMR seems to work above 93 percent of times, with this number coming close to 100 percent in SNR values of around 20 dB or more simulations can exhibit some degree of confidence.

Techniques applicable to the AMR problem are

- Spectral processing
- Instantaneous amplitude, frequency, and phase parameters
- Instantaneous amplitude, frequency, and phase histograms
- Combinations of spectral processing and instantaneous amplitude, frequency, and phase parameters
- Universal demodulators

As an example of two successful attempts to recognize modulation of intercepted signals automatically, summarization of a small subset of the excellent research work of Azzouz and Nandi[98] will be centered on the second of these approaches—instantaneous amplitude, frequency, and phase parameters. It is inexpensive to implement, does not require large memory capacity, and performs well in real-time. Azzouz and Nandi took two alternative approaches: decision-theoretical and neural-network based.

Decision Theoretical Approach

In the decision theoretical approach, specific signal features were defined for analog- and digitally modulated signals. The intercepted signal of L seconds duration was broken into successive segments, each with length of N = 2048 samples (equivalent to 1.707 ms). Several signal features were defined and extracted with real-time calculations. It is possible that segments are classified differently due to channel conditions and therefore majority rule has been brought into play, so in their work Azzouz and Nandi opted for the classification of the majority of segments to be the classification of the intercepted signal MR decision.[99]

Analog-Modulated Signals

In the analog-modulated signals approach, the extracted features included:

- g_{max} Based on the DFT (discrete Fourier transform) of instantaneous amplitudes, distinguishes between signals that carry amplitude information (like DSB) as opposed to signals that do not (for example, FM).
- s_{ap} Calculated as the standard deviation of the absolute value of the centered non-linear component of the instantaneous phase evaluated over the non-weak intervals of a signal segment; distinguishes between signals that have absolute phase information (when combined) and signals that have no absolute phase information.
- s_{dp} The standard deviation of the centered non-linear component of the direct (not absolute) instantaneous phase, evaluated over the nonweak intervals of a signal segment. (It is best to discriminate among AM, VSB, DSB, LSB, USB, FM, and combined AM-FM signals.)
- **P** A ratio intended to measure the symmetry of the signal spectrum around the carrier frequency and is calculated as the ratio of the difference over the sum of spectral powers of the upper and lower sidebands respectively. Discriminate the AM from the SSB and the latter from DSB, FM, and combined AM-FM signals for best results.

As the MR of real-life-modulated intercepted signals is usually classified, the examples shown in literature are mostly from simulated environments with more or less realistic signal, channel, and background contexts. The extraction of the signal features in a Monte-Carlo simulation environment for analog-modulated signals can be found in Azzouz's textbook.[100] The most important thing is that signal features can be extracted and, based on these features, a modulation decision is taken. It is striking how straightforward it is to immediately obtain the transmitted binary sequence in a straightforward, fast, and rather reliable way. It should then be evident how easy it is for a third party not only to recognize the modulation, but also to extract the information bit stream in real-time, given the appropriate resources.[101]

Digitally modulated signals

Likewise, in the case of digitally modulated signals Azzouz and Nandi defines several very pertinent signal features. The first three are the same as in the case of analog-modulated signals, namely: g_{max}, s_{ap}, s_{dp}. Two new features are added:

- s_{aa} The standard deviation of the absolute value of the normalized-centered instantaneous amplitude of a segment
- s_{af} The standard deviation of the absolute value of the normalized-centered instantaneous frequency, evaluated over the nonweak intervals of a signal segment

The time sequence of the extraction of these signal features as well as some real-time IF . . . THEN . . . ELSE evaluations have been shown to lead quickly to a high degree of confidence in the decision as to what modulation has been used on the

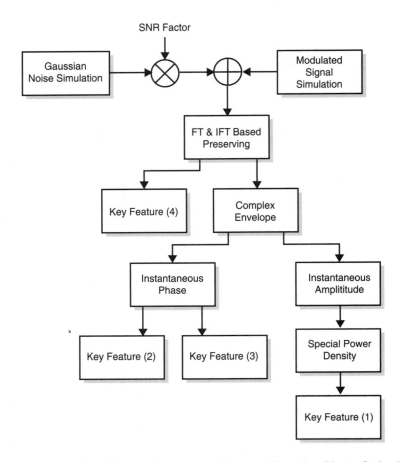

12-23 Extraction of signal features in a noisy environment based on Monte Carlo simulation.

intercepted signal. There is the need to estimate accurately the bit rate of the underlying bit stream as well, but Azzouz and Nandi have done an outstanding job documenting three different ways to do this: the level-crossing method, the derivative method, and the wavelet transform method.[102] The probability of estimating the symbol duration within 1 percent of its true value is 98 percent for the first method, 90 percent for the second and 99 percent for the third at a poor SNR of 10 dB. The wavelet transform method also has been shown to perform well on two, three, four, and even more levels of digital modulation, on top of the fact that it is simple computationally and therefore quite feasible to implement real-time processing hardware.

The overall level of the decision accuracy confidence (a function of the underlying SNR) has been found to vary above 93 percent when SNR is around 10 dB and well up to 100 percent when SNR is 20 dB.[103] The Azzouz and Nandi textbook contains many illustrations of this point as result of applying several possible algorithms. The rest of the process for the signal features extraction is identical to the analog case. You should by now recognize the odds that wireless transmission signals can be intercepted and analyzed in real-time.

Neural-Network-Based Approach

Because modulation recognition is a textbook case of classification, it was evident that neural network techniques could be highly probable candidates for a fast, inexpensive, and highly successful implementation of automatic modulation recognition systems. Azzouz and Nandi have shown that the order of applying each signal-features extraction creates different algorithms with varying degrees of accuracy and success. The simultaneous action of the whole neural network on the totality of an input signal segment ensures parallel operation, and with rather impressive results in terms of performance.

Neural network theory and real-time signal-processing practice techniques are very well documented in a series of excellent references.[104,105,106,107,108,109,110] Neural networks can operate supervised, nonsupervised, or in a self-organized way. Synapses weights are calculated periodically and dynamically refreshed while searching the optimal set of values. Choosing a neural network learning cycle architecture and topology and training a network (its learning cycle) is fundamental for a classification and regression task like automatic modulation recognition. For example, none, one-, and two-hidden layer configurations were tested and several learning methods considered: back-propagation learning, competitive learning, Hebbian learning, and Boltzmann learning.[111] The optimization criterion used was minimization of the sum-squared error, defined in terms of the difference between the calculated output corresponding to the data used in the training, and the actual target. The results show a clear and marked improvement of AMR decision confidence for more than 0 or 1 hidden layer even in low, SNR contexts. In a typical configuration of a two-hidden-layer neural network in a representative configuration, signal features (extracted as before) are applied as inputs in parallel and only one of the neural network outputs is activated showing a decision on the modulation recognition problem. Azzouz and Nandi's work contains a deeper discussion on the typical process for the training of a neural network with preexistent waveforms from which features are extracted by simulation or testing.[112]

Implications

Advanced Mobile Phone Services (AMPS)

If one pauses to contemplate the wireless security situation, one cannot but feel quite nervous about the current state of wireless security. Classical analog cellular in the United States and large part of the world in South America and Asia is still using AMPS, which is based on a simple FM modulation.

Time Division Multiple Access (TDMA) IS-136

TDMA, still sold to North American users by wireless operators and carriers with dubious performance claims, is based on the π/4-DQPSK (differential quadrature phase shift keying) modulation technique known to maintain spectral efficiency and to optimize the RF amplifier section.[113] To create a π/4-DQPSK modulated signal one combines two amplitude-modulated RF signals that are 90 degrees out of phase. This mechanism allows the transfer of information onto the carrier as different bit patterns at the modulator input, producing specific amounts of phase shift in the transmitted output. Therefore at the receiver or interception station if the received RF signal is sampled for phase transitions and amplitude at specific periods of time, it is possible to recreate the original bit pattern. The receiver looks for anticipated phase information, called a decision point. The four allowed phase shifts of +45, +135, −45, and −135 degrees represent the original binary information. Each two-bit input simulus has a corresponding phase shift. In IS-136 the transition period between decision points is 41.25 ms, resulting in a symbol rate of 24.3 thousand symbols per second. Since each symbol represents 2 bits in the IS-136 TDMA system, this corresponds to an input data rate of 48.6 Kbps.

GSM

GSM (originally Group Speciale Mobile, but now, Global System for Mobile Communications) transmits frequency-hopped *Gaussian Minimum Shift Keying* (GMSK) modulated signals. Since the GSM transmission is well documented and public information, the interception task is straightforward (with readily available commercial off-the-shelf equipment) and far from close to the difficulty of inter-cepting battlefield FH transmissions with unknown hopping schedules. The GSM FH algorithm is covered in several references listed in *Wireless Security*.[114,115,116,117] FH sequence for GSM is the same on both the uplink (from the mobile station or hand-set) and downlink (to the mobile station and handset).

The most straightforward way of implementing a GMSK modulator is to inject the data stream into a Gaussian *low-pass filter* (LPF) filter and use the resulting waveform to drive a *voltage-controlled oscillator* (VCO).[118] The VCO output is a FM signal with a Gaussian response. At the end of every bit interval a clean phase shift by π/2 is mandated, hence the LPF filter must have a narrow bandwidth and a sharp cutoff. Addressing the phase ambiguity problem, when trying to acquire a coherent local reference, Figure 12-24 shows that differential encoding is included in the transmitter as well as in the receiver (or interceptor).

Three ways to demodulate a GMSK signal have been documented:

- Differential detection
- Coherent detection
- FM discriminator detection

The latter is not desirable because it does not account well for phase changes. Coherent detection is done the same way classical MSK is done. The most common way of demodulating GMSK signals though is the differential detection method. The reason is that this technique does not require an absolute phase reference in the

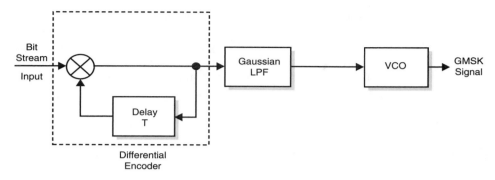

12-24 GMSK modulation signal generation using a differential encoder.

receiver (or interceptor) and therefore is a preferred method for signal recovery in multipath surroundings like urban areas with high-rise structures. One- and two-bit delay differential encoders have been tested and documented by Simon and Wang[119] and markedly improved results have been obtained, especially with the 2-bit case, as more energy is accumulated over 2-bit slots for the feedback loop of the differential encoding or decoding circuit.

Wideband and narrowband CDMA

CDMA as a spread-spectrum technique has been previously discussed. Of interest is how DH and FH PN codes are acquired, tracked, synchronized, extracted, and cracked. Once this is done either in an AMR context or by following the publicly available documentation one can demodulate the carrier and extract the underlying bit stream transmission. It is certainly a little more elaborate than an old analog wireless link, but only a little.

Spreading techniques used for the forward link (tower-to-handset) are different from the spreading used in the reverse link (from handset to tower). The reasons are numerous and can be found in any of the CDMA RF references provided earlier. In the IS-95 CDMA standard, forward and reverse are asymmetric links, meaning they have different structures altogether. The differences range from the modulation scheme used to the error control methods engaged. On top of this, the two links use different codes to channelize individual users. The forward link uses Walsh codes (one out of 64 Walsh codes) while the reverse link uses PN sequences. In the forward link, the IS-95 CDMA scheme has a pilot and a sync channel to aid synchronization, while on the reverse link things are very different. Walsh codes cannot be used on the reverse link, where the incoherent nature of the link requires another class of codes, namely PN sequences, for channelization. The reverse link is incoherent as the mobile stations (handsets) transmit at will and no attempt is made to synchronize their transmissions.

In reality the forward link also superposes a so-called short PN code, assigned uniquely to each base station in order to provide isolation among the different base stations. This is more than needed, as all base stations use the same 64 Walsh codes on their forward links. The short PN code in IS-95 CDMA is generated using a 12-stage LFSR and therefore has a length of $2^{15} - 1$ chips, which makes it easy to calculate. The reverse link uses the so-called long PN code, which has a length of $2^{42} - 1$ chips and is generated by an LFSR of 42 stages. In practice the receiver possesses a local copy of the PN code and when it requires acquiring an incoming sequence at an arbitrary phase, all it has to do is slide the incoming sequence against its own code replica and calculate the autocorrelation function. When the autocorrelation function reaches peak the two codes are in-phase and there is zero time shift between them. This is in reality how a CDMA handset acquires the unmodulated pilot channel. If the receiver is an interceptor who doesn't have a local replica of the code, it will simply create a replica by scanning the mathematical space of 42-bit codes and checking out by brute force which code correlates. From an engineering point of view it's an easy enough task.

Covert Transmission

We discussed in Chapter 5 the possibilities of steganographic hiding of information. Many schemes have been reported and evaluated on how to illicitly transmit information along covert channels.

The easiest example and the most straightforward way of embedding covert communications inside a suitable information carrier, say a transmitted picture or image, is to alter the LSB bit of each pixel (for example, if a pixel is encoded with 8 bits in a 256-color image, this technique implies changing the least significant bit) to one bit of the illicit transmission. Because the alteration happens at the lowest bit position of the legitimate picture one may not necessarily notice the change. On the other side on a 1024×1024 pixel-based image, for example, there are more than a million pixels (each color-encoded in this example with 8 bits) and simply using the LSB position of these million pixels allows a capacity of 1 MB of covert traffic. This means that an illegitimate 8-Kbps GSM telephone call can be run imperceptibly for more than two minutes piggy-backed onto one image like this example shows and to the unbeknownst of the image users. Of course the subject touches numerous aspects of statistical processing to avert such risks, special digital signal processing for when the covert information is smaller or larger than the carrier structure (for example, the image of this example), the spatial/temporal perceptivity of the existence of a covert channel that can spark suspicions in the mind of the legitimate user, etc. The principle is equally applicable on altered audio or wave files. Katzenbeisser and Petitcolas[120] in their book have combined a rich description of all these aspects. The principles of steganography imply more vulnerabilities exist during covert transmissions and further clarify the need for end-to-end security.

An interesting example of how vulnerable in this sense standardized packet-based information structures can be, Handel et al. [121] examined the *Open System Interconnect* (OSI) network model for possible covert channels that can be used to transmit secret information. Unused portions of data frames at the data link layer are only one of the multiple weaknesses they have identified. Similarly and even more subtle time-stamps of IP packets can be coded to account for illicit traffic. Packets sent on even time increments say can be made to correspond to a logical 1 while packets sent on odd time increments can be made to correspond to a logical 0 on the covert channel. One also should think twice about the 6 unused (reserved) bits in the TCP packet header, or the 2 reserved bits in the IP packet header. If appropriate filtering techniques are not in place to discard these reserved bits from further transmission, they represent some extremely easy channels to use for covert operations.

As another striking example of the covert channels that are available to illicit usage by attackers or devious designers, Westfeld et al. [122] report a system that can store messages into a lossy *discrete cosine transform* (DCT) based video compression scheme. In their paper, a whole GSM telephone conversation (at 8-Kbps rate) was imperceptibly piggy-backed onto an ISDN-based video conferencing system without severely degrading the video signal, thereby assuring the undisturbed presence of the covert GSM communication. Readers who are more interested in the aspects of embedding real-time covert communications onto transmissions of other nature are referred to and to the numerous references that it contains. [123]

The end-to-end secure communications methods and considerations that we examined in this chapter are a strong antidote against the risks associated with vulnerability of such covert channels.

Conclusions

In this chapter we defined end-to-end security and showed how its conception is a result of the evolution the communication industry at large has gone through the last 10 to 15 years. How the various techniques of classifying communications systems, techniques, and networks affect the definition of end-to-end security and what the ramifications are of half-baked solutions has been covered. It was then shown why end-to-end is the most comprehensive level of communications security one can seek, and to further corroborate our premise that if it can be transmitted it can be intercepted and analyzed, we have covered considerable length communication interception techniques, *electronic countermeasures* (ECMs) and *electronic counter-counter-measures* (ECCMs) as applied to communications systems (which is an altogether different issue from the corresponding radar designer's needs). It was expressly shown how *vulnerable to interception* are the *latest spread-spectrum techniques* and tangible methods with examples of automatic modulation recognition for wireless communications transmissions have been discussed. This chapter leads to the inevitable conclusion that interception vulnerability is probable and in fact likely in public and private networks, where the adversary can be either a properly equipped criminal or terrorist group or a well-funded enemy government.

Endnotes

[1]Nichols, Randall K., Daniel J. Ryan, and Julie J. C. H. Ryan, *Defending Your Digital Assets Against Hackers, Crackers, Spies and Thieves,* McGraw Hill, 1999.

[2]Black, Uyless, *Frame Relay Networks: Specifications and Implementations,* 2nd Ed., McGraw-Hill, 1996.

[3]Kumar, Balaji, *Broadband Communications: A Professional's Guide to ATM, Frame Relay, SMDS, SONET and B-ISDN,* McGraw-Hill, 1995.

[4]Doraswamy, Naganand, and Dan Harkins, *IPsec: The New Security Standard for the Internet, Intranets and Virtual Private Networks,* Prentice-Hall, 1999.

[5]Smith, Richard E., *Internet Cryptography,* Addison-Wesley, 1997.

[6]Kaufman, Charlie, Radia Perlman, and Mike Speciner, *Network Security: Private Communication in a Public World,* Prentice-Hall, 1995.

[7]Stallings, William, *SNMP, SNMPv2 and RMON: Practical Network Management,* Addison-Wesley, 1996.

[8]Stallings, William, *Cryptography and Network Security: Principles and Practice,* 2nd Ed., Prentice-Hall, 1999.

[9]Wittmann, Ralph, and Martina Zitterbart, *Multicast Communication: Protocols and Applications,* Morgan Kaufmann, 2001.

[10]Kosiur, David R., and Dave Kosiur, *IP Multicasting: The Complete Guide to Interactive Corporate Networks,* Wiley, 1998.

[11]Schneier, Bruce, *Applied Cryptography: Protocols, Algorithms & Source Code,* 2nd Ed., John Wiley & Sons, 1995.

[12]Goldberg, Randy, and Lance Riek, *A Practical Handbook of Speech Coders,* CRC Press, 2000.

[13]Minoli, Daniel, and Emma Minoli, *Delivering Voice over Frame Relay and ATM,* John Wiley & Sons, 1998.

[14]Minoli, Daniel, and Emma Minoli, *Delivering Voice over IP Networks,* Wiley, 1998.

[15]Bellamy, John C., *Digital Telephony,* 3rd Ed., John Wiley & Sons, 2000.

[16]Rabiner, Lawrence R., and Ronald W. Schafer, *Digital Processing of Speech Signals,* Prentice-Hall, 1978.

[17]Sklar, Bernard, *Digital Communications: Fundamentals and Applications,* Prentice-Hall, 1988.

[18]Mehrotra, Asha K., *GSM System Engineering,* Artech House, 1997.

[19]Groe, John B., and Lawrence E. Larson, *CDMA Mobile Radio Design,* Artech House, 2000.

[20]Proakis, John G., and Dimitris G. Manolakis, *Digital Signal Processing: Principles, Algorithms and Applications, 3rd edition,* Prentice-Hall, 1996.

[21]Madisetti, Vijay K., and Douglas B. Williams, eds., *The Digital Signal Processing Handbook,* CRC Press, 1998.

[22]Redl, Siegmund M., Matthias K. Weber, and Malcolm W. Oliphant, *An Introduction to GSM,* Artech House, 1995.

[23]ETSI/GSM Section 6.10, "European Digital Cellular Telecommunications System (Phase 2); Full Rate Speech Transcoding," September 1994.

[24]Webb, U.S. Patent No. 5101432, Signal Encryption Method.

[25]Perlman, Radia, *Interconnections, 2nd Ed.: Bridges, Routers, Switches & Internetworking Protocols*, Addison-Wesley, 1999.

[26]Halabi, Sam, Danny McPherson (contributor), *Internet Routing Architectures,* Cisco Press, 2000.

[27]Stewart, John W., *BGP4 Inter-Domain Routing in the Internet,* Addison-Wesley, 1999.

[28]Moy, John T., *OSPF Anatomy of an Internet Routing Protocol,* Addison-Wesley, 1998.

[29]Black, Uyless D., *IP Routing Protocols: RIP, OSPF, BGP, PNNI & Cisco Routing Protocols,* Prentice-Hall, 2000.

[30]Viterbi, Andrew J., *CDMA: Principles of Spread-Spectrum Communication,* Addison-Wesley, 1995.

[31]Wiley, Richard G., *Electronic Intelligence: the Interception of Radar Signals,* Artech House, 1985.

[32]Schleher, D. Curtis, *Introduction to Electronic Warfare,* Artech House, 1986.

[33]McDonough, Robert N., and Anthony D. Whalen, *Detection of Signals in Noise,* 2nd Ed., Academic Press, 1971.

[34]Schleher, Op. cit.

[35]Wozencraft, John M., and Irwin M. Jacobs, *Principles of Communication Engineering,* Waveland Press, 1990.

[36]Ojanperä, Tero, and Ramjee Prasad, eds., *Wideband CDMA for Third Generation Mobile Communications,* Artech House, 1998.

[37]Holma, Harri, and Antti Toskala, eds., *WCDMA for UMTS: Radio Access for 3rd Generation Mobile Communications,* John Wiley & Sons, 2000.

[38]Lee, Jhong Sam, and Leonard E. Miller, *CDMA Systems Engineering Handbook,* Artech House, 1998.

[39]Lee, Edward A., and David G. Messerschmitt, *Digital Communication,* 2nd Ed., Kluwer Academic Publishers, 1994.

[40]Yang, Samuel C., *CDMA RF System Engineering,* Artech House, 1998.

[41]Lipsky, S., "Find the emitter fast with monopulse methods," *Microwaves,* May 1978.

[42]Baron, A., K. Davis, and C. Hofmann, Passive Direction Finding and Signal Location, *Microwave Journal,* September 1982.

[43]Coppock R., R. Croce, and W. Regier, "Bragg cell RF signal processing," *Microwave Journal,* September 1978.

[44]Ibid.

[45]Campbell Colin, *Surface Acoustic Wave Devices for Mobile and Wireless Communications,* Academic Press, 1998.

[46]Ruppel, Clemens C. W., and Tor A. Fjedly, eds., *Advances in Surface Wave Technology, Systems and Applications* (Selected Topics in Electronics and Systems—Vol. 19), World Scientific Publishing, 2000.

[47]Sklar, Op. cit.

[48]Freeman, Roger L., *Telecommunication System Engineering,* 3rd Ed., John Wiley & Sons, 1996.

[49]Freeman, Roger L., *Radio System Design for Telecommunications,* 2nd Ed., John Wiley & Sons, 1997.

[50]Feher, Kamilo, *Wireless Digital Communications: Modulation & Spread Spectrum Applications,* Prentice-Hall, 1995.

[51]Lee, William C. Y., *Mobile Cellular Telecommunications; Analog and Digital Systems,* 2nd Ed., McGraw-Hill, 1995.

[52]Verdu, Sergio, *Multiuser Detection,* Cambridge University Press, 1998.

[53]Liu, Hui, *Signal Processing Applications in CDMA Communications,* Artech House, 2000.

[54]Fazel, Khaled, and Gerhard P. Fettweis, eds., *Multi-Carrier Spread Spectrum,* Kluwer Academic Press, 1997.

[55]Glisic, Savo, and Branka Vucetic, *Spread Spectrum CDMA Systems for Wireless Communications,* Artech House, 1997.

[56]Webb patent, Op. cit.

[57]Glisic, Op. cit.

[58]Kärkkäinen, Kari, *Code families and their performance measures for CDMA and Military Spread-Spectrum Systems,* Ph.D. Thesis, Dept. of Electrical Engineering, University of Oulu, Oulu, Finland, 1996, Acta Universitatis Ouluensis Technica C89, 1996.

[59]Kärkkäinen, Kari, "Correlation, Spread-Spectrum Multiple-Access and Linear Complexity Properties of Nonlinear Feedforward Logic (NLFFL) Pseudonoise Sequences," *Proc. IEEE MILCOM '93, Military Communications Conference,* Vol. 2, October 11–14, 1993, Boston, MA.

[60]Golomb, S. W., "Correlation Properties of Periodic and Aperiodic Sequences and Applications to Multi-User Systems," *Proc. NATO Advanced Study Institute on Multi-User Communications,* Norwich, U.K., 1980, pp. 161–197.

[61]Gong, G., Z. T. Dai and S. W. Golomb, "Criterion and Counting for Cyclically shift distinct q-ary GMW seqauences of period q^n-1," *IEEE Trans. on Inform. Theory,* Vol. 46, No. 2, March 2000, pp. 474–484.

[62]No, J. S., S. W. Golomb, G. Gong, H. K. Lee, and P. Gaal, "New binary pseudo-random sequences of period 2^n-1 with ideal autocorrelation," *IEEE Trans. on Inform. Theory,* Vol. 44, No. 2, March 1998, pp. 814–817.

[63]Sklar, Op. cit.

[64]Haykin, Simon, *Adaptive Filter Theory,* 3rd Ed., Prentice-Hall, 1996.

[65]Kay. Steven M., *Fundamental of Statistical Signal Processing, Vol. I: Estimation Theory,* Prentice-Hall, 1993.

[66]Kay, Steven M., *Fundamental of Statistical Signal Processing, Vol. II: Detection Theory,* Prentice-Hall, 1998.

[67]Rohde, Ulrich L., *Microwave and Wireless Synthesizers; Theory and Design,* Wiley, 1997.

[68]Mengali, Umberto, and Aldo N. D'Andrea, *Synchronization Techniques for Digital Receivers,* Plenum Press, 1997.

[69]Rohde, Ulrich L., Jerry Whittaker, and T. T. N. Bucher, *Communications Receivers, 2nd edition,* McGraw-Hill, 1997.

[70]Meyr, Heinrich, and Gerd Ascheid, *Synchronization in Digital Communications,* Vols. 1 and 2, John Wiley & Sons, 1990.

[71]Ibid.

[72]Sklar, Op. cit.

[73]Ward, R. B., "Acquisition of Psuedonoise Signals by Sequential Estimation," *IEEE Trans. Commun.,* COM13, December 1965, pp. 475–483.

[74]Simon, M. K., J. K. Omura, R. A. Scholtz, and B. K. Levitt, *Spread Spectrum Communications,* Vols. 1, 2, and more specifically 3; Computer Science Press, Inc., 1985.

[75]Spilker, J. J., and D. T. Magill, "The Delay-Lock Discriminator—An Optimum Tracking Device," *Proc. IRE,* September 1961.

[76]Spilker, J.J., "Delay-Lock Tracking of Binary Signals," *IEEE Trans. Space Electron. Telem.,* March 1963.

[77]Simon, M. K., "Non-coherent Pseudonoise Code Tracking Performance of Spread Spectrum Receivers," *Commun.,* Vol. COM25, March 1977.

[78]Sklar, Op Cit.

[79]Ziemer, R. E., and R. L. Peterson, *Digital Communications and Spread Spectrum Systems,* Macmillan Publishing Company, 1985.

[80]Holmes, J. K., Coherent Spread Spectrum Systems, John Wiley & Sons, 1982.

[81]Simon, M. K. and A. Polydoros, Coherent Detection of Frequency-Hopped Quadrature Modulations in the Presence of Jamming: Part I. QPSK and QASK; Part II. QPR class I Modulation, *IEEE Trans. Commun.,* Vol. COM29, November 1981, pp. 1644–1668.

[82]Azzouz, Elsayed E., and Asoke Kumar Nandi, *Automatic Modulation Recognition of Communication Signals,* Kluwer Academic Publishers, 1996.

[83]Polydoros, A. and K. Kim, "On the detection and classification of quadrature digital modulations in broadband noise," *IEEE Trans. On Commun.,* Vol. 38, No. 8, August 1990, pp. 1199–1211.

[84]DeSimio, M. P. and E. P. Glenn, "Adaptive generation of decision functions for classification of digitally modulated signals," *NAECON,* 1988, pp. 1010–1014.

[85]Soliman, S. S., and Z. S. Hsue, "Signal classification using statistical moments," *IEEE Trans. on Commun.,* Vol. 40, No. 5, May 1992, pp. 908–916.

[86]Nagy, P. A. J., "A modulation classifier for multi-channel systems and multi-transmitter situations," *MILCOM 1994 Conference,* 1994.

[87]Jondral, F., "Automatic classification of high-frequency signals," *Signal Processing,* Vol. 9, No. 3, October 1985, pp. 177–190.

[88]Brown, Robert Grover, and Patrick Y. C. Hwang, *Introduction to Random Signal and Applied Kalman Filtering,* 3rd Ed., John Wiley & Sons, 1997.

[89]Haddad, Richard A. and Thomas W. Parsons, *Digital Signal Processing: Theory, Applications and Hardware,* Computer Science Press, 1991.

[90]Orfanidis, Sophocles J., *Introduction to Signal Processing,* Prentice-Hall, 1996.

[91]Feher, Kamilo, *Advanced Digital Communications: Systems and Signal Processing Techniques,* Noble Publishing Corp., 1997.

[92]Feher, Kamilo, ed., *Telecommunications Measurements, Analysis and Instrumentation,* Noble Publishing Corp., 1997.

[93]Kailath, Thomas, Ali H. Sayed, and Babak Hassibi, *Linear Estimation,* Prentice-Hall, 2000.

[94]Brookner, Eli, *Tracking and Kalman Filtering Made Easy,* John Wiley & Sons, 1998.

[95]Ljung, Lennart, *System Identification: Theory for the User,* Prentice-Hall, 1999.

[96]Jeruchim, Michel C., Philip Balaban, and K. Sam Shanmugan, *Simulation of Communication Systems,* Plenum Press, 1992.

[97]Wysocki, Tadeusz, Hashem Razavi, and Bahram Honary, eds., *Digital Signal Processing for Communication Systems,* Kluwer Academic Publishers, 1997.

[98]Azzouz and Nandi, Op. cit.

[99]Ibid.

[100]Ibid.

[101]Ibid.

[102]Ibid.

[103]Ibid.

[104]Haykin, Simon, *Neural Networks, A comprehensive foundation; 2nd edition,* Prentice-Hall, 1999.

[105]Luo, Fa-Long, and Rolf Unbehauen, *Applied Neural Networks for Signal Processing,* Cambridge University Press, 1998.

[106]Kung, S. Y., *Digital Neural Networks,* Prentice-Hall, 1993.

[107]Fausett, Laurene, *Fundamentals of Neural Networks: Architectures, Algorithms and Applications,* Prentice-Hall, 1994.

[108]Glesner, Manfred, and Werner Pöchmüller, *Neurocomputers: An Overview of Neural Networks in VLSI,* Chapman and Hall, 1994.

[109]Proakis, John G., *Digital Communications,* 3rd Ed., McGraw-Hill, 1995.

[110]Ackenhusen, John G., *Real-Time Signal Processing; Design and Implementation of Signal Processing Systems,* Prentice-Hall, 1999.

[111]Azzouz, Op. cit.

[112]Ibid.

[113]Harte, Lawrence J., Adrian D. Smith, and Charles A. Jacobs, *IS-36 TDMA technology, Economics and Services,* Artech House, 1998.

[114]*ETSI/GSM Specification,* Vol. 2.20, Version 3.0.1, January 1990.

[115]*ETSI/GSM Specification,* Vol. 3.0.4, Version 4.0.0, October 1992.

[116]Mehrotra, *GSM System Engineering,* Op. cit.

[117]Redl, Op. cit.

[118]Hirade, Kenkichi, and Kazuaki Murota, "A Study of Modulation for Digital Mobile telephony," *29th IEEE Vehicular Technology Conf.,* March 1979.

[119]Simon, Marvin K., and Charles C. Wang, "Differential Detection of Gaussian MSK in a Mobile Radio Environment," *IEEE Trans. on Vehicular Technology,* Vol. VT-33, No. 4, November 1984, pp. 307–320.

[120]Katzenbeisser, Stefan, and Fabien A. P. Petitcolas, eds., *Information Hiding Techniques for Steganography and Digital Watermarking,* Artech House, 2000.

[121]Handel, T. G., and M. T. Sandford, "Data Hiding in the OSI Network Model," in *Information Hiding: First International Workshop, Proceedings*, Vol. 1174 of *Lecture Notes in Computer Science*, Springer-Verlag, Heidelberg, Germany, 1996, pp. 23–38.

[122]Westfeld, A., and G. Wolf, "Steganography in a Video Conferencing System," in *Proceedings of the Second International Workshop on Information Hiding*, Vol. 1525 of *Lecture Notes in Computer Science*, Springer Verlag, Heidelberg, Germany 1998, pp. 32–47.

[123]Katzenbeisser, Stefan, and Fabien A. P. Petitcolas, eds., *Information Hiding Techniques for Steganography and Digital Watermarking,* Artech House, 2000.

Optimizing Wireless Security with FPGAs and ASICs

Having defined the functionality and explained the need—as well as the merits—of end-to-end security in communications and more specifically relative to the wireless arena, this chapter elaborates on solutions in hardware versus software and discusses the two fundamental hardware categories, namely, configurable and non-configurable circuitry. Avenues of rapid implementations for highly integrated security solutions are investigated and various technologies are considered as enabling platforms, such as *digital signal processors(s)* (DSPs) and *system-on-a-chip* (SOC) with or without embedded DSP functionality.

Optimizing? Yes, But What?

Various aspects of security have been discussed, with the conclusion that interception is a real danger. The potential eavesdropper is the number one enemy. He or she can be casual or deliberate, well organized and financially-backed or not, highly trained and equipped or not, perhaps sponsored by a hostile government. Or the unwelcome listener may be a grade-school student who has just discovered the conversation by chance. Whatever the source of broken privacy, the need to protect the confidentiality, integrity, authentication, and potentially the non-repudiation of a communications session and its content is obvious. Ancillary aspects of wireless security, such as denial of service, assumes the form of signal level or application level jamming covered in the previous chapter and will not be addressed here.

As the designer of a wireless communications device (handset, PDA, and so forth) is confronted with several fundamental variables and parameters, his work should be examined *in situ* before defining an optimization. A circuit, for instance, can be designed to run faster, but it is not logical to expect that in the average case this will imply less power consumption. Likewise it would be at least absurd to think that packing extra functionality inside a microchip, all other things remaining identical (manufacturing plant, semiconductor process technology, clock rate, and so on), the size, and the cost of the chip are drastically reduced. Engineers learn by experience to keep in mind the harsh face of reality, also known as "there is no free lunch." One gains something by giving up something else. A circuit becomes more functional by becoming more complex, and therefore usually more costly to develop and/or sell. A circuit becomes faster by being allowed to draw more current from the power supply and hence consumes more power, or by becoming physically smaller whereby it can switch states more quickly.

There are 12 design parameters to be kept in mind as values to consider while deciding the appropriate value judgment on the merits of specific wireless security architectures, and on designing a secure wireless device. Without specific order of importance, these are

- Speed of real-time operation at negligible latency for the application at hand
- Power consumption
- Ease of integration and embedment
- Ease of engineering development
- Flexibility and upgradability
- Cost of development
- Acquisition cost for the user/customer
- Operational dependability on other external components of a wireless system
- Physical security (tamper-proof, plus intrusion detection)
- Robustness of the cryptography afforded
- Powerful and bidirectional authentication
- Randomness of key or *Initialization Vector* (IV) material generated.

It may be said that optimization attempts to improve efficiency; however, efficiency can be defined in many ways.

If an integrated system is built on an SOC platform around a standard CPU or DSP core (called here the main on-chip CPU), then security functionality is being executed as embedded SW, run generally from ROM by stealing cycles from the on-chip main CPU or an embedded DSP coprocessor. The application may be apportioned into modules, such as a stream cipher or a block cipher operating in the X or Y mode, coupled with a key generation mechanism. Then one checks the application's clock cycles, comparing oranges with oranges: Cipher X is found to be more efficient than Cipher Y by a fractional second. In addition to speed of execution, from which one can determine whether the application is power-hungry or power-conservative, one can look into silicon real-estate and compare solution A in X square millimeters with consequent cost of ownership as opposed to another in Y square millimeters, funding that X is significantly smaller or larger than Y. This does not have further value in most applications except that it clarifies the borders of acceptable performance for the implementation of specific solutions. A simple analogy would be if one considers using, say, a Ferrari sports car just to go to the corner store to . . . buy a bottle of milk. Can you do it? Of course, but it is rather exaggerated reasoning. Inversely, you can enter a car race with a . . . school bus or a tractor-trailer, but what are the prospects of winning?

Efficiency from the engineering point of view is ultimately the trade-offs among a series of requirements to come up with an optimal solution. The business point of view reveals a completely different story. Vendors will contort reality and push their square peg into the proverbial round hole to achieve commercial success. The only remedy for that is an informed market and open competition.

The 'Trust Nobody' Design Mentality

As mentioned earlier, embedded security SW is usually (and preferably) run out of ROM. This comes as clear contradiction to many electrical engineers who have learned to debug their designs by loading the code out of RAM, since, if a bug is found later on it would be straightforward to correct the source, recompile the pertinent modules, relink the appropriate code pieces and libraries, create the new executable image, and load the runtime environment into RAM. Next time one boots the embedded system, it will inevitably execute the corrected code. This seems so neat that one may be tempted to ask what is the problem with this picture.

The answer should not come as a surprise to anyone responsible for security. *You never know what code your system will be forced to execute when the code is loaded from outside every time you power up the system.* To put it crudely, someone may have planted a new memory module beyond your knowledge. We have built an elaborate case in this book around the premise that essentially nothing can be trusted inside someone's equipment if the stakes are high. Therefore depending on what level of security one needs to achieve, one must assume an opponent will engage the unthinkable. If a special PC adapter has to be installed inside your PC to steal information from your hard disk by malicious attackers and transmitted over the LAN or modem to an outside destination while you innocently browse the Internet or draft a spreadsheet, it can happen.

How many of us start our days by kneeling down under our desk each morning, unscrewing our PC cabinet, and checking out the actual HW configuration? How many of us even know how or what to look for? The situation is even more complex with a wireless device. It is usually highly integrated and unless physically held onto day and night, you cannot know who may have tinkered with it. We implicitly trust the manufacturer, but when the stakes are high, unusual things can be done. The reader is reminded of the well-publicized case of a Middle Eastern terrorist who was presumably targeted by the Israeli intelligence services. The Israelis apparently at some point took possession of his wireless phone, planted an explosive device in it, and returned it to him (obviously without his knowledge). At the appropriate moment a call activated the device and the phone literally blew him into pieces.

This same argument is one of the most fundamental of premises in the intelligence community. If someone wants to attack a secure link, the attacker will seek the weakest link, and usually this is not the cryptography (however good or bad it is) or even the cryptographic key management. It is the physical security, the access to system passwords (that some people have been known to write on Post-it® Notes stuck to their computer screen), the proverbial unlocked drawer where one may have neglected critical information, the secretary who can be more talkative than cautious, and so forth. Strong communications security implies that these basics have been addressed and taken care of. This realm then separates the professional from the dilettante.

It is a classical design philosophy in the communications security arena that essentially nothing can be trusted outside the cryptographic module. This is especially true in government-related applications where, for instance, *Federal Information Processing Standard* (FIPS)-compliant intrusion detection techniques must be provided. This is why code cannot be accepted for loading at will from outside (except in some specific and extremely well controlled environments), as one eventually will have to deal with the prospect of malicious or duplicitous code. The resulting philosophy is that ample functionality has to be integrated inside the cryptographic module. In the HORNET™ design for instance, the host device CPU (for example, a handset's master CPU) is not trusted. Keys, therefore, are generated inside the cryptography chip. Random numbers used for the production of initialization vectors (also known as seed values) for the random number generators are equally generated inside the chip. One minimizes the chances that trouble can be caused by excessive trust on another component.

The original issue then of ROM vs. RAM as the memory base for the execution source of code is outside the problem space for the embedded system designer. One will use RAM for prototyping development, one will even use PROM and EPROM memories in a board-level emulator for FPGA prototype, for debugging purposes, but the cryptographic system that must be delivered will actually have to use ROM for its code memory.

Evaluating Secure Design Architectures

When the task at hand is to evaluate a proposed secure wireless device or its architecture, one now has a quick list of criteria by which to judge the device or its architecture. Conversely, if the task is to maximize one or more parameters, again the 12-parameter model suggests a series of trade-offs that will facilitate the analysis of the device or its architecture, via specific constraints. By crude analogy, if one must travel from City A to City B in the least expensive way, the traveler had best be prepared for some risks, delays, and hardships along the way, as he or she is most probably not traveling in high style.

Reshuffling values for these parameters is a classical optimization problem, and some clearly require an agreed-upon method and technique of quantification. Engineers routinely are confronted with trade-offs and are bound by detailed budget or performance specification constraints.

In subsequent pages, this high-level approach is called the Wireless Embedded Architecture Security Evaluation List model, and for those who like funny acronyms, this one resolves to WEASEL. The model does not offer an exhaustive microelectronic design list of trade-offs, but does serve as the proverbial 50,000-foot view of architectural choices that one is expected to cope with.

'Weasel' Model Philosophy and Rationale

The authors are not discussing information security as this is understood in the world of INFOSEC. This discussion is not about securing e-mail content or encryption of computer files; these are operations that can be handled easily and inexpensively by software and, in most cases, offline. If one wonders what the system's user will say, the answer is that in most respects, no one cares whether his or her email message will be encrypted within 125 ms or in 500 ms. On the other hand, the user will certainly react and rightfully so if he or she must wait five minutes for a three-line e-mail message to be encrypted or decrypted. One also realizes from this small example that in real-time communications (especially when the transmitted content is large and unpredictable) the solution architect does not have the luxury of the offline-solution provider of passing twice over the data. This is the case for instance in a classical Lempel-Ziv type of compression algorithm, where the first pass allows the system to build the dictionary and the second pass over the data to be compressed actually encodes the content accordingly. In real-time communications things have to happen fast and correctly.

Incidentally, relative to potential user answers to exhaustive-detail questionnaires, the granularity between the extremes is the subject of traditional market analysis, where people will be asked what they need as response time, and some may say half a second, while others may say three seconds. The marketing department of the manufacturer charts these responses as a histogram and generates the appropriate answer in the market requirements document that they will submit to their business development department as the definition of a new product and business case. At the macroscopic level, the idea is: If we design something that looks like this and which does this and that, and if we manage to price it at that level, then that many people seem to be willing to buy it.

The market requirements document for a communications security system has several line items coherent with the 12 parameters of the *wireless architecture security evaluation list* (WEASEL) model. Market research tells the designer/manufacturer how many of these security systems one can expect to sell if they operate as specified at a given performance range and if they are profitably priced at specific levels. Business development teams then start working on these market requirements, first doing a feasibility analysis, where potential technologies are objectively reviewed and retained as candidates for the implementation of various pieces of the engineering puzzle that is eventually to be tackled. One can assume, for instance, that out of four technological know-hows needed to produce such a product, technologies 1 and 2 are available in house, technology 3 can be developed, but technology 4 is not available unless one licenses it from somebody who has it. Unless the designer/manufacturer acquires another company that possesses these attributes, economics will decide the latter part of this debate.

Assuming that all skills are made available inhouse and that the marketing department has decided based on its analysis that the market potential is real and attainable and this is corroborated by the feasibility analysis, the company decides this widget will become an actual product. Having done (irrelevant to our purposes) financial analysis on the business case that shows what it will cost and how much the company stands to gain if the product development and sales plan is achieved, the business development organization evaluates the market requirements and, based on their feasibility analysis, prepares a new document. This Functional Specification is a document showing in excruciating detail how the system will appear and how it will behave.

Based on the functional specification, the engineering department undertakes the project with three more levels of specification:

- An architecture
- A design
- An implementation specification

Now the actual design work begins. To a large extent the market requirements explain what parameters must be optimized. If one is to design an economical compact car for the low-income consumer, one does not dream about exotic body aerodynamics or huge cubic displacement engines usually found in an expensive sports car.

A Case Study

One may now proceed through the architectural options of a real-life example, designing an embedded security communications solution for a wireless device. We reveal the thought process in the architect's mind and play the traditional devil's advocate to show how he or she continually questions choices until the appropriate trade-offs have been settled and compromises are resolved. As this is not an engineering project management book, organizational detail is intentionally omitted. This is, as the chapter's title states, how one optimizes the solution.

Let's assume we want to secure wireless handsets and further assume that we want our design to be

- End-to-end secure for voice and data
- Operable at real-time speeds
- Tamper-proof and not easily susceptible to hacking
- Based on acceptable and robust cryptographic methods

Among several modules needed, the heart of this solution is a cryptographic engine. Encryption using DES or 3DES level of security, for example, is attractive for our example's architect.

The first decision to be made is whether to implement in software or hardware. If in software, DES requires a certain level of instructions to be executed per second. More specifically, a typical implementation of DES in Java will yield 1,656 32-bit instruction words when compiled onto a Pentium. Depending on the throughput and clock speed of the processor and assuming one instruction per clock cycle (not always the case), one can deduce what percentage of the processor's capacity is devoted to real-time encryption. Doubling roughly for decryption, one can estimate requirements for full-duplex operation. We say roughly, because the CPU does not just encrypt and decrypt. To switch between contexts, some household management chores are needed, such as flushing of registers to memory, reloading specific pointers, and so forth. In an actual design this switching overhead must be precisely quantified and optimized. For our purposes though it is more than adequate to assume that we just need to double the number of the instructions to be executed within a time-unit. Buffering will be needed so the processor can switch from context to context consistently for time-sharing. This operational capability was not available in current chips equipping handsets but will definitely be available on next generation SOC-based designs. Therefore to create a 3DES-level security one would have had to budget this same capability on another coprocessor CPU.

Literature indicates that this performance requirement is valid for a Pentium class CPU, but then we realize we cannot add a Pentium CPU to the handset for three reasons. First, it is expensive beyond consumer acceptance for such a handset; second, Pentium CPUs suffer from a heavy power consumption that although not noticeable in the desktop. PC, it would be prohibitive in the battery-lifetime-constrained handset; and third, even if the former two reasons were surmountable, no physical room is available on the handset's printed circuit board to integrate such a big chip, as it would make the ultimate product prohibitively large and therefore unacceptable to consumers as a physical form factor.

Thus, implementing 3DES encryption in software inside a handset must be ruled out, unless the current CPU is changed. Modern handsets use chips designed along an SOC architecture. We could change the core CPU inside the *main CPU unit* (MCU) and accommodate such a solution in software along with the baseband digital signal processer (DSP). The other solution that some manufacturers have taken is to create an external add-on module inside which 3DES runs on a separate CPU (with its own memory and power supply). This is NOT what we started to design. It is not embedded and it is NOT inside the handset. It is not a fast solution and it is most probably not tamper-proof.

The suitability of using 3DES in software for an inexpensive, real-time communications application suddenly seems to be evaporating. Before looking into a hardware approach, a few more minutes on the software approach may be in order in case we are not yet fully convinced as to its nonsuitability.

Inspecting the functionality the HW (usually a CPU and baseband DSP processor) has to deal with, and by doing so we budget the available MIPS in a typical 100-MIPS processor used in these environments for useful work at a predetermined baud rate of incoming or outgoing communications traffic, and we find some interesting figures.

The example shown in Table 13-1 is from a typical state-of-the-art U.S. IS-95 CDMA mobile handset compiled by Groe and Larson.[1]

These MIPS values decrease with improved (and more expensive) architectures, and further, the list of items in Table 13-1 is not exhaustive.

Adding real-time encryption obviously will strain the resources of the processor. If you also consider that, from the circuitry point of view, newer cryptography may not be symmetric, the message is rather loud and clear (using Rijndael in HW, as discussed later in this chapter, needs different circuitry at both ends of a link, as key scheduling is done differently at the encrypting and decrypting stations).

Table 13-1 MIPS Requirements for Some Common Algorithms Found in a CDMA IS-95 Mobile Radio

Algorithm	Implementation	Millions of Instructions per Second (MIPS) Needed
Correlator	Hardware	5
Automatic Frequency Control (AFC)	Hardware	5
Automatic Gain Control (AGC)	Hardware	5
Transmit filter	Hardware	30
128-pt FFT	Software	1
Viterbi decoder (length = 9, rate = $\frac{1}{2}$)	Software	6
Vocoder (8 Kbps Qualcomm code-excited linear prediction (QCELP)	Software	20
Vocoder (enhanced variable rate coder EVRC)	Software	30

Unless the MCU or baseband chip's computing capabilities can be upgraded, and the ensuing power consumption increase with commensurate decrease of useful battery lifetime and most probably increased cost as well remains acceptable, it will not be possible to run the contemplated 3DES encryption algorithm in software in a constrained device. The outlook is increasingly negative if 2.5G or third generation technology is considered, as multimegabit per second traffic (including streaming audio or compressed/encoded video content) is expected to flow back and forth.

This is incidentally the reason why 3DES encrypted phones do not exist at the corner store. Companies like Starium, SAGEM, Crypto AG, Siemens, and others (devices sold by Rohde & Schwartz) have tried doing it in several variations, but the best most have so far achieved is an externally mounted module that connects to the handset, with its own RISC CPU, memory, and power supply offering end-to-end security by software implementation of low-end cryptography and key management. This usually only works on compatible devices from the same vendor and it can only operate at low bit rates (telephony) while still at a cost varying from more than $100 per module to $44,000 for tamper-proof quality modules. This latter cost can be multiplied by an order of magnitude for specifying tamper-proof quality modules. When typical wireless customers struggle to meet $19.95 per month connection fee with their carrier or network operator, such an extra cost is prohibitive, and such a solution—besides not being convenient—is economically nonaccessible to the masses.

We now return to the hardware approach premise. What if we were to use a DES encryptor chip instead of software? There are several excellent DES encryptors in either silicon or IP core form. Why not license one of those numerous DES encryption IP cores that can be integrated easily into an ASIC? Why not design one of them into our handset?

Well . . . for the same reasons that a Pentium could not be integrated inside the handset, plus another consideration: DES is known to work in several cryptographic modes (one or more of which could be of interest for our configuration). The encryptor must go through 16 rounds of operations to run DES on a single key basis (single DES). During each round there are bit manipulations, rotations, shifts, Boolean operations, substitutions based on so-called S-box lookups, and so on, taking place. If we are to run 3DES (independently of whether we use two or three cryptographic keys, as explained elsewhere in this book and in the literature, there are some facts that our application designer will not like:[2,3,4]

- We will need to work block per block of incoming data to encrypt or digitize voice audio or video. Each block in this example is of 64 bits (in the newer AES-algorithm, namely Rijndael,[5,6] it is stipulated that the block can be 128, 192, or 256 bits at a time and not all combinations are part of the NIST-sanctioned FIPS standard, as apparently several cases have not been sufficiently attacked and cryptanalyzed).
- Incoming traffic must be buffered until processing of the immediate block has been completed. In general there is a certain paucity of time. We risk irritating our prospective user's patience, as one expects to hear something within 50 ms or the delay will be objectionable. When this block is completed, another can be read in from the input buffer. This illustrates the level of activity to be encountered if 3DES is to be run in software, even on a more powerful embedded CPU, especially since that CPU will not only be doing encryption in the handset.
- 3DES operation means 3×16 rounds $= 48$ rounds of operation. To curtail costs, commercially available DES encryptors are single-DES engines that can be configured into a 3DES mode of operation, effectively passing the work three times through the engine; not the solution for our high-speed connection. But as posited, this is real-time application of some rather heavy-duty content. Therefore the delay of execution and the economics of the implementation (in silicon real estate and power consumption) are of equally serious concern.

There are two choices to cope with the speed of execution:

- Use one single-round DES engine and run the block processing 48 consecutive times (called the *iterative approach*) through it.
- Design a huge pipeline of 48 stages that implement a fast 3DES silicon chip (in what is called the *pipelined approach*).

In reality these are both nonapplicable in our realm. The former exemplifies the quintessential definition of the bottleneck; having to block incoming (for example, multimedia) traffic to accommodate the currently processing chunk of traffic 48 times through the encryption engine. The latter choice is a silicon monster of unbelievable complexity. Sandia National Labs designed such a giant-pipeline 3DES chip but its obvious size, ensuing cost, and power consumption dooms it as a commercially viable candidate for the wireless handset we have in mind for a product platform.[7]

Our architect now begins to see that this approach is leading to nothing useful, realizing that classical analysis along this axis of choices is not enough to design a product in a rather revolutionary context. The analysis has failed to solve the speed requirement. The projected solution's cost has skyrocketed. Battery lifetime seems a lost cause. We may well be tempted to go back to the originator of the idea to report that it cannot be done with known technology.

The truth of the matter (and to conclude the case study) is that it *can* be done and in fact it *has* been done, for example in the design of the HORNET™ chip. Specific examples will be presented in some detail elsewhere in this book with comparison as to how things stand in terms of optimization against all the WEASEL-model requirements. These are ASIC and IP cores that are based on stream ciphering and/or block ciphering techniques that can be throttled at very high speeds, that occupy relatively little amount of silicon and that can be coupled with different mechanisms for random number generation and for a solid key production, scheduling, exchange, and management with the appropriate hooks for authentication and future PKI requirements of our society. These are cutting-edge designs implemented in very-low-power CMOS technologies and built to sell for only a few dollars. In a few words, we will show how to solve the problem we purported to solve.

Software vs. Hardware Implementation of Wireless Security

Recalling the taxonomy of the wireless communications systems (from a computing needs point of view) from the previous chapter, a quick classification of implementation approaches may be made, based on what needs to be secure:

- Large amounts of traffic to be processed, potentially in a high-speed network, especially when it is transmitted unpredictably in real-time.

  Typical examples are: telephone conversations, video conferencing, streaming audio or encoded video transmissions (video-on-demand for instance), telemetry data, and so forth. One does not usually have the luxury of processing leisurely this type of data in software, potentially executing double passes over the data (as in some compressing algorithms), as the data is coming in at significant line speeds and must be treated in real-time. Hardware resources are not close by, to temporarily swallow the mass of data, and consequently, buffer overflow leads to disaster unless the architecture of the system is such that full processing can be executed before the next incoming piece of data is presented at the input.

- Very small amounts of bit traffic to be processed in a moderately high-speed network, transmitted unpredictably and in real-time.

  Typical examples of this realm are e-commerce or m-commerce transactions, credit card number transmission, choice of a specific item to order, order placement with signature, issuing instructions to one's broker, bank account information extraction, making e-payments, and micro-browser-based (WAP-style) HTML page browsing (which in a handheld wireless device will, of course, be transmitted in lean WML).

Clearly the latter can be done (and in fact is done) usually in software on the wireless device's main CPU, usually via some SOC variation on a theme around an ARM or MIPS processor. If the information needs to be encrypted using say a 3DES encryption scheme (or in the near future Rijndael AES) it can be done leisurely in software by the embedded processor. The encryption routine is only used at a small percentage of a day's worth of using the system and does in no way hamper the economics of the overall offering and design if it is done in software. Not only this, but precisely the ability to do this type of operation without undue time pressure offers the possibility of iterative as opposed to pipelined processing for significant block ciphers like 3DES and Rijndael. The designer has the luxury and peace of mind to pass 10 times (if it were needed) over the processed data to come up with a Rijndael 28-bit key and block size run.

If on the other side, performance is the first objective, as in some multimedia networks for other types of applications, one would have to debate the choice between iterative or pipelined design, a decision that one way or the other would eat away the computational and financial resources of the design in order to cope with performance requirements.

Also in our example, when the transmitted traffic is secured using a symmetric-key algorithm (like Rijndael or 3DES) the key has to be communicated, securely, to the other party. This is the basis for a PKI-based solution on top of the symmetric encryption scheme.

This PKI-like structure is based on one of the following:

- A plain-vanilla *Diffie-Hellman* (DH) protocol
- A more elaborate elliptic-curve-cryptography-based ECC-DH (as specified for instance by IEEE P1363)
- A cryptologic scheme implemented on hyperelliptic curves
- An RSA system
- A lattice-cryptography-based solution like the NTRU system
- Some other solution either based on Abelian varieties, the latest trend in wireless security, or as a variation on a proprietary theme, like MQV™ key exchange, the RPK™ algorithm, the MUSE™ algorithm, and so on.

These variants and the hardware modules they map onto will be discussed later in this chapter, as well as the trade-offs their engagement entails.

For the moment these overlying PK schemes are a conceptual secure envelope. From time to time, the wireless device must be able to generate a digital signature, so a purchase order may be placed to the m-commerce supplier with whom the user is in touch or in session. This PK-based secure envelope will generate a session key at session setup time and the device will use it to communicate to the other party the first actual encryption key to be used with the underlying symmetric key algorithm at hand (Rijndael or 3DES on our example). It can and will also create digital signatures, which in realm as explained earlier are special encrypted hashes of some information. Why special? Special only in the sense that one uses one's own private encryption key (whether it be RSA- or ECC-based) to encrypt the hash one sends. If I encrypt something with a private key and everybody can decrypt it with my published public key (provided they are assured about the validity of the directory or source from which they obtained my public key), then this is living proof that I am the only one who could possibly have originated the message. (Assuming, of course, one has been sane enough to not share one's private key with . . . the rest of humanity.)

This should help clarify why many nontechnical people confuse the terms communications security, PK encryption, symmetric-key encryption, and so on. They see the term encryption and mistakenly assume the impossible. The author has heard, for example, some investment bankers asking how our company, a stream-ciphering ASIC design house, would compete with *elliptic-curve-cryptography* (ECC) toolkits provided by a rather well-known Canadian company, since "both are in the wireless encryption business." The discussion we have had so far, in conjunction with the earlier presentation of cryptography basics, must have shown the reader that the only thing in common is the term encryption, PK technologies are good for a secure envelope type of functionality and mathematically they cannot even come close to treating real-time processing of data with the speed of symmetric-key (also known as secret-key) encryption algorithms. Per definition then, there is no competition. The two technologies are applicable to different realms. A tractor-trailer, bus, bicycle, and camel are all ground transportation means, but they address different requirements, budgets and markets. Certainly one of them could fill in for some of the others in some cases, but this would hardly be an *optimal* solution, which brings us again to the title of this chapter.

People also usually misunderstand and mix up realm with realm above. Because somebody is able, with the latest handheld gadget, to quasi-securely place an order with his or her broker, this does not mean that he or she can securely download a video movie over the air in streaming mode, ensuring that nobody else can intercept the traffic and enjoy the content without paying the intellectual property owner the appropriate royalty or fee. Typical 40-bit encryption keys or red-bridge WAP solutions can hardly be called secure.

The big challenge is in the realm where the data flow rate is significant, the available time to get the job done is short, and the available computational resources scarce. Communications security in this context has traditionally been available only to those who can afford it. Things are changing rapidly, as alluded to in this book. The safest bet is that the sheer magnitude of the task cannot be satisfied (given the cost constraints of the platform and application) by software on a general purpose processor (CPU or DSP) as they are overloaded with other application-critical modules.

If software cannot do it, the alternative has to be hardware. The question now becomes What type of hardware?

Configurable versus Non-Configurable Hardware

By configurable hardware we mean a class of integrated circuits most commonly known as FPGAs field-programmable gate arrays,[8] although there are also other devices like *programmable logic devices* (PLDs) that could approach the same definition but not the capabilities) that can be bought off the shelf and reconfigured by the designer. Each configuration can be redone within a fraction of a second and along with it, the FPGA integrated circuit can be made to perform a completely different function. One thinks therefore about unlimited reprogrammability. The subject is highly elaborate as different vendors offer different architectures, different configuration loading techniques, based on different fusing technologies. Therefore, only a cursory view of the utility FPGAs play in the development of secure wireless communications systems will be given here. Large amounts of information in the form of white papers is readily available.[9,10,11,12]

FPGA devices can be reconfigured to change logical functions while resident in the target system.[13] This capability gives the systems designer an extraordinary degree of freedom not available with any other type of logic. Hardware can be changed as easily as software. Design updates or modifications are easy and can even be made in the field, directly to products already shipped. An FPGA can even be reconfigured dynamically to perform different functions at different times. Reconfigurable logic can be used in numerous types of systems to implement system self-diagnostics, create systems capable of being reconfigured for different environments or operations, or implement multipurpose hardware for a given application. As an added benefit, using reconfigurable FPGA devices simplifies hardware design and debugging and shortens product time-to-market. At the same time, in several contexts, designers use reconfigurable FPGA logic to implement in the same hardware *both* the public-key algorithm for the generation and secure exchange of a session key *and* the private-key algorithm traditionally used in the bulk encryption of the underlying traffic. This approach is of enormous utility in land-based systems, but due to cost and power consumption, it cannot be envisioned in small portable wireless systems. A small exception to this rule is potentially the large wireless installations or field-transportable devices like the ones favored by the signals intelligence community and the military.

Based on these fundamental characteristics of the technology, we can safely say that in the wireless realm the use of reconfigurable logic is limited to a certain set of contexts:

- For resource-constrained device design, an FPGA can be used as an emulator of the actual circuit, so once it is implemented on a special PCB adapter, for instance, one can plug it into a PC slot and with appropriate drivers and application software recreate a simulated environment for the demonstration, characterization, analysis and/or evaluation of the intended functionality.

- Due to their physical size, high power consumption and (for high degrees of integration as measured in available gates) low performance (as compared to ASICs in I/0 speed and computational power), and expensive price tag (some cost a few thousand dollars per FPGA device), FPGA devices cannot be even remotely contemplated for the delivery of functionality in either inexpensive consumer-oriented wireless devices like PDAs and handsets. Some recent models can be easily integrated into very-high-speed communication systems.
- FPGA devices are ideal for the debugging of a design, especially if the synthesized hardware description can be mapped by the design team from an FPGA realm onto an ASIC context.
- FPGA devices obviously can be contemplated on large wireless systems, big (transportable or not) transmitters and receivers, repeaters, spectrum-scanning devices, and intelligence equipment. The ease of integration into a larger platform, the straightforward modification of executable code and consequently of application and behavior is a worthwhile advantage, especially in areas such as government communications, where versatility, flexibility, and functionality in many cases are of primary importance, as opposed to cost or power consumption.

Besides shortening the design and development cycles, FPGA devices also offer the possibility of prototype manufacturing as well as a cost-effective solution for production rates up to around a few thousand systems per month. For even further lowering of the high-volume unit cost, FPGA manufacturers offer tools and processes for the design migration onto mask-programmed devices.

For the designer of a secure communications chip, the FPGA offers unprecedented systems design flexibility. The security architect can now experiment with different block or stream ciphers, with different hashing mechanisms, different interfaces with a main host CPU (the master device) until performance is analyzed and evaluated. Systems decisions are not just based on a hunch, or on software simulation, which may or may not yield all pertinent performance issues. The real product is realized in an FPGA and actual behavior can be documented. Sound decisions are then possible.

A quick, close look inside a typical FPGA reveals what makes them so flexible. FPGAs consist of thousands of universal building blocks, known as *Configurable Logic Blocks* (CLBs), arranged in a regular, flexible, programmable architecture. This is accomplished by a powerful hierarchy of versatile routing resources, and the whole sea of logic is surrounded by a perimeter of programmable input/output blocks. A CLB structure is shown in Figures 13-1 and Figure 13-2 while a programmable I/O block is shown in Figure 13-3. The routing resources around CLBs are shown in Figure 13-4 and the overall layout of a direct interconnect matrix is shown in Figure 13-5.

Loading configuration data into special internal memory cells customizes the FPGA devices. The FPGA can either actively read its configuration data from an external serial or byte-parallel PROM (master mode), or the configuration data can

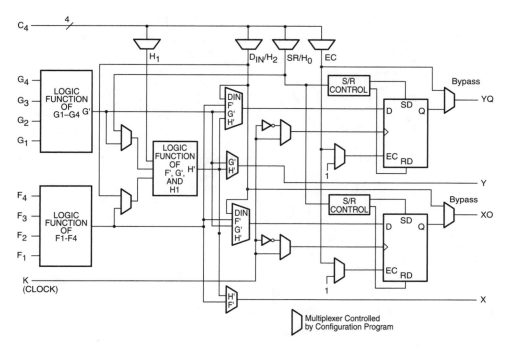

13-1 Internal structure of a Xilinx FPGA configurable logic block (CLB).

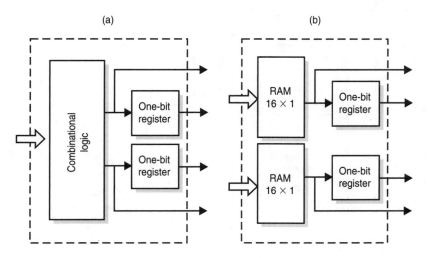

13-2 FPGA device. (a) Internal Structure of a CLB configured in the logic mode. (b) Internal Structure of a CLB configured in the memory mode.

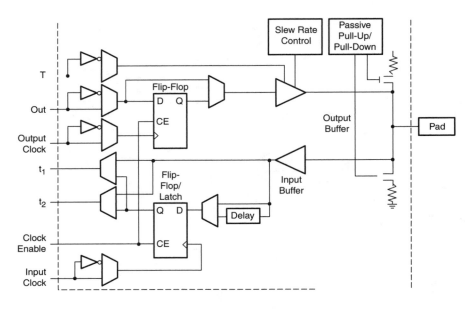

13-3 Typical Xilinx FPGA programmable IOB (input/output block).

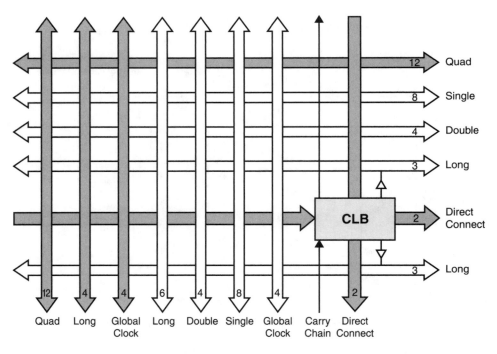

13-4 Typical routing resources available to each CLB inside a Xilinx FPGA.

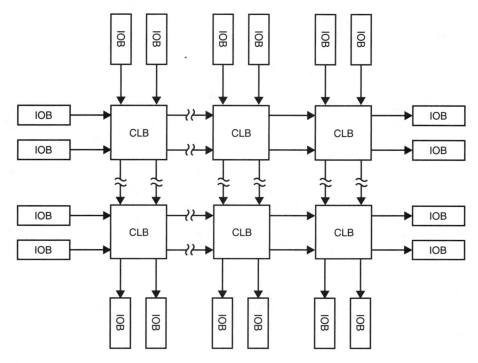

13-5 Direct interconnect and regular CLB/IOB layout matrix in a Xilinx FPGA.

be written into the FPGA from an external device (in slave or peripheral modes). The FPGA manufacturer usually provides powerful and sophisticated software covering every aspect of design, from schematic or behavioral entry, floor planning, simulation, automatic block placement and routing of interconnects, to the creation, downloading, and readback of the configuration bit stream.

During reconfiguration the function of each CLB is changed along with the connections between the CLBs, leading to a functionally new digital circuit. A CLB can be configured in two modes—as logic and as memory. This example is accomplished in the logic case by containing a small block of combinational logic, implemented using programmable *look-up tables* (LUT) and a couple of one-bit registers. In the memory configuration case, the combinational logic is replaced by two small memory arrays.

Configurable Logic Blocks

As an example of the *configurable logic blocks* (CLBs) of which FPGAs are made, xilinx's FPGA technology is exquisitely documented in their white papers and application notes.[14]

CLBs implement most of the logic in an FPGA. The principal CLB elements are shown in Figure 13-1. In this example of the Xilinx XC4000E and XC4000X series, two 4-input function generators (F and G) offer unrestricted versatility. Most combinatorial logic functions need four or fewer inputs. However, a third function generator (H) is also provided. The H function generator has three inputs. Either zero, one, or two of these inputs can be the outputs of F and G; the other input(s) are from outside the CLB. The CLB can therefore implement certain functions of up to nine variables, like parity check or expandable-identity comparison of two sets of four inputs. Each CLB contains two storage elements that can be used to store the function generator outputs. However, the storage elements and function generators also can be used independently. In specific FPGA device models these storage elements can be configured as flip-flops and/or optionally as latches. DIN can be used as a direct input to either of the two storage elements. H1 can drive the other through the H function generator. Function generator outputs can also drive two outputs independently of the storage element outputs. This versatility increases logic capacity and simplifies routing.

In this device example, thirteen CLB inputs and four CLB outputs provide access to the function generators and storage elements. These inputs and outputs connect to the programmable interconnect resources outside the block.

Four independent inputs are provided to each of two function generators (F1 to F4 and G1 to G4). These function generators, with outputs labeled F' and G', are each capable of implementing any arbitrarily defined Boolean function of four inputs. The function generators are implemented as memory *look-up tables* (LUTs). The propagation delay is therefore independent of the function implemented.

A third function generator, labeled H', can implement any Boolean function of its three inputs. Optionally, two of these inputs can be the F' and G' functional generator outputs. Alternatively, one or both of these inputs can come from outside the CLB (H2, H0). The third input must come from outside the block (H1).

Signals from the function generators can exit the CLB on two outputs. F' and H' can be connected to the X output. G' or H' can be connected to the Y output.

A CLB can be used to implement any of the following functions:

- Any function of up to four variables, plus any second function of up to four unrelated variables, plus any third function of up to three unrelated variables
- Any single function of up to five variables
- Any function of four variables together with some functions of six variables
- Some functions of up to nine variables

Implementing wide functions in a single block reduces both the number of blocks required and delay in the signal path, achieving both the increased capacity and speed. The versatility of the CLB function generators significantly improves system speed. In addition, the design-software tools can deal with each function generator independently. This flexibility improves cell usage.

The CLB can pass the combinatorial output(s) to the interconnect network, but it can also store the combinatorial results or other incoming data in one or two flip-flops, and connect their outputs to the interconnect network as well. The two edge-triggered D-type flip-flops have common clock (K) and clock-enable (EC) inputs and can be enabled together or separately. These CLB storage elements also can be configured as latches. Each flip-flop can be triggered on either the rising or falling edge of the clock. Multiplexers in the CLB map the four control inputs (C1 to C4 in Figure 13-1) into the four internal control signals that enable or disable internal modules.

The abundance of flip-flops in the FPGA device invites pipelined designs. This is a powerful way of increasing performance by breaking the function into smaller sub-functions and executing them in parallel, passing on the results through pipeline flip-flops. This method is seriously considered wherever throughput is more important than latency. Flip-flops can be used as registers or shift registers without blocking the function generators from performing a different and perhaps unrelated task. This ability increases the functional capacity of the FPGA devices.

Function generators can be used as on-chip RAM. Optional modes for each CLB make the memory look-up tables in the F' and G' function generators usable as an array of read/write memory cells. Available modes can be level-sensitive, edge-triggered, and dual-port edge-triggered. Depending on the selected mode, a single CLB can be configured as either a 16×2, 32×1, or 16×1 bit array. Edge-triggered designs are synchronous designs and synchronous RAM interfaces are characterized by a simplified system timing. Dual-port RAM effectively doubles the throughput of FIFO applications, something very common in cryptographic processing.

The on-chip RAM is extremely fast. The read access time is the same as the logic delay. The write access time is slightly slower. Both access times are much faster than any off-chip solution, because they avoid I/O delays.

All internal connections are composed of metal segments with programmable switching points and switching matrices to implement the desired routing. A structured, hierarchical matrix of routing resources is provided as shown in Figures 13-4 and 13-5 to achieve automated routing.

There are several types of interconnect fabric:

- CLB routing is associated with each row and column of the CLB array.
- IOB routing forms a ring around the outside of the CLB array. It connects the I/O with the internal logic blocks.
- Global routing consists of dedicated networks primarily designed to distribute clocks throughout the device with minimum delay and skew. Global routing also can be used for other high fan-out signals.

Different routing resources lend themselves to FPGA platforms with different capabilities. The designer therefore must identify the ideal FPGA onto which his or her design will most likely route automatically; this is a major concern when the design is large or when the design contains a great deal of interconnect. To facilitate use of placement and routing algorithms the CLBs are designed with inputs and outputs distributed on all four sides, providing maximum routing flexibility. In general, the entire architecture is symmetrical and regular as one can see in Figure 13-5. Inputs, outputs, and function generators can freely swap positions within a CLB to avoid routing congestion during the placement and routing operation when the designed logic is physically mapped onto different areas of the FPGA device.

The picture is completed with the *Input/Output Blocks* (IOBs) as shown in Figures 13-3 and 13-5. User-configurable input/output blocks provide the interface between external package pins and the internal logic. Each IOB controls one package pin and can be configured for input, output, or bi-directional signals. Figure 13-3 shows a simplified block diagram of the XC4000E FPGA-IOB.[15] A more complete diagram would also show the boundary-scan logic for the testability of the block. Inputs can be globally configured for either TTL (1.2V) or 5.0V CMOS thresholds, using an option in the bitstream generation software.

Inputs can be TTL-compatible and 3.3V CMOS-compatible. Outputs are pulled to the 3.3V power supply. The inputs of 5V devices can be usually driven by the outputs of any 3.3V device, if the 5V inputs are in TTL mode.

Distributed Arithmetic

One of the important advantages FPGA architectures offer to designers of DSP-based algorithms is the possibility of doing what has come to be known as distributed arithmetic.[16]

Distributed Arithmetic (DA), along with Modulo Arithmetic, is a computational algorithm that performs multiplication with *look-up table-based (*LUT) schemes instead of actually doing the calculations using multiplier and adder circuits. DA specifically targets the sum of products (sometimes called the inner product or dot product of multidimensional vectors) a computation that is at the heart of many important filtering and frequency-transforming functions used in DSP. The LUTs can be spread all over the die for all practical purposes inside numerous CLBs thereby allowing a better utilization of placement and routing resources, while enabling an unprecedented flexibility in embedding algorithms inside an FPGA that had not been contemplated until recently.

The derivation of the DA algorithm is most simple, but its applications are extremely broad.

FPGA vs. ASIC Approach in the Design Trade-Offs: A Business Context

Working with FPGAs is obviously a superb method for prototyping designs, a necessary step for low-budget demonstration units as well as for verification and debugging of a whole application. By low-budget we do not mean that the individual FPGAs cost little, as the more capable the FPGA (in terms of number of integrated gates it offers) the more expensive it is. The latest very-high integration and high-performance FPGA devices cost several thousand U.S. dollars each. As such even building three or four prototypes comes down (even for highly sophisticated large-scale designs) to something around $20,000 to $30,000 per run, as opposed to the $1 million you must spend to run an ASIC design from conception to manufacturing of prototypes. If the prototypes do not work, for any reason, one would have lost a significant amount of money (not to mention one's professional credibility and maybe . . . job) while experimenting. FPGAs therefore fulfill a tremendous need for low-budget prototypes, as well as for low-volume business cases.

For hardware implementations of cryptographic algorithms and protocols, the only choices (in decreasing order of cost of design) are Custom VLSI, Semicustom VLSI (also known as ASIC), and FPGA designs. The economics of these decision alternatives is extremely well documented and understood by the industry.[17,18,19,20,21]

Besides the full custom design that only makes sense when the designer's pockets are deep, as is the case usually in a national defense organization where the priority is to get it correctly, essentially no matter the cost, full custom designs are engaged in by major design houses when they expect to sell gigantic quantities of an integrated circuit in a highly competitive market where they must differentiate themselves from competition by a better or more efficient performance, speed, power consumption, smaller size and therefore smaller cost, and other factors. The expected return justifies the expenditure in the extra effort, time, people, and cost needed to come up with a fully functional full-custom VLSI design.

Semi-custom designs—better known as ASIC designs, or in some cases as *application-specific system product* (ASSP) designs—on the other hand are based on various forms of assembling a complete functional design using libraries of components that, properly combined, can build a custom system much faster and less expensively than full-custom design. Until only a few years ago, one could boast that only full-custom design with handcrafted placement and routing of modules can achieve the optimal design on a silicon die. This is no longer the case, as highly sophisticated breakthroughs in synthesis tools allow designers to distance themselves from the silicon and to concentrate more and more on the highest-value and complexity aspects of the design, namely the algorithm, the architecture, the dataflow, and so forth. EDA tools can come up with optimal designs that compete (if not outright beat) human designers. The cost of procurement of such tools can be easily written off by an organization that contemplates a couple of designs in a year or two, and therefore profit from expected sales should recover the significant investment rather quickly. Why, then, would a senior executive opt for full-custom design with all its associated direct and indirect costs? No wonder ASICs seem to be the best way to design and build a highly sophisticated system on silicon or (for the case of higher speeds) on *gallium arsenide* (GaAs).

If, however, you look at the third hardware alternative, FPGAs, you easily find that they offer some interesting advantages, namely that:

- Their shorter design cycle leads more quickly to fully functioning prototypes.
- The design tools for FPGA design, verification and testing are significantly less expensive to procure than for ASICs.
- By using FPGAs one has the potential for fast, low-cost multiple reprogramming, and experimental testing of a large number for considered architectures and revised versions of the same architecture.
- One achieves inherently a higher accuracy of comparison: in the absence of the actual physical design and fabrication, ASIC designs are usually compared only based on rather inaccurate pre-layout simulations, while FPGA designs are compared based on accurate post-layout simulations and actual experimental testing.

To get a better understanding of state-of-the-art cryptographic implementations of various algorithms on FPGAs the interested reader is referred to the NIST (National Institute of Science and Technology) Web site and more specifically to implementations submitted in the third AES conference.[22] Also, Altera has recently announced implementations of Rijndael in extremely high throughput implementations, so the field is rapidly evolving.[23]

On-Chip Modules Provide Wireless Communications Security

In general in a communications security system (and wireless is not an exception), one first of all needs a *good crypto engine* (also known in some circles as crypto logic) for the actual encryption and decryption. This can be based on block ciphers or stream ciphers.

For the integrity of traffic one would also expect a *strong hashing function* (as the presence of a simple MAC code is becoming rather antiquated as a standalone technique).

One should then add to the list a system that *generates good-quality keys*, *distributes keys*, and *verifies keys*.

One that allows the *optional generation* and *verification of digital signatures* with appropriate hooks to an overlying *public-key infrastructure* (PKI) entailing *certificate authorities* (CAs).

Random number generation is essential for good cryptography. Most systems use a pseudo-*random number generator* (RNG) and people can fool themselves into believing they are secure. From the sampling of RNGs one can generate random bits; hence, the notion of cryptographically strong *pseudo-random bit generators* (PRBGs) that was pioneered by Blum, Blum, and Shub,[24] and Yao.[25] The former, also known as the BBS PRBG scheme is also well presented in Schneier.[26] Informally, we can say that a PRBG is cryptographically strong if it passes all polynomial-time statistical tests, or in other words, if the distribution of sequence outputs by the generator cannot be distinguished from truly random sequences by any polynomial-time judge.[27] A PRBG is called *provably secure,* if its security can be reduced to a well-established conjectured hard problem such as factoring or computing discrete logarithms.

If the RNG module decides the quality of the keys the system generates, the system can be doomed at its birth. A *true random number generator* (TRNG) is essential and it must be self-sufficient, as the generation must be accomplished inside the chip package. Schemes whereby one has to go outside the chip, say to a host CPU and ask for seed values to calculate some pseudo-random number or sequence are *not* secure, as no one can really trust another CPU unless (to put it nicely) one has designed and built it by himself or herself.

A TRNG can or may degenerate as it operates in time. One can check a source for say 9,247 bits and find the group of bits perfectly random, but one will always wonder what will be happening after more testing. How can one prove to oneself that soon after, the RNG source will not start yielding straight 1's or straight 0's? Sufficient for the moment, let's just say that an *entropy accumulator* is a wise thing to have at the output of the TRNG. There may well be argument about *initialization vectors* (IVs), also known as seed values for the TRNG. If the RNG is a TRNG the statistical nature of the design takes care of the good seeding, at the same time.

If the TRNG in fact is a PRNG, then one has to worry about *a good IV generation mechanism.*

Another necessity in many cases is generating and verifying digital signatures and then the appropriate HW and API hooks should be available. For the bidirectional authentication of the communicating parties, one expects as a minimum a Diffie-Hellman protocol implementation with parameters that stand up to scrutiny or brute force. Alternative ideas are ECC-DH, RSA, Ntru's lattice cryptography, hyperelliptic curves, the RPK system, and Abelian varieties over finite fields, and so forth.

Ancillary devices also can be available for in-band or out-of-band key management, cryptographic synchronization preservation, recovery mechanisms, network management interface modules, and so on.

Required Modules in a Block-Cipher-Based COMSEC Chip

A symmetric block cipher (like 3DES, IDEA or Rijndael, and so on) in hardware is generically organized as shown in Figure 13-6. This organization contains the following modules:[29]

- **Encryption/decryption unit** Used to encipher and decipher input blocks of traffic data.
- **Key-scheduling unit** Computes a set of internal cipher keys based on a single external key.
- **Memory of internal keys** Stores internal keys computed by the key-scheduling unit, or loaded to the integrated circuit through the input interface.
- **Input interface** Loads blocks of input data and internal keys to the circuit, and to store input blocks awaiting encryption/decryption.
- **Output interface** Temporarily stores output from the encryption/decryption unit and send it to the external memory.
- **Control unit** Generates control signals for all other units in the engine.

In block-cipher cryptography as elsewhere detailed, there are two families of operating modes: *feedback modes,* such as the *Cipher Block Chaining* (CBC), *Cipher Feedback* (CFB), *Output Feedback* (OFB) modes, and *non-feedback modes,* such as the *Electronic Code Book* (ECB) mode and the counter mode.

In non-feedback modes, encryption of each subsequent block of data can be performed independently from processing other blocks, hence a high degree of parallelism can be exploited, and blocks can be encrypted in parallel. In the feedback modes, it is not possible to start the encryption of the next block of data until

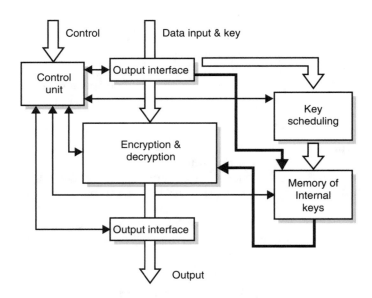

13-6 Block diagram of a hardware implementation of a symmetric-block cipher.[28]

encryption of the previous block is completed. The sequential computing structure that is by necessity imposed onto the design therefore excludes all ideas for parallel processing.

The current state-of-the-art in block cipher encryption shows that encryption of data is performed primarily using feedback modes, such as CBC and CFB. Nonfeedback modes, ECB for instance, are used mainly to encrypt session keys during key distribution. This in turn implies strongly that current encryption industry standards of usage do not permit full utilization of the performance advantage of hardware implementations of symmetric-key cryptosystems, based on parallel processing of multiple blocks of traffic data.

In terms of optimization of the behavior of a crypto-system in a wireless medium one must revisit the characteristics of each mode and make decision as to how the cipher behaves when transmitted bits are garbled (which is bound to happen at some point either due to noise or interference or shadowing or multipath fading, and so on) and when bits are dropped.

The behavior and performance of the crypto-logic is affected by the underlying protocols used in the communications infrastructure. Whether it is TCP or UDP on a data line, or whether it is the GSM stack or the IS-95 provisions which use a preponderance of error codes and interleaving prior to framing bits for transmission, it does affect the behavior, performance, and reliability of the encryption.

The following section summarizes how the various modes behave in various contexts. Later in this chapter these architectures are revisited for a closer look at their merits in terms of performance when confronted with HW/SW design and optimization inside an ASIC or FPGA.

Basic Architectures for Block-Cipher Crypto Engines in a COMSEC Chip

Relative to application of this approach on hardware-based designs, the following models of implementing block ciphers may be distinguished:[30]

- Basic architecture
- Loop unrolling
- Inner-round pipelining
- Outer-round pipelining
- Resource-sharing

Transmission Comparison of Cryptographic Modes of Operation

The *National Institute of Standards and Technology* (NIST) defined a set of four modes of operation for the *Data Encryption Standard* (DES). These standards were defined to be suitable for any 64-bit codebook, and, indeed, many other codebooks have used them. Table 13-2 summarizes those standard modes of operation, adds an additional mode for stream ciphers, and, finally, adds a mode for self-synchronizing a stream cipher system such as HORNET™.

Security Considerations for the Modes During Transmission

The two block-chaining modes, CFB and CBC, are of special interest because of their confidentiality and data integrity properties that make them ideally suited for some high security applications like financial transactions. However, they place stringent requirements on the data communications circuit and are totally intolerant to

Table 13-2 Modes of Operation

	Abbreviation	Mode	Block Chaining	Error Extension	System Security	Self Sync
1	ECB	Electronic Code Book	No	1 Block	Low	No
2	CFB	Cipher Feedback	Yes	2 Blocks	High	Yes
3	CBC	Cipher Block Chaining	Yes	2 Blocks	High	Yes
4	OFB	Output Feedback	No	None	Medium	No
5	STM	Stream cipher	No	None	High	No
6	PDC	Positive Data Correlation	No	None	High	Yes

dropped or garbled bits. While these chaining modes do provide an additional level of security, they come at a price that can be quite unacceptable in applications where dropped bits, garbled bits, and lost synchronization are a common occurrence. Thus, entire packets or frames must be resent until a completely accurate version of the message is received. This may not be appropriate or even feasible, for example in some RF applications such as voice-over-IP over wireless, or QoS-dependent scalable streaming compressed audio and video (especially MPEG-4) not only over the air but also on land lines, which may have to overcome these shortcomings by using nonchaining modes.

An example is Voice-over-IP transmitted over the unreliable-delivery UDP protocol. When encrypted, real-time VoIP systems performance will be dependent on the network transmission realm and can negate completely the mode of the cryptographic algorithm at hand.

Another example, as mentioned earlier, is streaming compressed video like MPEG4, where only symbols are being selectively transmitted and where images will be locally recreated at the receiver and where in scalable networks, QoS concerns may affect and vary the speed and content of the transmitted bit stream. Inappropriate buffer management, spanning several blocks of encrypted traffic, will create issues of faithful reconstruction of the video traffic locally. The results of such a crypto session are quite unpredictable and can vary from poor video quality and flickering (something that is at least irritating and most probably outright unacceptable to a pay-per-view consumer) all the way to a dropped session, if the receiver cannot decrypt the traffic within windows of timeout.

The clear message is that the secure link does not depend only on the cryptographic algorithm chosen, but on its mode and especially on the underlying protocol capabilities to recover from errors and the application at hand with its specified requirements. Some technologies, such as HORNET™, allow the optimation of the solutions depending on all systems variables and do not force the user to live with the proverbial "square peg in a round hole."

Yet another interesting example is the multicast environments, or conference calls (whether voice based or video or both). The need to be able to support a so-called late entry is obvious. A session can start with several parties and someone may come in later. A pay-per-view movie can be, for instance, securely broadcast and somebody dials in later than other viewers who were tuned in right from the beginning. If the key is scheduled to change often with the blocks of flowing traffic, the latecomer cannot possibly expect the secure movie or video broadcast to start again from the beginning upon his or her arrival to the session. The cryptographic system must be flexible enough to adapt to the context in such a realm and this is one more thing that HORNET™ and its various modes does enable. HORNET-SM™ is the standard mode of the cipher without correlation and HORNET-RF™ is the mode of the cipher when correlation is enabled. There is also a combined codebook and key-update mode as we will describe later.

The list of pertinent applications can go on and on. Systems constraints have a clear role to play on the choice of cryptographic algorithm. This turns out to be unexpected and rather surprising to many people, who only thought a cryptographic algorithm is chosen based on security specifications. This is not the case when the platform devices are constrained in terms of computational capabilities (for example, memory footprint and CPU horsepower) or cost (battery lifetime, physical size, cost of ownership, and so on).

In all these modes we assume that the underlying algorithm is secure against a known-plaintext and chosen-plaintext attack and that the key size is such that an exhaustive key search is computationally infeasible. However, regardless of the cryptographic strength of the block cipher itself certain modes of operation might leak information about the plaintext when encrypting many blocks under the same key. One should keep in mind that in an ideal cryptographic system the designer must be also careful among other reasons, because stereotypic message patterns can be preserved (as in the case with codebooks based on block ciphers like Rijndael and 3DES for instance) and selective message substitution can happen (which can be extremely devastating in data transmissions over some stream ciphers that use additive key material). It is noteworthy to mention that HORNET™ in its combination of modes addresses all of these issues in an optimal way.

The intention here is not to elaborate on HORNET™ modes, as an example of communications security optimization. We must mention, however, that Hornet can be easily configured also into a codebook made (called HORNET-CB™) (up to 320 bits wide and expected to be used mostly as a multiple of 8 bits, therefore most likely to be engaged as a 256-bit codebook) without extra computational overhead (in terms of silicon real-estate) or any further memory requirements. In this HORNET-CB™ mode, the cipher has all the advantages of the common NIST modes and at the same time:

- It does not preserve stereotypic message patterns as done with ECB (a classical weakness of block ciphers in that mode).
- It does not have the error extension and pipeline bottlenecks that the chaining modes (CFB and CBC) have. These latter are not security disadvantages, but are performance and error extension disadvantages.
- It does not have the message substitution possibility that OFB has (a clear security disadvantage).
- It allows a late entry into a secure conference call or secure multicast session.

This is a mode that combines codebook behavior and key-update mode. Through it the key is successfully updated with every new block of traffic and the cipher achieves all of the above without any computational cost or performance sacrifice.

For these cryptographic reasons and for the communications systems reasons mentioned here below, a designer frequently adopts a self-synchronizing stream cipher, such as HORNET™.

Recovery Properties for Garbled and Dropped Bits

When a bit is garbled during transmission, error recovery is sometimes referred to as finite error propagation, and when recovery cannot be obtained it is referred to as infinite error propagation. Beyond the garbling of a bit, the cases where a ciphertext block is lost or where an adversary inserts an additional block must be considered. The latter is susceptible to happen in a data transmission and much less likely in a secure voice communication. Ideally, we expect the system to recover from dropped bits and to guarantee that blocks inserted by the adversary will be rejected, and, indeed, a self-synchronizing error-recovering stream cipher like HORNET™ does this.

Block Size and Communications Protocol

Stream ciphers produce continuous key material that can be broken into any block size desired while block ciphers usually come in 64-bit or 128-bit sizes. These block sizes may or may not line up with the required blocking of the data within the communication protocol. This can be especially problematic in modes that require self-synchronization. If the communication protocol cannot guarantee correct byte boundaries, then CFB mode must operate in single bit feedback (CFB-1) mode to allow self-synchronization. This is inefficient because it requires the processor to generate 64 key bits for every one it uses. Similarly, if byte boundaries are preserved when the crypto can operate in 8-bit (CFB-8) feedback mode and provide self-synchronization (again less efficient). Stream cipher and Key OFB systems cannot recover from dropped bits unless they insert a synchronization pattern periodically in the cipher. Thus, these systems can employ either preamble synchronization where bits cannot be dropped or self-synchronization as mentioned above and as used by HORNET™. These considerations give rise to a different matrix of possible modes.

Comparison Matrix for Performance Optimization

Table 13-3 shows the comparison matrix contains a list of commonly used (or proposed) combinations of algorithms and modes and then matches that list with the other desired communications properties. The table below provides the reference set of symmetric algorithms and modes. The Garbling column refers to how many bits are lost if a single bit is garbled and the Dropped column refers to the effect of dropped or added bits.

From Table 13-4 it can be seen that a self-synchronizing stream cipher like HORNET™ has definite advantages in situations where the transmission medium causes dropped or added bits and in cases where such incidents will not be adequately handled by the underlying protocols. This is, for instance, the case with land-mobile radios but it is also the case with VoIP or with streaming compressed video like

Table 13-3 Modes of Operation and Synchronization Requirements

	Abbreviation	Mode	Cipher Block	IV Sync	Self Sync
1	ECB	Electronic Code Book	64	Yes	No
2	CFB-1		1	No	Yes
3	CFB-8	Cipher Feedback	8	No	Yes
4	CFB-64		64	No	Yes
5	CFB-128	Cipher Feedback	128	No	Yes
6	CBC	Cipher Block Chaining	64	No	Yes
7	OFB	Output Feedback	any	Yes	No
8	PDC	Stream Cipher Self Sync	any	No	Yes
9	STM	Stream Cipher Pre. Sync	any	Yes	No

Table 13-4 Comparison Table of Transmission Behavior

Algorithm	Mode	Applications	Garbling	Dropped
RC4	STM	SSL, WEP	1	Dead
DES	CBC	S/MIME, SSL, IPSEC	64	Dead
3DES	CBC	S/MIME, SSL, IPSEC	64	Dead
Irondale	CBC	S/MIME, SSL, IPSEC	128	Dead
Hornet	PDC	for example, VoIP, streaming MPEG4	1	OK
RC2	CBC	S/MIME	Dead	Dead
RC5	CBC	IPSEC	Dead	Dead

MPEG-4 which transmits symbols for the local regeneration of multiple images per second, and whose content and speed may depend and vary in real-time on QoS feedback obtained from the network. Unreliable delivery of these symbols may prohibit the faithful reconstruction of images and the impact can be anything from poor video quality and flickering (something irritating and potentially unacceptable to the consumer who subscribes to a pay-per-view service) all the way to inability to function on certain hours of the day, for example, when the transmission and delivery network happens to be loaded and over-solicited.

Voice-over IP (VoIP), for instance, is transmitted over UDP, which is characterized by a streamlined overhead that sacrifices the capabilities of ensuring a reliable delivery (as opposed to TCP) for a better throughput and real-time response. If you attempt to implement an end-to-end security scheme based on encrypting streaming traffic of VoIP, then these issues are major considerations for the designer.

In the latest computer telephony breakthroughs, SW-based telephone functionality is implemented inside handheld PDAs. A headset and microphone is plugged into the PDA jack and the handheld assistant now behaves like a telephone, potentially channeling telephony calls over IEEE 802.11b in a wireless LAN over to a gateway that either switches the call over to the *public switched telephony network*

(PSTN) or over an IP network like the Internet or some intranet with guaranteed available bandwidth and QOS arrangements.

Again the end-to-end security issue will confront the designer, who must judiciously weigh the available resources, namely *computational power* (measured as number of operations executed per second on real-time processing) and *power consumption* (measured as battery lifetime) before some major decisions are made. The argument should also show that you do not start the design process with an algorithm and then try to make it fit into a system's requirements. It is the other way around. You digest the system performance requirements (as discussed in the beginning of the chapter) and then accordingly decide which algorithm, in which mode of operation, in which configuration, and so forth. Cryptographic designs in the industrial sphere largely belong to the realm of wishful thinking as the average organization believes that it is a straightforward task and ordinary engineers should be able to do it properly. The average design team unfortunately replicates the wrong approach just mentioned, which is like putting the proverbial cart before the horse. The poor price/performance ratio of many pertinent products is the living proof of this sad fact.

Basic Architectures for Block-Cipher Crypto Engines in a COMSEC Chip

In the nonclassified world, block cipher communications security systems are usually built around some rather limited choices of algorithms. DES in single and triple modes is certainly for historical reasons the king of the road. This is likely to change in the next few years into block-cipher chips that use the AES Rijndael algorithm. A limited commercial success has been achieved by some designs embedding Ascot's IDEA algorithm from Switzerland, or Mitsubishi's MISTY from Japan, inside a chip. A marked exception is the Kasumi algorithm, a variation of Mitsubishi's MISTY, which has been adopted by the ETSI for the 3GPP (third-generation partnership project) handsets as the de facto standard algorithm in *wideband code-division-multiple-access* (W-CDMA) wireless handsets. We discuss about hardware-based Kasumi implementations later in this chapter.

As discussed earlier, the various modes of cryptographic operation of algorithms come into play in the designer's mind, especially in confrontation with optimizing objectives. Application of this approach to hardware-based designs involves structuring the possibilities. One distinguishes as shown in Figure 13-7 the following models of implementing block ciphers:[32]

- Basic architecture
- Loop unrolling
- Inner-round pipelining
- Outer-round pipelining
- Resource-sharing

Each is explained in the following sections. In the basic architecture of a secret-key block cipher, one round of the cipher is implemented in combinational logic and

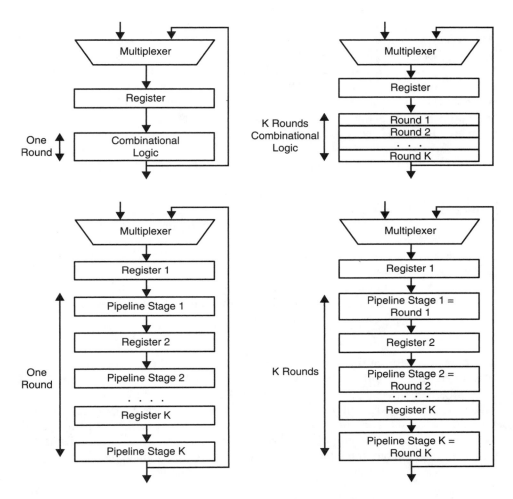

13-7 Four alternative architectures for implementation of an encryption/decryption unit of a block cipher: (a) basic architecture (top left), (b) architecture with k-round loop unrolling (top right), (c) architecture with the k-stage inner-round pipelining (bottom left), and (d) architecture with the k-stage outer-round pipelining (bottom right).[31]

equipped with a register and a multiplexer. The behavioral description of the algorithm's round coded in VHDL or Verilog will feed a synthesis tool like Design Compiler from Synopsys, and the synthesized sea of gates, represented as a netlist, is the combinational logic under discussion. In the first clock cycle, data is fed through the multiplexer into the register. In subsequent cycles, one new round of the algorithm is evaluated during every clock cycle and the result is fed back into the multiplexer and stored again into the register. The number of clock cycles it takes to encrypt a single block of plaintext traffic is equal to the number of rounds. The propagation delay of the incoming bits through the block of combinational logic gates must be less than the clock cycle, and the latter must reflect the input speed. It should also be clear that input clock and calculation-logic clock are essentially never the same. One can, for example, be reading in encrypted voice data arriving at 64 Kbps and processing the data internally with a logic that is clocked at 100 MHz, which amounts to a clock cycle of 25 nanoseconds (25 ns = $25 * 10^{-9}$ sec). If the *speed* of the cipher implementation is defined as the number of bits of plaintext encrypted in a unit of time (also known as circuit throughput), then the speed of the basic architecture is given by

$$\text{Speed} = 128/[(\text{Nr. of rounds}) \times \text{clock period})]$$

The good speed and rather modest gatecount requirements of the basic architecture can be improved by some of the alternative architectures.

An alternative architecture introduces loOp. unrolling into the basic architecture. If there are k stages of combinational logic, all k-rounds are implemented by this architecture in one pass. The number of clock cycles necessary to encrypt a single block of plaintext decreases by a factor of k. The minimum clock period increases by a factor slightly smaller than k, leading to an overall relatively small increase in the cipher implementation speed, which in this case is given by

$$\text{Speed(lu)/Speed(ba)} = (1 + \tau) / (1 + \tau / k)$$

where τ is the ratio of the sum of the multiplexer delay, the register delay and the register setup time to the delay of a single cipher round. Additionally, the number of internally needed keys used in a single block cycle increases by a factor of k, as k stages must be keyed simultaneously and hence working storage space must be foreseen for the preservation of these internal keys. In FPGAs this means k-times more CLBs (to implement the on-chip memory) and in an ASIC this means extra RAM. Not forgetting the combinatonal logic of k stages, this relatively small increase in speed is paid for by the substantial increase in gatecount (silicon space).

A third alternative architecture is based on inner-round pipelining. Pipelining is an excellent method for increasing the amount of data processed by a digital circuit in a unit of time. Evenly spaced registers are introduced into the datapath and therefore several blocks of data can be processed simultaneously by the circuit in a well-timed synchronous environment. In our case, shown in Figure 13-7, the circuit can encrypt simultaneously as many blocks as the number of pipeline stages it contains. In Kris Gaj and Pawel Chodowiec, there is a thorough presentation and analysis of the behavior of the pipeline given the number of stages and the clock frequency.[33] It is shown among other things that

- The speed of inner-round pipelining increases linearly with the number of pipelines.
- There is a maximum number of pipeline stages beyond which no further improvement in performance can be attained.

The latter is determined by the delay of the largest indivisible combinational logic component of the circuit. The area of the implementation increases only marginally and this by the length of the 128-bit registers needed at the boundary of each pipeline stage Another approach is the outer-round pipelining. This is implemented as shown in Figure 13-7 by introducing extra registers between parts of the combinational logic corresponding to each cipher round. The number of unrolled loops k is typically a divisor of the algorithm's number of rounds. In nonfeedback modes as in ECB the speed of the cipher increases proportionally to the number of pipeline stages. Therefore the designer can trade speed for silicon. In feedback modes (which are considered more secure) the speed of the cipher remains independent of the number of outer pipeline stages and therefore this design technique is not recommended.

The last alternative architecture we are looking into for the efficient implementation of real-time block ciphers in hardware is the one based on resource sharing. In Kris Gaj and Pawel Chodowiec, it is documented that by time-sharing some hardware resources it is possible to further decrease the circuit area.[34] The way one does this is by using the same functional unit to process two or more parts of the data block in different clock cycles. Such a use in real-life designs seems limited though because the

- Gain in circuit area is always smaller than the loss in circuit speed.
- Amount of area used by a basic implementation of a symmetric cipher is typically already quite small.

Comparison of the Block-Cipher Implementation Architectures

The performance of the various architectures heretofore described is obviously dependent upon the application at hand: real-time behavior, large quantity of streaming data, speed of traffic, cost sensitivity as measured by silicon real-estate, power consumption, and so on.

Figures 13-8 and 13-9 show for nonfeedback and feedback modes the speed versus silicon area characteristic for several levels of pipelining.[35] On one side, these figures show that the smallest possible area for nonfeedback modes can be obtained by using the basic architecture with resource sharing. The largest possible speed in non-feedback modes can be obtained by combining inner-round pipelining with outer-round pipelining. In feedback modes on the other side, it is again the basic architecture that offers the best value of speed/area ratio. Larger speeds can be obtained by loop. unrolling at the cost of very significant increase in area. Smaller area can be obtained using resource sharing at the cost of significant reduction in circuit speed. Inner-round pipelining decreases speed and increases circuit area. Outer-round pipelining in feedback modes is even worse: It does not increase the speed and it significantly increases the circuit area. No pipelining should be used in these modes.

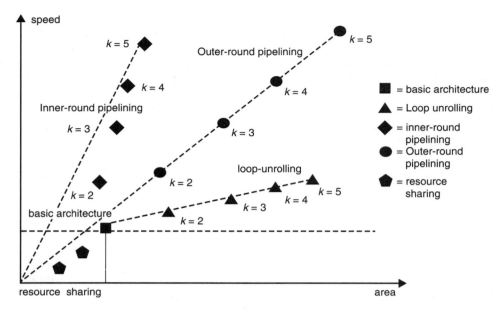

13-8 Hardware performance of various alternative architectures in nonfeedback modes (such as ECB and counter mode) for block cipher implementations in HW.

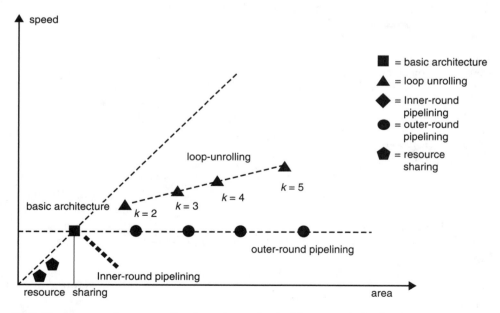

13-9 Hardware performance of various alternative architectures in feedback modes (such as CBC, CFB, and OFB) for block cipher implementations in HW.

Wireless devices (especially consumer-oriented devices like cellular telephones) fall into the category that requires minimum area. The performance bar seems to be raised, as speed requirements even in this class of products is projected to go rapidly up into broadband-speed realms, as heavy-duty multimedia content will soon need to be downloaded over the airwaves; for example, compressed video, CD audio, and similar content. There can be no doubts that we can expect to see significant VLSI circuits designed for higher-speed, implementing algorithms cleverly in smaller areas, and capitalizing on lower-power semiconductor technologies.

Required Modules in a Stream-Cipher Based COMSEC Chip

Stream ciphers have classically been described by the structure shown in Figures 13-10 and 13-11. The basic architecture of a stream cipher comprises a large state space structure, usually implemented as a cascade of various registers, which with a feedback mechanism creates a long period event. At the output of the state space, a nonlinear combining function generates so-called key material, which with an additive rule is XORed with plaintext traffic thereby generating cipher text. The additive rule is a MUST to avoid the error extension side effects. In some cases, another block is also available at the output of the stream cipher, as shown in Figure 13-12, that protects against the so-called catalog attacks. We come back to this point elsewhere in this chapter.

One might react to this classification by saying that instead of an additive XOR rule, the key material can be mathematically mapped somehow onto the plaintext. That is certainly true from an implementation point of view. Some people even think that because you map the combination of key-material bits and plaintext bits to the cipher text bit space, you are somehow more secure than in the additive rule case. Wrong! If there is a mapping function f(key, plaintext) (any function f, that is) that is used at the output of the combining function block with its own output directly

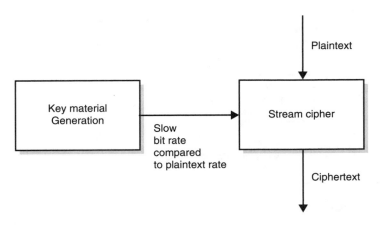

13-10 Stream cipher structure with key material production.

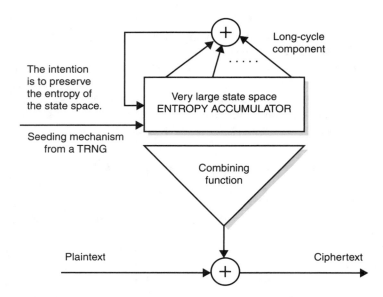

13-11 Production of additive key material in a stream cipher.

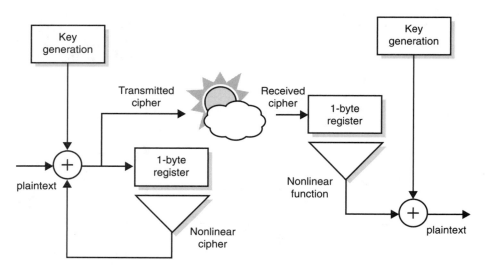

13-12 Sometimes a feedback loop based on a short register (usually 1-byte long) is used at the transmitter to further affect the transmitted stream against catalog attacks. The receiver can generate the plaintext in a straightforward fashion.

acting on the plaintext, it can be stated without exception that error extension becomes an issue and this is not good in a stream cipher case, as even a one-bit error will be propagated, ripple-effect, onto a series of subsequent bits. How many depends on the side size of the mapping matrix. This is a classical case of juxtaposition of block-cipher-inspired feedback modes, and desirable behavior in stream ciphers.

For example, if 8 bits of plaintext are combined into 8 bits of key material a mapping function is generated that combines 256 possibilities of plaintext with 256 possibilities of key material. Hence the 16-cell matrix of Figure 13-13 indicates the presence of 256×256 mapping possibilities.

This function matrix is a Latin square, meaning that each row is absolutely unique and therefore exhibits a strong mapping function. The same principle is used in codebook though, where a 64 bits input is combined with a 64-bit key and one has 2×64 bits possibilities at the output. Pretty impressive, one would say. The error extension trade-off is a side-effect as any bit error at the receiver will ripple-propagate itself and affect the deciphered plaintext for a period of length equal to the combination space. In the previous example of the byte-by-byte square matrix, 8 consecutive bits will be affected. In the case of 64-bit input, 64 bits (8 bytes) worth of traffic comprised of consecutive bits to the error will be affected.

Some people (supposedly in the name of computational efficiency) have thought to combine (say 8 bits of plaintext with 4 bits of key material repeated to fill in the 8 bit slots of the key material) input into the mapping function square. This is not a smart idea, since it cuts down the key generator state space and it will be immediately picked up in standard randomness and statistical tests run at the intercept level on the channel.

There seems also to be some confusion between a bit-level stream cipher and a bizarre concept of a byte-level stream cipher (whatever the latter term means). Some of this confusion may be coming from the concept of the RC-4 algorithm where keys are generated in bytes, but even then confusion usually comes from some telecommunication circuit architects, who think in terms of bytes, as their HW designs usually work in bytes (as opposed to bits). They therefore think that if 8 bits

	P1	**P2**	**P3**	**P4**	**P5**	**P6**	**P7**	**P8**
K1	x	x	x	x	x	x	x	x
K2	x	x	x	x	x	x	x	x
K3	x	x	x	x	x	x	x	x
K4	x	x	x	x	x	x	x	x
K5	x	x	x	x	x	x	x	x
K6	x	x	x	x	x	x	x	x
K7	x	x	x	x	x	x	x	x
K8	x	x	x	x	x	x	x	x

13-13 Mapping plaintext and key material onto the output (as opposed to using additive-rule XORing of key material with the plaintext). P1 through P8 are 8 consecutive plaintext bits and K1 through K8 are 8 consecutive bits of key material.

of key material are generated at a time and combined in parallel with 8 bits of plaintext at a time, a speed-up factor of 8 will result. Incorrect!

In fact, the argument could be made that if the TRNG source is not truly random, then by decimating the key stream to create these key bit positions, you run the risk of exposing yourself to other types of attacks.

Of course, if it is assumed that 8 parallel, simultaneously working, key generators can be combined in parallel as an 8-bit bus to produce 8 bits at a time, there is computational truth in the claim of speeding up the process bandwidth. However, the silicon real estate is 8 times larger and hence less affordable. Whether this is considered as a progress in the design alternatives depends on the market requirements, but it does not sound like the way to go say for a handset design. On the other side, it could very well be of interest to a designer of a wireless LAN system, where the communications happen over the air, but power consumption or space is not a problem to the same extent as with a handset, and therefore such an approach may be justified.

Protection Against Catalog Attacks

Risk of catalog attacks was mentioned in the previous section. The WEP algorithm in wireless LANs conforming to IEEE 802.11 has been documented as susceptible to catalog attacks. The reason for this type of attack is the combination of a bad randomizer and too short an IV (initialization vector) value. The former points to the need for a TRUE random number generator and not a pseudorandom number generator like most systems use. The latter is motivated by the fact that, in the case of WEP, the IV vector is 24 bits long, which means that after 2×12 words, repetitions may be expected on a statistical basis.

If the scheme of Figure 13-13 is used, it can be seen that no matter what happens on the channel, you can decipher, but you cannot attack the key generator. It is obvious that the original key generator state space (by feedback of the nonlinear function) is reduced to a smaller state space at the output of the transmitter. This sacrifice is justified as a means of protection against catalog attacks. It is also interesting to notice that the HORNET™ stream cipher does *not* suffer from this vulnerability, as the periodic DEK injection, coming from a TRNG continually alters and renews the state space, which would otherwise be limited to 2^{160} bits per session (by itself this is long enough for all practical purposes). To apply the same criterion, we see that HORNET™ has a true randomizer and the IV is 160 bits long.

Protection Against Power Analysis Attacks

A block-cipher system in a secure communications chip is more prone to be attacked by linear or differential power analysis, assuming the opponent has access to power supply pins in a chip bought and characterized in a lab. This is much more the case than that of a stream cipher. The reason can be easily seen if you note that in strong COMSEC chips, the encryption keys change relatively often.

This can happen either because:

- Chip is securing multiple sessions (each with its own key).
- Chip encrypts/decrypts only one session, but one where the actual block encryption/decryption key is changed at some point in time (hopefully in sync with the receiver, and usually after some new handshake occurs in the midst of the ongoing session).

If the generation of the key (as we know) incurs a certain and rather unusually high computational activity and overhead doing modular exponentiation, and so forth, which does not happen when the chip only churns traffic bits, the chip can be expected to draw more current from its power supply just to do these key-generation-related calculations. Correlating in time these current spikes, by parading bits in front of a network sniffer or wireless interceptor-generated bits stream, one can see where the handshake started, where the actual operands of a Diffie-Hellman were exchanged between the communicating parties. If you know the clocking frequencies of the chip, you can immediately deduce from this quick analysis the number of cycles the chip takes to calculate the key. Knowing the technique of modular exponentiation (to take the example of our case here), you can immediately know that the size of the exponent is say 512 or 1024 bits. You must have by now understood the implications of such vulnerability.

In an integrated circuit you in general have the ability to embed a computational functionality, which, if it cannot defeat this type of attack by power analysis, can render it extremely difficult to even conceive, making it highly unlikely to occur. The idea is to embed a small finite-state machine, which calculates dummy keys continuously in the background. When an actual key is needed it will have been generated and there will be no difference in the power-consumption pattern due to the sudden need for a new key. The engineering trade-off is obviously higher power consumption as the chip is executing a lot of dummy operations in the background. This latter issue may hint to the nonapplicability of such a design in all wireless devices, especially as the smaller, more inexpensive and battery sensitive ones may opt not to embed such functionality.

A realm where this would seem less of an issue is the military and intelligence communities whose equipment design is based on choices and decisions that are usually dictated by the seriousness and the nature of the task at hand, and less by battery-lifetime economics or the lifestyle and convenience of the user. This is especially true in the following case.

Literature is especially rich in proposing techniques against this type of attack. See the CHES conference proceedings for the years 1999, 2000, and 2001.

Protection Against Traffic Analysis Attacks

The average consumer in the street who uses his or her wireless telephone numerous times during the day may not necessarily feel threatened from this angle. Going back, however, to government circles, it should be obvious that some level of traffic analysis and load monitoring even on encrypted traffic can in many instances disclose a certain level of information. Before the invasion in Kuwait, a frenzy of wireless communications activity between their HQ in Baghdad and the Iraqi forces stationed at the Iraq-Kuwait border signaled to United States and Allied intelligence that some unusual event was happening and alerted them to the fact that maybe Kuwait was about to be attacked.

A solution to this problem is to use a COMSEC chip, which generates dummy fake traffic continuously even when idle from the regular communications point of view. An outsider who monitors the line or air medium then always sees the link busy and cannot deduce anything from the mere fact that the level of activity is high at some point in time. It is always high.

This implies several things. First, such a scheme cannot be commercially envisioned in the regular cellular communications world, as it will imply air-time that must be billed around the clock to someone most probably not willing to accept such a cost. Even in Europe where air-time cost is heavily subsidized by the carrier and billed to the caller exclusively, as opposed to what happens in the United States, this will mean that the fake extra calls must be filtered out of the system so they don't burden the network infrastructure. Even if the dummy calls are discarded, a heavy penalty can be paid on the signaling channels.

Second, the receiver must be able to know precisely at which bit dummy traffic is replaced by encrypted traffic so the decryption engine can be engaged. This implies a deterministic approach that remains elusive to an outsider, but which allows a corresponding party to be alert systematically and reliably for useful traffic. This usually means a programmable digital correlator is in place, loaded with reference values that somehow are tied to the cryptographic session key through irreversible functions (such as the SHA algorithm). The correlator scans the incoming traffic bit per bit until a specific value is detected, say over 128 bits, in which case an event is triggered. That event can be anything the system designer wants it to be. The HORNET™ system is an example of such behavior and functionality.

Common Techniques for Implementing Security Modules

Of course the design of pipelines, registers, latches, and so forth, needed to implement the mechanisms listed, are the bread and butter of electronics engineers and integrated circuit designers and there is a massive literature on the subject, starting from the conceptual level down to the detailed layout of the circuits.[36,37,38,39]

An overview here will suffice, of how things are implemented for the various modules that comprise a real-time communications security chip independently of whether it is an FPGA, an ASIC, or a full-custom design. You should remain alert to the fact that an SOC is a hybrid solution, in the sense that some (if not all) cryptographic functions can be implemented as embedded SW running on an IP core CPU inside the SOC, and that core CPU can be of either CISC, or most often RISC or even more recently, of DSP nature.

Initialization Vectors and Random Number Generation

It is well known that the robustness of most cryptographic schemes resides overwhelmingly on the quality of the random numbers that feed its structures. This is equally valid for both stream ciphers, which need good quality key material and block ciphers, which need good quality keys, calculated according to several rules based on what is the algorithm and what the overlying key exchange protocol dictates. Many people assume that a PRNG bank is enough and some initial value may be injected without too much thought. The consequences of such design negligence have been covered elsewhere in this book. Initialization values (also known as IV vectors, or seed values) are an important ingredient for pseudo-random number generators and they must be (for an outsider) random. The term random means a lot of things and so designers of embedded systems have traditionally looked into many different options trying to find such elusive random numbers. It is not an easy task.

Most random number sources are based on a *pseudo-random number generator* (PRNG), which (per definition) uses deterministic steps to generate its bitstream output based on some initial seeding value. Unfortunately, most systems (especially software based ones) use a known or predictable seed value, thereby allowing an attacker to predict the state of the PRNG. It is therefore of critical importance to use truly random sources of randomness for the initialization of a PRNG. Entropy is the key concept here and in a deterministic system, the entropy of the output only depends on the entropy of the initialization value.[40] Careful judgment is paramount, as it can be computationally infeasible to distinguish a good PRNG from a perfect RNG. Typical examples of PRNGs designed for cryptographic applications are SHA1Random (with 160 bits of state) and MD5Random (with 128 bits of state) in the BSAFE™ software toolkit available from RSA Data security, Inc. A PRNG seeded with 256 bits of state, has 256 bits of entropy, and cannot produce more than 256 bits of true randomness. If an attacker guesses the 256 bits of the seed, he or she can predict the entire PRNG output. Of course, computationally one can argue that guessing 256 bits is not easily feasible, hence the conclusion that a good reliable source seeding a PRNG can make a strong cryptographic combination.

Design issues and approaches for a good TRNG can be found in Vittorio Bagini's paper: A Design of Reliable True Random Number Generator for Cryptographic Applications.[41]

The Case of Stream Ciphers

In the case of stream ciphers, designers usually try to come close to the ideal case of a one-time pad, without the annoying overhead of having to manage pads, which is not a trivial task for a scalable design intended to work on a large-scale deployment of embedded devices, wherein handheld or transportable wireless devices mostly reside. To do this, designers use some source of random (or most often pseudo-random) number generation, which either feeds the cipher engine with additive material (using an XOR rule) or feeds an entropy accumulator which then in turn feeds the crypto engine either with additive or mapping material; all of this can happen in a codebook or noncodebook configuration.

We have referred in detail to the difference between random and pseudorandom numbers elsewhere in this book. Some people, especially SW designers without cryptographic background, believe that if they use something that they personally cannot attack, it cannot be attacked. You must by now have come to know that nothing is further from the truth than this. You should also keep in mind that if a certain bit sequence seems random that does not mean it is random. This is why there are usually whole batteries of randomness tests that check the sequence from many different angles.

As an example, if you change all the names of people and streets and numbers in the Boston telephone directory into their corresponding ASCII characters and keep this gigantic sequence of bits, you may be tempted to say that you have a random bit source of unpredictable bits to use as key material onto a stream cipher, especially if you do not tell a third party from which point the sequence is used. If two communicating parties agree to XOR their exchanged traffic with this bit sequence but not starting from page 1 of the directory, but instead they agree to start from page 67, second column from the left, 59th name from the top, then they have agreed to a very specific bit sequence that can be XORed with the actual traffic. If the receiver knows this information and applies it precisely by XORing this very same bit sequence in sync (as to denote synchronized operations) he or she will recover the original plaintext. What happens now when upon arrival at the end of the directory? The key material bit sequence that we had agreed upon has been exhausted. By prior agreement we move to the beginning of the directory and continue by using the front part of the Boston directory, which we had not used before, as if nothing has happened. Now we come to page 67, second column from the left, and finish the 58th name, concluding a full pass over the directory. What next? Some people will say, continue over and over again.

Well, one simply cannot continue and maintain a secure design.

Because, this is exactly what is meant by what seems random to the untrained eye may not necessarily be random. The Boston directory example clearly shows that a bitstream generated from directory, once through its entirety, if used again it is no longer random. One should have serious doubts as to whether the bitstream for a continuous bitstream segment that is subset of the same directory is pseudorandom at all, as letters in names are laid out alphabetically and therefore their sequence can be somehow correlated with the ASCII table progression. Now, by iterating the pass over the directory, it is clearly pseudo-random. In fact, the bitstream in this example is now periodic. It may be a long period for an 11-year-old to see, but it is periodic and most probably it can be seen by a 16-year-old. The question then becomes not whether it can be seen but what can be done against it. As there is plenty of high-quality, nonclassified, cryptanalysis-related material published showing how one goes about tackling the issue, we will not elaborate here. Pertinent references for deeper study have been provided at the end of the book.

The message the authors want to leave here for you is that because some manufacturer claims to offer random number generation, this does not automatically mean that what they offer is what they say they do or (unfortunately in some cases) that they even know what they mean. The latter argument can be easily expanded across the board onto essentially any cryptographic equipment. It is not too long ago that one of the authors of this book while attending a trade-show organized along with a major telecommunications congress asked the designer of a network encryptor which modes the company's DES chip could be configured into and was confronted with the astounding answer/question: I have no idea. The message is that many in the industry want to make believe that they know, when in fact they don't know, and it ultimately behooves the customer to become informed, to question, and to make the appropriate due diligence investigation before committing to a specific purchase.

Embedded Generation of Random Numbers

Obviously, many ideas have been tried for the generation of random numbers and it is not the topic of this book to exhaustively explain and document the various techniques of choice and the associated trade-offs. We will give a brief overview of some commonly used approaches and briefly cover their vulnerabilities or inapplicability in an embedded wireless world. The list can be rather long, but here the intention is to show some of the most common design options for an embedded cryptographic hardware system designer. We leave aside *true random number generators* (TRNGs) based on nuclear decay and so forth, which would not be feasible to integrate inside a portable wireless device.

LFSR- and Linear Congruence-Based Schemes

A seeding value or *initialization vector* (IV) is injected into an *linear feedback shift register* (LFSR) and runs sequentially. This category of PRNG is also called poor man's RNG because of the straightforward design and negligible cost, and many purportedly secure telephone and secure fax products are in wired and wireless markets, having given their users the impression that they are unbeatable. Unfortunately if the design is easy, the defense against attack is elementary in complexity and will not deter anyone (except maybe its designers!) from predicting its output easily. An RNG block whose output is predictable cannot be called random.

User-Initiated Information Collection

In some instances, usually in desktop software products like secure email, when setting up a user's profile the system asks the user to play around with the mouse or keyboard while the system gathers enough data to put together a proprietary non-documented random number. Human factors make the user in the majority of cases draw mouse circles that are more or less concentric. The annulus within which these typical circles lie is an excellent first value for an iterative attack on the random number the algorithm generates. No wonder that vendors usually don't want to disclose the algorithm (a characteristic that we would call SBO security by obscurity) which violates Kirckhoff's law.

In the keyboard case, the user is asked to type something rather long and random and the system will generate a random number. Needless to say, most people type in a more or less identical sequence to the one someone without a music background would play on a piano keyboard. Ample statistical information is available (for example, in password-guessing programs) to allow you to easily attack this source of alleged randomness. In fact, even for the most sophisticated keyboard environments, where not just the keys you hit are recorded, but also where the physical force with which the individual keys are pressed is recorded and therefore attackable. The writer of this chapter is personally aware of a spectacular neural-network implementation where the identity of a computer user can be decided based on the way someone logs on the computer. The system is based on history it has created itself derived from previous log-ins of the user, scanning a whole series of traits as to how one deals with the keyboard while the system is continuously learning about the user. It is currently at use daily in specific government and industry organizations and it will automatically flag to security anybody who logs on correctly (name and password) on the right workstation, but who does not seem to be hitting the keyboard as usual. Security then will be dispatched to check out whether the specific user at that workstation is having a bad day or whether something else more noteworthy is indeed happening.

In a wireless setting, this scheme (besides its weaknesses as discussed) is simply deemed not practical. Users will not spend time on their handset keyboard, which is infinitely less ergonomic than the desktop computer for fast and massive data entry, entering password phrases just to facilitate the encryptor's LFSR resetting. A pointer device will be equally non-practical for these reasons. Users, irrespectively of whether they are investors in NY City dialing up their broker down the street, or stranded travelers in Denver calling their home to say they are on the later flight, or soldiers in the desert calling a sister unit on the battlefield, will NOT be either interested or willing to know how the device works. The user wants secure communications and it must happen easily, transparently, reliably, consistently and to one's unbeknownst.

Nonlinear Diode-Based RNG

In some cryptographic systems with physically larger dimensions than a microchip, designers have used a PN diode with an unpredictably nonlinear I-V (current/voltage) characteristic, as a nice way of producing truly random values. Although this seems to be technically working for a one-off system, the business challenges that it causes are bordering the bizarre and unusual. More specifically, diode manufacturers cannot reproduce such products consistently and controllably out of specification and therefore procurement on an industrial TQM-scale is impossible. The technique is much less easy to contemplate in an integrated circuit; hence it is not considered a viable option for an ASIC/FPGA implementation.

Ambient Noise-Based RNG

In some rack-mountable communications security systems, the designers have ambient noise captured through a miniature microphone and internally digitized, filtered and then by applying it to some rudimentary proprietary (in almost all cases never publicly documented) digital signal processing routine, to generate a random number. Usually it is the case for systems that need to initialize certain registers with unpredictable material. It is the DES IV-generator for several current VPN products in the market.

Although at first blush a random source, if you take such a system into a noise-proof chamber, it may be driven towards specific and highly reproducible internal states, which, even if not explicitly known, can be cryptographically combined with specific types of attacks, such as a chosen text attack, known plaintext, known cipher, and so on.

It is also a fact of life that an attacker engaging in power analysis against such a system will know potentially, from the power consumption increases, when these infrequent signal processing algorithms are running, and therefore will know when in time new IV values are being generated and loaded into the registers, whose content the attacker is trying to predict.

Although a power analysis (usually executed against smart cards and other small devices) is not easily done against rack-mounted boxes with physical intrusion detection characteristics, it is to be expected that this will not be the case in the highly integrated designs of state-of-the-art embedded wireless devices, usually comprised of a couple of integrated circuits and a power supply, where an attacker can easily buy a like device, strip it apart to analyze how it behaves from a power consumption point-of-view when running in specific contexts. The attacker will then set up secure sessions, handshake a key exchange, exponentiate to calculate operands in a protocol, encrypt, and authenticate.

Sampling White Noise

A popular technique for generating embedded true random bit sequences is to sample presumably analog white noise after it has been quantized by means of a comparator. There may be offset value problems and bandwidth limitations, so the generated bit sequences usually suffer from bias and symbol correlations.[42] Different variations of sample-and-hold strategies have been documented in the literature and bit correlation is relatively well controlled by experimentation with the sampling frequency. Bagini and Bucci offer some interesting references for you who may care to delve more deeply into the subject.[43]

A typical design of this nature is shown in Figure 13-14. All components are easily integrated inside a microchip. Of course, the op-amp based comparator is an analog circuit and therefore the overall microchip must be built using a mixed-signal (analog and digital inside the same chip) mode technology that can combine analog and digital blocks in the same silicon die. This is not a low-cost solution; hence, chips like these are not readily available in low-cost wireless devices.

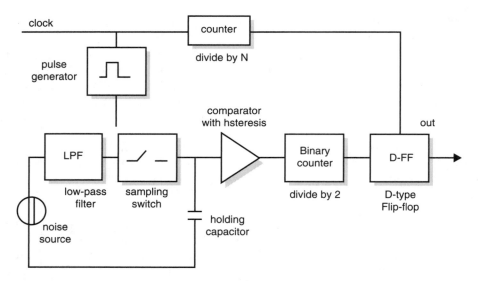

13-14 Block design of a TRNG based on sampling of white noise.[44]

Chaotic Processing-Based RNG

Chaos for our purposes can be described as a response that grows exponentially larger with time due to an arbitrary small perturbation. The combination of analog (so-called deterministic chaos) and a good analog noise source has been proposed as an interesting source of powerful and true random number generation.[45]

Maher and Rance claim that the reason why chaos is good for TRNG is that chaos guarantees that any noise contribution, no matter how small and how buried in deterministic interference, will ultimately significantly affect the output bits since the noise effects increase exponentially. Their specific design uses analog and digital circuitry, thus creating the same shortcoming (from an implementation point-of-view) that we mentioned in the previous section.[46] The principle is shown in Figure 13-15.

Other interesting efforts on the cutting-edge front of development on chaotic TRNG are more recently exploiting the analog behavior of purely digital CMOS transistors in an integrated form of the technology, where components inside the chip exhibit unpredictable and unique (for every chip manufactured) variations of electric behavior due to manufacturing tolerance of interlayer spacings, capacitances, and so on. Such an approach is robust mathematically for our wireless security purposes, as it cannot be altered or tapped into from the outside, and on top of that it can be inexpensively implemented as it is all happening in digital CMOS environment without need for mixed-signal designs and all the associated problems of crosstalk, coupling, isolation rings, and so forth.

Intel's Embedded RNG Source

The approach Intel has taken is based on thermal (also known as Johnson) noise. In an integrated circuit, various types of noise are present in all resistors, independent

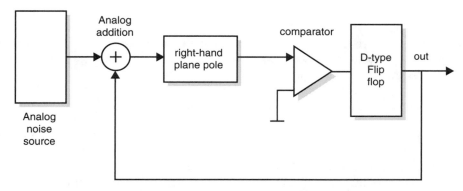

Negative feedback loop controls the instability created by the RHP pole circuitry

13-15 One approach to capitalize on chaotic behavior as a means to generate a TRNG.[47]

as to whether the resistors are implemented as epitaxially grown polysilicon strips or as parts of diffused and/or ion-implanted areas in a transistor-only circuit.[48] The latter is a rather common approach based on the so-called pull-up load of a CMOS circuit that ties specific nodes to VDD (the CMOS gate's drain supply connection).[49] Among these types of noise is thermal noise, shot noise and flicker noise. Noise in a resistor can be measured electrically and the associated circuit characteristics are dictated by the unpredictable and therefore random behavior of the electrons and the material itself.

As Jun and Kocher point out, the Intel RNG primarily samples thermal noise by amplifying the voltage measured across undriven resistors. Besides this being by itself a quite-random event, there is also a natural coupling with a locally produced pseudo-random environmental event, there is also a natural coupling with a locally produced pseudo-random environmental set of characteristics that include electromagnetic radiation and the ever-present variations of the power-supply. To avoid unwanted code coupling effects, Intel's RNG design compares and subtracts signals sampled from adjacent resistors. One must assume that special circuitry for the amplification of the detected signal and the subsequent signal processing must preserve as many components of randomness as possible. In such cases, you need to verify that a high degree of linearity and significant bandwidth is available so high-frequency components can be reliably passed onto subsequent stages of the circuit.[50]

In the Intel RNG design, the random signal originates from two free-running oscillators (binary clock signals), one fast and one much slower (in the Intel case this frequency ratio is of the order of 100). Thermal noise is used to FM-modulate the frequency of the low-frequency oscillator (slower clock). The variable-frequency noise-modulated slower clock then, when detected to be crossing a certain threshold, triggers sampling and measurement of the faster clock.

It is then clear that the drift between the two clocks is the source of randomness for the binary digits that are generated. If the clocks were found not to be drifting apart, sampled bits of the output would contain statistically colored traces of beat-periodicity (basic harmonic multiples).

Of course, there had existed other previous RNG designs based on the use of two oscillators but in all similar cases the slower clock frequency must be heavily modified by the noise effect for the scheme to be effective.[51,52]

The bit stream thus generated is fed into a modified von Neumann corrector to produce a (more or less) statistically balanced mix of 0's and 1's. A von Neumann corrector converts pairs of bits into single output bits by converting the bit pair [0, 1] into an output 1, converting the bit pair [1, 0] into an output 0, and outputs nothing for the bit pairs [0, 0] and [1, 1]. An immediate consequence of this design is that the aggregate output of the RNG is characterized by a variable bit rate. It has been documented that the Intel RNG in fact generates an average of one bit for every six raw binary samples translating into a performance of over 75 Kbps after the von Neumann corrector. This performance exceeds the classical requirements for most (but not all) standard cryptographic application requirements and the variable rate output must be handled with appropriate buffering techniques to ensure reliable random bit presentation to the application that needs it.[53]

In the Intel case, the customer for such a random bit stream is the software layer that will calculate keys for a block cipher like DES or Rijndael, or random operands for a Diffie-Hellman type of scenario, and so on.

To facilitate robustness and to maximize the RNG output's entropy quality, Intel is doing two things:

- There is an output mixing function based on the SHA algorithm, which as a mixer has beautiful characteristics. It combines variable size inputs and generates output bits with excellent statistical distributions. In fact, to quote Jun and Kocher, "the cryptograhpic properties of SHA destroy any remaining statistical structure and make it computationally infeasible to recover the seed state." To produce each 32-bit output, 32 bits of fresh data from the RNG must be supplied to the mixing function, which has 512 bits of state, as shown in Figure 13-16.
- Queuing the output into a 32-bit register ensures that no random outputs can be inadvertently read twice, ensuring that each READ operation executed by the application software always returns fresh data.

The small (and variable) bit generation capability of the Intel RNG makes it impossible to use as such for the implementation of an additive key material generator in a stream cipher environment that is meant to tackle real-time high-speed communications. If the traffic to be encrypted or decrypted is flying by at, say, 100 Kbps (streaming video case) or more (and it only gets worse for cable modems, xDSL connections and other broadband realms), then the slow performance of this type of an RNG generator cannot ensure enough random material to keep up with and to get XORed with the traffic. One would then have to use an entropy accumulator with appropriate state size and periodically reseed it with values taken from the low and variable speed TRNG. The entropy accumulator (as used in the HORNET™ system) not only creates a longer state space from the sparsely seeding TRNG, it also protects the cryptographic engine from a potential degeneration of the TRNG

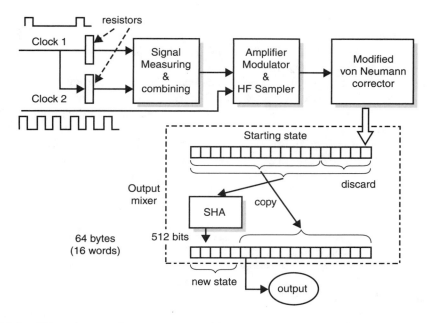

13-16 Intel™ random number generator architecture.

source, something that unfortunately can always happen and through a multitude of unforeseen and unexpected ways.

IBM Embedded RNG Source

IBM has used Gennaro's PRBG[54] as the base for the embedded random bit generator inside its 4758 Secure Crypto Coprocessor.[55,56] The IBM 4758 is a hardware module that plus into an industry-standard PCI-slot: it contains a 486-compatible CPU, custom hardware to perform DES and public-key cryptographic algorithms (RSA and DSS with SHA-1 implemented in hardware), a secure clock/calendar, and a hardware-based random number generator. It also has protective shields, sensors and control circuitry to protect against a wide variety of attacks involving probe penetration, power sequencing, radiation and temperature manipulation and it is certified to meet the U.S. Government's FIPS 140-1 Level 4 requirements.[57]

The basic element of protection is a multilayered grid of conductors, which is monitored by circuitry that can detect changes in the properties of the conductors, as well as in the inter-layer properties.[58] The conductors are not metallic and they resemble the material they are embedded into. This makes discovery, isolation, and manipulation of the conductors even more difficult. The grid is flexible and it is wrapped around the secure coprocessor as if it were gift-wrapped. The whole package is potted at the end of the manufacturing cycle in a way that will always denounce any attempted intrusion and it is enclosed in a grounded shield to reduce both its susceptibility to electromagnetic interference as well as any potentially detectable electromagnetic emanations.

During the final manufacturing step, the Coprocessor generates a unique public key pair, which is stored in the device. The tamper detection circuitry is activated at this time and remains active throughout the useful life of the Coprocessor, protecting the private key as well as other keys and sensitive data. The Coprocessor public key is certified at the factory by a global IBM private key and the digital certificate is retained inside the Coprocessor. Subsequently, the Coprocessor private key is used to sign the Coprocessor status responses that in conjunction with the public key certificate demonstrate that the Coprocessor remains intact and is genuine. From the time of manufacture, if the tamper sensors are ever triggered, the Coprocessor sets to zero its critical keys, destroys its certification, and is rendered inoperable. Extensive use of flash memory or even of protected memory with invisible bits that when set or reset by appropriate supervisory software can empty its banks, are some of the most common techniques used in the design of sophisticated cryptographic equipment.

The algorithm itself, which heavily uses modular arithmetic facilities in the IBM 4758 hardware, is well described in S. Smith and S. Weingart's article "Building a High-Performance Programmable Secure Coprocessor."[59] The efficiency analysis of this specific hardware implementation shows that the PRBG can produce random bits at a rate of 22.7 Kbps, which is the effective rate of communication between similarly encrypting 4758-equipped stations. It is considerably slower than SHA-1 based PRBG schemes as consistent with the key management scheme documented in ANSI X9.17 but is provably secure and in some circles this definitely carries a significant weight.

This brief exposition of the IBM approach in a FIPS 140-1 setting (something that is rather commonplace in the cryptographic community with numerous vendors) has been included here to show the nonspecialist reader the concerns with which a systems designer has to cope while designing a secure communications environment. One can then only imagine the multitude of dimensions the problem takes when the designer of an integrated circuit must compact this level of protection and functionality in a small and extremely constrained—from all points of view—microchip. It also shows the level of protection that the market will require as computational intelligence and connectivity make wireless devices of unprecedented power and capabilities, ubiquitous!

Other Designs

Another interesting rather hybrid approach is shown in Figure 13-17. One should imagine several branches of the same clock tree. Each branch contains a different number of inverters. The only two constraints of this construct are that the maximum propagation delay the incoming signal sees associated with each branch be shorter than one clock cycle of the master clock input and that the number of inverters on every branch be relatively prime to that on every other single branch. Translated into plain English, this means that one can have 3, 5, 11, 17, and, say, 29 inverters in a tree of five branches, but one cannot have 3, 9, 17, 21, and 25, since neither 21 nor 25 (nor even 9) are relatively prime to 3.

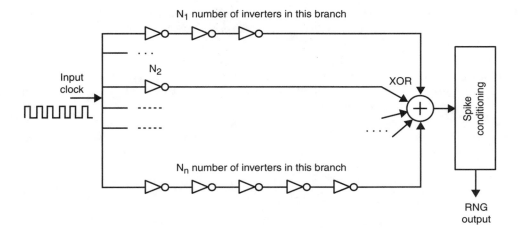

N_1 number of inverters in this branch

Input clock

N_2

XOR

Spike conditioning

RNG output

N_n number of inverters in this branch

(i) N_n, N_n, . . .N_n must be relatively prime to each other

(ii) N_n x Individual Inverter Propagation Delay < (1/f_{clock})

13-17 PRNG created by a special tree of inverter-induced propagation delays.

Binary Number Multiplication and Accumulation Engine

Until only a few years ago, traditional CISC and RISC *central processing units* (CPUs) possessed a classical multiplier unit as circuitry into which the *arithmetic logic unit* (ALU) would feed operands of 32-bit size and the result (with appropriate sign and overflow or error status information preserved) would be obtained in a short amount of time. Many different well-documented techniques are available for the realization of multiplication circuits using different algorithms like Booth, Wallace, and so forth.[60,61,62,63]

Modular Arithmetic Unit and Exponentiation Engine

There is often the need in a cryptographic chip to perform modular arithmetic. This is the case in the Diffie-Hellman key exchange algorithm, in the RSA algorithm, in the *Digital Signature Standard* (DSS), and in *Elliptic Curve Cryptography* (ECC). In the cryptography area, the most important examples are those of modular multiplication and modular exponentiation. A common algorithm that implements this technique is the Montgomery algorithm, which provides certain advantages and the question is whether it will be done in hardware or software within a certain implementation. Multiple designs of either approach have been proposed and can be found in the references.[64,65,66,67,68,69,70]

Several ASIC and FPGA implementations have been studied and reported. In cryptographic applications one usually encounters very large numbers. The precision required usually varies from 128 and 256 bits for the most current common forms of elliptic curve cryptography (especially applied on smart cards) to 1024 and 2048 bits based on exponentiation. Most designs for modular multiplication are of fixed-precision type. The literature also reports on designs that can handle operands of variable size as well.[71,72]

The basic features of a scalable Montgomery multiplier are

- The ability to work on operands of any precision at the kernel level
- Being adjustable to any chip area
- Using a pipelined architecture that reduces the impact on signal loads as a result of the potentially high precision of operands

Regarding the first of these issues, it is noteworthy that some researchers have approached the problem of long-precision numbers using short-precision operations, by employing a conventional multiplier and an appropriate control algorithm. This usually revolves around a standard 32 or 64 bit multiplier. The state-of-the-art in this approach as of early June 1001 is a precision that does not exceed 100 bits. The control algorithm is usually complex and the associated increase in parallelism leads to multiple datapaths and exceptionally high complexity at the system design level.

The second of these issues is a important characteristic as the scalable algorithm offers an unprecedented flexibility for the hardware to actually adapt to the operands' precision by adjusting both the word size and the number of processing elements. The more hardware there is the faster the performance, something of extreme importance in accelerator chips or infrastructure chips, as those used inside a server, switch, or router.

The high load on signals broadcast to several hardware components inside the chip is an important factor to slow down high-precision Montgomery multiplier designs. For this reason, some researchers have considered systolic designs.

Table 13-5 details the gatecount in NOR gates occupied by a scalable Montgomery multiplier as implemented by Tenca, Todorov, and Koç. The number of stages used in this pipelined approach is shown and at the same time one sees (in a normalized manner over the time it takes for a 15-stage design) to accomplish the computational task for the two shown precisions. The reason for not showing the absolute values of the computational time (which is of the order of 4 ms for 256-bit precision and 20 ms for 1024-bit operand precision) is that this research group from Oregon State University has used a 0.5μm technology library available to the academic world, which does not reflect the state-of-the-art in semiconductor manufacturing technology as it is engaged in deep submicron low power designs for the wireless industry. The state-of-the-art in the industry today is closer to 0.11μm transistor gate width. The same design ported onto a more sophisticated technology would obviously yield exceptionally stronger numbers.[74]

Table 13-5 Some Design Points for the Scalable Montgomery Multiplication Algorithm as Implemented in Custom VLSI HW Using 8 Bits Per Word by Tenca, Todorov and Koç[73]

Number of Stages	Gate Count	Computational Time Needed for 256-bit Operand Precision Normalized to the Time Needed for 15 Stages	Computational Time Needed for 1024-Bit Operand Precision Normalized to the Time Needed for 15 Stages
15	14,964	1	1
16	15,969	1	1.04
18	17,979	1.05	1.21
22	21,999	1.04	1.37
24	24,009	0.92	1.39
26	26,019	0.83	1.42

Nevertheless, the message from the table is clear. It can be seen that the design point with 22 as the number of stages is close to optimum, as the computational time for 256-bit precision is close to its minimal value. At the same time the computational time for 1024-bit precision is improved by 37 percent as compared to the computational-time point with 15 stages. You notice that with further increase of the number of stages towards 24 or 26, the computational time needed for 256-bit precision worsens while the computational time for 1024-bit precision does not improve significantly (only 2 percent per stage).

Typical performance of an off-the-shelf available hardware-based Montgomery exponentiation engine is 30 exponentiations/second for 1024 bits key size and it can be implemented with a circuit clocked at 66 MHz (minimum) and containing 40,000 gates.[75]

Hashing

Hashing is an extremely important function as we have seen elsewhere in the book. It is predominantly used for the integrity verification of a transmitted piece of information and it is also used for the generation and verification of digital signatures. In several systems like HORNET™ or in the Intel Random Number Generator, a one-way function, mostly a hashing function like the SHA, properly seeded, is used for generation of subsequent pseudo-random bit sequences used in key generation, DH-operands, and so forth. The importance and frequency with which such hashing functions are called upon to provide their valuable output to other circuitry in a COMSEC microchip, in conjunction with the speed within which this operation must be concluded, implies the need for several applications to provide a hashing function in hardware.

Typical cases are the *Secure Hashing Algorithm* (SHA), MD2, MD5, RIPEMD, and others that are covered in detail in many sources.[76,77] A hashing algorithm like

SHA can be implemented in an integrated circuit either in hardware or in software. The trade-offs for the optimal decision are mostly

- Performance measured in throughput speed
- Associated gate-count (hence silicon real-estate) cost. One could argue that this list of trade-offs should also contain one more variable, namely
- The ease and/or desirability to design such a block of VLSI circuitry.

Although this is certainly true the SOC revolution has facilitated the build-or-buy dilemma. If one does not know how to design SHA in hardware, one can license an IP core that implements the SHA algorithm from a multitude of companies and therefore spare oneself the VHDL and/or Verilog coding and verification of the function. One would then feed this hardware-description-language code along with specific synthesis scripts into a classical synthesis tool (such as, Design Compiler from Synopsys) and map the synthesis onto the technology library of the actual semiconductor foundry of choice. The result will be nothing short of a SHA-module in hardware. Of course there are interfacing issues with other circuits, buffers, I/O handling, timing, synchronization, and so forth, of this module to be designed into an SOC design, but these are all typical bread-and-butter SOC design issues that have nothing to do with cryptography or communications security. These are therefore integration and electronic design skills that the average chip design team should have in ample supply.

A typical hardware implementation of SHA can be done in 23,000 gates[78] with input and outputs clocked at higher than 133 MHz and giving an aggregate throughput of 846 Mbps by processing the input in 80 steps only. In our own company we have realized SHA-1 in an even smaller gate count. Nevertheless this referenced number is representative of a more or less typical implementation. These numbers can vary given specific assumptions about the implementation, clocking architecture, and latency-related throughput performance needed. For a typical CMOS implementation with four transistors per typical gate, this is immediately sized up to 92,000 transistors and depending on the semiconductor manufacturing process, which dictates the transistor size and the integration density of transistors per square millimeter, one sees immediately the impact such a decision will have on the chip die size. The semiconductor foundry then in turn will match the die size versus the projected yields and a dollar impact can be obtained that the solution architect will have to weigh against his or her marketing requirements, as noted earlier in this chapter. Likewise if you move into the latest NIST-proposed enhancements of the secure hashing algorithm using the SHA-256 proposal, you can typically find hardware implementations of SHA-256 attaining at a clock frequency above 133 MHz a throughput of 1.047 Gbps accomplished with 25,000 gates (100,000 transistors).[79] This hashing algorithm is not yet implemented in most environments, but it is mentioned here to show the direction things are taking from the HW implementation point of view. The SHA-256 algorithm operates on 512 bit inputs and generates a hash of 256 bits. In terms of computational efficiency the same circuit example implements the 65 rounds needed in 64 block periods, producing 8 bits per clock period.

On the other hand, if the integrated circuit is designed along the SOC principle and the SHA (for our example case) algorithm has to be implemented in embedded software, then the algorithm will have to be written in a major language like C, C++, or Java and, more rarely, in cases where performance has to be maximized, given meager computational resources in assembly. Code has to be developed and cross-compiled onto the SOC CPU platform. In true conformity to embedded software development, appropriate libraries will need to be generated and linked with the SHA application itself and then the instruction code will have to be burned onto the metallization-layer of ROM (after the appropriate debugging iterations over EPROM, PROM, and/or flash memory).

The trade-offs in this case (having assumed that the chosen data structures and the associated software internal structure is beyond reproach from the functionality point of view) are the

- Available skills (at hand with the design team) towards the easy and optimal coding of embedded software
- Size of the instruction memory, implemented in ROM, from where the code will have to be executed
- Size of data memory needed during calculations, also known as scratchpad memory, which is implemented in RAM

To give specific examples, the SHA algorithm of our example, implemented in software, typically fits the profile depicted in Table 13-6.

The numbers of this table have been produced by optimized Java coding. The significant difference in instruction memory needed between the core algorithm and the standalone algorithm is due to the overhead Java runtime requires to run the algorithm. This overhead for cryptographic applications adds as an average around 30 percent more code memory onto the algorithm required resources. In some cases, as in stream cipher engine implementations in software this can drop to a mere 10 percent. Java in such a realm is unfavorably compared with C, which provides approximately 15-percent better results in packing the code memory size. C++ in these functions is only by 5-percent worse than C in density quality of implemented code.

You should note that when implementation efficiency is mentioned, the same concept has two completely different connotations depending on the method by which an algorithm is inserted into an integrated circuit. When discussing hardware

Table 13-6 Hardware vs. Software Implementation of Typical Modules

	Core Algorithm in Pentium 32-Bit-Long Instructions	Total Slgorithm (with I/O and Libraries in Pentium 32-Bit Instructions)	Gate Count
SHA Diffie-Hellman 1024-Bits with a	2,006	2,232	23,000
Handshake Protocol	1,478	2,256	60,000
Finite-State-Machine 128-Bit Digital Correlator	270	383	25,150

implementation, usually the efficiency is the measure of how much useful bit output has been produced per clock period. This is very important in cases where throughput is the main issue. On the other side, when the algorithm is embedded in software inside an SOC design approach, the efficiency criterion (besides chip throughput) also assumes another form, namely that of the code footprint. In other words, the issue is then how much memory the implementation requires. This covers both the instruction memory out of which the algorithm is being executed and the data memory that the algorithm needs while executing, for intermediate calculations and data structuring.

Diffie-Hellman (DH) Key Exchange

One of the major breakthroughs in the proliferation of cryptography for the masses is the Diffie-Hellman protocol, described in detail elsewhere herein. Due to its simplicity and to the fact that the underlying patent that protected it when it was introduced has expired, it is an obvious choice for an inexpensive secure communications system. It certainly has its recognized and well understood weakness for a min-in-the-middle attack, which prohibit its use in classified or nonauthenticated data communications areas, but as long as one reliably recognizes the voice of the other party (something that unfortunately is only applicable in telephony and only when one knows the other party), the danger is mitigated and as such it allows the creation of inexpensive royalty-free designs.

The Diffie-Hellman protocol requires a couple of modular exponentiation operations of rather large numbers. It can be done in either software or hardware. The latter makes sense especially if one has the associated need for frequent execution of modular arithmetic operations. This is the case for instance if an RSA-based PKI is inside the wireless device. In a classical communications environment PK cryptography operations inside a wireless device seem realistically not something of exceedingly frequent use. A session key must be set up in the beginning and communicated to the other party, an authentication can happen in the beginning of the session or sporadically to various servers during a session, digital signatures may be required from time to time, rarely more than once per session and by session here we will dissociate the m-commerce transaction-based sessions from the real-time communications streaming sessions (voice, audio, or video). One can purchase something several times during a communications session with an e-commerce or m-commerce vendor. One would not necessarily need more than one digital signature (if any at all) during a real-time streaming communication session (for example, downloading a movie over the air from a video pay-per-view service).

This all points to the fact that DH naturally is mostly implemented in software. A hardware implementation may make sense in the future when one starts dealing with 4096 bits factors and larger. Typical cases today still use 512 and 1024 bit factors while it would really be a state-of-the-art implementation that provides 2048-bit exponents.

The Diffie-Hellman implementation mentioned in the last column of Table 13-6 is purely hardware-based, and as such, packs a Montgomery exponentiator and a *finite-state machine* (FSM) that looks for the appropriate operands to run the handshake between the communicating parties in hardware. This FSM can become quickly and astronomically larger in gate-count if it implements a reliable, quasi-fault-tolerant, and robust handshake protocol between communicating parties in a one-to-one session, or in a secure conference or multicast environment.

You can safely argue that since this handshake is only needed at session set-up time, this cannot justify the expensive hardware implementation of the protocol, nor would we argue against common sense. It is included here as an example of the complexity and trade-off decisions its availability implies to the designer as an option. You should keep in mind that the chip being designed has, by its functional specification, specific constraints that can negate several academically available options. If it is part of a custom-design where everything is designed in full-custom VLSI blocks, one cannot say that the DH protocol of this example will be implemented in embedded software, if there is no provision for an embedded CPU inside the chip.

It should be immediately obvious that to compare apples with apples, it is not a straightforward matter to observe how code is implemented on an exotic architecture (as for instance, a VLIW processor where one 240-bit instruction word compacts 11 to 13 different operations and has an essentially unfair advantage over traditional 32-bit CPUs) of either CISC or RISC variety.

During the last several years, *digital signal processors* (DSPs) have consistently pushed their presence expansively into mainstay computing. In the embedded world they have become the next generation super-microcontrollers by offering systems designers the

- Computational horsepower they need
- Availability of usually highly-optimized pipeline designs that allow optimal and efficient code implementation
- Potential multiple *multiply-and-accumulate* (MAC) circuits and other variations of what is known as Harvard architecture (contrary to classical Von Neumann architecture there are independent on-chip buses for data and program words allowing for high execution rate read/write instructions leading to a performance of one, if not more, instruction per clock cycle). Harvard architecture is shown in Figure 13-18.
- Embedded real-time operating system kernel that obviates the need in many cases of having to write system code, an art in which they may not be fluent.
- Possibility of embedding a highly powerful DSP core inside an SOC design, allowing the designer to tackle simultaneously both traditional digital signal processing and computational tasks within one chip.

Last but not least, there is no floating-point computation needed in the mainstream cryptographic realm, and hence the appropriate mathematical capabilities of an underlying core or CPU are largely irrelevant. Even to the extent that large number calculations are to be implemented, such a scheme is based on integer and/or modular arithmetic.

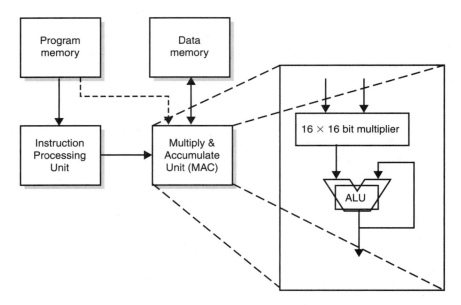

13-18 "Basic Harvard architecture" of DSP processors. This is different from von Neumann architectures, used in ordinary CPUs. The latter are usually characterized by one address bus, one data bus and one memory space. When the program memory, besides the instruction processing unit, also feeds the MAC unit (dotted line from ROM-based program memory to MAC), something that has high performance advantages for digital filtering, exemplified by loading coefficients (often stored in ROM), one talks about a "modified Harvard architecture."

Elliptic-Curve-Cryptography-Based Diffie-Hellman and Digital Signatures

A major area of work in public key cryptography is the *elliptic curve cryptography* (ECC) arena. Cryptosystems based on ECC were first introduced by Miller[80] and Koblitz.[81] There is ample literature on the subject.[82,83,84] The underling discrete logarithm problem seems to be much harder than in other groups. For the case of nonsingular curves there is no known subexponential-time algorithm for an attack on an ECC system. The direct result of this fact is that the keys used in ECC are much shorter than classical public-key cryptography based on RSA technology. Shorter key lengths for equivalent levels of security make ECC highly desirable in resource-constrained devices like wireless transceivers (cellular phones) and smart cards.

ECC implementations in FPGAs and ASICs are a field of very active research. Instead of addressing it comprehensively, we refer you to some excellent research papers on hardware and embedded software architectures published at the CHES'99, CHES'2000, and CHES'2001 Workshops, as well as specialized ECC implementation groups like the one run at WPI by Professor Christoph Paar.[85]

Many ECC implementations are either executed in software using specific cryptographic toolkits but others are implemented with optimized hardware architectures, where speed vs. area is the classical trade-off. For the designer of secure wireless equipment this very same argument sits at the heart of the design decisions and the dilemmas with which he or she is confronted. With small footprint embedded systems and only sporadic use of ECC techniques (which involve heavy loads of mathematical calculations), as for instance at session set-up when keys need to be exchanged between communicating parties, the hardware implementation is rarely justified. Designers therefore implement the ECC techniques in wireless basically as another set of routines to run on a timeshared DSP processor, which is available as an IP core in the baseband chip of wireless telephones.

The most fundamental ECC techniques used in the wireless arena are the ECC-DH, which is a variant of the Diffie-Hellman protocol as applied on elliptic curves. It can be used by two communicating parties for the secure generation and exchange of a session key, which will be used by them to start the actual encryption and decryption of traffic using some symmetric key technique (DES, Rijndael, stream cipher, and so on). It is well documented in IEEE P1363. The other equally important technique is the generation and verification of digital signatures based on the EC-DSA algorithm. The same hardware that can do the point additions and multiplications on elliptic curves over finite fields can be used for both ECC-DH and EC-DSA algorithms giving a strong resource sharing. The hardware implementation of ECC techniques is justified when real-time generation and verification of EC-DSA digital signatures based on elliptic curves is a requirement. This is also the base of a PKI-infrastructure, which in the entertainment industry has ramifications for *digital rights management* (DRM) of intellectual property, whether it be music, lyrics, movies, video, songs, pictures, graphics, and so on.

Hyperelliptic Curves

Hyperelliptic curves are a generalization of elliptic curves (which are simply hyperelliptic curves with genus one) and it has been shown that Jacobian groups of hyperelliptic curves can also be used to build discrete logarithm-based public key schemes. In fact, they were first suggested in 1988 by Koblitz.[86,87]

Cryptosystems based on *hyperelliptic curves* (HECC) allow for even shorter operands (50 to 80 bits depending on the curve genus) than classical public key cryptography schemes like RSA and DH and they are able to withstand known attacks. Special hardware-implemented architectures are required for the execution of addition (and doubling) on the Jacobian of a hyperelliptic curve over finite fields of arbitrary characteristic, and the two separate steps involved in the addition operation, namely composition and reduction.

The Jacobian is a finite quotient group of one infinite group of divisors of degree zero by another infinite group, namely that of principal divisors. Every element on the Jacobian is an equivalence class of divisors. Representation of elements and computation of operations are well documented.[88,89] These architectures are based on fundamental approaches regarding arithmetic on the underlying finite field as well as for arithmetic in the associated polynomial ring.

A nice work targeted on FPGA implementation of an HECC cryptosystem based on hyperelliptic curves of genus 4 over the Galois field $[2^{41}]$ is described in Thomas Wollinger's, *Computer Architectures for Cryptosystems Based on Hyperelliptic Curves*.[90] Plenty of references are also provided in Wollinger's thesis on theoretical analysis of the algorithm as well on various software implementations.[91,92,93,94]

NTRU Lattice Cryptography Engine

The NTRU cipher was invented in 1995 by J. Hoffstein, J. Piper, and J. Silverman,[95] and it is based on what is known as lattice cryptography. NTRU is a public-key cryptography scheme based on asymmetric key operations. In wireless communications it can be seen as a potential replacement of RSA or ECC or ordinary DH key exchange mechanisms. It does not affect the actual symmetric encryption of the transmitted traffic. As such even if NTRU is used as a secure envelope the designer must still address the issues we have seen in detail regarding choice of algorithm, block-cipher or stream cipher, modes of operation, and so forth. The fundamental computational task—which is expected to be difficult, thereby presuming the security of the NTRU cipher—is not aseasily described because it is not as elementary as prime factorization or discrete logarithms. One task that does remain difficult is to find the smallest vector in a lattice of high-dimensional vectors. The so-called *Shortest Vector Problem* (SVP) has been studied for more than a hundred years by the mathematical community[96] and both theory and experimentation suggest that it is difficult in lattices of high dimension. You can find ample material in a wide series of white papers that span the spectrum from the superficial to the truly detailed and esoteric, at the NTRU Web site.[97]

The interesting characteristics for purposes here of the NTRU cipher are *on the positive side.* Compared with RSA or *elliptic curves* (ECC), and for equivalent levels of afforded security, NTRU

- Runs many times faster
- Has much faster key generation
- Requires less memory

On the negative side, if one compares NTRU with ECC or RSA, NTR suffers from

- Requiring more bandwidth
- Larger key sizes than either ECC or RSA

The issue of bandwidth will be seen shortly, but first a cursory overview of the mechanics involved in key generation based on NTRU.

The cipher is best described using the ring of polynomials

$$R = Z[X] / (X^N - 1).$$

These are polynomials with integer coefficients that are multiplied together using the extra rule $X^N = 1$ so the product

$$c(X) = a(X) \times b(X)$$

is given by

$$c_k = \Sigma_{i+j} \equiv \text{kmodN } a_i b^j$$

with a, b and c the coefficients respectively of the polynomials. In particular if one writes the polynomials as vectors of their coefficients, then $c = a * b$ is the usual discrete convolution product of two vectors.

NTRU uses three public parameters (N, p, q) with $\gcd(p, q) = 1$ (greatest common denominator). Typical parameter sets that yield security levels similar to 1024-bit RSA and 4096-bit RSA respectively are $(N, p, q) = (251, 3, 128)$ and $(N, p, q) = (503, 3, 256)$. Coefficients of polynomials are reduced modulo p and modulo q. The inverse of $a(X) \mod q$ is the polynomial $A(X)\epsilon R$ satisfying $a(X) * A(X) \equiv 1 \mod q$.

NTRU Key Generation

For key generation, one chooses random polynomials F, $g \in R$ with small coefficients and set $f = 1 + pF$. One then computes the polynomial

$$h \equiv g \times f^{-1} \mod q.$$

The public key is h and the private key is f.

NTRU-Based Encryption

The plaintext m is a polynomial with coefficients taken $\mod p$. Choose a random polynomial r with small coefficients. The ciphertext is

$$e \equiv pr \times h + m \mod q.$$

NTRU-Based Decryption

Compute

$$a \equiv e \times f \mod q$$

choosing the coefficients of a to satisfy $A \leq a_i$, $A + q$. The value of A is fixed and is determined by a simple formula depending on the other parameters. Then $a \mod p$ is equal to the plaintext m.

It can be shown that NTRU transmits $(\ln q / \ln p)$ bits of ciphertext for each bit of plaintext. Since it is necessary that q . p to avoid losing information, this shows how NTRU uses more bandwidth than the older ciphers. In fact if we look at the two (N, p, q) examples mentioned earlier, we get

- In the RSA-1024 equivalent security case, bit rate increase of 4.416
- In the RSA-4096 equivalent security case, a required bit rate increase of 5.047

This means that in the former case, we will need 4.4 times more bandwidth and in the latter roughly 5.05 times more bandwidth. In some cases this can be OK, in some others though it can be unacceptable.

Another potentially interesting characteristic of this technology is that if and when quantium computers will be available and RSA will be broken based on Schor's discovery of quantum algorithms for fast factorization of large integers, NTRU would not be affected by such a prospect. [98,99]

The NTRU technology has already been included in the wireless security library of Texas Instruments OMAP platform[100] that is presumably going to be used by wireless communications systems designers to program functionality that runs inside a TI DSP chip in a wireless multimedia world. This implies that NTRU's advantages are perceived, at least by TI, to outweigh its disadvantages. It is also interesting to note that TI has not included ECC technology in its wireless security library, as of June 2001. The business truth is apparently somewhere in the middle, as there are applications where the extra bandwidth needed for NTRU, simply cannot be afforded by the infrastructure and hence NTRU cannot be accepted globally as the one-solution-fit-all. It does have its place under the proverbial sun and we believe that in many cases it will give a hard commercial time to elliptic curve implementations.

An interesting work was presented in April 2001 showing implementation of the NTRU engine on several constrained devices, from an FPGA through and ARM7TDMI core all the way down to a Palmtop computing platform based on the Motorola Dragonball microprocessor.[101] The performance of the algorithm is shown in Table 13-7 for several typical operations:

The same work reports that in an FPGA implementation on a Xilinx Virtex 100EFG860 clocked at 50 MHz the encryption time goes down to 5.17 ms allowing an encryption throughput of 48.52 Mbps. This implementation, which is estimated (as CLBs used in an FPGA implementation do not match automatically to useful gates) at 60,000 gates, is readily portable onto an ASIC platform, so it is only a matter of time before NTRU cores can be seen in wireless security COMSEC chips.

Other Alternative Techniques

There are several other techniques that could be considered as candidates for key generation and exchange in wireless communications systems. One of the most interesting and promising ones, as it can bring the operand sizes down even

Table 13- 7 NTRU Performance Results

Operation	MC68EX328 Dragonball (20-MHz palm Vx)	Intel 80386 (20-MHz RIM 957)	37-MHz ARM 7
Key Generation	1130 ms	858 ms	80.6 ms
Encryption	47 ms	39 ms	3.25 ms
Decryption	89 ms	72 ms	6.75 ms

further than hyperelliptic curves, is the cryptographic scheme based on Abelian varieties.[102,103,104]

A cryptographic scheme based on a two-dimensional Abelian variety over a finite field of size approximately 2^{87} can give security comparable to that achieved with an RSA system over a field of size 2^{1024} or an ECC system over a field of size approximately 2^{173}.

Abelian varieties are higher-dimensional versions of elliptic curves. An elliptic curve can be described in one third-degree equation as the elliptic curve space that can be considered as a one-dimensional space. Abelian varieties require many equations for their description. As an example, this means that over the complex numbers, for instance, two-dimensional Abelian varieties form a three-dimensional family. Three-dimensional Abelian varieties form a family of six-dimensions, four-dimensional Abelian varieties do the same in a ten-dimensional family, and so forth. In the case of a two-dimensional Abelian variety, it can be described by 13 quadratic equations. Therein lies the abundance of choices for a cryptographic protocol.

Yet another intriguing technique with solid mathematical backing is the braid-based algorithm owned and proposed by Arithmetica.[105,106]

RPK Key Protocol

Dr. William Raike of New Zealand invented the RPK cryptosystem and it is used today by Secure Media in its streaming products. The technology is well documented in Nichols.[107,108]

As Figure 13-19 shows the whole idea of the RPK system as a mixer that combines outputs from several LFSR-based sources in a quasi-random manner. Of course LFSRs are a straightforward data structure to code in software and/or design in custom-hardware with usual constraints to meet the silicon space one occupies or the required speed of performance. The usual way of explaining the RPK mixer is based on the so-called Geffe generator, which is equally easy to implement in shift register structures. We will not dwell on such a design here, but you are asked to keep in mind that this is an alternative technology of encrypting streaming media and it can be easily implemented in hardware or embedded software (see Figure 13-20).

Secure Repacketization of Information

We have discussed in the previous chapter how the original thinking along this line on the data link layer (frame relay, X.25, and so on) in the early to mid-90sgave birth to the IPsec effort on layer 3.

Here is where the transmitted IP traffic is repacketized in new packets with appropriate packet headers called AH and/or ESP for robust authentication, confidentiality and integrity; working in native or tunneling mode (a choice which sometimes obviously affects the network address translation possibilities at a site); with key generation, handshake, and key exchange mechanisms like IKE, ISAKMP, and Oakley that make intercompatibility between devices from various vendors come closer to reality; and making spoofing or playback attacks if not impossible, realistically difficult to execute.

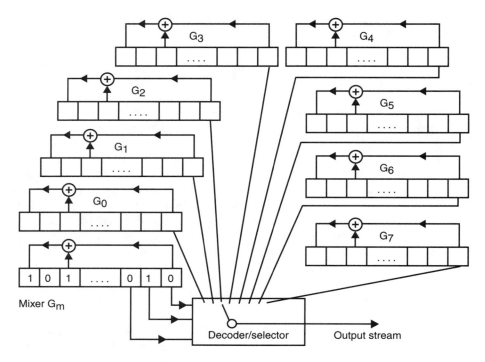

Figure 13-19 Principle of mixer in an RPK cryptosystem

IPsec functionality is available in a plethora of acceleration chips, from better known companies like Broadcom to new advanced architectural designs implementing fast IPsec as, for example, Corrent.[109] The latter's solutions purport to accelerate the multisession IPsec operation to links with online 2.3 Gbps connections in real-time. Impressive as those chips appear, they hardly fit the picture of our wireless devices and the WEASEL model of architecture evaluation. They are mostly $300 to $400 chips, rightfully power-hungry and heavily power-radiating, that can easily fit inside cooled routers or even servers where power supply is not an issue, but they cannot easily be contained inside small embedded power-constrained devices like handsets, PDAs, mobile radios, and so forth.

Some IP security purists, in a classical example of "when the only tool you have is a hammer, everything looks like a nail," believe that IPsec is the solution also for end-to-end secure mobile wireless communications. The opposite case is being made clear on the Voice over IP application example in the corresponding wireless VoIP chapter in this book, where you can see details of the overhead and latency imposed on the link by the excessive IPsec computational burden and associated overhead attached on packets carrying digitized voice. IPsec will have a definitive role to play on mobile and wireless communication security, but moreso on m-commerce or e-commerce types of settings where a few bytes of information need to be secured from an online transaction and the implementation can be easily taken

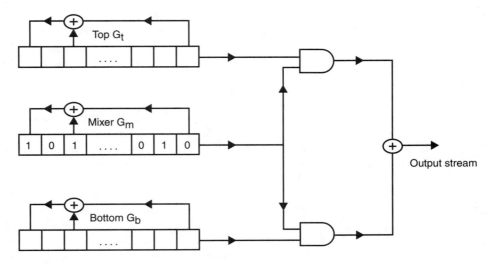

13-20 Geffe generator used for the explanation of the RPK mixer concept.

care of in software by the available computational resources of the wireless device itself. It will not be able to sustain real-time, unpredictable, heavy-duty, bidirectional traffic in streaming mode, like voice, audio, or video.

Leaving aside the land-network infrastructure, where hardware acceleration of IPsec operations will most likely be needed in several occasions, as the IPsec security scheme will be mostly executed in software, both in its current state of evolution as well as in the foreseeable future, with Rijndael AES slowly taking over the Triple-DES position, there is little to discuss about it in this chapter. It will not require any special hardware for the SOC designer who will be putting together a platform on which IPsec will run. Classical RISC CPU cores from ARM,[110] MIPS,[111] ARC,[112] and Tensilica[113] inside an SOC are equally competent in assembly and disassembly of packets as the more mathematically elaborate DSP cores from Texas Instruments,[114] Analog Devices,[115] Infineon,[116] DSP Group,[117] and others. In fact, the DSP cores must use their mathematical computation circuitry to justify their presence and IPsec formulation is not mathematical by itself (although it does call from time to time on some mathematical capabilities). The effort to design special circuitry to be added to a RISC core is mostly not worth the time and cost as one either has the need for such functionality and had better use an existing DSP engine as well, or one does not have that need at all. Again, purists may argue that the ensuing key generation (mostly through modular arithmetic, exponentiation, and so on) and the cryptography engine lend themselves ideally to the DSP core capabilities, a position that is certainly not without some merit.

You should, however, keep in mind two facts:

- The RISC core cannot handle these mathematical functions by itself on heavy-duty real-time streaming bit traffic.

- The associated DSP (when it is available in the SOC) will be sharing its processing cycles with numerous other tasks on the baseband signal processing side, for example, echo cancellation, channel equalization, filtering, and so forth, which need to happen in real-time as well, especially in devices like handsets.

This means that IPsec packet assembly and disassembly can be done by classical RISC computing, but the underlying cryptographic functions for encryption and authentication implemented in software will definitely require a DSP core as well.

The corresponding implementations and the actual inventory of tasks to run will be the ultimate evidence by which to judge as to whether specific products stand up to performance expectations of the users.

A hybrid but challenging solution is the potential use of powerful reconfigurable core CPUs inside the SOC. From one approach, Tensilica's Extensa as an example and from a different approach the Jazz VLIW CPU from Improv Systems[119] offer interesting possibilities for the implementation of cryptographic solutions without incurring the extra design cost and time-to-market to embed a separate core that behaves as a slave to the master CPU inside the SOC. From the designer's point of view, Tensilica's Xtensa processor reconfigurability make a COMSEC chip development much easier by adding custom hardware and (among other things) quasi-automatically generating customized development tools that can be optimized for a specific design. Improv's Jazz VLIW CPU processors are both scalable for straight-forward design in large multiprocessor chip designs without the hassle of embedding a multi-platform real-time operating system kernel. The design tools automatically map and configure the overall application (IPsec in this example) on the underlying processors, thus sharing the computational load and balancing the bandwidth resources.

These hybrid solutions are characterized as interesting because on top of their approach that bodes well for architectural optimization, they also offer the possibility of creating chips that have a smaller gate count, therefore occupying less silicon real estate. The fact that these CPU cores may be synthesized on many different technology libraries from various semiconductor manufacturers also clearly infers that the SOC designer has the ability to play with several variables and optimize the WEASEL choices to decrease the cost of design and manufacturing, therefore the cost of ownership as well.

Kasumi Algorithm

The *European Telecommunications Standards Institute* (ETSI) through its *Security Algorithms Group of Experts* (SAGE) group has adopted Kasumi as the international standard encryption algorithm for Third Generation Mobile Communications Systems, which will be based on W-CDMA (wideband CDMA) technology.

Kasumi (which means *mist* in Japanese) is a variant of the MISTY family of symmetric-key block ciphers developed by Mitsubishi Electric's R&D group. MISTY1 and MISTY2 are two quite similar block ciphers based on 64-bit blocks of data and 128-bit keys. The number of rounds can vary, but must be a multiple of 4 and Mitsubishi recommends 8. The original intention was to design an algorithm that has provable security against linear and differential cryptanalysis attacks, is compact (in low gate count and low-power consumption), and is easily implemented for sufficiently fast performance in both hardware and software.

With MISTY1 for instance implemented in software on a Pentium III (800 MHz) and written in assembly; the code encrypts at a sustained input/output rate of 230 Mbps. Using Mitsubishi's 0.35μ CMOS process a (presumably) pipelined version of the algorithm (meaning 8 cascaded stages in a pipeline) can sustain an 800-Mbps encryption rate, implemented over 50,000 gates. Likewise to show how compact the algorithm is, a minimal hardware version can be implemented in 7,600 gates (of the same CMOS semiconductor technology) and sustain an encryption rate of 72 Mbps. The rather safe assumption is that this difference is due to the rounds of operations executed using the same fundamental hardware in an iterative process. It is also of interest to know that ETSI had specified that 3GPP encryption for W-CDMA should be capable of implementation in hardware with less than 10,000 gates.[122]

MISTY1 and MISTY2 are variations on a theme of a recursive algorithm.[123] It is precisely this recursiveness that allows efficient implementation in either iterative or parallel (to take advantage of the computational quasi-independence of various rounds) hardware or in streamlined and compact software. Starting from the inside and climbing the complexity hierarchy at its heart are two families of substitution tables, S7 and S9. As seen in Figure 13-21, a codebook-like Feistel-cipher configuration of the S-boxes becomes the so-called FI function and a similar (but not identical) butterfly configuration of FIs becomes a more complex function called FO at the next higher layer of complexity. A further Feistel-cipher-like configuration of the FO and FI functions along with a third type called FL function combines the dataflow with parts of scheduled key material and completes the picture at the highest layer of complexity. The interested reader can consult several references and white papers by Mitsubishi.[124]

For SOC applications Mitsubishi has designed 44 IP cores with MISTY1 according to Table 13-8. Given the differences between algorithms, these numbers should provide a direct comparison with what one expects to achieve using Kasumi. To be more precise, Mitsubishi documents that Kasumi, implemented in MEL's 0.18μ high-speed CMOS technology, encrypts at a sustained throughput of 130 Mbps and is implemented in 6,500 gates. In configurable hardware, Mitsubishi has also integrated the same Kasumi algorithm in the Xilinx XC4000 family of FPGAs, in which the hardware reportedly sustains an encryption throughput of 35 Mbps and occupies 230 *configurable logic blocks* (CLB's).[125]

You should also notice that these cores implement the algorithm in ECB mode and the previous analysis of how the ECB mode behaves in an error-prone environment like wireless is equally applicable here.

Kasumi is organized in two modes of operation: Using the so-called f8 function for encryption (see Figure 13-22) and using the so-called f9 function that provides data integrity protection (see Figure 13-23).

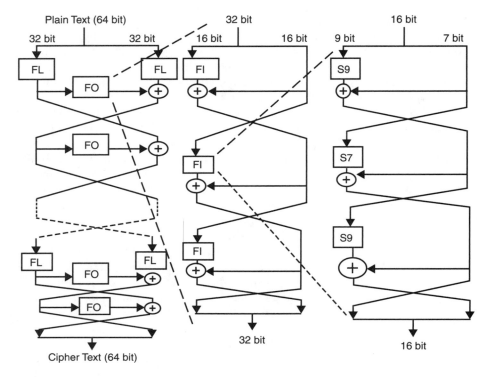

13-21 Structure of MISTY.[118]

Table 13-8 Mitsubishi Electric's MISTY1 IP Core[120]

IP Cores	Mode	Gatecount Using MEL's Middle-Speed 0.18μ Library	Encryption Rate (Throughput) with MEL's Middle-Speed 0.18μ Library	Gatecount Using MEL's High-Speed 0.18μ Library	Encryption Rate (Throughput) with MEL's High-Speed 0.18μ Library	Applications
C10	ECB	6K gates	80 Mbps	12K gates	600 Mbps	IC card, SOC-embedded CPU
101	ECB	10K	240 Mbps	19K	1.8 Gbps	Network devices
401	ECB	31K	1.0 Gbps	42K	2.6 Gbps	Network devices
801	ECB	51K	1. 0Gbps	71K	2.8 Gbps	Advanced networks, such as ATM and so forth

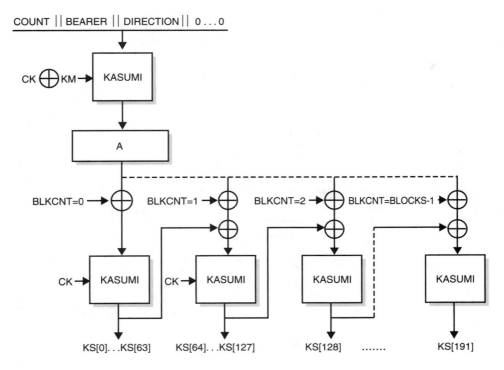

COUNT || BEARER || DIRECTION || 0 . . . 0

13-22 ETSI 3GPP stream cipher based on the F8 function.[121]

In encryption mode, Kasumi is structured as a stream cipher. This is based on an *output-feedback mode* (OFB) configuration, where the block count is added to prevent cycling and an initial extra encryption is added to protect against possible collisions and some chosen plaintext attacks. In integrity mode, Kasumi through the function f9 forms a CBC MAC (cipher block chaining, message authentication code) but with an unusual addition of a second feed-forward loop.

The major differences between MISTY and Kasumi are the number of so-called S7 boxes (2 versus 1 respectively) and the position of the so-called FO and FL functions. The other differences between MISTY and Kasumi are truly minor and the most significant among them is that the key scheduling in Kasumi is less complicated. The details of the Kasumi algorithm can be found at both Mitsubishi's and ETSI's 3GPP Web sites.[127,128] More specifically, the basic Kasumi algorithm is documented in PDF form and the two fundamental F8 and F9 functions are available in the references[129,130] (see Table 13-8).

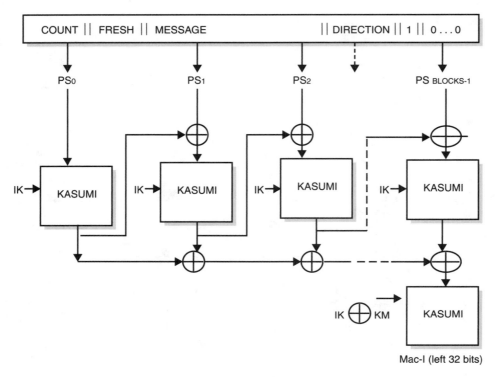

| COUNT ‖ FRESH ‖ MESSAGE | ‖ DIRECTION ‖ 1 ‖ 0 . . . 0 |

13-23 ETSI 3GPP integrity function F9.[126]

Hardware-Efficient Rijndael Implementations and Comparison with Alternative Technologies

As we have seen, the Belgian algorithm Rijndael has been chosen by NIST to become the *Advanced Encryption Standard* (AES) algorithm that is to replace DES and Triple DES as the cryptographic algorithm of choice in numerous applications, in both software and hardware, throughout the world. We do not intend to emphasize here the cryptographic advantages of Rijndael, especially in terms of increased security as opposed, for example, to DES or Triple DES, as there is ample literature available for anyone interested in the subject.[131,132,133,134,135] The basic structure for each round in Rijndael is shown in Figures 13-24 and 13-25.

We remind the reader in brief that Rijndael is a block cipher and that it will operate in one of the modes described at length in earlier sections of this chapter. One will recall that these cryptographic modes offer various levels of security against

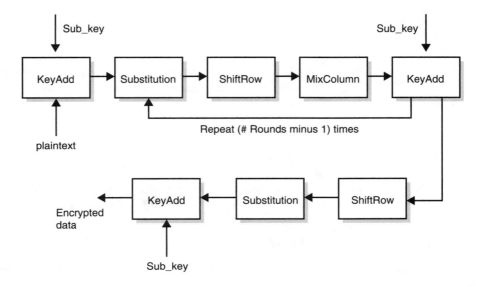

13-24 Basic structure of the Rijndael flow. For N rounds the top loop runs N-1 times and the last round uses the bottom branch.

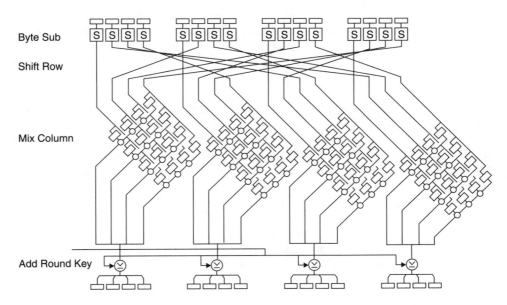

13-25 Overview of one round in Rijndael, showing the byte-long structures and the regularity of the algorithm.[169]

several types of attack with commensurate trade-offs in terms of performance in a transmission context, namely in terms of their ability to

- Preserve self-synchronization.
- Offer easy recovery from bit garbling or clock errors with or without error propagation to other bit positions in the transmitted stream.
- Guarantee the integrity of transmitted traffic.
- Ensure late-entry capabilities for users in a multicast or conference session, and so on.

All of that material is as applicable on the Triple DES as it is in the Rijndael realm. Before exploring this issue clarification is needed as to the underlying context of how power consumption constraints affect the available computational power, and therefore the applications, a system can handle reliably.

Power Consumption versus Performance

As control of power consumption is one of the absolute top priorities for the handset designer, a specialized and dedicated chip is available inside the already tight space of every cellular phone to ensure that the power consumption is regulated in an optimal way. Current cellular phones are equipped using an ARM7 CPU. It is interesting to note that although such a CPU is capable of running at 100 MHz, handset manufacturers usually have it running around 14 MHz and the reason is power consumption. This translates to a significant difference between nominal MIPS of the CPU (or DSP processor) and what is available to the handset designer. There is need for a coprocessor (independent of the main CPU or DSP processor) that can handle the end-to-end streaming communications security aspects along the lines we have painted in this book.

In third generation handsets the situation is likely to be different by a large extent. In that context, CPUs are scheduled to be much more powerful and simultaneously conservative in terms of low-power capabilities. This is the case, for instance, with both TI's OMAP™ platform, where a 200 MHz DSP processor handles the baseband functions next to a main ARM9 CPU inside the same chip, and the Intel 300MHz SA (which will combine the baseband functions in the same chip).[136,137] TI has stated that security will be running on the DSP baseband chip, because the main CPU's bandwidth will be solicited by numerous other applications and therefore cannot be handled reliably except if on the DSP. In both cases, consequently, the need for extra hardware to accommodate security can be strongly debated. In that realm the answer will be embedded software and in that case either a stream cipher approach like Hornet or Kasumi or a block cipher like Rijndael and Triple DES, can be envisioned as viable candidates. When one adds streaming compression capabilities in conjunction with other functions that reposition the whole system in terms of error recovery and other times, then the trade-off analysis we have had so far is more than appropriate.

Considering wireless LAN devices, the need for special coprocessors to run security in real-time is more than needed. Even if one achieves 11 Mbps throughput (not an easy thing to do) in a wireless LAN context, at our company we have estimated that slightly more than 500 MIPS are needed to sustain the I/O rates, the equivalent of more than 50 percent of an Intel 1 GHz processor. Few (if any) wireless devices will be equipped with such a processor.

If PDAs and their successors for wireless LAN access (including telephony based on voice-over-IP over wireless LAN) are considered, it is evident that the average PDA processor uses a 33 MHz CPU (such as Palm) and even in Windows-CE environments where a 160 MHz CPU is used (such as Cassiopeia) the fundamental application barely runs satisfactorily. How could we envision streaming security without an appropriate coprocessor onto which the COMSEC function is offloaded?

Further discussion about optimal implementations of the Rijndael algorithm and reflections on the state-of-the-art in performance and efficiency follow.

Software Implementations of Rijndael in an SOC

Typically for software run in equipment with less than top-of-the-line computational resources available, one would expect something similar to what has been reported, namely that Rijndael implemented on a Pentium 2000 Pro yields a throughput of around 100 Mbps.[138] This would be fine for some applications, but certainly not for high-speed routers or gateways in wireless applications where volumes of traffic comes in from numerous sources at the same time and where cryptographic contexts must be managed in real time. On the other side the state-of-the-art in performance for software-based implementations is Gladman's work.[139] On a 933 MHz Pentium III his 128-bit implementation achieves 325 Mbps throughput, his 192-bit implementation handles 275 Mbps, and his 256-bit implementation churns data at 236 Mbps.

One could argue that an Intel Pentium is certainly not a CPU one would expect to see in a wireless device, but it gives an indication of the computational horsepower required to sustain the stream of 100 Mbps speed and yet allow the code to fully process a block of 128 bits at a time, arriving for processing at that speed. It should also be clear that in a full-duplex mode, when the system encrypts *and* decrypts simultaneously in real time, you must divide this performance by 2, as there will be software code that handles each direction of the traffic. This certainly implies division of speed by 2, while potentially doubling the memory footprint, although one can contend that with appropriate software engineering this latter need for a combined program and data memory management can be significantly reduced by 40 to 50 percent.

Compiled in Table 13-9 are typical results obtained by the authors in the course of our their work while evaluating specific Rijndael implementations on various platforms. This table more specifically shows results obtained from embedded software running on a Texas Instruments C55x DSP simulator.

To avoid misperceptions and to clarify, although the physical device (such as a handset) may be encrypting and decrypting simultaneously as far as the user is con-

**Table 13-9 Rijndael Statistics Implemented in SW on a
TI C55x DSP Simulator (100-MHz Clock Case Only)**

Mode	Key Size (Bits)	Block Size (Bits)	Cycle Count	Instruction Memory Size (Bytes)	Data Memory Size (Bytes)	Execution Time in MMsec	Through-Put in Bits/sec
Encryption	128	128	1,803	—	—	0.01803	—
Decryption	128	128	1,793	—	—	0.01793	—
Encr. Key generation	128	128	1,529	—	—	0.01529	—
Decr. Key Generation	128	128	3,185	—	—	0.03185	—
Encryption + Decryption	128	128	3,596	—	—	0.03596	—
TOTAL in duplex mode	128	128	8,310	3,379	9,024	0.0831	1,540,313

cerned, this is *not* the case under the proverbial hood of this type of hardware (as opposed to the hardware of high-end switching devices as we will soon see). The encryption platform in this example was a Pentium. In a wireless handheld device (if the encryption and decryption algorithms are implemented in software) it would most likely be an ARM- or MIPS-based SOC chip, or a DSP baseband chip. These chips usually share the data bus in I/O mode; at some point in time the data bus behaves as an input and at some other moments it behaves as an output. Switching between these two modes happens millions of times per second, so the user clearly lives and operates at a different time plane altogether, thinking that the handset is encrypting and decrypting simultaneously when it clearly is not. The handheld device in fact switches its RF section between transmitting and receiving modes too fast and frequently per second for the user to perceive any annoying effect.

The reason this distinction is important here is that in a wireless handheld device performance must be carefully rated. Instruction memory will contain the code for both encryption and decryption, but the supervising CPU will only activate one part of the code at a time. Buffered plaintext data is read in from memory and encrypted. It is then stored in an appropriate output buffer or sent to memory, before the chip either continues with the encryption of further plaintext or switches into decryption mode, in which case it will read data in from a separate buffer and activate the decryption part of the program stored in the instruction memory. The performance numbers then (in this case), for throughput, pertain to encryption *only* or decryption *only*.

This is different from the case of a high-end device, such as a switch, where data enters in one port and simultaneously exits from another port, with ports handled by different data buses. In this latter case, assuming software implementation of the algorithms, the code must be reentrant, so that the same program can be accessed by different contexts and a CPU encrypting and decrypting at the same time. These performance constraints are much tighter to meet, because within one I/O clock cycle when 32 bits (or soon 64 bits) of traffic are coming in (assuming 32- or 64-bit wide parallel buses) the processing CPU must execute the encryption, or key generation cycle and switch context in time to handle for instance appropriate decryption on received data. This cascade of logical events executed in sequence is the main reason why dividing the quoted performance of the encrypting algorithms by 2 (or 4 or more in some cases) is appropriate depending on the context within which they are implemented.

To facilitate the use of the results shown in Table 13-9, some comments are needed:

- The first two rows show the numbers when the DSP operates in either encrypting or decrypting mode.
- There is but a slight difference in performance between the two. It is enough though to call one's attention to the ever-present need for appropriate buffering in real-time applications of streaming content (which in the case of software implementations can be almost taken for granted).
- The 3rd and 4th rows list the statistics involved in the generation of the keys. Notice that the generation of the decryption keys takes twice the time needed for the equivalent key generation at encryption time.
- The 5th row shows what computational power is needed so that the DSP will work in duplex mode (it encrypts and it then decrypts and so on). This is a real systems measure of ongoing lung capacity that the designer must apply by weighing this performance against I/O requirements of the application at hand (such as voice telephony over a wireless handset) and ultimately decide if this specific DSP can handle streaming encryption/decryption in real time along with other applications this same DSP will be called upon to run as well. The 5th row is the sum of the first two rows.
- The 6th row is an indication of performance in real life. It is the sum of what is needed to encrypt/decrypt (row 5) and what it takes to generate keys for encryption and decryption. It is therefore the sum of rows 3, 4, and 5. One can argue successfully that in most applications, the key scheduling will only execute once at the beginning of the session hence the rows 3 and 4 do not need to be added on an ongoing basis. This argument is correct except in cases where the application at hand requires dynamic modification of the session encryption/decryption key. This is for instance the case in switching equipment where blocks of traffic between users, from different sessions, with different cryptographic contexts must be handled sequentially.
- The empty cells (denoted by a bar "—") correspond to cases wherein disclosure of component numbers is almost superfluous, as we opted to do so for an integrated environment only. One can, however, easily calculate what is entailed to fill in those positions, based on the cycle count and the clock frequency of the DSP processor.
- Latency times are calculated based on a 100 MHz clock and the assumption that one instruction will be executed per cycle, as Rijndael does not make use of *multiply-and-accumulate* (MAC) instructions and hence will not use the extra multiplier hardware this DSP processor provides.

The numbers only show Rijndael as an stand-alone encryption algorithm and no other parts usually needed in a self-sustained COMSEC solution, like session key generation and exchange, hashing, digital signatures generation and verification, and so forth.

Comparing Rijndael with HORNET™ and DES/3DES in Embedded SW

As a comparison, under the identical conditions, the SHA-1-based HORNET™ approach implemented in embedded software running in this same TI DSP processor clocked at 100 MHz requires 12,573 bytes of instruction memory and 4,778 bytes of data memory. For 256 bits of input (equivalent to two Rijndael blocks) 9,973 cycles are required to fully process the input, hence although Hornet was not designed for software efficiency but for fast and inexpensive hardware-assisted performance (as its SOC implementation scales well into 16 Gbps and beyond of sustained throughput), it exhibits similar throughput and latency to Rijndael when implemented in lower-end DSP embedded software and it is slightly more demanding in memory footprint, as seen previously in Table 13-9.

With single DES running on this same TI DSP C55x based on the Texas Instruments simulator, again for the case of 256 bits input, one finds that the size of the instruction memory is typically 1,801 bytes and for the data memory 21,848 bytes. About 3,100 cycles for encryption and the same number of cycles are needed for decryption of the incoming 256-bit traffic example. The reader is reminded that DES was designed with hardware implementations in mind. Key initialization takes place in 97,024 clock cycles and the key setup takes 862 cycles. One cycle is 10 ns for this example.

In the case of 2-key *encrypt-decrypt-encrypt* (EDE) Triple DES, the size of the instruction memory is again 1,801 bytes and the data memory required is 21,848 bytes. About 9,455 cycles are needed for encryption and the same number for decryption of the incoming 256-bit traffic example. There is clearly a linear behavior as compared to single-key DES. Key initialization in Triple DES takes place in 194,048 clock cycles and the key setup takes 1,726 cycles. One cycle is again 10 ns for this example.

In both cases, throughput is an application-specific calculation, as the cryptographic key can be the same or change over time, or with every block of traffic; hence set up times vary and therefore a generic throughput number cannot be calculated for every DES or Triple DES use of this DSP chip. However, one can add the corresponding time components judiciously and calculate quite reliably what it takes to calculate the required performance.

One could rightfully ask in such a case, what are the advantages of using Hornet versus another more known block cipher like Rijndael or Triple DES? The answer is that if the specific algorithm choice is not mandated by the application, there are three main reasons to do so:

- The algorithm vs. protocol analysis, shown earlier in this chapter, in terms of error recovery remains intact and HORNET™ with its multiple cryptographic modes retains its superior error handling behavior and performance in (noisy environments such as wireless and RF, or in unreliable streaming transmission media (such as VoIP using UDP and so on).

- In terms of economies of implementation a very important argument working for Hornet is that since a robust hashing function is one way or the other needed for the generation and verification of digital signatures in next generation COMSEC chips, and since SHA is already an integral part of the most important digital signature algorithms and standards, one might as well use it for encryption as well as part of a powerful cryptographic engine. Implementing Triple DES or even Rijndael does not alleviate the need for SHA to be present in hardware or software inside the SOC design.
- When comparing platform cost, a DSP processor chip is known to cost several tens of dollars (if not more than a hundred in some cases) while a HORNET™ chip costs less than one-fifth (and sometimes even less than one-tenth) of the DSP's cost.

Going back to the Rijndael-on-a-DSP analysis, the conclusion to be drawn from this small example is that only about 4 percent of the processing capability of such a (relatively moderate-speed) DSP processor goes onto encryption and decryption using Rijndael. To the extent that the application's I/O rate allows handling of bidirectional traffic without choking, this would seem to allow enough computational horsepower to do several other tasks. If, however, the remaining tasks require an aggregate computational power in excess of what is available with this processor, then the encryption will obviously suffer. The baseband processor inside a wireless handset is tasked with an impressive multitude of signaling, encoding and signal-processing tasks that were covered in the previous chapter, implementation of which may hamper the other COMSEC functions needed in an end-to-end security scheme and some of which were generically enumerated in the previous paragraph. The handset must still function as a handset in a network infrastructure, when a session key is generated, or when a digital signature is being verified. Heavy cryptographic calculations, even if rarely used during a communications session, cannot hamper the other chores the baseband chip is expected to run faithfully and ceaselessly. In the newer handsets, there will be voice recognition, audio/video compression, and other features. The application itself will influence to a large extent what can and what cannot be done. One would then say that the proverbial jury is therefore still out as to what the optimal solution and platform is on most occasions when end-to-end security is contemplated.

Implementation of Rijndael on Configurable Hardware

Altera announced in May 2001 that they offer IP cores for embedding into customer-designed *system-on-a-chip* (SOC's) implemented in two versions.[140] The high-speed one is a parallel 128-bit wide bus unit, while the low-speed version is based on a 16-bit wide multi-cycle access bus for input/output. A high-speed implementation on Altera's APEX 20K100E FPGA device runs over 1.1 Gbps and the manufacturer says that it sells for $424 per piece in high-volume. A low-speed implementation on Altera's APEX 20K30E device encrypts/decrypts at 40 Mbps and is expected to sell at around $13 per chip in high-volume. The manufacturer has formally stated that they obviously try to compete with dedicated *application-specific standard product* (ASSP) chips that are expected to cost 70 to 80 percent more from other sources scheduled to be released by the end of 2001.[141]

McLoone and McCanny[142] recently reported a single-chip Rijndael implementation on a Xilinx Virtex-E FPGA. The design is a parameterized core (meaning that it can handle keys and data blocks of 128, 192 and 256 bits in length) and it handles a throughput of 7 Gbps when used with 128 bit keys, of 5.8 Gbps when confronted with 192 bit keys, and of 5.1 Gbps when the keys are 256 bits long. The 128-bit case is the *de facto* standard and it is interesting to note that this performance is 3.5 times faster than anything else designed in configurable hardware (excluding the fact that all other known FPGA implementations require more than one chip on which to map the pipelined algorithm) and 21 times faster than the best known software implementation.[143] In the same reference (for the reader who may be in a rush and is not ready to study the superb presentations of Rijndael's internals, one will find an overview of the mathematical operations needed to encrypt and decrypt traffic with Rijndael.[144,145,146]

Rijndael has 10, 12, and 14 rounds depending on the size of the key (128, 192, and 256 bits respectively). A pipelined design is obviously one approach, but one can also look at the other side of the spectrum for an iterative one, based on the underlying application requirements. This is something that the NSA team of Weeks, Bean, Rozylowicz, and Ficke had documented very well during the AES evaluation stage for the NIST contest, although to be fair to all finalist algorithms and just provide cryptographic assistance to NSIT, the NSA opted to not use truly cutting-edge silicon technology libraries to optimize these designs.[147]

The mode implemented in McLoone is ECB (whose design in trade-offs we have exposed earlier), which is easy to pipeline and is a mode that is often used although less secure than others. Several architectures have been contemplated.[148,149] The McLoone-McCanny design implements a fully pipelined approach with registers between the replicated hardware for the individual rounds to better control the data flow. In pipelined Rijndael designs memory is by far the biggest concern and therefore it is not surprising that it is the main consideration of this design as well.

The Rijndael s-box is implemented as a *look-up table* (LUT) or ROM.[150] This is less expensive than implementing the required multiplicative inverse operation and affine transformation in custom hardware. State bytes are operated on individually and each Rijndael round requires sixteen 8-bit to 8-bit LUT's. Clever utilization of BRAM cells allows the custom configuration of RAM at initialization time as either ROM or LUT. The ShiftRow transformation is hardwired as no decision logic is involved and the MixRow transformation is implemented as a matrix multiplication calculated by XORing the results of the multiplications in $GF(2^8)$ in accordance with equations shown in Máire McLoone.[151]

For key generation, when utilizing a 128-bit key, 40 words are created during the key expansion phase and every fourth word is passed through the s-box with each byte in the word being transformed. Therefore, 40 8-bit to 8-bit LUTs are required.

During decryption the inverse of the ByteSub transformation is also implemented as a LUT, albeit with a different content from the LUT used for encryption. This takes space if one implements a duplex design that handles bidirectional traffic. With a clever and efficient utilization of hardware resources in the FPGA the designers used BRAM cells as ROM, when the design is set to encrypt, with data read from a ROM containing the values required for encryption, and when the design is set to decrypt, the BRAMs are initialized with data read from a ROM containing the values required for decryption. A simple switch on a small two-way multiplexer activates the BRAM bank in the appropriate mode (encryption/decryption). The Inverse ShiftRow operation is also hardwired and the Inverse MixColumn operation is implemented by XORing results and multiplications in $GF(2^8)$ and multiplex-selecting again the values required for encryption and decryption.

The initialization process takes 256 cycles (as 256 values need to be read from ROM) for either encryption or decryption. With a system clock of 25.3MHz this means 10 ms is needed for initialization in this design. During encryption (assuming the same key is used during the whole communications session) keys are produced, as each round requires them. The encryption therefore takes 10 clock cycles corresponding to the 10 rounds needed when operating with a 128-bit key. During decryption however, the design requires 20 clock cycles to start, that is, 10 clock cycles for the required round keys to be constructed and a further 10 that correspond to the 10 rounds.

Looking at comparable FPGA implementations the McLoone-McCanny design achieves optimizing the best current efficiency when using S-boxes, as measured in Mbps/sec per *configurable logic block* (CLB) slice.[152,153,154,155,156] This is summarized in Table 13-10.

The numbers only show Rijndael as an standalone encryption algorithm without any of the other parts that are usually needed in a self-sustained COMSEC solution, like session key generation and exchange, hashing, digital signatures generation and verification, and so forth. This means that if we factor these ancillary security activities (as they occur usually only once per communications session) into a normalized

Table 13-10 Specifications of 128-Bit Key Rijndael Encryption Implementations[157]

	Type	FPGA Device	Area (GLB Slices)	Throughput Mbps	Throughput/ Area (Mbps)
Gaj *et al.*	Iterative looping	XCV1000	2,902	331.5	0.11
Dandalis *et al.*	Iterative looping	XCV1000	5,673	353	0.06
Elbirt *et al.*	Partially pipelined	XCV1000	9,004	1,940	0.22
McLoone-McCanny	Fully pipelined	XCV812E	2,222	6,956	3.1

latency time value by spreading their impact to the whole session (from a time penalty point of view), we can come up with an average estimate for this specific DSP processor saying safely that 0.04 ms is the latency time for real-time encryption/decryption in such an implementation. With typical CDMA telephony nowadays digitizing voice at 64 Kbps in a full duplex mode, the aggregate quantity of bi-directional data the DSP will see is 128 Kbps, or 1,000 blocks of traffic per second of combined input and output.

When confronted with low-baud data rates like voice telephony, the conclusion one can draw from this small example is that only about 2 to 4 percent of the processing capability of such a (relatively low-speed) DSP processor goes onto encryption and decryption using Rijndael. To the extent that the application's I/O rate allows handling of bidirectional traffic without choking, this apparently allows more than enough horsepower to do several other tasks.

If however, the remaining tasks require an aggregate computational capability in excess of what is available with the DSP processor in this example and similar cases, or if the incoming data is arriving at a much higher transmission speed (as is the case with third-generation handsets embedding, for example, MPEG4 video decompression and MP3 audio processing and working at multiple Mbps broadband speeds) then the encryption will obviously suffer, because a very significant amount of processing bandwidth will have to be assigned to these other responsibilities. One will find by working out the numbers that a predominant percentage of the computational power of the baseband chip will be sacrificed by encryption, negating other useful functionality.

Another interesting work on configurable hardware is a paper presented in May 2001 by Fischer and Drutarovský [158] wherein they also opted for a T-box implementation (proposed by Daemen and Rijmen originally) as opposed to the more common S-box work. Their results in throughput exceed those as their economic S-box version achieves a sustained encryption or decryption throughput of 212 Mbps, while their T-box economic design attains 115 Mbps. The corresponding numbers in the high-performance designs they presented are respectively 750 Mbps for their T-box version and 612 Mbps for the S-box version. The beauty of their work centers around the fact that their T-box is implemented in both Altera FPD devices of the 0.18μ APEX 20K400E family for high performance and ACEX 1K50E for low cost. Their S-box implementation is comparable to results obtained by others on Xilinx Virtex FPGA's. This work is a clear indication that clever and truly creative architecture implementation of the algorithm at hand can take advantage of the available hardware resources in an optimal way.[159,160,161]

As mentioned earlier in the chapter, the FPGA performance, as far as wireless is concerned, is only relevant to prototype development and infrastructure equipment (tower hardware for instance) where only the air part of the channel is secured (something that the end-to-end security scheme completely overturns). Such devices are not to be seen in consumer-grade portable devices like wireless handsets and PDAs. This brings us to the latter part of this section, namely custom VLSI ASIC hardware as the only other alternative to DSP-embedded software-based inexpensive implementations of Rijndael for wireless handheld or transportable devices.

As a measure of comparison with the DES world, we mention here the work by Trimberger *et al.* where in 4216 LUT's Single and Triple DES have been realized on Xilinx FPGAs.[162] On the XCV300-6 device using a 16-stage pipeline (for each DES round), a throughput of 6.4 Gbps is attained and on a 48-stage pipeline (3 DES runs times 16 rounds each) the throughput is 10.1 Gbps. On the XCV300E-8 device, the corresponding numbers are 8.4 Gbps and 12.0 Gbps respectively.

Full-Custom VLSI Hardware Implementations

The current state-of-the-art for custom-hardware implementation of Rijndael, as reflected in research work presented at conferences, is of interest.

Henry Kuo and UCLA's Prof. Ingrid Verbauwhede have designed a fast ASIC that implements Rijndael in 173,000 gates using a 0.18μ CMOS process and with a clocking rate of 100 MHz.[163] The throughput of the encryptor/decryptor is 1.82 Gbps. This specific design was the result of a research project in architecture optimization and in its CHES-2001 conference-presented version it does not implement a decryptor, as it was deemed that the silicon real estate penalty to be incurred was not acceptable. In real life, of course, one needs to encrypt and decrypt.

The Kuo-Verbauwhede Rijndael ASIC is designed around an encryptor module and a key scheduler (besides controllers for the input, output, and overall chip management). The encryptor module gatecount is 99,300 covering 1.39 mm², or 35 percent of the die. The chip area is about 3.96 mm². The paper analyzes well the trade-off reconciliation in critical paths between the two modules and identifies some areas for further improvement in the design.

Kuo and Verbauwhede generated subkeys on-the-fly. There are two fundamental ways for the generation of the round keys for encryption. The designer either generates all subkeys up front and stores them in a buffer from where they will be used during the encryption process, or on-the-fly and in parallel with the encryption process. The design approach chosen was the latter; hence the need for the two modules mentioned in the previous paragraph. If the subkeys had been generated in advance, the buffer memory requirements would have been prohibitively large for the requirements of this chip to minimize silicon real estate and cost, while maximizing throughput performance.

The design is heavily dependent on three types of *look-up tables* (LUTs):

- One with 256 entries (hence addressable by 8 bits) of 8 bits of content each for the implementation of the s-boxes with 48 copies of the table in the design, 32 in the encryption module and 16 in the key scheduling module. Using combinational logic the table is implemented with 2,200 gates in 51,000 μm². The access time is only 1.89 ns.
- The second table is used for the decision of the shift amount in the shift row module. The table has 24 entries and four copies of it are implemented in 55 gates using an area of 1,000 μm².

- The third type of table has 30 entries used to generate the round constant in the key-scheduling module. It is only accessed once in each round, so there is only one copy of the table, with 70 gates occupying 1,300 μm^2.

The datapath is 256 bits wide, precisely to allow parametric definition of the key size and block size, as one may recall that in Rijndael each of these entities can be 128, 192, or 256 bits long. This obviously allows for nine possibilities. The interested reader will find a description of the interesting series of architectural choices and trade-offs for the efficient handling of the various operations both in the encryption module and in the key scheduler.[164] An analysis of the critical paths in both modules in the same paper is equally informative as it shows clearly the steps one must take to improve the performance of an already quite optimized design.

If one wanted to embed decryption capability in the same chip, this could require an extra datapath (beyond the current two for encryption and key scheduling). It would imply more specifically that one either generate the entire set of sub-round keys up front, or a separate datapath implementing the inverse process of key scheduling. The former is estimated to require an additional 3,584-register storage, while the latter requires extra circuitry and more routing. Both would obviously require a much larger area.

Comparing this with so-called three-in-one iterative design documented in the NSA work, we see that NSA could accomplish this with a 1,029,054 transistor design (roughly 207,500 CMOS gates equivalent) sustaining a throughput of up to 447.55 Mbps for a key size of 128 bits, a throughput of up to 372,96 Mbps for a key of 192 bits size, and a throughput of up to 319.68 Mbps for a key of 256 bits.[165] The NSA design can also decrypt. This accounts for the approximately 35,000-gate count difference. One should also keep in mind that NSA used an old 0.5μm technology when synthesizing these designs, as opposed to the 0.18μm technology Kuo and Verbauwhede used. Also, to put things into perspective, a pipelined three-in-one design per NSA's estimates of Rijndael needs 7,130,697 transistors (roughly 1,782,675 gates) and can sustain an I/O of 5.33778 Gbps independent of block and/or key size.[166] The aforementioned NSA work also shows nicely the time quantification of computational asymmetricity in the Rijndael encryption and decryption modules and more specifically between the key setup times needed for encryption and decryption. In their implementation these two key-setup time parameters turn out to be 0 and 288.8 ns respectively for the iterative design, with 0 and 233.99 ns respectively for their pipelined design.

To complete the picture, one should also look at commercially available Rijndael cores.[167] ASIC International, for instance, has implemented a 128-bit key 128-bit block architecture in 28,000 gates, and clocked at 133 MHz can sustain a throughput of 1.5 Gbps by processing (11 rounds) 12.8 bits in each clock cycle.

To put things into perspective we will compare these custom-hardware achievements with some representative ones from the DES and Triple DES realms, as phasing out or replacing DES in many instances will inevitably take years. For this reason although the subject is certainly not as fashionable and trendy as Rijndael, covering it here is not completely inappropriate.

Leitold *et al.* reported the design of a 155 Mbps network encryptor clearly for real-time handling of ATM (asynchronous transfer mode) traffic cells.[168] Their chip for obvious reasons doubles the presence of encryption modules, for upstream and downstream handling. The DES controller can be switched into either single or Triple DES mode. As Triple DES (using two keys) encrypts with one key A, decrypts with another key B and reencrypts with the first key A, the encryption modules needed to be able to both encrypt and decrypt. A nice analysis is offered in their paper as to why the ideal mode of configuration for pipelined hardware is ECB and not CBC, because it affects the parallelism of the implementation. In the CBC mode of operation, the result of the previous encryption is required to process the current block. Hence one cannot partition computational tasks onto different units. More encryption modules can be used in parallel only in the ECB mode, which is less secure as discussed elsewhere.

Implemented in an old semiconductor technology by 0.6µ CMOS process from AMS International, the chip is implemented in 120,000 transistors operating at a clock of 250 MHz. Each of the two encryption modules comprises 32,000 transistors. The balance of the circuitry is the controller and CAM/RAM. The latter is a content-addressable memory, where the cryptographic context for each ATM cell (5 bytes of header information and 48 bytes of payload) is loaded. Every virtual connection in the ATM network is characterized by a 24-bit VCI (virtual connection identifier) address used in the encryptor chip to address the CAM/RAM positions. Each time a cell is processed, encryption parameters, like types of algorithm, mode, session keys, and initialization vectors, are retrieved from CAM/RAM.

In terms of performance, a Single-DES operation takes 42 clock cycles to load plaintext and encrypt.[170] In Triple-DES configuration, it takes 12 cycles for the loading of the plaintext and 108 cycles for encryption. The chip was designed using standard cells where possible and custom logic methodology based on the high-speed TSPL[171] technique (True Single-Phase Logic). This combines dynamic logic functionality with storage behavior and hence offers low transistor-count. On top of that it only uses a single clock and this simplifies generation and distribution of clocking signals.

Assuming a four-transistor mapping onto a CMOS gate, their Single DES module is implemented in 8,000 gates. Full-duplex operation calls for two of these, but again we offer some metrics only for comparison of alternative decisions and associated trade-offs. Of course, the discussion so far must have convinced the reader that to compare algorithms, one cannot just look at the encryption engine itself but should also take into consideration the ancillary logic needed for the generation of the cryptographic context.

Another indicative work for an ASIC implementation is the work by the Sandia National Labs team of Wilcox *et al.*, whose design is a fully pipelined 16-stage approach operating at 6.7 Gbps and simulated at 9.28 Gbps.[172] The chip was fabricated using a 0.6µ CMOS process and the die size is square with an 11.1 mm side. It contains 319 total pins (251 signals and 68 power/ground pins). It was designed to run at 105 MHz and is one of the rarest known nonclassified encryptor chips where the device may encrypt data with one key on one clock cycle, decrypt new input data with a different key on the very net clock cycle, potentially bypass the algorithm (pass the data unencrypted) on the following clock if required, then encrypt data with yet another independent key on the fourth clock cycle. It is also interesting to note that by that time, Sandia had already done their homework on porting the design to a (GaAs) gallium arsenide technology and potentially combined/cascaded six chips for Triple DES operation at 160-Gbps speeds of broadband network backbones. This is hardly a solution for wireless or low-power designs, however. It is mentioned here to round off the view of the state-of-the-art.

Last but not least, to conclude this section of hardware optimizations, we will remind the reader that we have covered elsewhere in this chapter the

- Gatecount for a typical SHA implementation in hardware
- Instruction memory and data requirements for an embedded SHA implementation in software running inside an SOC design

Therefore one can easily compare what it takes to implement Rijndael as opposed to implementing Hornet in custom silicon.

Authentication in Third-Generation Handsets

As this book is going to press, a few final notes are in place to document the latest status of authentication in the 3GPP handsets as of October 2001, and to steer the interested reader towards some pertinent links for further study about the subject.

Following the GSM evolution example, 3GPP designed a security scheme where not every carrier has to use the same *Authentication and Key-exchange Algorithm* (AKA). Under this methodology, instead of coming up with an imposed standard, 3GPP publishes a recommendation of an example algorithm, for those carriers who are not able to or do not want to design their own algorithms. The suggested algorithm is known as MILENAGE. It was originally introduced at the 16th meeting of the SA3 in December 2000, which is the *Technical Specification Group* (TSG) responsible for security[173] (in other words, that working group of the ETSI organization that produces security-specific documents). It was made official in March 2001 and is based on Rijndael, several aspects of implementation of which have been covered rather substantially in this book. ETSI's expert group (SAGE) has already released an evaluation of MILENAGE.[174]

It should be made clear that although the carriers have the choice of authentication algorithms, the air interface encryption and integrity algorithms must be the same for every carrier in the 3GPP realm, as the users must be able to roam into other carriers' territories without losing their ability to communicate with base stations there.

Conclusions

In this chapter we reviewed the definition of optimization and created a set of criteria and yardsticks, by showing how reshuffling parameters and coping with alternative approaches allow the designer of an integrated-circuit that implements communications security to come up with an ideal design, which satisfies requirements and technical or financial constraints. We have talked about *field programmable gate arrays* (FPGAs) and *application-specific integrated circuit* (ASIC) approaches to the trends towards the smaller, the more integrated, the faster, and the less inexpensive. These are the trends that seem to be driving wireless communications forward to an explosive growth making communications capabilities truly ubiquitous. We reviewed techniques of integrating block ciphers and stream ciphers in silicon as well as ancillary cryptographic modules like key generation engines, authentication engines and random bit generators. The reader has seen how the various pertinent COMSEC techniques discussed in depth in other chapters are implemented inside a silicon chip and therefore must have acquired both a sensitivity to the dangers associated with several of the available solutions and a degree of awareness of the dilemmas and trade-offs confronting the communications security microchip designer.

Endnotes

[1]Groe, John B., and Lawrence E. Larson, *CDMA Mobile Radio Design*, Artech House, 2000.

[2]Nichols, Randall K., *ICSA Guide to Cryptography*, McGraw-Hill, 1999.

[3]Schneier, Bruce, *Applied Cryptography: Protocols, Algorithms & Source Code, 2nd edition*, New York: John Wiley & Sons, 1995.

[4]Wilcox, D. Craig, Lyndon G. Pierson, Perry J. Robertson, Edward L. Witzke, and Karl Gass, "A DES ASIC Suitable for Network Encryption at 10Gbps and Beyond." *Cryptographic Hardware and Embedded Systems Int'l Workshop Proceeding, Lecture Notes in Computer Science, Vol. 1717*, pp. 37–48, Springer-Verlag, 1999.

[5]http://home.ecn.ab.ca/~jsavard/crypto/.

[6]http://www.esat.kuleuven.ac.be/~rijmen/rijndael/.

[7]Wilcox, D. Craig, Op. cit.

[8]Gaj, Kris, and Pawel Chodowiec, "Comparison of the hardware performance of the AES candidates using reconfigurable hardware." Paper presented at the 3rd AES Conference and available from the NIST Web site as http://csrc.nist.gov/encryption/aes/round2/conf3/papers/22-kgaj.pdf.

[9]Wolf, Wayne, *Modern VLSI Design, 2nd edition*, Prentice-Hall, 1998.

[10] Smith, Michael J. S., *Application-Specific Integrated Circuits*, Addison-Wesley, 1997.

[11]http://www.altera.com.

[12]http://www.xilinx.com.

[13]Ibid.

[14]Ibid.

[15]Ibid.

[16]Ibid.

[17]Weste, Neil H. E., and Kamra Eshragian, *Principles of CMOS VLSI Design—Second Edition,* Addison-Wesley, 1993.

[18]Kang, Sung-Mo, and Yusef Leblebici, *CMOS Digital Integrated Circuits—Analysis and Design,* 2nd Ed., WCB McGraw-Hill, 1999.

[19]Rabaey, Jan M., *Digital Integrated Circuits—A Design Perspective,* Prentice-Hall, 1996.

[20]Wolf, Wayne, *Modern VLSI Design,* 2nd Ed., Op. cit.

[21]Smith, Michael J. S. Smith, *Application-Specific Integrated Circuits,* Op. cit.

[22]http://csrc.nist.gov/encryption/aes/round2/conf3/aes3papers.html.

[23]Gaj, Kris, and Pawel Chodowiec, Op. cit.

[24]Blum, L., M. Blum, and M. Shub, "A Simple Unpredictable Pseudo-Random Number Generator," *SIAM J. Computing,* 15(2): pp. 364–383, May 1986.

[25]Yao, A., Theory and Applications of Trapdoor Functions, IEEE FOCS, 1982.

[26]Schneier, Bruce, Op. cit.

[27]Howgrave-Graham, Nick, Joan Dyer, and Rosario Gennaro, "Pseudo-Random Number Generation on the IBM 4758 Secure Crypto Coprocessor." *CHES 2001, International Workshop on Cryptographic Hardware and Embedded Systems, Proceedings,* pp. 97–106.

[28]Gaj, Kris, and Pawel Chodowiec, "Comparison of the hardware performance of the AES candidates using reconfigurable hardware, Op. cit.

[29]Ibid.

[30]Ibid.

[31]Ibid.

[32]Ibid.

[33]Ibid.

[34]Ibid.

[35]Ibid.

[36]Weste, Neil H. E., and Kamra Eshragian, *Principles of CMOS VLSI Design—Second Edition,* Op. cit.

[37]Kang, Sung-Mo, and Yusuf Leblebici, *CMOS Digital Integrated Circuits—Analysis and Design,* 2nd Ed., Op. cit.

[38]Rabaey, Jan M., *Digital Integrated Circuits—A Design Perspective,* Op. cit., and Wolf, Wayne, *Modern VLSI Design,* 2nd Ed., Op. cit.

[39]Smith, Michael J.S., *Application-Specific Integrated Circuits,* Op. cit.

[40]Shannon, Claude E., "A Mathematical theory of Communication." *The Bell System technical Journal,* Vol. 27, pp. 379–423, July 1948.

[41]Bagini, Vittorio, Marco Bucci, "A Design of Reliable True Random Number Generator for Cryptographic Applications." *Cryptographic Hardware and Embedded Systems Int'l Workshop Proceeding, Lecture Notes in Computer Science,* Vol. 1717, pp. 204–218, Springer-Verlag, 1999.

[42]Ibid.

[43]Ibid.

[44]Ibid.

[45] Maher, David P., Robert J. Rance, "Random Number Generators Founded on Signal and Information Theory." *Cryptographic Hardware and Embedded Systems Int'l Workshop Proceeding, Lecture Notes in Computer Science,* Vol. 1717, pp. 219–230, Springer-Verlag, 1999.

[46]Ibid.

[47]Ibid.

[48]Jun, Benjamin, and Paul Kocher, "The Intel® Random Number Generator." *Cryptography Research, Inc.* White Paper prepared for Intel Corporation, April 22, 1999, available for download at: http://www.cryptography.com/intelIRNG.pdf.

[49]Weste, Neil H. E., and Kamra Eshragian, *Principles of CMOS VLSI Design—Second Edition,* Op. cit.

[50]Jun, Benjamin, and Paul Kocher, Op. cit.

[51]Velichko, S., "Random-number Generator Prefers Imperfect Clocks." *EDN Access,* 1996.

[52]Hoffman, Eric, *Random Number Geneator,* 1996, U.S. Patent 5,706,208.

[53]Nichols, Randall K., *ICSA Guide to Cryptography,* Op. cit.

[54]Gennaro, R., "An Improved Pseudo-Random Generator Based on Discrete Log." CRYPTO'2000, LNCS 1880, pp. 469–481, Springer-Verlag, 2000. Also available in an updated version at: http://www.research.ibm.com/people/r/rosario/prng.ps.

[55]Howgrave-Graham, Nick, "Pseudo-Random Number Generation on the IBM 4758 Secure Crypto Coprocessor, Op. cit.

[56]Smith, S. and S. Weingart, "Building a High-Performance Programmable Secure Coprocessor." *IBM Research Report RC21102,* February 1998.

[57]National Institute of Standards and Technology, FIPS 140-1, *Security Requirements for Cryptographic Modules,* Available at: http://csrc.nist.gov/cryptval/140-1.htm.

[58]Howgrave-Graham, Nick, "Pseudo-Random Number Generation on the IBM 4758 Secure Crypto Coprocessor, Op. cit.

[59]Smith, S., and S. Weingart, "Building a High-Performance Programmable Secure Coprocessor," Op. cit.

[60]Ackenhusen, John G., *Real-Time Signal Processing: Design and Implementation of Signal Processing Systems,* Prentice Hall PTR, 1999.

[61]Koren, Israel, *Computer Arithmetic Algorithms,* Brookside Court Publishers, 1998.

[62]Schwartzlander, E. E., ed., *Computer Arithmetic,* Vol. I, Los Alamitos, CA: IEEE Computer Society Press, 1990.

[63]Parhami, Behrooz, *Computer Arithmetic—Algorithms and Hardware Designs,* Oxford University Press, 1999.

[64]Montgomery, P. L., "Modular multiplication without trial division." *Mathematics of Computation,* 44 (170): pp. 519–521, April 1985.

[65]Tenca, Alexandre F., and Çetin K. Koç, "A scalable architecture for Montgomery multiplication." In Ç. K. Koç and C. Paar, editors, *Cryptographic Hardware and Embedded Systems,* Lecture Notes in Computer Science No. 1717, pp. 94–108, Springer-Verlag, 1999.

[66]Koç, Ç. K.,, T. Acar, and B. S. Kaliski, Jr., "Analyzing and comparing Montgomery multiplication algorithms." *IEEE Micro,* 16 (3): pp. 26–33, June 1996.

[67]Tsai, W. S., C. B. Shung, and S. J. Wang, "Two systolic architectures for Montgomery multiplication." *IEEE Transactions in VLSI Systems,* 8 (1): pp. 103–107, February 2000.

[68]Todorov, Georgi, "Asic design, implementation and analysis of a scalable high-radix Montgomery multiplier." M.Sc. thesis, Dept. of Electrical and Computer Engineering, Oregon State University, December 2000.

[69]Walter, C. D., "Space/Time trade-offs for higher radix modular multiplication using repeated addition." *IEEE Transactions on Computers,* 46 (2): pp. 139–141, February 1997.

[70]Tenca, Alexandre F., Georgi Todorov, and Çetin K. Koç, "High-Radix Design of a Scalable Modular Multiplier." Proceedings of Cryptographic Hardware and Embedded Systems CHES-2001, May 2001, pp. 189–205, Paris, France.

[71]Blum, T., and C. Paar, "Montgomery modular exponentiation on reconfigurable hardware." In I. Koren and P. Kornerup, editors, *Proceedings, 14th Symposium on Computer Arithmetic,* pp. 70–77, Bath England, April 14–16, 1999, Los Alamitos, CA: IEEE Computer Society Press.

[72]Tenca, Alexandre F., and Çetin K. Koç, "A scalable architecture for Montgomery multiplication, Op. cit.

[73]Ibid.

[74]Ibid.

[75]http://www.asicint.com.

[76]Nichols, Randall K., *ICSA Guide to Cryptography,* Op. cit.

[77]Schneier, Bruce, *"Applied Cryptography: Protocols, Algorithms & Source Code,* 2nd Ed., Op. cit.

[78]http://www.asicint.com.

[79]Ibid.

[80]Miller, V. S., Use of Elliptic Curves in Cryptography, *Proceedings of Crypto '85, Lecture Notes in Computer Science,* Vol. 218, pp. 417–426, Springer-Verlag, 1986.

[81]Koblitz, N., "Elliptic curve cryptosystems," *Mathematics of Computation,* Vol. 48, No. 117, pp. 203–209, January 1997.

[82]Blake, I. F., G. Seroussi, and N. P. Smart, *Elliptic Curves in Cryptography,* Vol. 265 of *London Mathematical Society Lecture Notes Series,* Cambridge University Press, 1999.

[83]Menezes, A. J., *Elliptic Curve Public Key Cryptosystems,* Vol. 234 of The Kluwer International Series in Engineering and Computer Science, Kluwer Academic Publishers, 1993.

[84]http://www.certicom.com.

[85]Prof. Dr. Christof Paar's Web page at WPI with links to his group's papers and dissertations is found at: http://www.ece.wpi.edu/People/faculty/cxp.html.

[86]Koblitz, Neal, "A Family of Jacobians Suitable for Discrete Log Cryptosystems." In Shafi Goldwasser, ed., *Advances in Cryptology—Crypto '88,* Springer-Verlag, Lecture Notes in Computer Science, Vol. 403, pp. 94–99, Berlin 1989.

[87]Koblitz, Neal, "Hyperelliptic Cryptosystems." In Ernest F. Brickell, ed., *Journal of Cryptology,* pp. 139–159, 1989.

[88]Koblitz, Neal, *Algebraic Aspects of Cryptography,* Algorithms and Computation in Mathematics, Springer-Verlag, 1998.

[89]Wollinger, Thomas, *Computer Architectures for Cryptosystems based on Hyperelliptic Curves,* M.Sc. Thesis, Electrical & Computer Engineering Department, Worcester Polytechnic Institute, Worcester, Massachusetts, April 2001.

[90]Wollinger, Thomas, *Computer Architectures for Cryptosystems Based on Hyperellictic Curves, Op. cit.*

[91] Koblitz, Neal, "A Family of Jacobians Suitable for Discrete Log Cryptosystems," In Shafi Goldwasser, editor, *Advances in Cryptology—Crypto '88,* Springer-Verlag, Lecture Notes in Computer Science, Vol. 403, pp. 94–99, Berlin 1989.

[92]Koblitz, Neal, "Hyperelliptic Cryptosystems." In Ernest F. Brickell, ed., *Journal of Cryptology,* pp. 139–150, 1989.

[93]Koblitz, Neal, *Algebraic Aspects of Cryptography,* Op.cit.

[94]Wollinger, Thomas, *Computer Architectures for Cryptosystems Based on Hyperelliptic Curves,* Op. cit.

[95]Hoffstein, J., J. Pipher, and J. Silverman, NTRU: A new high-speed public-key cryptosystem. In J. Buhler, ed., *Lecture Notes in Computer Science,* Vol. 1423, Algorithm Number Theory (ANTS III), pp. 267–288, Springer-Verlag, Berlin, 1998.

[96]Coppersmith, D., and A. Shamir, Lattice attacks on NTRU, in *Advances in Cryptography—EUROCRYPT '97,* pp. 52–61, LNCS 1233, Springer-Verlag, 1997.

[97]http://www.ntru.com.

[98]Garrett, Paul B., *Making, Breaking Codes: Introduction to Cryptology,* Prentice-Hall, 2000.

[99]Schor, P., "Algorithms for Quantum Computation: Discrete Logarithms and Factoring," *Proceedings of the 35th Annual Symposium on the Foundations of Computing Science* (1994), pp. 124–134.

[100]http://www.ti.com.

[101]Bailey, Daniel V., Daniel Coffin, Adam Elbirt, Joseph H. Silverman, and Adam D. Woodbury, "NTRU in Constrained Devices." *CHES '2001, International Workshop on Cryptographic Hardware and Embedded Systems,* pp. 266–277, Paris, France, April 2001.

[102]Murthy, V. Kumar, "Abelian varieties—Optimal Cryptography for Wireless Communications?" *Wireless Security Perspectives,* Cellular Network Perspectives Ltd., Toronto, Canada, November 2000.

[103]Murthy, V. Kumar, *Introduction to Abelian Varieties,* CRM Monograph Series, Vol. 3, American Mathematical Society, Providence, Rhode Isalnd, USA, 1993.

[104]http://www.karthika.com.

[105]http://www.arithmetica.com.

[106] Garrett, Paul B., *Making, Breaking Codes: Introduction to Cryptology,* Op. cit.

[107] Nichols, Randall K., *The ICSA Guide To Cryptography,* Op. cit.

[108]http://www.rpkusa.com.

[109]http://www.corrent.com.

[110]http://www.arm.com.

[111]http://www.mips.com.

[112]http://www.arccores.com.

[113]http://www.tensilica.com.

[114]http://www.ti.com.

[115]http://www.analogdevices.com.

[116]http://www.infineon.com.

[117]http://www.dspg.com.

[118]http://www.security.melco.co.jp.

[119]http://www.improvsys.com.

[120]Either http://www.melco.co.jp. or http://www.mitsubishielectric.com.

[121]Ibid.

[122]Ibid.

[123]Ibid.

[124]Ibid.

[125]Ibid.

[126]Ibid.

[127]Ibid.

[128]http://www.etsi.org.

[129]http://www.etsi.org/dvbandca/3GPPSPECIFICATIONS/3GTS35.202.pdf.

[130]http://www.etsi.org/dvbandca/3GPPSPECIFICATIONS/3GTS35.201%20ver.1.2.pdf.

[131]ibid.

[132]http://fn2.freenet.edmonton.ab.ca/~jsavard/crypto/co040801.htm.

[133]Daemen, J., and V. Rijmen, "AES Proposal: Rijndael," Available at http://csrc.nist.gov/encryption/aes/rijndael/Rijndael.pdf. Plenty of pertinent material can also be found at: http://www.esat.kuleuven.ac.be/~rijmen/rijndael/.

[134]Barker, E., L. Bassham, W. Burr, M. Dworkin, J. Foti, J. Nechvatal, and E. Roback. "Report on the Development of the *Advanced Encryption Standard* (AES)," Available at: http://www.csrc.nist.gov/encryption/aes/round2/r2report.pdf.

[135]http://www.esat.kuleuven.ac.be/~rijmen/rijndael/.

[136]http://www.ti.com.

[137]http://www.intel.com.

[138]Daemen, J., and V. Rijmen, "AES Proposal: Rijndael," Available at: http://csrc.nist.gov/encryption/aes/rijndael/Rijndael.pdf. Plenty of pertinent material can also be found at: http://www.esat.kuleuven.ac.be/~rijmen/rijndael/.

[139]Gladman, Brian, "The AES Algorithm (Rijndael) in C and C++," April 2001, also available at: http://fp.gladman.plus.com/cryptography technology/rijndael/index.htm.

[140]http://www.altera.com.

[141]Ibid.

[142]McLoone, Máire, J. V. McCanny, "High Performance Single-Chip FPGA Rijndael Algorithm Implementations," *CHES 2001, Cryptographic Hardware and Embedded Systems Workshop, Paris, France, May 14–16, 2001, Proceedings,* pp. 68–80.

[143]Gladman, Brian, "The AES Algorithm (Rijndael) in C and C++," Op. cit.

[144]http://fn2.freenet.edmonton.ab.ca/~jsavard/crypto/co040801.htm.

[145]http://www.esat.kuleuven.ac.be/~rijmen/rijndael/.

[146]McLoone, Máire, Op. cit.

[147]Weeks, Bryan, Mark Bean, Tom Rozylowicz, and Chris Ficke (National Security Agency), "Hardware Performance Simulations of Round2 Advanced Encryption Standard (AES3) Candidate Conference," April 13–14, 2000, USA. Available as PDF file at: http://csrc.nist.gov/encryption/aes.round2/NSA-AESfinalreport.pdf and as a slide presentation at http://csrc.nist.gov/encryption/aes.round2/conf3/presentations/weeks.pdf.

[148]Ibid.

[149]Ichikawa, Tetsuya, Tonomi Kasuya, and Mitsuru Matsui, "Hardware Evaluation of AES Finalists," paper presented by Mitsubishi Electric at *2nd Round AES candidate conference,* April 13–14, New York, NY. Available at: http://csrc.nist.gov/encryption/aes.round2/conf3/papers/15-tichikawa.pdf.

[150]McLoone, Máire, Op. Cit.

[151]Ibid.

[152]Gaj, Kris, and Pawel Chodowiec, "Comparison of the hardware performance of the AES candidates using reconfigurable hardware," paper presented at *2nd Round AES Candidate Conference,* April 13–14, New York, NY, Available at http://csrc.nist.gov/encryption/aes.round2/conf3/papers/22-kgaj.pdf.

[153]Dandalis, Andreas, Viktor, K. Prasanna, and Jose D. P. Rolim, "A Comparative Study of Performance of AES Final Candidates Using FPGAs," paper presented at *2nd Round AES Candidate Conference,* April 13–14, New York, NY, USA.

[154]Fischer, Viktor, and Milos Drutarovsky, "Two Methods of Rijndael Implementation in Reconfigurable Hardware," *CHES 2001, Cryptographic Hardware and Embedded Systems Workshop, Paris, France, May 14–16, 2001, Proceedings,* pp. 81–96.

[155]Elbirt, A. J., W. Yip, B. Chetwynd, and C. Paar, "An FPGA Implementation and Performance Evaluation of the AES Block Cipher Candidate Algorithm Finalists," *The Third Advanced Encryption Standard (AES3) Candidate Conference,* April 13–14, 2000, New York, NY, Available at: http://csrc.nist.gov/encryption/aes.round2/conf3/papers/08-aelbirt.pdf.

[156]McLoone, Máire, Op. cit.

[157]Ibid.

[158] Fischer, Viktor and Milos Drutarovský, "Two Methods of Rijndael Implementation in Reconfigurable Hardware," *CHES 2001, Cryptographic Hardware and Embedded Systems Workshop,* Op. cit.

[159]Gaj, Kris, and Pawel Chodowiec, "Comparison of the hardware performance of the AES candidates using reconfigurable hardware," Op. cit.

[160]Elbirt, A. J., W. Yip, B. Chetwynd, and C. paar, "An FPGA Implementation and Performance Evaluation of the AES Block Cipher Candidate Algorithm Finalists," Op. cit.

[161]Dandalis, Andreas, Viktor K. Prasanna, and Jose D. P. Rolim, "A Comparative Study of Performance of AES Final Candidates Using FPGAs," Op. cit.

[162]Trimberger, Steve, Raymond Pang, and Amit Singh, "A 12 Gbps DES Encryptor/ Decryptor Core in an FPGA," Cryptographic Hardware and Embedded Systems CHES'2000, 2nd International Workshop, Proceedings, Lecture Notes in Computer Science, Vol. 1965, Springer-Verlag, Berlin, Germany, pp. 156–163.

[163]Kuo, Henry, and Ingrid Verbauwhede, "Architectural Optimization for a 1.82 Gbits/sec VLSI Implementation of the AES Rijndael Algorithm," private communication. Also presented at *CHES 2001, Cryptographic Hardware and Embedded Systems Workshop, Paris, France, May 14–16, 2001, Proceedings,* pp. 53–67.

[164]Ibid.

[165]Weeks, Bryan, Mark Bean, Tom Rozylowicz, and Chris Ficke (National Security Agency), "Hardware Performance Simulations of Round2 Advanced Encryption Standard (AES3) Candidate Conference," Op. cit.

[166]Ibid.

[167]http://www.asicint.com.

[168]Leitold, Herbert, Wolfgang, Mayerwieser, Udo Payer, Karl-Christian Posch, Reinhard Posch, and Johannes Wolkerstorfer, "A 155 Mbps Triple-DES Network Encryptor," *Cryptographic Hardware and Embedded Systems CHES'2000, 2nd International Workshiop, Proceedings, Lecture Notes in Computer Science,* Vol. 1965, Springer-Verlag, Berlin, Germany, pp. 164–174.

[169]Ibid.

[170]Ibid.

[171]Yuan, Jiren, and Christer Svensson, "High Speed Circuit Technique," *IEEE J. Solid-State Circuits,* Vol. 24, p. 62, 1989.

[172]Wilcox, D. Craig, Lyndon G. Pierson, Perry J. Robertson, Edward L. Witzke, and Karl Gass, "A DES ASIC Suitable for Network Encryption at 10 Gbps and Beyond," *Cryptographic Hardware and Embedded Systems CHES'1999, 1st International Workshop, Proceedings, Lecture Notes in Computer Science,* Vol. 1717, Springer-Verlag, Berlin, Germany, pp. 37–48.

[173]ftp://ftp.3gpporg/TSG_SA/WG3_Security

[174]The report on the design and evaluation by SAGE of the MILENAGE algorithm can be found at: ftp://ftp.3gpporg/TSG_SA/WG3_Security/2000_meetings/TSGS3_16_Sophia_Antipolis/Docs/PDF/S3-000730.pdf

ftp://ftp.3gpporg/TSG_SA/WG3_Security/TSGS3_17_Gothenberg/Docs/PDF/S3-010015.pdf.

http://www.research.att.com/~janos/3gpphtml (Explains the context rather nicely).

http://www.brookson.com/gsm/contents.htm.

http://www.isaac.cs.berkeley.edu/isaac/gsm.html. (A very good paper by UCal Berkeley's David Wagner with several interesting links to pertinent work.)

http://www.brookson.com/wap/li.htm. (Contains excellent links regarding legal contexts on communications interception and so forth.)

Bibliography

"3G—Third Generation Wireless Systems," http://www.info.gov.hk/digital21/eng/knowledge/3g.html, Digital 21, c/o Information Technology Services Department, 15/F, Wanchai Tower, 12, Harbour Road, Wan Chai, Hong Kong, webmaster@digital21.gov.hk.

"3G Device to Transmit and Rceive Wireless Voice Video and Data," http://www.info.gov.hk/digital21/eng/knowledge/3g.html: Digital 21, c/o Information Technology Services Department, 15/F, Wanchai Tower, 12, Harbour Road, Wan Chai, Hong Kong, webmaster @digital21.gov.hk.

1999 *Guide to Wireless Telecommunications Technology.* Arlington: ANSER, 1999. Available on INTELINK at: http://tesla.cia.ic.gov/regional/WirelessTelecomTech/Introduction.cfm, Accessed April 24, 2001.

2001 Guide to Wireless Telecommunications Technology, Arlington: ANSER, 2000.

Ackenhusen, John G., *Real-Time Signal Processing: Design and Implementation of Signal Processing Systems,* Upper Saddle River, NJ: Prentice-Hall, 1999.

Ackenhusen, John G., *Real-Time Signal Processing; Design and Implementation of Signal Processing Systems,* Upper Saddle River, NJ: Prentice-Hall, 1999.

Adamson, R. Brian (1994), Tactical Radio Frequency Communication Requirements for Ipng, (Memo) Naval Research Laboratory, Washington, D.C., Available at: www.cis.ohio-state.edu/cgi-bin/rfc/rfc1677.html, Accessed March 1, 2001.

Adamy, David, *EW 101: A First Course in Electronic Warfare,* Boston: Artech House, 2000.

Adcock, Gene, *Electro-Optical Surveillance,* Vol. 3, CCS Security Source Library, 2000.

Adleman, L., J. DeMarrais, and M. Huang, *A Subexponential Algorithm for Discrete Logarithms Over the Rational Subgroup of the Jacobians of Large Genus Hyperelliptic Curves Over Finite Fields,* Algorithmic Number Theory, Lecture Notes in Computer Science, Vol. 877, Springer-Verlag, pp. 28–40, 1994.

Advanced Mobile Phone Service (AMPS), *Dictionary of PC Hardware and Data Communications Terms,* http://www.ora.com/reference/dictionary/terms/A/Advanced_Mobile_Phone_Service.htm.

Advanced Mobile Phone Service (AMPS), *Wireless Local Loop Technology Standard Overview,* http://www.telecomresearch.com/overview.htm.

"Advanced Secure Wireless Integrated Networks," http://www.darpa.mil/ito/summaries 97/f390_0.html; Principal Investigator: Roy Stehle, SRI International, 333 Ravenswood Avenue, Menlo Park, CA 94025-3453, +1-650-859-2552, +1-650-859-5303 fax, stehle @erg.sri.com; Project Web site: http://www.glomo.sri.com/aswin/; Sponsor: *Defense Advanced Research Projects Agency* (DARPA), 3701 N. Fairfax Dr., Arlington, VA 22203-1714.

"Advanced Spectrum Technology," 4GNT's Network Design, http://www. 4gnt.com/technology.html, March 11, 2001.

Agnew, G., R. Mullin, and S. Vanstone, An Implementation of Elliptic Curve Cryptosystems over F_2^{155}, *IEEE Journal on Selected Areas in Communications,* Vol. 11, pp. 804–813, 1993.

Ahuja, Vijay, *Network & Internet Security,* New York: Academic Press, 1996.

Akdeniz, Yaman, *No Chance for Key Recovery: Encryption and International Principles of Human and Political Rights,* http://webjcli.ncl.ac.uk/1998/issue1/akdeniz.1. html.

Alderman, Ellen, and Caroline Kennedy, *The Right to Privacy,* New York: Alfred Knopf, 1995.

Althoff, John, *The Future Has Arrived: The Mobile Internet,* Presentation at Networld+Interop 2001, Las Vegas, NV, May 2001.

American Access to the European Standardization Process, Available at: http://www. ansi.org/public/library/eu_access/intro_1.html, Accessed June 27, 2001.

Amoroso, Edward, *Fundamentals of Computer Security Technology,* Upper Saddle River, NJ: Prentice-Hall PTR, 1994.

Amoroso, Edward, *Intrusion Detection,* Intrusion.net Books, 1999.

Anand, Nikil, *An Overview of Bluetooth Security,* SANS Infosec Reading Room, February 22, 2001.

Andersson, Christoffer, *GPRS and 3G WIRELESS Applications,* New York: John Wiley & Sons, Inc., 2001.

Anonymous, *Robert Philip Hanssen: Alleged KGB Mole Within the FBI,* Laguna Hills, CA: Aegean Park Press, 2001.

Anoto AB, The Anoto Web site on Bluetooth, http://www.anoto.com/, June 2, 2001.

Arehart, Charles, Nirmal Chidambaram, Ric Howell, et al., *Professional WAP,* Wrox Press, Inc., 2000.

Armitage, Grenville, *Quality of Service in IP Networks,* Upper Saddle River, NJ: Pearson Higher Education Publ., 2000.

Armstrong, Illena, "What's Happening with WAP,*" Security*, Vol. 12, No. 2.

Ask Dr. CT: *Installing VOIP Systems,* CT Labs, Inc., 1999, http://www.ct-labs. com/q42.htm, Accessed May 2001.

Atkins, Derik, et al., *Internet Security, Professional Reference,* Indianapolis, IN: New Riders Publishing, 1996.

Atkinson, R., *IP Encapsulating Security Payload ESP: RFC 1827,* Naval Research Laboratory, 1995, http://rfcl1827.x42.com, Accessed June 10, 2001.

Audin, Gary, "VOIP? A Question of Perspective," *Business Communications Review,* April 2001.

Aun, Fred, *Will Wireless Broadband Fry Slowpoke ISPs?* August 1, 2000, http:// www.zdnet.com/filters/printerfriendly/0.6061.2609999-2.00.html.

Austin, Marsha, "Wires Crossed at Columbine Scene," *The Denver Business Journal,* September 10, 1999, http://denver.bcentral.com/denver/stories/1999/09/13/story1.html.

"Authentication and Key Revocation Protocols for Wireless Networks," http://www.darpa. mil/ito/psum2000/j772-0.html, Principal Investigator: Agnes Chan, Associate Dean and Graduate Director, College of Computer Science, Northeastern University, Boston, MA 02115, 617-373-2464, 617-373-5121 fax, ahchan@ccs.neu.edu & Richard McNeil, Office of Sponsored Research, Northeastern University, Boston, MA 02115, 617-373-5600, 617-373-4595 fax, rjm@neu.edu; Project Web site: http://www.ccs.neu.edu/home/ahchan/wsl/ak_ protocols; Sponsor: *Defense Advanced Research Projects Agency* (DARPA), 3701 N. Fairfax Dr., Arlington, CA 22203-1714.

Avolio, Frederick M., *Firewalls and Virtual Private Networks,* TIS White Paper, 1998, www.tis.com.

Axis Communications, The Axis Communications Web site on Bluetooth, http://www.axis.com/products/index.htm, May 29, 2001.

Azzouz, Elsayed E., and Asoke Kumar Nandi, *Automatic Modulation Recognition of Communication Signals,* Dordrecht, The Netherlands: Kluwer Academic Publishers, 1996.

Bagini, Vittorio, and Bucci, Marco, *A Design of Reliable True Random Number Generator for Cryptographic Applications,* Cryptographic Hardware and Embedded Systems Int'l Workshop Proceeding, Lecture Notes in Computer Science, Vol. 1717, pp. 204–218, New York: Springer-Verlag, 1999.

Bailey, Daniel V., Danield Coffin, Adam Elbirt, Joseph H. Silverman, and Adam D. Woodbury, *NTRU in Constrained Devices,* CHES 2001, International Workshop on Cryptographic Hardware and Embedded Systems, pp. 266–277, Paris, France, April 2001.

Baker, Stewart A., and Paul R. Hurst, *The Limits of Trust: Cryptography, Governments, and Electronic Commerce,* Washington, D.C.: Kluwer Law International, 1998.

Barker, E., L. Bassham, W. Burr, M. Dworkin, J. Foti, J. Nechvatal, and E. Roback., "Report on the Development of the Advanced Encryption Standard (AES)," Available at: http://csrc.nit.gov/encryption/aes/round2/r2report.pdf.

Barlow, J. P., et al., "Forum: Is Computer Hacking a Crime?" *Harper's*, March 1990, pp. 46–57.

Barnes, Cheryl, and Brian Dooley, *Telecommunications in China,* Available on INTELINK at: http://doserve.mall.nsa.ic.gov/producer/refs/faccts/00017383.html, Accessed April 24, 2001.

Baron, A., K. Davis, and C. Hofmann, "Passive Direction Finding and Signal Location," *Microwave Journal,* September 1982.

Bass, Steve, "Net Phones: Dialing Without Dollars," *PC World*, November 2000, http://www.pcworld/com/resource/printable/article/0.aid.18623.00.asp, Accessed June 2001.

Bates, Regis J., and Donald W. Gregory, *Voice and Data Communications Handbook*, New York: McGraw-Hill, 1998.

Bates, Regis J., Jr., *Disaster Recovery Planning: Networks, Telecommunications, and Data Communications,* New York: McGraw-Hill, 1992.

Bath, Vivienne, and Cindy Chong, *China's New Telecommunications Regulations.* Available at: http://www.coudert.com/practice/chinanewtelecom.htm.

Bauer, F. L., *Decrypted Secrets: Methods and Maxims of Cryptology,* Springer, Berlin, 1997.

Beering, David, "The ARIES Project Prolog to Global Connectivity," *Oil and Gas Journal*, September 11, 2000.

Beker, Henry J., and Fred C. Piper, *Cipher Systems,* Wiley Interscience, 1982.

Beker, Henry J., and Fred C. Piper, *Secure Speech Communications,* Academic Press, 1985.

Bellamy, John C., *Digital Telephony,* 3rd Ed., New York: John Wiley & Sons, 2000.

Benedetto, Sergio, and Ezio Biglieri, *Principles of Digital Transmission with Wireless Applications,* Dordrecht, the Netherlands: Kluwer Academic Publishers, 1999.

Berkel, Bob, and Alred Kornbluth, *Electronic Surveillance and Counter-Measures,* Vol. 2, CCS Security Source Library, 1995.

Berkel, Bob, and Lowell Rapaport, *Covert Audio Interception,* Vol. 1, CCS Security Source Library, New York: CCS Security Publishing, Ltd., 1994.

Berkley Research, "Wireless LANs Have Serious Flaws," *Computerworld*, February 12, 2001.

Bernstein, T. A., B. Bhimani, E. Schultz, and C. A. Siegel, *Internet Security for Business,* New York: John Wiley & Sons, 1996.

Biggs, Maggie, "Unplugged Data Can Also Be Hack-Proof Data," *InfoWorld*, September 10, 1999, p. 61.

Biham, E., and A. Shamir, *Differential Cryptanalysis of the Data Encryption Standard, Journal of Cryptology,* Vol. 4, #1, pp. 3–72, 1991.

Bing, Benny, *High Speed Wireless ATM and LANs,* Boston: Artech House, 2000.

Biryukov, Alex, Adi Shamir, and David Wagner, *Real Time Cryptanalysis of A5/1 on a PC,* Proceedings of the Fast Software Encryption Workshop 2000, April 10–12, 2000, New York, http://cryptome.org/a51-bsw.htm, Accessed June 18, 2001.

Black, Uyless D., *IP Routing Protocols: RIP, OSPF, BGP, PNNI & Cisco Routing Protocols,* Upper Saddle River, NJ: Prentice Hall PTR, 2000.

Black, Uyless D., *Voice over IP,* Upper Saddle River, NJ: Prentice Hall PTR, 1999.

Blake, I. F., G. Seroussi, and N. P. Smart, *Elliptic Curves in Cryptography,* Vol. 265 of London Mathematical Society Lecture Notes Series, Cambridge, U.K.: Cambridge University Press, 1999.

Blaze, M., W. Diffie, R. Rivest, B. Schneier, T. Shimomura, E. Thompson, and M. Wiener, *Minimal Key Lengths for Symmetric Ciphers to Provide Adequate Commercial Security,* January 1996.

"Bluetooth and IEEE 802.11b Wireless Solutions from AmbiCom," no author provided, Ambicon Inc., 4829 Fremont Boulevard, Suite A, Fremont, CA 94538, (510) 249-0581, http://www.ambicom.com/products/air2net/btfaqs.htm.

"Bluetooth Chipset Projections," Source: Merrill Lynch Report: Bluetooth Handbook 1.1, June 29, 2000.

Bluetooth Security Architecture White Paper, http://www.bluetooth.com/developer/whitepaper/whiatepaper.asp.

Blum, L., M. Blum, and M. Shub, "A Simple Unpredictable Pseudo-Random Number Generator," *SIAM Journal on Computing*, 152: pp. 364–383, May 1986.

Blum, M., and S. Micali, "How to Generate Cryptographically Strong Sequences of Pseudo-Random Bits," *SIAM Journal on Computing*, Vol. 13, No. 4, pp. 850–864, November 1984.

Blum, T., and C. Paar, *Montgomery modular exponentiation on reconfigurable hardware,* In Proceedings, 14th Symposium on Computer Arithmetic, Koren, I. and Kornerup, P., eds., pp. 70–77, Bath England, April 14–16, Los Alamitos, CA: IEEE Computer Society Press, 1999.

Bologna, J., *Handbook of Corporate Fraud: Prevention, Detection, Investigation,* Boston: Butterworth-Heinemann, 1993.

Boneh, D., and R. Lipton, *Algorithms for black-box fields and their applications to cryptography,* Advances in Cryptology—CRYPTO '96, Lecture Notes in Computer Science, Vol: 1109, Springer-Verlag, pp. 283–297, 1996.

Bonisteel, Steven, "Mobile Content Rings Up Revenue, but United States is on Hold," *Computer User,* March 31, 2001, http://www.computeruser.com/news/01/03/31/news8.html, Accessed June 13, 2001.

Boran, Seán, *All About SSH—Part I/II,* 2/14/00, http://www.securityportal.com/research/ssh-part1.html.

Bosworth, Bruce, *Codes, Ciphers, and Computers: An Introduction to Information Security,* Rochelle Park, NJ: Hayden Books, 1990.

Bracey's, London.

Bradner, Scott O., and Allison Mankin, eds., *Internet Protocol Next Generation* (IPng), Reading, MA: Addison-Wesley, 1996.

Bray, Jennifer, and Charles F. Sturman, *Bluetooth, Connect Without Cables*, Upper Saddle River, NJ: Prentice Hall PTR, 2001, p. 5.

Brewin, Bob, "Computer World Wireless LAN Security Flawed Report: Systems Have Several Vulnerabilities," *Computerworld*, February 12, 2001, http://www.computerworld.com/cwi/story/0.1199.NAV47_ST057597.00.html.

Brewin, Bob, "Wireless LAN Security Flawed Report," Systems have several vulnerabilities, *Computerworld*, http://www.computerworld.com/cwi/story/0.1199.NAV47_STO57597.00.html, February 12, 2001.

Briedenbach, Susan, *A White Paper Convergence: A Strategic Analysis,* Sbreidenbach @usa.net.

Briefing slide obtained from SAIC John Allen's Ph.D., personal library.

"Broadband and Wireless Networking Laboratory (BWN-LAB)," The School of Electrical and Computer Engineering at the Georgia Institute of Technology, http://www.ece.gatech.edu/research/labs/bwn/.

"Broadband Wireless," *PCIA Washington Bulletin*, August 9, 1999.

Brodsky, Ira, "Don't Look Now—You're Being Followed," *Wireless Review*, February 15, 1998.

Broersma, Matthew, "Consumer Bluetooth on the Way This Year,*" ZDNetUK*, March 15, 2001, Available at: http://news.zdnet.co.uk/story/0.s2085025.00.html, Accessed June 18, 2001.

Broersma, Matthew, "Switching on Home Networks," *ZDNetUK*, April 12, 2001, Available at: http://news.zdnet.co.uk/story/0.s2085632.00.html, Accessed June 18, 2001.

Brookner, Eli, *Tracking and Kalman Filtering Made Easy,* New York: John Wiley & Sons, 1998.

Brooks, Jason, Reviews: *Bluetooth in Practice: Notebook PCs—Toshiba PC Cards Effectively Cut the Networking Cord; Spanworks Enables File Sharing and Chats,* ZDNet.com, October 30, 2000, http://www.zdnet.com/eweek/stories/general/0.11011.2645518.000.html, Accessed June 18, 2001.

Brooks, Michael, *Quantum Computing and Communications,* Springer-Verlag, 1999.

Brooks, Jason and Herb Bethoney, "The LAN, PAN, WAN Plan Wireless technologies Can Plug in Mobile Workers Securely as Long as Managers Act With Caution," *eWEEK*, January 15, 2001, 12:00 A.M. ET, http://www.zdnet.com/enterprise/stories/main/0.10228.2672836.00.html.

Brown, Peter, "Internet Over Satellite Soars," *Broadcasting & Cable*, March 20, 2000.

Brown, Peter, *Two-Way Data-Over-DBS Moves Stir Buzz,* Multichannel News, April 10, 2000.

Brown, Robert Grover, and Patrick Y. C. Hwang, *Introduction to Random Signal and Applied Kalman Filtering,* 3rd Ed., New York: John Wiley & Sons, 1997.

Browne, J. P. R. Air Vice Marshall, CBE and Wing Commander M. T. Thurbon, 1998, Electronic Warfare.

Buchmann, Johannes A., *Introduction To Cryptography,* Springer-Verlag, 2001.

Buckey, Sean, "IP Telephony: An Insider's War," *Telecommunications*, July 2000, http://www.telecoms-mag.com/issues/200007/tcs/ip.html, Accessed May 2001.

Buckingham, Simon, "Summary of This Current Evolution," Success 4 SMS White Paper, February 2001, Mobile Lifestreams Limited, http://www.info.gov.hk/digital21/eng/knowledge/3g.html, Digital 21, c/o Information Technology Services Department, 15/F, Wanchai Tower, 12, Harbour Road, Wan Chai, Hong Kong, webmaster@digital21.gov.hk.

Buckingham, Simon, *An Introduction to the Short Message Service,* Mobile Lifestreams Limited—Issued July 2000, http://www.gsmworld.com/technology/sms_success.html.

Burnett, Steve, and Stephen Paine, *RSA Security's Guide To Cryptography,* New York: Osborne, 2001.

Burrell, Barbaral, McCarty, Bill, and Yount, Arthur, *Jini Technology History,* http://www.emory.edu/BUSINESS/et/jini/.

By 2005, More Than 68% of Internet Users Will Use Wireless Devices to Go On-Line in Western Europe, Available at: http:///www.netscope.org.uk/scripts/hot_newspg.asp#63, Accessed June 12, 2001.

Byrnes, Cheryl, *Telecommunications: State of the World,* Faulkner Information Service. 2001, Available on INTELINK at: http://doserve.mall.nsa.ic.gov/, Accessed May 11, 2001.

Cambridge Silicon Radio, The Cambridge Silicon Radio Web site on Bluetooth, http://www.csr.com/pr/pr050.htm, Accessed June 15, 2001.

Campbell, Collin, *Surface Acoustic Wave Devices for Mobile and Wireless Communications,* New York: Academic Press, 1998.

Campen, Alan D., and Douglas H. Dearth, eds., *Cyberwar 3.0: Human Factors in Infirnation Operations and Future Conflict,* Fairfax, VA: AFCEA, 2000.

Campen, Alan D., Douglas H. Dearth, and Thomas R. Gooden, *Cyberwar: Security, Strategy and Conflict In The Information Age,* Fairfax, VA: AFCEA International Press, 1996.

Carne, E. Brian, *Telecommunications Primer: Signals, Building Blocks & Networks,* Upper Saddle River, NJ: Prentice Hall, 1995.

Cebrowski, Arthur K., Vice Admiral and John J. Garstka, *Network-Centric Warfare: Its Origin and Future,* October 1998, U.S. Naval Institute Proceedings, www.usni.org/Proceedings/Articles98/Procebrowski.htm.

Cellular Cloning, [article on-line] (Washington, D.C.: The Federal Communications Commission, 1998), http://www.fcc.gov/wtb/cellular/celfctsh.html, Accessed May 24, 2001.

"Cellular Networking Perspectives," no author provided, GSM TECHNOLOGY, http://www.irius-technologies.com/gsm_technology.htm, http://www.cnp-wireless.com/tdma.html.

"Cellular Networking Perspectives," no author provided, http://www.cnp-wireless.com/tdma.html, Motorola, Inc., CDMA Technology & Benefits, http://www.looksmort.com/r?page=/search/frames/index.html&isp=US&name=&bcolor=ffcc00&key=cdma&url=http%3a//www.mot.com/CNSS/CIG/Technology/cdma.html&pskip=&nskip=10&se=1000&index=.

Cellular Phone Supplies.com, http://cellularphonesupplies.ephones.com/resources/glossary.asp.

Cha, Ariana Eunjung, February 28, 2001, "Broadband's a Nice Pace if You Can Get It," *Washington Post,* p. G4.

Champness, Angela, *IEEE 802.11 is the path to high-speed wireless data networking,* Online document: www.parkassociates.com/events/forum99/F99papers/ieee802.11.htm, March 21, 2001

Champness, Angela, *Understanding the benefits of IEEE 802.11,* Online document: www.steinkuehler.de/wavelan_802_11_Benefits.htm, February 16, 2001.

Chapman, D. B., and E. D. Zwicky, *Building Internet Firewalls,* Sebastopol, CA: O'Reilly & Associates, 1995.

Chen, Elaine C.Y., "Comparison Report: It's a Small World After All," *Mobile Computing,* December 2000, http://www.mobilecomputing.com/printarchives.cgi?89.

Cheswick, W., and S. Bellovin, *Firewalls and Internet Security: Repelling the Wily Hacker*, Reading, MA: Addison Wesley, 1994. [Cheswick and Bellovin list 40 weak points in their book *Firewalls and Internet Security.*]

Chidi, Jr., George A., February 26, 2001, "Dataquest Says Satellite Broadband Will Surge by 2005," *InfoWorld*, p. 64B.

Chiong, John A., *Internetworking ATM for the Internet and Enterprise Networks*, McGraw-Hill, 1998.

Christensen, Gerald T., Paul G. Florack, and Robert Duncan, *Wireless Intelligent Networking*, Norwood, MA: Artech House, 2001.

Christensen, Gerald T., *Universal Mobile Telecommunications System*, Faulkner Information Services, 2000, Available on INTELINK at: http://doserve.mall.nsa.ic.gov/producer/refs/faccts/00016794.html, Accessed June 14, 2001.

Christensen, Gerald T., *Wireless Infrastructure Technologies*, Faulkner Information Services, 2001, Available on INTELINK at: http://doserve.mall.nsa.ic.gov/producer/refs/faccts/00017350.html, Accessed April 24, 2001.

Church, William, Managing Editor, CIWARS Intelligence Report—September 13, 1998: *1997–1998 Infrastructure Vulnerability Report*, Journal of Infrastructural Warfare and The Center for Infrastructural Warfare Studies, Vol. 2, Issue 23, pp. 5, 13–17. Available at: http://www.Iwar.org.

Cichocki, A., and R. Unbehauen, *Neural Networks for Optimization and Signal Processing*, New York: John Wiley & Sons, 1993.

Cisco Corporation, *SSL: Foundation for Web Security*, http://www.cisco.com/warp/public/759/ipj_1-1/ipj_1-1_SSL2.html.

Clarke, David James, IV, *CNE Study Guide*, San Jose: Novell Press, 1994.

Clayton, Jade, *Illustrated TELECOM Dictionary 3rd Edition*, New York: McGraw-Hill, 2001.

Clemens, C.W., Ruppel, and Tor A. Fjeldly, eds., *Advances in Surface Acoustic Wave Technology, Systems and Applications (Selected Topics in Electronics and Systems—Vol. 19)*, Singapore: World Scientific Publishing, 2000.

Collins, Daniel, *Carrier Grade Voice Over IP*, New York: McGraw-Hill, 2001.

Comerford, Richard, "Handhelds Duke It Out For The Internet," *IEEE Spectrum*, August 2000, p. 40.

Communications Security Establishment, *The Canadian Trusted Computer Product Evaluation Criteria Version 3.0e.*, Canadian System Security Centre, CSE, 1993, Available from Criteria Coordinator/S5B InfoSec Standards and Evaluations/Communications Security Establishment/P.O. Box 9703 Terman/Ottawa K1G 3Z4.

"Compatible Systems Partners with NETRIX to Offer voVPN: VoIP over VPN Provides Toll-Quality, Secure Voice Traffic on the Internet," *BusinessWire.com*, http://www.business-wire.com/webbox/bw.051099/191300795.htm.

Coover, Edwin R., *ATM Switches*, Norwood, MA: Artech House, 1997.

Copeland, Guy L., and Frederick G. Tompkins, *A New Paradigm for the Development of U.S. Information Security Policy, Computer Science and Corporation*, White Paper, Herndon, VA, September 1995.

Coppersmith, D., and A. Shamir, *Lattice attacks on NTRU*, Advances in Cryptography—EUROCRYPT '97, pp. 52–61, LNCS 1233, Berlin: Springer-Verlag, 1997.

Coppock, R., R. Croce, and W. Regier, "Bragg Cell RF Signal Processing," *Microwave Journal*, September 1978.

Cormen, Thomas H., Charles E. Leiserson, and Ronald L. Rivest, *Algorithms*, McGraw-Hill, 1990.

Council of Economic Advisors, *Annual Report of the Council of Economic Advisors to the President,* February 2000, pp. 97–127.

Counterpane Labs Press Release: *Flaw in Cell Phone Encryption Identified, Design Process Blamed,* March 20, 1997, http://www.counterpane.com.cmea-press.html.

Coutinho, S. C., *The Mathematics of Ciphers,* AK Press, 1999.

Cover, Robin, *The XML Cover Pages: WAP Wireless Markup Language Specification WML,* March 16, 2001.

Cox, D., 1995, "Wireless Personal Communications: What is It?" *IEEE Personal Communications.*

Cracking DES: Secrets of Research, Wiretap Politics & Chip Design, Electronic Frontier Foundation, O'Reilly, 1998.

Cravotta, Nicholas, "Voice Over Packet: Putting It All Together," *EDN,* March 16, 2000.

Csenger, Michael, A White Paper, *Convergence: A Strategic Analysis. Getting There, Trying to Do That,* Mcsenger@gte.net.

"Currents Shaping The Hardware Market," *PC Almanac,* 1st Ed., Winter 2000, p. 179.

Currin, Lisa M., *Wireless Application Protocol,* Faulkner Information Services, 2000. Available on INTELINK at: http://doserve.mall.nsa.ic.gov/producer/refs/facts/00017494.html, Accessed April 24, 2001.

Cybenko, George, et al., *The Mathematics of Information Coding, Extraction and Distribution,* Springer-Verlag, 1999.

CyLAN Technologies Inc., *CyLAN IPSec White Paper,* 1997, http://www.cylan.com/files.whpaper.htm.

daemon9/Route/Infinity, "IP spoofing Demystified: Trust Relationship Exploitation," [article online], *Phrack,* 1996, Available at: http://www.networkcommand.com/ docs/ipspoof.txt, Accessed May 30, 2001, Internet.Datapro Networking Report 2783, ISO Reference Model for Open Systems Interconnectikon OSI, p. 7, August 1991.

Daemen J., and V. Rijmen, "AES Proposal: Rijndael," Available at: http://csrc.nist.gov/ encryption/aes/rijndael/Rijndael.pdf. Plenty of pertinent material can also be found at: http://www.esat.kuleuven.ac.be/~rijmen/rijndael/.

Dam, Kenneth W., and Herbert S. Lin, eds., *Cryptography's Role In Securing The Information Society,* Computer Science and Telecommunications Board, National Research Council, National Academy Press, Washington, D.C., 1996.

Dandalis, Andreas, Viktor K. Prasanna, and Jose D. P. Rolim, "A Comparative Study of Performance of AES Final Candidates Using FPGAs," Paper presented at *2nd Round AES candidate conference,* April 13–14, New York, Available at: http://csrc.nist.gov/ encryption/aes/round2/conf3/papers/23-adandalis.pdf.

DAQ Software Inc., *Voice over Internet Protocol,* A White Paper by DSQ Software Ltd.

"DARPA Inded Server Search Form," http://www.darpa.mil/searchall/darpasearch.asp—search on term wireless, no author provided, Sponsor: *Defense Advanced Research Projects Agency* (DARPA), 3701 N. Fairfax Dr., Arlington, VA 22203-1714.

Datatec Systems, Inc., 23 Madison Rd., Fairfield, NJ 07004, Tel: 973-808-4000, 800-631-2524 Fax: 973-890-2888, e-mail: info@datatec.com.

"Datatec Systems," http://www.datatec.com/index.html.

Davie, Bruce S., and Yakov Rekhter, *MPLS: Technology & Applications,* San Francisco: Morgan Kauffman, 2000.

Deavours, Cipher A., and Louis Kruh, *Machine Cryptography and Modern Cryptanalysis,* New York: Artech, 1985.

DeCloet, Derek, "Plugged In," *Canadian Business,* June 25, 1999.

Defendis, Megan, "Regulatory Confusion May Cost Jobs," *Crain's Detroit Business*, October 20, 1997.

Deighton, Nigel, *Final Research Project IT for Management Bluetooth,* Gartner Group, http://students.som.yale.edu/ jmw68/Assignments/Final ResearchProject.htm, May 31, 2001.

Delaney, Helen, and Rene van de Zande, *A Guide to EU Standards and Comformity Assessment, Introduction to Europe: A Single Market,* Available at: http://ts.nist.gov/ts/htdocs/210/216/eu-guides/sp951/pg1.htm, Accessed June 26, 2001.

Denning Dorothy, Encryption Policy and Market Trends, May 17, 1997, www.cosc.georgetown.edu/~denning/crypto/Trends.html.

Denning, Dorothy, *Information Warfare and Security,* Boston: Addison Wesley, 1999.

Denning, Dorothy, *Thinking About Cyberweapons Controls,* February 1, 2000, Draft of an Unpublished Paper Presented to the Defense Science Board.

Department of Defense (DOD) Directive 5200.28-STD, Trusted Computer System Evaluation Criteria.

Department of Defense (DoD) Medium Assurance *Public Key Infrastructure* (PKI) Functional Specification DRAFT, Version 0.3, October 20, 1998.

Derfler, Frank J., Jr., "Wireless LANS," *PC,* Online document: www.zdnet.com/pcmag/stories/reviews/0.6755.2470130.00.html, March 28, 2000.

Derfler, Frank J., Jr., and Les Freed, "Wireless LANs," *PC,* April 18, 2000, pp. 226—28.

DeSimio, M. P., and E. P. Glenn, Adaptive generation of decision functions for classification of digitally modulated signals, *NAECON,* 1988, pp. 1010–1014.

Developers Zone, MobileSMS, Mobile Lifestreams Ltd., http://www.dataonsms.com/developers.asp.

Diba, Ahmad, "Voice on the Net," *Fortune,* Vol. 142, No. 8, October 9, 2000, p. 58.

"Digital 21: Knowledge Corner: 3G—Third Generation Wireless Systems" Digital 21, c/o information Technologies Services Department, 15/F, Wanchai Tower, 12, Harbour Road, Wan Chai, Hong Kong, webmaster@digital21.gov.hk, http://www.info.gov.hk/digital21/eng/knowledge/3g.html

Diffie, Whitfield, *Conventional Versus Public Key Cryptosystems,* Secure Communications and Asymmetric Cryptosystems, pp. 41–72, Boulder, CO: Westview Press, 1982.

Diffie, Whitfield, *The First Ten Years of Public-Key Cryptography,* Proceedings of the IEEE, Vol. 76, No. 5, pp. 560–577, May 1988.

Diffie, Whitfield, and M. Hellman, *New Directions In Cryptography, IEEE Transactions on Information Theory,* Vol. 22, pp. 644–654, 1976.

Diffie, Whitfield, and M. Hellman, *Privacy and Authentication: An Introduction to Cryptography,* IEEE proceedings, 673, pp. 397–427, 1979.

Diffie, Whitfield, and Susan Landau, *Privacy on the Line The Politics of Wiretapping and Encryption,* Cambridge, MA: The MIT Press, 1998.

Doble, John, *Introduction to Radio Propagation for Fixed and Mobile Communications,* Artech House, 1996.

DoD Information Infrastructure Public Key Infrastructure PKI Concept of Operations, Third Draft, October 24, 1997, Mitre/Disa/NSA.

Dodd, Annabel Z., *The Essential Guide to Telecommunications,* Upper Saddle River, NJ: Prentice-Hall, 1999.

Doolittle, Sean, "A Chat Room In Every PC," *Smart Computing*, June 2001, pp. 39–41.

Doraswamy, Naganand, and Dan Harkins, *IPsec: The New Security Standard for the Internet, Intranets and Virtual Private Networks,* Upper Saddle River, NJ: Prentice-Hall, 1999.

Douskalis, Bill, *IP Telephony, The Integration of Roust VoIP Service,* Upper Saddle River, NJ: Prentice Hall, 2000.

Dreher, Richard, Lawrence Harte, Steven Kellogg, and Tom Schaffnit, *The Complete Guide To Wireless Technologies: Cellular, PCS, Paging, SMR and Satellite,* APDG Publishing, 1999.

Duffy, Richard, *Sizing the Potential Market for Bluetooth Chips and Devices: Bluetooth '99,* The ARC Group, April 27, 1999.

"Dynamic Adaptable Modem and Cross-Polarization Interference Canceller for Point-to-Point Broadband Wireless Access," http://www.darpa.mil/ito/psum2000/h651-0.html; Principal Investigators: Brad Badke; 8515 E. Anderson Drive, Scottsdale, AZ 85255, 408-607-4812, 408-607-4807 fax, badke.brad@sicom.com & Renee Anderson, 8515 E. Anderson Drive, Scottsdale, AZ 85255, 408-607-4811, 408-607-4807 fax, anderson.renee@sicom.com; Project Web site: http://www.sicom.com.

Economist Technology Quarterly, "The Shape of Phones to Come," March 24, 2001, pp. 24–36, *E-Commerce, The Wall Street Journal Report,* December 11, 2000.

Egan, William F., *Frequency Synthesis by Phase Lock: 2nd edition,* New York: John Wiley & Sons, 2000.

Elachi, Joanna, *Standards Snapshot: The State Of The Big 3 in VoIP Signaling Protocols,* http://www.commweb.com/article/com 20001127S0008, Accessed July 01, 2001.

Elbert, Bruce R., 1997, Introduction to Satellite Communication, Artech Space Application Series.

Elbirt, A. J., W. Yip, B. Chetwynd, and C. Paar, "An FPGA Implementation and Performance Evaluation of the AES Block Cipher Candidate Algorithm Finalists," *The Third Advanced Encryption Standard (AES3) Candidate Conference,* April 13–14, 2000, New York, Available at: http://csrc.nist.gov/encryption/aes/round2/conf3/papers/08-aelbirt.pdf.

Electronic Privacy Information Center, *Cryptography and Liberty 1999: An International Survey of "Emerging Commercial Mobile Wireless Technology and Standards, Suitable for the Army?"* Author: Phillip M. Feldman, p. 69. Report sponsored by the United States Army under Contract No. DASW01-96-C-004, copyright 1998, RAND.

Encryption Policy, self-published, http://www.gilc.org/crypto/crypto-survey-99.html.

Emigh, Jacqueline, PlanetIT Ask the Experts, Mobile & Wireless, *Prediction: Your Dog Will Own a Cell Phone,* January 9, 2001, http://www.planeit.com/tec . . . /mobilewireless/expert/PIT20010109S000017.

Emigh, Jacqueline, "Where Should You Place Your Bets?" *ZDNet Mobile News,* December 23, 2000.

Enhanced Messaging Service White Paper, Ericsson Mobile Communications AB, 2001

Entrust Technologies, *Entrust Technologies Reinforces Commitment to WAP Via Its Certificate Interoperability.*

Entrust Technologies, *Entrust/Toolkit™ for SSL/TLS,* http://www.entrust.com/developer/tls/index.htm.

Epson, The Epson Web site on Bluetooth, http://www.epson.com/, June 7, 2001.

Ericsson, *Bluetooth Home Page,* http://bluetooth.ericsson.se/default.asp.

Ericsson Communications, WLAN Guard 2001.2, April 2001, http://www.ericsson.com/wlan/.

Ericsson Press Photo Library, http://www.ericsson.net/press/phli_paccess.shtml#.

ETSI/GSM Section 6.10, "European Digital Cellular Telecommunications System," (Phase 2); Full Rate.

ETSI/GSM Specification, Vol. 3.0.4, Version 4.0.0, October 1992.

ETSI/GSM Specification, Vol. 2.20, Version 3.0.1, January 1990.

European Union: Standards and the Role of the EU, Available at: http://www.pitt.edu/~wwwes/standards.guide.html, Accessed June 25, 2001.

"Executive Summary, FEDERAL OPERATIONS IN THE 1755–1850 MHZ BAND: The Potential for Accommodating Third Generation Mobile Systems," U.S. Department of Commerce—1401 Constitution Ave. N.W.—Washington, D.C. 20230—(202) 482-7002, http://www.ntia.doc.gov/osmhome/reports/imt2000/execsum.html.

Eyetek Surveillance, The Spy Shop, Chesterfield Derbyshire, England, http://ourworld.compuserve.com/homepages/eyetech/bugged.htm.

"Extensible Authentication Protocol (EAP)," no author provided, http://www.getesuite.com/content/Resources/esuite%20vpn/e-Suite_VPN_whitepaperp15.htm.

eZi Text, eZi Corporation Web Site, http://www.zicorp.com/technology1.htm.

Farley, Mary Ann, "PPV Encryption: A Wait-and-See Game," *Multichannel News*, May 11, 1998.

Farwell, Jennifer, "Something to Talk About: As Quality Improves, VOIP Becomes a Viable Communication Option," *Smart Computing*, Vol. 6, Issue 8, August 2000, pp. 44–49.

Faulkner Flash, Faulkner Information Service, February 24, 2000, Available on INTELINK at: http://doserve.mall.nsa.ic.gov/, Accessed May 11, 2001.

Fausett, Laurene, *Fundamentals of Neural Networks: Architectures, Algorithms and Applications,* Upper Saddle River, NJ: Prentice Hall, 1994.

Fazel, Khaled, and Gerhard P. Fettweis, eds., *Multi-Carrier Spread Spectrum,* Dordrecht, the Netherlands: Kluwer Academic Press, 1997.

FCC Adopts Annual Report on State of Competition in the Wireless Industry. FCC News, 2001, Available at: http://www.fcc.gov/bureaus/wireless/news_releases/2001/nrw10117.html, Accessed June 21, 2001.

FCC Takes Steps to Implement the Wireless Communications and Public Safety Act of 1999. FCC News, 2000, Available at: http://www.fcc.gov/bureaus/wireless/news_releases/2000/nrwl0029.html, Accessed June 21, 2001.

FCC Wireless 911 Requirements, FCC Fact Sheet, Available at: http://www.fcc.gov/e911/factsheet_requirements_012001.txt, Accessed June 21, 2001.

Fear Gates, http://WAP.com, March 5, 2001.

Feghhi, Jahal, Jahil Feghhi, and Peter Williams, *Digital Certificates: Applied Internet Security,* Addison Wesley, 1998.

Feher, Kamilo, ed., *Advanced Digital Communications: Systems and Signal Processing Techniques,* Tucker, GA: Noble Publishing Corp., 1997.

Feher, Kamilo, ed., *Telecommunications Measurements, Analysis and Instrumentation,* Tucker, GA: Noble Publishing Corp., 1997.

Feher, Kamilo, *Wireless Digital Communications: Modulation & Spread Spectrum Applications*, Upper Saddle River, NJ: Prentice Hall, 1995.

Feibel, Werner, *Complete Encyclopedia of Networking,* San Jose: Novell Press, 1995.

Field, Benjamin J., "Wireless Security Overview," April 25, 2000, bjfield@sunlightdesign.com, http://www.securityportal.com/research/wireless/wirelessgeneral20000421.html.

Feldman, Philip M., *Emerging Commercial Mobile Wireless Technology and Standards: Suitable for the Army?,* Arroyo Center, CA: Rand, 1998.

FIPS 113, Computer Data Authentication, specifies a Data Authentication Algorithm, based upon the DES, which may be used to detect unauthorized modifications to data, both intentional and accidental. The Message Authentication Code as specified in ANSI X9.9 is computed in the same manner as the Data Authentication Code as specified in this standard.

FIPS 140-1, Security Requirements for Cryptographic Modules, establishes the physical and logical security requirements for the design and manufacture of modules implementing NSIT-approved cryptographic algorithms.

FIPS 171, Key Management Using ANSI X9.17, adopts ANSI X9.17 and specifies a particular selection of options for the automated distribution of keying material by the federal government using the protocols of ANSI X9.17.

FIPS 180, Secure Hash Standard SHS, specifies a Secure Hash Algorithm SHA for use with the Digital Signature Standard. Additionally, for applications not requiring a digital signature, the SHA is to be used whenever a secure hash algorithm is required for federal applications.

FIPS 186, Digital signature Standard, National Institute for Standards and Technology, 1993, Available at: http://csrc.ncsl.nist.gov/fips/.

FIPS 186, Digital Signature Standard DSS, specifies a Digital Signature Algorithm appropriate for applications requiring a digital rather than a written signature.

FIPS 1985, Escrowed Encryption Standard (EES), Specifies a voluntary technology available for protecting telephone communications, for example, voice, fax, modem.

FIPS 46-2, Data Encryption Standard (DES), Provides the technical specifications for the DES.

FIPS PUB 190, Guideline for the Use of Advanced Authentication Technology Alternatives, FIPS PUB 46-1, National Bureau of Standards, Data Encryption Standard, 1987.

Fischer, Victor, and Milos Drutarovský, "Two Methods of Rijndael Implementation in Reconfigurable Hardware," *CHES 2001, Cryptographic Hardware and Embedded Systems Workshop, Paris, France, May 14–16, 2001, Proceedings,* pp. 81–96.

FLEETSATCOM Operations, www.fas.org/spp/military/program/com/fleet_ops.htm.

Ford, Warwick, *Computer Communications Security, Principles, Standard Protocols and Techniques,* Prentice Hall, 1994.

Ford, Warwick, and Michael S. Baum, *Secure Electronic Commerce: Building the Infrastructure for Digital Signatures and Encryption,* Prentice Hall, 1997.

Foreman, Michael, "Government Able to Demand Keys to Encrypted Data," *Technology News,* New Zealand, May 12, 2000.

Forsyth, Chris, "The Wireless Revolution," *Sybase,* Winter 2001 ed.

Fratto, Mike, "Tutorial: Wireless Security," *Network Computing,* January 22, 2001, http://www.networkcomputing.com/shared/printArticle?article+nc/1202/1202fldfull.html &pub.

Freeman, Roger L., *Radio System Design for Telecommunications,* 2nd Ed., New York: John Wiley & Sons, 1997.

Freeman, Roger L., *Telecommunication System Engineering,* 3rd Ed., New York: John Wiley & Sons, 1996.

Friedman, William F., *Advanced Military Cryptography,* Laguna Hills, CA: Aegean Park Press, 1976.

Friedman, William F., and Lambros D. Callimahos, *Cryptanalytics Part I—Volume 2,* Laguna Hills, CA: Aegean Park Press, 1985.

Friedman, William F., and Lambros D. Callimahos, *Cryptanalytics Part III,* Laguna Hills, CA: Aegean Park Press, 1995.

Friedman, William F., and Lambros D. Callimahos, *Cryptanalytics Part IV,* Laguna Hills, CA: Aegean Park Press, 1995.

Friedman, William F., and Lambros D. Callimahos, *Military Cryptanalytics Part I—Volume I,* Laguna Hills, CA: Aegean Park Press, 1985.

F-Secure Computer Virus Information Pages, http://www.europe.f-secure.com/v-descs/timofon.shtml.

Fulghum, David A., 1996, "Duplicating Enemy Voices Becoming a Combat Skill," *Aviation Week & Space Technology,* July 8, 1996, pp. 48–49.

Fulton, William, *Algebraic Curves—An Introduction to Algebraic Geometry,* Reading, MA: W. A. Benjamin, Inc., 1969.

Fusco, Patricia, "Hope for U.S. Encryption Policy?" *ISP Planet,* June 14, 1999, http://ispplanet.com/politics/encryption.html.

Gaines, Helen Fouche, *Elementary Cryptanalysis,* Dover, 1956.

Gaj, Kris, and Pawel Chodowiec, *Comparison of the Hardware Performance of the AES Candidates Using Reconfigurable Hardware,* Paper presented at the 3rd AES Conference and available from the NIST Web site at: http://csrc.nist.gov/encryption/aes/round2/conf3/papers/22-kgaj.pdf.

Garamone, Jim, Washington: American Forces Press Service, June 2, 2000.

Garfinkel, Simon, and Gene Spafford, *Web Security and Commerce,* O'Reilly, 1997.

Gartner Group Report, September 2000.

Gartner Group, *Wireless Application Protocol (WAP): A Perspective,* November 20, 2000.

Garrett, Paul B., *Making, Breaking Codes: An Introduction to Cryptology,* Upper Saddle River, NJ: Prentice Hall, 2001.

Gates, Bill, *Business @ The Speed of Thought: Using A Digital Nervous System,* Warner Books, 1999.

Geier, Jim, *Overview of the IEEE 802.11 Standard,* Wireless-Nets Consulting Services, Online document: www.wireless-nets.com/whitepaper_overview_802.11.htm, April 9, 1999.

Gennaro, R., *An Improved Pseudo-Random Generator Based on Discrete Log,* CRYPTO'2000, LNCS 1880, pp. 469–481, New York: Springer-Verlag, 2000. Also available in an updated version at: http://www.research.ibm/com/people/r/rosario/prng.ps.

Gerbig, Amanda, "AT&T Strategic Ventures invests $10 million in Nuera Communications to Speed Delivery of Broadband Voice to Customer Worldwide," http://www.nuera.com/news/pr081500.cfm.

Gerwin, Kate, "Voice Rises Up," *Tele.com,* November 27, 2000, http://www.teledotcom.com/article/tel2000127S0022/2, Accessed June 2001.

Gibilisco, Stan, *Handbook of Radio & Wireless Technology,* McGraw-Hill, 1999.

Gibson, Jerry, *The Communications Handbook,* Boca Raton, FL: CRC Press, 1997.

Gifford, James, "Wireless Broadband Networks for Voice & Data," *Computer Telephony,* March 1, 2000, http://www.computertelephony.com/article/printableArticle?doc_id=CTM 20000524S00009

Gillian, Stephen, *Vulnerabilities Within Wireless Application Protocol,* SANS Institute, August 31, 2000.

Gladman, Bryan, *The AES Algorithm (Rijndael) in C and C++,* April 2001, Available at: http://fp.gladman.plus.com/cryptography_technology/rijndael/index.htm.

Glesner, Manfred, and Werner Pöcchmüller, *Neurocomputers: An Overview of Neural Networks in VLSI,* London, U.K: Chapman and Hall, 1994.

Glisic, Savo and Branka Vucetic, *Spread Spectrum CDMA Systems for Wireless Communications,* Norwood, MA: Artech House, 1997.

"Global Information Infrastructure Report," The President's National Security Telecommunications Advisory Committee, May 2000, p. 27.

GN Netcom, The GN Netcom Web site on Bluetooth, http://www.gnnetcom.com/usa/9000.bt.html, June 10, 2001.

Gold, Steve, "5 Billion Text Messages a Month—and Counting," *Computer User,* June 1, 2001, http://www.computeruser.com/news/01/06/01/news11.html.

Gold, Steve, "No Strings Attached," *Security,* Vol. 12, No. 2.

Gold, Steve, *Sprint PCS—First To Market In US With 3G This Year*, http://www. newsbytes.com/news/01/163202.html.

Goldberg, Andy, "Bluetooth Teething Troubles," *The Standard*, March 22, 2001, http://www.thestandard.com/article/0.1902.23056.00.html.

Goldberg, Randy, and Lance Riek, *A Practical Handbook of Speech Coders*, New York: CRC, 2000.

Goldreich, O., *Modern Cryptography, Probabilistic Proofs and Pseudo-Randomness*, Springer-Verlag, 2000.

Golmie, Nada, IEEE p802.15 Working Group for Wireless Personal Area Networks, Dialog with FCC, National Institute of Standards and Technology, IEEE document 802.1501/00144r0, March 2001, http://www.ieee802.org/15/pub/TG2.html, May 30, 2001.

Golmie, Nada, R. E. Van Dyck, and A. Soltanian, *Bluetooth and 802.11b Interference: Simulation Model and Systems Results*, IEEE 802.11b Working Group for Wireless Personal Area Networks, http://www.ieee802.org/15/pub/2001/May01/01195r0P802-15_TG2-BT-802-11-Model-Results.pdf, Accessed June 18, 2001.

Golomb, S. W. Correlation Properties of Periodic and Aperiodic Sequences and Applications to Multi-User Systems, *Proc. NATO Advanced Study Institute on Multi-User Communications*, Norwich, U.K., 1980, pp. 161–197.

Goncalves, Marcus, *Voice over IP Networks*, New York: McGraw-Hill, 1999.

Gong, G. Z. T. Dai, and S. W. Golomb, Criterion and Counting for Cyclically shift distinct q-ary GMW sequences of period $q<V>n-1<V>$, *IEEE Trans. on Inform. Theory*, Vol. 46, No. 2, March 2000, pp. 474–484.

GPRS Gb Protocol Stack, Overview, Hughes Software Systems, http://www.hssworld.com/products/gprs/stacks/gprs_gb/gprs_home.htm.

Graff, Jon C., *Cryptography and E-Commerce*, John Wiley & Sons, 2001.

Green, Andy, "Internet Focus: Taking The First Steps To VOIP," *Teleconnect*, March 5, 2001, http://www.teleconnect.com/article/printableArticle?doc_id=TCM20010227S0011, Accessed May 2001.

Greiner, Lynn. *Mobile Commerce*, Faulkner Information Services, 2000, Available on INTELINK at: http://doserve.mall.nsa.ic.gov/, Accessed May 11, 2001.

Griffin, Andrew, Osha, Joseph and Dennis, Ron, *Bluetooth Handbook 1.1*, Merrill Lynch, Pierce, Fenner & Smith, U.S., June 29, 2000, p. 4.

Grewal, Mohinder S. and Angus P. Andrews, *Kalman Filtering: Theory and Practice*, Englewood Cliffs, NJ: Prentice-Hall, 1993.

Groe, John B., and Lawrence E. Larson, *CDMA Mobile Radio Design*, Boston: Artech House, 2000.

Grust, Don, *Developing Wireless Applications*. Presented at Networld+Interop 2001. Las Vegas, NV, May 2001.

"GSM—An Introduction to WAP," *GSM World*, http://www.gsmworld.com/technology/yes2wap.html, February 1, 2001.

"GSM Association CEO Backs WAP Success," *GSM World*, http://www.gsmworld.com/news/press_2001/press_releases_3.html, February 6, 2001.

"GSM—Optima WAP Bearer," *GSM World*, http://www.gsmworld.com/technology/wap_05.html#ussd.

Guidelines for the Security of Information Systems, http://www.oecd.org/dsti/sti/it/secur/index.htm.

Gupta, Narij K., *Wireless Broadband 4G: 100 Mbps in Your Palm*, Available at: http://www.voicendata.com/content/columns/fromcell/101010301.asp, Accessed June 8, 2001.

Gupta, Rajarshi, *Cellular Digital Packet Data* (CDPD), February 24, 1998, April 2, 2001, http://www.cs.berkeley.edu/~adj/cs294-1.s98/CDPD/.

Gustafson, H., E. Dawson, W. Caelli, Comparison of Block Ciphers, In *Proceedings of AUSCRYPT '90,* J. Seberry and J. Piepryzk, eds., pp. 208–220, 1990.

Hac, Anna, *Multimedia Applications Support for Wireless ATM Networks*, Upper Saddle River, NJ: Prentice-Hall, 2000.

Haddad, Richard A., and Thomas W. Parsons, *Digital Signal Processing: Theory, Applications and Hardware,* New York: Computer Science Press, 1991.

Hagenauer, J., 1987, *Forward Error Correction Coding for Fading Compensation in Mobile Satellite Channels,* IEEE Journal On Selected Areas in Communications.

Hager, Nicky, 1997 *Exposing the Global Surveillance System,* No. 59—Winter *1996–1997*, pp. 21–26.

Halabi, Sam, and Danny McPherson (contributor), *Internet Routing Architectures,* San Jose, CA: Cisco Press, 2000.

Hammar, Sven, "PKI Enables Digital Signatures," [Web article], *NWFusion.com,* http://www.nwfusion.com/news/tech/2000/1030tech.html, Accessed March 05, 2001.

Harte, Lawrence, J. Adrian, D. Smith, and Charles A. Jacobs, *IS-136 TDMA Technology, Economics and Services,* Norwood, MA: Artech House, 1998.

Harte, Lawrence, Richard Levine, and Geoff Livingston, *GSM Superphones,* McGraw-Hill, 1999.

Harte, Lawrence, Steve Prokup, and Richard Levine, *Cellular and PCS: The Big Picture,* McGraw-Hill, 1997.

Harte, Lawrence, Tom Schaffnit, Steven Kellogg, *The Comprehensive Guide to Wireless Technologies,* ADPG Press, August 1999.

Hasselmeyer, Peer, et. al, *Pay as You Go—Associating Costs with Jini Leases,* April 2, 2001, http://www.ito.tu-darmstadt.de/publs/papers/edoc00.pdf.

Haykin, M. E., and R. B. J. Warnar, *Smart Card Technology: New Methods for Computer Access Control,* NIST Special Publication 500-157, September 1988.

Haykin, Simon, *Adaptive Filter Theory,* 3rd Ed., Upper Saddle River, NJ: Prentice-Hall, 1996.

Haykin, Simon, *Neural Networks, A Comprehensive Foundation,* 2nd Ed., Upper Saddle River, NJ: Prentice-Hall, 1999.

Hearing before the Select Committee On Intelligence of the United States Senate One Hundred Fourth Congress Second Session on Current and Projected National Security Threats to the United States and its Interests Abroad, Thursday, February 22, 1996.

Hedy, Lamar photograph from www.imdb.com.

Heile, Robert F., *IEEE 802.15_WAPNs,* Presentation at Networld+Interop 2001, Las Vegas, NV, May 2001.

Held, Gil, *Data Over Wireless Networks: Bluetooth, WAP & Wireless LANs,* McGraw-Hill, Inc., 2001, p. 212.

Hermelin, M., and K. Nyberg, *Correlation Properties of the Bluetooth Combiner,* Proceedings of the ICISC '99, Springer-Verlag LNCS 1787, 1999, pp. 17–29, Available at: http://citeseer.nj.nec.com/271131.html, Accessed June 18, 2001.

Hewitt, Rod, *North American MPEG-2 Information,* 1999, Published at: http://www.coolstf.com/mpeg/.

Hirade Kenkichi, and Kazuaki Murota, "A Study of Modulation for Digital Mobile Telephony," *29th IEEE Vehicular Technology Conf.,* March 1979.

Hirsch, Herbert, *Statistical Signals Characterization,* Artech House, 1991.

Hoffman, Eric, *Random Number Generator,* 1996, U.S. Patent 5,706,208.

Hoffstein, J., J. Pipher, and J. Silverman, *NTRU: A New High-Speed Public-Key Cryptosystem,* J. Buhler, ed., Lecture Notes in Computer Science, Vol. 1423, Algorithmic Number Theory, ANTS III, pp. 267–288, Berlin: Springer-Verlag, 1998.

Hogan, Monica, "DBS Turns Eye Towards Two-Way Data Services," *Multichannel News,* February 12, 2001.

Holma, Harri, and Antti Toskala, eds., *WCDMA for UMTS: Radio Access for 3rd Generation Mobile Communications,* New York: John Wiley & Sons, 2000.

Holmes, J. K., Coherent Spread Spectrum Systems, New York: John Wiley & Sons, 1982.

Horak, Ray, *Communications Systems and Networks,* IDG Books Worldwide, 2nd Ed., 2001.

Horak, Ray, *How Secure Is Your Connection?* New York: M&T Books, 2000.

How to Build a Wireless Office: The Next Wireless Revolution, Gartner, February 4, 2000.

How Voice Travels over IP [article on-line], http://www.dqindia.com/cgi-bin/printer. asp?id=23008, Accessed May 30, 2001.

How Will WAP Work With GPRS? WAP FAQ for Developers: 9.4, http://wap.com/cgi-bin/wapfaq.cgi?chapter=9.4.

Howe, Dennis, *The Free On-Line Directory of Computing,* 1999, http://wombat.doc.ic. ac.uk.

Howgrave-Graham, Nick, Dyer, Joan, and Gennaro, Rosario, *Pseudo-Random Number Generation on the IBM 4758 Secure Crypto Coprocessor,* CHES 2001, International Workshop on Cryptographic Hardware and Embedded Systems, Proceedings, pp. 97–106.

http://allnetdevices.com/faq/?pair=01.004.

http://biz.yahoo.com/rf/010222/123508129_2.html, March 5, 2001.

http://www.cisco.com/warp/public/759/ipj_1-1_SSL1.html.

http://www.ericsson.com/3g/how/index.shtml, February 12, 2001.

http://www.gsmworld.com/technology/yes2wap.html#3.

http://www.hostuffworks.com/.

http://www.wapforum.org, March 7, 2001.

http://www.wirelessinanutshell.com/wap/whatis_wap.shtml.

HuiChan, Agnes, DARPA Quad Chart; "Security Protocols for Wireless," http://www. darpa.mil/ito/Quad_Chart2000/J7720-20000726110124.PPT, Sponsor: *Defense Advanced Research Projects Agency* (DARPA), 3701 N. Fairfax Dr., Arlington, VA 22203-1714.

Huovinen, Lasse, *Authentication and Security in GPRS Environment: An Overview,* Department of Computer Science and Engineering, Helsinki University of Technology, http://www.hut.fi/~lhouvine/netsec98/gprs_access.html.

Hutt, A. E., S. Bosworth, and D. B. Hoyt, eds., *Computer Security Handbook,* 3rd Ed., New York: John Wiley & Sons, 1995.

Hyatt, Richard, SMSgt and Korte, Thomas, *VoIP Holds Promise but Implementation Issues must be Addressed,* Intercom, Air Force Communications Agency Scott Air Force Base, May 2001, pp. 30–31.

IBM, The IBM Web site on Bluetooth, http://www.ibm.com/, June 9, 2001.

IEEE 802.15 WPAN™ Task Group 2 TG2, http://www.ieee802.org/15/pub/TG2.html, Accessed June 18, 2001.

i-Mode FAW, WestCyber Corporation, http://imodelinks.com/desktop/faq.html#1, March 5, 2001.

Infrared Data Association, Commonly Asked Questions About irDA, http://www.irda.org/use/faq.asp, Accessed June 18, 2001.

Inglis, Andrew F., and Arch C. Luther, *Satellite Technology: An Introduction,* 2nd Ed., Focal Press, 1997.

Initiative, 1/23/01, http://www.entrust.com/news/files/01_23_01_673.htm.

Innes, Stuart, "No Excuse For Being Late at the Airport," *The Advertiser,* May 30, 2001, http://www.theadvertiser.com.au/common/story_page/0.4511.2054410%5E2682.00.html.

Inventel, the Inventel Web site on Bluetooth, http://www.inventel.com/bluedsl.html, June 11, 2001.

IP Telephony Opportunities, http://www.ipaxs.com/images/Iptel-opportunities.pdf, Accessed June 13, 2001.

IPsec [encyclopedia online] (Needham, MA: Whatis.Com, 2001), http://whatis.tech target.com/definition/0.289893.sid9_gci214037.00.html, Accessed June 10, 2001.

ITworld.com, *802.11b Satisfies High-Speed Wireless LAN Requirements,* Online document: http://www.itworld.com/Net/1749/ITnet-geier-0323/, March 22, 2000.

Jamiol, Christine, "Medium Access Control Functions," http://www.iol.unh.edu/training/vganylan/teach/vgconcepts/mac/macsum.html

Jerome, Marty, "Wireless: Business Will Never Be The Same," *PC Computing,* www.pccomputing.com, April 2000, p. 78.

Jeruchim, Michel C., Philip Balaban and K. Sam Shanmugan, *Simulation of Communication Systems,* New York: Plenum Press, 992.

Johnson Consulting, http://www.abc.se/~m10183/bluet00.htm, Accessed June 18, 2001.

Johnson, Dana J., Bryan C. Gabbard, and Scott Pace, *Space,* New York: The Rand Corporation, 1998.

Johnson, Don B., "Future Resiliency and High Security Systems," *ECC,* March 30, 1999.

Joint Chiefs of Staff JCS1995, Joint Publication 6-0, Doctrine for Command, Control, Communications and Computer Systems Support to Joint Operations.

Joint Chiefs of Staff JCS2000, Joint Publication 3-51, Joint Doctrine for Electronic Warfare.

Joint Chiefs of Staff JCS 2001, Joint Spectrum Vision 2010.

Jondral, F., "Automatic Classification If High-Frequency Signals," *Signal Processing,* Vol. 9, No. 3, October 1985, pp. 177–190.

Jones, Jennifer, "Fixed Wireless Goes After DSL," *InfoWorld,* pp. 34–35, February 26, 2001.

Jormalainen, Sami, and Jouni Laine, *Security in the WTLS,* 10/1/00, http://www.hut.fi/~jtlaine2/wtls/.

Juha, Vainio, *Bluetooth Security; Encryption,* http://www.niksula.cs.hut.fi/~jiitv/bluesec.html, copyright 2001-05-25.

Jun, Benjamin, and Paul Kocher, *The Intel® Random Number Generator,* Cryptography Research, Inc., White Paper prepared for Intel Corporation, April 22, 1999, http://www.cryptography.com/intelRNG.pdf.

Kahn, David, *The Codebreakers: The Story of Secret Writing,* 2nd Ed., New York: Macmillan, 1997.

Kailath, Thomas, Ali H. Sayed, and Babak Hassibi, *Linear Estimation,* Upper Saddle River, NJ: Prentice-Hall, 2000.

Kamerman, Ad, *Coexistence Between Bluetooth and IEEE 802.11 CCK—Solutions to Avoid Mutual Interference,* in IEEE P802.11 Working Group Contribution, IEEE P802.1100/162r0, July 4, 2000, http://grouper.ieee.org/groups/802/15/arc/802-15-2list/msg00048.html.

Kamerman, Ad, and Nedim Erkocevic, *Microwave Oven Interference on Wireless LANs Operating in the 2.4 GHz ISM Band,* Lucent Technologies, March 30, 2001 http://www.palowireless.colm/infotooth/knowbase/othernetworks/17.asp.

Kang, Sung-Mo, and Jusuf Leblebici, *CMOS Digital Integrated Circuits—Analysis and Design,* 2nd Ed., New York: WCB McGraw-Hill, 1999.

Kant, Shri, "Application of Pattern Recognition in Cryptology Proc," Of INFOSEC Bangalore, pp. 104–118.

Kant, Shri, *What Help a Classification Technique Can Provide to a Cryptanalyst,* Proc. 3rd Int. Conf. on Pattern Recognition and Digital Technique, I.S.I Calcutta, 1993, pp. 651–660.

Kant, Shri, and Laxmi Narain, "Analysis of Some Stream & Block Ciphers: Using Pattern Recognition Tools," *NSCR '98*, July 9–10,1998, C10–C21.

Kant, Shri, and Neelam Verma, *An Effective Source Recognition Algorithm: Extraction of Significant Binary Words, Pattern Recognition Letters,* 21, 2000, pp. 981–988.

Kant, Shri, and Verma Neelam, "Recognition of the Type of Polynomial and Coding Scheme," *NSCR '98*, July 9–10, 1998, C1–C9.

Kant, Shri, Laxmi Narain, and D. K. Garg, "Evaluating the Strength of Cryptoalgorithm: Souvenir," *INFOSEC-99*, MCTE Mhow, 1999.

Kant, Shri, T. L. Rao, and P. N. Sundaram, *An Automatic and Stable Clustering Algorithm Pattern Recognition Letters,* 15, 1994, pp. 543–549.

Kardach, James, *Bluetooth Architecture Overview,* Intel Technology Journal, 2nd quarter, 2000 Ed., http://developer.intel.com/technology/itj/q22000/articles/art_la.htm, Accessed June 18, 2001.

Kärkkäinen, Kari, *Code Families and Their Performance Measures for CDMA and Military Spread-Spectrum Systems,* Ph.D. Thesis, Dept. of Electrical Engineering, University of Oulu, Finland, 1996, Acta Universitatis Ouluensis Technica C89, 1996.

Kay, Steven M., *Fundamental of Statistical Signal Processing, Vol. I: Estimation Theory,* Upper Saddle River, NJ: Prentice Hall, 1993.

Kay, Steven M., *Fundamental of Statistical Signal Processing, Vol. II: Detection Theory,* Upper Saddle River, NJ: Prentice Hall, 1998.

Nonlinear Feedforward Logic (NLFFL) Pseudonoise Sequences, *Proc. IEEE MILCOM '93, Military Communications Conference,* Vol. 2, October 11–14, 1993, Boston.

Kassel, Amelia, "Internet Access by Satellite," *Online*, July–August 1998.

Katz, Gregory, *As Europe's Wireless Market Booms, Lack of Single Standard Bogs Down U.S.,* Available at: http://www.siliconvalley.com/docs/news/tech/059878.htm, Accessed June 7, 2001.

Katzenbeisser, Stephan, and Fabien A. P. Petitcolas, *Information Hiding—Techniques for Steganography and Digital Watermarking,* New York: Artech House, 2000.

Kaufman, Charlie, Radia Perlman, and Mike Speciner, *Network Security: Private Communication in a Public World,* Upper Saddle River, NJ: Prentice Hall, 1995.

Kaufman, Jerry, "Introduction—Analysis of Customer Demand and Requirements for Mobile Internet and Third Generation Wireless Products and Services," 2000, Alexander Resources (online) at: www.alexanderresources.com.

KDD Okinawa Service Co., Ltd., Microsoft Internet Services Network, http://www.microsoft.com/ISN/case_studies/kdd.asp.

Kent, S. and R. Atkinson, *IP Authentication Header RFC 2402,* 11/98, http://www.ietf.org/rfc/rfc2402.txt.

Kent, S., and R. Atkinson, *IP Encapsulating Security Payload ESP RFC 2406,* 11/98, http://www.ietf.org/rfc/rfc2406.txt.

Kent, S., and R. Atkinson, "Security Architecture for the Internet Protocol: RFC 2401," *Internet Society*, 1998, http://www.ietf.org/rfc/rfc2401.text, Accessed June 10, 2001.

Kent, Stephen, *How Many Certification Authorities are Enough?* BBN Technologies, unclassified Presentation, Cambridge, MA 1997, Presentations at RSA Data Conference, 1996 and DIMACS Workshop on Trust Management, 1996.

Kent, Stephen, *Let a Thousand 10,000? CAs Reign,* Keynote for Defense Information Management Seminar DIMACS Workshop on Trust Management, September 1996.

Kent, Stephen, *Reasoning About Public-Key Certification,* Presentation at RSA Data Security Conference, January 1996.

Keyware Technologies, Inc., http://www.l.slb.com/smartcards/associates/members/keyware.html, 500 West Cummings Park, Suite 3600, Woburn, MA, 01801, POC Mr. Eric Anderson, 781-933-1311, www.keywareusa.com.

King, Rachel, "Broadband Wireless Battles To Get Grounded," *Inter@ctive Week*, September 19, 1999, Retrieved from the World Wide Web, February 25, 2001, http://www.zdnet.com/filters/printerfriendly/0.6061.2339034-2.00.html.

Kipnis, Barry, *Wireless Web Access Market Trends*, Faulkner Information Services. 2000, Available on INTELINK at: http://doserve.mall.nsa.ic.gov/, Accessed May 11, 2001.

Kippenhahn, Rudolf, *Code Breaking: A History and Exploration,* Overlook Press, 1999.

Klander, Lars, *Hacker Proof: The Ultimate Guide to Network Security,* Las Vegas, NV: JAMSA Press, 1997.

Knudsen, Jonathan, *Java Cryptography,* O'Reilly, 1998.

Knuth, Donald E., *The Art of Computer Programming in Three Volumes,* 1997.

Koblitz, Neal, *A Course in Number Theory and Cryptography,* 2nd Ed., Springer-Verlag, 1994.

Koblitz, Neal, *A Family of Jacobians Suitable for Discrete Log Cryptosystems,* In Shafi Goldwasser, ed., Advances in Cryptology—Crypto '88, Springer-Verlag, Lecture Notes in Computer Science, Vol. 403, pp. 94–99, Berlin, 1989.

Koblitz, Neal, *Algebraic Aspects of Cryptography,* Algorithms and Computation in Mathematics, New York: Springer-Verlag, 998.

Koblitz, Neal, *CM-curves with good cryptographic properties,* Advances in Cryptology —CRYPTO '91, Lecture Notes in Computer Science, Vol. 576, Springer-Verlag, pp. 279–287, 1992.

Koblitz, Neal, *Elliptic Curve Cryptosystems,* Mathematics of Computation, Vol. 48, pp. 203–209, 1987.

Koblitz, Neal, "Hyperelliptic Cryptosystems," In Ernest F. Brickell, ed., *Journal of Cryptology*, pp. 139–150, 1989.

Koblitz, Neal, A. J. Menezes, and S. A. Vanstone, "The state of elliptic curve cryptography, Design," *Codes and Cryptography*, 19 2/3: pp.173–193, March 2000.

Koç, Ç. K., and C. Paar, eds., *Cryptographic Hardware and Embedded Systems,* Lecture Notes in Computer Science, No. 1717, pp. 94–108, Berlin, Germany: Springer-Verlag, 1999.

Koç, Ç. K., T. Acar, and B. S. Kaliski, Jr., "Analyzing and comparing Montgomery multiplication algorithms," *IEEE Micro*, 16 3: pp. 26–33, June 1996.

Koç, Ç. K., and C. Paar, eds., *Cryptographic Hardware and Embedded systems,* Lecture Notes in Computer Science, No. 1717, pp. 94–108, Berlin, Germany: Springer-Verlag, 1999.

Koç, Ç. K., T. Acar, and B. S. Kaliski, Jr., "Analyzing and comparing Montgomery multiplication algorithms," *IEEE Micro,* 16(3): pp. 26–33, June 1996.

Komagan, Chan, "allNetDevices:—Wireless 3G: The Future of Wireless—Page 4," ckomagan@scient.com, Senior Associate, http://www.scient.com, http://www.allnetdevices.com/developer/white/2000/06/30/wireless3g4.html.

Kondisetty, Sudhakar. *VoIP in Your Contact Center—Much More than Cheap Phone Call,* http://www.computerworld.com/cwi/story/0.1199.NAV47_STO59262.00.html, April 5, 2001.

Kong, Deborah, "FCC To Allow Tracking of Wireless Calls," *Mercury News*, August 28, 1999, 69://http://www.mercurycenter.com/svtech/news/indepth/docs/074697.htm.

Kosiur, David R., and Dave Kosiur, *IP Multicasting: The Complete Guide to Interactive Corporate Networks*, New York: John Wiley & Sons, 1998.

Koren, Israel, *Computer Arithmetic Algorithms,* Amherst: Brookside Court Publishers, 1998.

Korhonen, Juha, *Introduction to 3G Mobile Communications,* Boston: Artech House, 2001.

Krechmer, Ken, "Communications Standards Review," http://www.crstds.com.

Krechmer, Ken, "World Standards Day 1995," krechmer@csrstds.com, Communications Standards Review, 757 Greer Road Palo Alto, CA, 94303-3024, +1-650-856-8836, http://www.csrstds.com, http://csrstds.com/gih.html.

Krüger, Gerhard, *The Digital Battlefield of the Future,* April 5, 2000, retrieved from the World Wide Web, March 12, 2001, http://www.ccii.co.za/COMPANY/Press%20Releases/digitb.html.

Kumar, I. J., *Cryptology: System Identification and Key-Clustering,* Laguna Hills, CA: Aegean Park Press, 1997.

Kumar, Murthy V., *Abelian Varieties—Optimal Cryptography for Wireless Communications?* Wireless Security Perspectives, Toronto, Canada: Cellular Network Perspectives Ltd., November 2000.

Kumar, Murthy V., *Introduction to Abelian Varieties,* CRM Monograph Series, Vol. 3, Providence, RI: American Mathematical Society, 993.

Kumar, Balaji, *Broadband Communications: A Professional's Guide to ATM, Frame Relay, SMDS, SONET and B-ISDN,* New York: McGraw-Hill, 1995.

Kung, S. Y., *Digital Neural Networks*, Englewood Cliffs, NJ: Prentice Hall, 1993.

Kuo, Henry, and Ingrid Verbauwhede, "Architectural Optimization for a 1.82 Gbps VLSI Implementation of the AES Rijndael Algorithm," private communication, also presented at *CHES 2001, Cryptographic Hardware and Embedded Systems Workshop, Paris, France, May 14–16, 2001, Proceedings,* pp. 53–67.

Labovitz, Bruce, *Voice-over-IP VOIP Arrives in the Last Mile in Philadelphia,* http://www.neura.com/news/pr042401.cfm.

Lai, Xuejia, *On the Design and Security of Block Ciphers,* ETH Series in Information Processing, Vol. 1, 1992.

Lake, Anthony, *6 Nightmares,* Little, Boston: Brown and Company, 2000.

LaMacchia, B. A., and A. M. Odlyzko, "Computation of Discrete Logarithms in Prime Fields," *Designs, Codes and Cryptography*, Vol. I, pp. 47–62, 1991.

Lamm, Gregory, Gerlando Faluto, and others, *Security Attacks Against Bluetooth Wireless Networks,* Self-published Internet report, December 4, 2000, http://www.people.virginia.edu/~gal4y/Bluetooth.doc.

Landau, Susan, *Eavesdropping and Encryption: U.S. Policy in an International Perspective*, http://www.ksg.harvard.edu/iip/iicompol/papers/landau.html.

Larson, Lawrence E., ed., *RF and Microwave Circuit Design for Wireless Communications,* Norwood, MA: Artech House, 1998.

Lee, C. Y. William, *Mobile Cellular Telecommunications,* New York: McGraw-Hill, 1995.

Lee, Chris, *Bluetooth to Grow Steadily,* ZDNetUK, June 1, 2001, Available at: http://news.zdnet.co.uk/story/0.s2088048.00.html, Accessed June 18, 2001.

Lee, Edward A., and David G. Messerschmitt, *Digital Communication,* 2nd Ed., Norwell, MA: Kluwer Academic Publishers, 1994.

Lee, Jhong Sam, and Leonard E. Miller, *CDMA Systems Engineering Handbook,* Norwood, MA: Artech House, 1998.

Lee, L. H. Charles, *Convolutional Coding Fundamentals and Applications,* Norwood, MA: Artech House, 1997.

Lee, Wei Meng, Soo Mee Foo, Karli Watson, and Ted Fugofski, *Beginning WAP, WML & WMLScript,* Wrox Press, Inc., 2000.

Legard, David, "Citibank, M1 bring mobile banking to Asia," *Computerworld*, IDG News Service, Singapore Bureau, Hong Kong, January 14, 1999, http://www.cw.com.hk/News/n990114002.htm.

Legard, David, *Spain, Brazil to Join Forefront of 3G,* Available at: http://www.idg.net/idgns/2001/03/07/Update1InternetworldSpainBrazelTo.shtml, Accessed May 15, 2001.

Leitold, Herbert, Wolfgang Mayerwieser, Udo Payer, Karl-Christian Posch, Reinhard Posch, and Johannes Wolkerstorfer, "A 155 Mbps Triple-DES Netowkr Encryptor," Cryptographic Hardware and Embedded Systems CHES'2000, 2nd International Workshop, Proceedings, Lecture Notes in Computer Science, Vol. 1965, Berlin, Germany: Springer-Verlag, pp. 164–174.

Levitt, Jason, "Wireless Devices Present New Security Challenges—Growth in Wireless Internet Access Means Handhelds will be Targets of More Attacks," *Information Week*, October 23, 2000, p. 120.

Levy, Stephen, "Crypto: The Story of How a Group of Code Rebels Saved Your Privacy On The Internet," *Newsweek*, January 15, 2001.

Lewis, Frank W., *Solving Cipher Problems—Cryptanalysis, Probabilities and Diagnostics,* Laguna Hills, CA: Aegean Park Press, 1992.

Liberti, Joseph C., Jr., and Theodore S. Rappaport, *Smart Antennas for Wireless Communications: IS-95 and Third Generation CDMA Applications,* Upper Saddle River, NJ: Prentice-Hall, 1999.

Lidl, R., and H. Niederreiter, *Introduction to Finite Fields and their Applications,* 2nd Ed., Cambridge, U.K.: Cambridge University Press, 1994.

Lipsky, S., "Find the emitter fast with monopulse methods," *Microwaves,* May 1978.

Liu, Hui, *Signal Processing Applications in CDMA Communications,* Norwood, MA: Artech House, 2000.

Ljung, Lennart, *System Identification: Theory for the User,* Upper Saddle River, NJ: Prentice-Hall, 1999.

Long, Cormac, *IP Network Design,* Osborne/McGraw-Hill, 2001.

Lu Stout, Kristie, *China Mobile Only has Eyes for 2.5G,* Available at: http://asia.cnn.com/2001/business/asia/06/05/hk.chinamobile2.5g/index.html, Accessed June 7, 2001.

Lu Stout, Kristie. *DoCoMo 3G Tests H it by Email Hiccup,* Available at: http://asia.cnn.com/2001/business/asia/06/04/tokyo.docomoemailglitch/index.html, Accessed June 14, 2001.

Luby, Michael, *Pseudorandomness and Cryptographic Applications,* Princeton CSN, 1996.

"Lucent Technologies Wireless Networks," http://192.11.229.3/search.vts?querytext={_wireless}%Cand%3E+end+to+end&topic=_wireless&BU=wireless&collection=LU&resulttemplate=default.hts&action=Filtersearch&filter=filter.hts&resultmaxdocs=100&sortfield=score&sortorder=desc&displayformat=full&resultcount=10&Yourquery=end+to+end&P1=y.

Luo, fa-Long, and Rolf Unbehauen, *Applied Neural Networks for Signal Processing,* Cambridge, U.K.: Cambridge University Press, 1998.

Lusher, Betina, *Slow Down Hits Germany's Mobile Market,* Available at: http://asia.cnn.com/2001/TECH/05/23/germany.mobiles/, Accessed June 7, 2001.

Lutz, W. E., *Wireless LAN Technologies,* Faulkner Information Services, 2000, Available on INTELINK at: http://doserve.mall.nsa.ic.gov/, Accessed May 11, 2001.

Lutz, W. E., *Wireless PBX Systems,* Faulkner Information Services, 2000, Available on INTELINK at: http://doserve.mall.nsa.ic.gov/, Accessed May 11, 2001.

Lutz, W. E., *Wireless Standards and Protocols,* Faulkner Information Services, 2000, Available on INTELINK at: http://doserve.mall.nsa.ic.gov/producer/refs/facts/00021009.html, Accessed April 24, 2001.

Lyons, Richard G., *Understanding Digital Signal Processing,* Addison Wesley, 1999.

Madisetti, Vijay K., and Douglas B. Williams, eds., *The Digital Signal Processing Handbook,* Boca Raton, FL: CRC Press, 1998.

Maguire, Jr., G. Q., *Module 9: Voice Over IP VOIP,* Stockholm, Sweden, University of Stockholm—Lecture Notes for 2G1305 [Internetworking], March 3, 1999, http://www.it.kth.se/edu/gru/Internet/Lectures/VOIP.fm5.pdf., Accessed June 2001.

Maguire, Richard, *Reviewing The Basics Of The General Packet Radio Service,* Wireless Systems Design, August 2000, http://wsdmag.com/2000/aug2200/38-45.html.

Maher, David P., and Robert J. Rance, *Random Number Generators Founded on Signal and Information Theory,* Cryptographic Hardware and Embedded Systems Int'l Workshop Proceeding, Lecture Notes in Computer Science, Vol. 1717, pp. 219–230, New York: Springer-Verlag, 1999.

Maitra, Amit, and Brian J. Dooley, *Telecommunications in the Pacific Rim,* Faulkner Information Service, Available on INTELINK at: http://doserve.mall.nsa.ic.gov/producer/refs/faccts/00017382.html, Accessed April 24, 2001.

Mammone, Richard J., ed., *Computational Methods of Signal Recovery and Recognition,* New York: John Wiley & Sons, 1992.

Mannell, Robert H, *Principles of Text-to-Speech and Speech Synthesis,* Sydney, Australia, Macquarie University—Lecture notes from SLP807, 2001, http://www.ling.mq.edu.au/~rmannell/slp807/vocoders/, Accessed May 2001.

Marjalaakso, Mike, *Security Requirements and Constraints of VOIP* [article online], http://www.hut.fi/~mmarjala/voip, Accessed June 4, 2001.

Market Grows as Prices Sink, http://www.germanyinfo.org/newcontent/be/ phonfeb.htm, Accessed May 15, 2001.

Martin, Frederick Thomas, *Top Secret Intranet: How the U.S. Intelligence Built INTELINK—The Worlds Largest, Most Secure Network,* Prentice Hall, 1997.

Masey, James L., *On The Optimality of Safer+* Diffusion, Cylink Corporation, Sunnyvale, CA, http://csrc.nist.gov/encryption/aes/round1/conf2/papers/massey.pdf, Accessed June 18, 2001.

Massey, J. L., G. H. Khachatrian, M. K. Kuregian, *SAFER+* Candidate Algorithm for AES—Submission Document, Cylink Corporation, June 1998.

Matsui, M., *Linear Cryptanalysis of DES Cipher,* in Proceedings Eurocrypt *'93,* 1993.

McCabe, Karen, *Bluetooth Specification Serves as Foundation for IEEE 802.15 WPAN Standard,* http://standards.ieee.org/announcements/bluespec.html, Accessed June 18, 2001.

McClendon, James W., Col., *Information Warfare: Impacts and Concerns*, Battlefield of the Future: 21st Century Warfare Issues, www.airpower.maxwell.afr.mil/airchronciles/battle/bfatc.html.

McClure, Stuart, et al., *Hacking Exposed,* 2nd Ed., McGraw-Hill, 2001.

McDaid, Cathal, *Bluetooth Security,* Cathal's Corner, http://www.palowireless.com/ infotooth/cathalscorner.asp, March 2001.

McDonough, Robert N., and Anthony D. Whalen, *Detection of Signals in Noise,* 2nd Ed., San Diego, CA: Academic Press, 1971.

McGree, Chas, 2nd Lt., *Voice-over Internet Protocol Enhances Telephone Service,* Intercom, Air Force Communications Agency Scott Air Force Base, Ill, 618-256-4396, May 2000.

McKeever, Susan, *The Dorling Kindersley Science Encyclopedia,* New York: Dorling Kindsersley, Inc., 1994.

McKitrick, Jeffrey, James Blackwell, Fred Littlepage, George Kraus, Richard Blanchfield, and Dale Hill, *The Revolution in Military Affairs.* Battlefield of the Future: 21st Century Warfare Issues, Published at www.airpower.maxwell.afr.mil/airchronicles/batle/bftac.html.

McLarnon, Barry, "VE3JF Wireless LAN MAN MODEM product directory," Last updated: November 28, 1999, http://hydra.carleton.ca/info/.

McLaren, Tim, and Stephen Myers, *MCSE Study Guide: TCP/IP Systems Management Server,* Indianapolis, IN: New Riders, 1996.

McLaughlin, Kevin, *Bluetooth Reality Check*, http://www.business2.com/content/ channels/technology/2000/12/20/23958.

McLaughlin, Kevin, "Bluetooth Wireless Technology," kmclaughlin@business2.com, Business 2.0, 5 Thomas Mellon Circle, Suite 305, San Francisco, CA 94134, 415-656-8699, http://www.business2.com/content/channels/ technology/2000/12/20/23958.

McLoone, Máire, and J. V. McCanny, "High Performance Single-Chip FPGA Rijndael Algorithm Implementations," *CHES 2001, Cryptographic Hardware and Embedded Systems Workshop, Paris, France, May 14–16, 2001, Proceedings,* pp. 68–80.

McMurry, Mike, *Wireless Security,* SANS Information Security Reading Room, 2001, Available at: http://www/sans.rg/infosecFAQ/wireless/wireless_sec.htm.

McNulty, F. Lynn, *Encryption's Importance To Economic and Infrastructure Security,* Published at: www.law.duke.edu/journals/djcil/articles/DJCIL9P427.htm.

McNurlin, Barbara C., and Ralph H. Sprague, Jr., *Information Systems Management In Practice,* Upper Saddle River, NJ: Prentice-Hall PTR, 1998.

Mehrota, Asha K., *Cellular Radio: Analog and Digital Systems,* The Artech House Mobile Communications Series, Artech House, May 1994.

Mehrotra, Asha K., *GSM System Engineering,* Norwood, MA: Artech House, 1997.

Mehta, Princy C., *Wired Equivalent Privacy Vulnerability,* SANS Information Security Reading Room, 2001, Available at: http://www/sans.org/infosecFAQ/wireless/equiv.htm.

Mel, H. X., and Doris Baker, *Cryptography Decrypted,* New York: Addison Wesley, 2000.

Menezes, Alfred J., *Elliptic Curve Public Key Cryptosystems,* Vol. 234 of The Kluwer International Series in Engineering and Computer Science, Boston: Kluwer Academic Publishers, 1993.

Menezes, Alfred J., Paul van Oorschot, and Scott A. Vanstone, *Handbook of Applied Cryptography,* New York: CRC Press, 1998.

Menezes, Alfred J., Tatsuaki Okamoto, and Scott Vanstone, *Reducing Elliptic Curve Logarithms to Logarithms in a Finite Field,* IEEE Transactions on Information Theory, Vol. 39, pp. 1639–1646, 1,993.

Mengali, Umberto, and Aldo N. D'Andrea, *Synchronization Techniques for Digital Receivers,* New York: Plenum Press, 1997.

"Messages Can Freeze Popular Nokia Phones," by Laura Rohde, September 1, 2000, *CNN.com*, http://www.cnn.com/2000/TECH/computing/09/01/nokia.freeze.idg.

Meyr, Henrich, and Gerd Ascheid, *Synchronization in Digital Communications, Volumes 1 and 2,* New York: John Wiley & Sons, 1990.

Michalewitz, Z., and D. B. Fogel, *How to Solve It: Modern Heuristics,* Springer-Verlag, 1998.

"Microsoft 2000 Annual Report," *The Wall Street Journal,* November 27, 2000.

"Microsoft is Ready to Supply a Phone in Every Computer," *New York Times*, New York, June 12, 2001.

"Microsoft's ICSA—Internet Cellular Smart Access, The Platform for Going Places," *System Overview,* 2000.

Microsoft Corporation, http://mobile.microsoft.se.

Miles, Rae, "Top 10 Technologies," *Credit Union,* July 2000.

Mileva, Rali, "TIA Comments to FCC Urge the Allocation of Additional Spectrum to Support 3G Wireless Services, Address Difficult Technical Issues Contact," 703-907-7721, rmileva@tia.eia.org, February 23, 2001, http://www.tiaonline.org/pubs/pres_releases/index.cfm?paralease=01-17.

Miller, Brent A., and Chatschik Bisdikian, *Bluetooth Revealed,* Upper Saddle River, NJ: Prentice Hall, 2001.

Miller, Jr., Mark A., *Voice Over IP: Strategies for the Converged Network,* Foster City, CA: M&T Books, 2000.

Miller, V. S., *Use of Elliptic Curves in Cryptography,* Proceedings of Crypto '85, Lecture Notes in Computer Science, Vol. 218, pp. 417–426, New York: Springer-Verlag, 1986.

Millman, Howard, "Give Your Computer the Finger," *Computerworld,* March 27, 2000, http://www.computerworld.com/cwi/story/0.1199.NAV47_STO44211.00.html.

Minoli, Daniel, and Emma Minoli, *Delivering Voice Over Frame Relay and ATM,* New York: John Wiley & Sons, 1998.

Mintzer, L., *FIR Filters With the Xilinx FPGA,* presented at FPGA '92, ACM/SIGDA Workshop on FPGAs.

Mitchell, Dan, "Did Breaking the News Network Break the Law?" *Wired News,* August 28, 1997, http://www.wired.com/news/topstories/0.1287.6455.00.html.

Mitel Corporation, IP Telephony, *The TCO Value Proposition,* www.mitel.com. 2000.

Miyaji, A., *An Ordinary Elliptic Curve Cryptosystems,* Advances in Cryptology— ASIACRYPT '91, Lecture Notes in Computer Science, Vol. 218, Springer-Verlag, pp. 460–469, 1993.

Mobile Penetration to Exceed 250 Million Subscribers by 2005, http://www.wireless-comm.globalsources.com/magazine/wc/0101/outch01.htm, Accessed May 15, 2001.

Mobile Phone R520: Features, http://www.ericsson.com/r520/presentation/index.html, Mach 5, 2001.

Mobile to Overtake Fixed Communications, http://www.globalsources.com/magazine/wc/0101/sg02.htm, Accessed June 15, 2001.

Mollin, Richard A., *An Introduction to Cryptography,* Chapman & Hall/CRC, January 2001, 371 pages.

Molta, Dave, *Cisco Aironet 350 Series Tightens Wireless Security,* Network Computing, February 5, 2001, http://www.networkcomputing.com/shared/printArticle?article=nc/1203/1203spl.html&pub=nv.

Montgomery, P. L., *Modular Multiplication Without Trial Division,* Mathematics of Computation, 44 170: pp. 519–521, April 1985.

Morris, Jr., John B., *Broadband Backgrounder: Public Policy Issues Raised By Broadband Technology.* Center for Democratic Technology, December 2000, http://www.cdt.org/digi_infra/broadband/ackgrounder.shtml.

Moy, John T., *OSPF Anatomy of an Internet Reading Protocol,* Reading, MA: Addison_Wesley, 1998.

Muller, Nathan J., *Bluetooth Demystified,* Washington, D.C.: McGraw-Hill, 2000, 16.

Muller, Nathan J., *Satellite Communications Market Trends*, Faulkner Information services, 1999, Available on INTELINK at: http://doserve.mall.nsa.ic.gov/, Accessed May 11, 2001.

Muller, Nathan J., *Telemetry Applications*, Faulkner Information Services. *2000.* Available on INTELINK at: http://doserve.mall.nsa.ic.gov/, Accessed May 11, 2001.

Muller, Nathan J., and Bruce Kramer, *Telecommunications in the U.S.: State of the Marketplace,* Synopsis. Available on INTELINK at: http://doserve.mall.nsa.ic.gov/producer/refs/facts/000174999.html, Accessed June 13, 2001.

Muller, Thomas, *Bluetooth Security Architecture version 1.0,* July 15, 1999.

Munro, Neil, *The Quick and the Dead—Electronic Combat and Modern Warfare,* New York: St. Martin's Press, 1991.

Murray Associates Counterespionage Consultants to Business and Government, http://spybusters.com.

Naccache, David, ed., *Topics in Cryptology—CT RSA 2001,* LNCS 2020, RSA 2001 Conference, Springer 2001.

Nagy, P. A. J., "Modulation classifier for multi-channel systems and multi-transmitter situations," *MILCOM 1994 Conference,* 1994.

National Bureau of Standards, Federal Information Processing Standards Publication 46: *Data Encryption Standard,* January 15, 1977.

National Bureau of Standards, Federal Information Processing Standards Publication 74: *Guidelines for Implementing and Using the NBS Data Encryption Standard,* April 1, 1981.

National Bureau of Standards, Federal Information Processing Standards Publication 81: *DES Modes of Operation,* December 2, 1980.

National Computer Security Center, Rainbow Series, *Montographs on Many Aspects of Information Systems Security,* 1983.

National Information Systems Security—INFOSEC Glossary, National Security Telecommunications Information Systems Security Instruction NSTISSI #4009, June 5, 1992.

National Institute of Standards and Technology, *Approval of Federal Information Processing Standards Publication 185,* Escrowed Encryption Standard, Federal Register, Vol. 59, No. 27, Washington, D.C., February 9, 1994.

National Institute of Standards and Technology and National Security Agency, *Memorandum of Understanding Between the Director of the National Institute of Standards and Technology and the Director of the National Security Agency Concerning the Implementation of Public Law 100-235,* Washington, D.C., March 24, 1989.

National Institute of Standards and Technology, FIPS 140-1, *Security Requirements for Cryptographic Modules,* Available at: http://csrc.nist.gov/cryptval/140-1.htm.

National Institute of Standards and Technology, Publication XX: *Announcement and Specifications of a Digital Signature Standard DSS,* Washington, D.C., August 19, 1991.

Natural and Technological Disaster Threats to National Security and Emergency Preparedness NS/EP Telecommunications, National Communications System, http://www.ncs.gov/n5_hp/Information_Assurance/NAT96-2.htm.

Naval Air Warfare Center 2000, *Electronic Warfare and Radar Systems Engineering Handbook TP 8347*, http://ewhdbks.mugu.navy.mil/freqspec.htm.

NAVSTAR GPS Overview, 1991 Report, Los Angeles, ARINC Research Corporation.

Nebabin, V. G., *Methods and Techniques of Radar Recognition,* Artech House, 1995.

Nee, Richard Van, and Ramjee Prasad, *OFDM for Wireless Multimedia Communications,* Norwood, MA: Artech House, 2000.

Neil, Stephanie, "Tuning In To Wireless Broadband," *eWEEK,* June 4, 2000, http://www.zdnet.com/eweek/stories/general/0.11011.2579419.00.html.

NetLine Communications Technologies NCT LTD., http://www.c-guard.com/.

NeTrue Communications, *NeTrue Delivers VoIP Network to KPT,* October 16, 2000, http://www.netrue.com/ . . . eTrue_News/2000Oct16/2000Oct16.html.

Neumann, Peter G., *Computer Related Risks,* New York: Addison-Wesley, 1995.

Neurosurgeons Prescribe Red-M Bluetooth Network as Mobile Cure for Doctors, May 2, 2001, http://www.mobil.com/news/2001/05/neurosurgeons_prescribe_red.htm, October 30, 2001.

Newmarch, Jan, *Chapter 12: Security Contents,* April 2001, http://www.javacoffeebreak.com/books/extracts/jini/Security.html.

Nguyen, Thuan, et al., "Voice Over IP Service and Performance in Satellite Networks," *IEEE Communications,* March 2001.

Nichols, Randall K., *Classical Cryptography Course Volume I,* Aegean Park Press, 1995, and *Classical Cryptography Course Volume II,* Aegean Park Press, 1996.

Nichols, Randall K., *ICSA Guide to Cryptography,* New York: McGraw-Hill, 1999.

Nichols, Randall K., Daniel J. Ryan, and Julie J. C. H. Ryan, *Defending Your Digital Assets Against Hackers, Crackers, Spies, and Thieves,* New York: RSA Security Press and McGraw-Hill Professional Books, 2000.

No, J. S., S. W. Golomb, G. Gong, H. K. Lee, and P. Gaal, New binary pseudo-random sequences of period 2^{n-1} with ideal autocorrelation, *IEEE Trans. on Inform. Theory,* Vol. 44, No. 2, March 1998, pp. 814–717.

No author, *00Q4—Forecast Revenues and Shipments of Bluetooth Enabled Devices, Including Cell Phones, Desktop and Laptop Computers and PDAs,* http://www.infotechtrends.com/cgi- . . . 1?ux=846&quar=01Q2&01212031.htm=on, June 10, 2001.

No author, *01Q2—Forecast Shipments and Revenues for Bluetooth Enabled Devices, Worldwide,* http://www.infotechtrends.com/cgi- . . . 1?ux=846&quar=01Q2&01212031.htm =on, June 10, 2001.

No author, *1999 Guide to Wireless Telecommunications Technology,* Arlington: ANSER, 1999, Available on INTELINK at: http://tesla.cia.ic.gov/regional/Wireless TelecomTech/Introduction.cfm, Accessed April 24, 2001.

No author, *2000 IEC Conference Explores Rapid Growth and Impact of Broadband Wireless Services,* September 15, 2000, Press release, International Engineering Consortium, http://www.iec.org/news/pr200000915.html.

No author, "A LAN Line, The Wireless Internet," www.economist.com/business/display Story.cfm?Story_ID=473081, *The Economist,* January 11, 2001.

No author, *African Cellular: Bluetooth Short Range Radio System,* April 2, 2001, http://www.cellular.co.za/bluetooth.htm.

No author, *American Access to the European Standardization Process,* Available at: http://www.ansi.org/public/library/eu_access/intro_1.html, Accessed June 27, 2001.

No author, *An Introduction to Encryption and PKI* [Web site], IT Security.com, http://www.itsecurity.com/papers/upaq.htm, Accessed March 3, 2001.

No author, *An Introduction to Information Security,* ECC Whitepapers, http://www.certicom.ca/research/wecc1.html, July 2000.

No author, *Analog Cellular Systems Outside the US TACS Variants,* http://www.iit.edu/~diazrob/cell/tacsvar.html.

No author, AT&T Strategic Ventures invests $10 million in Nuera Communications to speed delivery of broadband voice to customers worldwide, http://www.nuera.com/news/pr081500.cfm.

No author, Berkley Research, "Wireless LANs Have Serious Flaws," *Computerworld*, February 12, 2001.

No author, "Bluetooth and IR Will Work Side by Side," *Personal Computer World*, June 21, 2000, http://www.thechannel.vnunet.com/News/1103833, Accessed June 18, 2001.

No author, *Bluetooth Architecture,* http://www.xilinx.com/esp/bluetooth/tutorials/architecture.htm, Accessed June 18, 2001, The power point slides on this page were used for the segment. You cannot access the slides directly with an URL.

No author, *Bluetooth Architecture Overview,* http://filebox.vt.edu/users/sangle/bluetooth/architecture.htm, Accessed June 18, 2001.

No author, *Bluetooth Specification Volume 1 Version 1.1,* Bluetooth SIG, February 22, 2001.

No author, "Broadband Wireless," *PCIA Washington Bulletin*, August 9, 1999.

No author, *Business Case for Secure VPNs,* TimeStep Corporation, Kanata, Ontario, 1998, Available at: www.Timestep.gov.

No author, *By 2005, More Than 68% of Internet Users Will Use Wireless Devices to Go On-line in Western Europe,* http://www.netscope.org.uk/scripts/hot_newspg.asp#63, Accessed June 12, 2001.

No author, *Cellular Summary,* Washington, D.C.: The Federal Communications Commission, 2001, http://www.fcc.gov/wtb/cellular/celfctsh.html, Accessed May 24, 2001.

No author, *Cellular Telephone Cloning,* Washington, D.C.: The Federal Communications Commission, 1998, http://www.fcc.gov/cib/consumerfacts/cellfra1.html, Accessed May 24, 2001.

No author, Cisco Corporation, *SSL: Foundation for Web Security,* http://www.cisco.com/warp/public/759/ipj_1-1/ipj_1-1_SSL2.html.

No author, "Citibank Goes Public with Y2K Satellite Contingency," *Computer Weekly*, May 20, 1999.

No author, "Compatible Systems Partners with NETRIX to Offer VoVPN: VoIP over VPN Provides Toll-quality, Secure Voice Traffic on the Internet," *Business Wire.com*, Texas: Frost-&-Sullivan, http://www.businesswire.com/webbox/bw.051099/191300795.htm, May 10, 1999.

No author, Cornell University, Cell Phone Security, http://www.cit.cornell.edu/cellphone/security.html.

No author, *Cylink Secures Bluetooth™ Wireless Networking Technology—Cylink's SAFER+ Algorithm Provides User Authentication for Emerging Wireless Networking Standard;* Cylink Corporation Web site press release September 20, 2000; http://www.cylink.com/news/press/pressrels/92000.htm, Accessed June 18, 2001.

No author, "DARPA Leads Assault on Batteries," *Jane's International Review,* Vol. 34, February 2001, p. 27.

No author, *DoCoMo launches test of 3G mobile phone services,* http://www.wireless-comm.globalsources.com/MAGAZINE/WC/0107/WN060101.HTM, Accessed June 26, 2001.

No author, Entrust Technologies, *Entrust Technologies Reinforces Commitment to WAP Via Its Certificate Interoperability Initiative,* January 23, 2001, http://www.entrust.com/news/files/01_23_01_673.htm.

No author, Entrust Technologies, *Entrust/Toolkit™ for SSL/TLS,* http://www.entrust.com/developer/tls/index.htm.

No author, *European Union: Standards and the Role of the EU,* http://www.pitt.edu/~wwwes/standards.guide.html, Accessed June 25, 2001.

No author, *Fact Sheet #2: Wireless Communications,* Cordless/Cellular Phones, Privacy Rights Clearinghouse, http://www.privacyrights.org.

No author, General Packet Radio Service, Product Overview, Nortel Networks, http://www.nortelnetworks.com.

No author, "Gone in 60 Seconds GSM Phone Hack Recovers Key In One Second," *Hack Watch*, December 7, 1999, http://www.iol.ie/~kooltek/gsmpaper.html.

No author, *Government-Industry Forum on Encryption and Law Enforcement: A Partnership With Industry,* http://www.homeoffice.gov.uk.

No author, *GPRS Speeding Up 3G Uptake in Britain,* http://www.globalsources.com/MAGAZINE/WC/0106/MOBIN02.HTM, Accessed June 7, 2001.

No author, *GSM—An Introduction to WAP,* http://www.gsmworld.com/technology/yes2wap.html, February 1, 2001.

No author, *GSM Association CEO Backs WAP Success,* http://www.gsmworld.com/news/press_2001/press_releases_3.html, February 6, 2001.

No author, *Guide to the Wireless Local Loop Industry.* Arlington: ANSER, 1999.

No author, *HiperLAN2 Global Forum, FAQs,* http://www.hiperlan2.com/web/, Accessed June 18, 2001.

No author, HiperLAN2 Resource Center, Palowireless.com, http://www.palowireless.com/hiperlan2/about.asp, Accessed June 18, 2001.

No author, *How A Wireless LAN Works,* http://www.zdnet.com/pcmag/stories/reviews/0.6755.2482910.00.html.

No author, *How Does Bluetooth Work?*, http://www.xilinx.com/esp/bluetooth/tutorials/bt_how_works.htm, Accessed June 18, 2001.

No author, *How to Build a Wireless Office: The Next Wireless Revolution,* Gartner, February 4, 2000.

No author, http://standards.ieee.org,wireless/overview.html, Accessed June 18, 2001.

No author, http://www.palowireless.com/bluearticles/intro.asp, Accessed June 18, 2001.

No author, http://www.palowireless.com/infotooth/tutorial/baseband.asp, Accessed June 18, 2001.

No author, *IBM Comprehensive Guide to Virtual Private Networks,* Vol. I, IBM Redbooks, 1999, www.redbooks.ibm.com/sg245201/sg240006.htm.

No author, *I-mode: Japanese Version of WAP,* [article online], http://www.cellular.co.za/imode.htm, Accessed March 16, 2001.

No author, *International Multimedia Teleconferencing Consortium,* San Ramon, CA, 1999, Published at: http://www.imtc.org/.

No author, Interview with Ron Sperano, Program Director for the Mobile Market Development Department of IBM, Available at: http://www.itradionetwork.com/scripts/speranor.html, conducted October 18, 2000, Accessed June 18, 2001.

No author, *Jini™ Software Simplifies Network Computing,* http://www.sun.com/980713/jimi/feature.jhtml.

No author, *Laws Governing Radio Monitoring in the United States,* http://www.nf2g.com/scannist/us_laws.html.

No author, *Marshall Brains How Stuff Works, Question of the Day,* 70/http://www.howstuffworks.com/question309.htm.

No author, *Mobile Penetration to exceed 250 Million Subscribers by 2005,* http://www.wirelesscomm.globalsources.com/magazine/wc/0101/outcho01.htm, Accessed May 15, 2001.

No author, *Mobile to overtake fixed Communications,* http://www.globalsources.com/magazine/wc/0101/outsg02.htm, Accessed June 15, 2001.

No author, *Motorola Launches Its Latest Satellite Series Phone with Starfish TrueSync Software Capabilities,* Cambridge Telecom Report, January 10, 2000.

No author, *New bug floods German cell networks,* ZDNet Germany August 4, 2000, http://www.zdnet.com/zdnn/stories/newsbursts/0.7407.2612018.,00.html.

No author, *Novarra Partners With Certicom To Deliver Fully Secure, Instant Wireless Solutions for Enterprise.* February 22, 2001, http://www.individual.com/network/headline . . . &level=82luid=Secur10&afid=k1KNTL1GPxc.

No author, *Product Expected to Start the Mass Market for Bluetooth,* ARC Group Bluetooth Industry Survey, http://www.thebluelink.com/section.asp?page=survey, June 1, 2001.

No author, *ProFit International has the Answer for Mounting Your Wireless Phone,* http://www.pro-fit-intl.com.

No author, *See How Carnivore Gathers Data for the FBI,* CNN 2000, August 25, 2000, Available at: http://www.cnn.com/2000/tech/computing/08/25/carnivore/index.html.

No author, *SK Telecom Deplays CDMA2000,* http://www.globalsources.com/magazine/wc/0012/wn101301.htm.

No author, *Smartcard Developer Association Clones Digital CGM Cell Phones,* press release from SDA, Hack Watch, April 13, 1998, http://www.ioe/~kooltek/gsmhack.html.

No author, *SMS Continues to Take Message World by Storm,* http://cyberatlas.internet.com/markets/wireless/article/0.10094_733811.00.html.

No author, *Synopsis of Wireless Telecommunications Technology,* Available on INTELINK at: http://www/01wf.ic.gov/pages/Support/Guide_to_wireless_Technology/synopsis.htm.

No author, "Technology Framework for Data-Broadcasting," *Multichannel News,* June 21, 1999.

No author, "The Shape of Phones to Come," *Economist Technology Quarterly,* March 24, 2001, pp. 24–36

No author, *The Telecommunications Act of 1996 and the Changing Communications Landscape,* The Benton Organization, http://www.benton.org/library/landscape/landscape.html.

No author, "To Jam or Not to Jam? Debate Heats Up on Silencing Pesky Cell Phones," *News-Journal Wire Services,* News-journal online.com, April 22, 2001, http://www.news journalonline.com/2001/Apr/22/STECH1.htm, June 15, 2001.

No author, "Verisign Japan Adapts Encryption Technology to I-Mode," January 23, 2001, *AsiaBizTech,* http://www.nikkeibp.asiabiztech.com/wcs/leaf?CID=onair/ababt/moren/121657.

No author, "VOIP Shapes Multi-Million Dollar Future for PBX Market," *Business Wire.com,* Texas: Frost-&-Sullivan, http://www.businesswire.com/webbox/bw.012400/200240118.htm, January 24, 2000.

No author, *What is 3G?,* http://www.ericsson.com.au/3G/3g_what_is_3g.asp, March 5, 2001.

No author, *What the 3G Challenge Means for U.S. Competitiveness: Why 3G?* Available at: http://www.ntia.doc.gov/ntiahome/threeg/3gintro.htm.

No author, *What's Behind Ricochet: A Network Overview* [Web site], Metricom.com, http://www.metricom.com/ricochet_advantage/tech_overview/index.html.

No author, *Will LAS-CDMA Lead the 4G Evolution?* Available at: http://www.globalsources.com/MAGAZINE/WC/0012/WCDMA.htm.

No author, *Wireless Application Protocol WAP: A Perspective,* Gartner Group, November 20, 2000.

No author, "Wireless Glossary," *Government Technology*, May 2000.

No author, *Wireless LAN Security, 802.11b and Corporate Networks,* Internet Security Systems, http://documents.iss.net/whitepapers/wireless_LAN_security.pdf, Accessed June 18, 2001.

No author, *Xilinx, Products—HiperLAn2,* www.xilinx.com/esp/home_networking/networking_technologies/wireless/wireless_lans/hiperlan2.htm, Accessed June 18, 2001.

Nobel, Carmen, "Still Waiting for Bluetooth," *ZDNet eWeek*, April 23, 2001, Available at: http://www.zdnet.com/eweek/stories/general/0.11011.2710689.00.html.

Nocella, Judith, *Security and the National Infrastructure in the Computer Age,* Fall 1996, Computers and Law, http://wings.buffalo.edu/Complaw/CompLawPapers/nocella.html.

Nokia 8260 User's Guide, http://www.nokia.com.

Nokia Artuse USSD Center—fast messaging services to nearly any existing mobile terminal, Nokia Networks.

Nokia, *H.323—The Standard*, http://www.helike.com/nokiaip/h323.html, Accessed July 1, 2001.

"Nokia Launches New Multipoint Mobile Chat Application for a New Era of Mobile Messaging," *Business Wire*, September 1, 2000, Nokia Networks, Communications Department, http://www.businesswire.com/webbox/bw.090100/202452049.htm.

Nonproliferation and National Security Institute, *Vulnerability to Technical Operations*, www.nnsi.doe.gov/C/Security_Guide/V2comint/Telephon.htm#Penetrating%20Telephone%20Systems.

Nordwall, Bruce D., "1998 'Navywar' Expands EW Challenge," November 23, 1998, *Aviation Week & Space Technology*, pp. 57–58.

Norwood Systems, The Norwood Web site on Bluetooth, http://www.norwoodsystems.com/frameset5-news.html, Accessed June 14, 2001.

"Novorra Partners With Certicom To Deliver Fully Secure, Instant Wireless Solutions for Enterprise," *Individual News*, February 22, 2001, http://www.individual.com/network/headline . . . &level3=82luid=Secur10&afid=k1KNTL1GPxc.

NTT DoCoMo Launches Test of 3G Mobile Phone Services, Available at: http://www.wirelesscomm.globalsources.com/magazine/wc/0107/wn060101.htm, Accessed June 26, 2001.

Nyberg, K., and R. Rueppel, "Message Recovery for Signature Schemes Based on the Discrete Logarithm Problem," *Designs, Codes and Cryptography*, Vol. 7, pp. 61–81, 1996.

O'Hara, Bob, *Security and 802.11,* Presentation at Networld+Interop 2001, Las Vegas, NV, May 2001.

O'Leary, A. and P. Gallagher, Bragg Cell Spectrum Analyzer, *Military Microwave Conference,* London, U.K., 1982.

Oberle, Richard, *Fourth Generation Wireless,* Available on INTELINK at: http://doserve.mall.nsa.ic.gov/producer/tnn/101/4gw.htm, Accessed April 24, 2001.

Ojanperä, Tero, and Ramjee Prasad, eds., *Wideband CDMA for Third Generation Mobile Communications,* Norwood, MA: Artech House, 1998.

"On-line Simulation and Control for Advanced Wireless Networks," http://www.darpa.mil/ito/psum2000/k147-0.html; Principal Investigators: Gary D. Warren, 1710 SAIC Dr., T1-5-2, McLean, VA 22102, 70-676-2611, 703-676-2613 fax, gary.warren@saic.com; Project Web site: http://projects.time.saic.com/nmands/, Sponsor: *Defense Advanced Research Projects Agency* (DARPA), 3701 N. Fairfax Dr., Arlington, VA 22203-1714.

Openwave Systems Japan: No More 'WAP vs. i-Mode,' http://www.mobilemediajapan.com/newsdesk/openwave, March 5, 2001.

Orfanidis, Sophocles J., *Introduction to Signal Processing,* Upper Saddle River, NJ: Prentice Hall, 1996.

Orozco, Lance, *Cell Phone Spying,* CBS Channel 2, February 1999, 61/http://www.channel2000.com/.ew-specialassignment-990203-190523.html.

Orubeondo, Ana, 2001, "Six Ways to Connect Your Telecommuters," Periodical *InfoWorld,* March 21, 2001, p. 51.

Pacuraiu, Calin, "Handspring, Inc.," *Presentation at Networld1Interop 2001*, Las Vegas, NV, May 2001.

Pandya, Raj, *Mobile and Personal Communication Systems and Services,* New York: Institute of Electrical and Electronics Engineers, Inc., 2000.

Parhami, Behrooz, *Computer Arithmetic—Algorithms and Hardware Designs,* New York: Oxford University Press, 2000.

Parker, Donn B., *Fighting Computer Crime,* New York: John Wiley & Sons, 1999.

Parkinson, Richard, *Cracking Codes,* California Press, 1999.

Pattan, Bruno, *Robust Modulation Methods & Smart Antennas in Wireless Communications,* Upper Saddle River, NJ: Prentice Hall, 2000.

Patterson, Wayne, *Mathematical Cryptology for Computer Scientists and Mathematicians,* Rowman & Littlefield, 1987.

Pecar, Joseph A., and David A. Garbin, *The New McGraw-Hill Telecom Factbook,* 2nd Ed., New York: McGraw-Hill, 2000.

Pelton, Joseph N., *The How To of Satellite Communications,* 2nd Ed., Sonoma, CA: Design Publishers, 1995.

Pelton, Joseph N., *Wireless and Satellite Telecommunications: The Technology, The Market, and the Regulations,* Upper Saddle River, NJ: Prentice Hall, 1995.

Perera, Rick, *CeBit: Bluetooth Devices A Mixed Bag,* IDG.net, March 27, 2001, http://www.cnn.com/2001/TECH/industry/03/27/cebit.bluetooth.idg/index.html, June 12, 2001.

Perlman, Radia, *Interconnections, 2nd edition: Bridges, Routers, Switches & Internetworking Protocols,* Reading, MA: Addison-Wesley, 1999, Pfitzmann, Andreas, Birgit Pfitzmann, Matthias Schunter, and Michael Waidner, *Vertrauens—wfirdiger Entwurf portabler Benutzerendger Ate und Sicherheitsmodule; VerIABliche IT—Systeme* VIS '95; Dul FachbeitrAge, Vieweg, Wiesbaden 1995, pp. 329–350.

Pfitzmann, Birgit, *Digital Signature Schemes: General Framework and Fail-Stop Signatures,* Berlin, Germany: Springer, 1996.

Phrack Staff, *On the Morality of Phreaking,* E-Journal of Writing and Technology, Vol. 2, 1998, Node 9, August 1998, http://node9.phil3.uni-freiburg.de/1998/phrack.html.

Pidwerbetsky, Alex, DARPA Quad Chart, "Very High Spectral Efficiency Radio;" Lucent Technologies Bell Laboratories, http://www.darpa.mil/ito/Quad_Chart2000/H6480-200000726144935.PPT; Sponsor: *Defense Advanced Research Projects Agency* (DARPA), 3701 N. Fairfax Dr., Arlington, VA 22203-1714.

Pitorri, Peter, *Counterespionage for American Business,* Butterworth-Heinemann, 1998.

Pocit Labs, The Pocit Labs Website on Bluetooth, http://www.pocitlabs.com/, June 15, 2001.

Polydoros, A., and K. Kim, On the Detection and Classification of Quadrature Digital Modulations in Broadband Noise, *IEEE Trans. on Commun.,* Vol. 38, No. 8, August 1990, pp. 1199–1211.

Powell, Thomas, and Joe Lima, "The Challenges of a Wireless Web," *Network World*, March 20, 2000.

Prasad, Ramjee, Werner Mohr, and Walter Konhäuser, eds., *Third Generation Mobile Communication Systems,* Norwood, MA: Artech House, 2000.

Press Release, http://www.bluetooth.com/news/signal/2000/3_42.asp.

Press Release, http://www.cin.com/jini/overview.

Privacy Rights Clearinghouse, Fact Sheet #9, *Wiretapping/Eavesdropping on Telephone Conversations: Is There Cause For Concern?* August 2000, http://www.privacyrights.org.

Proakis, John G., *Digital Communications,* 3rd Ed., New York: McGraw-Hill, 1995.

Proakis, John G., and Dimitris G. Manolakis, *Digital Signal Processing: Principles, Algorithms, and Applications,* 3rd Ed., Upper Saddle River, NJ: Prentice-Hall, 1996.

Project Bluetooth Technology Developments, ANSER, 2000, Available on INTELINK at: http://doserve.mall.nsa.ic.gov/, Accessed May 11, 2001.

Proxim Inc, *Range LAN 802.11, The IEEE 802.11 Wireless Standard,* A White Paper, December 1997.

Proxim, What is Wireless LAN? 2001.2, April 2001, http://www.proxim.com/wireless/whitepaper/whatwlan.shtml.

Putscher, Joyce, "Bluetooth Is For Real," *Electronic News,* May 7, 2001.

Rabaey, Jan M., *Digital Integrated Circuits—A Design Perspective,* Upper Saddle River, NJ: Prentice-Hall, 1996.

Rabiner, Lawrence R. and Ronald W. Schafer, *Digital Processing of Speech Signals,* Englewood Cliffs, NJ: Prentice-Hall, 1978.

Radding, Alan, "Crossing the Wireless Security Gap," *Computerworld,* January 1, 2001, http://www.computerworld.com/cwi/story/0.1199.NAV47_STO55583.00.html.

Radding, Alan, *Fly and Be Free,* Midrange Systems, May 12, 1995.

Radio-Communications Theory, Retrieved from the World Wide Web, February 17, 2001, http://209.207.236.112/spp/military/docops/afwa/U2.htm.

Raju, Chebium, *US Supreme Court Hears Arguments in Cellular-Wiretapping Case,* December 5, 2000, http://www.cnn.com/2000/LAW/12/05/scotus.wiretapping/index.html.

Randkl W., and W. Effing, *Smartcard Handbook,* New York: John Wiley & Sons, 1997.

Rao, Madanmohan, *Asia Leads World In Wireless Internet Technology, Markets,* Available at: http://www.electronicmarkets.org/electronicmarkets/electronicmarkets.nsf/pages/emw_0104_.

Rappaport, Theodore S, *Cellular Radio and Personal Communications,* Vol. 2, Piscataway: The Institute of Electrical and Electronics Engineers, Inc., 1996.

Rappaport, Theodore S., *Wireless Communications: Principles and Practice,* Upper Saddle River, NJ: Prentice-Hall PTR, 1999.

Rappore Technologies, The Rappore Technologies Web site on Bluetooth, http://www.rappore.com/home.cfm, June 15, 2001.

Rathbun, Elizabeth, "Satellite Radio Shoots for June Launch," Broadcasting & Cable, April 17, 2000, Intertec, *Satellite Communications.*

Rautpalo, Jussi, *GPRS Security—Secure Remote Connections over GPRS,* Helsinki University of Technology, Department of Computer Science, http://www.hut.fi/~jrautpal/gprs/gprs_sec.html.

Razavi, Behzad, ed., *"Monolithic Phase-Locked Loops and Clock Recovery Circuits: Theory and Design,"* New York: IEEE Press, 1996.

Razavi, Behzad, *RF Microelectronics,* Upper Saddle River, NJ: Prentice Hall, 1998.

Rysavy, Peter, "The Evolution of Cellular Data: The Road to 3G," *GSM Data Knowledge Site,* www.gsmdata.com.

Redl, Siegmund M., Matthias K. Weber, and Malcolm W. Oliphant, *An Introduction to GSM,* Norwood, MA: Artech House, 1995.

Remarks on the Security of The Elliptic Curve Cryptosystem, Certicom White Paper, September 1997.

Rhee, Man Young, *CDMA Cellular Mobile Communications and Network Security,* Upper Saddle River, NJ: Prentice Hall, 1998.

Rhee, Man Young, *CDMA Network Security,* Prentice Hall, 1998.

Rhee, Man Young, *Cryptography and Secure Communications,* McGraw-Hill, 1994.

Richelson, Jeffrey T., *The U.S. Intelligence Community,* 3rd Ed., Westview, 1995.

Rescorla, Eric, *SSL and TLS: Designing and Building Secure Systems,* Upper Saddle River, NJ: Addison-Wesley, Pearson Education, 2001.

Richharia, M., *Satellite Communications Systems: Design Principals,* New York: McGraw-Hill, 1995.

Riezenman, Michael J., "The Rebirth of Radio," *IEEE Spectrum,* January 2001, p. 64.

Riku, Mettala, *Bluetooth Protocol Architecture,* http://www.bluetooth.com/developer/whitepaper/whitepaper.asp, copyright August 25, 1999.

Rivest, Ron, A. Shamir, and L. Adleman, *A Method for Obtaining Digital Signatures and Public Key Cryptosystems, Communications of the ACM,* No. 2, February 21, 1978, pp. 120-126.

Roberts, Randy, *Everything in One Box,* Presentation at Networld+Interop 2001, Las Vegas, NV, May 2001.

Roberts, Randy, "Introduction to Spread Spectrum," *Spread Spectrum Scene,* February 16, 2001, http://sss-mag.com/ss.html.

Roberts-Witt, Sarah L., "Sound Bits: Carriers Have Plans for VOIP Services But Does Anyone Need Them?" *Internet World,* May 15, 2001, http://www.internetworld.com/051501/05.15.01internettech1.jsp, Accessed May 2001.

Robinson, Daniel, "Bluetooth for Pentium III Notebooks," *IT Week,* April 28, 2001, http://news.zdnet.co.uk/story/0.s2085898.00.html, May 31, 2001.

Robinson, Sara, "Design Flaws in Mobile Phone Protocol Opens Security Hole," *IT Week Analysis,* 2000, http://www.zdnet.co.uk/itweek/analysis/2000.

Rodbell, Mike, "Standards & Protocols: Bluetooth—Baseband and RF Interfaces," *Communications System Design,* April 2000, Available at: www.csdmag.com/main/2000/04/0004stand.htm#bluetab, Accessed June 18, 2001.

Rogers, Donna, "The ? Of Encryption," *Law Enforcement Technology,* March 2000, Vol. 27, No. 3, p. 62.

Rohde, Ulrich L., *Microwave and Wireless Synthesizers; Theory and Design,* New York: John Wiley & Sons, 1997.

Rohde, Ulrich L., Jerry Whittaker, and T. T. N. Bucher, *Communications Receivers,* 2nd Ed., New York: McGraw-Hill, 1997.

Rosenblatt, K. S., *High-Technology Crime: Investigating Cases Involving Computers,* San Jose, CA: KSK Publications, 1995.

Rosing, Michael, *Implementing Elliptic Curve Cryptography,* Manning Press, 1999.

Rowlett, Frank B., *The Story of Magic: Memoirs of An American Cryptologic Pioneer,* Aegean Park Press, 1998.

RSA Data Security, Inc., *Cryptographic Message Syntax Standard,* PKCS-7, November 1, 1993.

"RSA Security's Role in WAP and WTLS," The WAP Forum is an industry body founded in 1997 to provide a worldwide standard for delivering Internet-based services to mass market mobile devices. WAP architecture is therefore optimized for wireless users, networks, and devices. RSA Security has made significant contributions to different security standards within WAP, including *Wireless Transport Layer Security* (WTLS)—the wireless version of the Internet security protocol *Secure Socket Layer* (SSL)/*Transport Layer Security* (TLS). Ideal for wireless devices with limited power and memory and the need to optimize battery life, WTLS provides all of the critical security features of authentication, data privacy, and data integrity, http://www.rsasecurity.com/products/bsafe/wtlsc.html.

Rudy, Roger J., "IP Service Level Agreements Bringing Light to the End of the IP Network Tunnel," *Quick Eagle Networks*, March 22, 2001.

Rueppel, R., *Design and Analysis of Stream Ciphers,* Springer-Verlag, 1986.

Russell, Deborah, and G. T. Gangemi Sr., *Computer Security Basics,* Cambridge, MA: O'Reilly & Associates, 1992.

Ryan, Jerry, "QoS in the Enterprise," *The Technology Guide Series*, http://www.techguide.com.

Rysavy, Peter, *Wireless Broadband and Other Fixed-Wireless Systems*, http://www.networkcomputing.com/shared/printArticle?article=nc/netdesign/bbl.html&pub=nv, 1999.

Samsung Builds 3G R&D Center in Beijing, http://www.globalsources.com/magazine/wc/0101/wc112201.htm.

Schirokauer, O., *Discrete Logarithms and Local Units, Philosophical,* Transactions of the Royal Society of London A, Vol. 345, pp. 409–423, 1993.

Schleher, D. Curtis, *Electronic Warfare in the Information Age,* Boston: Artech House, 1999.

Schleher, D. Curtis, *Introduction to Electronic Warfare,* Dedham, MA: Artech House, 1986.

Schlumberger Delivers Full-featured, Secure Wireless Mobile Banking Solution to Microcell, Schlumberger Press Release, November 7, 2000, http://www.1.slb.com/smartcards/news/00/sct_microcell0811.html.

Schneider, Fred B., *Trust in Cyberspace: Public Telephone Network and Internet Trustworthiness*, [book online] National Academic Press, 1999, http://nap.edu/html/trust/trust-2, Accessed May 19, 2001.

Schneiderman, Ron, *A Manager's Guide to Wireless Telecommunications,* New York: Amacom Books, 1999.

Schneiderman, Ron, "Bluetooth's Slow Dawn," *IEEE Spectrum*, November 2000, p. 62.

Schneier, Bruce, *Applied Cryptography: Protocols, Algorithms & Source Code,* 2nd Ed., New York: John Wiley & Sons, 1996.

Schneier, Bruce, *e-mail Security,* New York: John Wiley & Sons, 1995.

Schneier, Bruce, et al., *The Twofish Encryption Algorithm,* New York: John Wiley & Sons, 1999.

Schneier, Bruce, *Secrets and Lies,* New York: John Wiley & Sons, 2000.

Schor, P., "Algorithms for Quantum Computation: Discrete Logarithms and Factoring," *Proceedings of the 35th Annual Symposium on the Foundations of Computing Science* (1994), pp. 124–134.

Schramm, John, *Security Issues in WAP and I-Mode,* December 2, 2000, Sans Institute, http://www.sans.org/infosecFAQ/wireless/WAP4.htm.

Schroeder, M. R., *Number Theory in Science and Communications: With Applications in Cryptography, Physics, Digital Information, Computing and Self Similarity,* 3rd Ed., Springer, 1999.

Schuchart, Steve J., Jr., "The Bluetooth Invasion Begins," *Network Computing*, March 19, 2001, http://www.networkcomputing.com/1206/1206ws3.html, Accessed June 18, 2001.

Schwartau, W., *Information Warfare*, 2nd Ed., New York: Thunder's Mouth Press, 1997.

Schwartz, Ephraim, "Handful of Wireless Solutions Set to Boost Data Analysis, Security, Shopping Preferences," *InfoWorld*, February 26, 2001, p. 69.

Schwartzlander, E. E., ed., "Computer Arithmetic," Vol. I, Los Alamitos, CA: IEEE Computer Society Press, 1990.

SCM Microsystems Teams with NOKIA to Develop Terrestrial Broadband Receiver for the PC. February 24, 2000, http://www.scmmicor.com/corporate/p_report.html?release=&&year=2000.

Securant Technologies™, *Support for WAP White Paper,* January 2001.

"Securing the Mobile Enterprise," PACKET™, *Cisco Systems Users*, 1st Quarter 2001, pp. 14–15, The Forrester Report—Mobile Internet Realities, Forrester Research, May 2001, Introduced in article, "Self Configuring Wireless Transmission and Decentralized Data Processing for Generic Sensor Networks," http://www.darpa.mil/ito/psum2000/k257-0.html; Principal Investigator: Stephen Wicker, College of Engineering, 386 Rhodes Hall, Ithaca, NY 14853, 607-255-8817, 607-255-9072 fax, wicker@ee.cornell.edu & Weber Mary, 225 Phillips Hall, School of Elect. and Comp. Eng., Ithaca, NY 14853, 607-255-1442, 607-254-4565 fax, maryw@aniseee.cornell.edu; SPONSOR: *Defense Advanced Research Projects Agency* (DARPA), 3701 N. Fairfax Dr., Arlington, VA 22203-1714.

Seltzer, Larry, *The Standards Industry, Corporate consortia are supplanting traditional rule-making bodies*, http://www.internetworld.com/041501/04.15.01 internettech1.jsp.

Shankar, Hari, "Emerging Technology Series #1," *CSD*, Communication System Design, Available at: http://www.csdmag.com/main/2000/01/0001feat2.htm, January, 2000.

Shannon, C. E., "The Communication Theory of Secrecy Systems," *Bell System Technical Journal*, Vol. 28, October 1949.

Shannon, Claude E., "A Mathematical theory of Communication," *Bell System Technical Journal*, Vol. 27, pp. 379–423, July 1948.

Sharma, Chetan, *Wireless Internet Enterprise Applications*, New York: Wiley Computer Publishing, 2001.

Shaw, James K., *Strategic Management in Telecommunications*, Boston-London: Artech House, 2000, p. 231.

Shim, Richard, *Bluetooth Bite Blunted by MS Pullout*, ZDNetUK, April 6, 2001, http://news.zdnet.co.uk/story/0.s2085512.00.html, Accessed June 18, 2001.

Short Messaging Service Center (SMSC), FAQ, Hughes Software Systems, http://www.hssworld.com/products./smsc/smsc_faq.htm.

Shoup, V., *Lower Bounds for Discrete Logarithms and Related Problems*, Advances in Cryptology—EUROCRYPT '97, Lecture Notes in Computer Science, Vol. 1233, Springer-Verlag, pp. 256–266, 1997.

Sicap Mobile Payment, Product Description, Sicap Ltd., http://www.sicap.com.

Siep, Tom, *An IEEE Guide: How to Find What You Need in the Bluetooth Spec,* New York: The Institute of Electrical and Electronics Engineers, Inc., p. 19.

Silje Beite Loken, *i-mode and WAP Harmony,* http://www.wap.com/share/osas/cache/artid550419.html, March 5, 2001.

Simon, M. K., Non-coherent Pseudonoise Code Tracking Performance of Spread Spectrum Receivers, *Commun.*, Vol. COM25, March 1977.

Simon, M. K., J. K. Omura, R. A. Scholtz, and B. K. Levitt, *Spread Spectrum Communications*, Vols. 1, 2, and more specifically 3; Rockville, Maryland: Computer Science Press, Inc., 1985.

Simon, M. K., and A. Polydoros, Coherent Detection of Frequency-Hopped Quadrature Modulations in the Presence of Jamming: Part I. QPSK and QASK; Part II. QPR class I Modulation, *IEEE Trans. Commun.*, Vol. COM29, November 1981, pp. 1644–1668.

Simon, Marvin K., and Charles S. Wang, "Differential Detection of Gaussian MSK in a Mobile Radio Environment," *IEEE Trans. on Vehicular Technology*, Vol. VT-33, No. 3, November 1984, pp. 307–320.

Singer, Edward N., *Land Mobile Radio Systems*, 2nd Ed., Upper Saddle River, NJ: Prentice Hall, 1994.

Singh, Simon, *The Code Book: The Evolution of Secrecy from Mary, Queen of Scots to Quantum Cryptography*, Doubleday, 1999.

Sizer, Tod, *Bluetooth Coexistence Working Group Liaison Report, document IEEE 802.1501/158r0,* March 2001, http://www.ieee802.org/15/pub/TG2.html, Accessed June 18, 2001.

SK Telcom deploys CDMA2000, Available at: http://www.globalsources.com/magazine/wc/0012/wn101301.htm, Accessed June 7, 2001.

Sklar, Bernard, *Digital Communications, Fundamentals and Applications,* Englewood Cliffs: Prentice Hall, 1988.

Smith, Michael J. S., *Application-Specific Integrated Circuits,* Reading, MA: Addison-Wesley, 1997.

Smith, Richard, *Internet Cryptography,* New York: Addison Wesley, 1997.

Smith, S., and S. Weingart, "Building a High-Performance Programmable Secure Coprocessor," *IBM Research Report RC21102*, February 1998.

SMS Continues to Take Message World by Storm, Available at: http://cyberatlas.internet.com/markets/wireless/article/0.10094_733811.00.html, Accessed May 15, 2001.

Snyder, Edward F., "A Framework for the Wireless World," edward.snyder@chase.com, *Connected*, Vol. 4, Issue 3, October 2000, Exhibit 15, 16 & 17, http://connected.jpmhq.com/issue43/5.html.

"Speech Transcoding," September 1994.

Spilker, J. J., "Delay-Lock Tracking of Binary Signals," *IEEE Trans. Space Electron. Telem.,* March 1963.

Spilker J. J., and D. T. Magill, "The Delay-Lock Discriminator—An Optimum Tracking Device," *Proc. IRE,* September 1961.

Soliman, S. S., and Z. S. Hsue, Signal Classification Using Statistical Moments, *IEEE Trans. on Commun.,* Vol. 40, No. 5, May 1992, pp. 908–916.

Solinas, J., *An Improved Algorithm for Arithmetic on a Family of Elliptic Curves,* Advances in Cryptology—CRYPTO '97, Lecture Notes in Computer Science, Vol. 1294, Springer-Verlag, pp. 357–371, 1997. Sony Develops New Memory Stick for Bluetooth Called 'Infostick,' January 11, 2001, http://www.nikkeibp.asiabiztech.com/, June 9, 2001.

Spec Watch, The ATM Forum, http://www.atmforum.com/pages/aboutatmtech/specwatch.html.

"Spectrum Ware," http://www.darpa.mil/ito/psum1997/d013-0.html; Principal Investigator: John Guttag, Laboratory for Computer Science, 545 Technology Sq. Room 515, Cambridge, MA 01239 617-253-6022, 617-253-2673 fax, guttag@lcs.mit.edu; Project Website: http://www.sds.lcs.mit.edu/SpectrumWare/; Sponsor: *Defense Advanced Research Projects Agency* (DARPA), 3701 N. Fairfax Dr., Arlington, VA 22203-1714.

Spread Spectrum Background, http://www.sss-mag.com/bkgnd1.html, Tel: 865-717-1019, fax: 865-717-1044, e-mail: Staff@SSS-mag.com, This site © 1995–2001 by SSS Online, Inc., All rights reserved.

Spring, Tom, "Net2Phone Brings Voice Over IP to Telephone," *PCWorld.com*, June 6, 2001, http://www.pcworld.com/resource/printable/article/0.aid.51864.00.asp, Accessed June 2001.

SSH, [encyclopedia on-line] (Needham, MA: Whatis.Com, 2001), http://whatis.tech target.com/definition/0.289893.sid9_gci214091.00.html, Accessed June 16, 2001.

SSH Transport Layer Protocol, T. Ylonen, 07/31/1997, http://www.ietf.org/internet-drafts/draft-ietf secsh-transport-09.txt.

SSL, [encyclopedia on-line] (Needham, MA: Whatis.Com, 2001), http://whatis.tech target.com/definition/0.289893.sid9_gci343029.00.html, Accessed June 16, 2001.

Stallings, William, *Business Data Communications,* 4th Ed., Upper Saddle River, NJ: Prentice Hall, 2001.

Stallings, William, *Cryptography and Network Security, Principles and Practice,* 2nd Ed., 1999, 569 pages.

Stallings, William, *Networking Standards: A Guide to OSI, ISDN, LAN, and MAN Standards,* New York: Addison Wesley, 1993.

Stallings, William, *Protect Your Privacy: A Guide for PGP Users,* Prentice-Hall PTR, 1995.

Stallings, William, *SNMP, SNMPv2 and RMON: Practical Network Management,* Reading, MA: Addison-Wesley, 1996.

Stein, Penelope, *The Cell Phone Handbook,* Newport, RI: Aegis Publishing Group, 1999.

Stewart, Bruce, *WAP Security: Little Browsers Need Big Protection* [Web article]. Webtools.com, http://www.webtools.com/story/servers/TLS20001106S0001, Accessed March 3, 2001.

Stewart, John W., *BGP4 Inter-Domain Routing in the Internet,* Reading, MA: Addison-Wesley, 1999.

Stiroh, Kevin J., *Information Technology and the U.S. Productivity Revival: What Do the Industry Data Say?* A White Paper, January 24, 2001, Federal Reserve Bank of New York, 212-720-6633.

Street, Michael, 1998, *Software Radios: What are they and how do I write one?* White Paper Institution of Electrical Engineers, USAF White Paper, 1995, Cornerstones of Information Warfare Department of the Air Force.

Sutherland, Ed, "War of the Standards: GSM vs CDMA," http://www. mcommercetimes.com/ Technology/95, March 8, 2001.

Suvak, Dave, *IrDA and Bluetooth: Complementary Comparison,* Extended Systems Inc., 2000.

Swartz, Nikki, "Bluetooth Not Falling Out," *Wireless Review*, May 1, 2001.

Sweatt, Richard, "ATM's Pivotal Role," *Telecommunications*, October 2000, http://www. telecoms-mag.com/issues/200010/tci/atms_pivotal_role.html, Accessed May 2001.

Sweetman, Bill, "HALE Storms to New Heights," *Jane's International Review*, Vol. 34, March 2001, p. 50.

Synopsis of Wireless Telecommunications Technology, Available on INTELINK at: http://www/01wf.ic.gov/pages/Support/Guide_to_wireless_Technology/synopsis.htm, Accessed April 24, 2001.

T9 Text Input Home Page, http://www.t9.com/.

Taylor, S. C., *The Archimedes Satellite System*, In a Collection of Technical Papers for the 14th AIAA International Communication Satellite Systems Conference and Exhibition, 1992.

Technet International 2001, Washington, D.C., June 5–7, 2001, Air Force Technology Booth.

Technet International 2001, Washington, D.C., June 5–7, 2001, Siemans Technology Booth.

Tecnomen eZoner Web Site, http://www.ezoner.com.

Telecom Weekly, October 22–27, 2000, Faulkner Information Services, Available on INTELINK, Last referenced on June 13, 2000.

Tenca, Alexandre F., and Cetin K. Koç, *A Scalable Architecture for Montgomery Multiplication,* Proceedings of the Workshop on Cryptographic Hardware and Embedded Systems—CHES '99, August 12–13, 1999, Worcester, MA.

Tenca, Alexandre F., Georgi Todorov, and Cetin K. Koç, High-Radix Design of a Scalable Modular Multiplier, Proceedings of Cryptographic Hardware and Embedded Systems CHES-2001, May 2001, pp. 189–205, Paris, France.

Terplan, Kornel, and Patricia Morreale, *The Telecommunications Handbook,* Danvers: CRC Press, 1999.

Terra Voice over Internet Protocol VOIP Technology Industry Background, White Paper, Customer Alternatives and Technology Issues by Tierra Telcom.

Terrajella, Frank, U.S. Monitoring Laws, Monitoring Times, 1995, http://grove-ent. comLLawbook.html.

The American Heritage Dictionary of the English Language, 4th Ed., Houghton Mifflin Company, 2000.

The Defense Advanced Research Projects Agency, http://www.darpa.mil/baa/ baa00-29.htm, SPONSOR: *Defense Advanced Research Projects Agency* (DARPA), *Contract Management Directorate* (CMD), 3701 N. Fairfax Dr., Arlington, VA 22203-1714.

The Elliptic Curve Cryptosystem For Smart Cards, Certicom White Paper, May 1998.

The International Engineering Consortium, Universal Mobile Telecommunications System UMTS Protocols & Protocol Testing Tutorial, Available at: http://www.iec.org/tutorials/ umts/topic01.html, last updated December 1, 2000, Accessed June 18, 2001.

The International Multimedia Teleconferencing Consortium, Inc., http://www.imtc. org/h323.htm, 2001.

The Joint Security Commission, *Redefining Security*, A report to the Secretary of Defense and the Director of Central Intelligence, Washington D.C., February 28, 1994.

The Nokia 6210 and 6310 at a Glance, The Nokia Web site, http://www.nokia.com/ phones/index.html, Accessed June 20, 2001.

The Orange Book, DOD 520 0.28-STD, published December 1985 as part of the Rainbow Book series, Department of Defense, National Security Agency, ATTN: S332, 9800 Savage Road, Fort Meade, MD 20755-6000.

The Reader's Digest Great Encyclopedic Dictionary, Reader's Digest Association, 1968.

"The Seven Layers Model," no author provided, "Network Architecture based on the OSI model," http://www.rad.com/networks/1994/osi/layers.htm.

"The Symbian Platform Version 6.0: Power and Innovation; Reference Designs and Generic Technology," Corporate Web site, no author provided; www.symbian.com/ technology/v6-papers/sp/papers-sp.html "THE IS-54 DIGITAL CELLULAR CHANNEL" http://www.eecs.utoledo.edu/general/Cadence/channel.html, no author provided; references from within the article: [1] EIA/TIA IS-54 Interim Standard 1992. [2] Jerry D. Gibson, The Mobile Communications Handbook, CRC Press Inc., 1996.

The Telecommunications Act of 1996 and the Changing Communications Landscape, The Benton Organization, Available at: Jbenton.org/library/landscape/ landscape.html, Accessed June 19, 2001.

"The WAP Forum," http://www.phone.com/, http://www.wapforum.org/what/index.htm, no author provided, The WAP Specifications, http://www.wapforum.org/what/technical.htm.

The Wireless Networking Industry's Information Source, WLANA: The Learning Zone for Wireless Networking, April 2, 2001, http://www.wlana.com/learn/security.htm.

Tobkin, Vince, and Dave Sanderson, September 1, 1999, *Broadband Wireless—The Next Telecoms Gold Rush,* Global Telecoms Business, Bain Publications, http://www.bain.com/bainweb/about/insights/pract_insights_read.asp?article_id=244.

Todorov, G., *ASIC Design, Implementation and Analysis of a Scalable High-Radix Montgomery Multiplier,* M.Sc. Thesis, Dept. of Electrical and Computer Engineering, Oregon State University, December 2000.

Tompkins, Fred G., *U.S. Information Security Policy—How Should the Government Approach the Post Cold War Environment,* Eastern Michigan University, Ypsilanti, MI, September 22, 1995.

Torrieri, Don J., *Principles of Military Communication Systems,* Artech, 1981.

Torrieri, Don J., *Principles of Secure Communications Systems,* 2nd Ed., Artech House, 1992.

TRADOC Pamphlet 525-69, August 1, 1995, Department of the Army, Headquarters, United States Army, Training and Doctrine Command, Fort Monroe, VA.

Transilica Inc., The Transilica Inc Website on Bluetooth, http://www.transilica.com/news.cfm?PR=6, June 15, 2001.

Tranter, William H., Brian D. Woerner, Jeffrey H. Reed, Theodore S. Rappaport, and Max Robert, *Wireless Personal Communications: Bluetooth and Other Technologies,* MA: Kluwer Academic Publishers, 2001, p. 252.

Trimberger, Steve, Raymond Pang, and Amit Sing, "A 12 Gbps DES Encryptor/Decryptor Core in an FPGA," *Cryptographic Hardware and Embedded Systems CHES '2000, 2nd International Workshop, Proceedings, Lectures Notes in Computer Science, vol. 1965,* Berlin, Germany: Springer-Verlag, pp. 156–163. TROY XCD Inc. Web site on Bluetooth, http://www.troyxcd.com/, June 11, 2001.

Tsai, W. S., C. B. Shung, and S. J. Wang, *Two Systolic Architectures for Montgomery Multiplication,* IEEE Transactions in VLSI Systems, 8 1:103–107, February 2000.

Turner, William Bennett, "What Part of 'No Law' Don't You Understand?" *Wired,* March 1996, Published at: http://hotwired.lycos.com/collections/censorship/4.03_william_turner1.html.

U.S. Senate, *Vulnerability of Telecommunications and Energy Resources to Terrorism,* Hearings before the Committee on Governmental Affairs, Senate Hearing 101-73, February 7–8, 1989, Washington, D.C.: USGPO, 1989.

U.S. Patent No. 5101432, Signal Encryption Method.

United States Marine Corps (USMC) 2000, *Concepts and Issues 2000: Leading the pack in a new era.*

United States Merchant Marine Academy (USMMA) 2000, author's class notes from GMDSS Certification Course, personally taken December 6–15, 2000.

United States Signals Intelligence Directive [USSID] 18, Legal Compliance and Minimization Procedures, Department of Defense, Washington, D.C., July 27, 1993.

Vacca, John, *Internet Security,* Rockland, MA: Charles River Media, 1997.

Vacca, John, *Internet Security Secrets,* New York: IDG Books, 1996.

Vacca, John, *Satellite Encryption,* San Diego, CA: Academic Press, 1999.

Vainio, J. T., *Bluetooth Security,* Proceedings of Helsinki University of Technology Telecommunications Software and Multimedia Laboratory, Seminar on Internetworking: Ad Hoc Networking, Spring 2000, http://www.niksula.cs.hut.fi/~jiitv/bluesec.html, May 25, 2000, Accessed June 18, 2001.

Vakman, David, *Signals, Oscillations, and Waves*, Artech House, 1998.

Varshney, Upkar, and Ron Vetter, "Emerging Mobile and Wireless Networks," *iMP*, http://www.ciscp.org/imp/june_2000/06_00vetter.htm#reference12, June, 2000.

Velichko, S., *Random-number Generator Prefers Imperfect Clocks*, EDN Access, 1996.

Verdu, Sergio, *Multiuser Detection*, Cambridge, UK: Cambridge University Press, 1998.

Vergara, Michael, *Securing the Mobile Internet*, Presentation at Networld+Interop 2001, Las Vegas, NV, May 2001.

"Very High Spectral Efficiencies for Wireless Channels," http://www.darpa.mil/ito/psum2000/h648-0.html, Principal Investigators: Alex Pidwerbetsky, 67 Whippany Rd., Room 15F-242, Whippany, NJ 07981-0903, 973-386-3839, 973-386-7859, fax, pidwerbetsky @lucent.com; Laura Tutterow, CID26, P.O. Box 26049, Greensboro, NC 27420-6049, 336-279-5366, 336-279-5367 fax, tutterow@lucent.com.

Viterbi, Andrew J., *CDMA: Principles of Spread-Spectrum Communication*, Reading, MA: Addison-Wesley, 1995.

"VoIP Shapes Multi-Million Dollar Future for PBX Market," *Business Wire.com*, Texas: Frost-&-Sullivan-5, Available at: http://www.businesswire.com/webbox/bw.012400/200240118.htm, January, 2000.

Voice over Internet Protocol, [article online], http://www.anixter.com/techlib/pdf/0w0078x0.pdf, Accessed June 13, 2001.

Voice over IP Calculator, [article online], http://www.voip-calculator.com/protocols.htm, Accessed May 14, 2001.

Voice over IP (VOIP) [article online], http://protocols.com/papers/voip.htm, Accessed June 14, 2001.

Voice/Network Test, [article online], 2/http://www.empirix.com/Empiri . . . test/resources/qos+testing+for+voipp.htm, Accessed June 14, 2001.

Walter, C. D., *Space/Time Trade-Offs for Higher Radix Modular Multiplication Using Repeated Addition*, IEEE Transactions on Computers, 46 2: pp. 139–141, February 1997.

Waltz, Edward, *Information Warfare: Principles and Operations*, Norwood, MA: Artech House, 1998.

WAP™ Architecture: *WAP-210-WAPArch, Proposed Version*, October 17, 2000, http://WatchIT.com, Program 09042000, September 4, 2000.

WAP—Frequently Asked Questions, WAP Forum, http://www.wapforum.org/faqs/index.htm.

"WAP Infrastructure Overview," no author provided, http://www.cellular.co.za/ wap_technical_details.htm.

"WAP Security & Mobile eCommerce," no author provided, http://www.cellular.co.za/wap_security.htm.

"WAP SmartPhones and Companions," no author provided, http://www.cellular.co.za/wap_hardware.htm.

War in The Information Age, Institute for Foreign Policy Analysis, MA, 1996.

Ward, R. B., Acquisition of Pseudonoise Signals by Sequential Estimation, *IEEE Trans. Commun.*, COM13, December 1965, pp. 475–483.

Warren, Gary, DARPA Quad Chart: "Online Simulation and Control for Advanced Wireless Networks," http://www.darpa.mil/ito/Quad_Chart2000/K1470-20000726110729.PPT, Sponsor: *Defense Advanced Research Projects Agency* (DARPA), 3701 N. Fairfax Dr., Arlington, VA 22203-1714.

Washington, D.C., 1996, General Services Administration (GSA), National Communications System, Technology & Standards Division, Information Technology Service, *Telecommunications: Glossary of Telecommunication Terms; Federal Standard—1037C*.

Washington, D.C., Director of Central Intelligence, 2001, *The Annual Report of the United States Intelligence Community.*

Washington, D.C., Government Printing Office, Office of Technical Assessment, 1994. *Information Security and Privacy in Network Environments*, OTA-TCT-606.

Washington, D.C., National Intelligence Council NIC 2000-02, Office of the Director of Central Intelligence, 2000. *Global Trends 2015: A Dialogue About the Future With Non-government Exports.*

Wayner, Peter, *Digital Cash: Commerce on the Net,* New York: AP Professional, 1996

Wayner, Peter, *Digital Copyright Protection,* Academic Press, 1997.

Wayner, Peter, *Disappearing Cryptography,* New York: Academic Press, 1996.

WCAI 2001, LMDS overview, Machine readable data file, retrieved from the World Wide Web, March 4, 2001, http://www.wcai.com./lmds.htm.

WCAI 2001, MMDS Overview, Machine readable data file, retrieved from the World Wide Web, March 4, 2001, http://www.wcai.com/mmds.htm.

WCAI 2001, Others, Machine readable data file, retrieved from the World Wide Web, March 4, 2001, http://www.wcai.com/others.htm.

"We Trading at Schwab," no author provided, 101 Montgomery Street, San Francisco, CA 94104, Corporate Communication at 415-636-5454, http://www.schwab.com/Schwabnow/navigation/mainFrameSet/0.4528.781.00.html.

Webb, Warren, "Bluetooth Vendors Bite the Bullet," *EDN*, March 29, 2001.

Weeks, Bryan, Mark Bean, Tom Rozylowicz, and Chris Ficke (National Security Agency): "Hardware Performance Simulations of Round2 Advanced Encryption Standard (AES3) Candidate Conference," April 13–14, 2000, New York, Available as PDF file at: http://csrc.nist.gov/encryption/aes/round2/NSA-AESfinalreport.pdf and as a slides presentation at: http://csrc.nist.gov/encryption/aes/round2/conf3/presentations/weeks.pdf.

Weiner, Nancy, *Wireless LAN Market Trends,* Faulkner Information Services, 1999, Available on INTELINK at: http://doserve.mall.nsa.ic.gov/.

Welsh, Dominic, *Codes and Cryptography,* New York: Oxford Science Publications, 1993.

"Welcome to 724 Solutions—A Global Leader in Delivering Secure, Scalable Mobile Transactions," no author provided, http://www.724.com/.

Wesel, Ellen Kayata, *Wireless Multimedia Communications; Networking Video, Voice and Data,* Reading, MA: Addison-Wesley, 1998.

Weste, Neil H. E., and Kamra Ashragian, *Principles of CMOS VLSI Design—Second Edition,* Reading, MA: Addison-Wesley, 1993.

Wexler, Joanie, "WAP Under the Hood*,*" *Network World Wireless in the Enterprise Newsletter*, October 16, 2000.

What is 3G?, http://www.ericsson.com.au/3G/3g_what_is_3g.asp, March 5, 2001.

What is WAP?, Security in WAP [Web site], Baltimore.com, http://www.baltimore.com/telepathy/securityinwap.html.

"What is Wireless LAN/ 2001," *Wireless LAN.com*, April 2, 2001, http://www.wirelesslan.com/wireless.

"What the 3G Challenge Means for U.S. Competitiveness: Why 3G?" Available at: http://www.ntia.doc.gov/ntiahome/threeg/3gintro.htm. Accessed June 22, 2001.

Wicker, Stephen R., DARPA Program Quad Chart, "Self Configuring Wireless Sensor Networks," Cornell University College of Engineering, http://www. darpa.mil/ito/Quad_Chart2000/K2570-20000831105002.PPT; Sponsor: *Defense Advanced Research Projects Agency* (DARPA), 3701 N. Fairfax Dr., Arlington, VA 22203-1714.

Wiener, M., *Efficient DES Key Search—An Update, RSA Laboratories Cryptobytes,* Autumn, 1997.

"Wi-LAN and 4G Network Technologies," *TeTon Financial*, June 7, 2000, http://www.tetonfinancial.com/060700A.html.

Wilcox, D. Craig, Lyndon G. Pierson, Perry J. Robertson, Edward L. Witzke, and Karl Gass, *A DES ASIC Suitable for Network Encryption at 10Gbps and Beyond,* Cryptographic Hardware and Embedded Systems Int'l Workshop Proceeding, Lecture Notes in Computer Science, Vol. 1717, pp. 37–48, New York: Springer-Verlag, 1999.

Wilcox, Joe, *As Bluetooth Nibbles, Competition Lurks,* CNET News.com, September 15, 2000 Quote of Rebecca Diercks, http://technews.netscape.com/news/0-1003-200-2784702.html?tag=rltdnws, Accessed June 18, 2001.

Wiley, Richard G., *Electronic Intelligence—The Analysis of Radar Signals,* 2nd Ed., Artech House, 1993.

William, C., and Y. Lee, *Mobile Cellular Telecommunications; Analog and Digital Systems,* 2nd Ed., New York: McGraw-Hill, 1995.

William, Lee, Mobile Cellular Telecommunications Systems, McGraw Hill, 1989, p. 2.

Williams, Paul, and Robert Darlington, *2001 CISA Review Technical Information Manual,* Illinois: Information System Audit and Control Association, Inc., 2000, p. 381.

"Will LAS-CDMA Lead the 4G Evolution?" Available on the Internet at: http://www.globalsources.com/magazine/wc/0012/wcdma.htm, Accessed May 15, 2001.

Wilson, Stephen G., *Digital Modulation and Coding,* Englewood Cliffs, NJ: Prentice-Hall, 1996.

Wireless Data Communications: Security [Web site], Metricom.com, http://www.ricochet.com/ricochet_advantage/resource_center/security.html, Accessed March 6, 2001.

Wireless Mobile ATM Task Force, Introduction, http://www.delson.org/tf-wmatm/intro.htm.

Wireless Mobile Data Study, ANSER, 2000, Available on INTELINK at: http://doserve.mall.nsa.ic.gov/.

"Wireless Standards Compared," *PC*, Online document: http://www.zdnet.com/pcmag/stories/reviews/0.6755.2475113.00.html.

Wireless Telecommunications Bureau & Consumer Information Bureau, FCC Consumer Facts: Cellular Telephone Cloning, Washington D.C., http://www.fcc.gov/cib/consumerfacts/cellfra1/html.

Wittmann, Art, *Brush Up on Bluetooth,* June 1999, http://www.networkcomputing.com/1013/1013colwittmann.html.

Wittmann, Ralph, and Martina Zitterbart, *Multicast Communication: Protocols and Applications,* San Francisco, CA: Morgan Kaufmann, 2001.

Wolf, Wayne, *Modern VLSI Design,* 2nd Ed., Upper Saddle River, NJ: Prentice-Hall, 1998.

Wollinger, Thomas, *Computer Architectures for Cryptosystems Based on Hyperelliptic Curves,* M.Sc. Thesis, Electrical & Computer Engineering Department, Worcester, MA: Worcester Polytechnic Institute, April 2001.

Wolaver, Dan H., *Phase-Locked Loop Circuit Design,* Englewood Cliffs, NJ: Prentice-Hall, 1991.

Wood, Ben, *Explaining the Phenomenal Growth Rates of SMS Usage and the future of Messaging,* IBC—Mobile Message Forum, January, 2001, Millennium Conference Centre, London, Mobile Lifestreams Ltd.

Wood, Joel B., *What is a Wireless LAN,* April 2, 2001, ftp://ftp.netlab.ohio-state.edu/pub/jain/courses/cis788-95/wireless_lan/indax.html.

Wozencraft, John M., and Irwin M. Jacobs, *Principles of Communication Engineering,* Prospect Heights, IL: Waveland Press, 1990.

Wriston, Walter B., *The Twilight of Sovereignty,* New York: Charles Scribner's Sons, 1992.

Wrixon, Fred, *Codes and Ciphers & Other Cryptic Clandestine Communication,* Black Dog and Leventhal, 1992, 704 pages.

Wrolstad, Jay, *DoCoMo to Launch Intro 3G in Japan,* Available at: http://www.wireless-newsfactor.com/perl/story/9269.html.

wysiwyg://20/http://www.networkcomputing.com/nedesign/1109voip3.htr.

Wysocki, Tadeusz, Hashem Razavi, and Bahram Honary, eds., *Digital Signal Processing for Communication Systems,* Norwell, MA: Kluwer Academic Publishers, 1997.

Xiong, Fuqin, *"Digital Modulation Techniques,* Norwood, MA: Artech House, 2000.

Yang, Samuel C., *CDMA RF System Engineering,* Norwood, MA: Artech House, 1998.

Yao, A., *Theory and Applications of Trapdoor Functions,* IEEE FOCS, 1982, wysiwyg://ww.echoplex.net/Knowledge_Base/VOIP.htr.

Yolen, T., et al., *SSH Transport Layer Protocol,* Network Working Group Internet Draft, January 9, 2001, http://www.ietf.org/internet-drafts/draft-ietfsecsh-transport-09.txt.

Yomogita, Hiroshi, Staff Editor, *Bluetooth Devices Unable to Communicate with Each Other: Solution Unlikely to Appear In 2001,* AsiaBizTech, Nikkei Business Publications, Inc., March 19, 2001, Available at: http://www.nikkeibp.asiabiztech.com/wcs/leaf?CID=on-air/asabt/fw/125958, Accessed June 18, 2001.

Yuan, Jiren, and Christer Svensson, "High Speed Circuit Technique," *IEEE J. Solid-State Circuits,* Vol. 24, 1989, p. 62.

Zambenini, Linda, *High Speed Management, Tacit Knowledge, Creative Chaos, and Cultural Changes: The Incredible Transformatikon of NTTDoCoMo Under Keiichi Enoki, Mari Matusunaga, and Tadeshi Natsuno* [research paper online], January 19, 2001, http://php.indiana.edu/~lzambeni/L571/imode/paper.html, Accessed March 12, 2001.

Zeller, Tom, "Security Still Up in the Air," *Network Computing,* zeller@indiana.edu, February 5, 2001; http://www.networkcomputing.com/1203/1203ws1.html.

Zeller, Tom, "The Future Solution: 802.1x," *Network Computing,* zeller@indiana.edu, February 5, 2001; http://www.networkcomputing.com/1203/1203ws13.html.

Ziemer, R. E., and R. L. Peterson, *Digital Communications and Spread Spectrum Systems,* New York: Macmillan Publishing Company, 1985.

Zuccherato, R., *New Applications of Elliptic Curves and Function Fields in Cryptography.* Ph.D. Thesis, University of Waterloo, Canada, 1997.

Zyren, Jim, and Al Petrick, *IEEE 802.11 tutorial,* Online document.

Zyren, Jim, *Reliability of IEEE 802.11 WLANs in Presence of Bluetooth Radios,* document IEEE 802.15-073r0, September 1999, http://www.manta.ieee.org/groups/802/15/pub/1999/Sep99/, June 15, 2001.

Press Release, *2000 IEC Conference Explores Rapid Growth and Impact of Broadband Wireless Services,* September 15, 2000, International Engineering Consortium, http://www. iec.org/news/pr20000915.html, Accessed July 16, 2001.

Trademarks

SSH is a registered trademark of F-Secure Incorporated (www.f-secure.com) and Secure Shell is a trademark of SSH Communications Security Corp. (www.ssh.com).

Unpublished Articles

Denning, Dorothy. "Thinking About Cyberweapons Controls." (February 1, 2000, Draft of an Unpublished Paper Presented to the Defense Science Board).

Public Documents

Massachusetts: 1996, Institute for Foreign Policy Analysis. *War in The Information Age.*

Washington, D.C., National Intelligence Council NIC 2000-02, Office of the Director of Central Intelligence, 2000. *Global Trends 2015: A Dialogue About the Future With Non-government Experts.*

Washington, D.C., Director of Central Intelligence, 2001, *The Annual Report of the United States Intelligence Community.*

Washington, D.C., U.S. Government Printing Office, Office of Technical Assessment, 1994. *Information Security and Privacy in Network Environments.* OTA-TCT-606.

Washington, D.C., 1996, *General Services Administration* (GSA), National Communications System, Technology & Standards Division, Information Technology Service, *Telecommunications: Glossary of Telecommunication Terms; Federal Standard—1037C.*

Index

Symbols

A

Q–R

X–Y